# The History and Haunting of the Palace of Versailles

Rebecca F. Pittman

*A History and Haunting Of* series book.

Published by Wonderland Productions LLC in the USA and Paris, France



A special thank you to my editors:

Dan Scherer & Rusty Judd

Cover design and creation by Rebecca F. Pittman



ISBN-13: 978-0-9983692-3-5

## *DEDICATION*

As always, I dedicate this book to my family who support my creative efforts and inspire me every day.

And—

To my "Second Family" that offered me a safe place to land:

James, Jayden, and Eli Mayberry

&

To Heidi, Garrett, Macy, Maddy & Grady Kluth for your unconditional support.

To my editors who put in copious hours to read, edit, and suggest: Dan Scherer and Rusty Judd.

Love you all "long time."

RFP

# Table of Contents

## *ACKNOWLEDGMENTS*

I would like to thank Sandy Lakdar for being my Paris consultant concerning reports of paranormal activity at the Palace of Versailles. I'd also like to thank Karine McGrath for sharing her insights as a Versailles' on-site historian on some of the secret locations and information about the palace. Special thanks to Dan Scherer and Rusty Judd for their editing acumen. All sources used for the writing of this book are listed in the Bibliography section. These authors are highly accredited experts in their field, and I am indebted to their years of research.

Finally, a grateful nod to the Château de Versailles for their permission to write this book and their ongoing efforts to maintain, refurbish, and constantly discover new secrets of the palace of the French kings.

Merci beaucoup!

**Note:** All spelling and grammar contained within quoted material has been retained without editing. The French spelling for parliament is "parlement." The words king, queen, prime minister, etc. are lower case unless followed by a proper name. French words have been translated where it impacts the understanding of the sentence. All efforts were taken to make clear all references to the confusing number of people with the same name. The quotes in the story concerning Moberly and Jourdain in the Haunted section of the book were not edited but reported in their original format.

# The History

# Prologue

*He walked ghostlike along the long gallery turning from time t time to see his reflection in the seventeen mirrored arches. Candle from the hanging chandeliers and gold candelabras threw light int the silvered glass, which in turn sent it out in bursts that glinted o the gold gilt, silver furnishings, statuary, and ochre-colored parque flooring. The effect transformed the area into a glowing universe o golden light enveloping the soul and giving the illusion of floatin in brilliance.*

*His royal blue frock and Rhinegrave breeches broke th ubiquitous reflection of gold in the mirrors. Elaborate brocad infused with pearls bordered the frock coat that reached down pas his knees. The red and gold silk thread of his waistcoat wer reflected in the war scenes painted above his head. A diamon broach at his neckline anchored the jabot's explosion of lace. I twinkled in the candlelight, as did his jeweled fingers, and the silver buckles adorning his square-toed metallic shoes. He flourished a lace-cuffed sleeve, enjoying the delicate movement of the fine cloth. The red heels of his shoes flashed in the mirror as he adroitly swung his right foot in front of his left. With graceful movements he adjusted the long dark curls hanging over his shoulders and lifted his chin in appreciation of the total effect the mirrors declared.*

*Twirling once in memory of a studied dance move, he stopped and lifted his eyes to the painting directly above his head. It was an image of himself, portrayed as the Greek god Apollo. The cartouches of the lengthy ceiling murals showcased the wars and triumphs of his reign as King of France. He had accomplished all he set out to do. He had created a palace that was the envy of every monarch, and a successful war campaign that had made him the terror of Europe. He had fathered an heir to the throne, and countless other children through a long line of mistresses. The world he created shone as bright as his name: the Sun King. And yet, as his eyes traveled across the central mural above him, he felt a shiver. The weight of his decisions and the loneliness he often felt, even in the midst of thousands of adoring courtiers, were summed up in the four printed words staring back at him:*

*"The King Governs by Himself."*

# Chapter One
# "OF PALACES AND KINGS"

It rose impossibly from marsh land and thickets, this palace of gold gilt, brick, stone, and blue slate roofs. Before its blueprints rolled over the area like a juggernaut, there was only a small village boasting a castle, church, and a scattering of humble dwellings culled from the wilderness in the Ile-de-France region of France. The village was called Versailles, a word meaning to "turn the soil." Never has a definition been more applicable than it would be to the events about to eradicate this small hamlet.

The earliest mention of Versailles is from a document dating back to 1038 called the Charte de l'abbaye Saint-Pere de Chartres (Charter of the Saint-Père de Chartres Abbey). One of the signatories on the charter was Hugo de Versaillis (Hugo de Versailles), who was a seigneur of Versailles. As the village's local lord, he governed it as a feudal estate, meaning the peasantry of the area were charged taxes or exchanged their agricultural production and labor in exchange for land and their living.

The village of Versailles was located on a road from Paris leading to Dreux and Normandy and so the small town flourished for a time from the trade the road brought to its small inns, stables, and market. During the outbreak of the Plague and the Hundred Years War, the village was all but destroyed. In 1575, Albert de Gondi, a Florentine who became a favorite at the court of Henry II, purchased the seigneury of Versailles.

The palace that would adopt its name from this rustic settlement and forever stamp Versailles on the map of world history, was not the chateau that was the originator of the village denizens' destiny. It was from the royal residence of Saint-Germain-en-Laye, six miles north, that ultimately shone a spotlight on the forests surrounding the village and changed its course forever.

Saint-Germain-en-Laye

Henry XIV, the first king of the Bourbon line, adored Saint-Germain and invested vast amounts of money into the refurbishing of it. Gardens had always played a role in royal residences and Henry spared no expense in expanding the flower beds and lawn designs of the chateau until they reached down to the river Seine. Perched on a hill overlooking the river, the large home commanded breathtaking views of the Seine, a comparison that would find the later palace of Versailles sadly lacking. For most of the seventeenth century, Saint-Germain was a favorite retreat for the royal house of Bourbon. Anne of Austria, King Louis XIII's queen, gave birth to Louis XIV inside its walls. It offered a retreat from the dirty and overcrowded city of Paris, some 40 miles away. In the 1670s, Louis XIV spent at least ten months a year at Saint-Germain while the construction of Versailles was underway. He would visit the building site often, especially in the summer when La Notre's Garden was in full bloom. For now, Saint-Germain remained the seat of power.

It was, with the popularity of Saint-Germain that our story begins. It is also with the popularity of the "sport of kings" that the wheel of fortune turned in favor of the forests flanking the village of Versailles. The royal hunt was a time-honored tradition, not just among French nobility. Balmoral Castle in Scotland is a favorite hunting retreat for the Queen of England's family. Studley and at least seven other hunting lodges dotted England. Russia, Austria, Germany…they all boasted hunting lodges, although it may be fair to say, none of them dreamed of turning that sporting retreat into a royal palace of power.

There was something noble about the bagging of a handsome stag. Perhaps it was the pitting of royalty against the creature who reigned within the pediments of forest walls—a challenge of cunning and skill between man and beast. The primary animals hunted were fallow deer, red deer, roe deer, and wild boar. The establishment of hunting forests peaked between the end of the 12$^{th}$ and middle of the 14$^{th}$ centuries in England. Game was often enclosed within a park pale (a massive fenced or hedged bank), sometimes with an internal ditch and hunting lodges—usually moated—were built in the forests to provide temporary accommodation for visiting royalty and nobility.

But it was here, to the forests of Versailles, that King Henry IV guided his horse, along with a gathering of friends, and found the hunting plentiful and varied. Our main concern here is the importance of Henry’s fondness for the hunt that put him within the eyeline of the future court of Versailles.

## The Foundation of the Palace of Versailles Begins

It was with Louis XIII, heir to the throne after his father Henry IV’s assassination in 1413, that took the royal family’s fondness for the hunting area to a new level. During Louis XIII’s visits to Saint-Germain, Albert de Gondi, the seigneur of Versailles, invited the king to hunt in his forests that had so amused Henry IV. Louis became enchanted with the untamed wilderness, the plethora of deer, and the small feudal village. In 1624, Louis ordered the building of a small hunting lodge there to house himself and his friends as they indulged their sporting pursuits. The small lodge was designed by Philibert Le Roy. It was a modest chateau made of stone and red brick, with a raised roof. It sat atop a small hill, surrounded by forest, swamp, and a fledgling village. In 1632, Louis bought the seigneury from the Gondi’s and began to enlarge his remote hunting lodge.

The new lodging took on the details of a more traditional chateau, complete with a dry moat and exterior towers on all four corners.

Dry moats were a means of protecting a castle or royal residence from attack. Some were filled with water, but that water had to come from a nearby spring, which Versailles was sadly lacking. A dry moat did thwart the enemy's ability to tunnel under the fortress and attack from within. The new chateau sported an entrance court with a *corps de logis (*principal block of the chateau with its rooms and entry*)* on the western end, flanked by secondary wings on the north and south sides, closed off by an entrance screen. There were two service wings creating a forecourt with a grilled entrance heralded by two round towers. On the western side of the chateau was a garden with a fountain on the central axis and the ubiquitous rectangular shaped *parterres* (an ornamental garden with paths between the beds) on each side. This pattern of garden layout would become an elaborate composition of compartmented foliage, flowers, and fountains beneath Louis XIV's feverous hand.

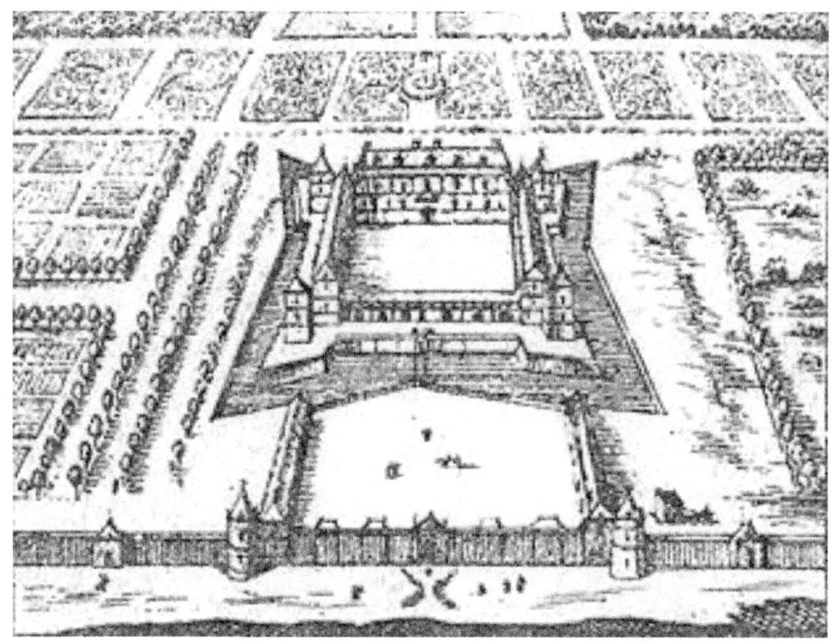

The Chateau, c. 1630-1640 as shown on the map of Jacques Gomboust.

## The Louvre & The Tuileries

In 1639, Louis XIII was also adding to the royal residence in Paris, the Louvre. This massive complex occupied the site of the Louvre castle: a 12th century fortress built by King Philip Augustus and inhabited by King Charles V until he suffered a humiliation at the Palais de la Citè. Charles abandoned his need for a large fortress with a towering keep and decided a royal residence in the fashionable form of a chateau would be better. You can still see the old castle's foundations today at the Louvre Museum in the basement level known as the "Medieval Louvre" department. This transformation from castle to palace took place from 1360 to 1380. Impenetrable walls gave way to windows, new wings were added to the courtyard, and wonderful chimneys, turrets, and pinnacles were added to the top. It became known as the *joli Louvre* ('pretty Louvre') and was nicknamed "Charles V's pleasure palace."

King Francis I razed the keep in 1528 and built what would become the royal residence of every consecutive French monarch, that is until Louis XIV came along. At another royal residence, the Palace of Fontainebleau, Francis acquired what would become the focus of the modern Louvre Museum today—Leonardo Da Vinci's *Mona Lisa*. In 1546, Francis commissioned the architect Pierre Lescot and sculptor Jan Goujon to modernize the Louvre and turn it into a Renaissance-style palace. Francis I died in 1547, at which time Henry II continued the building in 1549. During the reigns of François II and Charles IX in 1559-1567, Lescot created a four-sided chateau the same size as the old Louvre with a third wing to the north and a lower entrance wing on the east. He also created the *Petite Galerie* which ran from the southeast corner of the Louvre to the Seine.

In the late 1560s, all work on the Louvre stopped, as the Wars of Religion took center stage. In the meantime, Catherine de' Medici, widow of King Henry II, began to build another imposing edifice to the west of the Louvre. It became known as the Palais de Tuileries due to it being constructed on the site of an old tile factory (*tuileries*). It would play prison to King Louis XVI and Marie Antoinette in the decades to come.

The *Palais des Tuileries* became a royal and imperial palace in

Paris which stood on the right bank of the river Seine. It was the usual Parisian residence of most French Monarchs, from Henry IV to Napoleon III, until it was burned by the Paris Commune in 1871. It must be noted that these palaces housed the royals on a rotating basis. Often one chateau was chosen over another due to the season, the hunting, the gardens, or the need for certain entertainments or political agendas. Therefore, there could be long stretches of time when a residence sat empty, awaiting the king and his entourage's return.

Catherine de' Medici

The royal house of Bourbon took control of France in 1589 at the time of Catherine de' Medici's death and would give us the names we associate most with Versailles, namely, a long line of Louis's. Henry IV, son-in-law to Catherine de' Medici (he married her daughter Marie de' Medici) came to the throne in 1589 and completed a gallery at the Tuileries that Catherine had only begun. While still hunting in the forests of Versailles at the time, Henry began his "Grand Design" to remove remnants of the medieval segments of the Louvre and create an amazing two-story gallery that would stretch all the way from the Louvre to Medici's Tuileries palace. The architects were Jacques II Androuet du Cerceau and Louis Metezeau. It was a quarter of a mile long and built along the bank of the river Seine. At the time of its completion, it was the longest building of its kind in the world. Henry was an enthusiastic patron of the arts and invited hundreds of artists and craftsmen to live and work in the building's lower floors. Napoleon ended this tradition 200 years later.

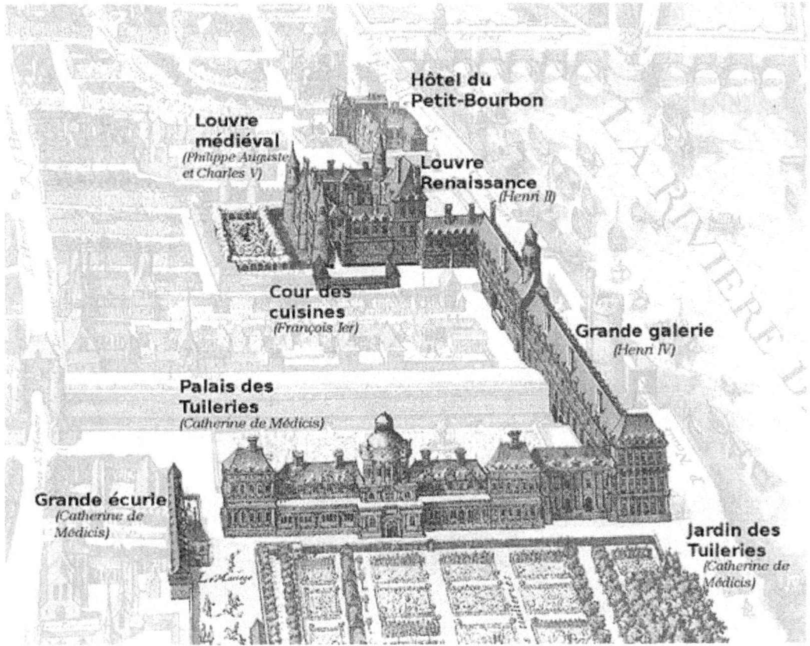


The Tuileries Palace connected by the Grande Galerie
to the Renaissance Louvre as seen on Merian's map of Paris, 1615.

Louis XIII, along with Cardinal Richelieu, built the Lemercier Wing in 1639 as the Louvre once again underwent transformations. In 1642, his central pavilion, known as the Pavillon de l'Horloge, boasting an exterior clock, was added. Louis XIV, who resided at the Louvre until his obsession with Versailles took center stage, completed the *Cour Care*, which was closed off to the city of Paris by a colonnade. This Louvre comprised 8 wings with 8 pavilions and covered 520 feet. It was also the home of the royal treasury. In 1659, Louis XIV began a phase of construction at the Louvre with his dream team: the architect Louis Le Vau and painter Charles le Brun. Le Vau also saw the remodeling of the Tuileries Palace. Andre' Le Nôtre, the third party of Louis' team of creators, redesigned the Tuileries Garden in the French style, as Catherine de' Medici had originally created it in the Italian tradition. These three men, Le Vau, Le Brun and Le Nôtre would be the chief creators of Versailles, under Louis XIV's demanding vision.

Meanwhile, the Versailles palace was in a constant flux of building, tearing down, expanding, and remodeling. A wall or gardens erected today, could be torn down and redesigned tomorrow. Many courtiers and visiting politicians stated that Versailles was a continual building site. Noise and plaster filled the air as hapless inhabitants picked their way through scaffolding, tarps, buckets, workmen, and debris.

West façade of the Louvre, c. 1644.
Engraved by Israel Silvestre.

Many of the King's paintings were placed in the Cabinet du Roi on the upper floor of the remodeled Petite Galerie. It became a kind of museum, open to art lovers. In 1681, after the court moved to Versailles, 26 of the paintings were transferred there. The collection of Louis XIV showcased works of Da Vinci, Titian, Veronese, Bernini, and many other famous artists of the time. The metamorphosis of the Louvre continued under Louis XIV, morphing into symmetrical wings and the Louvre Colonnade, its most distinctive feature. Le Vau, Le Brun and Claude Perrault designed the east face of the Louvre beginning in 1667 and it was mostly completed by 1674. The baroque manner, which has been emulated in grand edifices in Europe and America was honed to perfection in the Louvre's facades.

Louis XIV's business manager, Jean-Baptiste Colbert set about remodeling the Louvre with expensive decorations, state rooms, paintings, and furnishings in readiness for the king to make it his center of operations in Paris. He was aware of Louis' fascination with Versailles and the amount of time the young King was spending there, but everyone assumed the Louvre would be the royal residence and seat of power. As we shall see later, disruptive events that happened there while the king was but a young boy changed the course of history. And so, in 1678, Colbert gave up his dream of the Louvre and trotted off after Louis to begin the exhaustive expansion of what would become quite simply "Versailles."

East wing of the Louvre (1667-1674), one of the most influential classical facades ever built in Europe.

The Louvre and Versailles was not Louis XIV's only focus—it appeared the King would continually work on several massive projects at a time. In 1659 to 1661 Louis extended the Tuileries

Palace to the north by adding the *Theatre des Tuileries.* The Sun King's love of the theater, opera, and dance were part of his signature pursuits as he built several venues in which to showcase the talents of France and beyond. From 1664 to 1666 his chief architect Louis Le Vau and his assistant Francois d'Orbay made other significant changes. They transformed Philibert de l'Orme's facades and central pavilion, replacing its grand central staircase with a colonnaded vestibule on the ground floor and the Salle des Cents Suisses (Hall of the Hundred Swiss Guards) on the floor above, while adding a rectangular dome. This grand staircase and Hall of a Hundred Swiss Guards would be the backdrop to the bloody attack that saw the slaughter of the guards as they tried to keep the revolutionary mobs from Louis XVI and Marie Antoinette in 1789.

A new grand staircase was installed in the entrance of the north wing of the palace, and lavishly decorated royal apartments were constructed in the south wing. The King's rooms were on the ground floor, facing toward the Louvre, and the Queen's on the floor above, overlooking the garden. At the same time, Louis' gardener, Andre Le Notre, redesigned the Tuileries Garden. The court moved into the Tuileries Palace in November 1667, but left in 1672, and soon after went to the Palace of Versailles. The Tuileries Palace was virtually abandoned with this departure to Versailles and used only as a theatre; its gardens became a fashionable resort for Parisians.

Gardens at the Tuileries Palace

The Tuileries Palace

Louis XV, heir to the throne after the Sun King's death, was moved from Versailles to the Tuileries Palace on January 1, 1716, four months after ascending to the throne. He was six years old. He moved back to Versailles on June 15, 1722, three months before his coronation at the age of 12. Both moves were made at the behest of the Regent, Phillip II, duc d'Orleans, nephew to Louis XIV. Louis XV also resided at the Tuileries for short periods during the 1740s.

Louis XVI's interaction with the Tuileries Palace will be covered under his reign and the fallout of the French Revolution of 1789.

## Other Royal Residences of the Kings of France

### The Palace of Fontainebleau

The Palace of Fontainebleau is located 34 miles southeast of the city of Paris and is one of the largest French royal chateaus. The medieval castle and subsequent palace served as a residence for the French monarchs from Louis VII to Napoleon III. Francis I and Napoleon were the monarchs who had the most influence on the palace as it stands today.

In the 12th century, as with the origins of other famous palaces, Fontainebleau began as a royal hunting lodge for the kings of France due to its abundant game and many springs in the surrounding forest. It took its name from one of these springs, the fountain de Bliaud. It was used by King Louis VII, for whom Thomas Becket consecrated the chapel in 1169; by Philip II; by Louis IX (later canonized as Saint Louis and the name sake for the chapel built at Versailles), who built a hospital and a convent, the *Couvent des Trinitaires*, next to the castle; and by Philip IV, who was born and died in the castle.

During the 15th century, the Renaissance found its way to the sweeping oval courtyard of Fontainebleau. Francis I (1494-1547) commissioned the architect Gilles Le Breton to build a palace in the new Renaissance style, recently imported from Italy. Le Breton preserved the old medieval *donjon* (a massive inner tower in a medieval castle), where the King's apartments were located, but incorporated it into the new Renaissance-style Cour Ovale, or oval courtyard, built on the foundations of the old castle. A monumental Renaissance stairway, the *portique de Serlio*, gave access to the royal apartments on the north side.

In 1528, Francis constructed a lengthy gallery that allowed him to pass directly from his apartments to the chapel of Trinitaires. He brought the architect Sebastiano Serlio from Italy and the Florentine painter Giovanni Battista di Jacopo to decorate the new gallery. They filled the hall with murals glorifying the King. This elaborate gallery with its cartouches of paintings emulating the royal conquests would be outdone when Louis XIV designed his own shrine to himself in Versailles' Hall of Mirrors. However, Francis I held the bragging rights to the first great decorated gallery built in France. Historically speaking, the Palace of Fontainebleau introduced the Renaissance to France.

Other inspirations used for the creation of Versailles were first implemented at Fontainebleau: the first grotto in France was built at Fontainebleau (Versailles later boasted the Grotto of Thetis); pavilions, minister's wings and other outbuildings that surrounded courtyards and elaborate parks.

Following Francis I's death, King Henry II and his wife Catherine de' Medici chose to expand the chateau using the same architect Catherine used for the creation of the Tuileries Palace, Philibert de l'Orme, along with Jean Bullant. It was here, between 1547 and 1570, that many of the iconic structures were added, namely, the magnificent horseshoe-shaped staircase that swept up to the entrance of the palace. In the oval court, they transformed the loggia into a Salle des Fetes, or grand ballroom, with a coffered ceiling. Facing the courtyard of the fountain and the fishpond, they designed an opulent building, the Pavillon des Poeles, to contain the new apartments of the king.

As with most French kings, Henry II had a mistress, Diane de Poitiers. He commissioned artist Benvenuto Cellini to create the Nymph de Fontainebleau and asked that it be installed at Diane de Poitiers' Chateau d'Anet. This bronze lunette is now in the Louvre, with a replica in its place at the Chateau d'Anet.

The Chateau d'Anet and Diane de Poitiers (top), mistress of Henry II.

At the death of Henry II in a jousting accident, his widow, Catherine de' Medici, continued the construction and decoration of the chateau. The wing of belle Chemiee, noted for its elaborate chimneys and two opposing stairways, was one of her more influential donations to Fontainebleau. In 1565, the Wars of the Religions broke out and Catherine ordered a moat dug around the chateau to protect it. As the French did not allow queens to sit the throne, Fontainebleau fell into the hands of the heir, Henry IV. It was said Catherine's memories of her husband's betrayal while living at the chateau caused her to build her own palace, the Tuileries, an amazing symbol for a determined and strong Queen.

The horseshoe-shaped staircase at Fontainebleau built for Henry II by Philibert de l'Orme (1547-59), then rebuilt for Louis XIII by Jean Androuet du Cereau in 1632-34.

From 1570-1610, **King Henry XIV** made more additions to the chateau than any king since Francis I. He extended the oval court toward the west by building two pavilions, called Tiber and Luxembourg. Between 1601 and 1606, he remade all the facades around the courtyard, including the Chapel of Saint-Saturnin. On the east side, he built a new monumental gateway with a dome, called the porte du Baptistere. A new courtyard was built between 1606 and 1609 called the *Cour des Offices* or the *Quartier Henry IV*, to provide a place for kitchens and residences for court officials. Two new galleries, the *Galerie de Diane de Poitiers* and the *Galerie des Cerfs* (a nod to the honored stag), were built to enclose the old garden of Diane. He also added a large *Jeu de paume*, or indoor tennis court, the largest such court existing in the world. Not to be outdone by his grandfather, Louis XIV would build one later at Versailles. Tennis had become a fashionable sport of the royals. Henry VIII's indoor court still stands today in his Hampton Court Palace in England.

Gallery of the Cerfs (Stags) created by Henry XIV at Fontainebleau.

More painters were hired and went to work on the interiors. Heroic paintings were added to the salons by artists Ambroise Dubois and Toussaint Dubreuil. A new wing, named for its central building, 'La Belle Cheminee,' was built next to a large fishpond.

Henry IV next turned his attention to the gardens and parks. His mistress, Diane de Poiters, inspired him, after having done something truly remarkable at her Chateau d'Anet. She had introduced France to a gardening layout using angles and symmetry. It was called *parterres*: large geometric shapes of flower beds separated by paths and usually adorned with statuary, sheets of water and fountains. Henry IV borrowed Poitiers' gardener, Claude

Mollet, and created his own parterres, decorated with ancient statues. The fountain of Diane and a grotto were made by Tommaso Francini. On the south side of the park, he planted pines, elms, and fruit trees to create a lovely sanctuary, and laid out a grand canal 1200 meters long, sixty years before Louis XIV built his own canal at Versailles.

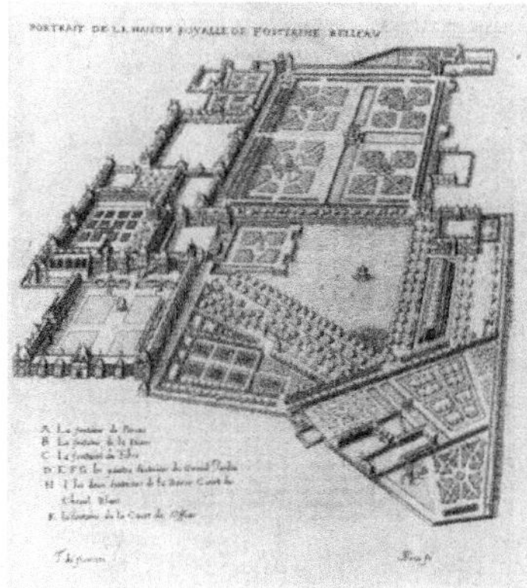

Comparison of Versailles parterres layout (l) and Fontainebleau's (r).

Looking at the side-by-side illustrations of the garden layouts of Fontainebleau and Versailles, it is clear the chateau had a great impact on Louis XIV's vision for Versailles, complete with a grand canal, partitioned gardens, grottos, fountains and statuary. The gallery created by Henry II, showcasing his great conquests, and salons boasting heroic figures, were yet other inspirations for the Sun King.

The Chateau's transformation from **Louis XIII** through **Louis XVI** were not as impactful as those of Francis I and Henry IV. **King Louis XIII** was born and baptized at the chateau, and continued the works begun by his father, Henry IV. He completed the decoration of the chapel of the Trinity and assigned the court architect Jean Androuet du Cerceau to reconstruct the horseshoe-shaped staircase. After Louis XIII's death, his widow, Anne of Austria, redecorated the apartments within the Wing of the Queen Mothers next to the Court of the Fountain, designed by Primatrice.

King Louis XIV spent more days at Fontainebleau than any other monarch; he liked to hunt there every year at the end of summer and the beginning of autumn. He made few changes to the exterior of the chateau but did build a new apartment for his companion Madame de Maintenon. This would signify that his visits to Fontainebleau came after the creation of the Hall of Mirrors at Versailles and well into his reign there. A chance to escape the confines of court life, along with the press of as many as 10,000 courtesans, would routinely find the Sun King spending time away from Versailles at Marly, Fontainebleau, and Compiegne chateaus.

Louis XIV demolished the old apartments of the baths under the Gallery of Francis I to create new apartments for the royal princes, and he made some modifications to the apartments of the king. Architect Jules Hardouin-Mansard, the genius creator of parts of Versailles, including the Hall of Mirrors, was called upon to create a new wing alongside the Galerie des Cerfs and the Galerie de Diane to provide more living space for the court. He also brought along the rest of his dream team and commissioned Louis Le Vau and Andre Le Nôtre to redesign the large parterre into a French formal garden. He destroyed the hanging garden his grandfather Henry XIV had built next to the large fishpond, and instead built a pavilion, designed by Le Vau, on a small island in the center of the pond.

A monumental piece of paper was signed here at Fontainebleau; one that would almost bankrupt the French economy. Louis XIV signed the Edict of Fontainebleau at the chateau on October 22, 1685, revoking the policy of tolerance towards Protestants begun by his grandfather, Henry IV. Henry had put into place the Edit of Nantes in 1598, after the deadly Wars of Religion that had pitted Catholics against Protestants, each trying to eradicate the other from the face of the earth. The Edit of Nantes allowed Protestants to practice their faith with certain caveats: they could not worship their religion within Versailles, the city of Paris, within schools, universities, special tribunals, and a few fortified cities. The Protestants, mostly worshiping in private, were grateful to a Catholic monarchy for its tolerance, albeit a restricted one.

With Louis XIV's swish of a quill, the Protestant freedoms were redacted, and hell broke loose. It was the final straw for a people who were overburdened with taxes, unfair salaries, squalor, and segregation. In a word, they took off. And by leaving France, they crippled the labor sector and the economy. It would become one of Louis XIV's most tragic mistakes.

May 19-20, 1717, another great monarch appeared at

Fontainebleau. Louis XIV had died, and the Russian Czar **Peter the Great** came calling. The Regency governing the young future king, Louis XV, welcomed the Czar. A hunt for stags was organized for him and an impressive banquet. Despite Fontainebleau's hospitality, the Czar was underwhelmed. In his memoirs he noted that he disliked the French style of hunting and that he found the chateau too small compared to other royal French residences. The everyday routine of the chateau also found no favor in his eyes as he preferred to rise early, and the French court preferred a more languid awakening. He also stated that he preferred beer to wine.

Peter the Great, Czar of Russia

Once **Louis XV** came of age, he too turned his eyes to the chateau beloved by his ancestors. His ambitions for the chateau even outshone his father's, Louis XIV. The new king had many courtiers and so he needed more lodging for them when they accompanied him to Fontainebleau. In 1737-38 the king built a new courtyard call the *Cour de a Conciergerie* or the *Cour de Princes*, to the east of the *Gallerie des Cerfs*. New wings went up, and old ones came down. The wing of the Gallery of Ulysses was torn down and gradually replaced by a new brick and stone building, built in stages in 1738-1741 and 1773-74, extending west toward the Pavilion and Grotto of the Pines.

The building continued. Between 1750 and 1754, the king commissioned the architect Ange-Jacques Gabriel to build a new wing along the Cour de la Fontaine and the fishpond. The old Pavilion des Poeles was demolished and replaced by the Gros Pavilion, built of cream-colored stone. Lavish new apartments were created inside for the king and queen. A new meeting room for the Royal Council was decorated by the leading painters of the day: Francois Boucher, Carle Vanloo, Jean-Baptiste Marie Pierre, and Alexis Peyrotte. An impressive small theater was created on the first floor of the wing of the Belle Cheminee.

King **Louis XVI** also made additions to the chateau to create more room for his courtiers. A new building was constructed alongside the Gallery of Francis I; it created a new large apartment on the first floor, and several small apartments on the north side of the Gallery of Francis I. The apartments of **Queen Marie-Antoinette** were redone, a Turkish-style salon was created for her in 1777, a room for games in 1786-1787, and a boudoir in the arabesque style. She was sadly imprisoned only a year later. She and King Louis XVI made their last visit to Fontainebleau in 1786, on the eve of the French Revolution.

During the French Revolution, the Chateau was spared any structural damage, but the furnishings were sold at auction. **Napoleon I** installed a military school there as he prepared to become Emperor. Napoleon chose Fontainebleau as the site of his historic meeting with **Pope Pius VII**, who had traveled from Rome to crown Napoleon Emperor.

Pope Pius II

Napoleon refurnished and decorated the chateau in the new Empire style for which he became associated. *The Cour du Cheval Blanc* was renamed the *Cour d'Honneur*, or Courtyard of Honor. The gardens of Diane and the Grotto of the Pines were replanted and turned into an English landscape garden.

Napoleon Bonaparte at his study at the
Tuileries Palace, 1812.

Napoleon's visits to the chateau were sporadic as he was heavily involved with military campaigns. Between 1812 and 1814, the chateau served as an elegant prison for Pope Pius VII. On November 5, 1810, the chapel of the chateau was used for the baptism of Napoleon's nephew, the future Napoleon III, with Napoleon serving as his godfather and the Empress Marie-Louise as his godmother.

Napoleon spent the last days of his reign at Fontainebleau, before abdicating there on April 4, 1814, under pressure from his marechals, Ney, Berthier, and Lefebvre. On April 20, after a failed suicide attempt, he gave an emotional farewell to the soldiers of the Old Guard, assembled in the Court of Honor. Later, during the One

Hundred Days, he stopped there on March 20, 1815.

The table at Fontainebleau where Napoleon signed his abdication on April 4, 1814, before his exile to Elba.

While in exile on Saint Helena, he wrote about his time at Fontainebleau; "the true residence of Kings, the house of the centuries. Perhaps it was not a rigorously architectural palace, but it was certainly a place of residence well thought out and perfectly suitable. It was certainly the most comfortable and happily situated palace in Europe."

Fontainebleau went on to house other monarchs from **Louis XVIII** to **Charles X**. They added minor touches such as stained-glass windows and decorations in the neoclassical style. Napoleon III, who had been baptized at the chateau, resumed the custom of long stays, particularly in the summer. Due to a fire destroying the old theater built by Louis XV, **Napoleon III** built a new theater in the style of Louis XIV. The **Empress Eugenie** built a small but rich museum on the ground floor of the Gros Pavilion, containing gifts from the King of Siam in 1861. Close by, in the Louis XV wing, the emperor established his office, and the Empress made her Salon of Lacquer. These were the last rooms created by the royal residents of Fontainebleau. In 1870, during the Franco-German War, the Empire fell, and the chateau was closed.

The Chateau Fontainebleau is today open for tours.

## The Chateau de Marly

The **Chateau de Marly** was one of the royal residences built for Louis XIV. It was situated on the northern edge of the royal palace and park of Versailles. It was here that Louis XIV escaped from the formality and crowds of Versailles. At Marly, he could invite select groups of the nobility to join him for a less-restricted protocol. The invitations to join the king at Marly were coveted and many of the nobility jostled to gain Louis' favor. The chateau was a mere 4 ½ miles north-west of Versailles—an easy escape.

Marly boasted a revolutionary design in that it offered twelve small matching pavilions flanking the central sheets of water. Marly had what Versailles did not—a water source. The ponds were fed one from the other by formalized cascades. This water source, the river Seine, would later feed the massive Machine at Marly, created to pump much-needed water to Versailles to satiate the king's need for over 55 fountains on the property, a grand canal, and facilities for up to 10,000 courtiers.

The work at Marly was begun in the spring of 1679; three years before Louis XIV moved his court permanently to Versailles from Paris. The king wanted a well-wooded retreat between Versailles and his other residence at Saint-Germain-en-Laye that touted water resources and a fetching view. Louis' head architect—after the death of his original designer, LaVau—was Jules Hardouin-Mansart.

Mansart, along with Dream Team member number two—the painter Charles Le Brun—worked on Marly. They concurrently were also working on the Hall of Mirrors, or *Galerie des Glaces,* at Versailles. The two men created a richly Baroque chateau with frescoed exteriors, statuary, hanging gardens, and Olympian symbolism which Louis favored. Apollo, the Sun King's iconographic persona, was featured in the pavilion du Roi, and Thetis. These two themes of Apollo and Thetis would appear at Versailles as well.

The Sun King attended the opening of the completed hydraulic works in June 1684 and by 1686 Marly was sufficiently completed to allow Louis to begin spending time there with a select entourage. The chateau was yet another hunting lodge for Louis XIV.

Versailles had morphed into a city-like labyrinth where his every move had become a ceremony. Over the years, Louis continued to embellish the beautiful park surrounding Marly, with wide straight rides, in which ladies or the infirm might follow the hunt (at some distance) in a carriage. There were more prolific waterworks than the waterless Versailles could offer.

Chateau de Marly painted by Pierre-Denis Martin in 1724.

When Louis XIV died in 1715, it trumpeted the demise of Marly as well. The king's heirs found the north-facing slope made Marly damp and dreary, and they rarely visited. In 1799, Marly was sold to an industrialist, Sagniel, who installed machinery to spin cotton thread. When the factory failed in 1806, the chateau was demolished, and its building materials sold. Napoleon bought back the estate the following year. The empty woodlands and park still belong to the State. During the Revolution that sent Louis XVI and Marie Antoinette to the guillotine, the marble horses by Guillaune Coustou the Elder, the *Chevaux de Marly*, were transported to Paris (1794) to flank the opening of the *Champ-Èlysèes* in the soon to be renamed *Place de la Concorde*. They are now in the Louvre Museum. You can visit the park at Marly today and view a small ruin of the chateau.

The Versailles' court diarist, the Duke of Saint-Simon, summed up Louis' need for Marly in his *Memoires*:

"In the end the King, tired of grandeur and the crowds, decided he would sometimes like to have simplicity and solitude."

## Chateau de Compiegne

The **Chateau de Compiegne** is a royal residence built for King Louis XV and restored by Napoleon. Compiegne was one of the three seats of royal government, the others being Versailles and Fontainebleau. It is in Compiegne in the Oise department and is open to the public.

The Chateau de Compiegne seen from the garden.

Even before the Chateau was constructed, Compiegne was the preferred summer residence for French monarchs, primarily for hunting given its proximity to Compiegne Forest.

The first royal residence in Compiegne was built in 1374 for **Charles V**, and a long procession of successors both visited it and modified it. **Louis XIV** resided in Compiegne some 75 times. **Louis**

**XV** was perhaps even more favorably impressed. His passion for the place was recorded by the Comte de Chevergny:

"Hunting was his main passion...and Compiegne, with its immense forest, with its endless avenues amongst the trees, where it stretches down which you could ride all day and never come to an end, was ideal place to indulge his passion."

In 1750, prominent architect Ange-Jacques Gabriel, who also worked on Fontainebleau and Versailles, proposed a thorough renovation of the chateau. Work began in 1751 and was finished in 1788 by Gabriel's student Le Dreux de La Chatre. Due to the town's ancient town ramparts the chateau took on a triangular plan. The building covers about 5 acres and is in the Neoclassical style.

During the French Revolution, the chateau passed into the jurisdiction of the Minister for the Interior. In 1795 all furniture was sold and its works of art were sent to the Museum Central; it was essentially gutted.

In 1799 **Napoleon** visited the chateau and again in 1803. In 1804 the chateau became an imperial domain and in 1807 he ordered it be made habitable again. Architects, painters, and decorators restored the chateau to its former glory. Its layout was altered, a ballroom added, and the garden was replanted and linked directly to the forest.

The result is an example of First French Empire style (1808-1810), though some traces of the earlier décor survive. The writer Auguste Luchet remarked that "Compiegne speaks of Napoleon as Versailles does of Louis XIV." From 1856 on, **Napoleon III** and **Eugenie** made it their autumn residence, and redecorated some rooms in the Second Empire style.

## Saint Cloud

The **Chateau de Saint-Cloud** was a palace in France, built on a site overlooking the Seine, about 3 miles west of Paris. Phillipe of France, Duke of Orleans (King Louis XIV's brother), expanded the site in the 17$^{th}$ century. Marie Antionette further enlarged it in the 1780s. Napoleon 1 and Napoleon III resided there until the chateau was destroyed during the Franco-Prussian War.

It began with the Hotel d'Aulnay which was expanded into a grand chateau in the 16$^{th}$ century by the Gondi banking family. These were Florentine bankers established at Lyon who arrived at the French court in 1543 along with Catherine d'Medici. In the 1570s, the Queen offered Jerome de Gondi a dwelling at Saint-Cloud, the Hotel d'Aulnay, which became the nucleus of the chateau with a right-angled wing that looked out on a terrace. Of all the royal residences, Saint-Cloud resembles the palace of Versailles in almost every detail: from the wings to the stonework, the blue-slate roof to the gardens. It had one thing Versailles did not—a magnificent view of the river.

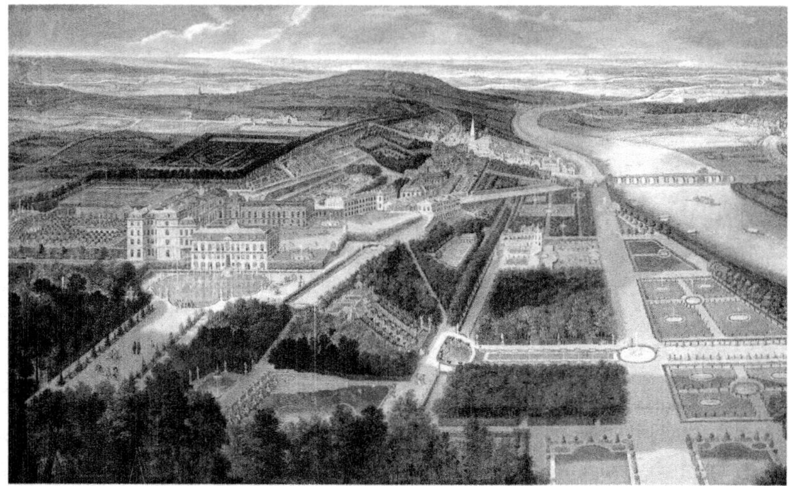

Saint-Cloud overlooking the Seine River.

The remarkable resemblance of Saint-Cloud (above) to Versailles.

Henry III of France was ensconced at Saint-Cloud while he

conducted the siege of Paris during the Wars of Religion, and it was here he was assassinated by the monk Jacques Clément. The chateau passed through several of the Gondi family's hands, before being bought by Barthélemy Hervart in 1655, a banker of German extraction. He enlarged the park to twelve hectares (a unit of area equal to 10,000 square meters) and did considerable rebuilding.

On October 8, 1658, Hervart organized a sumptuous feast at Saint-Cloud in honor of the young Louis XIV (20-years-old at the time), his younger brother Philippe of France, Duke of Orleans ("Monsieur), their mother Anne of Austria, and Cardinal Mazarin. It must have made an impression on young Philippe as he purchased Saint-Cloud only two weeks after the feast for 240,000 livres. It was to this chateau that Philippe often retreated when the politics and confines of Versailles became too much for him. He and his brother, King Louis XIV, often locked horns, although their devotion to each other remained steadfast.

Philippe's sumptuous additions to Saint-Cloud were unveiled in October 1677, with five days of magnificent feasts in honor of his brother Louis XIV. The impressive Galerie he had created was preceded by, and followed by, a salon on each end. Not to be outdone by his younger brother, Louis began creation in 1678 on the astonishing Hall of Mirrors at Versailles, ironically preceded by the Salon of War on one end, and the Salon of Peace at the other. The brother's rivalry never really dimmed, whether it was in the form of accolades for victorious war campaigns, or in the architecture of their chateaus.

Other similarities between the two chateaus were noted, including the building of a grand staircase in the left wing of Saint-Cloud in the manner of the sweeping Ambassador's Staircase at Versailles. Andre Le Notre, Louis' master gardener, was hired to redesign Saint-Cloud's gardens. Even Louis' architect, Hardouin-Mansart added the basin and lowermost canal in 1698.

Philippe's love for the chateau was apparent. He spent 156,000 livres over the years. His first wife, Princess Henrietta of England ("Madame") had her apartments in the left wing. Anne Marie d'Orleans, the last child born to Philippe and Henrietta, was born here in 1669. She would become the maternal grandmother of Louis XV of France. Princess Henrietta tragically died at Saint-Cloud in 1670. Much rumor circulated as to the cause of her death. A plethora of poisonings had been going on at Versailles, and it was whispered that may have been the cause of her demise. Henrietta had never been particularly hearty, although she loved to swim in the ponds.

Henrietta had just returned from England where she negotiated the Secret Treaty of Dover with her brother, King Charles II, at King Louis XIV's request. Upon returning, she complained of a sharp pain in her side. In April 1670 she began having digestive problems so severe that she could consume only milk. On June 29th, she drank a glass of iced chicory water. The pain magnified after drinking it and she reportedly screamed out, "Ah! What a pain! What shall I do! I must be poisoned!" The doctors were called in and the king and queen were called from Versailles. At 2 o'clock in the morning of June 30, 1670, Princess Henrietta died at the age of 26. While an autopsy report cited "death from cholera morbus (gastroenteritis) caused by heated bile," many still surmised she had been poisoned. The Chevalier de Lorraine, Philippe's long-time lover, was one suspected, as was the local apothecary and witch, Marquis d'Effiat, who had provided poisons to many of the Versailles court. It was also rumored that Henrietta had affairs with King Louis XIV, Philippe's own brother, so the list of suspects was a long one.

Henrietta of England, Philippe's wife & Princess of France

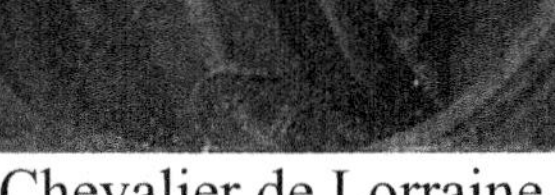

Chevalier de Lorraine　　Philippe, duc d'Orleans

It was from the chateau Saint-Cloud that Louis XIV, France's Sun King, lead a procession of nobles to Versailles to begin his royal dream of a new power seat for France's rule. This monumental exodus has always been dated as May 6, 1892. Versailles was ready, in Louis's opinion, to being housing the nobility of Paris, along with those of royal blood. The *Gazette de France*, that purveyor of royal gossip, announced, "On the sixth of this month, the Court left Saint-Cloud to go to Versailles, where Madam la Dauphine was carried in a sedan chair because of her pregnancy, which is far advanced." Indeed, Maria Anne Victoire of Bavaria, wife of the Grand Dauphin Louis (son of Louis XIV and Marie Therese) was second only in importance to the Queen, and gave birth to Louis de France on August 16, only three months after being carried into the royal courts of Versailles. This infant would go on to father the future King of France, Louis XV.

## Creation by Masters

The magnificence of each of these royal places boggles the mind. The fact that most, if not all, were undergoing construction, remodeling, and expansion at the same time is even more overwhelming to contemplate. The favored architects, gardeners, painters, and sculptors were moved from site to site. These skilled artists employed a legion of workers to carry out their designs and plans, yet it was they who still had to sit down at the drawing board or render templates and miniature murals to be recreated on ceilings in massive scale, or models of buildings on an even broader scope. It is so easy to throw some words on a page describing how a palace or chateau was built between this year and that, but the reality of what went into their creation, in that era, is simply astonishing.

The stone had to be brought from a quarry, only after being cut from massive blocks or from the face of a mountain or cliffside. The art of breaking large chunks of stone into smaller ones was done with several methods, one being the ***plug and feathers***. Multiple sets of plug and feathers are typically used to split a single, large piece of stone. The stone is first examined to determine the direction of the grain and to identify any potential defects. After the location of the intended split is chosen, a line is scored on the surface of the stone. Several holes are cut or drilled into the stone face along the scored line approximately 10-20 cm apart. Plug and feather sets are then inserted into the holes with the "ears" of the feathers facing the direction of the desired split. The plugs are then struck with a hammer in sequence. An audible tone from the wedge changes to a ringing tone when the wedges are tight. Between each series of strikes, a pause of several minutes allows the stone to react to the pressure. Eventually, a crack appears along the line that was scored on the surface and the stone splits apart. Attempting to split the stone too quickly may cause the stone to "blow out" at the site of the plug or split at an undesirable section. While the stone might be recoverable, it requires additional work.

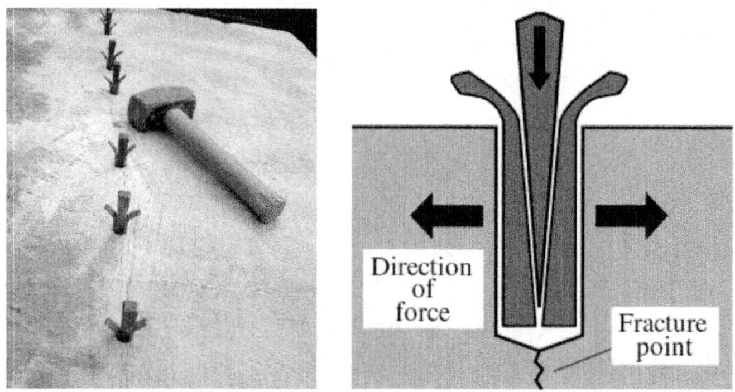


Plug and feathers technique on stone.

After looking at the size of these chateaus and palaces, envision each of those square stones comprising the structure being cut like this one at a time. That doesn't include the chiseling it down to the correct size, or the carting of it by wagon along rutted roads, and finally hefting it into place using rickety wooden scaffolding. This was long before the industrial revolution. The fine moldings and carved plasters were done by hand with various tools; everything from chisels to gouges.

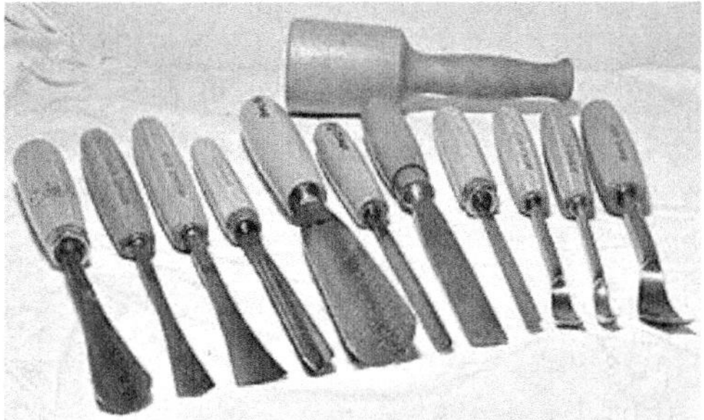

Hand tools like those used in the creation of the chateaus.

Doing it by hand, one section at a time.

Paints for the murals and décor were made from hand-crushed pigments. Fragile gold leaf sheets were applied in small squares to each surface and tamped down. Cobblestones, wooden beams, parquet floors, mirrors, tapestries, carriages, marble columns and fireplaces…hand cut, hand stitched, and hand polished. The perfection of the results from these skilled laborers still stands today.

# CHAPTER TWO
# **LOUIS XIII**

To say that the French monarchy was fond of the name Louis, would be akin to saying George Foreman's sons had something in common. The long line of Bourbon's and Navarre's christening their sons with "Louis" can get confusing. It is no wonder that each Louis was typically given a number and a moniker. We begin with Louis XIII.

Louis XIII, whose moniker was "The Just," was born on September 27, 1601, and died on May 14, 1643. He was the King of France from 1610 to 1643, and King of Navarre (as Louis II) from 1610 to 1620, when the crown of Navarre was merged with the French crown.

Posthumous portrait of Louis XIII by Philippe de Champaigne.

Besides being the founder of the hunting lodge that became the Palace of Versailles, Louis XIII was the father of the future King Louis IX and Phillipe I, Duke of Orléans. Louis XIII was known to have a rather complicated relationship with his wife, Anne of Austria. In short, Louis preferred the company of men, relegating Anne to two purposes for their marriage: a favorable alliance with Austria, and to produce an heir. As we will see, this was the common impetus for kings marrying foreign royal blood. In France, the pressure for the queen to produce an heir was even more intense—it had to be a boy. Unlike England, where a woman could sit a throne, in France there were no French queens reigning as monarchs. If a girl was the outcome of a pregnancy, she still had her purpose; she could be used to guarantee an alliance with a favorable prince or king and thus further the crown's ambitions. Basically, women were pawns in an elaborate game called "The Conquest of the World."

Louis XIII, age 10, by Frans Pourbus the Younger (1611)

Louis XIII became King of France shortly before his ninth

birthday, after his father Henry IV was assassinated. His mother, Marie d' Medici, acted as regent during this minority and basically created chaos. Ceaseless political intrigues by her Italian favorites and mismanagement of the kingdom led the young king to exile his mother and execute her followers when he took power in 1617. This was an audacious move by such a young ruler. Concino Concini, the most influential Italian at the French court, was one of those executed.

Louis XIII, a taciturn and suspicious youth, assigned a chief minister to help him navigate the troubled kingdom of France. He first called Charles d'Albert, duc de Luynes and then Cardinal Richelieu, to help him govern his new realm.

## Cardinal Richelieu

Cardinal Armand Jean du Plessis, Duke of Richelieu (September 9, 1585-December 4, 1642) would prove to be a good choice for the young king. Richelieu had advanced politically by faithfully serving the Queen-Mother's favorite, Concino Concini, the most powerful minister in the kingdom at the time. In 1616 Richelieu was made Secretary of State and was given responsibility for foreign affairs. He was also a close advisor to Louis XIII's mother Marie de Medici. The Queen had become Regent of France when the nine-year-old Louis ascended to the throne; although her son reached the legal age of majority in 1614, she remained the effective ruler of the realm. As mentioned, her policies (as well as those of Concini's) and intrigues proved unpopular with many in France. When Louis XIII ordered Concini murdered, Richelieu lost his power, was dismissed as Secretary of State, and removed from court. Marie d'Medici was exiled.

In 1619, Marie escaped from her confinement in the Chateau de Blois and became the leader of an aristocratic rebellion. The king and duc de Luynes recalled Richelieu, believing he would be able to reason with the Queen. He was successful, proving himself an able mediator between the Queen and her son. The result was the Treaty of Angouleme. Marie was given complete freedom and reconciled with the king. The Queen-Mother was subsequently restored to the royal court. After the death of Louis' favorite advisor, the duc de Luynes in 1621, Richelieu rose to power quickly. The year after, the king nominated Richelieu as a candidate, which Pope Gregory XV granted in September 1622.

Cardinal de Richelieu by Phillippe de Champaigne (1642)

Richelieu, also called the king's "Chief Minister" and "the Red Eminence," due to his red shade of a cardinal's clerical dress, sought to consolidate royal power and crush domestic factions. The French nobility, always a thorn in the monarch's side, rose in rebellion against the notion of their king wielding absolute power. Wealthy, privileged and proud, this class rebelled against being taxed and any usurping of their power. This uprising would play out throughout the successive reigns of kings named "Louis." Richelieu restrained their power and transformed France into a strong, centralized state. His chief foreign policy objective was to check the power of the Austro-Spanish Habsburg dynasty and to insure French dominance in the Thirty Years' War that engulfed Europe.

Although Richelieu was cardinal, he negotiated with Protestant rulers to further his goals. Yet, as with all who rise to power, that lofty view can be taken away just as quickly as it is given. This was clear concerning a day in November 1630 that became known as the *Day of the Dupes.* Marie d'Medici, never content to sit quietly by, verbally attacked the cardinal in a stormy scene at the Luxembourg

Palace. Richelieu had many enemies, as does anyone who has the king's ear and confidence. These enemies believed they had succeeded in persuading the king to dismiss Richelieu from power. When Louis refused to listen to them, Marie exploded at the cardinal in the king's presence, demanding he be dismissed. As Louis waffled, she thundered that the king must choose between her or the cardinal.

Louis' answer was to head off to his hunting lodge at Versailles. The king's departure made Richelieu believe his political career was over. The apartments at the Luxembourg Palace were filled with the sounds of rejoicing as Medici joined in with Richelieu's enemies to celebrate the cardinal's fall. What they hadn't counted on was the number of Richelieu's friends who came to his defense, or that the cardinal would head to Versailles himself to plead his case. There, at the private confines of Louis's hunting lodge, Richelieu was assured of the king's continued support. When word reached Marie, she decided not to await her judgement and exiled herself to the Chateau Compiegne.

Cardinal Richelieu continued to impact Louis XIII's reign. He founded the *Academie française*, the learned society responsible for matters pertaining to the French language. He also founded the *Compagnie des Cent-Associés* and saw the Treaty of Saint-Germain-en-Laye return Quebec City to French rule. The city would prove to be the heart of Francophone culture in North America.

In 1614, the clergymen of Poitou asked Richelieu to be one of the representatives to the Estates-General. The Estates-General represented the three classes of French citizens: the Clergy (first estate); the nobility (second estate); and the commoners (third estate). He became a vigorous advocate of the Church, arguing it should be exempt from taxes and the bishops should have more political control. The commoners were his biggest opponents. After the Estates-General was dissolved, Richelieu became almoner to King Louis XIII's wife, Anne of Austria.

Richelieu's power and influence in the court of the king filled his coffers, as was the case with all ministers who served the kings. He built himself a palace called the Palace-Cardinal. After Richelieu's death, King Louis XIII took over residency and it became the Palais-Royal. When Louis died a year later, his Queen, Anne of Austria pocketed the keys. Richelieu had filled the palace with works of art, books, and manuscripts. His manuscripts alone numbered 900, bound in red Moroccan leather with his cardinal's arm stamped upon them. His unequaled library was transferred to the Sorbonne in 1660. The fittings of his chapel at the Palais-Cardinal were solid gold set with 180 rubies and 9,000 diamonds. He funded the literary careers of many writers and was a lover of the theater. A palace was not enough, however. The Palais-Royal's architect, Jacques Lemercier, also received a commission to build a chateau and a surrounding town in Indre-et-Loire; the project culminated in the construction of the Chateau Richelieu and the town of Richelieu. The chateau housed one of the largest art collections in Europe, including Leonardo da Vinci's *Virgin and Child with Saint Ann*, and paintings by Veronese, Titian, and Rubens. To top it off, he owned two of Michelangelo's *Dying Slave* sculptures that are now on display at the Louvre. The *Richelieu Bacchus* is still admired today by neoclassical artists and is also at the Louvre. In his will, Richelieu left his magnificent Palais-Royal to Louis XIII's wife and Queen, Anne of Austria.

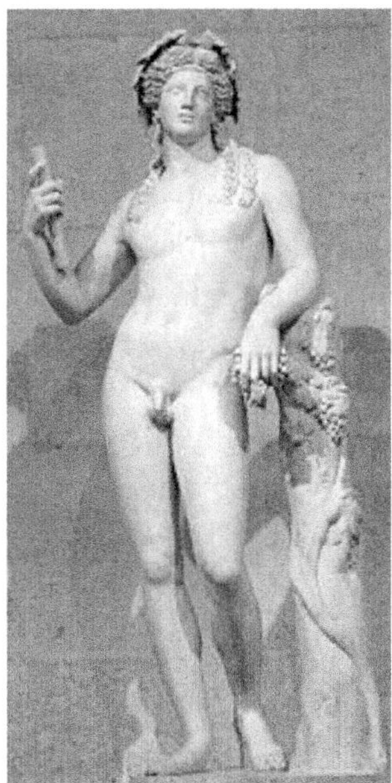

The *Richelieu Bacchus* in the Louvre.

Palais-Royal, across from the Louvre in Paris.

Richelieu's influence cannot be downplayed. He impacted a crucial period of reform for France. Earlier, the nation's political structure was largely feudal, with powerful nobles and a wide variety of laws in different regions. Parts of the nobility periodically conspired against the king, raised private armies, and aligned themselves with foreign powers. It was during one such turbulent attack that the young Louis XIV witnessed first-hand how powerful these noblemen could be when forming an alliance against the monarchy. The memories of having to flee his home to escape an attack gave the boy nightmares for the rest of his life. It was the major impetus for the future King Louis XIV to move the seat of power from Paris to a protected palace called Versailles.

For now, the system by which the nobles could rebel gave way to a centralized power under Richelieu. Local and even religious interests were subordinated to those of the whole nation, and of the embodiment of the nation—the king. Louis XIV would once proclaim, "I AM the state!" Louis XIII and Richelieu are remembered for ending the French revolt by the nobility. They systematically destroyed the castles of defiant lords, and denounced the use of private violence (dueling, carrying weapons, and maintaining private armies.) Equally critical for France was Richelieu's influence in Europe. Richelieu did not survive to the end of the Thirty Years' War. However, the conflict ended in 1648, with France emerging in a far better position than any other power, and the Holy Roman Empire entering a period of decline.

Richelieu's successes reached far beyond the throne of Louis XIII; they were highly important to his successor, King Louis XIV. The Sun King continued Richelieu's work of creating an absolute monarchy; in the same vein as the cardinal, he enacted policies that further suppressed the once mighty aristocracy and destroyed all remnants of Huguenot (French Calvinist Protestants) political power with the Edict of Fontainebleau. Moreover, Louis took advantage of his nation's success in the Thirty Years' War to establish French hegemony in continental Europe. Thus, Richelieu's policies were the requisite prelude to Louis XIV becoming the most powerful monarch, and France the most powerful nation, in all of Europe during the seventeenth century.

## Louis XIII and War

Louis XIII Crowned by Victory (Siege of La Rochelle, 1628)

Like all good kings, Louis XIII was active in launching expeditions into foreign territories and going to war when it was warranted. Like a stain spreading across a parchment map, France's troops, throughout the Bourbon reign, seeped across boundaries and planted flags on conquered turf. These acquisitions and alliances could be fortuitous for the succeeding king, or a blight to be dealt with. Wars were costly. They drained the treasury, left carnage in their wake, and often-times pitted relative against relative. Yet, power was everything. There was also the pragmatic aspect of war: conquered kingdoms filled the coffers with needed money.

The money came from taxes and from their colonies, or from plundering and raiding. France and Britain were huge rivals for control of the seas, and it was customary for each to raid the other's ships and steal their cargo. A portion of that plunder was handed over to the state, ergo, the king. This was also a time of colonial expansion and France had usurped a lot of countries that paid tribute and/or taxes to France. That accounts for the copious amount of money poured into the building of the Palace of Versailles.

Each succeeding monarch was left strapped with the decisions his predecessor had made. If the treasury had been depleted, bad treaties drawn, or formidable enemies made, these albatrosses were passed along just as surely as the crown jewels. While one king laid down his crown and rested inside a satin-enclosed casket, the next in line ran a nervous hand through his lustrous wig and tackled the inherited mess, usually with his trusted counsel by his side.

## Morocco

Louis XIII began his ambitious foray into worldly acquisitions with an expedition to Morocco. This area had first been looked at by Louis' father, Henry IV who was interested in a colonial venture. A French fleet was sent under Issac de Razilly in 1619 who explored the Moroccan coast as far as Mogador. In 1624 he was given charge of an embassy to the pirate harbor of the Salé in Morocco. In 1630, Razilly was able to negotiate the purchase of French slaves from the Moroccans. He visited again in 1631 and helped negotiate the Franco-Moroccan Treaty. This treaty gave France preferential treatment, known as capitulations: preferred tariffs, the establishment of a Consulate, and freedom of religion for French subjects.

## Americas

Meanwhile, across the Atlantic lay a new world, the result of an uprising in England. Wanting religious freedom, scores of dissatisfied men, women, and children boarded ships bound for the promised land. The eastern segment of this newly founded continent consisted of an area called New France. It was made up of colonists and natives who were finding it hard to co-exist. Louis XIII and Cardinal Richelieu sent people to encourage a peaceful co-existence. Indians, converted to Catholicism, were considered "natural Frenchmen" by the Ordonnance of 1627:

"The descendants of the French who are accustomed to this country (New France), together with the Indians who will be brought to the knowledge of the faith and will profess it, shall be deemed and renowned natural Frenchmen, and as such may come to live in France when they want, and acquire, donate, and succeed and accept donations and legacies, just as true French subjects, without being required to take letters of declaration of naturalization," stated Cardinal Richelieu.

Acadia was also developed under Louis XIII. Acadia was the land originally settled by the Acadians, the first permanent French colony in the New World. They called it "L'Acadie," which was believed to come from a native Miqmac word meaning "Land of Plenty," and was later Anglicized to Acadia. French Acadie was North American Atlantic seaboard owned by France in the 17$^{th}$ and 18$^{th}$ centuries. It was centered in what is now New Brunswick, Nova Scotia, and Prince Edward Island. It was probably intended to include parts of Maine (US) and Quebec.

In 1632, six decades before the Salem Witch Trials broke out down the coast in Massachusetts (USA), Isaac de Razilly became involved, at the request of Cardinal Richelieu, in the colonization of Acadia, by taking possession of the "Habitation at Port-Royal" (now Annapolis Royal, Nova Scotia) and developing it into a French colony. The king gave Razilly the official title of lieutenant-general for New France. He took on military such a taking control of Fort Pentagouet at Majabigwaduce on the Penobscot Bay, which had been given to France in an earlier treaty, and to inform the English they were to vacate all lands north of Pemaquid. This resulted in all the French interests in Acadia being restored. When ships of people leaving England began docking in the New World, carrying such groups as the Massachusetts Bay Colony in the latter part of the 1600s, the Indian tribes from Acadia assisted the French in attacking the settlements of these Puritans who were still living under English rule.

In **Brazil**, the colony of Equinoctial France was established in 1612, but only lasted 4 years until it was eliminated by the Portuguese.

### Asia

Louis XIII instigated communication with Japan in 1615 when Haskura Tsunenga, a Japanese samurai and ambassador, sent to Rome by Date Masamune, landed at Saint-Tropez for a few days. In 1636, Guilaume Courtet, a French Dominican priest, reciprocated when he set foot in Japan. The France-Japan relations were established.

In 1615, Marie dé Medici incorporated the merchants of Dieppe and other harbors to found the Company of the Moluccas. In 1619, an armed expedition composed of three ships (275 crew, 106 cannons) and called the "Fleet of Montmorency" under General Augustin de Beaulieu was sent from Honfleur to fight the Dutch in the Far East. In 1624, with the Treaty of Compiégne, Cardinal Richelieu obtained an agreement to halt the Dutch-French warfare in the East. The Dutch and French would face off again under King Louis XIV's reign.

### Blood Brothers

As mentioned before, when it came to thrones and power, the term "blood is thicker than water" was a converse concept. Conspiracies, plots, and subterfuge were the rule of the day. In fact, those closest to the one in power were to be feared most. They knew his vulnerabilities, his habits, and knew just where in his soft "underbelly" to plant the knife.

Gaston, duc d'Orleans, Louis XIII's brother

Gaston, Duke of Orléans, was Louis XIII's younger brother. As the king's brother, his title was "Monsieur." Twice, he had to leave France for conspiring against his government and for attempting to undermine the influence of his brother and Cardinal Richelieu. After waging an unsuccessful war in Laguedoc, he took refuge in Flanders. In 1643, on the death of Louis XIII, Gaston became Lieutenant-General of the kingdom and fought against Spain on the northern frontiers of France. It was common for a Prince of the Blood to be reinstated, even after conspiring against the crown. Perhaps the adage "Keep your friends close, and your enemies closer," came into play here. We do know Louis XIV would take that sententiae to another level.

## Long Live the Queen

Louis XIII married Anne of Austria, daughter of Philip of Spain and a Spanish Habsburg, on November 24, 1615. This was not the first political marriage alliance for these two countries. Louis XII and Constance Castile cemented two Catholic royal families of those two regions earlier. For Louis XIII, the marriage seemed to be strictly a pragmatic move rather than a romantic one. As mentioned earlier, Louis showed a proclivity for male companionship and the union seemed doomed from the start.

Anne of Austria, Queen of France, by Peter Paul Rubens (1625)

Four still births, separated by lengthy lapses of time, showed both the king's infrequent visits to the Queen's bedroom, as well as a problem with producing a living heir. In 1619, 1622, 1626, and 1631, the Queen went into labor only to deliver a baby devoid of life. It was no secret that King Louis XIII went to great lengths to avoid her. In fact, the realm was beginning to fear that an heir to the throne was even possible. A greater concern for Louis was that his brother, Gaston, would inherit the throne and set about destroying all the policies and platforms he had put in place. The Queen's great fear was being sent home due to her inability to produce an heir. A barren Queen could be returned to her homeland for lack of fulfilling the marital contract just as one returns a car today for not living up to the seller's proclamation. In short, this was not going well.

And so it was, on a dark and stormy night, on December 5, 1637, the planets aligned, and a series of events transpired that unexpectantly put the king in the queen's bed.

One of the events leading to this unusual occurrence, was a young woman by the name of Louise de la Fayette. She had been a maid-of-honor for Anne of Austria at the court. Her mother, Marguerite de Bourbon-Busset was a member of an illegitimate branch of the royal house of Bourbon. Through her grandmother, Louise de Bourbon-Busset, she came to the French court in Paris. In 1635, Cardinal Richelieu conspired to put Louis XIII and Louise de la Fayette together, but his attempt at providing the king with a mistress failed miserably. Louis did appreciate Louise's "innocence and piety" and she became his trusted confidante. In the end, Louise entered the convent Order of the Visitation of Holy Mary, where she continued to correspond and support Louis XIII.

Louise de la Fayette

It was to visit Louise in the convent that set about the chain reaction of events that December day. Louis was traveling from his hunting lodge in Versailles on his way to Saint Maur where he planned to spend the night. Anne of Austria was wintering at the Louvre. He stopped at the convent in Paris to see Louise and stayed longer than he anticipated. His bedding and other necessities had gone ahead of him to Saint Maur, as was the custom for king's traveling to other royal residences. It was also common to take along furnishings, plate, and even tapestries as the chateaus sat relatively empty when the royals were not in attendance.

While visiting with Louise, a freezing rainstorm slashed against the buildings of Paris and turned outlying roads into muddy obstructions. By the time Louis departed the convent, his entourage were encouraging him to shelter in Paris rather than continue his journey. It was now evening. Louis waffled as the rain fell in torrents. His captain of the guard, M. d Guitaut, pressed the suggestion that his majesty should spend the evening at the Louvre instead of risking the roads and demanding his escort endure such vile weather. Louis, repulsed at having to pass the night in the company of his Queen, persisted by pointing out all his bedding had been sent to Saint Maur and his room would be empty at the Louvre. Possibly swallowing hard, Guitaut offered that perhaps the king could share the queen's bed for the evening.

Despite several more protests, Louis was finally swayed. Anne of Austria was no doubt surprised to see her recalcitrant king arriving suddenly in a storm. Even more surprised to find him disrobing by her bed. We do know, that exactly nine months later, the future King of France, Louis XIV, bounced into the world with a cry that filled the hearts of France with joy! It was a miracle, they proclaimed. After twenty-two years of marriage, four still births, and a husband who went to great lengths to avoid her, Anne of Austria produced a son at the age of 38, and not just one, but two! Philippe of France, Duke of Anjou (later Duke of Orléans), was born two years later on September 21, 1640. Obviously, Louis found encouragement to "give it another go" after a living heir was born from that fateful December evening at the Louvre.

A Venetian ambassador, Alvice Contarini was present at the birth of Louis XIV. The child was named Louis-Dieudonné, "Louis, the Gift of God." Contarini reported that "His Majesty went today four or five times to "Monseigneur" the Dauphin's room to see him breastfeeding." Monseigneur was the court name given to the infant and he was indeed the new Dauphin of France. A wet nurse was always used for breastfeeding, and so the Queen was probably not in the room. Contarini went on to say, "Monsieur (the court name given to the king's brother…in this case, Gaston) was stunned when Mme Péronne (the midwife) showed him that the Queen had given birth to a son." Gaston was no doubt feeling more than surprise. Laying within the bassinette was the future King of France, thus thwarting any ambition he had toward fulfilling that role himself.

King Louis XIII's joy was immense. He took Ambassador Contarini himself to the boy's crib, and gushed, "Here is a miraculous effect of the grace of our Lord, for that is how one must describe so beautiful a child born after my twenty-two-years of marriage and my wife's four unhappy miscarriages."

Mme de Motteville, Anne of Austria's faithful lady-in-waiting summed up the Queen's joy over the events begun on that stormy night in Paris: "It has been said that the encounter gave us our present king. When the queen received this grace from Heaven, she badly needed it to save her from all the sufferings which seemed to await her." Marie Antoinette would face those same fears in the years to come as wife to Louis XVI.

## Funerals and Regents

Louis XIII was not a beloved king. He was often sullen, remote, and suspicious. His speech impediment may have had much to do with his awkward associations with his court and the public in general. Sir Edward Herbert, an ambassador sent to the French court by King James I of England to present his credentials, remarked on Louis' extreme congenital speech impediment caused by his double row of teeth:

"I presented the King a letter of credence from the King (James) my master; the King (Louis) assured me of a reciprocal affection to the King (James) my master, and of my particular welcome to his Court: his words were never many, as being so extreme a stutterer that he would sometimes hold his tongue out of his mouth a good while before he could speak so much as one word; he had besides a double row of teeth, and was observed seldom or never to spit or blow his nose, or to sweat much, 'tho he were very laborious, and almost indefatigable in his exercises of hunting and hawking to which he was very much addicted..."

Louis' distrust of the people around him extended to his son, Louis XIV, heir to the throne. This was not uncommon between monarchs and sons, as heirs were always being encouraged to champion this cause and that, to the point of leading a coup against their fathers sitting the throne. Mme de Motteville wrote the following: "Monseigneur the little Dauphin was not even three before he apparently worried and annoyed the King. One day, coming back from some hunting trip, he saw his father wearing a night cap; he began to cry because he was frightened as he was not used to seeing him like that. The King was as angry as if it had been a thing of much consequence; he complained to the Queen, accused her of teaching his son to feel aversion for him and threatened her very roughly with removal of both children from her care."

Queen Anne begged the king not to have the young heirs removed from her and was finally successful. This not only assured her that she could continue on in her role as nurturing mother, but it put her in a position of power should the king die. King Louis XIII was often sick; in fact, many had bet on the monarch's death on more than one occasion. It was with the great Cardinal Richelieu's illness that the court's future prospects came into question. Thus, when Richelieu succumbed to one of the many illnesses with which he had been dealing, the court was stunned. The date was December 17, 1642. The palace was abuzz with questions. King Louis XIII had relied heavily on this cardinal's counsel and machinations. Who would succeed him? Would a new Council be chosen? Would the king change his political strategies? It seems Richelieu's influence reached far beyond the grave, for the man Louis elected to take his place was the very man the cardinal suggested before his death: Guilio Mazarini. In 1639, Mazarini became Mazarin after his naturalization as a Frenchman. Mazarin was made a cardinal by the Pope and became prime minister.

King Louis continued with the same political practices he had endorsed under Richelieu. Taxes remained high and the commoners disgruntled; the nobility was still excluded from the Council (causing continual threats of an uprising); and the war with Spain rolled on. Louis' continued placement in the crosshairs of both branches of the House of Habsburg—Spain and Austria—had been the king's primary focus. Mazarin picked up where Richelieu left off and supported Louis' wars with the two great Houses.

Cardinal Mazarin

The last month of 1642 saw the king's health worsen. By February of 1643, it became certain that his demise was imminent. The burning question was what was to be done with the five-year-old heir, Louis XIV? A regent would have to be named. The two choices were the young boy's mother, Anne of Austria, or his uncle, Gaston d'Orléans. The king trusted neither of them. His own mother, Marie d'Medici had all but ruined his reign as his acting regent after his father's assassination, and his brother Gaston had plotted and revolted against him more times than he could count. If Gaston got hold of the regency, it was a sure bet all of Louis' hard fought-for policies would go by the wayside, not to mention his influence over the dauphin. He was not happy with this two-sided coin. No matter the toss, he felt he would lose.

When by April 19 it was clear the king was at death's doorstep, he called for the principal players to gather around his bed. The

Queen, Gaston, the two young princes, the Princes of the Royal Blood, the Dukes, and other officials stood in silent anticipation of the King's words. One of the servants present recorded the following words: "...the King, after having ordered that the curtains of his bed be opened, and having spoken to the Queen, Monsieur, his brother, and Monsieur le Prince (the King's cousin, the prince of Condé), raised his voice and made a very beautiful speech to all who were present, and then ordered M. de la Vrilliére (Secretary of State) to read aloud the act proclaiming the Queen's regency... The Queen was at the foot of the King's bed, seated in a chair... She kept weeping... All the others also cried... The King who, that day, had a pink complexion and looked pleased and unworried, showed that he had no fear of death. Everyone could see the greatest king on earth, after so many victories and conquests, leaving his scepter and his crown with as little regret as if it had been a bundle of rotten straw."

Perhaps "a bundle of rotten straw" was not a bad analogy, as was the responsibility, battles, and stress endured by this king. The weight of it all would soon be over. Yet, his final act did not go without instilling anger and fear in those stationed about his death bed. Yes, Anne had gotten her regency, but Louis had also made Gaston Lieutenant General. This position carried with it a great deal of power. Not only that, but Louis also installed a council that would run the government, led by Mazarin, whom the queen distrusted. She had won the regency, but the power laid elsewhere. She was guaranteed the promise of her children remaining by her side, and that was her trump card. For whomever ruled the future king, ruled the throne of France.

A. Lloyd Moote, Louis' biographer, summed up the king's ailments: "...his intestines were inflamed and ulcerated, making digestion virtually impossible; tuberculosis had spread to his lungs accompanied by a habitual cough. Either of these major ailments, or the accumulation of minor problems, may have killed him, not to mention physiological weaknesses that made him prone to disease or his doctors' remedies of enemas and bleedings, which continued right to his death." Many believed the act of bleeding the patient in the hopes of purging the disease caused more death than hindered it.

Louis III died on May 14, 1643, at three in the afternoon, at the age of 41 on the 33rd anniversary of his father's death. Sadly, his death was not mourned. A magistrate by the name of Oliver Lefèvre d'Ormesson summed up the feelings of the hour: "He died… after having reigned for thirty-three years less two hours. He never had any contentment in his life and always met with crisis. He accomplished some things, but only under the leadership of his favorites, especially the Cardinal (Richelieu) who, for twenty years, always had to force him to do things so that, during his illness, he said that the way the Cardinal had constrained him had reduced him to his present state."

Few that day thought of the king who loved the lute and played it for his mother at the age of three. Or that in 1635, Louis composed music, wrote the libretto and designed the costumes for the "Ballet de la Merlaison." He himself danced in two performances of the ballet the same year at Chantilly and Royaumont. Nor, perhaps, was anyone crediting him at the time for his influence in the world of French fashion. It was he who introduced the wearing of wigs among men in 1624, the same year he built a modest hunting lodge in Versailles. For the first time, since antiquity, wigs became fashionable and would be the dominant style among men in European-influenced countries for nearly 200 years; until the French Revolution brought about changes in fashion. It was his ineffectual, brooding nature and his reliance on a domineering cardinal they remembered.

Upon his death, the nobility rejoiced, hoping to gain concessions under the new ruling forces; ministers began positioning themselves for favor; and the poor prayed for relief from taxes. Before the final sounds of funeral rites were barely silenced, the queen left Saint-Germaine-en-Laye the day following Louis' death and headed back to the Louvre with her young princes in tow. Five-year-old Louis XIV looked out through the window of his couch at the country he would soon govern. The young Sun King would lay aside his wooden horses and soldiers and soon take command of the real thing. He was destined to leave his mark on the world in ways his mother would never have imagined; even now as she rode over the rutted roads of the French countryside and planned her next move.

# Chapter Three
## Obsessions Are Born

The young king Louis XIV inherited more than the crown of France when his father died. Louis XIII's reign had been beleaguered with war, debt, and plagued by civil struggle for almost a century. It was the same conflicting theologies that had caused so many fields and scaffolds of France to be drenched in blood: the Catholic church versus the French Protestants, or "Huguenots." At the head of this Protestant rebellion were two notables: the duc de Bouillon and the notorious duc de Rohan. The clash between the monarch and the nobility was also bequeathed to the adolescent king, along with the silver, plate, lands, chateaus, and treasury.

Many enemies of the late king saw Anne of Austria's regency as a good thing. She was known to be kind, benevolent, and fair. Cardinal Richelieu was gone, along with his influence. The nobles and Huguenots could see the tides turning in their favor. After all, Anne did not carry a king's authority and she was only a woman. How much trouble could she be? They were about to find out.

Before she barely patted her hair into place after the journey from Saint-Germain to the Louvre, Anne called a *lit de justice*. This French name, meaning literally "bed of justice," was a formal session called by the king, or in this case, the regent of the new king. As the young boy sat beneath the baldachin, perched on satin pillows embroidered with the gold fleur-de-lis, his mother called the Parlement of France to order to hear the reading of King Louis XIII's will and have it legally entered into the register. The Parlement was unlike the Parliament of England. The French version was comprised of judges who had basically bought their titles and positions. They had neither a law background nor the vote of the people whom they professed to protect. They were rich nobles who had inherited their positions under Henry XIV's law that these positions would be handed down from family to family and remain exempt from yearly taxes. Their main purpose was to enter a record of edicts and important proclamations into the register for posterity. They could oppose a king's edict and voice their concerns, but the throne had the final say. The parlement was notably a thorn in the monarch's side.

Baldachin, or canopy, above the throne.

Anne of Austria proved a cleverer regent than Gaston, duc de Orleans, or any of the nobility gave her credit for. Following Louis XIII's death, she called Cardinal Mazarin to be her new prime minister. If Gaston was unnerved by this move, he did not show it outwardly. Mazarin was thought to be weak, vacillating, and a pleaser. He was not the cutthroat Richelieu had been and therefore not a threat to the Huguenots or nobles waiting for their chance to pounce. Yet, these attributes of Mazarin were exactly the reason Anne chose him. He was not surrounded by a powerful family like Richelieu had been. He was not forceful, greedy for power, and combative. He would do her bidding and offered no threat to her policy or agenda. Mazarin was hers and had the same goal—to make her son Louis XIV *le plus grand roi du monde*, "the greatest king in the world." Anne believed that kings and queens were called of God, and therefore semi-deity; a belief she instilled in her young son.

Declaring herself, as had Marie de Medici before her, the young king's regent, and placing Mazarin solidly beside her was only the beginning in a series of surprises. Anne was Spanish...she was a Habsburg. All expected her to begin a quick campaign of peace with her brother Philip IV and Ferdinand III to bring to close the ongoing war between France and Spain. She was expected to lower taxes and bend to the will of the crush of men lobbying for a change in the rules that Louis XIII and Richelieu had forced down their throats. But Anne proved to be made of sterner stuff. She turned her face not toward Spain, but to France, and most-importantly, its new king.

Her tunnel vision to raise her first-born son high on the world platform eclipsed the role her other son would play as the king's brother. Philippe, duc d' Anjou was cut from a different cloth than his brother. At a young age he showed more interest in fashion than he did in battle. Mme de Motteville, Anne's Lady in Waiting, summed it up in her usual appraising tone:

"That prince had wit as soon as he learned to talk. The clearness of his thoughts went along with two praiseworthy inclinations... generosity and humanity. It might be wished however, that the idle amusements he was allowed had been forbidden him. He liked spending his time with women and girls dressing them and doing their hair: he knew what would make them look elegant even better than most curious women... He was well built; his features were fine... His eyes were black, shiny and beautiful; their expression was sweet yet grave... His black hair, which curled naturally, suited his complexion; and his nose, which looked like it might become aquiline, was then handsome. One could think that, if the years did not lesson his beauty, he could dispute its crown with the fairest ladies; but it already seemed as if he could not be tall."

Louis XIV was described as having "handsome features of his face, the sweet yet serious look in his eyes, the whiteness of his complexion together with his hair which was then very fair, adorned him even better than his costume. He danced admirably; and although he was then only eight years old, one could say of him that he was one of those who had the grandest air, and certainly the most beauty."

Louis and Phillipe's father, King Louis XIII, had shown a proclivity for men. It was probably not shocking to his family then to see the young prince's interest in a more effeminate existence. It may have been Anne's lack of interference that nurtured this sensitivity. Philippe remained dressed in flowing gowns after the time of "breeching" had passed. As shown in portraits at the time, Louis had advanced to coats and breeches, while Philippe remains in dresses.

Louis XIV (l) with Philippe and Anne of Austria.

The world of kings and queens was a ruthless one in the Ancien Régime ("old rule") which was the political and social system of the Kingdom of France from the Late Middle Ages (circa 15$^{th}$ century) to the French Revolution of 1789. Bonds of family and blood went by the wayside if power was to be had. Husbands executed wives, brothers betrayed brothers, cousins slandered, and children revolted against their parents. It was a time of suspicion and plotting where loyalties were always in flux. While today it seems monstrous that members of a family would imprison and slay each other, it was done with shocking regularity when all the marbles were at stake.

One such story is that of the two princes, Edward V, King of England, and Richard of Shrewsbury, Duke of York. The two brothers were the only sons of Edward IV, King of England and Elizabeth Woodville surviving at the time of their father's death in 1483. When they were 12 and 9 years old, respectively, they were lodged in the Tower of London by the man appointed to look after them, their uncle, the Lord Protector Richard, Duke of Gloucester. This was supposedly in preparation for Edward's forthcoming coronation as king. However, before the young king could be crowned, he and his brother were declared illegitimate. Their Uncle Richard ascended to the throne. The boys disappeared. It was assumed they were murdered, perhaps by Richard in an attempt to secure his hold on the throne. Many theories were posited, but without evidence, the story remained a mystery. In 1674, workmen dug up a wooden box containing two small human skeletons found under the staircase in the Tower of London. They were widely accepted to be those of the princes. King Charles II had the bones buried in Westminster Abbey, giving credibility to the story that the bones were of royal blood.

The Two Princes in the Tower, Edward and Richard.

Louis XIV and Philippe I

Is it any wonder Anne of Austria kept her two sons close? Their uncle, Gaston duc d' Orleans, was a devious player in this game of power, who had already fought hard for the right to govern their young lives. He missed being the little King's regent by a hair. Would he have schemed against the young boy? The mortality rate for children in those days was astronomical. If a child lived past his seventh birthday, it was a cause to celebrate. If an adolescent suddenly died, would anyone look into the cause past a brief medical appraisal? These were dangerous times. This would become all too clear in a very short time.

What of Anne, their mother? Did she encourage Philippe in his affinity for dresses and graces, rather than have him become a threat to his brother's reign? Brothers pitted against brothers was as common as croissants at the *boulangerie*. The rivalry between the two would last throughout their lifetimes, yet they were the main constant in each other's company as the world plotted against them.

## Education and Nurturing

And while Anne's rule started off with promise, it was soon recognized that the regent was not the most educated of women. Caring nothing for architecture, reading, the arts, or sciences, Anne preferred to enjoy herself and was seen frequently about Paris. She was not a slave to fashion and made do with her collection of jewelry, preferring a strand of pearls over lavish gemstones. She could hide her lack of intellect through shrewd conversation, playful flirting, and her adroit skills as hostess. Entertainments she could handle. Discussions on politics and diplomacy were fielded over to Mazarin.

It is perhaps due to the regent's own lack of education that meager emphasis was placed on the young king. His old Governess, which he had while his father was still alive, was dismissed by his mother, partly due to the fact the woman had been chosen by Richelieu while he was alive. And so, Mme de Lansac was out and Mme de Sénéce was in as Governess of the Children of France. Sénéce was chosen primarily because she was a friend of Anne's. All positions held within the upper echelon of the royal family came with perks, including money, gifts, and usually a nice apartment. The new Governess was more interested in her place at court than she was with nurturing small minds. It was the Sub-Governess, Mme Lassalle, who actually gave Louis and Philippe the attention they craved. She was happy and fun, often playing make-believe war games, which Louis adored. With fake swords they attacked the royal nursery and sent invisible bad guys to the Bastille. Philippe may have been more enamored with the costumes than the weaponry, yet he too one day would show his merit on the battlefield.

At the age of seven, when the dresses came off and the breeches were buttoned instead, Louis was handed over to a Governor. It was obvious the boy had spent more time in play than in books. He was practically illiterate. He was tutored on all things decorous; how to walk, address an assembly, bow, maintain an air of authority, and defer to the regent. He was praised for his maturity and confidence at such a young age, and his mother would parade her two sons in front of gatherings in all their splendid clothes. The court would applaud the little brothers and especially flourish praise upon the young king. Yet, once they had been displayed, they were shuffled off to their room where the fancy gold embroidered costumes were replaced with simple threads. It was a show, one that Louis took note of, even at the age of seven. He and his brother saw their mother only during her morning *lever* and then they were taken away to be molded by governors and governesses. It was often easier to let the boys play, than to commit them to their studies. Sadly, the brothers would play the same roles in their own children's lives, leaving their sons and daughters to the care of others, only to be trotted out for royal appearances, or when it became time to learn the ways of a king, or become the bride of a political ally.

Anne eventually made Cardinal Mazarin the superintendent of the king's education. Mazarin chose marquis de Villeroy to be the new governor. Villeroy was considered very intelligent, had led armies, and knew the kingdom well. He appointed Abbé de Beaumont to be the little king's tutor. And so, young Louis began his new studies. According to Mme de Motteville: "At that time, he was taught to translate Caesar's Commentaries; he learned how to dance, to draw, to ride horses, and he was as good at all bodily exercises as a prince, whose profession they aren't, should be… The Queen took great care to nurture, in the soul of that young prince… feelings of virtue, wisdom, and piety; she preferred preventing the alterations of his innocence by other men of his age, rather than seeing him more aware of all the things which normally free youth from a certain shyness."

Later reports, including Louis' own words, lamented his lack of education. To learn the arts and dance was one thing, but this child would become the head of a nation. He later showed a fascination with science, and perhaps wished he had been schooled more in its mysteries. He did enjoy learning about French history and its wars.

## A Tragic Move

Anne of Austria's first foray into the political arena met with restrained popularity. The members of the royal family who had been exiled during Louis XIII's reign began to return to Paris, encouraged that Anne's rule would be a more benevolent one. Her old friend, the duchesse de Chevreuse, was reinstated, although watched closely. Marie de Rohan, duchesse de Chevreuse had been embroiled in frequent conspiracies against the monarchy. She was once accused of pressuring Queen Anne to play boisterous games in the corridors of the Louvre while Anne was pregnant. A miscarriage followed. She went on to conspire against the throne and Richelieu, aligning herself with the nobles. Marie went as far as to hatch a plot to replace King Louis XIII with his brother Gaston duc d' Orleans. Her lover, the comte de Chalais, was her co-conspirator and it cost him his head in 1626. Marie fled to Lorraine. Even after her next lover, Charles IV, Duke of Lorraine, intervened on her behalf to have her allowed to return to court, she continued her subversion of royal power. She was at the heart of every intrigue that involved foreign powers against France. Mazarin had also been in her crosshairs during the *cabale des Importants* led by the marquis de Châteauneuf. It seems a strange thing then, that Anne would allow this woman back into the bosom of France. Was the young king watching closely as his mother kept her enemies close to her? Is it a lesson he would remember and implement as he created his new seat of power—Versailles?

Marie de Rohan, duchesse de Chevreuse

If allowing subversive nobles to gain access to her was a questionable move, her next decision could have cost her, and her young sons, their lives. In 1644, Anne moved from the Louvre fortress to the new and relaxed halls of the Palais-Royal; Richelieu's opulent chateau that had been left to the crown in his will. Centered in the heart of Paris, it offered Anne more freedom and a less-restricted schedule. Many saw the move as a dangerous one. There was no moat, defensive outbuildings or walls surrounding the grounds. She may have taken her popularity and the relative quiet Mazarin's station brought to her for granted. Nothing in 17th century France ever remained quiet for long.

Beneath the surface, an underbelly of derisive activity was bubbling and brewing. Old foes reunited to create a unified front against the throne. The nobles, never happy to play a subservient role to anyone, not even a king, put their cards and purses on the table as they plotted their next move. The lower-class poor of Paris went to bed with rumbling stomachs and growing anger at the burden with which the monarchy shackled them. Protestants read their bibles while fearing Catholic reprisal. How many of them had burned at the stake for practicing their religion?

By 1646, it was becoming clear that the sleeping dragons were stirring in their nests. The aristocracy and the parlement, not usually allies, were now joining forces to oppose an absolute monarchy. The aim was to begin by getting Mazarin fired. While not as bombastic and ruthless as Richelieu had been, he continued to support heavy taxes and, like Richelieu, he was Italian. If they toppled Mazarin, surely Anne would be in a weak position and needing a new minister—one they could get behind. But again, they underestimated the regent. Her resolve to see Louis king, and a great king, was all that mattered. In that goal, Mazarin was fully onboard.

Rumors began to fly that perhaps the Queen and her minister had feelings that went beyond running a kingdom. This fueled the fire of hatred toward Mazarin. His powerful alliance with the Queen and her fondness for him gave him, in their view, a dangerous platform of power. It was clear the man wasn't going anywhere.

In 1646, a new force entered the stage of conflict. The old prince de Condé had died. Taking his place as the new Grand Master of France was an arrogant young man called the duc d' Enghien. This new Monsieur de Prince was the King's closest relative except for Louis' uncle, Gaston duc d'Orleans. He was Governor of Burgundy, Berry, and Champagne, and the wealthiest man in the country.

Adept on the battlefield, he wanted control of the navy and army. Flanders was his next obsession and he sought to conquer an independent municipality there.

It was no secret that Condé, as he was now known, hated Mazarin. It was also obvious that he would be a huge ally in the "Topple the Monarchy" camp. The often-underestimated Mazarin sent him off to besiege Lerida, west of Catalonia, Spain, bearing the new title of Viceroy of Catalonia.

Meanwhile, the Parlement continued its campaign to subvert the throne. To garner fractured denizens of France, it became the defender of the poor and oppressed. Here was a body of wealthy men showing an interest in the ragged and ignored body of laborers and common people. The fact that they were exempt from taxes while the unfortunates could barely put bread on the table was overlooked. Outside the shimmering walls of the Palais-Royal, the muddy streets of Paris were teeming with angry mobs.

Anne may have seen the waters of discontent churning, but there would be no compromise. The monarchy would stand. Her son would be the absolute ruler of the people of France. No other governing body would have a say in the infrastructure of taxes, titles, and affairs of state. She and Mazarin held a collective finger to the air, and while feeling the increasing winds that presaged a storm, chose to ignore it. It would be the catalyst of an event that not only haunted Louis XIV for the rest of his life but was the impetus to create a formidable palace *outside* the walls of Paris.

# Chapter Four
# The Fronde

The plots against the Queen, her Prime Minister Mazarin, and a young king permeated into the nooks and secret crannies of Paris. Nobles gathered at their fancy tables and schemed, while the Parlement garnered new recruits to their cause. The tipping point was coming as the Queen balanced precariously on the edge. It was not the time for illness to come calling at the Palais-Royale.

In late September 1647, Philippe, the young prince became ill and for a time it was whispered he might not survive. At seven years of age, any illness in those days could prove fatal and the Queen was beside herself. Her fondness for the boy was never questioned, yet here there was a greater concern when it came to the affairs of the crown. If the young duc d'Anjou died, the scheming Gaston would become heir to the throne should something happen to Louis. The duc d'Orleans had been enough of a threat as the uncle who had plotted to gain control of the young king as his regent, but should Philippe die, Gaston was one step closer to wearing a crown.

To the relief of all but the boy's uncle, Philippe recovered. The happiness was short-lived, as only two months later, on November 10, the young king himself became ill. At first, it seemed a minor ailment, but the next day he was suffering from a high fever. Two days later, it was reported to be smallpox. The Queen was inconsolable as his symptoms worsened. Mme de Motteville duly reported the situation as fear gripped the court:

"The Queen, on this occasion, carried away by her feelings, was unable to put on a public face; and her anxiety showed that she felt a very great love for the king, more so than that for her younger son. The king was given to her by God, after a thousand unfilled longings [four miscarriages], and when she had given up hope. He had rescued her from the wretched state to which Cardinal Richelieu's persecution had brought her. He had made her the regent; and finally, he had been the first to claim her love, so that she only had that left for Monsieur [Philippe] with which nature provides all good mothers."

Francoise Bertaut de Motteville, memoir writer and
Anne of Austria's Lady in Waiting. (1629-1689)

It is interesting to note here that Motteville, who was very close to the Queen, knows that Philippe was perpetually in his older brother's shadow. The television mini-series *Versailles* summed it up in the scene where the two brothers are arguing and Philippe reminds King Louis of the time, they were small and had thrown porridge at each other, which escalated into them "pissing on each other." It was Philippe who got into trouble and not Louis. As Philippe stated in this scene, "You pissed on your brother; I pissed on the King."

Motteville continues in her *Memoirs* concerning the 9-year-old king's illness and the Queen's distress:

"The King's illness now caused her to become ill herself. The feelings of her heart were plain on her face, and I have never seen her so changed in so little time. Two or three days later, she was reassured when the king's fever suddenly went down, and pustules came out abundantly… On the twenty-first, as she was hearing Mass at Notre Dame, suddenly the king felt worse. His fever rose rapidly; he fainted and remained unconscious for three quarters of an hour.

"When the Queen returned and found him thus, she felt the strongest pain, and nearly died herself. For the rest of the day, according to the physicians, he remained in great peril and the Queen never stopped crying. The duc d'Orleans [Gaston] stayed with her, which made her feel even worse; she found neither relief nor consolation in crying in front of him. That evening, the king felt a little better; but the next morning, his illness grew far graver again. On the Sunday, the fourteenth day of his illness, he felt so ill that the physicians no longer expected him to live because since the time of his faint, three days before, the pustules had all gone back in; and although he had been bled four times, his fever was no lower…"

Gaston hovered about the boy's chamber, like a vulture nestled in the frame of the bed's canopy. The physicians placed a bowl beneath the boy's arm and cut it, allowing the blood to freely flow into the vessel. This was supposed to purge the body of the toxins causing the illness. More times than not, it led to the patient's weakening and sometimes death.

The Queen "fainted that day by the King's bed…finally at midnight God gave her back the child who was so dear to her and whose life was so necessary to France."

Gaston, no doubt was making big plans before he heard of the young King's recovery. This was perfect! Both Philippe and Louis had been seriously ill within two months of each other, the Queen herself had become ill from worry, and even now, it was predicted the young King would not survive. Plans began to be put into motion and there was every reason to believe there would be a new King Gaston very soon. His allies rejoiced. They would finally oust that foreigner Mazarin. The Parlement was in discussions to make Gaston and the prince de Condé co-regents over little Philippe once his brother was dead. The nobles would be free to return to their feudal supremacy without being taxed due to the monarch's need for money. The promise of a new France was heady, and the wine flowed.

When the sun rose, the celebration ended. The King was very

much alive, and Mazarin still held the reins to power. The minister had outlasted them again. It had all been within their reach, and as they saw it snatched away again, their anger reached the boiling point. A young boy, laying upon his death bed, had not been oblivious to the fickle and false protestations of love some of his relatives had shown him. It was a lesson he would not forget, and as the days progressed and lightning filled the gathering storm clouds, it would cement in his mind that no one was to be trusted…no one.

## A Dangerous Game

On January 15, 1648, Anne of Austria called together the Parlement in another *lit de justice.* She put before the disgruntled assembly more edicts for registration. But the voice "of the people" rose higher in opposition than normal. The Thirty Years' War had all but drained the country dry from taxes needed to support the ruinous cost of battle. Mazarin, as all ministers, looked to be living in opulence. The fact that the money came from the benefits he derived as a cardinal and were ecclesiastical and not derived from taxes, fell on deaf ears. The finances were a mess. People were breaking beneath the yoke of continuing taxation for a war that seemed as if it would never end.

The Parlement took a stand, shocking the Queen. Omer Talon stood and declared there would now be a different way to handle things. The Parlement would look over new edicts and *they* would decide if they would be enforced or not. It was an unprecedented move against the monarchy. The king had always had final say. As young King Louis XIV sat upon his cushion and listened to the betrayal around him, Talon continued, touting the immense burden the poor of France were suffering. They were just getting warmed up.

The Parlement took its most dramatic stand yet. It ignored the *lit de justice* and refused to enter the new edicts into registration. One must wonder if such a rebellion would have occurred if an adult king stood before them instead of a female regent and a boy monarch. Anne's authority appeared more as a paper crown, and Louis seemed hardly a threat at such a tender age. The Queen, enraged, shot back. She announced the edict declaring the Parlement's offices hereditary (as put into effect by the late Henry XIV) was no longer in force. This was a huge blow. These offices assured the members' families financial support in perpetuity. They were also exempt from taxation. Now, with a flourish of her gown's sleeve, the Queen took it all away.

The gauntlets had been tossed down. The Parlement retaliated by reaching out to three other councils: the Grand Conseil, the Cour des Comptes and the Cour des Aides. They proposed that all four councils join forces and become one body to protest the right of the throne to act as a supreme monarchy. While Mazarin declared that what they were doing was illegal, they ignored him and on June 16, the new merger was in place. Their first bold move was to set forth new regulations concerning the king. He could no longer arrest or detain people at his will; the Parlement would vote on the legality of any proposed taxes; and, even more disastrous to the French monarchy's continued emphasis on conquests, it took away a quarter of the money going toward the military's expenses. The Parlement had moved its game piece and was ready to declare Check Mate. Anne and Mazarin had other plans.

To stave off further revolt, Anne gave the appearance of accepting the constitutional reforms put forth by the Parlement with its new union of the sovereign courts of Paris. Meanwhile, Louis II de Bourbon, Prince de Condé and Louis XIVs cousin (also known as the duc de'Enghein), who was leading France's largest army, attained another victory for the throne by capturing Lens. Within three months, the *Treaty of Westphalia* was signed, finally extinguishing the hopes of the Austrian Habsburgs. France also garnered the province of Alsace and won the role of arbiter in a divided Germany. Strengthened by the victory, Mazarin suddenly arrested the leaders of the Parlement and had them imprisoned on August 20, 1648. Paris broke into insurrection and barricaded the streets.

The noble faction demanded the calling of an assembly of the Estates General which had not been convoked since 1615. The Estates General represented three classes: the clergy, the noble, and the lower class or *bourgeois* element. Anne and Mazarin were outnumbered without any military force at their disposal. She had no choice but to release the prisoners as Paris erupted around her.

The situation had become threatening. Mobs surrounded the Palais-Royal as royal troops were blocked by chains and barricades. Anne called on Monsieur le Prince (Condé) to return to Paris now that he was no longer needed on the battlefront. Condé was a Prince of the Blood. His father, Henri II, was a first cousin-once-removed of Henry XIV, the King of France, and his mother was an heiress of one of France's leading ducal families. He was of the house of Bourbon. He would defend the Queen, but not without cutting out a piece of victory for himself. He rounded up his vast army and headed back toward Paris.

Louis II, Prince d'Condé

While Condé was Anne's man, he was also a man of immense ambition. His victories in war, his wealth, properties, and heritage only inflated an already greedy disposition. The Queen needed him. He knew the primary players in the Fronde; indeed, many were his relations. Why not take the opportunity to play both fields and come out the hero? He approached the Parlement and played the role of arbiter between the monarchy and the incensed body of officials. What he negotiated was not what the Queen had hoped for. Anne, with tears flowing, was forced to sign a declaration accepting the constitution put forth by the Parlement on October 22nd. Mazarin began plotting his next move.

Although the Parlement rejoiced over its new concession by the throne, tensions remained high. The Queen and her small king were basically powerless at the moment. The hatred about them was palpable. They had returned to the Palais-Royal, but it was still within Paris' boundaries. They needed to secretly escape.

Anne of Austria protects her son Louis XIV during the Fronde.

On January 5, 1649, the plan was put into motion. According to Mme de Motteville, who witnessed it all, it began with the closing of the gates of the Palais-Royal. "The necessary orders were given to the captains of the guard… The maréchal de Villeroy allowed the king to sleep until three in the morning; then he roused him, along with Monsieur [Gaston], and brought them to the carriage which was waiting for them at the garden gate of the Palais-Royal. The Queen joined the King and Monsieur."

It must have been a stressful arrangement to have Gaston accompany them. It was no secret that he backed the Parlement. Still, the late King had given him certain rights and powers, and his place was wherever little Louis XIV went. Mazarin had arranged a rendezvous point at the Cours la Reine, away from the walls of Paris.

He, along with the rest of the royal family were waiting there. The others had been given no warning as to the escape plans, and as they stood there in the chill of the early morning hours, they were ignorant of the trying days ahead. As the King's furnishings and household goods tended to travel with him and the Court as they moved from residence to residence, there were no accommodations waiting for them at the other end of the secret escape route.

Mme de Motteville continues: "Once all the royal House was assembled, they drove off to Saint-Germain-en-Laye. The king, the Queen and the Court found themselves there without beds, without attendants, without linens, without any of the things needed for the service of the royal family. The Queen, upon her arrival, went to sleep in a small bed which Cardinal Mazarin had sent out from Paris a few days earlier for this purpose. In the same way, he had provided for the king, and there were further, two small camp beds, one of which he gave Monsieur [Gaston] and the other which he kept for himself. Madame la duchesse d'Orleans [Gaston's wife] slept that night on a bunch of straw as did Mademoiselle [Gaston's oldest daughter]. All those who had followed the Court shared the same fate; and within a few hours, straw had become so expensive in Saint Germain that it could no longer be found at any price."

In February, news reached the Queen that a civil uprising in England had just resulted in the beheading of King George I. This must have struck terror in the regent as it was no less than a civil war that had driven her from Paris. Condé's army was there, maintaining some sense of control, yet that very prince had let power go to his head. In front of the little king, he treated the Queen with total disrespect and took control of the situation at Saint-Germain. Young Louis watched as this all played out. Due to the civil uprising in Paris, no taxes were being paid and the royal family was reduced to penury. The royal jewels had to be pledged in order to buy food and supplies.

Of all the lessons Louis XIV learned as a youth, it was this one that would forge his resolve for his future reign. He had watched the nobles exert authority over him...HIM...ordained by God to lead France! He was forced to flee in the night and live like a prisoner, while his cousin strutted about with total disdain for the Queen, and therefore, to himself as well. Louis XIV declared to himself he would create an empire so impenetrable and so absolute in its authority, that these rich lords of France would bow before him, and indeed, turn to him for the very food they ate.

The Parlementary Fronde (1648-1649)

The Second Fronde, the Fronde of Princes ran for three years from 1650-1653. It was a scramble for power and control of patronage, losing all trace of its first constitutional phase. The leaders were discontented princes and nobles: Gaston, Duke of Orleans [the king's uncle]; the great Louis II, Prince de Condé and his brother Armand, Prince of Conti; Frederic, the Duke of Bouillon and his brother Henri, Viscount of Turenne. There were also female conspirators, namely Gaston's daughter, Mademoiselle de Montpensier; Condé's sister, Madame de Longueville; Madame de Chevreuse [back to her old tricks]; and the astute intriguer Jean Francois Paul de Gondi, the future Cardinal de Retz.

These were the nobles surrounding the Queen and Louis XIV; traitors living in their Court while conspiring behind their backs. The merry-go-round of loyalties was dizzying. One moment, a close intimate had your back. The next, he had put together an army against you. Louis, who was now eleven years old had front row seats to the deception and betrayal from his relatives and entire families of nobility. It was a first-hand education not found in dusty books or at a tutor's knee.

The two warring parties signed *The Peace of Rueil* on March 16, 1649; it lasted until the end of 1649. Once back at court, the princes renewed their intrigues against Mazarin. On January 14, 1650, Cardinal Mazarin, having come to an understanding with Monsieur Gondi and Madame de Chevreuse, suddenly arrested Condé, Conti, and Longueville. Turenne, who had led many wars for the realm, was now against it. He headed an armed rebellion to rescue Madame de Longueville's brothers, particularly Condé, who had fought beside him in the battles of Freiburg and Nördlingen. War broke out between Tureen and his army and Mazarin's troops alongside Plessis-Praslin. The battle of December 15, 1650 was severe and for a time doubtful, but Turenne's Frondeurs gave way in the end, and his army, as an army, ceased to exist. Turenne himself, undeceived as to the part he was playing in the drama, asked and received the young king's pardon, and meantime the court, with *maison de roi* and other loyal troops, had subdued the minor risings without difficulty (March-April 1651).

Condé, Conti, and Longueville were released, and by April 1651 the rebellion had everywhere collapsed. Then followed a few months of hollow peace and the Court left Saint-Germain and returned to Paris. It was not to say that anarchy was not still rife. Mazarin, hated still, was forced to leave Paris twice, as small rebellions continued, with Condé leading the fray. It was the lower classes, quarreling with the princes that permitted the king to enter the city on October 21, 1652. King Louis XIV asked Mazarin to return, unopposed, in February 1653.

While the two Frondes entailed many more battles and skirmishes during the Franco-Spanish War, with Turenne and Condé squaring off against each other continually, the rebellions finally gasped their last as resources and passions were depleted.

Another event which occurred during this time did much to change the circumstances of France—Louis XIV turned thirteen on September 5, 1651 and was now eligible to take over the crown. For France, tired and direly in need of guidance, this was a moment to celebrate. According to Mme de Motteville a great parade passed along the streets of Paris to herald the new king. "His Majesty, dressed in clothes so heavily embroidered with gold that one could see neither the fabric nor the color, seemed so tall that it was hard to believe he was not yet fourteen." Anne of Austria officially handed over the reins to her son during a séance royale in front of the Parlement, ending her regency. Louis XIV modestly said to her within the hearing of all gathered, "Madame, I thank you for the care you were pleased to take of my education and the administration of my realm. Pray continue giving me your advice; I wish that after myself, you be the head of my Council." And with that, Louis XIV looked out at his battle-weary Paris, damaged and broken, and took the helm.

Before the age of fourteen, the king was demonstrating just how formidable he could be. He had witnessed the humiliations born by his mother at the hands of Parlement, and the civil wars to which they had been party. Thus, to the surprise of many in attendance at a recent delegation, Louis took the remonstrances the Parlement handed him and tore them up without reading them. Likewise, when the royal princes sent their embassies to him with propositions that would result in their favor, Louis told them to take it up with his Prime Minister, Mazarin. Infuriated, they told the king they were told not to deal with the minister. The king quietly told them to follow him, and he led them, in person to Mazarin.

Louis XIV was proving he was no puppet king. He witnessed the destruction all about him caused by the civil war. Villages were decimated, innocent lives taken, rape, pillaging and utter destruction of homes, farms, and businesses had left the country shell-shocked. This was his France. He would be absolute in his power. Looking out on the suffering of his people touched him deeply. His displeasure was poured out in an April letter to Turenne who was acting as his Commander in Chief as the War continued:

"I receive complaints from every quarter," Louis wrote, "about the extreme disorders caused by the troops in my army… who pillage through towns and country and do not even spare noble houses." In May, he wrote again: "It is with great displeasure that I have received a complaint from the inhabitants of Melun, which is that on the eleventh of this month sixty to eighty German calvary men, or some other foreign troops belonging to my army, of which you are in command, took a hundred and fifty cows from the neighborhood of the same town whose inhabitants had already lost several plow horses which were taken from them; and when several of the most notable men of this town went with the poor people to whom the cows belonged, all of them unarmed, to recover them from the soldiers who had stolen them, offering money, they killed in cold blood several of the said inhabitants and of the poor people who were with them."

On October 20, 1652, the King, Queen and the Court were met in Paris with "the acclamations of the crowds and shouts of "Long Live the King" from all the people, who surrounded his Majesty's return with all the greater affection that he was bringing them the only possibility of living in peace after so many calamities." Oliver Lefevre d'Ormesson, a magistrate continued: "The next day, the King met his Parlement in the Gallery of the Louvre; he had a general amnesty registered in his presence, as well as the reunion of the two Parlements, that of Paris and that of Pontoise; he declared the exile of some twelve conseillers who had been particularly violent Frondeurs; he forbade the Parlement ever to discuss the affairs of the state again without his permission; he ordered that no one serve the princes or accept a pension from them; and finally he called the great nobles to come and render their respects to him within three days... The very next day, the Bastille was turned over to the King. This return of the King's is a miracle, a work of God," Ormesson declared in his diary.

Louis was just warming up. The duc d'Orleans, his very Uncle Gaston, was ordered to leave and retire to his castle in Blois, where he remained for the next six years. We can almost hear Anne and Mazarin's collective sighs of relief. Gaston's daughter, Mademoiselle de Montpensier, was exiled to her estate at Saint Fargeau after leading several insurrections against the king. The estate was a week's ride away from Paris, where she had tried in vain, to remain. Also in the king's crosshairs were the ducs de Beaufort and de Rohan who were also exiled.

After enduring years of poverty and neglect, "the King settled into the Louvre for good, having learned from the untoward events of the Palais Royal that private, moat-less houses were not for him." As for Condé, that royal prince who had instigated so many rebellions against the king, he was now called forth. Louis remembered how the prince had openly humiliated Mazarin in front of the Queen and himself by mocking the minister, pulling on his beard, and even slapping him. At first, Condé was forced to leave France to be appointed Commander in Chief of the Spanish armies. Louis wasted no time banishing him. His estates in France were seized and, on March 27, 1653, the Parlement ordered him to be beheaded for treason, showing once again how fickle the winds of politics could be.

And Mazarin, that hapless yet determined minister, found himself besieged with requests from the Parlement for his protection—the very men who had refused to see him or declare his authority only a short time earlier. To prove just how cemented the prime minister was now in public opinion and the Court's, his Italian niece married Condé's brother, the prince de Conti, who had been paramount in the Fronde uprising. The carousel of intrigues that constituted the Frondes had come full circle. It would not be the last time rebellions broke out in Paris, but it would be the last time the nobles tried to usurp the supreme monarchy of France.

Execution of Charles I, King of England

Louis XIV had accomplished what Charles I of England had not;

he had crushed the civil uprising and restored the crown. The gory painting showing the beheading of that English King would haunt the monarchs of France and even find its way into the bedroom of the future king, Louis XVI as a warning of what happens to kings who ignore their subjects' plights.

Condé escaped execution as he allied himself with Spain. Despite victory over Turenne at Valenciennes in 1656, a defeat at the Battle of Dunes in June 1658 led to the *Treaty of the Pyrenees* in 1659. This included a pardon for Condé and restoration to his previous titles, but his power was largely broken, and he did not hold another military command until 1667.

The Franco-Spanish War lasted until 1659, at which time Louis had turned twenty-one. He was mature beyond his years even as a teenager, but now, he had grown into his crown and taken the lessons he learned from the Fronde with him into what would become one of the more-audacious moves in history.

"Louis XIV Crushes the Fronde" by Gilles Guerin 1654

# Chapter Five
# **The Sun King Rises**

Louis XIV's childhood came to an end with the outbreak of the Fronde. He had witnessed betrayal, fear, and poverty at the very hands of those who should have protected him as the future king. Only his mother and Mazarin had kept him safe and fought to keep his throne intact. He realized there was no surety in a handshake or title; that a friend today would stab you in the back tomorrow; and that even bloodlines meant very little. For a young boy, it was a lot to try to comprehend. His family home had, at times, become a prison and he had to flee Paris, the very seat of the monarchy. The Fronde years instilled in Louis a hatred for Paris and consequent determination to move out of the ancient capital as soon as possible, never to return.

1655 portrait of young Louis, the Victor of the Fronde, portrayed as the god of Jupiter.

For now, Louis XIV was firmly ensconced in the Louvre. The civil war was over, and he felt peace for the first time. In 1652, the young man did what most youth do at the age of fourteen in that era, he hunted, danced, enjoyed music, and plays, and…discovered the pleasures of the female sex.

While engaging in sexual affairs at fourteen may sound a bit promiscuous to modern standards, people in that era were often married at that age, as was the case with Marie Antoinette. Louis XVI was only fifteen when they were wed in 1770. In France especially, a king's virility was a sign of strength and encouraged, within reason. And so, with all vigilance, Louis began a few dalliances and enjoyed his new freedom.

Meanwhile, Mazarin, who began life at Court as a meek and malleable minister to first Louis XIII and then to Anne of Austria, had let his recent victories go to his head. Suddenly, he was the man to see. He was approached with requests for promotions, pensions, and other honors, often delegating them without the Queen's consent. As with royal cardinals before him, his coffers filled. Richelieu's wealth had been demonstrated in luxurious chateaus, rare works of art, gold, silver, and jewels. Cardinal Woolsey, Henry VIII's right-hand man, had amassed such wealth that Ann Boleyn often hissed into Henry's ear that his minister was the richest man in England. Indeed, Cardinal Woolsey's home, Hampton Court, was a marvel, and after his arrest, was handed over to Ann Boleyn and became a royal residence. Today, it is the only royal home that hosted all six of Henry VIII's wives during their individual reigns.

Mazarin, by 1658, was pulling down a salary of 793,570 livres (equal to $6.5 million) yearly. His cumulative wealth, not counting his own respectable collection of art, rare books, and artifacts, was over 8 million livres (about $65 million). As his power and status grew, close confidants of the queen noticed she was showing a slight cooling toward the cardinal.

It was in 1653 that Mazarin played many roles in the 15-year-old king's life. Louis was content to let the minister handle the boring day-to-day running of the court, while he indulged in more pleasurable pursuits. This is not to say that he was not still being tutored by the minister. Indeed, Louis could hardly have asked for a better education than to be privy to Mazarin's machinations at the helm of the monarchy. This was the education the young man needed—hand's on exposure to politics and negotiations.

## The Coronation of Louis XIV

Louis XIV's Coronation 1654

On June 7, 1654, Louis was crowned king in Reims, at the young age of fifteen. As you can see in his coronation painting, he still had the face of a young teen, yet he was touted as being confident and imposing. The coronation ceremony was filled with the pomp and tradition associated with the induction of a new realm. Louis XIV was anointed with the oil from the Holy Ampulla, a balm that was reported to have been brought down by an angel a thousand years earlier. This oil gave the king a specific status and it was even believed that he was able to heal a type of skin disease (scrofula) with his touch. The scepter and the hand of justice were given to him by the Archbishop of Reims, the crown placed upon his head, and a new era in the French monarchy began. *"Vivat Rex in aeternum"* filled the Reims Cathedral as those present raised their voices in celebration of the new king. Louis was now truly "God Given" as his mother had always told him. The reign of Louis XIV is often referred to as "Le Grand Siècle" (the Great Century). As he took the throne, Louis swore to defend the Catholic faith, a declaration that would result in anarchy within the walls of his perfect Palace of Versailles.

It was Anne of Austria who gave Louis his belief in the absolute and divine power of his monarchical rule. A passage in his journal proved his love and appreciation for his mother's guidance and unwavering love:

"Nature was responsible for the first knots which tied me to my mother. But attachments formed later by shared qualities of the spirit are far more difficult to break than those formed merely by blood."

King Louis XIV's Royal Monogram

Louis still leaned heavily on Mazarin's advice. He had much to learn, and a war was still going on against Spain. He had survived two civil uprisings, exile, and a reversal of fortune, only to suddenly be hailed as "Louis, the God Given." Yet, the king was far from being a "playing card king," as his mother had once lamented during the Parlement's betrayal during the Fronde. That body of law would get its first taste of what a teenage king would tolerate.

Mme de Motteville took to her pen and recorded a faithful account of one such event. It was the spring of 1654:

"The Parlement, which felt humiliated only because it could no longer resist the king's power, tried, now and again, to recover its strength; there were even some occasions when police measures and the king's service forced it to come together; but since these assemblies had been so harmful to France, and that very word 'assembly' being odious to the Minister, the King stopped them, and came from the Vincennes forest wearing his riding boots to forbid these assemblies.

"As he walked in, His Majesty showed only too clearly in his expression the anger he felt in his heart. 'Everyone knows,' he said in a voice less pleasant and graceful than usual, 'the troubles your assemblies have brought upon the state, and the dangerous consequences they have had. I have learned that you expect to go on with them, taking as your pretext a deliberation on the edicts which have been read and published in my presence. I have come here for the sole purpose [pointing directly at the Messieurs of the Enquêtes, one of the tribunals of the Parlement] of forbidding you to go on with them, as I do now absolutely; and I forbid you, Monsieur le Premier president [the chief magistrate appointed by the king to whom he also pointed] to allow or grant them no matter how much the Enquêtes may ask for them.' After that, His Majesty, having risen immediately before anyone else had spoken a word, returned to the Louvre and from there to Vincennes."

The Parlement may well have been shocked to see the new king in his hunting apparel, as indeed, he had come straight from the hunt in the woods of Vincennes to dispel yet another assembly of the grumbling Parlement. There was no warning, no show of pomp, only a young 15-year-old king who had had enough! With anger in his voice and a jabbing finger in their direction, Louis left no doubt who was in charge. Mazarin, no doubt looked on with approval. It would not be the last time the king's bellowing voice thundered against the several *chambres* composing the Parlement.

As the war with Spain continued, it was apparent that both provinces were battle-weary and practically bankrupt from the military expense. France did finally regain all the territory it had lost while the double fronde's were assaulting Paris. Louis XIV was learning more about the military and the strategies of war. He met with his troops in person and spent a great deal of time with them, learning more in their midst than he would have from home. He was kept away from the front lines, as his role as king was to be safeguarded.

A major victory was won on August 25, 1654, as the Spanish army was besieging Arras. Turenne returned the favor by besieging the Spanish army and won. None other than the Grand Condé was heading the troops for Spain, and after a frenzied effort, was forced back and defeated. Thus encouraged, Mazarin to set his scope on England as an ally to finally wrap up this ongoing war. Cromwell had made England a powerful country, one to be contended with. Mazarin put together his proposal and presented it to England, wrapped up in a pretty bow. If England would help the French, they would take Dunkerque together. France would then gift that city to England, giving them a port in Flanders. The treaty was signed on November 8, 1655.

From there, the English navy, under the command of Admiral Blake overtook Spanish treasure ships near the Canary Islands and scuttled them. This was a death blow to Spain who was in financial ruin. Without the treasure ships, they were left without funds for the troops fighting in Flanders. Following hard on the heels of this victory, the English blockaded Dunkerque as six thousand of its soldiers joined Turenne. On June 14, 1658, the Battle of the Dunes' death knell sounded for Spain. The Franco-British, under Turenne, had crushed the army of Don Juan of Austria, and Spain waved the white flag of defeat.

The cries of victory were still ringing throughout Paris when the unthinkable happened: Louis XIV fell gravely ill. It happened only a week after the Spanish defeat at the Battle of the Dunes. The king was at Calais and was diagnosed with scarlet fever. His condition remained perilous for two weeks, with the Court in perpetual fear. Those who were majorly suffering the pain and fear for his life were his mother, Anne, and his younger brother, Philippe. Motteville recounts:

"...the Queen felt all the anguish which her great love for him was bound to cause... Monsieur [Philippe was now given the tile of Monsieur as his brother was crowned King] showed her the greatest affection possible and seemed very frightened of losing his brother. When the Queen told him he must no longer visit for fear of catching his disease, he started to cry and...it was a long time before he could say a word."

The vultures once again circled, and despite Philippe's grief, took this opportunity to begin trying to sway him to begin means to dispatch the minister should the king die. To Philippe's credit, he shunned their entreaties, even though one of the men pushing him was his closest friend, the comte de Guiche.

The king, to the delight of his mother and brother, recovered. Balls were held at the Louvre, and sometimes Louis came masked so that he could amuse himself without the typical etiquette that followed him everywhere. He played the part of Apollo in several ballets and hosted extravagant equestrian contests and performances.

Louis XIV, in 1655, was now sixteen. He had already noticed Mazarin's nieces who were often at court. He had had a short fling with Hortense Mancini in 1653, before she was married off to the comte de Soissons of the House of Savoy. Mazarin's other niece, Marie Mancini would soon prove a more formidable conquest. In the meantime, Anne of Austria kept the young king entertained and allowed his forays into innocent flirtations. There did come a time, however, when the royal mother had to remind her cub of his duties. According to Mme de Motteville, there was a royal gathering thrown by the Queen where young Louis rebelled against etiquette:

"One evening, the Queen asked the Queen of England to come and see the King dance in private... and made sure that the company, though small, was worthy of the royal guests. The king, who was all too accustomed to putting the cardinal's nieces first, asked Mme de Mercoeur to dance to the first *branle* with him. The Queen, who was surprised by this mistake, rose quickly from her chair, pushed Mme de Mercoeur away from him and told him to go back and ask the princess of England [Henrietta of England]. Later that evening, he was again scolded by his mother, but he answered that he did not like little girls."

## Marie Mancini

In 1658, Louis began an intrigue with one of Mazarin's nieces, Marie Mancini. He was now nineteen years old. Anne, for a time, thought little of it. It was a young man's fancy, not unlike his friendship with Hortense Mancini in 1653, but it soon became clear this was no passing fling. The king had fallen in love. The two were inseparable, and if they were parted, the love letters flew back and forth as fast as the courier could bring them. As their romance heated up, Anne and Mazarin began to despair. Marie was not a political alliance that was sought as a bride for Louis. The two were parted on two separate occasions, only to continue declaring their love in writing.

Marie Mancini by Jacob Ferdinand Voet.

Cruelly, Marie was used by the queen and the minister in an attempt to force Anne's brother, Philip IV of Spain, to pledge his daughter in marriage to Louis by seeing Marie as a possible contender for his affections. They allowed Marie to travel with Louis and be seen by his side. This only gave Marie hope, and she felt assured she would be the next Queen of France. Louis had even mentioned marriage to her. As Philip IV hesitated, looking over his political and military positioning, the situation between Marie and the king continued to heat up. He gave her an expensive string of pearls worth 70,000 livres (over half a million dollars). Finally, Anne put a stop to it. She convinced Mazarin that it was necessary to marry Marie off and get her "out of town." The candidate was an Italian prince, Lorenzo Onofrio Colonna and they were duly married in Italy. The prince remarked after their wedding night that he was surprised to find Marie still a virgin. The bridegroom had not expected to find a conquest of Louis XIV's still "untouched."

While one might suppose Mazarin would have been in favor of Louis' love for his niece, he supported the queen's position for both dynastic and political reasons. He knew her support for his power and his foreign policy depended on making peace with Spain from a strong position and on a Spanish marriage. All of Louis' tears to his mother did not make her change her mind. The Spanish marriage was very important both for its role in ending the war between France and Spain, and because many of the claims and objectives of Louis' foreign policy in the next 50 years would be based on this union.

# Chapter Six
## Dynasties and Marriages

Louis XIV suffered the loss of Marie Mancini long after she was sent away. They continued corresponding until Mazarin appealed to the king in a letter shortly before they were to set off for Saint Jean de Luz to sign a treaty with Spain which became known as the Treaty of the Pyrenees. A major clause would be the marriage of the Spanish Infanta to Louis XIV. On July 12, 1659, Mazarin wrote to the heartbroken king and reminded him of his love for him, and the position given him by the late King Louis XIII and Anne of Austria to lead and protect the king. The letter was written in a soft tone, yet one that left no room for misunderstanding.

"…in the present situation, you owe it also to yourself," Mazarin wrote, "you are about to set off to carry out something which cannot occur if you continue this sad relationship, which causes you a greater wrong than if the person in question were at court and if you were behaving to her as you did in Paris…And since I care even more for your honor than for that which can affect me the most directly, I cannot refrain from telling you this…I beg your pardon if I press you to do something which, at first will go against your inclinations and hope you will believe I would give my life so as to be able only to suggest things that would be pleasant to you."

This may have been the first realization for a king just turning twenty-one years of age, that although the crown sat firmly upon his head, his will fell within the parameters of duty. In the seventeenth century, duty was paramount. The pages of history have relentlessly stamped in ink the rise and fall of monarchs who lead with their hearts and not their heads. It was a lesson in reality for a young leader who had only just felt the heady sense of power his title, looks, and prowess bestowed upon him. A hand had been put before his face, and no demonstrations of rebellion would move it. He would marry the Infanta of Spain, and Marie would remain in Italy as another man's wife.

On August 13, 1659, Mazarin met the Spanish Prime Minister Don Luis de Haro, on an island in the middle of Bidassoa, a symbolic and literal geographic divider between France and Spain. Even as the minister negotiated the terms of the treaty, Louis, who had not yet joined him, continued to write to Marie. He spoke of nothing but her to those in his confidence. He was in agony. When Mazarin found out and remonstrated the king in letters, in which he criticized his niece for her thoughtlessness in continuing with the romance, Louis began to rebel. Mazarin had even threatened to resign as Louis' prime minister if the affair continued. They underestimated a proud king in love.

Mazarin had assigned M. du Terron to look after his niece Marie in Italy. When the minister found out Terron had actually been encouraging Marie's correspondence with the king, he erupted. He wrote to Jean-Baptiste Colbert, his assistant, in a rage:

"So, a relationship which had altogether ended after all the efforts I made to that end (going even so far as to tell the King I would resign and meant to leave everything and take ship with my nieces to go wherever I could if he did not break with her) is now about to start again, more than ever, because of the said Terron who, in one word, has tried thus to make his fortune," Mazarin wrote to Colbert.

Mazarin's blackmail failed. Louis, incensed at his minister's continual meddling and threats, did the unthinkable. In a heated moment, Louis accepted Mazarin's resignation. Mazarin, standing on an island with the Spanish mediator, negotiations flying that would impact the future of France, gritted his teeth, and continued on as if Louis had said nothing to him. Once the cardinal was alone, he went after his niece who finally gave in to his insistence that the affair end for the good of France and the king's duty. Marie sent off a letter to her beloved, and renounced her claim to his heart, freeing him finally to marry elsewhere. Louis broke into tears and was inconsolable.

On November 7, 1659, the Treaty of Pyrenees was signed. With the flourish of a pen, Louis XIV was betrothed to the Infanta of Spain and became the most-powerful monarch in Europe. The king, far from feeling celebratory, gave way to his feelings of despair.

Treaty of the Pyrenees November 7, 1659.

While 1659 may have ended in ruins for Louis XIV in the department of romance, all the other planets in his reign seemed to be aligning in readiness for the year 1660. The Treaty of Pyrenees had been skillfully crafted by Mazarin, despite the drama that played out between king and cardinal over the Marie Mancini affair. France now owned two Mediterranean provinces—Roussillon and Cerdagne—and an important northern province, Artois, along with six or so fortresses. A key clause, artfully inserted into the treaty by the cardinal, would prove to be a huge military coup for Louis in the coming years. The caveat stated that the Infanta, upon marrying Louis XIV, would give up her rights to Spain and its empire, along with rights of succession for any of her offspring. In exchange, Philip IV would pay France a dowry of 500,000 gold ecru. Reasonable enough. Large dowries were always attached to the bride's concessions. The problem, for Spain anyway, was that the

Thirty Years' War had left it bankrupt. The dowry was not paid, perhaps pledged when the coffers filled again, but the salient point is that this left the door open to future demands from France. Philip IV was in poor health, as was his only son. Mazarin had done well, and France was now in a powerful position for future expansion of its empire.

The details of the marriage between King Louis XIV and Maria Thresa of Spain now began in earnest. As was the custom, the marriage by proxy was the first part of the ceremonial itinerary. This was held in Fuenterrabia. Her father and the entire Spanish court accompanied the bride to the Isle of Pheasants on the border of France and Spain in the Bidasoa river. Louis and his court met her in the meeting on the Isle of Pheasant on June 7, 1660. She had now entered France and her new country. On June 9, the marriage took place in Saint-Jean-de-Luz at the recently rebuilt church of Saint Jean the Baptist.

The Treaty of the Pyrenees with Louis XIV and Philipe IV of Spain at the meeting on the Isle of Pheasants.

Mme de Motteville gives us our usual snapshot of the occasion as the bridegroom and bride first see each other. "After Louis XIV had looked at the Infanta, he left... As he went out, he told M. le prince de Conti and M. de Turenne that, at first, he had been surprised by the frightful coiffure and dress of the Infanta; but once he looked at her carefully, he had realized that she was quite beautiful."

Maria Therese of Spain was fair of complexion with blue eyes and blond hair. She was rather short and had a prominent nose and lower lip, but all-in-all, Louis found her pleasing to look at. She was nothing like his lost Marie, who had been described as thin and tall, with dark eyes and hair. Marie's smile was said to dazzle, and she sparkled with intelligence and wit. Louis' new bride was rather dull-witted and docile. She gave the air of being totally malleable to the king's will, which many saw as perfect attributes of the future queen. There would be no plotting or dominating personality to deal with. Yet, it was this lack of fire and spunk that would lead Louis to find that challenge and excitement in others' beds as his reign progressed.

One other obstacle was that Maria spoke no French, and Louis only a smattering of Spanish. Even in later years, when Maria had mastered the French language, her heavy Spanish accent left no doubt as to her origin.

On June $6^{th}$, the two kings met and before a glittering assembly declared to uphold the peace the recently signed treaty had demanded. On the following day, the Infanta made her regal entrance into France in a golden carriage, dressed in crimson silk with gold and silver embroidery. The Church of Saint Jean de Luz was draped in finery as Louis XIV arrived wearing gold cloth covered with a black veil. The court was still mourning the recent loss of Gaston d'Orleans, Louis' rebellious Uncle, hence the black veil.

For the actual ceremony, Maria Therese had changed into a silver brocade dress along with a velvet purple cloak embroidered with the French fleur-de-lis and was wearing a crown. Anne of Austria, dressed in black, looked on with pride at a union she had worked so hard to facilitate. All her protection of her son, through uprisings and illness, had culminated in this historic wedding day. It was a political union, but so much more. Producing an heir would be the key focus of the young couple, and hopefully, years of stability and love. Anne may have thought back to her own unhappiness with Louis XIII—a husband that despised her, and of her many miscarriages. She may have offered a silent prayer that this marriage would be blessed and happy.

Marriage ceremony of Louis XIV and Maria Therese

If Anne of Austria heaved a sigh of relief and celebration at the carefully orchestrated nuptials of her son and his Spanish queen, it was short-lived. Louis, fresh from the altar, threw his mother and Cardinal Mazarin a curveball.

Wedding celebration at Saint Jean de Luz

It seemed as if everything was going to plan. The king and his new bride were put to bed early on their wedding night. Breaking with tradition, Anne made sure they were left alone, rather than the usual humiliating bedding ceremony where half the court watched the newlyweds climb into bed. Louis, it was said, seemed eager for the consummation of the marriage to begin.

The following morning, as Anne and the rest of the court eagerly awaited signs that the couple had found favor in each other's company, Louis announced they would share a room on the long journey back to Paris. Maria looked flush with victory, and it was said she had fallen deeply in love with her new husband. As the convoy of coaches made its way back to the Louvre, people lined the streets and cheered. At every stop there were celebratory banquets and fetes. To all appearances, Louis was happy and content in his new role as husband. And so, it was with much surprise and fear that his next announcement was received. During the wedding celebrations, Louis dropped his bombshell.

One of the stops along the route home was Saintes, near Bourdeaux. The king told the royal wedding party that the queens (his mother and Marie) were to journey on to Saint Jean d'Angély without him. Taking only four of his men with him, he announced he would take a side trip and visit the city of La Rochelle, where a strategic port was located. While a king pausing to inspect an important seaport would hardly raise an eyebrow, it was La Rochelle's close proximity to Brouage, Marie Mancini's former residence, that caused the Queen Mother's heart to race. All felt that the marriage was a sure sign that Louis's affections for Marie were in the past.

After inspecting the fleet at La Rochelle, Louis did indeed make the short trip of only a few miles to Brouage. Here, he walked the beach throughout the night and wept. When news of it was relayed to the Queen Mother and the cardinal, they feared the worst. It didn't matter that Marie had been married off. So had her sister, yet Olympe had become Louis' mistress despite being someone else's wife. No one doubted that Marie, with her heart still filled with love for the king, would follow suit. Once again, Mazarin and Anne of Austria resorted to trickery to thwart any attempts by the pair to get together.

Gossip began to fly that Marie's heart was now devoted to

another—Prince Charles of Lorraine. The rumors had her throwing herself at him with wanton abandon. For Louis XIV, a man of great pride who had never lost a conquest in the romantic arena, it was enough to douse the flames of passion he had for the Princess Colonna. The fact that the rumors were lies, concocted by his scheming mother and prime minister, were not known to him. He believed it all. Marie, ignorant of what had happened, was confused by Louis' cold demeanor to her when she met the king at the Chateau of Fontainebleau. It was over.

The wedding procession moved on and entered the gates of Paris on August 26. To the sound of cheers and fireworks, Louis, upon a prancing horse, and Marie sitting in an open golden coach, waved to the crowds. Speeches were made and the denizens of France saw in this strikingly handsome and charismatic man, all their future hopes for a prosperous and peaceful country. Former enemies who had instigated the Frondes now cheered and praised the monarch whom they had diligently tried to root out only a few years prior. It was a triumph not only for the king, but for the two people who had plotted and fought so hard to see this day unfold—Anne of Austria and Cardinal Mazarin.

Louis had done his duty. He had married a diplomatic and strategic pawn, one in whom he seemed to find some happiness. Yet, it was soon apparent this docile and accommodating queen would not be enough to satisfy a man whose need to hunt and conquer went beyond the forests and stags of his estates. The couple had little in common other than the desire to produce a royal heir to the throne. In addition to the earlier language barrier, Maria had few pursuits other than discovering the delights of French cuisine and the collecting of dwarves. Her hours were spent in fervent prayer and her ladies-in-waiting were her closest friends. The French court barely noticed she was there, except on state occasions when she was trotted out.

As expected of most kings, Louis XIV soon began the acquisition of a long line of mistresses. With humble resolution, Maria accepted it. Louis continued to frequent her bed and do his royal duty. It was a habit of hers to show her pleasure at his routine trips to her chamber by clapping her hands the morning after during her *lever*. She was like the tapestries of the palace—stitched only for posterity to admire, and without animation.

# Chapter Seven
# **Louis XIV Begins His Reign**

Louis XIV had begun his reign with landmark victories: he had defeated two civil wars against his monarchy, and married Maria Theresa of Spain on August 26, 1660. The marriage was a highly strategic move that would prove to be one of his greater achievements, and one that would later bear fruit in his reign.

Maria Theresa circa 1660-1661

Louis and Maria were actually cousins. Her new mother-in-law, Anne of Austria, was also her aunt. In this older woman, Maria found a friend at court. It had made her transition into a foreign country more bearable. She was soon taught the delights of the French Court's favorite pastime—cards and gambling. Although she could be found sporadically at the salon tables, she paled in comparison to the rouged courtesans who sparkled with their flirtations and opulent gowns. Her obsession with having dwarves (the uglier the better) around her was just one of many oddities that became the topic of court gossip. As for Louis, he remained faithful to her for the first year of their marriage. He commanded the Grand Maréchal du Logis that "the Queen and himself were never to be set apart, no matter how small the house in which they might be lodging." It would be later that year on October 25th, that Maria first set eyes on the modest hunting lodge that would transform into the greatest palace in Europe—Versailles.

## Cardinal Mazarin Nears the End

The man who had been so instrumental in the machinations behind the scenes that resulted in so many triumphs, including the negotiations for the marriage of Louis XIV and Maria Therese, was strangely absent from the marriage promenade that made its way into Paris that late August of 1660. Cardinal Mazarin's health was declining, and he was forced to watch the celebrations from a distance.

Giulio Raimondo Mazzarino (Mazarin) was an Italian cardinal, diplomat and politician who served as the chief minister to the kings of France, Louis XIII and Louis XIV from 1642 until his death in 1661. He was Queen Anne's minister and faithful supporter, and private tutor and minister to Louis XIV.

The last years of Mazarin's life, between 1657 and his death in 1661, were marked by a series of major diplomatic victories. In 1657 he made a military alliance with England. In 1658 he unveiled the League of Rhine: a new group of fifty small German principalities which were now linked by a treaty with France. In the same month, Marshal Turenne decisively defeated the army of Condé at the Battle of the Dunes in Flanders. Between February and June 1659, Mazarin conducted intensive negotiations with the Spanish. On November 7, 1659, Spain signed the Treaty of the Pyrenees, which added Artois, the Cerdagne and Roussillon as new provinces of

France. This was followed in June 1660 by an even more important diplomatic event carefully arranged by Mazarin; the marriage of Louis XIV and Maria Therese of Spain. This marriage ended, at least for a time, the long and costly wars between the Habsburgs and France.

Mazarin was second only to Louis XIV as a patron of the arts in France in the 17th century. In 1648 he founded the Royal Academy of Painting and Sculpture. After his death in 1661, the inventory of his art collection at the Mazarin Palace recorded 858 paintings, 128 statues, 185 busts, plus 150 carpets, 514 pieces of jewelry and fine silver, and 317 precious stones, not counting the famous Mazarin diamonds, which he left for Louis XIV.

His collection included works by Poussin, Rubens, Corregio, Van Dyck, Titian, and Raphael. Just before his death, he visited his gallery for the last time with his deputy Brienne, and told him: “Ah, my poor friend, I must leave all this. Farewell, dear paintings, which cost me so much and which I so much loved.” Many of the paintings hang today in the Louvre.

Mazarin seated within the Gallery of his Palace (1659)

In his last months, Mazarin resided mainly at the Louvre Palace. A large fire broke out in the Gallery of Apollo, the main picture gallery of the Louvre, and destroyed many paintings, greatly upsetting Mazarin. It was the beginning of his decline. When his doctor informed him that his end was near, Mazarin asked, "How long?" The doctor replied, "two months." Mazarin responded, "That's enough."

The cardinal had already prepared several wills. Knowing that his enemies at court were telling Louis XIV that he was taking money that belonged to the King, his first will, which he made public, cleverly left all his fortune to Louis XIV. Mazarin probably calculated that the King would be too embarrassed to take all of his mentor's and chief Minister's wealth. Louis waited three days, then refused to accept it. Mazarin had also prepared a different will, which left a large sum for the establishment of the Collège des Quatre-Nations, founded for students from the four new provinces which he added to the territory of France by the Treaty of Westphalia.

The College, now the *Institut de France*, was eventually built directly across the Seine from the Louvre, where it is visible from the Palace. Mazarin asked that his remains be interred there, where they rest today in a marble monument beneath the dome. Exhausted by his diplomatic efforts, Mazarin died on March 9, 1661, at the age of 58. He had been dealing with gall stones, gout, and a failing heart.

Tomb of Mazarin in the *Institut de France.*

## A Changing of the Guard

Cardinal Mazarin was gone. "As soon as the Cardinal was dead," Brienne, one of the junior ministers scribed, "the King, with tears in his eyes, came into the wardrobe where I stood waiting with the principle members of the Court and, leaning on the maréchal de Grammont, he told him: 'We have just lost, you and I, a true friend."

It was now that the King put into action the move that would set him apart from each reigning French monarch since Henri IV: he would rule without a prime minister.

"No sooner was the Cardinal dead," Brienne continued, "than the King sent for MM. Fouquet (the new minister of Finance), Le Tellier (Secretary of State for War and the Navy), and de Lionne (Minister of State including overseer of Foreign Affairs) and gave to them alone his trust for the most secret part of the state's business." It was the first rumblings of the fallout from the Frondes. No prince of blood, duke, or member of the royal family was selected to be among Louis' private cabinet of ministers. The lessons the young king had learned concerning treason and rebellion during those frightening days, when members of his own family set out to overthrow him, were now coming home to roost. He would never again put someone in a position of trust based simply on the faded ink of a family tree. That included his mother, Anne of Austria.

Brienne, now assembled with the members of the Council, continued: "As soon as we had entered, "the King, who was already there, said gravely: "Messieurs, I have gathered you here to tell you that henceforth I intend to rule my state alone. M. le Chancelier, and M. le Surintendant will no longer sign any decree or any *ordonnance de comptant* (a piece of paper signed by the Superintendent des Finances ordering the payment of sums from the Treasury) without first telling me, and the Secretaries of State will no longer issue any papers, and I mean not even a passport or a spending authorization of a hundred écus, without having first received my orders to do so. Whenever one of you gentlemen has criticism of my decisions, I mean concerning the legal forms which I have yet not had time to learn, I will gladly listen to the good advice of my faithful servants."

The three ministers—Fouquet, Le Tellier, and de Lionne, were then informed they would meet together on Mondays and Thursdays to discuss state business. Brienne, the elder, who was also involved in Foreign Affairs, was invited to attend if he had something to contribute. As it turns out, a twice-weekly meeting with the ministers proved inadequate, and for the time being, council meetings were held daily.

On March 10, Louis went over the funeral arrangements for Cardinal Mazarin, and then sent for the clergy's representatives. They were told to make an appearance at his *lever* the following morning. It was common for the King to conduct business during his dressing ritual (*lever*) each morning, and it was also a coveted time for members of the court to try and gain an audience with him in attempt to gain favor. The representatives waited as the King's dressing gown was removed and his many layers of clothing adroitly draped about him. As valets tucked, ruffled, and buckled, Louis conducted business. The clergy were taxed with providing a full account of the garrisons in all the fortified cities. He then instructed them to get a message to the Spanish Ambassador condemning Philip IV's handling of a recent Italian dispute.

Then, on the same day, only one day after Mazarin's passing, Louis (doubtless with much satisfaction) "gathered in the Queen Mother's bedroom, where the Councils had been held, all the people who usually attended them, the princes, the dukes, and the ministers of state; there, he told them that he had decided to rule his state alone without trusting to any cares but his own (those were his very words) and sent them away very politely telling them that he would call for them when he needed good advice." Brienne, the younger, had captured in this narration the face of a monarch determined to rule on his terms. What must have felt like a slap in the face was his exclusion of his mother, who was directly responsible for much of his rise to power. After some licking of her wounds and a few protests, she resigned herself to her role *behind* the throne.

## A New Routine for the King

During Mazarin's adept handling of the affairs of the state, Louis XIV had been free to pursue entertainments in various arenas. An hour a day at the minister's side, learning about everything from war strategies to politics and finances, had been enough to keep the young king abreast of things. Now, without his formidable ally by his side, Louis's day became regulated down to the last hour. We look once again to Mme de Motteville to apprise us of his new routine.

Françoise Bertaut de Motteville, Queen Anne's Lady-in-Waiting & Court Scribe

"He decided to rise between eight and nine even though he went to sleep very late. When he left the Queen's bed, he went to his own; then he said his prayers and was dressed. His business then forced him to close the door of his bedroom… Around ten, the King went into the Council and stayed there until noon. Then he attended Mass; and he gave the rest of the time before dinner [2 p.m.] to the public and especially to the Queens.

"After the meal, he usually stayed a rather long time with the royal family, then he went off to work with one of his ministers. He gave audiences to those who required them, patiently listening to those who spoke to him. He took written requests from those who presented them to him and answered them on certain days which were reserved for this; in the same way a day was set apart for the Council of Conscience [a body for advising the king on ecclesiastical appointments] which had been set up at the beginning of the regency and which he now revived.

"As he set himself to work, he began to enjoy it and the desire he had to learn the things he needed to know soon made him very knowledgeable... He became politic in the affairs of state, a theologian as regarded the Church, precise when it came to the finances. He spoke well, always made the right decision in Council; he was sensitive to private people's interests but hated intrigues and flattery; he was harsh to the great nobles because he suspected they wanted to rule him.

"In person he was kind, polite, and of easy access to all, but with a serious and majestic mien which made him feared and respected and prevented even those closest to him from taking liberties even in private, though he was friendly and cheerful with the ladies."

Although the King's younger brother Philippe (Monsieur) was still his biggest supporter, Louis allowed him only so close. The sad reality of a monarch was that someone was always lurking, ready to take away from you what they could...even the crown. History was littered with accounts of brothers and sisters doing just that. There was also a jealous rivalry between the brothers. More than once, Louis passed Philippe over for advancement or to allow him to shine in battle. It was a subservient role the younger brother had played all his life. There would be no more flinging porridge at this king!

Louis rolled along like a juggernaut, making sure all who had seen him as puppet king in his youth would now look upon this 22-year-old monarch as totally in charge of his kingdom. He ordered Brienne to notify all the French ambassadors and ministers, who would in turn relay the message to the princes in their jurisdiction, that King Louis XIV would rule France alone. These were not the only people put on notice. His next move struck fear in the hearts of nobility; that very faction that had betrayed him while hiding behind the frock coats of Parlement.

On March 21, not even two weeks since Mazarin's death, Louis ordered that all nobility in his court must present proof of their titles. The nobility had been living tax-free, building opulent homes, and living off the fat of the kingdom. If it were proven they had lied about their lineage and were in fact, commoners, they would not only be without a place at court but would be subject to taxation. What followed the edict was a scrambling of richly attired denizens of France looking about wildly for papers with official stamps declaring their birthrights as nobility. Many were embarrassed publicly by the King when it was made clear they were not who they professed to be. The most-dreaded sentence in the French Court was the one made by the King when he dismissed someone from his presence, and hence his palace: "I do not know this man!"

After the purging of the noble class, the King also abolished the tax levied on drinks from Normandy, which the overly taxed lower class were in favor of. Louis had looked over every paper, edict, and government codicil with an eagle eye. Those around him could not have been more shocked at the transformation from a pleasure-seeking youth into a formidable monarch who intended to let nothing fall between the cracks. His brother Philippe was also in the crosshairs of his vision to build his kingdom. Through Louis' communication with the recently restored Charles II to the throne of England, Philippe was now engaged to marry Henrietta, Charles' little sister, thus uniting two great countries.

It was a whirlwind of new changes. Many barely caught their breath before a new ruling was put in place. If they thought Louis had played his hand by this point, they would be surprised to see he was just warming up. Perhaps none was caught more off-guard than Louis' new Minister of Finance: Nicholas Fouquet.

## The King's Finance Minister: Nicholas Fouquet

Nicholas Fouquet, marquis de Belle-île, vicomte de Melun et Vaux was born February 23, 1615, and was the Superintendent of Finances in France from 1653 until 1661 under King Louis XIV. He had a glittering career and acquired enormous wealth. He fell out of favor, accused of peculation (maladministration of the state's funds) and lése-majesté (actions harmful to the well-being of the monarch).

From 1642 to 1650, he held various intendancies, at first in the provinces and then with the army of chief minister Cardinal Mazarin. Coming thus in touch with the court, he was permitted in 1650 to buy the important position of *procureur général* to the *parlement* of Paris. During Mazarin's earlier exile during the Fronde, Fouquet kept him apprised of the situation at court and protected his property.

But as with all relationships with Fouquet, there were always strings attached. Upon Mazarin's return, Fouquet demanded and received as reward, the office of Superintendent of the Finances. This position was a powerful one. He who controls the purse strings controls the Treasury, and hence, the very foundation beneath the king. In the unsettled condition the government was in, in 1653, the title threw into his hands not merely the decision as to which funds should be applied to meet the demands of the state's creditors but also the negotiations with the great financiers who lent money to the king. Fouquet counted on the fact that the debts carried over from the Fronde and the hodge-podge of old systems and outdated paperwork would make it impossible for a new monarch to unravel it all. Some notes had been sold off at five or ten percent during the past upheavals but could now be cashed in for full value. Taxes had been changed in some areas, neglected in others…it was a royal mess. But to the man who knew how to take advantage of the loopholes, it meant vast wealth.

Fouquet's impressive title also landed him a wealthy wife. In 1651, he married Marie de Castille, who belonged to an affluent family of the legal nobility in Spain. Fouquet received around 160,000 livres from the marriage dowry.

Nicholas Fouquet, painting by Charles Le Brun.

Fouquet, at times, met the demands for money placed upon him while in the office of Minister of Finance by borrowing upon his own credit, but he soon turned this confusion of the public purse with his to good account.

The disorder in the accounts became hopeless; fraudulent operations were entered into with impunity, and the financiers were kept in the position of clients by official favors and by generous aid whenever they needed it. Fouquet's fortune now surpassed even Mazarin's, but the latter was too deeply implicated before his death in similar operations to interfere and was obliged to leave the day of reckoning to his agent and successor, Jean-Baptiste Colbert.

It was his confidence, arrogance and spending that became Fouquet's undoing. That it climaxed due to a fete thrown in honor of the king at his opulent chateau, the Vaux-le-Vicomte, was something straight out of a Shakespearean drama.

Fouquet's Vaux-le-Vicomte chateau

Upon Mazarin's death in 1661, Fouquet expected to be made head of the government; but Louis XIV was suspicious of his poorly disguised ambition, and it was with Fouquet in mind that he made the well-known statement, upon assuming government, that Louis would be his own chief minister. Colbert, perhaps seeking to succeed Fouquet, fed the King's displeasure with adverse reports upon the deficit and made the worst case against the finance minister.

As if flying his wealth in the face of all, Fouquet bought the port of Belle-île-en-Mer and strengthened the fortifications with a view to taking refuge there in case of disgrace. He had spent enormous sums in building a magnificent chateau on his estate of Vaux-le-Vicomte, which in its magnificence and splendor of decoration, was a forerunner of the Palace of Versailles. Here, he brought together three artists that would later become paramount to Versailles' creation: Andre le Notre (the landscape designer), Charles Le Brun (famous artist), and Louis Le Vau (talented architect).

The Vaux-le-Vicomte became home to the rarest manuscripts, paintings, jewels, and antiques. Everywhere one looked was a profusion of opulence and taste. Fouquet's tables served artists and authors with the fare from his famous chef, François Vatel. His coat of arms was found throughout the chateau and applicably bore the image of a squirrel with the motto, "What heights will he scale?" (Quo non ascendet?) The choice of this small animal derives from the name *foucquet*, which in the dialect of Angers (in the west of France) means *squirrel.*

Fouquet's Coat of Arms

By August 1661, Louis XIV was already set upon Fouquet's destruction. The king penned his frustration and anger in a letter ten years after Fouquet's fall. "The sight of the great positions [Fouquet] was preparing for himself, and the insolent purchases he had made convinced me that his ambition was boundless; and the general sufferings of all my [overtaxed] people were a constant call for justice. But what made him guiltier toward me was that, far from recognizing the kindness I had shown him by retaining him in my Council, he had thought that proof he could fool me; far from becoming wiser, he merely tried to be cleverer.

"No matter what stratagems he practiced, however, I soon noticed his bad faith. For he was unable to stop his excessive outlays, fortifying his own fortresses, building palaces, forming cabals, and putting under his friends' names important offices which he bought at my own expense in the hope of making himself the supreme arbiter of the state."

The Vauban Citadel in Le Palais, Belle-île, owned by Fouquet.

It was with this knowledge that Louis laid low to determine how to handle Fouquet. The Superintendent had allies and headed enormously wealthy and influential corps of *partisans* (tax farmers), who, if challenged as a group, could have caused the king serious trouble. By crafty devices, Louis began his subtle undoing of the minister. Fouquet was induced to sell back his office of *procureur général,* thus losing the protection of its privileges, including arrest, and he paid the price of it into the royal Treasury. The king and Colbert had convinced Fouquet that once the aging Séguier died, the post of Chancellor of France would be his. Since this office was at the head of the judiciary, Fouquet could not hold both offices and would need to relinquish the lesser post of *(attorney general*). Fouquet fell for it and gave up the lesser position, thus losing the protection the post held. Perhaps, sensing trouble in the ranks, and with the view of flattering the King with an outpouring of admiration and pomp, Fouquet made his final mistake.

On May 4th, 1661, Fouquet threw a great fete at his opulent chateau. It was a party that rivaled any France had seen, and Louis was the guest of honor. The wine flowed, tables were laden with delicacies and displays of food that were jaw-dropping. Moliere's *Les Facheux* was produced here for the first time, all in the hopes of showing Louis XIV Fouquet's gratefulness for his support of him as Minister of Finance. It backfired in a huge way! As the King looked about him at the extravagance portrayed everywhere, he was aghast at the wealth demonstrated before him; wealth gleaned from his very coffers. With much restraint, the monarch smiled throughout the lengthy evening, and Fouquet retired to bed feeling triumphant in his conquest of the King's favor.

To Louis' credit, the way he handled the situation belied his youth. A young man of 22 might be excused a royal outburst of indignity and anger that would have leveled the minister's manicured gardens. Even now, the King was showing he could be someone who took a measured and mature pace to get what he wanted. This resolve of will, would serve him greatly in military strategies that lay ahead. For now, he had a plan in place for his dear Minister of Finance.

After his visit to Vaux, the King announced that he was going to Nantes for the opening of the meeting of the provincial estates of Brittany. He required his ministers, including Fouquet, to go with him. When Fouquet was leaving the council chamber, flattered with the assurance of the King's esteem, he was arrested by Charles de Batz-Castelmore d'Artagnan, Lieutenant of the king's Musketeers. The trial lasted almost three years, and its violation of the forms of justice is still the subject of frequent monographs by members of the French bar. Louis acted throughout "as though he were conducting a campaign, evidently fearing that Fouquet would play the part of Richelieu."

During the trial, French public sympathy turned to support Fouquet. La Fontaine, Madame de Sévigné, Jean Loret, and many others wrote on his behalf; but when Fouquet was sentenced to banishment, the king, disappointed in the ruling, "commuted the sentence to imprisonment for life." In December 1664, Fouquet was taken to the prison fortress of Pinerolo. There, Eustache Dauger, the man identified by historical research as the Man in the Iron Mask, but whose name was never spoken or written, served as one of Fouquet's valets. The minister's wife was denied permission to write him until 1672; she was allowed to visit him only once, in 1679. The former man of wealth bore his imprisonment with fortitude and composed several translations and devotionals in prison.

The Man in the Iron Mask

According to official records, Fouquet died in Pinerolo March 23, 1680. A year after his death, his remains were removed from Pinerolo to the family crypt in the Ѐglise Sainte-Marie-des-Anges in Paris.

# Chapter Eight
# **Policies, Plays and Passions**

Within a mere three weeks of Cardinal Mazarin's death, Louis XIV had given notice to France that there was a new game in town. It would be ruled by an absolute monarch who had dispatched with the need of a prime minister. He had seen his brother advantageously married to the sister of the King of England, thus uniting two strong kingdoms. With the arrest of Fouquet, Louis had taken control of the Treasury's purse strings. The theft of monies he found there as he went over the convoluted records of the former Minister of Finance was staggering. In 1662 over 16 million livres in tax money and financiers' loans never reached the treasury! No wonder Fouquet could afford to buy an entire port and bling out a chateau that rivaled any in France.

Louis decided at this time to surround himself with a Council, instead of ministers, as had always been the way of things. In this new Council the matters of state were discussed with only three men: Colbert, Le Tellier, and Lionne. On occasion the Chancellor in charge of the judiciary would attend if direct concerns needed airing. Lionne, who had effectively elbowed aside Brionne, was in charge of Foreign Affairs; LeTellier was the head of all military concerns and was aided by his son, Lavois; and Colbert, that faithful and tireless friend to the King, wore many hats, including finances, public works, the colonies, the arts, police, and the running of the King's Household.

Louis never made the mistake again, however, of letting others run the ship. He oversaw every decision made and would spend up to five hours daily meeting with Council and running the business of his kingdom. He kept all the financial records of the Treasury in a little notebook bound in red Moroccan leather and stamped with a gold fleur-de-lis. It traveled with him always in the pocket of his coat.

The King, with his new knowledge of the actual financial standing of his estate, took measures to replenish the coffers. He then turned his attention to the overtaxed lower classes of his realm. "Nothing seemed more urgent to me," he wrote, "than to relieve my people. The state of my finances seemed to preclude this, and, in any case, made for delay; but one should always be in a hurry to do good… I therefore ignored every other consideration and immediately forgave three million on the *tailles* which were about to be collected." The *bourgeois* classes took note and the King's popularity swelled. Under his strict helmsmanship, the Treasury filled, and by 1664, the French financial situation was touted as the healthiest in Europe. After being in the hole by the tune of $30 million, the King had a surplus of over a half -million livers in under two years.

If there were any left in doubt as to the determination of this new king to take the reins of his realm and be the greatest monarch in history, the end of the year put the final stamp on his ambition. On November 1, 1664, Maria Therese gave birth to a son! All this and an heir to the throne. Louis XIV, in a very short time, had risen as high as his name: The Sun King.

## The World is Watching

Louis XIV first laid eyes on Versailles when he was three years of age. Once old enough to hunt, he would frequent the forests surrounding his father's hunting lodge while staying at Saint-Germain. It was not until 1661, when he was now a twenty-three-year-old King, that he began to empty funds into the hunting lodge and gardens. Many believed Louis' sudden interest in the remote chateau was due to a need to carry on romantic interludes away from the prying eyes of the court and the two queens (Maria Therese and Anne of Austria).

Louis had begun what would be known as a series of affairs. The first was rumored to be with his own sister-in-law, Henrietta, his brother Philippe's wife. This was the same young lady that he distained dancing with when she was little. But the sister to the King of England had blossomed over the years and captured Louis' attention. According to Mme. Motteville, Queen Anne's lady-in-waiting, "The Princess of England was rather tall: she was very graceful, and her figure, which not free of faults, did not then seem as spoiled as it actually was [Henrietta had a malformation of the spine, causing her to limp and carry one shoulder higher than the other]; but her whole person, although it was not shapely, was still altogether attractive because of her manner and her charm. She had a very delicate and very white complexion, mixed with a natural blush similar to a rose and jasmine. Her eyes were small, but brilliant and inviting; her nose was not ugly; her lips were very red and her teeth as white and as fine as anyone could wish; but her face was too long and she was too thin, which seemed to indicate her beauty would not last. She dressed and arranged her hair in the most becoming way…and already showed much intelligence and reason."

Henrietta Stuart, Henrietta of England, and Henrietta wife of Philippe duc d'Orleans (Monsieur) was one of many women used as a pawn in the game of politics. She had married Philippe due to a pact between Louis XIV and Charles II of England as a military alliance. It was well-known Philippe was gay, although it has been reported he may have been bi-sexual. He admitted later that he never loved Henrietta and carried out high-profile affairs with a number of male courtiers, the most famous with the Duke of Lorraine. Louis took notice of her in 1661, although she was only 16 years old, and fell head over heels in love.

What Henrietta lacked in physical appeal, she made up for in her adroit handling of herself. She was witty and intelligent, knew how to amuse, flirt, and entertain, and had an air of mystery about her. Louis' wife was entirely the opposite. She was malleable, dull, lacking in wit or intelligence bred from reading. Her days were relegated to prayer, dwarves, and an occasional card game. For someone with Louis' insatiable drive in everything, here was a woman that challenged

Henrietta of England

and excited him. The fact that he and his brother always competed may have added a delicious spice to the illicit affair. We do know, when Philippe found out, the Louvre's walls reverberated with his wrath. Never one to hide his feelings, he let it be known that this was unacceptable, despite the fact he had no feelings for his wife other than those required by duty.

Philippe was short and lacked his brother's dignity and presence. He was emotional and prone to rages and scenes that frequently embarrassed the king and the Queen Mother. He adored fashion, perfume, and jewelry, and could be counted on to join in juicy gossip. His line of male conquests was paraded beneath the nose of his mother and wife. The only solace taken from Monsieur's behavior was that he would never be one to lead a civil rebellion against his brother. He was no Gaston.

Queen Maria Theresa also made her disdain clear by suddenly ignoring Henrietta at dinner and other occasions when the two women were in each other's company. Louis exploded and demanded his wife show his sister-in-law the respect she deserved. Maria Therese always knew that fidelity would not be found in the fine print of her marriage agreement. At 23, Louis was described as incredibly handsome, with a flair and presence that awed any room he occupied. Henrietta was but the first of the scandals to come.

Louis XIV at 23 years of age. Painting by Charles le Brun.

In his way, the king demanded respect for his wife Maria Therese. She was the Queen of France and had just produced an heir to the throne. Louis acknowledged that she had certain rights and slept with her at regular intervals. It was rumored that one knew when the king had favored her with a nocturnal visit, because besides the hand clapping the following morning, she would attend a special Mass.

It was not long before Louis' eye wandered once more to Henrietta's lady-in-waiting, Louise de La Vallière. "Mlle de la Vallière was very amiable, and her beauty was much enhanced by her dazzling pink and white complexion, her blue eyes which had a very sweet expression and the attraction of her silvery blond hair which made her face still more appealing," wrote one courtier. Another claimed, "She has a handsome figure and a noble look; there is something majestic in the way she walks; her eyes have a kind of languor which must charm all those who have a tender heart. She has the most beautiful hair in the world, and in great abundance. She is kind, has taste, likes books, and is a good judge of them. She is polite, generous, helpful."

Louise de La Valliere

Henrietta (Madame) may have seen Louis' new infatuation as a relief. The strain of being his mistress beneath the glaring eyes of the Court was not an easy role to play. Besides, La Valliere was her maid, and would guarantee Louis would still be lurking in the hallways outside her apartments. No one believed the intrigue with this penniless girl without title or rank would be anything but a fling. They were to be surprised, and not for the first time, at who could capture the King of France's heart.

It was in 1661 and 1662 that Louis began his campaign of introducing himself to the world as the great entertainer. He had always been enamored with plays and music, dance, and theatrical fetes, and he decided to use them to full advantage. At an early age, the king learned how to put a "spin" on the activities of his court and made sure his entertainments found their way into the gossip rag of Paris—the *Gazette de France.*

"On the 8th of this month," the *Gazette* reported, "Their Majesties, accompanied by M le prince and Mme la princesse de Conte and many other lords and ladies were entertained on the canal in barges while trumpet fanfares sounded, and the King gave a splendid supper to all present. That same day, the princess of Tuscany along with Mademoiselle [the King's cousin] and several other persons of quality arrived at Court...and the next day accompanied Their Majesties to an outing on the same canal and to the Comédie Française.

"On the 10th, the King offered her a very splendid dinner...The illustrious company then went on an outing and, when they returned, were offered a ball."

It is interesting to note here that Louis XIV had begun his campaign to bring the nobility to heel. Mademoiselle, the very nobility he was wining and dining was none other than the daughter of the King's vile Uncle, Gaston, former duc d'Orleans. Known as Mlle de Montpensier, she, along with Conde, had led the insurrection against the King during the Fronde and almost cost him his crown. Like a spider spinning a finely orchestrated web, Louis drew them in, not with threats or demands, but through lavish fetes and a soon-to-begin fashion protocol that would leave them all but bankrupt. The trumpets heard on the canal at the Louvre on the evening of May 8th were quite possibly the announcement of a plan so clever, the nobles weren't even aware of the cage enclosing around them.

Along with the fine dinners and entertainments, Louis now introduced his own array of fashions. In 1662, Louis designed a special coat to replace the shorter bolero-like jacked that opened over a white shirt infused with lace. The new coat was made of blue silk or velvet and was embroidered with gold and silver. It was called the *justaucorps a brevet* and special permission had to be granted for anyone to wear one like it. Here we begin a systematic honing of the Court. Soon, the fashion rules and regulations of Louis XIV's palace would bring the nobility to their knees.

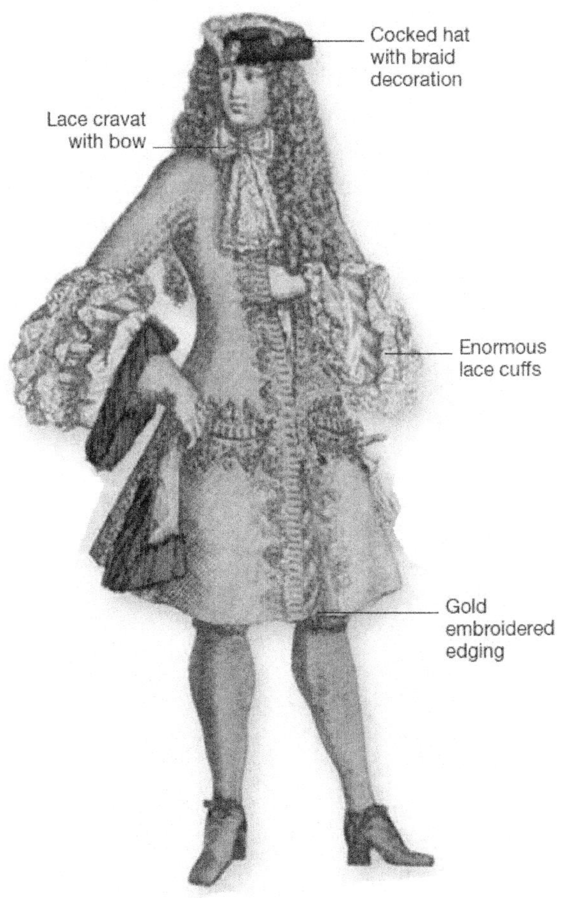


*Justaucorps* jacket that went below the knee. Lace adorned the neck and sleeves of the cravat and cuffs.

Louis was about to throw an enormous party to celebrate the birth of his son, Louis, Grand Dauphin who was born on November 1, 1661. He was born at the Chateau de Fontainebleau. As a Fils de France (Son of France) he was entitled to the name of Royal Highness. He was baptized on March 24, 1662, at the chapel of the Chateau de Saint-Germain-en-Laye and given his father's name of Louis.

Alas, Louis XIV secretly nursed the same suspicious jealousy of the Grand Dauphin that Louis XIII had once shown to himself. No prince could have been less deserving of such feelings. "Monseigneur," as the heir to the throne was now known, had inherited his mother's docility and low intelligence. All his life he remained petrified with admiration of his formidable father and stood in fear of him even while lavish proofs of "affection" were showered upon him. The young boy was handed over to a repellent tutor, the Duc de Montausier, who was so ruthless in his teachings the Dauphin developed a lasting horror of books, learning, and history. It was said that when the Grand Dauphin was an adult, he could pass an entire day simply tapping his cane against his foot in the armchair.

Louis, the Grand Dauphin

Louis was one of six legitimate children born to Louis XIV and Maria Therese. The others all died in early childhood; the second longest-lived, Marie Therese of France, died at the age of five when Louis was 11. He lived to be 49 years of age, married twice, and had three children. He did not outlive his father, and so never made it to the throne. It was his son, Louis, Dauphin of France, who became Louis XV and succeeded to the throne.

Louis XIV had a low opinion of his son. He found him indolent, fatuous, and dull. His only saving grace of his bourgeois morals kept him from outraging the pious people about him. He enjoyed the hunt as his father did, but that was the only way in which he resembled his famous namesake.

## The Carrousel of 1662

Carrousel of 1662 between the Louvre & the Tuileries

Louis XIV was on a crusade to make his mark in French history. It was safe to say that no one in mid-17th century Europe was not aware of this man that many considered bombastic and a megalomaniac. Hosting a grand carrousel to celebrate the birth of his son and heir to the throne the year before was not unheard of in France, but few had been hosted since tournaments were banned after the tragic death of Henri II. He had been wounded by a splintered lance in a tournament celebrating the marriage of his daughter and died shortly after. It was with Louis XIV's grandfather, Henri IV, that the first French Carrousel took place at the Hôtel de Bourgogne and was quite the sight to see.

A carrousel was a competition of horsemanship. It's a mix of a parade with outlandish and spectacular costumes, ring-races, and a tournament. The Carrousel of 1662 was not just to celebrate the birth of the Grand Dauphin; it was Louis' notice to the world that after the death of Cardinal Mazarin, he was now sole monarch. For the large audience of people attending the event, it was a precursor to the magnificence that would become synonymous with the Sun King.

It took months of preparation to construct the arenas and platforms for the grand performance. Not only did hundreds of elaborate costumes need to be made, but every segment of the tournament and parade had to be choregraphed down to the last detail. The area between the Louvre and the Tuileries palaces was turned into a giant arena with bleachers for up to 1500 spectators. A special raised dais, decorated in purple velvet and golden fleur-de-lis, for Louis' XIV's mother and Queen Maria Therese, along with the high-ranking ladies of court was set up in front of the central pavilion of the Tuileries, from which the ladies could behold the prancing horses and noble gentlemen in all their finery. There were also a few women sitting a horse. Two other tribunes were constructed near-by, creating a Roman-style theater. These were for the royal Princes and foreign ambassadors.

On June 5, 1662, the event began with a choreographed ballet/parade in which the entire court participated. It started at the Hôtel de Vendôme and consisted of 1297 people; 655 of whom were on horseback. The crowds cheered as the parade moved through the streets towards the Tuileries. Here, several quadrilles of riders entered the arena. First were the Romans, in outfits of red and gold and lead by the twenty-five-year-old king. Louis was dressed in a dazzling suit of silver brocade embroidered with gold and precious stones that winked in the sunlight. The harness of his horse was the color of flames and lit up beneath the sun's rays. Around his shoulders was a golden cloak that shimmered like molten gold as it flapped about him. As he approached the dais where the two queens and the ladies of the court sat all a-flutter with delight, musicians played as the horses pranced in step to the cacophony of sounds. The Sun King had never looked more dazzling.

Louis XIV at the Carrousel of 1662.

Philippe, the King's brother, must having been bursting with excitement at this chance to dress up in such a costume. Monsieur's Persian quadrille wore red and white and sparkled with jewels and fine threads. Ribbons and diamonds decorated their horses, and Philippe himself wore a golden suit with a headdress that defied gravity. His riders all bore turbans as their salute to the Persians.

Philippe, leading the Persian quadrille

Prince de Condé led the next quadrille of Turks. Their colors were black and blue. The next quadrille was led by the Duc d'Enghien, the oldest son of Prince de Condé. Their attire was a nod to the Indians with colorful fabrics and flesh-colored suits. The last quadrille was led by Duc de Guise wearing odd costumes of feathers and leaves.

At the conclusion of the parade of quadrilles, the horsemen moved into a staged fight and fired little colorful and scented balls at one another. Louis XIV displayed a golden sun, anchoring his moniker as the Sun King. Thus ended Day One of the Carrousel. Day Two, June 6th, began with more fighting. This event took the form of ring races where the galloping riders had to pierce a ring with their lances. This was a challenging sport and an exciting one with cheers erupting from the spectators as each rider took his turn. The Comte de Sault was the victor and rode proudly up to the royal dais to receive his prize from the queen: a small and richly decorated box covered in diamonds, containing a portrait of the king.

The next event was a bizarre one where puppet heads were attached to something resembling an Oriental warrior. They were speared by a rider riding at full gallop. The Marquis de Bellefonds was triumphant here. Louis XIV's Romans claimed the victory during the staged fight, and all cheered their new hero. The entire event was such a success, that a few years later, Louis created another carrousel that would outshine the one of 1662. It would be held at his newest obsession, Versailles, and would literally throw France into a tizzy of excitement. He named it *The Pleasures of the Enchanted Island.*

As for the Carrousel of 1662, it was chronicled in rich engravings and put together in a large book by the head of the Petite Académie, Perrault, who spent the next eight years following Louis' Carrousels and sharing their opulence with the world. It was published in 1670 by the King's official publisher and it was filled with illustrations and descriptions of each event.

Years later, Napoleon built his Arc de Triomphe du Carrousel on the exact spot where the Carrousel of 1662 was hosted to commemorate *his* victories.

# Chapter Nine
# **Versailles Makes Its Debut**

While the royal princes and noblemen pranced upon their decorated steeds before the adoring crowds at the Carrousel of 1662, they had no idea that the fete was far more than a celebration of the birth of the Grand Dauphin; it was a piece of propaganda for Louis to make his mark upon the world stage. Beyond that, the King had, in fact, begun his subtle corralling of the nobility that had threatened his court and his throne. If the royal bluebloods had looked more closely at the cost of the opulent costumes demanded for their participation in the Carrousel, they would have felt the soft tug of a royal tether being inextricably tied to their persons. It was an insidious strategy to empty their wallets until they were totally dependent on the largesse of the king.

Before the first costume design or arena layout was agreed upon for the Carrousel, Louis sat in secret with his head of finances, Colbert. The king was well aware of the ruinous cost of the attire (which included jewel-encrusted liveries and jackets), and the build-out and arrangements needed to create the various seating platforms and arenas. Colbert, taking pen to paper, assured the king that the huge influx of tourists to Paris to witness the event would fill the coffers. There were seats surrounding the arena to accommodate over 1500 spectators. It was a two-day event where people would require food and lodging. In short, the Carrousel's revenue far outweighed the cost of the event…at least, for the king.

There was more to Louis XIV's strategy to host the large entertainment; it was a three-legged stool of control upon which Versailles would later build its political foundation. Firstly, the nobles wishing to participate in the tournament would have to leave their various estates [some at great distances] and travel to Paris. Here, they were under Louis' watchful eye. Secondly, if the rebellious faction was too busy designing their costumes and practicing their horsemanship in an effort to shine, they were too busy to be planning a revolt. And, thirdly, the cost of the trip to Paris, the purchasing of such expensive costumes for themselves and their horses, was exorbitant. While Louis raked in the money, the nobles' resources were vastly depleted.

It was with this Carrousel that Louis XIV began his systematic reigning in of the nobility. It was well known that to gain the king's favor meant being constantly in his presence and adhering to a new dress code that could exclude you from court by only the inappropriate choice of a shoe buckle. From 1662 on, fashion would rule France, and those not wishing to be left out in the cold would find themselves ensconced in fine threads, lace, stockings, and platform shoes.

Louis now began a regular routine of balls, receptions and fetes. Many were held at Fontainebleau at this time, and the halls and gardens glittered with gowns and jewels. The conundrum was whether to go into debt to buy the different outfits demanded by certain occasions, or to be absent from court and lose all hope of social standing and advancement. Each fete became more splendid than the last as Louis threw himself into proving to the world that this Sun King shone above all other monarchs. Besides the attire, the nobility was also judged by their carriages, the number of servants accompanying them, their horses' livery, the state of their trunks bearing their outfits and necessities, etc. You were on display 24/7 and in the French Court, the gossip was fierce. Someone wearing a cheap gown or sporting last season's hairstyle became a social pariah. Finally, there was the cost of the gambling. At all court functions, the playing of cards for high stakes was the featured entertainment. Many lost as much as half a year's income at one night wagering against the odds.

In order to be seen at court—the center of all society—most of the nobility went into debt rather than lose face. Without funds, and being far from their estates, one-by-one they had to rely on the generosity of the King. A typical way for the monarch to bestow a monetary gift was to give the supplicant an office that carried a salary or pension. This office would, of course, become another tether tying the person to the court's parameters. The king could also grant a loan, wherein the nobleman or noblewoman, were in his debt. Without force or coercion, His Majesty broke the nobility as surely as one breaks a wild horse: by making it completely dependent upon him for its every need. There was no time, and no money, for this dangerous class of rebels to go about planning another insurrection. Little did they know, it was only the beginning of Louis' plan to bring them utterly to their knees.

One of the engravings of a 1662 Ball given by Louis XIV.

The Carrousel of 1662 placed a glaring spotlight on more than the Sun King's flare for entertainment, it proved that the Louvre—acting for now as the King's main residence—was far too inadequate to host the fetes Louis had planned. There had been grumblings from the nobility, some who had traveled great distances for the grand tournament, that there were no proper lodgings to house them. Louis looked about him at the shabby outdated interior of the Louvre Palace and decided it would not do. There were unfinished wings and architecture dating back to 1550. It lacked a grand entrance and impressive gardens.

The undertaking to put a pretty face on this sagging relic was too daunting. Therefore, Colbert and Louis looked across the grounds to the Tuileries Palace and decided it would be the new seat of power. Catherine de Medici's haven would have to undergo a major renovation. Begun in 1560, much of it was still uncompleted in 1661. Louis, in his usual hurry for results once he made up his mind, commissioned Le Vau to turn the Tuileries into something suitable to showcase the King of France, and to waste no time. The thought of the nobles suggesting that he, or his residences, were lacking in any detail, was painful to this monarch.

And so, the work began to create the perfect façade for the impatient monarch. Le Brun, the banished Fouquet's accomplished artist, decorated the ceilings with murals and brought in tapestries from the Gobelin Manufactory in Paris. Aubusson carpets decorated newly polished floors while wood paneling sparkled in white-and-gold. While La Vau oversaw the massive remodeling inside, Le Nôtre rolled up his cambric sleeves and tackled the gardens. A grand entrance located near the eastern end of the Louvre was added, forming one side of an inner courtyard. Louis XIII and Henri IV had already built a southern wall on the western side, leaving only a northern wing to be constructed to encase the new courtyard.

While the Tuileries was getting a face lift, the court carried on with its amusements and frolicked at the other palaces. Louis, looking about him at the run-down condition of Fontainebleau and Compiegne, grew more and more impatient with his surroundings. The court spent much of its time at Saint-Germain-en-laye, and although needing renovating as well, it was in better condition and in a spectacular setting overlooking the Seine. It was also close to a hunting lodge that had become an obsession with the young king.

Even as the Tuileries was undergoing a massive transformation, Louis would find his way to the small park surrounding the lodge he had inherited from his father, Louis VIII. It was here he felt connected to nature. As the miles melted away from the weight of Paris to this quiet hunting reserve where the sound of birds filled the air instead the shriek of commerce, he felt reborn. If Colbert had breathed a sigh of relief that the king had finally settled on the Tuileries as his palace of power, he must have felt the niggling of trepidation as Louis began pouring money into this untamed wilderness. Before Colbert could finish the summing up of all the costs being laid out for fixing up the Tuileries, Fontainebleau, and Compiegne, the ledger was filling up with over half a million livres a year on La Nôtres transforming of the park around the hunting lodge at Versailles.

## Louis XIII's Hunting Lodge Takes Center Stage

When Louis XIII built his humble hunting lodge, he laid out a hunting-park; the ground was filled with marshes, and it formed a circle bounded to the right and left by rounded hills. When the Sun King stood atop an abutment in the surrounding hills and envisioned a grand garden, no one would have imagined the immense cost of the designs he had in mind. Versailles was but a scattering of rudimentary buildings and farmland. The space the hunting lodge commanded was untamed foliage, swamp, and the problematic sloping of terrain. La Nôtre must have looked upon the deserted and wild expanse of acreage and wished he were back at the Tuileries where at least there had been some semblance of civility.

With sheer will power and an army of men, the talented landscape architect began. Swamps were drained, mountains of earth moved and brought in as the sloping hill upon which the lodge sat was terraced. Over the years, as Louis continued to expand the grounds around this chateau, small villages were relocated as the Grand Canal, parterres, walkways, and theater-like enclaves rolled out across the expanse like a juggernaut. Foundations were laid, mature trees in every specimen transported from long distances, an Orangery created, and symmetrical gardens claimed the earth where once there had been only chaos. Perhaps most impressive of all were the sheets of water that replaced murky marshland. These dazzling ponds, complete with bronze sculptures, reflected the mood of the sky and the skyline of the evolving chateau. It was a Herculean effort, to be sure. And acting as a promenade of green velvet was the *Tapis Vert*, a long stretch of manicured lawn flanked by pathways and architectural groves, or *bosquets* . These groves were designed as one would design a set for a play. They sported ponds in different geometrical shapes, where statues played among cascading fountains. Terraces composed of greenery played backdrop to stages and stone steps. It was a wonderland for the senses and a foreshadowing of the grand palace that would arise here and transfix the world.

## Blueprints and Bosquets

As the gardens were being crafted into works of art, Louis XIII's hunting lodge began the first phase of expansion in 1661. Louis Le Vau, that formidable architect Louis XIV absconded with from Fouquet's court, was now tasked with building something that would provide adequate accommodations for the king's planned parties. At this point, it was only seen as a "pleasure palace" for the entertainment of the court. It was also a place where Louis could carry out clandestine affairs and retreat from the glare of Paris. Le Vau began by adding two wings to the forecourt: one for the servants' quarters and kitchens, the other for the stables.

The garden façade of Louis XIII's hunting lodge 1660-1664.
(Engraving by Israel Silvestre.)

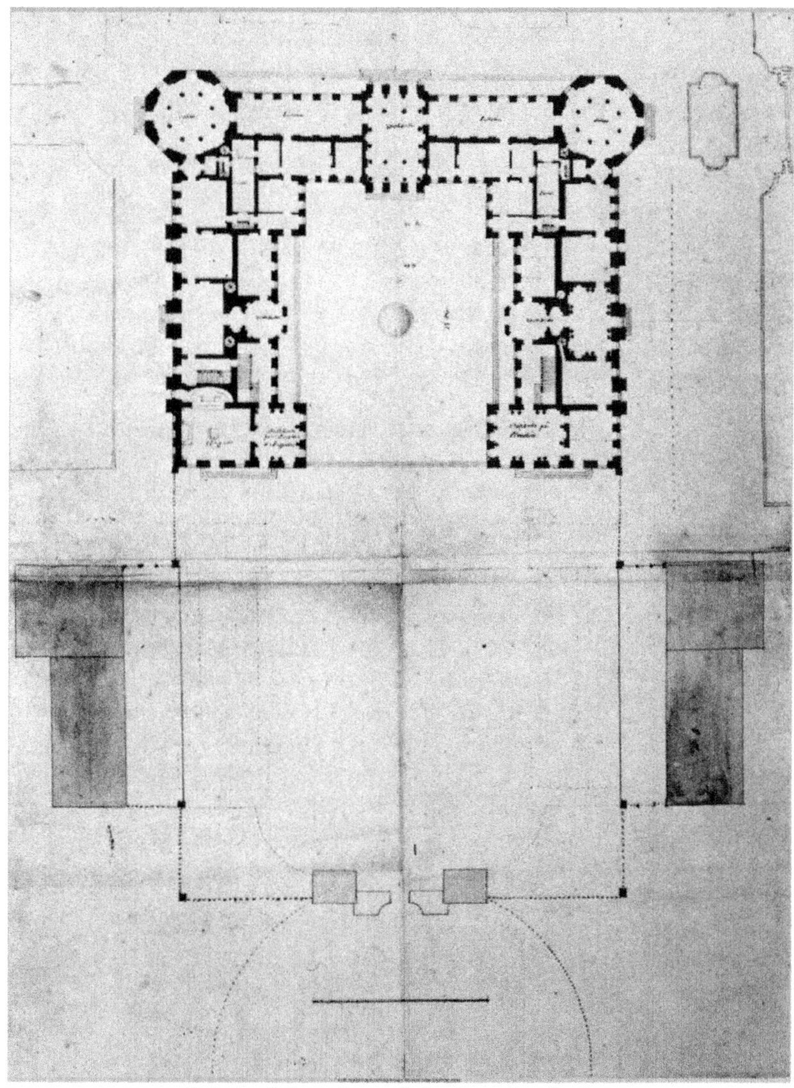

Original drawing of the hunting lodge.

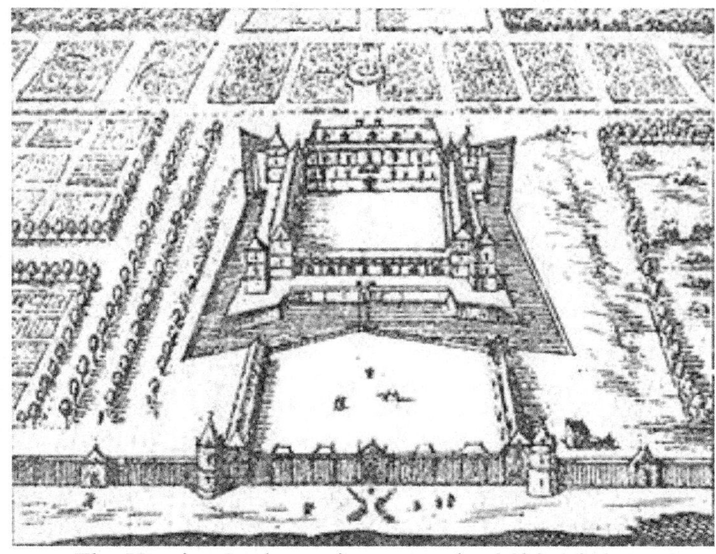

The Hunting Lodge as it appeared c 1630-1640.
Drawing by Jacques Gomboust. It is surrounded by a dry moat.

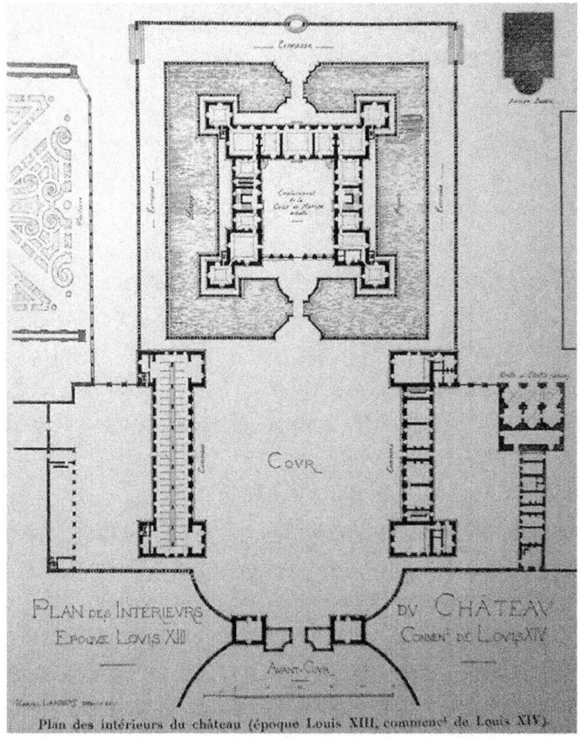


Hunting Lodge with new wings added by Le Vau, c 1662-1664.

## The Orangery and the Menagerie

**Menageries** were found throughout the seventeenth century to provide entertainment and study for the courts of France and other countries. In the 1660's, Louis XIV constructed two new menageries: one at Vincennes, next to a palace on the eastern edge of Paris, and an elaborate one at Versailles which became the model for menageries thereafter. Most of the Menagerie at Versailles was constructed in early 1664 when he brought in the first animals. It was his first major project at Versailles and one of several structures built for pleasure around the palace. It touted a Baroque-style pavilion in the middle of its circular layout. Around the pavilion was a walking path abutted by seven cages and enclosures for birds and exotic animals. Each of these enclosures had a house or stable for the animal with three walls and one barred barrier facing the pavilion. The menagerie was in the south-west area of the park and would almost touch the south arm of the Grand Canal, after its construction in 1667.

The Menagerie at Vincennes, built in 1661, housed tigers and elephants, and other ferocious beasts that were mainly used in battles against each other. These were bloody attacks that amused visiting dignitaries, such as the ambassador of Persia, who watched a fight to the death between a tiger and an elephant. Versailles' menagerie did away with the gory battles and when the Vincennes' Menagerie was discontinued in 1700, its animals were brought to Versailles. When any of the animals died, Louis XIV donated their bodies to science.

Marie Adelaide of Savoy, Louis' favorite daughter-in-law, adored the Menagerie and he gave her free run of it as a gift. She often held parties here for her guests in the daytime and evening hours. Courtiers loved to visit this part of the park and watch the foreign animals. Sharp cries from exotic birds filled the air, and the roar of some ferocious beast sent delightful shivers along the spine.

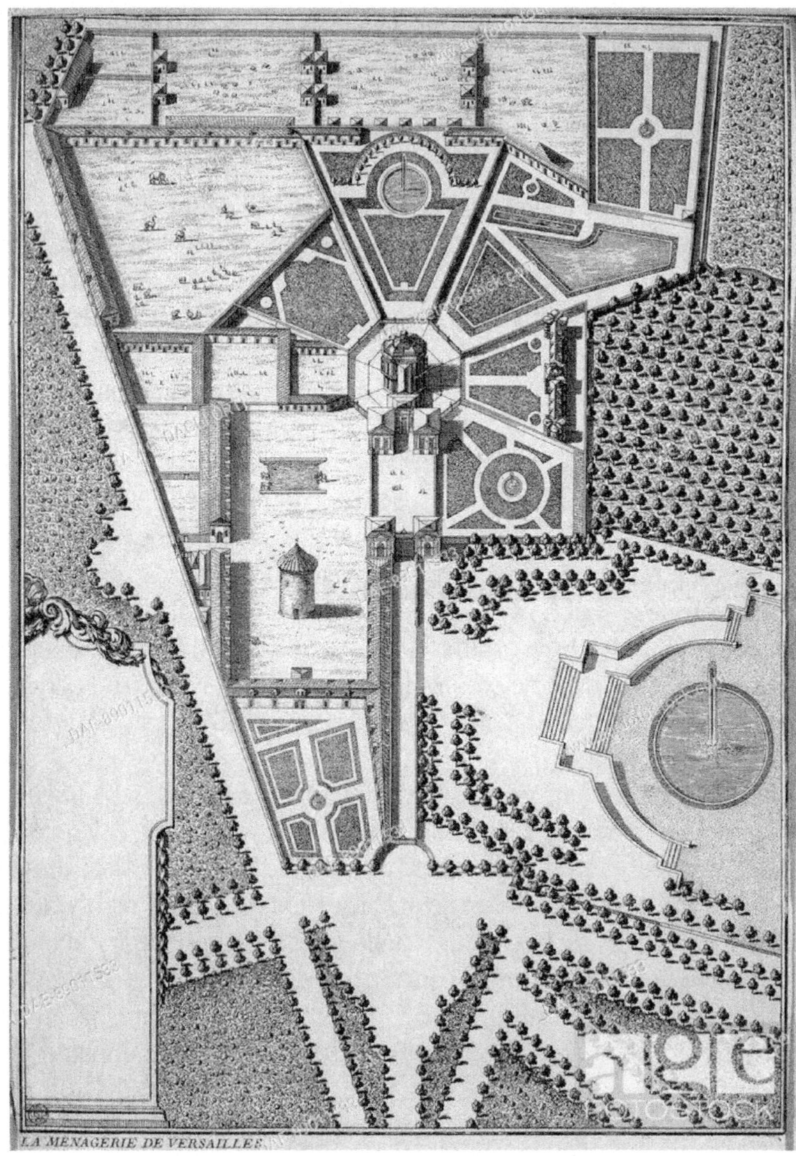


Menagerie at Versailles, begun in 1664 and completed in 1668-1670. Aerial view of the Menagerie. After 1667, you can see the tip of the Grand Canal at the right.

Once the Grand Canal was begun in 1667, romantic evenings sailing along it in gondolas would send one to the landing at the Menagerie. It was one of the courtiers' favorite attractions.

**The Orangery** at Versailles was begun in 1663. Louis XIV's chief architect, Louis Le Vau built it, selecting the perfect location to ensure the trees' longevity. It faces directly south and is situated just below the South Parterre, protecting it from wind. Jules Hardouin-Mansart replaced Le Vau after his death and twenty years after the Orangery's beginnings, Mansart doubled the length and breadth of the building in 1684 that housed the trees during the winter months. It boasts a central gallery 150-metres-long with ceilings rising to 13-metres-high. Beneath the exterior Hundred Steps staircase are two side galleries. The walls are 4-5-metres-thick with double windows and a south-facing position. The temperature of the gallery is never lower than 5° C. The trees were housed inside the Orangery building during the cold months, and then spread out across the parterres in the warmer seasons, filling the air with the scent of orange blossoms. It was rumored that after the Grand Trianon was built, one occupant found the heady scent of flowers and oranges too cloying to bear, even within the walls of the building.

The Orangery and South Parterre at Versailles.

Louis XIV, with the help of La Nôtre and Mansart, gathered all the orange trees from the royal houses; in fact, many courtiers relinquished their own orange trees to the king after it was hinted that it was considered good manners to do so. Trees from Portugal, Spain, and Italy were brought in at great expense. When Louis' restless nature demanded delivery even during the winter months, many trees did not survive the journey. Lemon trees, oleander, palm, and pomegranate were some of the trees found in Versailles' collection. It soon became the largest assembly of such trees in Europe.

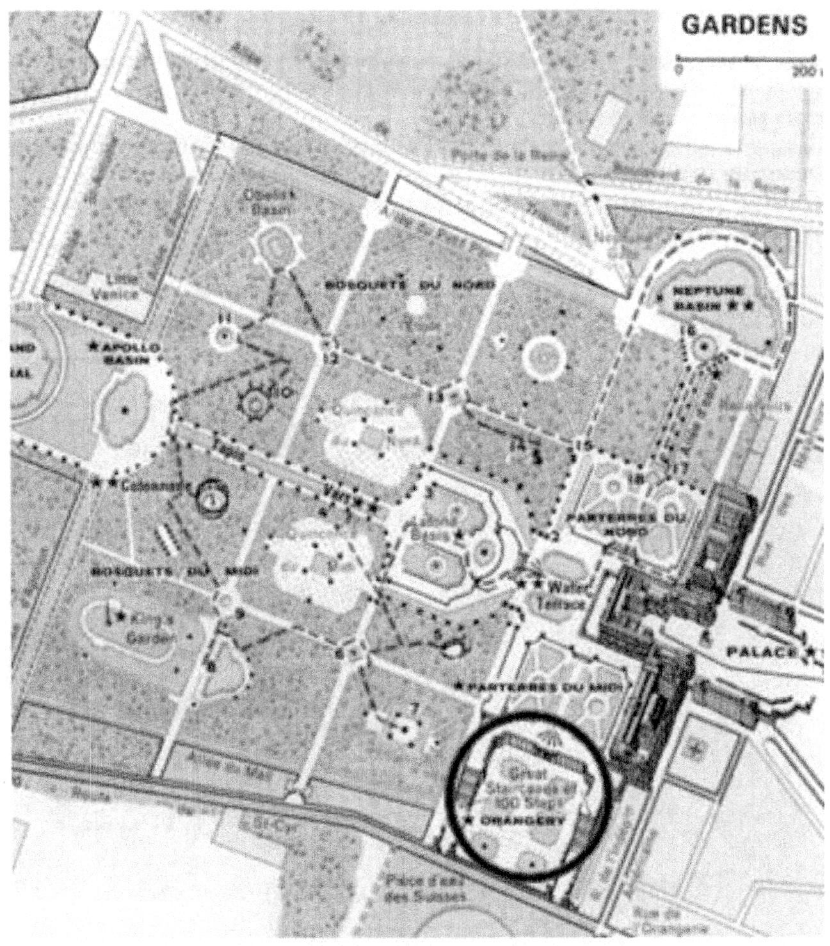


The location of the Orangery (circled) on the Garden side of the Palace, facing East.

## Women at the Forefront

Louis XIV had burst into the early 1600s as a great steed thundering through a thicket. The briars and entanglements of the Fronde and Parlement's subterfuge were behind him. He had weeded out the traitors in the midst, as exemplified by the imprisonment and death of his Chief Minister of Finances, Nicolas Fouquet. His wife had born him an heir to the throne, and his first fete, the Carrousel of 1662 had been a huge success; heralded throughout Europe. The cherry on the top was the beginning of his campaign to bring the French nobility to heel. The Sun King had made notice that he was his own man, and no one would control him. Perhaps no single person felt that more keenly than his mother, Queen Anne of Austria.

Louis had forcefully removed his mother from any inclusion in conducting the affairs of state. He conducted all business in the Council chamber to which she was excluded. He loved her, as indeed he loved his brother Philippe, but they would not participate in his ruling of the government of France. That the feelings Louis had for his mother were of real affection were never doubted. It was during a crisis concerning his mother that his devotion was brought to the foreground.

In April and May of 1663, the Queen Mother became ill. She was stricken with a high fever. Fever was always an indicator of smallpox and other fatal diseases in that era and all within the court held their breath. According to one spectator, "The King stayed up watching her for several nights when it was feared that the fever would be more violent. He had a mattress brought in, which he had put down on the rug by the queen's bed, and sometimes slept on it without undressing. He also looked after her with the greatest of care; he helped her to change beds and served her better and more gently than the maids."

To the relief of all, the queen recovered. The crisis averted; Louis went back to running his kingdom. If Queen Anne took his recent attention to her as a sign of him softening his resolve, she was mistaken. It was during 1663 that the entire court was made aware of Louis' affair with Mlle de La Vallière. Marie Thérése suffered inwardly, not daring to make a scene. The Queen Mother was more inclined to be recalcitrant about the situation. Anne stopped speaking to La Vallière. The young King confronted his mother and demanded that she respect his wishes and his new mistress. The two locked horns until the Queen Mother dramatically announced she would rather retire to a convent—an acceptable solution for myriad issues during the day. After much emotion and tears, Louis persuaded her to stay. From that point on, Anne greeted the new focus of her son's affection with civility, once again proving Louis controlled the court and its denizens.

The blow-up between mother and son brought about an admission of guilt from the head-strong king. He admitted to his mother that he knew he was committing adultery and exposing his wife to shame and misery, yet he announced in all candor: "I know my problem, I sometimes feel sorry and ashamed, I have done what I could to stop offending God and resist my passions, but I am forced to admit that they have become stronger than my reason. I can no longer resist them, and do not even feel the desire to do so."

It is interesting that the retelling of this quote was attributed to Mme de Motteville, Queen Anne's lady-in-waiting. Had she overheard the conversation or had the Queen Mother repeated it to her? It is an astonishing declaration on the king's part. At such a young age, and so quickly within his reign, he had laid claim to his God-given alliance with the Almighty and yet was above the laws that governed mere mortals. Anne had pounded it into his head since his infancy that he was Louis Dieudonné: "Louis the God-given;" that he was blessed by deity to rule here on earth. It was evident that he had accepted that mantle, in all its complicities.

# Chapter Ten
# The First Fête at Versailles

It has been said that we owe the opulent fêtes of Versailles in the early 1660s to Nicolas Fouquet. It was his elaborate party at his chateau Vaux-le-Vicomte in honor of the Sun King that was his downfall and an impetus to Louis to create something similar. The king recruited the three men responsible for Fouquet's splendid home and they became inextricably linked to the creation of Versailles: Louis Le Vau, Charles Le Brun, and André le Nôtre. Fouquet's chateau bears a striking resemblance to the early hunting lodge at Versailles, but it was the fete he threw for the royal guests that inspired Louis to create a party that would dazzle the world.

Nicolas Fouquet's Vaux-le-Vicomte chateau.

## The Theater King

Louis XIV had what is known as a "showman's flair." P.T Barnum would have been proud. His attire became more and more flamboyant, he adored the theater and dance, composed his own music, and was a major patron of the arts. It was to no one's surprise that his love of the dramatic and theatrical would find its way into his entertainments.

The world's focus turned to the small hunting lodge at Versailles when Louis began a series of nocturnal fêtes in 1664. Le Nôtre had transformed the marshland and wilderness into symmetrical gardens and ponds with parterres filled with spiraling hedges and bursting with flowers. The scent of blossoms from the Orange Gallery and the guttural growls of the Menagerie's occupants filled the night. Versailles was ready to shine.

Louis hired only the best to create the party he would host at Versailles in 1664; the first of several fêtes he had planned. Actors, playwrights, musicians, artists, set builders, costume designers, florists and the most-skilled pyrotechnic engineers he could find were all on the payroll. Invitations went out to the nobility, ambassadors and other notable and distinguished foreigners, along with the Parisian bourgeois. All who opened the wax seal of their parchment invitation felt a flutter of excitement. If Louis was throwing a party, it was going to be epic!

## Pleasures of the Enchanted Island

The small hunting box Salomon de Bronc had created for Louis XIII was slowly eclipsing into something magnificent. This was now the Sun King's "pleasure palace"—a place to host large parties with the theatrical flair he envisioned. Twenty minutes outside Paris, it was far enough away for the King to have illicit affairs or to throw opulent parties. He could control every aspect of the comings and goings of the guests while impressing the rest of the world with his showmanship. Here was his three-ringed circus, complete with thrills and spectacle, where the dancing bears were cleverly disguised as the nobles.

The Royal Court would follow the King to Versailles from the

Tuileries or Saint-Germain for sumptuous banquets after the hunt, or the latest play, or carefully orchestrated balls. And there to record every delicious moment was the *Gazette de France*.

Versailles, as the king's new entertainment site was inaugurated in a grand fête that lasted from the 7th to the 9th of May 1664. Louis was now 25 years old, and his affair with Louis La Vallière was in its zenith. It was no secret that the grand party was really to impress Vallière, although it was advertised as an entertainment in honor of his mother Queen Anne, and his wife Queen Maria Therese. When Louise's brother, the Marquis de La Vallière won the coveted prize for the tilting of the rings, the courtiers winked at one another conspiratorially.

One of those in attendance at the fête commented upon the chateau: "Although, it has not the great size that is to be remarked in some of his Majesty's other palaces, it is charming in every respect, everything smiles within and without, gold and marble vie with one another in their beauty and brilliancy… It's symmetry, the richness of its furniture, the beauty of its walks and the infinite number of its flowers and orange-trees, render the surroundings of this spot worthy of its own remarkable beauty." One wonders how many of the those in attendance had seen the mosquito-infested swamp and tangle of underbrush before Le Vau and La Nôtre whipped it into submission and formed something truly magical?

More than six hundred guests arrived via carriages and horseback. Added to that number were all the artists, actors, and workmen who had come from Paris to facilitate Louis' grand plans. One guest remarked "it had the appearance of a small army." The details for the event were arranged by Carlo Vigarani, "a gentleman of Modena," who was very clever in matters of decoration and mechanism. Louis dubbed him the "King's Engineer" and thenceforth he would manage all the entertainments at Versailles.

The magnificent fête was called *Pleasures of the Enchanted Island.* The Duc de Saint-Aignan, first gentleman of the chamber, was charged by the king to unite the various entertainments by a common idea. M. de Benserede and President de Périgny arranged the ballet and the topical verses which included an episode from *Orlando* where the king himself played the lead role of Roger. The theme went as follows: Roger, along with his brave knights are detained in the island of the enchantress Alcina, until the moment when Angelica's ring, placed on Roger's finger, releases him from the witchcraft that holds him captive to pleasure. This was the theme of the three days' entertainments, in which the scenes were richly engraved in a collection of illustrations by Israel Sylvestre under the title *Pleasures of the Enchanted Island.*

There were three points within the Versailles gardens where the entertainments that fell beneath the Island theme were carried out. Th Royal Walk, narrower today than the existing *tapis vert*, was reserved for the various incidents in the fête. Thanks to eye-witness reports, we can discern where in the gardens these events took place.

Frontispiece engraving of *The Pleasures of the Enchanted Island* by Israel Sylvestre for a commemorative booklet.

To begin the festivities on the first day of the 3-day fête, the guests watched as a parade of horsemen, dressed in lavish costumes, pranced along the Royal Walk (tapis verte), followed by Apollo's golden chariot. Louis, playing the role of Roger, was dressed in brilliant fire-colored attire. His horse's harness was in gold and silver and encrusted with gems. The promenade made its way to Alcina's Palace, which was built on the *grand rondeau*, a fine sheet of water at the end of the Royal Walk that would later become known as Apollo's Fountain, or the Basin of Apollo.

The first event was the tilting of the rings, and its location was described as follows:

"The great path that is at the end of the parterre leads to a very spacious circle, which is traversed by another path of the same width. This spot, which is five or six hundred paces from the Palace, was chosen as the most suitable for the display of the first entertainments in Alcina's enchanted palace." This was nearly in the middle of the Royal Walk, which widened into a circular space. The riders used lances to try and spear a ring secured to frames. This was similar to the tournament held at the Carrousel of 1662, with much fanfare and horsemanship. As already mentioned, La Vallière was the victor and the prize ceremoniously handed to him by Queen Anne. It was a sword of gold enriched with diamonds. He was also awarded valuable belt-buckles.

An illustration of *The Pleasures of the Enchanted Island* layout in 1664. In the background is the Versailles chateau. In the foreground is the Round Pool that would later become the Fountain of Apollo.

As the skies darkened and the torches were lit, the garden took on a fairytale setting. Night fell: "the camp was lit up, and, all the Knights having retired, the Orpheus of our day appeared—you will easily understand that I refer to Lully—at the head of a large troupe of musicians, who, having approached slowly in time to their instruments, separated into two bands, to the right and left of the high dais, close to the hedges of the circle."

Violins played during the entrance of the four seasons, Spring being mounted upon a Spanish horse, while the others rode respectively an elephant, a camel, and a bear. Forty-eight people, dressed suitably to the season they accompanied, bore upon their heads basins full of viands and fruit for the banquet. Pan and Diana, supported on a little rock planted with trees, also appeared, with attendants who offered meats derived from Pan's menagerie and from the hunting of Diana. Pan was represented by Molière. New verses were recited to the queens, and then the king, Monsieur (Philippe), the queens and the ladies sat down at the great table covered with flowers and shaped like a crescent, which was a fine sight.

The Four Seasons. You can see the elephant, camel, etc.
Engraving by Israel Sylvestre.

"In the night, close to the high green hedges, a countless number of chandeliers painted green and silver, each of them furnished with twenty-four candles and two hundred tapers of white wax and held by an equal number of people in masks, shed a light that was nearly as bright and was more agreeable than that of day. After the banquet their Majesties and all the Court went out by the portico opposite the barrier, and in a great number of much-adorned carriages they returned to the Palace."

On the second day, the guests were treated to a large outdoor theater at the end of the Royal Walk. "A large theater had been put up at about a hundred yards below the circular space where the Knights had tilted at the ring." Louis XIV, dressed as Roger, performed in a ballet written especially for the occasion by Molière and Lully, called La *Princesse d'Elide*, or the Princess of Elis. It was nightfall and Lully's music filled the air. The spectacle of lights, performers and an orchestra set the bar for all entertainment to come. Never before had opera, comedy, theater, and literature come together in such perfect harmony. The heady music of flutes and violins wafted on the night breeze as shepherdesses and animals frolicked on stage.

The theater set for *The Pleasures of the Enchanted Island* for the *Princess of Elis* performance. Engraving by Israel Sylvestre.

Finally, for the third day, "the palace of Alcina, which was consumed by fireworks, was built on the grand rondeau, the fine sheet of water at the bottom of the park, afterwards called the Basin of Apollo, which already had its present proportions, but was adorned by no group of figures nor jet of water."

On Day Three, the evening of May 9, the most-remarkable performances of Vigarini's machines were on display. In the middle of the lake (Basin of Apollo) rose the castle of the enchantress on a rocky island, before which were extended two lines of illuminated rocks, where some tapestry fixed on spars formed the two sides of a sort of stage upon the water. Here the musicians took their places when the court was seated near the bank. "But the most surprising thing was to see was Alcina coming from behind the rock, carried by a marine monster of prodigious size. Two of the nymphs of her suite started at the same time, and they approached the banks of the lake, and Alcina began some verses, to which her companion responded, and which were composed in praise of the Queen, the King's mother.

"Two excellent actresses, Mademoiselle de Bric and Molière's wife, represented the nymphs of Alcina, who was Mademoiselle du Parc. When they had finished their recital the monsters took them back towards the enchanted island where stood the enchanted castle, which, opening as they arrived, agreeably surprised the spectators by architectural beauties of so marvelous a nature that they would have been thought to be the creation of Vigarani, if they had not been declared beforehand to be due to Alcina's enchantments. Then the musicians redoubled their harmonious efforts, and there became visible within the Palace some giants of prodigious size, who performed the first figure of the ballet."

Suddenly, a theatrical clap of thunder followed by lightning marked the end of the enchantress's spell; and the palace of Alcina sank into ruins amid a splendid exhibition of fireworks, the effect of which was doubled by the water which reflected the rockets, and by the echoes which repeated the noise of the mortars."

The "prodigious monsters" have been described as a large artificial whale and two male calves, who carried Mademoiselle de Bric, Molière's wife, and Alcina away.

The fireworks display as Alcina's Enchanted Castle burns. Engraving by Israel Sylvestre.

While the three-day production of *The Pleasures of the Enchanted Island* was over, the party was not. The king prolonged the festivities for a few days more with opulent entertainments. On May 10th, he offered the game he had added to the Carrousel of 1662—the "hunting of the heads," in the German fashion. The knights who took part in the game endeavored to carry off successively, at full gallop, with the lance, the javelin, and the sword, the dummy head of a Turk, a Moor, or Medusa. The tournament took place in the dry moat surrounding the little chateau.

"The whole court had taken up its position on a balustrade of gilded iron, which ran round the pleasant home of Versailles and overlooked the moat in which the lists had been set up and barricaded." The King carried off the prizes in two contests, but he at once gave back one, which was offered by the Queen to the Knight who had been in his troupe: it was a diamond, and the Marquis de Noislin, who won it, received it from the hands of the Queen."

On the following day, there was an expedition to the Menagerie, where the king demanded admiration for the new buildings he had just built there and for the large number of rare birds. It is probable that the elephant, bear, and the camel that were featured in the Four

Seasons segment of the Enchanted Island fête were also housed here.

In the evening, the king ordered a performance on a stage in his salon of *Les Facheaux*, by Molière, interspersed with ballets. On the following day, after dinner, the king made the ladies draw lots for "jewelry, ornaments, silver, and other similar things; and although it is customary for presents of the kind to be distributed at a fête, it was no doubt in accordance with His Majesty's desire when the most fortunate number fell into the hands of the Queen."

The spectators then saw a challenge exchanged between two of the nobles who had figured in the proceedings of the first day: the Marquis de Soyecourt and the Duc de Saint-Aignan. They tilted for heads in their costumes, and many wagers were laid among their partisans. M. de Saint-Aignan won the contest.

"In the evening, His Majesty ordered the performance of a comedy called *Tartuffe*, which the Sieur de Molière had written against hypocrites…" The play, Moliere's astute mirror of society, greatly pleased the king but outraged others who felt the playwright's quill hit too closely to home. It underlined Louis XIV's complete control of all within his reach. The line *"Nous vivons, sous un roi ennemi di la fraude"* translates to "We are ruled by a king who will not tolerate injustice." As many of the post-Fronde nobles were in the audience, it was sure to have ruffled some ruffs.

On May 12th, the king wished to tilt at heads again and in the evening the comedy of *Le Mariage Forcé* was played. On May 14th, a satiated and tired court headed back for the chateau at Fontainebleau where, no doubt, they collapsed, clutching their prizes, souvenirs, and sore feet.

As Louis congratulated himself on a monstrous success, one he was sure had never been attempted or accomplished with so much expense and theatrical brilliance, the same accolades were missing among many who had attended. One such lady was Madame de Sévigné. In his memoirs, Oliver d'Ormesson reported: "Madame de Sévigné described to us the entertainments at Versailles, which lasted from Wednesday to the Sunday, and included tilting at the ring, ballets, plays, fireworks, and other very fine conceits; and told us that all the courtiers were in a fury because the King did not take care of any of them, and MM. de Guise and d'Elbeuf had scarcely a hole to take shelter in." The Village of Versailles, with its inns only fit for carriers, offered few resources for the courtiers who followed the king. Twenty years later, a large town would appear here, dedicated to the whims and needs of the biggest palace in Europe.

When the grumbling of the court reached Louis' ears, he was furious. The Carrousel of 1662 had offered up the same complaint, albeit on a smaller order, as Paris offered infinitely more places to lodge than the hovel that was at that time the small village of Versailles. Colbert and Le Vau caught the largest extent of Louis' wrath as he demanded that designs begin to offer accommodations to his guests who would visit his "Pleasure Palace" in the future.

Perhaps it would be the Queen-Mother who would look back at *The Pleasures of the Enchanted Island* with much feeling. Old and struggling with health issues that had yet to be named, the matron had bent over from her place on the royal dais to bestow the treasured prices won in the contests by the triumphant knights. In a gown straining from the extra girth of age, and certainly weary from the whirlwind of activities that stretched out across the week, she may have guessed it was to be her attendance at such events was coming to an end. It was possibly the last time she saw Versailles, for Queen Anne of Austria would succumb to breast cancer just one year later.

# Chapter Eleven
## A Queen Dies and War Begins

As 1666 found its way into the astrological charts and almanacs, the Sun King had every reason to celebrate his victories. All who had stood to defy him had been made to bow before him. This included a mother who, while being given the respect her title demanded, had been relegated to a back seat and repeatedly reminded of her place *behind* the king. While it was obvious to all the Queen-Mother's health had been failing, it took a tragic turn in early 1665. The courtiers and newspapers were still buzzing over the extravagant *Pleasures of the Enchanted Island* fête held at Versailles.

The court had returned to the Louvre, and doctors were called in to attend to the ailing queen. After much deliberation, the cause of her suffering was announced. It was breast cancer. In an era where surgery and infection often killed the patient faster than a lingering ailment, this was a major blow. A complete mastectomy would, no doubt, cause the end of her life. It was therefore determined to opt for a semi-ablation that would be complete torture. For an entire year, the Queen-Mother was subjected to smaller operations that literally involved cutting away pieces of each breast along with parts of the tumor. There was no anesthesia in this era, nothing to dull the pain other than imbibing strong drink. There were no reports suggesting the queen resorted to strong spirits to distance herself from the pain. Instead, she endured the bloody bandages adhering to raw wounds, only to have them pulled away along with pieces of her flesh. It was an agonizing torture that lasted throughout 1666.

Anne of Austria, once renowned for her elegant, lovely hands, now looked at the swollen fingers ravaged by cancer and whispered, "I can see it is time I went." Those around her marveled at her courage and resolve. It was clear she was fading fast, and the court readied itself for the passing of a monarch. She was a Queen in her own right. She had become the Royal Regent after her husband's death and raised a son who now ruled France. Her second son, Philippe, was a Royal Prince and would assume the throne should anything happen to Louis. She had fulfilled her duty and perhaps faced the darkness of night with calm. Surely, the suffering she endured daily, lying there with the bosom of her nightgown, stained crimson, might have made death feel like a welcome angel.

The usual milieu that occurs when one with property is about to pass ensued. Quarrels broke out between those who would inherit as to who was entitled to what. Louis lay claim to his mother's famous pearls as Monsieur (Philippe) angled for his share of the soon-to-be late queen's possessions. Meanwhile, courtiers came to her bedside to pay their respects and weep quietly. Anne went deeper into her faith and spent much of the days in fervent prayer. On January 20, 1666, as the golden mantel clock chimed out the hour between four and five A.M., the great lady died.

As it is with death, even when protracted illness has heralded its imminent arrival, the finality of the queen's passing hit her sons hard. The court went into mourning as Louis XIV and Philippe knelt by her still body still prone upon her bed. The tears flowed from both brothers without any regard to those who stood about them. Philippe, always the more emotional of the two, was inconsolable. Thanks to the memoirs of Mme de Motteville, who was close to the situation, we see how the brothers handled their grief:

"I was told by people who slept in the King's bedroom that he wept in his bed for almost the entire night. The next day, speaking to the duchesse de Montausier about the Queen Mother, she said that he had the consolation of knowing that he had never disobeyed her in anything of real consequence; and, continuing to extol her merits, he added that the Queen, his mother, was not only a great

Queen but that she deserved to be ranked with the greatest Kings."

We can see here in Louis' words that his ability to see things only through his lens is intact. To him, the recent admonitions of his mother to give up a mistress (La Valliere), declaring he was committing adultery, a very real sin in her eyes and God's, was now filed under nothing of "real consequence." It was not a problem in Louis' eyes, therefore there had been no disobedience to his mother's pleadings. It was a convenient filter through which the Sun King would run many annoyances.

Philippe, with perhaps sudden clarity, realized he had just lost the only person who would take his side against his brother the king. It was obvious Louis was intent on keeping his younger brother bereft of rank or duties, other than those bestowed in family trees. The betrayal of his Uncle Gaston was still fresh in his memory. He knew how easy it was for a brother to move in and try to usurp authority, with force if necessary. There would not be another Fronde if Louis had his way. He mollified Philippe with properties, cash, jewels, and an allowance to facilitate the young man's obsession with fashion and fine things, while making sure he remained compliant and without any real power to be a threat. It was an impossible position for the subservient brother, and now, his one ally that could have helped him was dead.

Louis paid tribute to his mother in very eloquent words in one of his many letters and journals: "Nature," he wrote, "had formed the first links which tied me to the Queen, my mother; but the closeness resulting from a kinship of the soul is much harder to end than that due only to blood. To explain both the extent and the justice of my sorrow, I would have to set out here the full merit of this Queen, and that would be a very difficult undertaking.... The respect I paid her was not of that forced kind of duty we owe to appearances. The habit I made of living in the same house and eating at the same table with her, the assiduity with which I could be seen to visit her several times a day were not an obligation I imposed on myself for reasons of state but a sign of the pleasure I found in her company; and in fact the way in which she had freely transmitted the sovereign power to me showed me clearly enough that I had nothing to fear from her ambition to allow me to dispense with insincere marks of affection."

Here again, we witness Louis' unique filter through which he processed life. It was not his mother's sacrifices for him throughout her regency, including removing him from danger and likely saving his life, that he extols in this writing. It is her submission to *his* will and the relinquishing of power that is uppermost in his praise. We see a young man suspicious of the bonds associated with family and the ultimate need to control all who could be a threat to his throne. There is a mantle of self-serving desperation to make all—family and nobles uppermost—firmly obedient and restrained.

The reading of the will took place, at which time Louis headed off to Versailles to hunt. Protocol demanded that a king not remain in the same house with a dead body, due to fear of disease and contagion. The final assault on his mother's person was done as he made his way to his favorite retreat. "On the twenty-first, at 7 A.M., the Queen's surgeon took out her heart through her side as she had ordered; they embalmed her body though she had forbidden it, but it was so gangrened that it had to be done, since the body had to stay at the Louvre for a few days to allow enough time to prepare the coaches… She was put into a lead coffin, which was put in a covering of black velvet and white satin and…topped with a crowned canopy bearing at each corner the Queen's arm embroidered.

"On the twenty-second the coffin was put on a platform… with many silver candlesticks holding white candles bearing the Queen's arms… All the room, including the ceiling, was draped in black on a black velvet cushion at the head of the coffin."

Throughout the ceremony, the members of the royal bloodline jockeyed for precedence in the proceedings. At times, Louis had to step in and decide who was entitled to what according to rank and etiquette. It would be a role he would exploit many times. The queen was laid to rest in the Abbey of Saint Denis. As Louis' wife, Maria Therese looked on through a black veil. She, like Philippe, said goodbye to one of the few allies she had at court. It was a gift knowing Anne was her aunt as well as her mother-in-law and had commiserated with her over Louis' flagrant affair with Louise La Valliere. Without the glare of the Queen-Mother looking over the King's shoulder, what would happen now? The last of any parental conscience had just been interred.

Even as the queen suffered throughout 1666, Louis campaigned and plotted. The Habsburgs had been the enemies of the Bourbon line for generations. The marriage of Maria Therese had been a political move, and had served its purpose, but casting any loyalty or fondness his wife might have to her native country, Louis put the Spanish Empire in his crosshairs. As it was, events would fall into place that literally laid the Empire at his doorstep.

Last known portrait of Anne of Austria, by Charles Beaubrun.

## Into Spain We Go!

The shadow of the late Cardinal Mazarin had far-reaching fingers. It was now that the clever caveat he had attached to the marriage of Louis XIV and Maria Therese rose to collect its dividends. Anne's brother, Philip IV had died before her the previous year on September 17, 1665, leaving only a mentally challenged four-year-old as heir to his throne. Philip had died without honoring the huge dowry pledged for Maria Therese—just as Mazarin had planned. *The Treaty at Pyrenees* all those years before now called in its chips. Maria would have to renounce her Spanish inheritance. To tie it up with a bow, Louis had his lawyers resurrect a "right of devolution" from the past which stated Queen Maria was entitled to Flanders, Brabant, Luxembourg and the Franche-Comté.

Still not satisfied, Louis drew up a secret treaty with Emperor Leopold I that in the event the sickly heir of Philip IV, Charles II, should die without leaving an heir of his own, the provinces mentioned become French. Leopold's prize was that he would obtain the rest of the Spanish Empire for Austria. Another treaty was signed with Portugal on March 31, stating that Spain could be attacked from the rear if the situation was necessary. Finally, Louis bribed German princes not to attack France. He had tied it all up and in May 1667, the French army headed into Flanders beneath the guise to simply claim Maria Therese's property as was their right under *The Treaty of Pyrenees*. Mazarin was still serving his monarch, even from the grave.

Louis tapped Turenne, his most-experienced general to lead the attack. Like dominoes falling, one after another, the Spanish fortresses toppled. Ath, Tournai, Oudernarde, Furnes, Armentiers, Courtrai, and Douai were conquered by August. Lille, a city that held out to the end, finally fell on August 27. On the thirty-first, Louis quite inexplicably called the war off after the marechal de Crequi defeated the last of the Spanish army. He had captured enough of the Spanish frontier for now. A fortress was built up around Lille and Louis turned his attention to making the most of his victory.

Fireworks exploded throughout France while the King's accolades were trumpeted in pamphlets and newspapers. For once, Louis shared the spotlight with his wife, who had remained almost invisible at court. It was, after all, her territories he had just vanquished. Ceremonies were held at each conquered city. The court was invited along to worship at the feet of the conquering hero. The artist Le Brun was commissioned to design commemorative tapestries from the Gobelin Factory, spotlighting all the war's victories. Engravings would later be made. Murals, tapestries, coins, other artwork, writings, verse, and all manner of propaganda were used with aplomb to show all of Europe which monarch ruled with the greatest success.

The artwork began piling up, and once again Louis lamented the perfect showcase to display his magnificence. As Colbert was entreated again by the king's impatience for a proper palace and image, he may have felt the purse strings open wider. He knew the signs. As it was, money was pouring into Versailles. The first of endless statues were put into place in the gardens that were expanding and morphing into a fairyland in 1665. An amazing structure called the Grotto of Tethys (Thetis) was begun at this same time. It was just to the south of the chateau and became a masterpiece of design and mechanical wonders. In 1667, work began on the Great Canal. There would be no turning back from the hunting lodge in the small hamlet of Versailles.

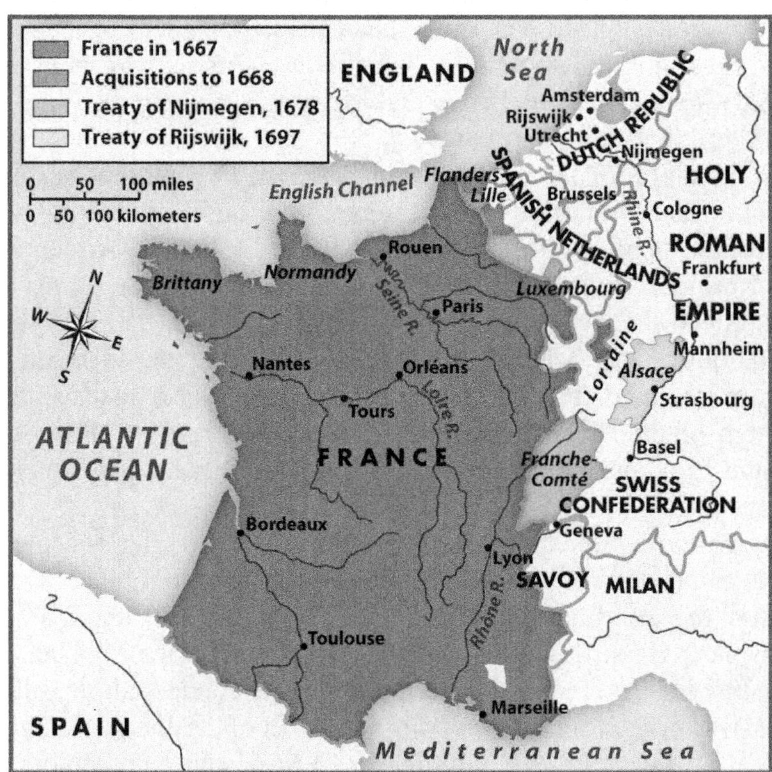

Louis XIV's Acquisition of Spanish Territory.

# Chapter Twelve
# **All Eyes Are on Versailles**

As Queen Anne dealt with her health issues in 1665, Louis stayed several times at Versailles, becoming more and more obsessed with turning it into something extraordinary. Sketches of his visions for the grounds filled journals as he peered out across the vast expanse of garden taking shape under Le Nôtre's experienced hand. It seemed the more the talented gardener created, the more Louis' mad scribblings pushed his imagination out even farther.

Early 1663 drawing of Versailles' gardens.

While André Le Nôrte feverously pushed his small army of gardeners into ever-expanding acres around the evolving Chateau of Versailles, Louis contented himself with hunts, balls, plays, and feasts, each one adroitly organized and orchestrated. A play was given on June 13th, followed by a ball in a large salon built of foliage in the Royal Walk *(tapis vert)* by Vigarani, and lighted by a hundred crystal chandeliers.

In the month of July, the Queen of England, who had come to France for the confinement of her daughter, Madame (Henrietta, Philippe's wife), paid a visit to Versailles, remaining there for five days with her household. Louis threw down the red carpet, eager to impress his British allies with the brilliance of his chateau and hospitality. In September, the court kept the Feast of St. Hubert at Versailles which lasted four days. A hunting expedition was included, in which Queen Maria Therese, Madame (Henrietta), Mademoiselle (the eldest daughter of Louis' late Uncle Gaston; she was also called Mlle de Montpensier), Mademoiselle d'Alençon, and the other ladies appeared dressed as Amazons. A play with a ballet was acted, which was the first performance of Molière's *L'Amour Mèdécin.* The Queen-Mother's name does not appear on the reports of the activities at Versailles in 1665. Her deteriorating health probably precluded it, and as already stated, she died early the next year.

It was obvious from the beginning that one of Versailles' major shortcomings was going to be the lack of a nearby water source. To facilitate the need for water, one of the most-admired features of Europe was added to the chateau's grounds, not far from the King's bedroom window.

## The Grotte de Thétys

The Thetis Grotto (also spelled Thétys) was one of the original wonders of the Versailles gardens. Started in 1664, it played a critical role in the hydraulic system that supplied water to the garden. The roof of the grotto supported a reservoir that stored water pumped from the Clagny pond which fed the fountains lower in the garden via gravity. Three reservoirs sat next to it. Although the outside of the building was a stunning piece of architecture, consisting of intricate grill work and arches, it was the interior that caused visitors to stand and stare in wonder.

Symbolically, the "Grotte de Thétys" related to the myth of Apollo, Louis XIV's favorite avatar. The Grotto represented the cave of the sea nymph Thetis, where Apollo rested after driving his chariot to light the sky. The Sun God's imagery aligned with Louis' image of himself, and solar images can be seen throughout the Grotto. Apollo would feature again in the Basin of Apollo at the other end of the garden. The Thetis Grotto was a free-standing structure located just south of the chateau. The statuary created and installed for the Grotto would come later; Gilles Guérin, François Girardon, Thomas Regnaudin, Gaspard Marsy, and Balthazard Marsy were the sculptors. The interior, which was decorated with shell-work to represent a sea cave, contained the statue group by the Marsy brothers depicting the Sun God attended by nereids and his horses being groomed by attendants of Thetis. Originally, these statues were featured in three art niches at the back of the Grotto and surrounded by various fountains and water features.

Exterior of The Thetis Grotto by Jean Le Pautre, 1672.

The Grotto's whimsical, under-the-sea interior was decorated with precious stones, shells, mirrors, mosaics, and masks. Louis was fond of taking special guests to see it and demonstrate its most-incredible feature. He would gather his select group around one of the tranquil fountain bases and pause for dramatic effect. Then, with the clap of his hands, the fountains would spring to life and fill the cave-like structure with the fine mist and smell of water. Smiling broadly, like a child displaying his new toy, he would clap his hands again, and to the amazement of all, the fountains filled the room with the sound of bird calls. It was a feat of underground machinery and magic the people of France had not witnessed before.

The Thetis Grotto was not completed until 1675, when the three statues' groupings were placed in their niches at the back of the room. Despite its great success, the Grotto was demolished in 1684 to make room for the north wing of the expanding palace. The statues were saved and moved first to the Grove of the Domes and then into a rock Grotto at the Baths of Apollo, where they can still be seen today. The Thetis Grotto comes to life thanks to twenty detailed engravings published in the 1670s.

It was with the Grotto's emphasis on Apollo and the solar image of the sun, that the gardens of Versailles, and indeed the chateau itself began to take on the iconic imagery that would be forever linked with Louis XIV. Everywhere one looked, statuary, grillwork, and murals depicted Louis as the Sun King and Apollo. Even the radiating lines of the bosquets and walkways mimicked the rays of the sun spreading its light throughout the manicured grounds of Versailles.

Interior of The Thetis Grotto, by Jean Le Pautre, 1676.

Apollo attended by nymphs by François & Thomas Regnaudin, 1675.

Apollo's Horses Groomed by Two Tritons by Gilles Guérin

Apollo's Horses Groomed by Two Tritons, by Gaspard & Balthazard Marsy

The Thetis Grotto at Versailles (white arrow). It was directly behind the Minister's Wing. The Chateau is in the upper-left corner. The Grotto roof captured rainwater and shows as blue in color photos.

## An Explosion of Creation at Versailles

It was during this time that Louis' frenetic quill drafted idea after idea and pressed them into Le Nôrte's calloused hands. In 1665, the first of the statues began to fill the freshly laid-out parterres, bosquets and walkways. Fountains sprang up, their mists encircling bronzes from the most-revered sculptors in Europe. A report was given by an unknown source that perfectly encapsulates this frenzied period of creative genius:

"Louis XIV transformed the wild and deserted spot into this region of life and beauty, but we shall never know how much was spent in the way of will-power, labor, and money in raising all these terraces, the earth for which had all to be brought from elsewhere, and in strengthening the foundations and approaches of the great Palace. It stands up superbly, in all its whiteness and wealth of decoration, spreading out before the gardens the broken but symmetrical lines of its façade, which can be seen from afar."

The great terrace before the Palace was an albatross about Le Nôtre's neck, as it was constantly changing. In the beginning, it was only a way across the dry moat like a drawbridge, with balustrades here and there, leading into a formal carpet-patterned parterre. This is what Boyceau designed and what Le Nôrte found. He does not appear to have altered it at all for some time, because the first water-parterre is seen in the pictures after Le Vau begins enlarging the chateau. Originally, only gently inclined walks of semicircular shape led from the great terrace to the Latona parterre, which from its form got the name of the Horseshoe. The Latona fountain would not be installed until 1670, even though the pond existed under Louis XIII. It was in 1666 that Le Nôtre laid down the imposing steps which gave the feature an immense size to the show-garden, which again, derives much of its importance and justification from the buildings of Le Vau. It was Le Vau's *envelope* that would alter the small hunting lodge forever.

Early Versailles with Orangery to the right below the slope, and Le Nôtre's steps.

One description given of the overall theme of the gardens, was this: "If the cult by courtiers of the "Roi Soleil" had already begun in the grotto, the brotherhood of earthly and heavenly Sun-Kings had purposefully united, so that the whole garden could be converted into a veritable temple of the sun."

In 1667, one of the more grandiose designs of Louis XIV's began. He envisioned a canal that would traverse the gardens in the form of a cross.

Its sheer vastness would boggle the mind, especially for an area so devoid of a natural water supply.

## The Grand Canal

The Grand Canal was begun in 1667-1668 and completed in 1680. It is a breathtaking 5118 feet long and 394 feet wide, intersected a third of the way down by a branch 3376 feet long forming the "cross" section. This branch stretches north towards the site of the Menagerie, and just south of the location of what would become the Grand Trianon. It was described as "one of the finest sights in the gardens. It is exactly in a line with the central point of the Palace, from whose windows it may be seen sparkling and quivering in unison with the waters of the Parterre d'Eau." Above and beyond the decorative and festive aspects of this garden feature, the *Grand Canal* also served a practical role. Situated at a low point in the gardens, it collected water it drained from the fountains in the garden above. Water from the *Grand Canal* was pumped back to the reservoir on the roof of the *Grotte de Thétys* via a network of windmill-powered and horse-powered pumps.

"It was first designed in 1667, when the Basin of Apollo was no more than a Basin of Swans, without any kind of ornamentation. [This was the location of the fireworks finale during the 1662 *Pleasures of the Enchanted Island*, where the fantasy castle burns.] In order to enlarge the view, the king had the happy idea of forming this Canal, which should drain the marshy places of this low-lying ground. The gentlemen of the Academy of Sciences were consulted and declared that the operation would drain the plain while at the same time beautifying the Park. The Canal was gradually enlarged and at last reached the fine proportions that we see today."

The Canal was formerly surrounded by a border of stone, level with the ground. The sheet of water near the Basin of Apollo served as a port for the numerous pleasure boats. As early as 1669 great "naval" pageants were held here, and guests at the Palace could navigate the ever-expanding gardens using ornate boats and gondolas. Flotillas could float along the Canal and bank at various locations, including the Menagerie. At night, lanterns adorned these vessels, reflecting in the water like a mirror of stars. It was an incredible sight to see. In 1687, several Venetian gondolas sailed this stretch of water, and were housed in small buildings north of the Fountain of Apollo. Today, it has been nicknamed "Little Venice."

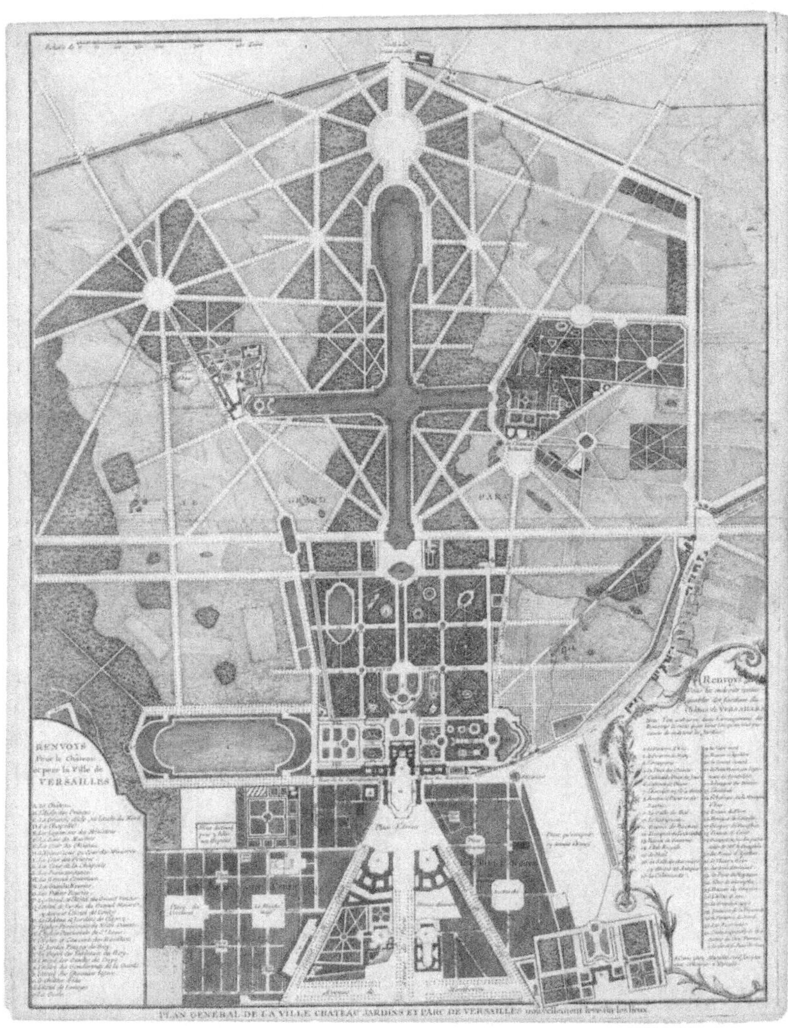


The Grand Canal can be seen at the top of the photo. You can see the Menagerie at the left of the cross branch of the Canal. This map shows the later additions of the north and south wings added to the chateau and the Grand Trianon, which was begun in 1670 as the Porcelain Trianon, shown at the right-hand side of the cross branch. The section of gardens south of the beginning of the canal in the photo was called the Petite Parc, and the area comprising the Canal, Menagerie and Trianon was called the Grand Parc.

"Little Venice" was a nautical city that grew up on the borders of the Canal, a sort of corporation with its own regulations and customs. It began when in 1674, Venice sent the Grand Roi some brilliantly gilded gondolas for use in his Canal. They were manned by costumed gondoliers. Other Venetians joined them, attracted by the advantages offered them, and these, together with men of Provence, composed the regular crews of the Canal boats. The small town of "Little Venice" sprang up, which was enclosed by walls, the families of the Italian immigrants multiplied and lived there in peace until the end of the 18th century. There were boats of every description, built by the architects of the Royal Navy. Every vessel was a gem of decoration.

Louis XIV was well on his way to creating his "Pleasure Palace" that would host fêtes unrivaled in the world. The gardens were shaping up nicely. Now it was time to show them off.

## The Grand Fête of 1668

The year 1668 would be a momentous one for the young king. As the work at Versailles continued, Louis signed the *Treaty of Aix-la-Chapelle* or Aachen which ended the War of Devolution between France and Spain. This was the fallout of Louis XIV's claim that large parts of Spain "devolved" to him by right of marriage to Maria Theresa of Spain. The provinces included parts of the Spanish Netherlands and Franche-Comté. In the fighting, the French encountered minimal resistance; however, Louis was more concerned to assert his inheritance rights in the Spanish Empire, and consequently returned much of his gains in the May 1668 *Treaty of Aix-la-Chapelle.* The terms were agreed by Emperor Leopold in January 1668, and reinforced by the Triple Alliance of England, Sweden, and the Dutch Republic.

The conflict marked the end of the long-standing Franco-Dutch alliance and was the first of the French wars of expansion that dominated Europe for the next 50 years. Louis went to war in 1667 because he believed the Dutch would never voluntarily agree to the concessions required. He now decided capturing the Spanish Netherlands required him to first defeat the Republic and began planning the Franco-Dutch War.

France withdrew from Franche-Comté and the Spanish

Netherlands, with the exception of eleven towns and their surrounding areas. Lille, Armentières, Bergues and Douai were considered essential to reinforce France's vulnerable northern border and remain French to this day. The retention of Tournai, Oudenaarde, Kortrijk, Veurne, Binche, Charleroi and Ath made future offensives much easier as would be shown in the Third Anglo-Dutch War of 1672. Concern over French ambitions revived the Orangist party, increasing internal political conflict with De Witt's republican faction. One result was the deliberate neglect of the Dutch army, generally seen as bolstering the power of the Prince of Orange, leading to catastrophic repercussions in 1672.

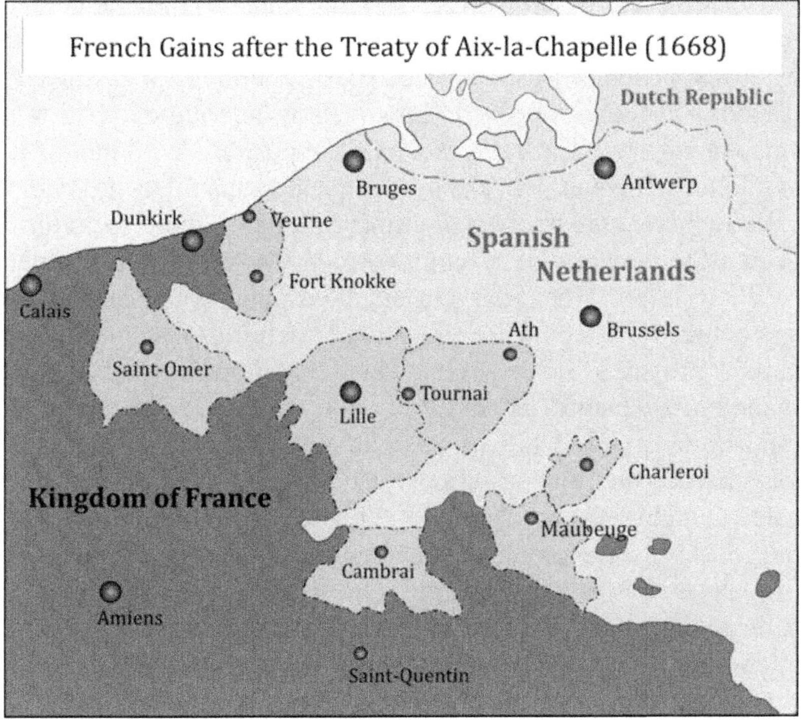


The Treaty of Aix-la-Chapelle (1668) showing French Gains (Medium-grey color).

Two-and-a-half-months after the *Treaty of Aix-la-Chapelle*, the king wished to compensate the court for the loss of the festivities of

Carnival, which the war had interrupted. Therefore, on the evening of July 18, 1668, Versailles was the scene of the grandest fête—the most sumptuous he had ever given. It came at the cost of more than a hundred thousand French livres for an evening of entertainment. Five large prints engraved by Le Pautre commemorated the event. The party marked the most brilliant moment of Louis XIV's youth.

While the *Pleasures of the Enchanted Island* fête had clearly been hosted to impress Louis' mistress at the time, Louise de La Valliére, this party was to delight the new lady in Louis' life, Madame de Montespan. Louis XIV, because of his position as king, could literally have any young lady he chose, and he chose often. While he became devoted to only a few, his conquests were so numerous that a full count was never made. La Valliére, fearing the loss of his love, committed the ultimate error—she clung to him fiercely and drove him farther away. Her suffering became evident in her physical appearance as she became pale and thin in court. She cried, pleaded, and found no pity in him. His wandering eye had found someone who was La Valliére's exact opposite. A woman of fire, his intellectual equal, witty, confident, and as lustful as he was.

While there were many grumblings in France about the return of the Franche-Comté, the *Treaty of Aix-la-Chapelle* was heralded a French triumph. Not everyone shared Louis' enthusiasm. Many were enraged that Louis had given back territories that an expensive war had garnered France. What was the point of it? Yet, Louis, in his indomitable style declared it a major success and celebrated in grand-Louis style. The party would showcase all the wonders Le Nôtre had created in the gardens, and the new expansions to the chateau, including an elaborate forecourt. As the eager guests arrived, they were greeted with straight alleys leading to hidden bosquets, groves, statues, playing waters, latticework structures, and nearer to the palace, gardens of brightly colored flowers in intricate patterns and symmetry. The patterns of the floral arrangements mimicked embroidery and abstract works of art.

Specially built fountains were everywhere. If anyone doubted Louis XIV's ability to command nature, it was obvious in the way he had commandeered water from foreign sources to decorate his gardens with jets of sparkling mists. The groves were even more enchanting, as each became its own salon, as if the rooms of Versailles had been moved outdoors. One such room, a cabinet de verdure, was made of greenery and built to house five tables set up for a light meal. One of these tables resembled a mountain containing several grottos filled with cold meats. Another housed a fake chateau made of almond cakes and candies; one was made up of pyramids of candied fruit, and yet another was filled with vases filled with a variety of liquors. A fifth room offered caramel creations. Separating the tables were orange and other fruit trees such as pears, and bushes offering gooseberries, with fruit adorning their branches, ready to be plucked. Dominating the center of these delights was a thirty-foot-high jet of water.

Fête of 1668 in the garden of Versailles. Engraving by Le Pautre.

The king himself chose the parts of the garden that were to be used, and decided upon the entertainments, in which the water that had lately been brought in at great expense was the chief interest. These beautiful waters had contributed more than any other device to the remodeling of the decorations of Versailles and this was an excellent occasion to show them sparkling everywhere in these lovely gardens where, ten years earlier, nothing was to be seen but marshes. The members of the various organizers were appointed to them. The Duc de Créqui, first gentleman of the Chamber, was charged will all that concerned the stage; the Marshal de Bellefond, first maître d'hotel to the king, was to manage the banquet and supper; and Colbert, as superintendent to of the king's buildings, was entrusted with erecting various structures and the fireworks. He distributed the work between the architects of the theatre, the supper-room, and the ballroom.

The king had arrived earlier in the day from Saint Germain to dine at Versailles with the queen, the Dauphin (who had been brought from Compiegne for the occasion), Monsieur (the King's brother Philippe), and Madame (Henrietta of England, Philippe's wife). The rest of the Court arrived in the afternoon and the officers of the King's household offered refreshments to everyone in the rooms of the ground-floor. The principle ladies were shown to private rooms where they might rest. At about 6 o'clock, the king, the queen, and the entire court went out to the Grand Parterre, and in a moment, this charming multitude of beautiful and richly dressed people dispersed into every part of the gardens. With them, the king passed in front of the Grotto of Tethys, that marvel of rockwork and playing waters, and went down and across the grass to the Basin of the Dragon, to point out the figures of gilded lead that had just been placed there. This fountain was north of the North Parterre at the end of what would be called The Water Avenue. When Louis XVI became king, the dragon's mouth spouted a jet of water 90-feet- high. When the king was not in residence, it was lowered to 35 feet.

Basin of the Dragon at Versailles.

The party then passed through a grove of young trees, the shade of which was fairly thick, and assembled in a sort of labyrinth, the center of which was arranged as an open-air room, at the junction of five paths. It was here that the delighted group attacked the five rooms of meats, cakes, fruits, and caramels, much to the king's delight. At the end of each path was a flowered niche adorned with the king's cipher, and sheltering gilded figures of sylvan divinities, which showed well against the green background of hedges.

After the party had devoured the delicacies, the king stepped into his *calèche*, the queen into her chaise, and the court into carriages, and they drove around the Basin of the Fountain of Swans, which is at the end of the Royal Walk opposite the palace. Here, though the group of statues containing Apollo's chariot was not yet set up, there was a large spout of water composed of a number of jets. Behind them, in the Grand Parc, they would have seen the beginnings of the Grand Canal, then under construction. Following other paths, they arrived at the space where Vigarani had put up the theater. The hall was capable of holding nearly three thousand spectators. The outside was entirely of foliage, the inside was hung with the most beautiful tapestry belonging to the crown, and lighted by thirty-two crystal chandeliers.

Fete of 1668 theater in the gardens of Versailles.
Print engraving by Le Pautre.

On the two sides of the stage two statues, Victory and Peace, did homage to the fortunate conqueror of Flanders and Franche-Comté. Refreshments were again offered at the entrance to the theater. A musical comedy by Molière was performed, called *George Dandin*. The music was once again by Lully.

"On leaving the theater, the Court made its way to another junction in the paths of the park, there to watch from afar another illumination of an octagonal room composed of foliage, covered with a dome, and adorned with gilded figures, trophies, and bas-reliefs. The interior was a magic scene, with its endless effects of water and light. In the center of the room a large rock, surmounted by a figure of Pegasus and studded with silver figures of Apollo and the Muses, represented Parnassus. Flowing cascades bubbled from its summit, forming little rivers that ran out upon the grassy lawns. The whole building was made of foliage, with the exception of eight pilasters at the angles, which supported marble shells by which the water was returned." Flowers, crystal balls, and garlands adorned the room suspended by silver gauze.

Banquet in the domed room. Pegasus can be seen center adorning the rock. Engraving by Le Pautre

Opposite the entrance was the principle buffet in an arbor of considerable size, on it was the king's most beautiful china and plate, with twenty-four enormous basins of chased silver; divided from each other by as many large silver vases, cressets, and candelabra. High silver stands, recently made from Gobelins, held candelabras with ten candles each. The king took up his position in front of the rock, round which tables had been arranged to accommodate sixty people.

"The banquet was of five courses, each of fifty-six large dishes! In the neighboring paths the Queen's private table was laid under awnings, and many other tables were prepared for the ladies. There were three for the ambassadors in the Grotto of Tethys, and there were other profusely laden tables in various parts of the park, where anyone might eat." Madame de Montespan, the king's new favorite, was seated with the beautiful Madame de Ludres, Mademoiselle de Scudéry, and Madame Scarron, afterwards known as Madame de Maintenon. It is Maintenon who will later shock the court when she secretly marries Louis XIV.

At the king's table was seated, the suffering Louis de La Valliére, at the time, still considered the mistress of choice, although most of the court was aware that her popularity with the king had waned. Joining them was the Marquis de Sévigné with her daughter, and Madame de Grignan.

After the banquet, the king rose, and the court followed him through a portico facing the palace. In a couple of hundred paces the party reached a ballroom. This was not like the banquet room they had just departed. It was a magnificent eight-walled building, faced outside and in with marble and porphyry, and ornamented with garlands of flowers. "There is no palace in the world," cried Mademoiselle de Scudéry, "that has a room so fine, so large, so high, and so superb!" There were six rows of seats arranged in the form of an amphitheater, the back of which was a grotto of rockwork. It was here that the effect of the water was most curious. It flowed from the pedestals of statues representing Arion and Orpheus singing among nymphs holding various musical instruments. The water flowed along a path that opened out on one side of the hall. This path, which was flanked by little rooms appeared to go back a long way.

There were chandeliers and pyramids of candles in the great hall, reflecting off the water while the sound of fountains harmonized with the playing violins.

Ballroom at the Fête of 1668. Engraving by La Pautre.

Louis XIV loved to dance. He was known for his adroit moves and composing some of the dances performed at court. Yet, only two years later, it was noticed that while he would partake in royal dances on state occasions, he no longer participated in ballets and carnival performances where he once took center stage. He turned his mind to ruling France as a monarch and laid aside the flippant pageantry that had once amused him.

After the ball, the king and court climbed the steps of the Horseshoe round the Basin of Latona. Latona was mother of Diana and Apollo. Jupiter, the father of her children, turned the peasants of Lycia into frogs when they scoffed at Latona. While the pond had been there since Louis XII built his hunting lodge, it wasn't until two years after the Fête of 1668 that the statue of Latona along with its fountain was placed into the Basin.

It was here that the ubiquitous fireworks would end the grand Fête. "After having passed along several paths whose comparative darkness served to increase the brilliancy of the sight that followed, and on arriving at a magnificent terrace whence both the palace and the terraces that form the amphitheater of gardens are visible, the spectators saw a prodigious change which had taken place in everything. It may be affirmed that no night was ever made so beautiful and so brilliant as that one. For indeed the palace seemed to be a veritable Palace of the Sun, for it was luminous everywhere, and all the windows seemed to be filled with the most beautiful statues of antiquity, but statues that were luminous and of various colors, which shed a great light.

Fireworks at the Basin of Latona, Fête of 1668, by La Pautre.

Abruptly, "the crash of a thousand mortars was suddenly heard, and was followed by a thousand jets of fireworks, which were seen rising from the basins, the fountains, the flowerbeds, the green woods, and a hundred different places. The two elements: water and fire, were so closely mingled together that it was impossible to distinguish them. Then everyone, thinking that this marvelous show of fireworks must be the end of the fête, were returning towards the palace, when suddenly the sky was filled with flashes and the air with a noise that seemed to make the earth shake. Everyone stood still to see the fresh surprise, and immediately a huge number of large rockets shot into the air. There were even some that marked out the king's cipher as they turned and twisted, tracing the double

"L" brilliantly in the air in vivid and clear light."

**Layout of the gardens at Versailles**. 1. Basin of Latona. 2. Fountain of the Dragon. 3. Basin of Apollo. 4. Future home of the Labyrinth. 5. Orangery. 6. Palace of Versailles.

And so ended the grand Fête of 1668. It put Versailles on the map for unequaled pageantry and entertainment. Almost immediately afterwards, the order was given to remodel the palace and its gardens. It was at this period that the Louis XIV began to dream of preparing a more glorious future for Versailles and of moving the court and the government there. The parties at Versailles became more numerous and formed one of the chief titles to the fame of the French Court, which was envied and imitated by foreign courts for its magnificence and good taste. The fêtes by Louis XIV, and later by Louis XV, were copied in the same way that palaces and gardens in imitation of Versailles were built everywhere in Europe, and especially in the principalities of Germany.

In truth, even as the court frolicked in the heady burst of fireworks that July evening, Louis had already tasked La Vau with designing the enlargement of the Palace with a grand design that became known as "The Envelope."

# Chapter Thirteen
## The Envelope

The first building campaign (1664-1668) was launched by the *Pleasures of the Enchanted Islands* fête in 1664. The celebration is often regarded as a prelude to the War of Devolution, which Louis waged against Spain. This first building campaign involved alterations to the chateau and gardens to accommodate the 600 guests invited to the party. The fêtes of 1664 and 1668 did more than just entertain—they impressed upon the king the need for more lodging at the chateau to accommodate his guests. The huge outdoor ballroom erected for the 1668 party had been enormously expensive. Constructing walls and bringing in tapestries and statuary, candelabras and seating for such a temporary structure could hardly be economical. He planned many more spectacular events and needed a permanent place to showcase them. France received a good deal of rain which created another concern for his outdoor festivities.

Louis wheeled about on his platform heels and faced his father's chateau. It would have to come down. He wanted to demolish the original hunting lodge and add huge wings to the north and south to house a ballroom, theater, and lodgings for the members of his court who were worthy of such accommodations. Bringing the nobles to him had been a high priority for the king since the days of the Fronde. Besides, the grumblings of poor accommodations by his guests during his fêtes still bristled.

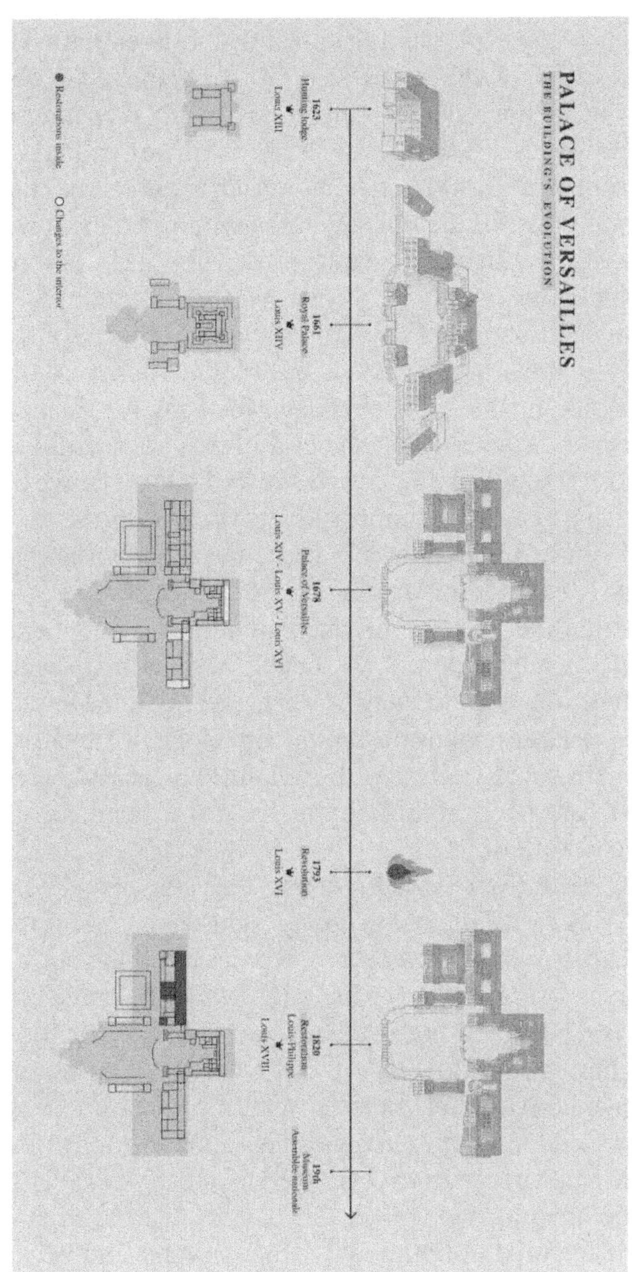


The evolution of Versailles. Eyleen Camargo, Density Design Research Lab.

It was now that Louis and Jean-Baptiste Colbert butted heads over the destination of the royal seat of government. A fortune had already been poured into the Louvre in preparation for the monarch's needs. It was, besides, in the heart of Paris where the king's residence should be. The treasury was there. His ministers were there. Most of the nobility lived within the Paris walls or had estates nearby. Besides, tearing down the old chateau to build something new would be a vast waste of money. Finally, a compromise was reached. Louis would forsake his idea of demolishing the original chateau built by his father Louis XIII, and Colbert (with great reluctance) began focusing the finances on what Louis insisted would be the new seat of power: Versailles.

Louis Le Vau was called in and showed the challenge before him: how to keep the little hunting lodge yet enlarge it for the grand design the king had in mind. The architect finally returned with his drawings. He designed wings and courts that would literally envelope the old chateau, giving Louis the room, he craved. The Envelope, as it became known, or the *chateau neuf* would enclose the hunting lodge on the north, west, and south. Le Vau's design imagined a large extension of the Envelope westwards, enabling huge galleries and staircases to be built. In 1669, the design was approved. The new lodgings for the King and members of his family would be as follows:

On the main floor (which was actually the second floor of the chateau) was called the *piano nobile.* This area was for the king and queen. The *grand appartement du roi* occupied the northern part of the *chateau neuf* and was for the king, while the grand *appartement de la reine* occupied the southern part for the queen's use. The western part of the Envelope was given over almost entirely to a terrace, which was later enclosed with the construction of the Hall of Mirrors (*Gallerie des Glaces*). The ground floor of the northern part of the *chateau neuf* was occupied by the *appartement des bains*, which included a rare sunken tub of rose marble in an octagonal shape. It featured hot and cold running water and became one of Louis XIV's and Madame de Montespan's favorite meeting places. The bath apartments took up five rooms. This area later became the apartments for one of Louis XV's daughters, Madam Victoire, and the tub was moved to the Orangery gallery for storage.

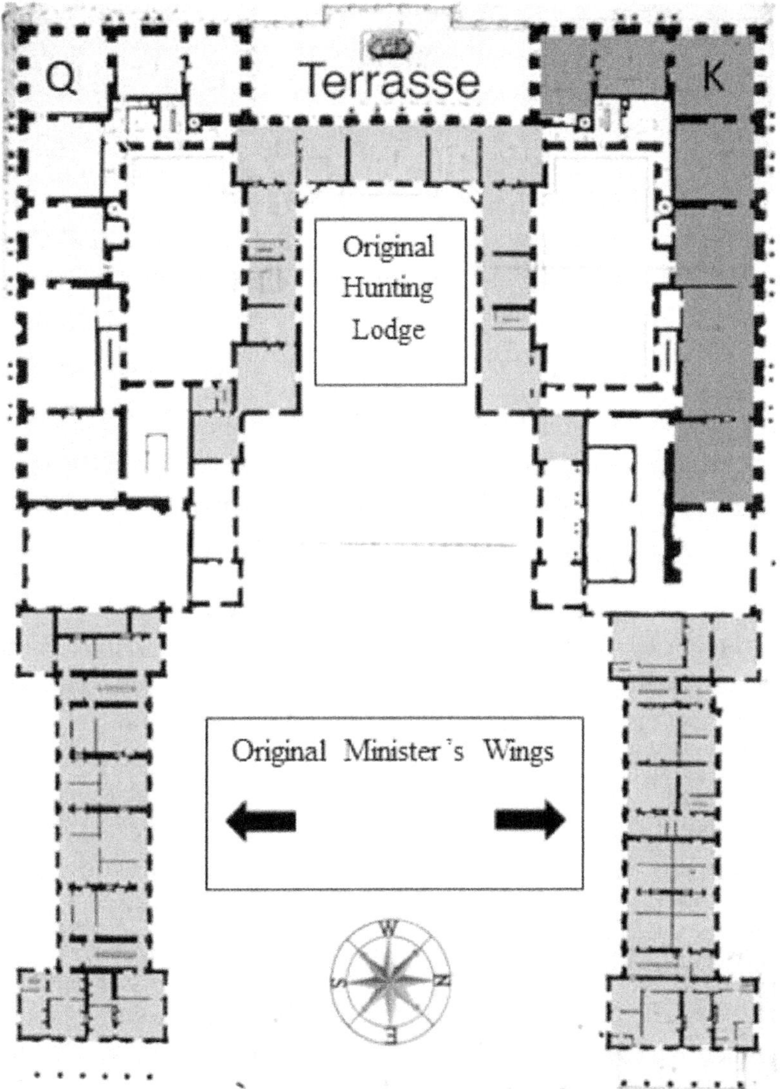


The main floor of Louis XIV after the Envelope was created. The original hunting lodge is shown in medium grey, along with the two minister's wings that were built during the first building campaign of 1664. The King's (K) new apartments are shown upper right in dark grey, and the Queen's (Q) apartments are in the upper left in light grey. The terrace that connected the two royal wings is top center and faced the gardens.

The ground floor also housed the rooms for Philippe (Monsieur, the king's brother) and his wife Henrietta of England. They were known as the Duke and Duchesse d'Orleans. Their sumptuous apartments were on the south side of the chateau. The upper story of the *chateau neuf* was reserved for the private rooms of the king to the north, and rooms for the king's children above the queen's apartments to the south. The upper story, or attic, went a long way to satisfy the king's wish to house his courtiers. Today, we are able to see remnants of these rooms showing the original décor which included painted ceilings and sculpted cornices—elaborate designs for that era.

The Envelope allowed for inner courtyards enabling servants to traverse the growing building without navigating through private rooms. Recent research has also showed that it is possible there were inner carriage ways that allowed the inhabitants to travel under the cover of a *porte cochere* of types. Archeologists have found compacted roadwork material beneath the Dauphin's apartment's area that leads them to believe there were inner court passages for carriages to access the large palace.

On the Paris side of the palace (East) the original minister's wings were converted into more lodgings for courtiers and joined up with the side wings of the old chateau. This created an enormous forecourt. To accommodate his four chief ministers of state, their families and servants, Louis created four pavilions that flanked the courtyard.

A perpetual challenge facing Louis and Le Vau was the discord between the facades of the new palace. The face of the palace facing Paris (East) and that of the garden side (West) were very different. The Paris side's façade was dominated by the old chateau's design. The newer garden side was Le Vau's Italianate façade with Ionic columns, bright creamy stone, and classic lines. It jarred horribly with the French construct of the front of the palace created in the French style with mansard roofs of blue slate, and duller stonework. Le Vau tried to fix the problem by flattening the mansard roofs on the Paris side to harmonize with the garden exterior. However, Louis' growing need for more room won out. Only a year or two later, Le Vau rose the roofs dramatically to provide two attics filled with lodgings. You can still see remnants of Louis XIII's chateau windows in the attic after the Envelope devoured them.

Versailles in 1668. The Minister's new pavilions can be seen flanking the entrance court to the left and right. The Envelope is not yet represented in this painting by Pierre Patel.

## The Salons

With the king and queen's apartments taken care of, and the rooms given to the other notables at court, it was now time for Louis to turn his attention to the north wing. Here he would create a row of salons, one opening into the other that would culminate at the entrance to the open terrace overlooking the gardens. These salons would serve various functions, all destined to impress. From a throne room for the king to receive dignitaries, to fêtes, gambling and cards, this enfilade arrangement allowed an uninterrupted flow of guests and a sweeping view of each room from one end of the hall to the other.

Louis decided to create each salon in the theme of planets with each planet represented by the mythological deity associated with it. Le Brun, the official First Painter for Louis XIV, was tasked with painting the ceiling murals and other room décor. The paintings, in keeping with the propaganda of comparing Louis XIV to the heroic gods, used subjects such as Caesar and the Persian King Cyrus. It was not lost on the public that the scenes melded nicely with Louis' own conquests. It was with the creation of the Hall of Mirrors that the King dropped all semblance of subtlety and had his face painted upon the formidable embodiment of gods and heroes.

These King's Grand Apartments were entered at that time in a systematic order. The Ambassador's Staircase had not yet been constructed, nor had the Hercules drawing room or the Drawing Room of Plenty. These were added under Louis XV's reign. Under Louis XIV's design, one would enter the long line of salons by beginning at the **Venus Drawing Room.**

On the ceiling of the Venus Drawing Room is an oval painting by Houasse portraying Venus crowned by the three Graces as "the Goddess of Love subjugating the Gods and Powers." The corners of the room depict famous lovers in ancient history. Tromp-l'oeil murals were seen everywhere in Europe at this time. Tromp-l'oeil means to "trick the eye." You could paint a statue rather pay the expense of having one made or create a fake window or doorway looking out onto incredible views or imaginary rooms. In the Venus Drawing Room, artist Jacques Rousseau used this technique to paint fake statues of Meleager and Atlanta.

Another useful creation was that of forced perspective. A talented craftsman could make an area appear taller or wider by a clever use of perspective that would trick the eye to see something grander than it was. By using diminishing dimensions, it might seem like the wall was taller. This trick was used in Cinderella's Castle at Disneyland and elsewhere in the other Disney theme parks to make the castles appear taller than they really were. Basically, the area was created or painted smaller toward the top, making one see a false sense of proportion.

The Venus Drawing Room offered the entering guests' light meals. Here, surrounded by gold-leaf molding and accents, the room was a busy juxtaposition of rose and green marble vying for attention. The ceiling murals added to the feeling of opulence but also a sense that the room was too heavy and too much for the senses to take in all at once. Holding court over it all was the only life-size statue of Louis XIV by Jean Warin. He is dressed as a Roman emperor, muscular and commanding, atop a marble pedestal residing in a large niche, a golden seashell rising above it like a canopy. The golden hues of the parquet floor added to the feeling of richness and tone. There was no mistaking whose palace you were in.

The Venus Drawing Room with the statue of Louis XIV (r).

The next room one entered is the **Diana Drawing Room**. Here, the bust of Louis XIV by the famous sculptor Bernini is on full display. The murals decorating the ceiling in the Diana Drawing Room were painted by Gabriel Blanchard and depict the goddess "presiding over hunting and navigation." These two themes were replicated in the coves showing Audran and Lafousse engaging in the two sports. Diana was the sister of Apollo, the sun god that Louis XIV now used as his moniker. The large room, once again created in rose and green marble with heavy gold molding and cartouches, spotlighted a painting by Charles de Lafousse depicting Diana saving Iphigenia. Opposite it hangs a painting by Blanchard showing the goddess watching over a sleeping Endymion. Adorning the ornate fireplace is a bas-relief by Sarrain of the *Flight into Egypt.* Other classical busts, including one of Diana, adorn slender pedestals around the room.

This is the room Louis relegated to one of his favorite pastimes—billiards. He was extremely good at the game and many a courtier learned not to wager against him. Two tiers of seating were arranged to allow guests to watch him play. A large billiard table was set up in the middle of the room. When not in use, it was covered with a large crimson velvet carpet.

Bust of Louis XIV by Bernini in the Diana Drawing Room.

Diana Drawing Room with the bust of Louis XIV (l).

The Venus and Diana Drawing Rooms served as vestibules to the King's State Apartment and were entered from the Ambassador's Staircase when it was added a few years later.

**The Mars Drawing Room** carried the theme of the God of War and marked the beginning of the King's Apartment. This room served as a ballroom and backdrop for concerts, despite the overall theme of war and conquest. Up until 1682, it had been used as a Guard Room, a more fitting use of a room touting war. The cornice surrounding the room is decorated with gold sports helmets and war trophies. The ceiling showcases the God of War on a chariot drawn by wolves. It was painted by Audran. In 1684, galleries for musicians were installed on either side of the fireplace but these were removed in 1750 under Louis XV. Louis XV also decorated the room with large portraits: *The Tent of Darius* by Lebrun and two portraits of by Van Loo of Louis XV and his bride Marie Leszczyńska. Above the doors are paintings brought in from the chateau of Saint-Germain-en-Laye, painted by Simon Vouet. The original paintings that hung here are now at the Louvre.

The Mars Drawing Room today as Louis XV decorated it.

The Mars Drawing Room today is as Louis XV left it—rich red wall coverings, green and white marble, and heavy gold frames housing famous works of art. At the back of the room hang portières—draperies that covered doors or alcoves.

**The Mercury Drawing Room** represented the god of trade, commerce, and liberal arts. It was here under Louis XIV that the gaming was made available. Cards was the court's favorite form of amusement and lost wagers often bereft many a courtier of his purse. At the time, the Mercury and Apollo Drawings Rooms were the most luxurious of the salons. The Mercury Room was also used as an antechamber and became the state bedchamber in 1882. The red-damask draped walls swathed the room in deep tones depicting the opulence of royalty. Chandeliers and candelabras were seen everywhere, their gold and glass dancing in the candlelight. This was the *Ancien Régime* and the height of Louis XIV's glory.

The Mercury Room houses a rare and wonderful piece of craftsmanship—the Automaton Clock presented to Louis XIV by Antoine Morand in 1706.

The Automaton Clock in the Mercury Room.

The Mercury Room showing the Automaton Clock
and acting as a royal bedchamber.

**The Apollo Room** came after the Mercury Room and as mentioned, their use transitioned with the needs of the king. The Apollo Room was a bedchamber until it was repurposed as Louis XIV's throne room. An imposing silver throne rose eight feet high here until 1689. Red damask wall coverings mirrored those of the Mercury Room. A portrait of Louis XIV hung here, painted by Rigaud. Later, a portrait of Louis XVI by Callet was added. Adorning the ceiling was one of Louis XIV's favorite avatars—Apollo. The large fountain of the god sat at the end of the tapis vert in his garden, and he would make another appearance in the ceiling décor of the Hall of Mirrors.

The Apollo Room houses six original candelabras made for the wedding of Louis XVI and Marie Antoinette. There were 24 ordered for the Hall of Mirrors in honor of their wedding. The gold pedestals are replete with fine detailing in the figures seen supporting the columns.

The Apollo Room with the portrait of Louis XIV above the fireplace and an idea of the throne dais, although the king's silver throne had a back that rose 8 feet high. The candelabras are from the Hall of Mirrors and were created for the marriage of Louis XVI and Marie Antoinette.

The salons were designed for amusement, and Louis's *"les soirees de l'apparetement"* were evening receptions given three times a week: Monday, Wednesday, and Thursday evenings. The food was plentiful, the gaming feverous, and the music could be heard throughout the long gallery of salons. All the rooms were decorated by Charles LeBrun and were filled with silver furniture that glinted beneath the candle's glow. When the War of the League of Augsburg broke out, the silver furnishings throughout the chateau were melted down to finance the war. Everywhere was gold and silver, red damask, and rich paintings. At this time, the Apollo Room ended with the king's room on the north side. This room gave out onto the long terrace overlooking the gardens. It later became the War Drawing Room when the Hall of Mirrors replaced the open terrace. A large fountain was in the center. At the opposite end to the south was the Queen's Room, which was replaced with the Peace Drawing Room after the Hall of Mirrors was erected. Construction began on the Hall in 1678.

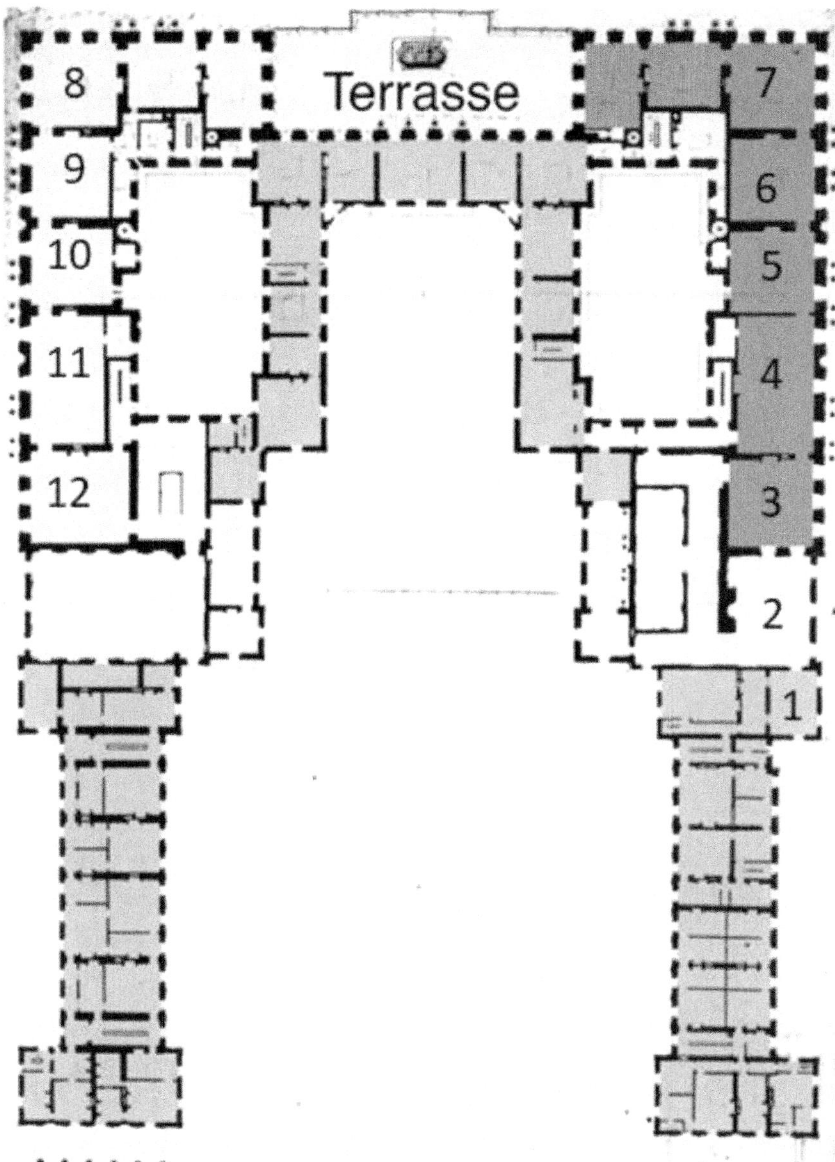


**State Apartments**: 1) Drawing Room of Plenty; 2) Venus Drawing Room; 3) Diana Drawing Room; 4) Mars Drawing Room; 5) Mercury Drawing Room; 6) Apollo Drawing Room; 7) War Drawing Room; 8) Peace Drawing Room; 9) Queen's Bedchamber;10) Salon des Nobles; 11) Antechamber of the Grand Couvert; 12) Guard Room

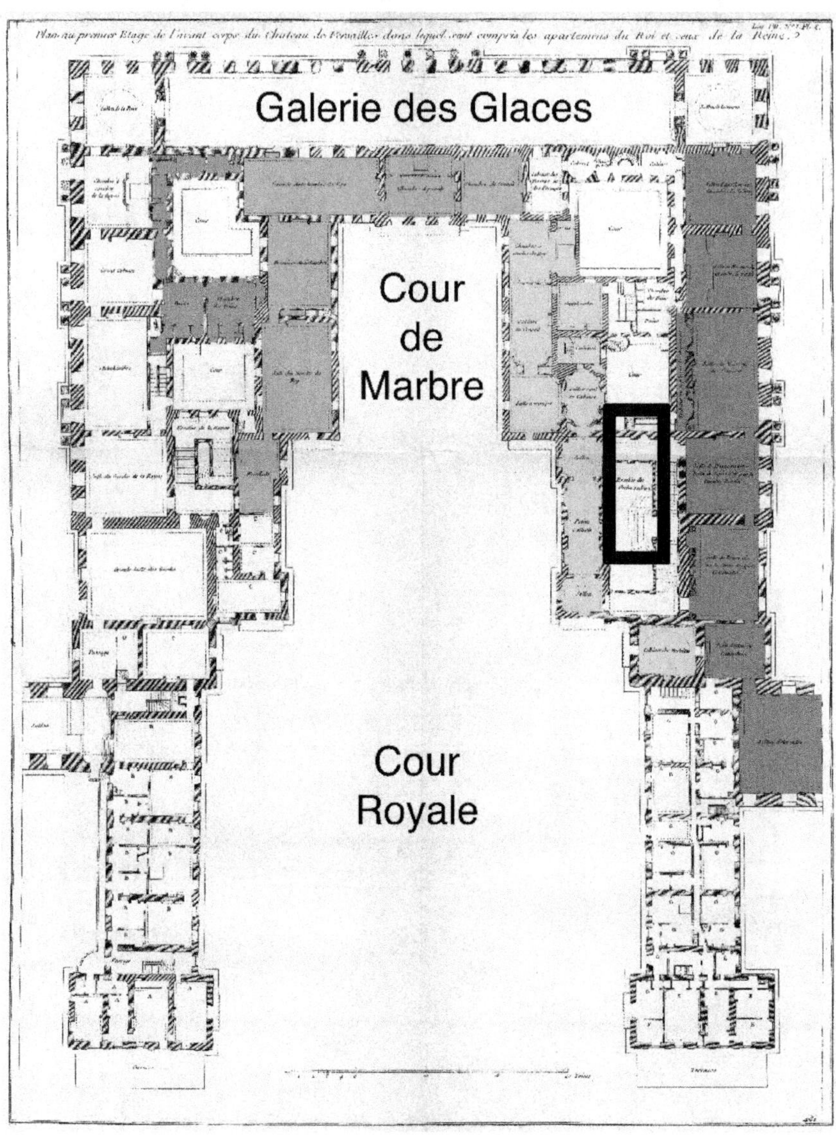


Ambassador's Staircase (*The Grand Escalier*) is seen outlined in black. This illustration also shows the new layout once the Hall of Mirrors (*Galerie des Glaces)* was created.

**The Ambassador's Staircase** was one of two grand designs that put Versailles on the map for architectural achievement. A triple entrance in the brick and stone palace façade offered exterior access to the ceremonial Ambassador's Staircase. It was built to impress and introduce visiting dignitaries to the glories of the Sun King. On the day of their formal audience, overseas diplomats would have been escorted from the Ambassador's Salon across the marble courtyard to enter the imposing vestibule and climb the stairs leading to the King's State Apartment. Designed by the architect Louis Le Vau, the staircase was decorated between 1674 and 1679 with polychrome marbles and an elaborate program of illusion paintings by Charles Le Brun, all lit by a glass roof. Visiting dignitaries were duly impressed by the spectacle that unfolded before them while climbing the stairs that led to the King's State Apartment. Bernini's bust of Louis XIV was first found here at the top of the stairs in an impressive niche. The staircase was destroyed in 1752 by Louis XV who wanted more room for apartments.

The Ambassador's Staircase at Versailles.

So grand was the Sun King's staircase that it was copied literally by King Ludwig II of Bavaria. Although Linderhof castle is much smaller than Versailles, it is evident that the palace of the French Sun-King Louis XIV (who was an idol for Ludwig) was its inspiration. The staircase, for example, is a reduction of the famous Ambassador's Staircase, which would be copied in full in Herrenchiemsee. Ludwig also constructed a Hall of Mirrors, a Grand Trianon and the Petit Trianon based on Versailles' creations.

Ludwig II's reproduction of the Ambassador's Staircase at the Herrenchiemsee Palace.

Louis XIV and his Ambassador's Staircase

## The Hall of Mirrors

While the Ambassador's Staircase was torn down due to King Louis XV's need for more apartments for his daughters and other uses, the jaw-dropping Hall of Mirrors remains. Louis had already shed his ill-disguised nod to his greatness touted in the Salon's ceiling murals. Beginning with the Ambassador's Staircase, he began to have his face portrayed on the various art creations that highlighted his conquests and victories. With the Hall of Mirrors, all reticence to proclaim himself victor of all and the greatest monarch to sit a throne was tossed into the river Seine. This would be the monument to all he had achieved.

Boasting a length of 240 feet, the ceiling murals were to be of prime importance as their sole purpose was to glorify the king. The Counsil of State were called into the Cabinet Room to deliberate the proposed drawings by Le Brun. Sprawled across the table was a detailed arrangement of how the cartouches and main murals would be laid out. Louis was to be portrayed as either Apollo or Hercules, all against the background of his actual victories against his European neighbors.

The bombastic approach of the Sun King to literally thumb his nose at visiting dignitaries who would look up at the propaganda and feel the sting of defeat anew, was one that Louis had been warned about by his right-hand man, Colbert. Saint-Simon, a prolific keeper of journals and diaries at the time of Louis XIV, noted that the ceilings of Versailles had helped to turn Europe "against the King's person rather than his kingdom." Arrogance over one's foes has never been a popular move, but for Louis, his glory and legacy were all he cared about.

Thirty painted tableaus adorned the ceiling, depicting Louis XIV's reign, beginning in 1661. One of these tableaus highlighted the Canal of the Two Seas. This canal, begun in 1666, allowed French's ships to navigate between Sète and the Bay of Biscay on France's south coast. Ten thousand workers engineered the 150 miles of waterway. Just as the Marly Machine had been built to satisfy Louis' demand for more water to feed the fountains and grounds of Versailles, so the Canal of Two Seas bowed beneath his determination to control an inadequate waterway.

Battle after Battle is splashed across the ceiling of the Hall of

Mirrors, trumpeting Louis' victory of wars he had instigated up to this point. It is perhaps the depiction of Louis crossing the river Rhine in 1672 that showcases the Sun King's narcissism. Dressed in Roman attire, hair flowing as if blown by Mother Nature herself, he grips a thunderbolt in one hand while seated atop a silver chariot pushed by none other than Hercules. Enemy towns are seen in a subservient view as they are basically run over. For the Dutch, who had flooded Amsterdam by opening the sea dikes to avoid the onslaught of the Rhine crossing, this mural depiction was an affront.

The Hall of Mirrors was built during the third building phase between 1678 and 1684. The paintings adorning the Ambassador's Staircase were just wrapping up. Before Charles Le Brun could rinse out his brushes from the staircase artwork, he was tasked to begin work on the Hall of Mirrors. Jules Hardouin-Mansart was asked to head the design development and construction of this monumental hallway. The hallway would be flanked by the two new salons—the Salon of War on the king's end, and the Salon of Peace on the queen's. The exterior walls of the Salons date from the time of Le Vau's envelope encasing of the old chateau and were given their current appearance after the installation of the Hall of Mirrors by Mansart.

With its height of 40 feet, the Hall reaches to the attic floor of the Corps de Logis. The square windows of the attic that can be seen from outside only serve aesthetic purposes, as there are no rooms inside. No fireplaces for the Hall were ever considered as it was just too large to heat.

There are 17 tall windows that line the Hall and open in the direction of the park. On the opposite inside of the Hall are 17 equally large mirrors, which are composed of more than 350 individual mirror surfaces. These mirrors reflected the garden façade outside, bringing the colors and grandeur into the chateau. It also reflected the candlelight, setting all the gold and silver accoutrements ablaze. The mirrors served yet another purpose as they spoke to the wealth of the King of France. Mirror glass was very expensive…especially the flawless glass that Louis demanded. The manufacturing of these mirrors was the first major order for the Manfacture royale de glace de miroirs, a glass factory founded by Jean-Baptiste-Colbert, the later Compagnie de Saint-Gobain. The Venetian monopoly on the manufacturing of mirrors fell beneath this new French factory.

The tragic loss of the stunning silver furnishings that lined the Hall of Mirrors is something still mourned today. As mentioned, the furnishings were melted down to finance the War of the League of Augsburg. The furnishings seen today were manufactured during the $19^{th}$ century after most of the original furnishings were lost during the French Revolution.

Besides the paintings and furnishings, there were sculptures of rare beauty lining the lengthy hallway. The gilded bronze capitals of the Rouge de Rance marble pilasters are decorated with the Fleur-de-lis and Gallic roosters. The gilded bronze trophies, which adorn the green marble Pier glasses, were manufactured by goldsmith Pierre Ladoyreau.

The marble and porphyry busts of eight Roman emperors are accompanied by sculptures of Greek and Roman deities, and Muses, such as Bacchus, Venus, Modesty, Hermes, Urania, Nemesis and Diana. The latter (Diana of Versailles) moved to the Louvre in 1798. A copy was placed in Versailles in 2004 to 2007 during the restoration of the Hall of Mirrors.

The Hall of Mirrors at Versailles

Chandeliers hung from the 40-foot-high ceilings and could be pulled up during the day so that the murals could be seen unobstructed. Candelabras lined the hall, seated atop ornate gold pedestals. The cost of candles alone needed to light just this area of the palace was formidable. Balls were held here, treaties signed, dignitaries glad-handed, as the beautiful and famous walked beneath Louis' image shining in all his glory above their heads. Thomas Jefferson and Benjamin Franklin were guests who would go back to England and look askance at the modest stone walls of the royal palaces. The Hall of Mirrors was perhaps Louis XIV's crowning success. It has been copied and admired for centuries.

A royal ball held in the Hall of Mirrors

# Chapter Fourteen
# **The Court**

The Sun King had proved to France, and indeed the world, that he was to be set above all who had come before him, and, if he continued with his vision of Versailles, all who would come after.

Although his affair with Mlle de La Vallière had been prominently displayed for some time, she remained an ornament without status. By 1667 she had given the king two daughters, only one of whom survived infancy. In the registry of births, their parentage was listed as "unknown." Louis XIV, with his usual thumbing of his nose at protocol, reinstated his grandfather's custom: La Vallière was given the title of duchess and her daughter by Louis—Marie-Anne de Bourbon, was officially declared as the king's issue in front of the Parlement. This officially made La Valliere Louis XIV's first *maîtresse déclarée.* the recognized mistress of the king. This title would be given to several mistresses in Louis XIV's and Louis XV's reigns. Louis XVI never offered Marie Antoinette a rival, something practically unheard of in the French aristocracy.

Louise La Vallière may have hoped that this official title and recognition of her daughter as the king's offspring was a good sign that she held his sole regard. It was very apparent to the court and the queen that Louis's only interest in his wife was purely one of duty and giving her the tributes, she was entitled to. Maria Therese had never had the wit, cunning, or sexual appetite that could hold a man like Louis XIV's interest. She had held a certain hatred in her heart for La Vallière as her lady-in-waiting had clearly betrayed her. How difficult it must have been to watch a woman's belly swell with the child of her husband and king. These cruelties were inflicted on royal wives throughout the annals of history, not just in France.

The court gossip spoke not of Louise's new status as official mistress as a raising of rank but thought it a sign that Louis was foisting her off with a title and acknowledgement of her daughter. It was no secret that the King had turned his attentions and affections to another: marquise de Montespan. Louise was not naïve; she had seen the change in Louis and his visits to her bedchamber had declined over the weeks and months. Rather than accept her fate and be satisfied with her rank in the court and the luxuries it brought, she panicked and clung to him. Weeping openly, she began wasting away as she tried without success to regain the attention he had once lavished upon her. This did nothing but diminish her in his eyes, and he pulled further away. She was in love with him, but Louis was capable of loving more than one woman at a time. While he had few official mistresses, his sexual conquests could fill a ledger. No pretty thing was out of reach for the King.

Madame de Montespan

In 1667, Louis began his affair with Mlle de Montespan. The fact that she was the friend and confidant of Louise La Vallère made it all the more painful for the long-suffering lady who was once again pregnant with Louis' child. Louis was now spending his evenings with Montespan, but he kept the poor Louise dangling on a thin thread of hope. Louis refused to cut her loose. What was his would always remain his, and he continued on with both women beneath the queen's nose. It was now Montespan he sported about the grounds and paid homage to, even though that fall Mme de La Vallière bore him a son.

As the courtiers continued to fill the halls at either Saint Germain or the newly completed Tuileries, Louis grew more impatient to have his shining palace in the wilderness completed. It was fine to host extravagant fêtes there, but he wanted it to be home base—the French seat of power. Colbert, his trusted advisor, poured over blueprints and financial assessments morning, noon, and night. It didn't help the bottom line that Louis often changed his mind after a room or garden component had been built. The palace chapel underwent several changes and locations before the one that stands today was completed. It was akin to dealing with a child who enjoys the thrill of building something out of blocks, only to tear it down and start again when a new idea strikes. It was costly and prolonged the finished project longer than it should have.

Colbert's tireless loyalty to Louis did not go unnoticed by the Sun King. On January 1, 1667, Louise wrote to the duc de Chaulnes, a great man of a prominent French family, that he was arranging the marriage of the man's nephew, the sieur de Chevreuse, to Colbert's elder daughter. Here again, Louis played his hand, showing the aristocracy that the line of nobility had been blurred. Colbert's father had been a mere clothier. They were what the French called *bourgeois*. Here, Louis had elevated his faithful minister to a rank equal to any nobleman, giving notice to the elite that those who served him loyally could be elevated as high as those of noble birth. It was a tremendous shaking of the aristocratic scaffolding that had been their foundation and right since time began. Colbert was greatly honored, while the nobility looked about them with the new understanding that their place at court was not only perilous, but as fragile as the parchment upon which their coveted invitations had been printed.

The campaign to bring the nobles to heel was done so adroitly, that few realized the manipulation behind the new court etiquette. What seemed to be merely a desire for decorum and high fashion was actually Louis' way of keeping them tied to him through rules and spending. If they were kept busy learning the new dance routines, or table etiquette, or the latest length of lace cuff, they would not have the time, or money, to revolt against him.

His taming of the Protestant church was much more obvious and still foremost in the king's mind. He kept track of each conversion to the Catholic faith and discreetly rewarded those who "changed lanes," either in a written letter or advancement at court. It was made patently clear that no Protestant would be elevated in the service of the Sun King.

During all of Louis' machinations, both in front of and behind the throne, his sole heir to the throne was largely forgotten. The Dauphin, housed away at Compiègne with the king's other children born outside the royal bedchamber, was never visited by his father. The maréchale de La Mothe, the boy's governess, received a letter from Louis concerning his six-year-old son on May 21, 1667: "I am very glad that my children should have arrived at Compiègne in good health and that my son should be well-behaved; use the time in which you are alone with him to make him fear you. I can see nothing more needed at the present time."

Queen Maria Theresa with Louis, the Dauphin

While Louis XIV cared for his son and kept in contact with La Mothe concerning his happiness, it was uppermost in the King's mind that his son obey authority, and that he remained in good health. He was heir to the throne. Unfortunately, the young boy was of a passive nature, without his father's fire or passion. Louis was also aware that sons can rise up as enemies to the throne. For the boy, it was a cold and remote upbringing.

The young Dauphin was not the only one feeling the mercurial love of the Sun King. Louise La Vallière was now in an impossible position. The King loved her in his way. She had born him children and remained a pliant and obedient mistress. But there was another, more heartless need to keep Louise nearby—she acted as a shield for his burgeoning affair with Mme de Montespan. For Montespan was a married woman. Not only married but wed to a jealous man of temper. To bed Montespan was to commit double adultery. Even the French Court was shocked at this audacious move of Louis'. How his queen must have felt is not hard to imagine.

Yet, it was little Louis La Vallière that was treated with the most cruelty. In order to keep the adulterous affair with Montespan under wraps a while longer, Louis placed her apartment behind Vallière's so that he could pretend to be seeing Louise, while in actuality, he would go into her room, dismiss her servants, and hurry to the door leading to Montespan's chambers. It wasn't long before Montespan became pregnant. Her labor and delivery were carried out in utmost secrecy.

Little by little, the veil of secrecy fell away, and Mme de Montespan was ensconced at court, dazzling all who came near her. With her blonde hair, full bosom and beautiful face, she was said to outshine every woman in Louis' ample court. She outdressed them—a feat in itself for the French noble women. Dripping in jewelry, she went about enjoying the entertainments at court with abandon. Whether dining on rich pastries, whirling about the dance floor, or gambling at the tables, she demanded the spotlight. The apartments given her by the king were fitted with every luxury. By the time she was moved into Versailles, she had more rooms appointed to her than the queen, including the royal bath apartments that filled five rooms!

**To the Victor Go the Spoils**

In 1670, when Louis XIV looked about at what he had created, he must have felt the pride of great accomplishment. His court with its etiquette and fashions was the finest in Europe. Even his long leonine wig was being copied by the rest of Europe, as were his fashions, many of which he designed himself. Louis had cultivated the finest minds of his era and unleashed them to create unprecedented marvels: Mansart the architect; Lully the musician; Molière and Racine with their theatrical productions; and Le Brun, who was rivaling the finest Italian artists. The French fashions dominated the world boutiques. The richness of fabric and abundance of lace wasn't enough for Louis to demonstrate his wealth; jewels were sewn into the clothes, hats, and shoes. Adding to that were the tiaras and jewels adorning fingers, ear lobes, and wrists. It was all a dazzling masterpiece that would become synonymous with Versailles.

In that same year, Louis looked with pleasure at the royal treasure chest. His coffers had swollen from 63 million livres in 1664 to 74 million in 1670, and all while keeping taxes stable. His army and navy were given 16 million and 9.5 million respectively, boundaries were fortified, and new buildings sprung up to the tune of 5 million. Colbert oversaw it all. Knowing his chief minister was always there, ready with the ledgers, the advice and the loyalty, Louis looked ahead with the confidence of a man who dominated all he saw.

Colbert, perhaps feeling his oats, took the brave stance in 1671 to admonish the king against a strategy he was considering regarding war. Louis ignored him, perhaps to keep the minister in his place, and also because he had been listening to other counsel at the time. Colbert, surprised at the transference of Louis' usual trust in his sole counsel, reacted as a jilted lover would. The King put pen to paper to reassure him, while keeping the lines of authority securely in place:

"Do not think that my regard for you can be abated as long as your services continue, that will never happen, but you must render them such as I wish, and believe that I do it all for the best. The preference you fear my giving others must not worry you. I only wish to avoid injustice and work for the best of my service."

While the other ministers served the King in their specific roles, it was Colbert who intervened in other, not-so-official matters. He would keep the King apprised of his children should one fall ill, and make sure he was aware of any close relations or friends who were indisposed or absent from court for unusual reasons. Perhaps a more uncomfortable role occurred pertaining to the King's brother, Phillipe.

Philippe, duc d'Orleans

Phillipe, the duc d'Orleans (Monsieur), had never tried to hide his affinity for the male sex. He had married Henrietta out of duty but sought affection elsewhere. Phillipe had fallen madly in love with a penniless young man who was related to the Lorraine family, and hence, entitled to attend court. There, the chevalier de Lorraine, wooed both men and women alike with his good looks and charming personality. He, in fact, got by on his cunning and seductive nature. Once aware that the royal brother had fallen for him, he wasted no time in reciprocating the affection, seeing the golden goose literally handed to him. Their affair was flouted before the court, enraging Louis and embarrassing Phillipe's poor wife who doubled her efforts to annoy him. Despite the fact that Henrietta had carried on a long affair with her husband's own brother, she felt insulted and humiliated.

Henrietta of England

Louis, needing to mollify Phillipe to keep him in line, finally came to terms with the two men's affair, even granting certain privileges to the chevalier from time to time. When the news of the death of the Bishop of Langres reached the ears of the court at St. Germain, Philippe promised the dead Bishop's two abbeys to his lover, Lorraine. Phillipe went to Louis to confirm the transaction. There were things Louis was willing to do to keep Phillipe dependent upon him and happy enough not to ever commandeer an uprising against him but giving two abbeys to a man of Lorraine's reputation was too much to ask. He declined to grant Philippe the abbeys.

Monsieur, acting with his usual flare-up of emotions, announced that he was moving out! He ordered his apartments packed and made ready to leave. Louis sent M. L Tellier to talk to him, but Philipe continued to rant and said he would go as far away as possible.

Memories of his late Uncle Gaston d'Orleans surfaced in Louis' mind. An unhappy brother could start a civil rebellion. This was a serious matter. Phillipe was an emotional man, and emotional men are irrational men. What Philippe didn't count on was Louis' next move.

Feeling that M. le chevalier de Lorraine had encouraged Philipe to leave court, Louis had the chevalier arrested. The guards surrounded Philippe's apartments at St. Germain where Lorraine was staying and took him into custody. Philippe embraced him but knew there was nothing he could do. Lorraine was sent to Montpellier. Philippe made good his promise to leave and departed St. Germain palace with Madame, stopping for a day or two in Paris. On January 30$^{th}$, they went on to Villers-Coteret, one of his castles twenty miles north of Paris. Only three days later, a miserable Philippe appealed in a letter to the one man he knew would have the king's ear—Colbert.

"Monsieur Colbert," Philippe wrote, "since for some time now I have thought you one of my friends, and since you are the only one among those who have the honor of being close to the King who has also showed concern for me in my present dreadful circumstances, I think you will not be sorry that I ask you to tell the King: that I have come here feeling the greatest pain at having either to go away from him or to be covered with shame if I remained at his Court. That I beg of him to think of what the world would say if I were observed cheerful and at peace in the pleasures of St. Germain during Carnival while an innocent prince [the chevalier de Lorraine], my best friend on this earth, and one truly attached to me, languishes for the love of me in a wretched prison; further, the manner in which he was seized was an insult to me, uncertain as I was whether it was not myself who was to be arrested, as my room was, for quite some time, surrounded by guards… Further, the King sent to ask my wife what she wanted to do; this shows he was inclined to allow her to fail in her duty to me by deserting me…

"If M. le chevalier de Lorraine were guilty, I would be the first to send him away, but he never thought of anything but deserving the King's good graces and esteem; I can answer for this, to the shame of my enemies, that I love the King better than myself if only he will give me the means of reconciling my love for him and my honor, and in this I beg him to remember I am his brother."

It is astonishing that a royal prince would reach out to a commoner such as Colbert to entreat Louis' forgiveness. Colbert's approach to Louis must have worked, or it was the heartfelt effort of Philippe's letter, but by March 3rd, it was accomplished. A contrite Philippe and a relieved Henrietta arrived back at St. Germain and soon after, Lorraine was released. His return to Court was not instantaneous, but when he did return, much of his haughty manner was missing. He appeared humbled and submissive.

Louis had presented a powerful lesson to Philippe, and the rest of the world. Not even his own brother was safe in his Court. He held all the cards and made all the rules of the game. Philippe accepted his role; despite how well he had shown bravery and skill during the campaign in Flanders, he would remain in his brother's shadow and be totally dependent on the crumbs thrown him.

The chevalier de Lorraine

A possible coup had been averted, but Louis XIV was cognizant of the fact that sands can shift beneath one's feet at any moment. His son Louis, the Dauphin, was not exactly made of the stuff of great kings. He needed an insurance policy that should he die, his legacy would live on. He ramped up his efforts to find one.

Louis, the Grand Dauphin at a young age.

# Chapter Fifteen
# The Gilded Cage of Versailles

Mark Twain defined the 19th century as the Gilded Age of America. He called it a period "that was glittering on the surface but corrupt underneath." Louis XIV's reign was certainly glittering; as were the hallways, furnishings, and attire. Yet, beneath the surface lay treacheries, adultery, greed, and even murder. It was a time of manipulation and avarice. No one was safe. You could obtain the King's good favor one moment and incur his wrath the next. People and relationships were discarded as easily as an obsolete piece of lace.

In the forefront, especially from the 1670's on, was Louis' one obsession—Versailles. The very name was recognized now as the palace that morphed into new lines and structures as if by magic. Yet this magnificent structure was not created using alchemy or by the waving of a wand. It came with a terrible cost in human life. With the grand creations needed to host Louis' fête of 1664, six men were crushed by stage machinery that had lost their mooring and fallen. It was common knowledge that workers were being injured almost daily, partly due to Louis' need to rush things that should have taken a longer period to create.

While the King was in the midst of a public audience at nearby Saint Germain, a mother recently bereft of her son who was killed while working at Versailles, accosted the king verbally where all could hear. She screamed that he was a "king of machines," that he surrounded himself with whores, and that he was a "tyrant!" Louis's surprise is perhaps a glimpse into just how removed he was from public opinion. He asked if the woman was referring to him? She shouted "Yes!" and continued on with her rants until she was restrained and arrested. She was publicly whipped as an example, but it did little to settle the disquiet surrounding Louis' feckless drive to have his palace completed at all costs.

In the early 1680's, the peak of the building frenzy, tens of thousands of workers labored day and night. Extra lighting was supplied to allow them to work through the darkness. There were no safety ropes in place, and many workers plunged to their death from the rickety scaffolding. To make matters worse, the water situation at Versailles added to the death toll. The ponds Louis had put in place to catch the rainwater and help supply needed water to his property, became a breeding ground for mosquitoes. These small insects were not only the bane of visitors to the site but carried with them typhoid and marsh fevers. Those exposed most often to the flying carriers were the workers, some building in near proximity to water features and stagnant swamp areas. The death toll was so high, that the bodies were removed at night in the hopes that the healthy workers wouldn't see them. Some blamed it on the "air" of Versailles. Over three thousand workers were injured to the point that they could no longer work. Their families were paid a small indemnity as recompense, but it amounted to not more than enough to sustain a small family for several weeks.

Louis' fevered pace to see his creation realized and the court moved to Versailles resulted in extravagant waste of not only lives but money. One area was built, only to be torn down when Louis changed courses. An example is the royal chapel, a building that changed location and façade several times during his reign. In 1672, the king commissioned a new chapel that was larger than the original one at Versailles. It would be built on the south side of Le Vau's Envelope. It later became the Grand Guardroom and finally, the Coronation Room. This was due to Louis's desire for an even bigger and grander chapel. Only six years after the smaller chapel had been created, it was decided it was obstructing entrance into the new south wing. Mansart was once again instructed to design something worthy of the chapel of Versailles. Unfortunately, this would require a new north wing, the building of which required the destruction of the wonderful Thetys Grotto.

In 1682, it was stated in the *Mercure Galant* that Louis XIV's vision "has always been that the Chapel of Versailles would be the most magnificent part of this sumptuous and brilliant palace." While the designs were being drawn up, a temporary chapel was built in what is today the Salon of Hercules. It was decorated in suitable elegance, with an altar and religious paintings, gold guilt trimmings and matching parquet floor. Le Brun, however, was not commissioned to paint a ceiling mural here as it was only to be in use until the grand chapel was completed.

It is useful to note, that 1682 is also the official recorded date that the court was finally moved from Saint Germain to Versailles. The palace was still very much a building site, and nobles, seeking out their rooms on various floors, flecked pieces of plaster from their fine clothing and wiped sawdust and debris from their effusive wigs. The clamoring of hammers and pickaxes went on throughout the day. Feet encased in the latest Parisian shoe stepped over tarps and buckets. The smell of new paint was cloying, as was that of wet plaster. Dust floated in the sunlight that found its way through rippled window glass. Yet, there was an air of excitement as the noble guests were given their room assignments—some not quite as happy to find they had been relegated to the much smaller apartments on the attic floor.

It is no wonder that when the day was fine, many new inhabitants of Versailles found their way outside into the gardens, as far away from the noise and pollution of building supplies as they could get. In awe, they watched as the new foundation was laid in 1688 for the Grand Chapel. It was enormous. Yet, as with so many of Louis' grand plans, it was halted before it had even really begun. Not due to a change of mind by the king, but to a change in the political climate. In short, France was at war. It was called the War of the League of Augsburg. The chapel was not completed until a decade later in 1710, but by that time, Louis had a new vision for it. Mansart licked the tip of his worn pencil and began on the new blueprints.

This design would entail a tall, elongated building in Baroque style, two stories high. It dominated the front courtyard, and while its façade was sometimes at war with the original design of the small hunting lodge, it was considered a triumph of architecture and Versailles' crowning glory. The second story of the building was the king's private area, or "tribune," where he could watch the services below, along with selected members of his royal family. It was on the same level as his living quarters. The altar and was on the main floor and the court assembled there for worship. The chapel was dedicated to Saint Louis, Louis IX, who was a source of great pride to the Bourbon dynasty. The interior of the chapel was resplendent with paintings, gold gilt, and marble. Two relics of Saint Louis were installed.

The Royal Chapel looming over the roofline of Versailles

Critics of the design thought its height jarring as it disrupted the usual horizontal flow of the palace roofline. Saint Simon, the prolific court diarist, called it an "enormous catafalque." But none could deny the breathtaking beauty of the interior. The King's tribune was entered through the Salon de la Chapelle. Here, classic Corinthian columns ascended in a colonnade of marble. The Salon de la Chapelle is decorated with white stone and the bas-relief sculpture *Louis XIV Crossing the Rhine* by Nicolas and Guilaume Coustou that forms the focal point of the room's décor.

Main floor and organ of the Royal Chapel

The floor of the chapel itself is inlaid with polychromatic marbles, and at the foot of the steps leading to the altar is the crowned monogram of an interlaced double "L" alluding to Saint Louis and Louis XIV. The sculptural and painted decoration uses both Old Testament and New Testament themes. Paintings of *God the Father in His Glory Bringing to the World the Promise of Redemption*, *The Resurrection of Christ*, and *The Descent of the Holy Ghost Upon the Virgin and the Apostles* were some of the magnificent artwork adorning the altar area and elsewhere. The magnificent organ of this fifth chapel of Versailles was built by Robert Clicquot and Julien Tribuot in 1709-1710. The organist was Jean-Baptiste Buterne. The chapel was finally completed in 1710, near the end of Louis XIV's reign.

Painting in the domed ceiling of the Chapel.

During the 18th century, the chapel witnessed many court events. *Te Deums* were sung to celebrate military victories and the births of children (*Fils de France and file de France*) born to the king and queen. Marriages were also celebrated here, such as the wedding of Louis XV's son the dauphin Louis with Infanta Marie-Therese d'Espagne of Spain on February 23rd, 1745, and the wedding of Louis XVI to Maire Antoinette on May 16, 1770. Of all the celebrations hosted in the chapel, those associated with the Order of the Holy Spirit were among the most elaborate.

Today, the chapel, after having been de-consecrated in the 19th century, is now a venue hosting both private and state events. Musical concerts are often held in this glorious chapel of Versailles.

## Did the Cost of Versailles Bankrupt France?

There are two sides to the French livre when it comes to sizing up the vast sums spent in the creation of the Sun King's dream. Some believe the almost 91 million livres spent on the palace and grounds was the reason for the food shortages and the French Revolution. Others point to the fact that the building of the royal seat of power needed to showcase wealth and power as part of the message to the world that France was the undeniable poster child of military and economic strength. When the ledgers were balanced sometime later, it was shown that the cost to build Versailles was not much more than one percent of the annual total expenses of the royal government. In contrast, in 1692 alone, the total cost of the military and war efforts equaled 114 million livres. And so, the debate continues. It is known that the feeling of the lower classes of France was that the royalty and nobility at Versailles were living in opulence while they were begging for scraps of food.

## Louis' Open Door Policy

To the amazement of much of Europe, Louis XIV believed that all should be able to enjoy the pleasures of Versailles. The doors to the palace remained open to the public. The only cost of admission was that you were respectfully dressed. Male visitors had to wear swords. Indeed, there was a cart stationed at the gates where you could rent a sword for your visit. The nobility wore swords as a symbol of their rank. Peasants were not allowed, including the gardens where the King often escaped the crowds within his palace. The guards opened the gates at six in the morning and closed them again at midnight. For those of the *bourgeoise* set (not one of the court elite), it gave them ready access to the King—perhaps not close enough for conversation, but close enough to view him in all his glory.

To reach the palace in the early days was to endure a rutted cattle path. By 1680, Louis had vastly improved the road, including its shape. Gone was the irregular twisting and turning pathway that bent to the will of the wilderness. Under Louis' hand, the earth was moved, and a straight road leading from the Champs-Elysees to a new bridge that crossed the Seine at Sevres, and finally a broad avenue known as the avenue de Paris culminated at the palace.

There were several means of transportation depending on your pocketbook. If you had money, you could buy a seat in a carriage that seated four and took roughly two hours from Paris to Versailles. The court in the 18$^{th}$ century could hire a two-seater carriage that had been nicknamed, oddly enough, the "chamber pot." Finally, there was a large omnibus that could seat twenty at the cost of twenty-five sols. These typically carried the less well-to-do. These buses left the Tuileries twice a day. It was as close as ferrying visitors to Disneyland as the century came. Speaking of ferries, you could take a ferry to the new bridge at Sevres, and a horse the rest of the way. Some were reduced to walking the 12 miles from Paris, and risked robbers who were still very much a threat in those days.

The irony of Louis XIV's open door policy was that his desire to create the seat of power at Versailles was his need to get away from the crowds and threats of civil unrest to which living in Paris exposed him. Yet, here, in his sanctuary in the wilderness, he flung open his palace to anyone who observed the court etiquette and didn't appear in rags. It was obvious that his real goal was to impress, and those he wished most of all to dazzle were the nobility, foreign diplomats, ambassadors, and leaders of state. Where it backfired for Louis, and his successors, was it isolated him from the common daily activities of Paris. After Louis' permanent move to Versailles, he visited Paris only eight times in thirty-three years!

He was encapsulated within his marble fortress and his subjects felt he had not only abandoned them by moving away from the capital city, but that he was completely unconcerned with their welfare as he spent fortunes on food, entertainment, and fireworks. This discontent and anger would fester and grow until it exploded in 1789, culminating in the beheading of Louis XVI and his Queen, Marie Antoinette in 1793.

### A Gilded Cage or a Prison?

While the Sun King may have thought his subtle maneuvering of the nobility went unnoticed, there were some who saw all too clearly the clever fitting of the golden bit into the aristocratic mouths. Saint-Simon, the court historian was one such person. He was not pleased with the king's methodical stripping away of power from these noble men. He also saw another, insidious reason for Louis' need to build a palace away from Paris. According to Simon "The awkward situation with his mistresses and the dangers involved in conducting such scandalous affairs in a busy capital, crowded with people of every kind of mentality, played no small part in deciding him to leave."

Louis, once the lodgings at Versailles were large enough to house his formidable entourage, made known that he expected the court (emphasis on the nobility of the court) to be in attendance upon him on a permanent basis. The household, entertainments, strict etiquette, lodging arrangements, and schedules were to ensure that those who benefited from his largesse, room, board, stables, and even religious services, never forgot to whom they were to pay homage.

Saint-Simon was well aware that the infrastructure of Versailles' dress code, gambling, and office pensions were to impoverish the nobility through lavish spending, including their carriages and servants needed to keep face. The outcome was a subservient noble class that would be brought even lower when the King's *lever* and *coucher* were introduced. They would go from merely trying to keep up with the demands of court, to squabbling over who had the right to hand the king his shirt.

And so, Louis XIV's vision of a palace grand enough to house his entire court was realized. In the 1670s, Saint-Germain-en-Laye could only house sixty-three lodgers. Most of the courtiers were forced to find rooms in town, just as they had in Paris. As the court swelled, so did the complaints as to lack of places to stay, or the rudimentary lodgings they were forced to take. A noble lady who had spent a fortune on gowns and jewelry could find herself sleeping on a hay mound.

Louis knew the hook needed to lure the prey to the court. It was himself. Their need to be in his proximity and a chance to advance themselves and their families depended on being at Versailles. Many palace offices were handed down through family lines, insuring wealth and privilege. In his memoirs, Louis stated that the "shared pleasures of the court entertainments, which give the members of the court an honest familiarity with us, touch and charm them more than one can say."

The marquise de Sèvignè summed up how well Louis's plan had worked, "I have seen those beautiful apartments, I am charmed by them...Everything is grand and magnificent, and the music and dancing are perfect...But what pleases me above all is to spend four hours with the sovereign, to share in his pleasures and he in ours."

She went on to state better than most could, the culmination of Louis' progress in reining in the nobility: "Formerly, the queen's ladies of honor were marquises, and all the great offices of the king's household were mere lords: now they are all held by dukes or marshals of France, and everything has gone up."

Alexandre Bontemps, 1st Valet to Louis XIV

It was not just the etiquette and rules of the court that lay within the king's control. He knew everything that went on behind closed doors. Louis' First Valet, Alexandre Bontemps, was feared for his exceptional access to the king. Through him, Louis set up a vast network of spies. The gossip among the courtiers was also a grapevine of information. It was well known that few secrets lasted withing the golden gates of Versailles. Saint-Simon stated that they used Swiss Guards "to frequent the corridors and passages, courts and gardens by day and night, morning and evening, to hide, observe people, follow them, see where they went and when they returned, overhear their conversations and report exactly on everything."

The invisible golden tether attached to each member of Louis XIV's court was as tangible as if it had been made of leather and attached to each person's waistband. Having everyone under one roof assured the Sun King of knowing who was in attendance and who had strayed back to his own estate or to Paris. If one was away for any amount of time, they could hear the King's words that sounded a death knell for the recipient, "I do not know him!"

# Chapter Sixteen
# A Wheel Within a Wheel

As Versailles' court swelled in numbers, so also did the rivalry between families and office holders. The number of household stations needed to accommodate the King alone was staggering:

King's Cabinet (*Cabinet du roi*)
King's Music (*Musique du roi*)
Ceremonies (*Ceremonies*)
Lodgings (*Lodgements*)
Buildings (*Batiments*)
Faculty (*Faculte*)
King's Wardrobe (*Garde-robe du roi*)
Furnishings (*Garde-meubles*)
Entertainment (*Menus Plasirs*)
Provostship of the King's Hotel (*Prevote de l'Hotel du roi*)
King's Mouth (*Bouche du roi*)
King's Bedchamber (*Chambre du roi*)
Grand Stables (*Grande Ecurie*)
Small Stables (*Petite Ecurie*)
Hunt (*Venerie*)
Grand Falconry (*Grande Fauconnerie*)
Wolf Hunt (*Louveterie*)
Boar Hunt (*Vautrait*)
Chapel-Oratory (*Chapelle Oratoire*)
Chapel-Music (*Chapelle Musique*)
Commons Chapel (*Chapelle du Commun*)
Valets
Pages
Wig makers
Guards
Chefs and Kitchen staff

Gardeners
Ministers and their underlings
Artists & Craftsmen
Cleaning Staff
Lords and Ladies-in-Waiting
Scribes
Clergymen
and more

Louis had accomplished his mission to create a city within his marbled walls. Merchants were invited to set up their wares inside the palace. On the upper-floor room of a small building linking the south wing to the central block, licensed tradesmen catered to the wealthy nobility of Versailles with their offerings of lace, perfumes, gloves, dress goods, fans, hats, books, small ornaments, and more. The palace had now furnished everything the residents could desire. They were fed, housed, entertained, offered sports, hunting, tennis, bathing, opulent gardens, music, dancing, and religious services. There was no need to go outside the golden gates of Versailles; just as the Sun King had planned.

Yet, as every caged bird knows, no matter the beauty of the bars, the fineness of the food, or the toys offered it for its amusement, it is still held captive. There comes a time when its need for freedom overcomes its complacency. Within the confines of Versailles, as the numbers of the court would sometimes swell to 10,000 souls, Louis' system of hierarchy soon began to foster discontent. Beyond discontent, it evolved into jealousy and competition for advancement, and beyond that, murder.

## Poison

An environment born of protocol and a strict routine may breed adherence to the dictates of the monarch, yet it can also give a dangerous familiarity with the day-to-day movements of the king and court. Most inhabitants of Versailles were well aware of each other's routine and secrets. Louis was the most well-informed of all.

According to Primi Visconti, an Italian observer in 1673, "Never was a prince less ruled by others. He wants to know everything through his ministers the affairs of state; through the presidents those of the Parlaments; through the judges the least little things; through his favorite ladies the latest fashions; in a word, there seldom occurs, in the course of a day, an event of which he is not informed and there are few people whose names and habits he does not know. He has a penetrating glance, knows everyone's most private business, and, once he has seen a man or heard about him, he always remembers him.

"Besides that, he is very orderly in all his actions. He always rises at eight, remains at the Council from ten to twelve-thirty, at which time he goes to mass, always together with the Queen and his family. Because of his intense and persistent desire to control all the state's business, he has become very clever... He has an extraordinary talent and can often resolve problems which neither the ministers nor their secretaries could understand... At one, after having heard the mass, he visits his mistresses until two, and then he invariably dines with the Queen in pubic. During the rest of the afternoon, he either hunts or goes for a walk; most of the time, he holds another Council when he returns. From nightfall until about ten, he talks to the ladies, or plays cards, or goes to the theater, or attends a ball. At eleven, after his supper, he visits his mistresses again. He always sleeps with the Queen."

A routine so stringent and unvarying allowed an enemy a strong insight into insidious strategies. But it was not only the king who risked attack. Those who circled in his orbit and attended upon him within those advertised timelines were also within the crosshairs of those who paid attention. What Louis set-up as a mantra to a well-structured government and lifestyle soon became the blueprint for evil machinations.

Perhaps the catalyst for a sudden string of poisoning inquisitions at the court of Versailles began with the marquise de Brinvilliers. She was the daughter of a wealthy nobleman but suffered a string of financial reversals while married to Antoine Gobelin de Brinvilliers. According to the charges laid against her in 1675, in 1666 Marie Madeleine-Marguerite de Brinvilliers had conspired with her lover, Captain Godin de Sainte-Croix to poison her father Antoine Dreux d'Aubray, and in 1670 she had likewise killed two of her brothers, Antoine and François d'Aubray, in order to inherit their estates. The poison in question was Tofana poison: a powder or liquid containing arsenic, lead, and belladonna. Fearful that poisoning her close family members could backfire on her if they survived and suspected her, Brinvilliers opted to try a few trial runs on unsuspecting outsiders. She volunteered at the Parisian hospital, the Hôtel Dieu, to help with the care and feeding of some of the patients there. When many of her patients began dying within weeks of her careful tending, she felt she was ready to begin her campaign to sudden riches.

Rather than give the concoction to her male relations all at once and cause suspicion, she administered the poison in small doses over a certain period of time. Her father and two brothers finally succumbed. Natural causes were suspected and so far, all went as planned.

Mme de Brinvillers

Then it all went wrong. Sainte-Croix suddenly died in 1672, and letters and diaries found in his possession pointed to the poison plots between himself and Brinvilliers. Rumors began circulating and reached the ears of Louis XIV who had been dealing with suspicions of poisoning within his court. The king wrote Colbert, saying "As to the business of Mme de Brinvillers, I think it important that you tell the Premier president and the Attorney General from me, that I expect them to do all that honorable people like them must do so as to pursue everyone, no matter what their rank, who are involved in such wickedness. Write me what you hear; it is said that there are many solicitations and that much money is being spent."

Louis had reason to look into the rumors of poison beyond the widespread reports inside his palace. Gossip had suggested it may have been behind the death of his dear sister-in-law, Henrietta of England, Philippe's wife.

Henrietta had been one of Louis XIV's first mistresses of the court, despite the fact she was married to his brother. With Philippe's interest in men, and his obvious distaste for her, it had been easy to be tempted by Louis' attention and affection. As the years went on and Louis lost interest in her, Henrietta's hatred for her marriage escalated and she made it a point to make Philippe's life hell. It was rumored she indulged in extramarital affairs. He in turn threw his usual tantrums, making it clear to the court and to the king that the situation was intolerable.

In 1670, Louis, with his usual lack of tack or sympathy, decided Henrietta could be of use to him. She was the sister of the King of England, King Charles II. Louis sent her across the ocean to act as an intermediary between himself and Charles, a tactic that was highly successful, resulting in the Treaty of Dover. Due to her victory, Henrietta gained a certain notoriety at court and Louis lavished his praise upon her, further alienating his brother. Philippe needed no reminding that he was last on the totem pole and now the woman he had come to hate had risen above him.

On the afternoon of June 29, 1670, Henrietta was out strolling the terrace of St. Cloud, the palace she and Philippe called home when away from Versailles. She asked one her ladies to bring her a glass of chicory water. This was sometimes used to calm upset stomachs and Madame had been suffering from stomach ailments for some time. Within an hour of drinking the mixture, she doubled over in pain and was carried to her bed, where she fell into violent convulsions. After hours of excruciating pain, the princess died.

Immediately, due to other rumors of poisonings going on at court, it was thought that perhaps Philippe had played a part in her passing, a suggestion that dogged him even after an autopsy showed Madame likely died of peritonitis, a form of tuberculosis. The findings showed that one of her lungs was adhered to her ribs and her liver was spilling bile into her stomach. Despite the physicians' announcements of the princess' poor state of health, the gossip mills churned with suspicions of poisoning.

It was no wonder then that Louis was most anxious to find out from Mme de Brinvilliers how she obtained the poison and if she knew of others in his court practicing this insidious form of ridding themselves of relatives, unfaithful lovers, or anyone standing between themselves and advancement. Hearing of her imminent arrest, Brinvilliers fled to England in 1675, then on to the Netherlands and finally to a convent near Liege, where she was arrested by a policeman pretending to be a priest. On July 17, 1676, she was tortured with the "water cure." This form of torture consisted of tying the victim to a rack, tilting them backwards and forcing sixteen pints of water down their throat until they felt they were drowning and confessed. This she finally did, and that confession, along with the documents left behind by her dead lover, Sainte-Croix, resulted in a sentence of death.

The torture of Mme de Brinvillers

Louis was desperate to find out who else may be dealing with poisons. But the woman refused to talk. He finally assigned the condemned lady to a confessor, the Abbe Pirot, in hopes she would tell the priest who else was involved. Pirot promised her that he would only pass on the information to the king after her death. Still, she stubbornly refused, stating "Half the people of quality are involved in this sort of thing, and I could ruin them if I were to talk." She was finally decapitated and burned. However, her crimes had opened a Pandora's box. The inquiry into the misdeeds of France's nobility had only just begun. Called the *Affair of the Poisons*, many aristocrats over the course of two years were found guilty and executed.

While potions and black magic were not new to the court of Versailles, this mainstream dispatching of obstacles was. People had been purchasing concoctions for decades to ensure love, heightened sexual pleasures, remedies for every ailment, and today's equivalent of uppers and downers. Vials filled every trunk and pocket. Poison rings had been in use since the 1500's. These handy little pieces of jewelry contained a hidden compartment where a powder could be secreted and poured easily into someone's food or drink.

Poison Ring

Once the investigations were begun, it was not long before the names of those selling the poisons (and those administering it) began to pile up. Versailles had become a haven of Lucretia Borgias. Chief among these poison merchants were two women, Catherine La Voisin and La Vigouroux; the former's lover, Lesage; and incongruously, two priests by the names of the abbes Mariette and Guilbourg. La Voison was also a fortune teller and very popular amongst the nobility. On April 10, 1679, Louis created a special task force to seek out all among his court who were involved in poisoning plots. Terror descended on the court as the *chambre ardente* slithered through the nobility in search of the guilty. The above-mentioned practitioners were promptly arrested, alerting all that there would be no mercy shown. When the dust settled, 442 noble gentlemen and ladies had been arrested! An astounding number. It appeared that arsenic had been as prevalent as table salt during the buffets at Versailles.

Catherine La Voison, fortune teller & poisoner

Perhaps the hardest thing for Louis to face pertaining to his pet nobility was the list of names coming to the forefront—people who had been close to him and holding stations of importance:

The Comtesse de Soissons, Mazarin's niece and Louis' love interest in the 1650's. She was now the Superintendent of the

Queen's Household.

The duchesse de Bouillon, Louis' great general, Turenne's relative; the princess de Tingry; the marechale de La Ferre, and the marquise de Polignac were accused.

In 1680, the providers of the poisons, Voisin, Vigouroux and their accomplices were executed. Some of the accused, such as Comtesse de Soissons fled, while others were sent to the Bastille. For Louis, it was a form of betrayal. These were his people, his chosen to live within his gilded cage, to form a perfect society of France's elite. It had turned into a wholesale slaughterhouse. If his heart was pierced by this new spotlight on what he had created, it was about to turn into something that toppled him from his high station.

Marguerite Voisin, the daughter of the accused and executed poisoner, came forth with one more name. A name that would shock the monarch to his soul. Perhaps with great fear for the repercussions to come, Marguerite gave up her testimony. One of her mother's clients had been none other than Louis' current mistress, his favorite, Madame de Montespan. Mme de Montespan was accused of using potions to keep, enhance, or regain Louis' love for her. Such aphrodisiacs were not uncommon, yet this came at a time when Louis was obsessed with Montespan. There would have been no need for such enhancements. It was further reported that Montespan had gone further and joined in black masses where she lay prostrate on an altar naked, while a baby's blood (or that of an animal) was poured upon her during Satanic rites. This too was to insure the king's love for her. Several people collaborated these accusations. Other rumors included Montespan not only adding love potions to the king's food, but that she had contemplated poisoning him as his attention, once again, began to wander from her.

Louis, perhaps through embarrassment or his love for her, kept the findings quiet. There was enough reasonable doubt to the charges that allowed him to put it on the back burner. But the reports had done their damage regardless. He was already having an affair with Mlle de Fontanges during 1679. Alas, she died while miscarrying the king's child. Montespan's possible involvement in wanting him tied to her through Satanic means, and the rumor she had thought to have him killed, finished the king's feelings for the mistress he had loved the longest. He was no longer a young man. He had seen too much war, and too much betrayal in his life. And while it came as a complete shock to the court, it was perhaps not an unusual thing that Louis's next choice of consort was a pious woman; one who was widowed and devout in her religion: Madame de Maintenon.

## The War of the League of Augsburg

The War of the League of Augsburg, also called the Nine Years War and the War of the Grand Alliance, lasted from 1688-1697. A full accounting of it would fill a small book on its own. It was a conflict between France and a European coalition which mainly included the Holy Roman Empire (led by the hated Habsburg Monarchy), the Dutch Republic, England, Spain, Savoy, and Portugal. It was fought in Europe and the surrounding areas, in North America, and in India. It is sometimes considered the first global war.

The conflict encompassed the Williamite War in Ireland and Jacobite risings in Scotland, where William III (known as William of Orange) and James II struggled for control of England and Ireland, and a campaign in colonial North America between French and English settlers and their respective indigenous allies, today called King William's War in America.

The main fighting took place around France's borders in the Spanish Netherlands, the Rhineland, the Duchy of Savoy, and Catalonia. The fighting generally favored Louis XIV's armies, but by 1696 his country was in the grip of an economic crisis. The Maritime Powers (England and the Dutch Republic) were also financially exhausted, and when Savoy defected from the Alliance, all parties were keen to negotiate a settlement. This resulted in the Treaty of Ryswick where Louis XIV retained the whole of Alsace but in exchange had to return Lorraine to its ruler and give up any gains on the right bank of the Rhine. Louis XIV also recognized William III as the rightful King of England, while the Dutch acquired a Barrier fortress system in the Spanish Netherlands to help secure their borders. With the ailing and childless Charles II of Spain's death approaching, a new conflict was soon to embroil Louis XIV and the Grand Alliance in the War of the Spanish Succession.

Map of the War of the League Augsburg

While the loss of lives from the war totaled around 9,000 men for France, there was a much more devastating figure concerning the denizens of France and Italy. In 1693-1694, over two million people died from famine. Severe harvest failures had decimated the land. France was hit with an economic disaster. By the time the Treaty of Ryswick was signed in May 1697, many rulers looked about them at the wreckage inflicted on their territories and their people. Hanging above their heads like a vulture was the unsettled question of the Spanish inheritance once Charles II died, which he did only three years later. It was three years of reasonable peace before Louis would once again take up arms.

Louis XIV returned to Versailles after nine years of war and immediately picked up where he left off—to finish the Grand Chapel.

# Chapter Seventeen
# Secret Passages, Gardens and Ciphers

The intrigues at the court of Versailles were many. It was almost impossible to find a royal, noble, or courtier who didn't have an agenda. Bribes were wanton as chambermaids were asked to look through their mistresses' belongings for papers, poisons, or precious jewels. Gossip replaced mundane conversation. And throughout the palace of Versailles, secret passages, and assignations abounded.

Within the undecorated back hallways and passages of Versailles nefarious plots and secret rendezvous were carried out. Lovers met in shadowed corners, notes were passed concerning the insidious underpinnings of the court's dealings, and the king's mistresses and dalliances were conducted to his quarters. By far, the most talked about and long-lived affair at court was that of King Louis XIV and Madame de Montespan. Long before she was involved with the *Affair of the Poisons*, this beauty dominated the King's heart and bed for ten long years.

## Madame de Montespan

Françoise-Athénaïs de Rochechouart de Mortemart, Marquise of Montespan, better known as Madame de Montespan, was the most celebrated of *maîtresse-en-titre* of King Louis XIV, by whom she had seven children. She was born October 5, 1640, and died on May 27, 1707, at the age of 66. Her children by Louis were: Marie Christine de Pardaillan de Gondrin; Louis Antoine, Duke of Antin; Louis Auguste, Duke of Maine; Louis César, Count of Vexin; Louise Françoise, Duchess of Bourbon; Louise Marie Ann,

Mademoiselle de Tours; Françoise Marie, Duchess of Orléans; and Louis Alexandre, Count of Toulouse. The common repeated usage of first names created much confusion among historians and scholars. Monikers were often given to differentiate who was who.

Madame de Montespan

Born into one of the oldest noble families of France, the House of Rochechouart, Madame de Montespan was called by some the "true Queen of France" during her long romantic interlude with the king. She ruled the court in sheer personality, wit, and cunning. Her conversation was dazzling and seduced many a noble. In France, a woman's ability to charm and banter was highly regarded. Many a beauty fell by the wayside due to her dullness and lack of verve. For Montespan, all of France was laid at her jeweled feet. Her acumen at cards was also remarked upon. It was this same instinct for cunning and manipulation that would be her downfall.

Montespan's reign as Louis XIV's favorite lasted from around 1667, when she first danced with Louis XIV at a ball hosted by his younger brother, Philippe I, Duke of Orleans, at the Louvre Palace, until her alleged involvement in the notorious *Affaire des Poisons* in the late 1670s to early 1680s.

The fortuitous dance with the King was probably not by accident. Montespan had been trying to replace the hapless Louise de La Valliére as mistress since 1666. While pretending to befriend Louise, Montespan ingratiated herself with the king and even the king's son, the Dauphin, who was very fond of her. To hedge her bets, Françoise befriended the Queen Maria Teresa, often helping the retiring queen come out of her reclusiveness where the court was concerned. When both Louise de La Valliére and the queen were pregnant with Louis' child, it was Montespan who was asked to help entertain the king during private dinners. They soon regretted their decision as Montespan upped her game and enticements. They had basically thrown the steak to the wolf, and Louis responded with his ravenous appetite for the conquest. It was said, Madame de Montespan's enjoyment of sex equaled his. The rumor was that "her powder was easily lit."

It was not long after, that Louise's place as head mistress was diminished to second place. Heartlessly, Louis continued to see them both—one night favoring Louise's bed, the next night, Françoise's. The fact that he had to enter Montespan's room by traveling through Louise's was even more despicable. Louise suffered greatly, more so it appears than the queen, who was not in the dark as to Louis' constant infidelities. Blissfully, perhaps, the queen's rooms were in the other wing of the palace, while Louise endured watching him scurry across her floor in his haste to reach the new favorite.

It is interesting to note how Montespan's living quarters were rearranged as her powerful position as the King's favorite began to falter. While the *Affair of the Poisons* was certainly her swan song, Louis had, as he always did, began to lose interest in her. She had gone through seven pregnancies and births and her body was no longer the youthful playground the king had enjoyed. As with Louise, he refused to completely cut Montespan loose, and so, her rooms were relocated.

Beginning in 1678, Louis XIV began to modify the rooms near his royal apartments for his personal and private needs. The configuration of the rooms dating from the time of Louis XIII was repurposed. The most significant alteration for this era was the relocation of the *degré du roi* (staircase) from the exterior *cour de marbre* (marble court) to the interior *cour de roi* (King's Court). This gave the King private access to his rooms and precipitated the rearrangement of rooms in this part of the chateau to become the *petit appartement du roi.* In 1684, as the influence of Françoise-Athénaïs, marquise de Montespan waned, the King attached her rooms to his petit appartement. Later, she was moved to the ground floor into the *appartement des bains* which consisted of five rooms of marble relegated to the royal bath.

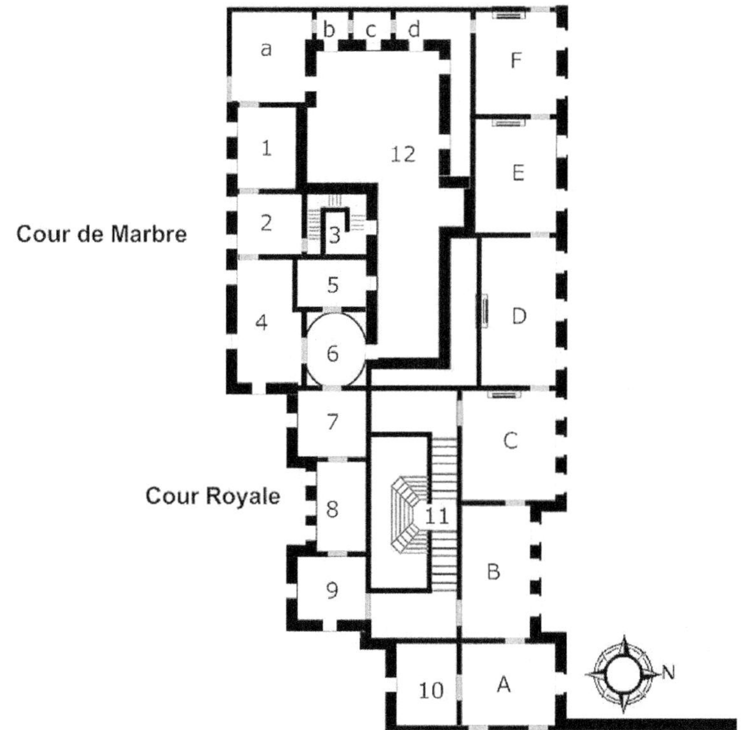


Plan du petit appartement du roi - 1693

A-F were the king's Private Apartments, also known as the Salons. Rooms 7, 8 and 9 were Montespan's rooms before she was moved to the ground floor bath apartments. These rooms, after her removal, became the King's galleries that housed famous works of art, including the Mona Lisa.

As for the rejected Louise La Valliére, she joined a convent after passing her crown to the 25-year-old Francoise-Athénaïs de Montespan. As for Athénaïs (as she was called at court), during her early affair with Louis, she was still married. Despite this, in 1673, her first three living illegitimate children by the king were legitimated by Louis XIV and given the royal surname of de Bourbon. Their mother's name, however, was not mentioned in the legitimization documents, as she was still married to her husband. Other children followed, and as Montespan was busy dazzling the court, the children fell under the love and guidance of a quiet and pious governess, Madame Scarron, or more widely known as Madame de Maintenon. This unassuming widowed woman would later play one of the biggest roles in Louis' life.

In 1691, after watching other mistresses come and go, Montespan accepted her fate that she was no longer in royal favor. She retired to the Filles de Saint-Joseph convent, in the rue Saint-Dominque in Paris, with a pension of half a million francs. In gratitude for her departure, the king made her father the governor of Paris and her brother, the duc de Vivonne, a marshal of France. In her long retirement, Madame de Montespan donated vast sums to hospitals and charities. She was also a generous patron of the arts and letters.

The last years of Montespan's life were given up to a very severe penance. Real sorrow over her death was felt by her three youngest children. She died at the age of 66 on May 27, 1707, while taking the waters at Bourbon-l'archambault in order to try to heal an illness. The king forbade her children to wear mourning for her.

It is a sad testament to a woman who had been capable of exciting the king's affections for a decade—a feat unequaled among his mistresses. During the height of their passion, Louis built a pleasure pavilion called the Trianon de Porcelaine surrounded by gardens as a hideaway for their trysts. This was a plot of land near Versailles Louis had purchased. Because of the fragility of the earthenware tiles used to create the Trianon de Porcelaine, it was demolished in 1687 and replaced by the Grand Trianon of pink marble which stands today. The Trianon de Porcelaine's destruction came at a time when Montespan had been displaced and disgraced within Louis' lavish court. It may have been a sad testament to the lady that all things are temporary.

## The Royal Bathtub

The bath apartments that Madame de Montespan had been relegated to once held a marvel of Europe—a octagonal rose marble bathtub brought to the palace just for Louis XIV during the height of his passion for Montespan. It was large enough for ten people to share in the enjoyment of it. Sunken into the floor, it was surrounded by marble opulence in the walls and flooring, intricately carved basins, gold statues, and aquatic cartouches. Five rooms were dedicated to these incredible apartments of the bath.

The octagonal rose marble tub in its final resting place within the Orangery.

This royal tub was installed in 1674. It measured 3 meters wide and 1 meter deep. Marble steps led down into where one could sit on the shelving. It cost the equivalent of $235,000 in today's dollars. The entire 5-room apartments of the bath ran a staggering $5 million.

During this time, Louis XIV was amassing the world's largest collection of orange trees, sending emissaries all over Europe to bring back the finest specimens in order to create his favorite perfume, the odeur de Nerolie, a floral essence produced from the blossom of the orange tree. Louis filled his bath water with the essence. The king so loved the smell of oranges that he built a garden cathedral, the Orangery, to house them—over 2,000 trees.

While Europe was trying to rid itself of the plaque, bathing in natural water was thought to be a great risk, fearing contaminants in the water would be absorbed through the skin. For Louis, splashing about in a giant tub filled with orange essence seemed a perfect solution. He not only smelled wonderful, but he also felt safeguarded against the evils of a rudimentary medical era. Today, orange is one of the most widely used oils in aromatherapy. A few drops will do it. Swimming in it may have been a tad overwhelming.

Louis XIV and Madame de Montespan spent many secret hours in this fabled tub. It must have been bittersweet to find this section of apartments her new home. The tub was covered over with the ubiquitous parquet flooring and her bed was placed above it. During Louis XV's reign, it was uncovered, dug up and transported to his own mistress's garden, that of Madame de Pompadour, where it was displayed as a pleasure pool at Fontainebleau.

Oddly, the tub found its way west of Paris to the home of a French poet in Neuilly. It was called The Pink Palace and it was built in 1899, appropriately inspired by the Grand Trianon of Versailles. In 1934, the bathtub was finally returned to Versailles and placed inside the Orangery, a fitting place for the perfumed bathtub of Louis XIV.

## Sealed Letters

In the court of Louis XIV, the denizens were basically cut off from the world they knew. They had left behind estates, friends, relations, the affairs of Paris, and their ability to communicate quickly about important matters. They therefore wrote copious letters that were carried outside the golden gates of Versailles. This $17^{th}$ and $18^{th}$ century mail system had some major drawbacks. The courtiers were at first unaware of its existence. It was Louis XIV's surveillance system and it involved spies and an entire system of trusted people, secreted away in a private room, to open and read the letters coming and going from his domain.

The operation was quite elaborate. Once a letter was written and folded, the writer would then take a wax crayon, light the wick and drip the wax (usually red) onto the folds of the letter. Small spoons were also used, held over a flame with a bit of wax in the bowl of the spoon. A stamp made of bronze or brass with a special insignia would then be pressed into the hot wax, sealing the letter closed. Different stamps represented the crest or insignia of different families.

Sealing Wax Stamp of brass with the French Fleur-de-Lis insignia.

But just because letters are sealed didn't mean they were secure. The secret spies would hold the letter over a heated lantern to soften the wax, carefully slit the seal, thus unfolding the letter, and read it. It would be placed in a pile if the information contained within was deemed important to report to the king or his ministers. The letters would then be resealed using a special mixture of mercury and other components that could be poured upon the seal and a copy of the writer's stamp pressed into it. It now held the original shape and appearance of the seal. This system was used to keep tabs on the nobility and know their every move, the important gossip, their displeasure with the king or his government, plots, and much more.

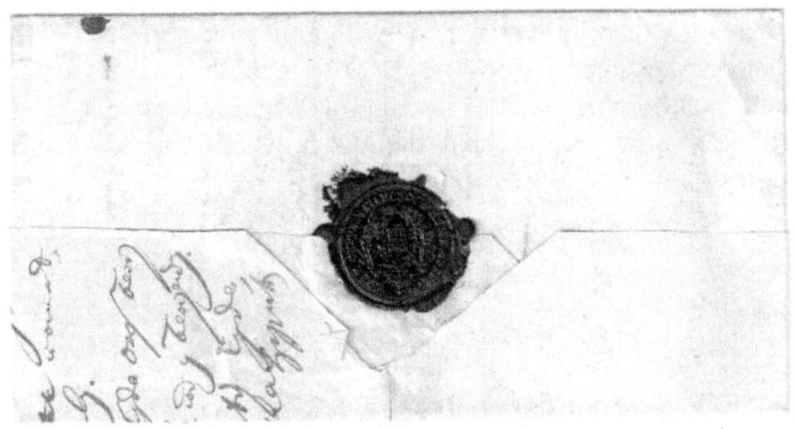

A sample of a sealed letter

## Ciphers & Secrets

With letters and important document seals being breeched, the nobility, military, and the king turned to more nefarious means of corresponding in secret: ciphers. While ciphers had been around a long time, it was Louis XIV who finally found a cipher that was unbreakable, allowing him to send important information to his militia and friendly foreign diplomats.

The father-and-son team of Antoine and Bonaventure Rossignol invented the "Great Cipher" for Louis XIV to encrypt the empire's most secret messages, protecting details of his plans, plots, and political schemes. While the nature of the Great Cipher was simply an enhanced monoalphabetic cipher with homophones, it seemed implausible that it remained unbreakable for two centuries. However, there were two main factors that led to such a secure cipher:

The most significant one was considered to be the Rossignol's ingenuity and resourcefulness. Including 587 different numbers, the Great Cipher was obviously not a straightforward substitution cipher. There are only 26 letters in the alphabet, so obviously each letter was not being substituted for a single number. But when Etienne Bazeries, a distinguished cryptanalyst tried to crack it as a homophobic cipher, he failed. He then came up with the idea that each number might represent a digraph, or a pair of letters. Although his efforts to this deciphering approach again yielded nothing, it enlightened him on the possibility that some numbers corresponded to syllables. After a few attempts, he made a breakthrough, with the discovery of "les-en-ne-mis-s" represented by a cluster of numbers (124-22-125-46-345), and thus the idea eventually proved to be right. It was a phonetic code. The cluster spelled out "les enemis" … the enemies.

The Great Cipher. A letter written by Louis XIV in code.

During a time when cryptology was mainly about encrypting plain alphabets with cipher alphabets, it was creative of the Rossignol's to use syllables for the complexity of homophones. More importantly, they also laid traps for codebreakers, adding numbers which deviously deleted previous numbers instead of representing any meaningful letters or syllables.

After the death of the father and son, the Great Cipher fell into disuse and many details about it were lost; therefore, for those who wanted to break the codes they had to start from scratch. The Great Cipher was known as one of the strongest ciphers in the history of cryptography.

## Secrets in the Gardens of Versailles

It was not just within the secret passageways of Versailles that intrigue was carried out. The vast gardens of Versailles had continued to grow throughout the 1670s and 1680s. The Grand Canal, 5118 feet long and 394 feet wide, was finally completed in 1680. In 1687, several Venetian gondoliers were put in charge of the flotilla which sailed this long sheet of water and lived in small buildings north of the Fountain of Apollo. This small area is called Little Venice due to these housings.

The giant Fountain of Apollo was created in 1671, made of lead sculptures from sketches by Le Brun and created by Tubi. Here, the God of the Sun, Apollo, rises from the water on his golden chariot. The fact that he is seen rising from the West and heading towards the East, Versailles, was a nod to Louis XIV and against the normal course of nature.

The Fountain of Apollo

The 1670s exploded with a wealth of new fountains, ponds, and garden bosquets being erected at Versailles. In 1676, the Fountain of Enceladus was created by Marsy. This sculpture depicts the giant who attempted to scale Mount Olympus and dethrone Jupiter. Jupiter defeated Enceladus and buried him in a mass of rocks. An 85-foot-high jet of water shoots from the giant's mouth as he struggles to release himself from his rock imprisonment.

The Fountain of Enceladus

In 1677-1678, Hardouin-Mansart built two Greek pavilions facing one another, whose fountains still exist. This area was called the Bosquet des Dômes (Grove of the Domes) and it was altered more than the other features in the garden. A statue of Fame stood in the center of the octagonal pond until 1684, and for a time it was known as that name. In 1686, statues from the Thetys Grotto were placed here after the Grotto was torn down to make way for the new north wing of the palace. The statue of Apollo with his horses, once housed in the Grotto stood here, but were moved in 1704. They were replaced on their pedestals created for them by Caffieri at a later date.

The Bosquet des Dômes

The Fountains of Spring and Summer, parallel to the fountains of Autumn and Winter, are dedicated to Flora and Ceres. Tubi created Flora, seated before a bed of flowers in a circular pond during 1672-75. Ceres, in an octagonal pool, was created by Regnaudin 1672-74. Le Brun was once again the artist designing the sculptures.

The Fountain of Spring with Flora

The Children's Island, known at the *Ile des Enfants* once graced the Porcelain Trianon during the time of Louis XIV and Madame de Montespan's secret trysts. It is a whimsical display of children splashing about in a fountain. The sculptured group is the work of Hardy. It was moved from the site of the Porcelain Trianon in 1710 to where it sits today in the lavish gardens of Versailles.

The Children's Island Fountain

The North Parterre sat in perfect symmetry to the South Parterre where Louis' orange trees flourished. Louis loved showing this part of the garden to his visiting guests and courtiers. Here one could find statues, crowns, and the Pyramid fountain, which dominated the area. The North Parterre is different from the South Parterre in its use of the grounds. Here we find triangular lawns and paths. In 1669-1670, Giradon created the Pyramid Fountain after Le Brun's designs. Further on, one can see the beautiful fountain of the Bathing Nymphs, also by Giradon. This bas relief shows the sensuality and playfulness of the Nymphs beneath gentle waterspouts.

The layout of Versailles allowed select residents of the palace to look out from their apartment windows onto these amazing grounds. Usually relegated to Princes of the Blood and the Royal Family, this side of Versailles was breathtaking. The Paris side, whose view from the windows entailed marbled courts and an avenue that stretched out as far as the eye could see, was relegated to the lesser privileged denizens of the palace.

The North Parterre of Versailles

The South Parterre of Versailles w/the Orange Trees in silver buckets.

The Bathing Nymphs Bas Relief

*The Allée d'Eau* (Water Avenue) is a fascinating corridor of groups of children cast in lead, once again inspired by Le Brun's drawings. The 14 groups of children playing amongst fountains was created by Claude Perrault, brother of Charles Perrault, the famous author of Mother *Goose.* The figures were cast in lead and installed in 1670. In 1678 eight more groups were added. Once again, owing to the changing nature of Louis' vision, the 26 groups were replaced by bronze copies by Le Gros, Le Hongre, Lerambert, Mazeline and Buirette.

The Water Avenue at Versailles w/children's statues.

The Obelisk Fountain was built in 1706 and is the work of Hardouin-Mansart, Louis XIV's premier architect. It replaced the Banquet Hall that was situated upon this site, also known as the Salle du Counseil (Counsel Chamber). One would assume from the name that a giant marble obelisk akin to the one in Washington DC or associated with Egypt would stand here. But it was the work of 230 jets of water shooting up as high as 85 feet that created the obelisk shape. The pond actually rises above the ground in terraces, culminating in a circle of reeds acting as the fountain's spouts.

The Obelisk Fountain at Versailles.

The Colonnade was the masterpiece designed by Hardouin-Mansart and Le Notre. The architect and master landscaper collaborated to create one of the most unique features at Versailles. This Bosquet comprised a circular peristyle of 32 Ionic-order columns made of various types of marble. The columns, coupled with Languedoc marble pilasters, support arches crowned each with a white marble cornice and 32 urns in line with the columns. The tympani are decorated with reliefs depicting cupids playing music. Beneath each arch is a basin surrounding a fountain spout. A sculpted group by Girardon depicting the Rape of Persephone (1699) stood in the center of the floor where now sits a pedestal. It was removed to preserve it and will be replaced by a copy. This was where Louis held concerts and when the area was lit with candles beneath the evening stars, it rivaled anything Paris could offer in the way of concert halls.

The Colonnade at Versailles

The Rape of Persephone statue at the Colonnade

The Royal Avenue, or the *Tapis Vert*, was covered in an earlier chapter when we spoke of Louis' grand fetes. It was a carpet of grass running between the Fountain of Latona and ending with the Basin of Apollo. It is 1100 feet and 210 feet wide, lined by 12 vases.

The Royal Avenue or *Tapis Vert*

The Water Parterre is reached by going down the steps of the terrace flanking the main building. It is decorated with two marble statues: the War Vase by Coysevox and the Peace Vase by Tubi. Two large rectangular pools dominate this parterre, giving it its name. Bronze statues by the Keller's were installed between 1683 and 1690 representing the main rivers and streams of France.

The War Statue at the Water Parterre

The Peace Statue at the Water Parterre

These two ponds with their themes of Peace and War beautifully complemented the two drawing rooms flanking the Hall of Mirrors within the Palace: The Peace Drawing Room and the War Drawing Room. It was a nod to Louis' reign and his triumphs both on the battlefront and bringing short periods of peace to his people.

The Fountain of Latona plays a significant role in the layout of Versailles's gardens. Louis had taken on the persona of Apollo, the Sun King, both in his opinion of his reign, and in the many details depicting a golden sun that were seen throughout the palace, grounds, and gates. Latona was the mother of Diana and Apollo by Jupiter. The pond, where this amazing statue grouping is located, just below the Water Parterre, was already there under Louis XIII's rule. In 1670 the central fountain by Marsy was built. It originally faced the Chateau, but now faces west, down the *tapis vert* toward the Basin of Apollo.

Latona, according to Roman mythology, was the goddess of motherhood and modesty. She was scoffed at by the peasants of Lycia, infuriating Jupiter, who deftly turned them into frogs. The three levels of the pond, built by Mansart, show the metamorphosis of the Lycians into frogs. On either side of the fountain are two ponds each with a fountain also depicting the metamorphosis of the Lycians.

Eighteen statues, created from sketches by Le Brun, line the two ramps or the central staircase that leads to the Fountain of Latona. Jets of water shoot from the mouths of the frogs surrounding the base of the fountain immediately animating this unique portrayal of this Greek and Roman goddess.

One wonders if Louis chose Latona not only due to her maternal connection to Apollo, but perhaps also as nod to the mother who had given birth to the Sun King.

The Fountain of Latona at Versailles

*Le Bosquet des Rocailles* (Rockwork Grove) was created between 1681 and 1683 and is arguably the most spectacular area in the gardens of Versailles. In the center of this grove was once a marble floor where balls were held in the opulent splendor Louis XIV's Court had come to expect. Near the entrance to the grove were tiers where those who were not dancing could sit and watch. The other semi-circle is decorated with rockwork cascades above which rise gilt-lead vases by Leconte and Le Hongre, marking the spot where musicians stood. The large candlestands by Le Gros, Mazeline, and Jouvenet were designed to hold candelabras.

*A Little Chaos* (2014) starring Kate Winslet and Alan Rickman gave a fictionalized account of the creation of the Rockwork Grove, but it nonetheless gave us great insight into the Herculean efforts needed to create something of this scale and brilliance.

*Le Bosquet des Rocailles* (Rockwork Grove)

The Queen's Grove was originally the location of a fantasy world called the Labyrinth. The bosquet was made of a labyrinth of foliage and groupings of whimsical statues. Designed by Le Notre, it was created on this site in 1673 and contained 39 fountains, each depicting a theme from Aesop's Fables. Some of these lead sculptures are housed in the Musée de l'Oeuvre inside the Grand Ecurie (Grand Stables) at Versailles. It was great fun for the courtiers to wander these walls of greenery only to discover the surprises of fairytale fountains at every turn.

The Labyrinth at Versailles

It became the Queen's Grove when the labyrinth was replanted in 1774-1775 by Hubert Robert at the beginning of Louis XVI's reign.

One of the Fables' fountains inside the labyrinth.

The Queen's Grove

The Mirror Pond was shaped like a farthingale and was built in 1672. It later became a garden surrounded by fences, trees, statues and vases completed in 1674-1683 along with the Royal Island. By the 1800s, the area had become a swamp and abandoned until Louis XVIII commissioned his architect Dufour to restore Versailles and planted a garden and lawns here, along with winding paths and flowering shrubs. It was then renamed the King's Garden.

The Mirror Pond/King's Garden

*La Salle des Marronniers* (Hall of Chestnut Trees) was a grove called the Hall of Classical Statues at one time, and then the Water Gallery, and was originally lined with yew trees and decorated with ponds and statues. It was a long alley running near the Colonnade. It was redesigned in 1704-06, and numerous classical busts were placed here at the time. The bright yellow of the yew trees in the fall was a surprising burst of color from the evergreens that lined most of the pathways of the garden.

La Salle des Marronniers (Hall of Chestnut Trees)

The Fountain of Winter

The Fountains of Autumn and Winter were begun in 1672 following the designs by LeBrun, and they represent the season of the Gods who symbols are showcased here. Autumn is represented by Bacchus and is the work of Marsy (1673-1675) and shaped in an octagon. Winter, depicted by Saturn, was executed by Girardon (1675-1677) and is circular in shape. These two fountains lie on the other side of the *Tapis Vert* from their counterparts representing Spring and Summer.

The Fountain of Autumn

While this is but a sampling of the many creations that filled Louis XIV's grand gardens, it gives an insight to the astronomical amount of dirt being moved, trees planted, water regulated, plumbing installed, swamps drained, and statues created. Le Brun must have gone through a lifetime's worth of pencils and paper as he created each new design, with Louis at his elbow. For the king oversaw every nuance and tree, each water jet and placement. Known to scribble his own ideas and designs, he engineered the layout and juxtaposition of each grove and pathway as surely as his architects and gardeners.

It was here, in these shaded pathways and hidden enclosures of green that many of Louis' court found secret places to carry out salacious rendezvous or hatch schemes within the palace. What better place to meet someone clandestinely than to pass a note or a whisper saying, "Meet me at the Labyrinth at midnight." Beneath the delicious darkness of night, they wedged themselves into the leafy shadows, away from the pressing closeness of Versailles' overly crowded hallways and carried out their plans of love or espionage.

Within the palace, the many passageways and staircases that combined one wing to another or were a segue from one apartment cluster to the next, served as perfect meeting places if one knew the other's habits and preferred means of transportation. The palace was so vast, that many of the nobles were transported by sedan chair; a contrivance that involved a seat and two or more servants carrying it throughout the palace and gardens. Even cloistered within a sedan chair or traveling along candle-lit corridors presented impediments. Servants often carried torches to light the way. More than one noble lady had come close to having her gowns or powdered wigs set ablaze. There was also the smell. Orange blossoms or not, the aroma of sweat mixed with that of urine wafted through the glittering hallways. The palace was void of public bathrooms and if one could not get back to one's chamber pot, or was merely visiting for the day, they would go into a recess, or behind a curtain or screen, and relieve themselves.

The Sedan Chair used at Versailles

Versailles during the 1670s and 1680s morphed into a veritable city—a city with everything to facilitate its needs. But a city contained within palace walls can be dangerous. Nobles, who had at times been at war with one another—and many who commanded their own armies—were now thrown together and vying for the right to buckle Louis' red-heeled shoes. If the poisonings had taught the king one thing, it was that his gilded cage could also represent a prison and keeping people captive could lead to disaster. A change was coming. He could feel it in his age, in the dissatisfaction of his courtiers, in the pull he felt from the church to amend his adulterous ways, and the distance he felt from his children. Louis XIV looked about at the golden fortress he had created and wondered if the Sun King's brilliance was still as bright as it had been at the beginning. It came to him through subtle rumblings at court, and at night when he was alone with his valet Bontemps. The head valet may have been surprised to see the King do something he had never done before…doubt himself.

Louis XIV in 1701

## Chapter Eighteen
## **A Change in the Air**

The 1670s heralded major changes in the royal court of Louis XIV. In November of 1671, Philippe, the king's restrained brother, took a new wife. This was once again a diplomatic move. It is doubtful that any female would have pleased him, as his ongoing affair with Lorraine was openly flaunted. The woman chosen for him set off a new volley of tantrums from the emotional duc d'Orleans. Madame Elizabeth-Charlotte von der Pfalz was a Bavarian princess. She was stout, big-boned, loud, and exhibited more masculine qualities than feminine. The ladies at court did not quite know what to make of her. Many warmed to her quickly as they found her direct conversation a breath of fresh air. There was no intrigue with this lady who adored the hunt and could sit a saddle as well as any man. Charlotte, as those close to her called her, looked about her with amusement at the pompous regalia of the court and promptly made her way to the gambling tables where her intellect benefited her greatly.

It was during her marriage to Philippe that Charlotte found a new purpose in her role as wife. Strangely enough, she became friends with not only Philippe, but his lover, Lorraine. Here, Philippe came the closest he had come to true female companionship. The Princess Palatine truly cared for him and gently tried to steer him through the politics at court. He found a friend without agenda. The woman he had ridiculed as "a fat German reeking of sausage," was now a safe harbor—perhaps the first he had known.

Princess Elizabeth-Charlotte Palatine

In 1674, Louis threw another of his famous fêtes. He was celebrating the capture of a region of Franche-Comté. The celebration would contain five parties in all from July 4th through August 31st. Much of the festivities were hosted outside to show off the expansion of the gardens. The theme was honoring music and plays. The Marble Courtyard was the stage for the play "Alceste," for which a large fountain was created in the center of the court. The Porcelain Trianon, that fragile structure of Delft tile Louis had created for his trysts with Madame de Montespan, was the backdrop for "L'Eglogue de Versailles" by Lully. Even the Grotto of Thetis for used to host the play "Du Malade Imagine" by Moliere and Charpentier. (The Grotto of Thetis was demolished in 1684.)

The usual candlelit dinners abounded, as well as sailing on the Grand Canal, which was illuminated throughout as musicians serenaded the guests upon the floating flotilla. Racine's play "Iphigene" took place in front of the Orangery. The newly completed Apollo Fountain was the dramatic focus of an evening of fireworks on August 18th to end the lengthy parade of parties. No less than 5000 rockets lit the night to the delight of the courtiers…one in particular, Madame de Montespan, who was the guest of honor as the King's *maitresse-en-titre*. The amazing cost of the festival was a 1/3rd of the sum spent on the construction of Versailles—117,000 livres!

The Marble Court with a fountain for the play "Alceste."

The fete was reminiscent of the one Louis threw to honor his first official mistress, La Valliére in 1668. Did Montespan look about her at the royal festivities and feel a niggling of doubt? If one mistress could be cast off, might not another one? As time passed, it was clear Louis was tiring of her. If Madame de Montespan had seen the writing on the wall in the late 1670s, so Louis was facing shifting sands. All through 1679 he had carried on an affair with Mlle de Fontanges who was a lady in waiting to Philippe's new wife Elizabeth Charlotte, Princes Palatine. Marie Angelique de Scorailles (Fontanges) was a French noblewoman and only eighteen years of age when she caught Louis' eye. Her beauty was apparent early on, and her parents saved up their money in order to send her to Louis' court in hopes of restoring the family fortunes.

Marie arrived at the court of Louis XIV in 1678 and became maid of honor to the Duchess of Orleans. At the time Louis had appeared to be losing interest in his long-time established mistress Marquise de Montespan and turning to the governess of their children, Madame de Maintenon. Infatuated by the beauty of the young girl, the King suddenly abandoned both women and the stand-off between the two was eclipsed by a new passion which appeared to threaten them both equally.

Despite her physical charms, Marie Angelique was said by the court to be "as stupid as a basket." The Duchess of Orleans wrote "she is a stupid little creature, but she has a very good heart...she is loyal as an angel, from head to foot." As Marie now waited on the Charlotte, it was easy for Princess Palatine to observe her at close quarters. She may have realized the naïve young girl was out of her depth with the King.

La duchesse de Fontages

For Louis, this bright young thing made him feel years younger. He began sporting more diamonds, ribbons, and feathers, and presented her with a pearl grey carriage with eight horses.

During a hunt in the forest of Fontainebleau, her hair clung to a branch, and she appeared before the king with her hair loosely tied in a ribbon, tumbling in curls to her shoulders. The king found this rustic style delightful, and the next day many courtiers adopted the new "fontage" hairstyle; except the Marquise de Montespan, who thought it was in "bad taste." As if by Providence, two pet bears of de Montespan's escaped their cage at the Menagerie and managed to find, and destroy, Marie's apartment in Versailles. The event was the favorite laugh at court for weeks to come. Some may have surmised whether the good Marquise had perhaps planted meat in the naive young woman's apartments as enticement.

Montespan's anger over the new rival escalated when it became apparent Marie was pregnant. Montespan, in a rare moment of candor, confided to Maintenon that the king had three mistresses: herself in name, this girl in his bed, and Maintenon in his heart.

In January 1680, Marie gave premature birth to a stillborn boy, and was said to have been "wounded in the service of the King." In April, Louis granted her the title Duchess of Fontanges and a pension of 80,000 livres, as was his usual habit on ending love affairs. Unwell after the birth, she retired to the Abbey of Chelles. In 1681, Marie suffered a high fever and was sent to the Abbey of Port-Royal, where, according to some, she gave birth to a stillborn girl in March.

Realizing she was going to die, she asked to see the king, who touched by her suffering, wept while at her deathbed. Fontanges is reported to have said, "having seen tears in the eyes of my King, I can die happy." This story was deemed untrue by many at Versailles because according to them, the king had, in fact, already forgotten her. The duchess died on the night of June 28, 1681. She was not yet 20 years old. While rumors of poison were rampant, the autopsy showed she died probably due to pleuro-pneumonia induced by tuberculosis, not dissimilar to the diagnosis of Philippe's first wife, Henriette of England.

## Marquise de Maintenon

Long before Françoise d' Aubigne came onto the radar of the Sun King, she had lived among the shadows of his court. Françoise had met an accomplished poet by the name of Paul Scarron, who was 25 years her senior. He counted King Louis XIII's among his patrons and offered Françoise marriage. Although Scarron suffered from chronic and crippling pain, Françoise accepted his proposal and the two married in 1652. The match permitted her to gain access to the highest levels of Parisian society, something that would have otherwise been impossible for a girl from an impoverished background. For nine years she was more a nurse than a lover to her husband. In turn, he gave her exposure to education and a vocation as a teacher.

After Paul Scarron's death in 1660, Queen-Mother Anne of Austria, continued his pension to his widow and even increased it to 2,000 livres a year, thus enabling Françoise to remain in literary society. When the Queen-Mother died in 1666, Louis XIV suspended the pension. Once again in straightened circumstances and having spent several years living off the charity of her friends, Madame Scarron prepared to leave Paris for Lisbon as a lady-in-waiting to the new Queen of Portugal, Marie-Francoise de Nemours. Before setting off, however, she met Madame de Montespan, who was secretly already the king's mistress. Montespan took such a fancy to Scarron that she had the king reinstate her pension, which enabled the latter to stay in Paris.

Françoise Scarron, ne Aubigne, in younger days.

In 1669, Madame de Montespan placed her second child by Louis XIV with Madame Scarron in a house on Rue de Vaugirard and provided her with a large income and staff of servants. Scarron took care to keep the house well-guarded and discreet, doing many duties as secretary and caretaker. Montespan and Scarron found in each other kindred spirits as far as both were highly intelligent. It is there the similarities end. Françoise Scarron was a pious, highly religious woman who thought nothing for frivolity and wanton acts of lust. It was her care of the infant Louis Auguste, Duke of Maine (born 1670) that first brought her to the attention of Louis XIV, though he was initially repelled by her strong temper and strict religious practice. After Louis Auguste and his siblings were legitimized on December 20, 1673, Francoise moved to Chateau de Saint-Germain and became the royal governess; one of very few people permitted to speak candidly with the king as an equal. Madame de Sevigne observed that Louis XIV was pleased to have someone who would speak to him in this way. This was not a cowering doormat out to please him at all costs. This was a woman of substance.

The Widow, Madame de Maintenon

Due to her hard work, the king rewarded Scarron with 200,000 livres, which she used to purchase the property at Maintenon in 1674. In 1675, Louis gave her the title of Marquise de Maintenon after the name of her estate. Such favors incurred the wrath of Madame of de Montespan who began to spar openly over the children and their care. Maintenon (as she was now known) was 40 years of age in 1675. This was past the age of eligible women in that era. She had the respectability of being a widow rather than a spinster, but she had probably put thoughts of any future romances from her mind.

It was true that Madame de Maintenon looked much younger than her age. She was thought attractive with a more seasoned appearance. Françoise exuded an air of calm, so different from the turbulent tantrums of Montespan. Another drastic comparison to the king's former mistress was her style of dress. She was always in mourning black, unlike flamboyant Mme de Montespan. Modesty and piety were her keystones. The king also found in her a high intellectual acumen that fascinated him. She could talk about complicated theological passages for hours. Something was awakening in the Sun King—his ties to deity. Suddenly before him was a woman who could bring him back to his calling as an emissary of God. His double adultery with Montespan had been haunting him for years. Perhaps he could once again shine as the ruler he was born to be.

As with our metaphor of the Gilded Age pertaining to the corrupt underbelly of Versailles' glittering façade, it too can be applied to this seemingly pious woman who had gently insinuated herself into Louis XIV's crosshairs. The temper which had at first repulsed the king was still there, as was a secret thirst for power. Being raised in a penniless existence by a father who saw his fair share of jail time had instilled in the lady a true desire for stability that went beyond the mundane. The smitten king had not yet seen this side of her, nor her increasing habit of perpetually complaining. By the time he did, it would be too late.

Soon after the *Affair of the Poisons*, Madame de Montespan left the court. Maintenon adroitly stepped into her place as the king's confidant, while holding him at bay in the bedroom. She also befriended the almost invisible queen, who had been relegated to the shadows cast by Montespan's glaring spotlight. Queen Marie

Therese openly declared she had never been so well-treated as at this time. Had she known the machinations going on within the well-oiled wheels of Maintenon's mind, she may have seen things differently.

## The Dauphin Comes of Age

The Grand Dauphin

The year 1680 brought with it some major changes to the court. Saint-Germain was still the favored gathering spot for Louis's jeweled nobility as Versailles morphed into more and more rooms and gardens. Impatient to move his entourage there permanently, the king pressed the workers through the night and cracked an invisible whip over his dream team of architects, artists, and landscapers. This is not to say that the chateau had not been in constant use for fêtes and other functions, but it was still not recognized at the seat of power for France. Many still held out hope that the Sun King would return to the Tuileries and keep Paris as his permanent residence. If one thing should have become apparent by now, it was that Louis XIV never did what was expected of him. He may as well have had the motto "I will not be a foregone conclusion" stamped on the royal stationary letterhead.

Louis, the Grand Dauphin was suddenly thrust into the spotlight from the shadows where he had been kept when in 1680 when he turned nineteen. Finally, moving from beneath the iron thumb of his governor, he was given his own establishment. He was also handed a wife as part of the package. The lady was Maria Anna Victoria of Bavaria. She became known in France as Dauphine Marie Anne Victoire.

Primi Viconti had this to say of the event: "The Dauphin took a wife as obediently as he learned his lessons. His governor was the duc de Montausier, an elderly man of austere mores and severe principles. The Dauphin seemed to have become wholly passive; no one could say anything in his ear. There were even some who said that the marquis de Crequi, having taught him a certain bad habit, Milet, his under governor, would stand with a rod near his bed, and when he saw the Dauphin move his hands under the blanket, he would strike him.

"For his wedding, his First Valet de Chambre, a friend of Mme de Beauvais, who had given the king his first love lesson, was ordered to enlighten him." While the Dauphin's marriage freed him finally from the tyrannical grasp of the duc de Montausier, he was still held at arm's length by his father, the king. Rather than given the expected name of: Monsieur le Dauphin," "*mon fils*" (my son), or "Your Royal Highness," Louis XIV dubbed his son "Monseigneur," a title no better than "Your Lordship." Even ministers and princes were called "Monseigneur" by those below them. But for the Sun King's only legitimate son and heir, the title that would follow him was a constant reminder he would never rise in his father's opinion.

The King need not have worried that his son might raise an army against him or incite civil unrest. The Dauphin's early indications of being slow-witted and without his father's drive and ambition had not improved with age. The young man's sole interests seemed to be eating, hunting, and occasional trysts with lower-class women. He was passive, lazy and not at all thrilled with the prospect of marriage. It is quite possible she too was underwhelmed with the groom presented to her.

"The Dauphine," Primi noted, "from the moment she arrived, seemed to know about the Court, ready to flatter the King and obey all his wishes. The offices of her Household were sought in preference to those of the Queen's. The duchesse de Richelieu, who was dame d'honneur to the Queen, became that of the Dauphine, thus incurring a lowering of her rank, and her husband the duc became chevalier d'honneur, but that was all the result of an intrigue of Mmd de Maintenon's, the governess of Mme de Montespan's children, who was made a lady of the wardrobe, first under the marechale de Rochefort, and was then declared her equal, which infuriated the latter; but the most furious of all was Mme de Montespan, who, as a result of Mme de Fontange's illness, had hoped the King would come back to her." It was the beginning of Maintenon's insinuation into the inner sanctions of Louis' court.

Maria Anna Victoria of Bavaria, the Grand Dauphine

The Dauphine was an interesting mix of attributes. While tall and regal in appearance, it was at once noticed that she was of average intelligence when she spoke. One was more impressed with her perfect teeth and flawless complexion that with her wit or drive.

Indeed, she much preferred the seclusion of her private rooms with a small circle of friends than she did to the chaos of court life. None of this mattered once she began bearing sons, which she did with regularity: Louis, duc de Bourgogne made his appearance on August 6, 1682; Philippe, duc d'Anjou was born December 19, 1683; and Charles, duc de Berry bounced into the world on August 31, 1686. The King could rest assured the royal lineage was intact. As three of his illegitimate children had died by 1683, it was comforting to know the royal bloodline was secure.

**Death of the Queen**

During the last week of 1683, Maria Theresa fell ill, perhaps from childbirth complications, and, as her illness worsened, her husband ordered for the sacraments to be kept nearby. She died a painful death on July 30, 1683, at Versailles. The court had only been moved to the massive chateau one year earlier. She had barely had time to order new tapestries for the changing of the seasons. Upon her death, Louis XIV said, "This is the first chagrin she has ever given me."

Maria-Theresa, Queen of France

A grandiose funeral was carried out befitting a queen. Marc-

Antoine Charpentier composed dramatic motets H.409, H.189 and H.331. Jean-Baptiste Lully, the toast of France, composed his *Dies irae.* The funeral prayer was by Bossuet. And so marked the life of the woman Louis XIV had married in 1660. She had tolerated his affairs and watched as first La Valliére and then Montespan were paraded throughout the court, often with swollen bellies. The king left her to her devices, yet reprimanded Montespan when her behavior at court too flagrantly disrespected the queen's position.

There have long been rumors that Marie Theresa had an illegitimate daughter, Louise Marie Therese (The Black Nun of Moret). Allegedly, the queen gave birth to a black daughter in 1664. The rumors were that the child was the result if some interlude between the Queen and a black dwarf servant named Nobu. That Maria Theresa was fond of dwarves and had them around her was no secret. The child was handed over to a nunnery and became convinced as she grew that she was of royal blood. Saint-Simon, the infamous court scribe, stated that she once greeted the Dauphin as "my brother." The fact that King Louis XIV granted her a pension of 300 pounds on October 15, 1695, "to be paid to her all her life in this convent or everywhere she could be, by the guards of the Royal treasure present and to come" suggest that she may well have had royal connections.

Nobu, the proffered offender of the king's wife, was later found dead in the fountain in front of the palace, implying he was the father and either killed to keep the secret or out of Louis' vengeance for cuckolding him under his own roof.

Louise Marie Therese, the Black Nun

Of the queen's six children, only one survived her, Louis, le Grand Dauphin, the oldest one of her children, who died in 1711. One of her younger grandsons eventually inherited her claim to the Spanish throne to become King Philip V of Spain in 1700.

# Chapter Nineteen
## Versailles Takes Center Stage

The 1680s held up a mirror to Louis XIV and all he saw was full sail ahead. The queen was dead. This alleviated a sense of guilt for his numerous trysts and opened certain doors. His brother had been married off and while it had done nothing to reduce Philippe's love affair with the chevalier de Lorraine, he was not out trying to usurp the King. The nobles had been brought effectively to heel, he was known throughout the world as the dominating military force, and his palaces shown like jewels in the sun. But there was one residence that he wanted to become synonymous with glory and opulence—Versailles. It was time to complete his vision.

Louis Le Vau, that talented French Baroque architect who had designed the Envelope and so many other facets of Versailles, died October 11, 1670. Louis had been entangled with wars and intrigues at court and the building program had not advanced much. He therefore hired a new architect to take his plans to the heights he imagined—Jules Hardouin-Mansart. Mansart was also of the French Baroque style. In 1674, four years after Le Vau's death, he became one of the groups of royal architects working for Louis XIV. His first important project was the Chateau de Clagny, built for the king's consort, Madame de Montespan. He quickly showed he was a master of bureaucratic diplomacy as well as design and construction; he gained the protection and support of Madame de Montespan, then François-Michel le Tellier, Marquis de Louvois, the Minister of War. He studied under and then collaborated with landscape designer Andre Le Notre, before finally working with the king himself.

Jules Hardouin-Mansart

In 1677 Mansart began working on the expansion of the royal Palace of Versailles, a project which occupied him for the rest of his life. He was named First Architect of the King in 1681 and was raised to nobility in 1682. He owed his rise not just for his ability to please his patron with his designs, but especially because of his ability to manage enormous and complex projects with many elements and designers. He would sketch out an idea, stand back and intervene and adjust when needed, from time to time visit the site, and see to it that the budget was kept under control.

### The Ambassador's Staircase

Perhaps two of the most celebrated works at Versailles during the beginning of Mansart's period were the Ambassador's Staircase and the Hall of Mirrors. The grand staircase leading to the King's apartment was called the Grand degrè or the Ambassador's Staircase. Louis Le Vau designed the staircase, but it was built by his successor, Francois d'Orbay (who was brought on-board before Mansart took the reins) and decorated by the painter Charles Le Brun between 1672 and 1679. The staircase was built to impress. A glass ceiling lit the expensive polychrome marble, glit bronzes and paintings. The paintings were to celebrate the victory of the king in the Dutch wars (1672-1678). The landing highlighted several illusionistic paintings also touting the military victories of the Sun King. Holding center court was the bust of the King by Warin, his long hair and cloak blowing around the proud uplifted face of Europe's most-prominent ruler. It is as if the bust itself held Louis' restless energy and motion.

The Ambassador's Staircase let to enfilade of state rooms (salons) and acted as the first impression for visiting dignitaries and ambassadors. It was created to dazzle and impress…and it did.

Ambassador's Staircase at Versailles

## The Hall of Mirrors

Mansart also tackled the Hall of Mirrors. As already mentioned, it was built during the third building phase between 1678 and 1684. It became synonymous with the name Versailles. It replaced the long terrace that opened towards the gardens. The terrace was originally situated directly outside of the king's and the queen's apartments. Le Vau's terrace was considered to be a rather misplaced architectural element with open exposure to the elements.

Eventually, it was decided to turn it over to Jules Hardouin-Mansart for something more utilitarian and worthy of a monarch's palace. Mansart did not disappoint.

The Hall of Mirrors is flanked at the far ends by the Salon of War (Salon de la guerre) in the north and the Salon of Peace (Salon de la paix) in the south, respectively. This dazzling Hall of Mirrors connects the two Salons, which were assigned to the king's apartments in the north and the queen's apartments in the south. Both Salons are accessible via the Hall of Mirrors through wide opening passageways. Visitors to the palace, who had already been wined and dined through the long line of salons on the King's side, would find themselves in the Salon of War and turn to the left. Before them stretched a gallery of such magnitude and dazzling light that it left many in shock and awe.

The Hall and the two Salons were identically furnished and decorated to form a stylistic and functional unit. The exterior walls of the Salons date from the time of Le Vau's encasings of the old chateau and were given their current appearance after the installation of the Hall of Mirrors by Hardouin-Mansart.

The Hall of Mirrors at Versailles

The mirrors not only reflected the outdoors, but they also hid the king's chambers on the other side. One could enter the antechambers through the hinged mirrored door. Even more dazzling was the effect the mirrors had on the plethora of lit candles floating overhead in chandeliers and mounted on gold gilt candelabras lining the length of the room. The mirrors were also a silent nod to the King's wealth. Mirror glass was expensive in the 17th century and could only be produced with great effort. The manufacture of the mirror surfaces was the first major order for the Manufacture royale de glaces de miroirs, a glass factory founded by Jean-Baptise Colbert, the later Compagnie de Saint-Gobain, with which the Venetian monopoly on the manufacture of mirrors was broken.

The elaborate ceiling murals decorating the vault of the hallway are the work of Charles Le Brun, Louis' favored artist. Nine large murals and numerous smaller cartouches are dedicated to the idolization of the Sun King and praise his successes for the first 20 years of his reign. The most prestigious scenes were painted on canvas and glued to the vault by Le Brun himself, aged 60 when work began on the ceiling. The painting *The King Governs by Himself* highlights the claim to absolute power. Further topics include the *Peace of Nimegen* and the *Conquest of France-Comté*. A rumor at the time was that architect Jules Hardouin-Mansart had deliberately created mirrored surfaces in the 17 large arches to prevent Le Brun from having even more areas to decorate and impress the king.

The Hall of Mirrors with Louis XIV, 1675

*The King Governs by Himself* by Charles Le Brun

1682 saw the installation of the Court permanently at Versailles. Yearly visits to Fontainebleau were still held, but prolonged stays at Saint Germain, Chambord, or Compiegne were virtually eliminated. It became clear to the residents of Paris that their monarch had removed himself to the wilderness of Versailles. Louis never again resided at the Tuileries or the Louvre. Only one bridge separated him from the city that had instilled such fear in him as a child during the Frondes. He had built a fortress and he had conquered Europe.

Yet, as the early 1680s plowed ahead with new improvements to his palace, the court saw a change in the air. Louis was now in his forties. The double adulterous affair with Madame de Montespan had cost him both in the respect of the pious people in attendance upon him and in his own reckoning with his conscience and God. It was now that the heavily ritualized routines of his etiquette system began to tire on the nobility. Standing in wait upon Louis's morning and evening rituals of the *lever* and the *coucher*; watching for hours as he ate or dressed or hunted; endless routines to where each minute of the day was regulated, even the endless rounds of card games had dulled the shine of what had been a "palace of pleasures."

The homage paid to the king had gone to new levels. The custom of bowing to his food as it was transported to his table must have ruffled a few feathered adornments. The cost of all the different outfits demanded for court functions had not lessened, and many courtiers grumbled over the lack of toilet facilities, the smells from people openly urinating in corners, the heat in the summer and the cold in the winter. In short, Versailles' gilded cage had begun to lose its enticement.

Louis XIV saw all and knew all. He could see through flattery and intrigue, much to the detriment to those who used either. He took his hat off to every female, including the staff, and was known for his impeccable manners until the day of his death. He could gain attendance at holy services or ceremonies by simply remarking how pleased he would be to see so-and-so show up at the next event. It was subtle but effective.

It was in the early 1680s that one saw the biggest change in the Sun King. He became much more interested in religious beliefs and placed more importance on attending communion in the chapel. A devout Catholic, he began to live the long-held belief that he was "God Given," to the point that he took on the responsibility of calling others to their knees. In Olivier Bernier's book *Louis XIV: A Royal Life*, he states: "These so-called Gallican principles were combined with a radical extension of the *regale.* This was the King's right, first, to select all ecclesiastical dignitaries, subject to canonical ordination by the Pope; and, finally, to appropriate the revenues of all benefices while they were unoccupied, i.e., between the death of one holder and the appointments of the next. Taken together, these rights made Louis XIV virtually absolute in Church matters; and that was a good deal more than the Pope could bear."

Innocent XI, elected in 1676, became Louis' nemesis. Influenced by the Jansenists, who believed salvation came from God's grace and not works, the Pope went after the Sun King. He claimed all religious rights, including the deposing of a king. He refused to accept the king's extension of the regale and the French bishops' declarations from the Assembly of 1682. From April 1682 on, he sanctioned Louis' appointments to vacant seats. Thirty-five bishoprics were vacant by 1688.

Typical of Louis, he continued on without missing a step, secure in the self-knowledge that he was above any law but of his own making. To him, he was in good standing with God as he was, after all, he was an extension of His divine power on earth.

Another show of power was his organization of a new way to capture territories without the hassle of war. He called it the *chambres de reunion.* Basically, he searched the archives for towns and territories that were taken from him during certain wars and went about collecting them one by one. These were in or near the Trois Eveches (Metz, Verdun, Toul) and Alsace. They had all once belonged to France but had been lost. He then cited those who oversaw these smaller principalities and simply took them back. The fact that the sovereigns were of a lesser rank such as small German princes was one thing. He also took back Strasbourg in 1681, which was a thriving city. Surrounding it with 20,000 French troops didn't hurt to motivate the turnover. Not one canon was fired.

As many of his former enemies, such as William of Orange, had disbanded their militia, no one really wanted to take Louis on in a costly war. He was feared, not only for a formidable army and resources to back them up, but perhaps for his ego that saw no bounds and would not hesitate to go after what he wanted. He had reached the pinnacle, and everyone seemed to know it. Those teetering on the mountain top, however, can sometimes lose sight of the precipices beneath them.

As the jeweled court continued to feel less and less enthralled with the new religious Louis, expansion continued. Two long wings were added to the forecourt to house the Royal Children (in the South Wing—1678-1682) and the Princes of Blood (in the North Wing—1684-1689 when the Thetis Grotto was destroyed). These royal families and the ministers who were housed in two buildings near the main court, totaled a staggering 4,000. Colbert, who never ceased to worry about the ongoing building, looked with concern at the flooring of the passageways in 1680 and wondered if they could withstand the constant traffic of all those people. Versailles was a labyrinth of passages, salons, state apartments, and well-traveled hallways. At times, the number of people crammed into the palace numbered 10,000.

Due to the poor lighting that candles facilitated, the shadowy recesses could be dangerous. More than one fight would break out among sparring nobles: often over lost wages from a card game. One such note was made by Saint-Simon who said the light from his torchbearers suddenly revealed his enemy, the duc de Vendome, feeling his way down a staircase in the darkness. The candles were replaced by oil lamps, but not until 1747, long after Louis XIV was gone. Right up until the Revolution, Saint-Simon scribed that courtiers and royal alike moved about in the gloom lit only by their servant's torches.

Versailles resembled a small city, with interior streets and throughfares. Many courtiers grouped their families together for their lodgings. The Noailles family took up so much of the attic rooms in the north wing that the corridor there became known as Noailles Street. It became so territorial that if you were seen in a part of the palace lodging areas where you had no rooms, you were suspected of nefarious reasons. Spies abounded, whether the king's, or servants belonging to the nobility who had been slipped a coin to go and listen at doors or hide out in passageways. Spies could also detect who was visiting whom, as the visitor's assistant or guard remained outside the door in their telltale uniforms. Knowing the layout and location of certain rooms and staircases also allowed the inmates to maneuver "chance encounters." It was a place of non-stop machinations for advancement, romance, and even murder.

# Chapter Twenty
# **Rituals and Regrets**

In 1684, Jules Hardouin-Mansart began work on the Orangery at Versailles. It replaced an earlier design by Louis Le Vau in 1663, before the palace began to morph into the structural splendor it had become in the early 1680s. It is an example of many such prestigious extensions of grand gardens in Europe designed both to shelter tender plants and impress visitors. Louis XIV's gardens were no longer just a sanctuary for him to stroll, but also a setting for grand fêtes, although one had not been presented since the grand party of 1674.

In the winter, the Versailles' Orangery housed more than a thousand trees in boxes. During the cold months the trees were housed in a cathedral-like space and if the temperatures were extremely cold, the gardeners would burn fires to heat the housing of the trees. In 1689 gardener Valentin Lopin created a device to transport and move the large orange trees. Most of the trees are citrus and originally shipped from Italy, but there were many tender Mediterranean plants including oleanders, olive, pomegranate, and palm trees, totaling over 1,055 altogether. From May to October, they are put outdoors in the "Parterre Bas."

The new Orangery was modeled on the theories of the horticulturalist Jean-Baptiste de La Quintinie, the master gardener of the Potager du roi, whose writings detailed a system for protecting exotic plants from the cold without the use of artificial light.

As Louis XIV grew older, he became allergic to flowers and

preferred the smell of oranges and other citrus trees. He had them potted in silver tubs and placed throughout the state rooms of the palace to perfume the air—something, no doubt, much appreciate. The specimens supplied the Court with fruit year-round.

The Orangery at Versailles

Inside the Orangery at Versailles

As Mansart toiled away on the Orangery for two years, other signs of cultivation were going on inside the walls of the palace. The Sun King was showcasing his daily ritual to the world.

## A Palace Run Like Clockwork

The marquis de Dangeau, a devoted courtier, began taking notes concerning the king and court life. In 1684 (before Montespan departed), as the smell of orange blossoms permeated the air, he set down in writing the unusually public routine of Europe's most infamous monarch. You will see similarities from Louis' earlier routine, but the change of names is interesting.

"He usually rose between eight and nine; as soon as he was dressed, he closeted himself with his ministers and stayed with them until twelve-thirty; at that hour, he came out of the study, had Mme la Dauphine warned that he was ready for mass, and the whole family went to mass, where the music is very beautiful. The mass usually ended between one and two and the King went to visit Mme de Montespan until his food was ready. His Majesty then took his dinner in Mme la Dauphine's antechamber [the Salon of Peace]. The appointed noblemen served him. Monseigneur (the Dauphin), Mme la Dauphine (the Dauphin's wife), Monsieur (Philippe), and Madame (Charlotte), Mlle and Mme de Guise (the daughter and granddaughter of the king's uncle, Gaston, due d'Orleans) ate with the King and so, occasionally, did the princes of the blood royal."

Here we see roughly the same schedule the King maintained in earlier times, but the parties have changed. Whereas he used to dine in the queen's bedchamber, he now dines with his daughter-in-law, the Dauphine, in the Salon of Peace…the antechamber to her private quarters. Louis' wife died, and the Dauphine took over her apartments. We see his visit to Madame de Montespan, where before, it was simply stated that he would see "his mistresses" at that hour, those ladies being La Valliére and Montespan. In 1684, this changed.

Madame de Maintenon was from the first given an apartment on the same level as the royal family, namely Philippe, Charlotte and the Dauphin Louis. At that time Louis XIV had been using Madame de Montespan as a smoke screen to pass through her apartment to see Maintenon, just as he had used La Valliére to see Montespan. Now that longest-reigning mistress of the king suffered as she watched him enter her room, dismiss her servants, and then enter through another door to see his new favorite, the widow

Maintenon—the very woman Montespan was responsible for bringing to the court.

Montespan had been losing favor for years. It was now, in 1684, that she was finally asked to vacate her lovely apartments and move to the lower level that had once been the apartment of the baths.

The marquis de Dangeau continued: "After dinner, the King visited with Mme la Dauphine for a moment, then he either closeted himself to work or went out. At seven or eight, he went to Mme de Montespan's, where he usually stayed until midnight; and the *petit coucher* was ordinally over by twelve-thirty or one at the latest.

"On the days of *appartement* (two to three times a week when the king entertained the Court in the State Apartments or Salons), one went into the State Apartments at seven. The King played at billiards until nine with M. le dc de Vendôme, M. le Grand, the duc de Grammont and M. Chamillard; after billiards, the King went into his cabinet with Mme de Maintenon or visited her in her apartment until supper. Mme la Dauphine watched the King play for a few minutes, then went and listened to the concert for a quarter of an hour and then opened the ball. Monseigneur played cards with Mme la Dauphine or attended a play with her."

These evenings of *appartement* were not the crowded fêtes for which Versailles was famous. They were smaller affairs of perhaps 300 people. On July 19, 1684, there was "a big supper to which forty ladies sat down at two tables." The men stood, along with ladies who did not rank high enough in favor or title to sit at the table with the king. On these evenings, Louis would sometimes hold a lottery with prizes ranging from finery to expensive jewels. At other times he would honor his guests with a play or concert. Despite the lavishness of the food and entertainment, the constant routine and the same faces and conversation began to wear on the court. Many began to complain of the rigid routines and boring repetition of festivities. If you have Christmas every day, it loses its magic.

And of course, there were the non-stop meetings with his ministers and counselors: "On Sundays, there was a meeting of the Council of State attended by the King, the Chancellor [in 1684, Le Tellier, Louvois's father], M. de Louvois [Military], M. de Croissy [Colbert's brother in charge of Foreign Affairs], and M. Pelletier, who replaced Colbert after his death in 1683 as Controller General of Finances. On Mondays, again Council of State. On Tuesdays,

Council of Finances, attended by the King, the Dauphin, the Chancellor, M. le marchal de Villeroy, the Controller General, M. Pussort, and M. Boucherat. Wednesday, Council of State. Thursday, Council of State. Friday, Council of Conscience [church affairs] with the Archbishop of Paris first, then with the Pere de la Chaise [Louis' confessor], each separately. Saturday, Council of Finances. Every other week on Monday was held a Council of Dispatches, and on those days there was no Council of State; this Council was attended by the King, Monseigneur, Monsieur [neither of whom had much input], the Chancellor, M. le maréchal de Villeroy, the four secretaries of state, who present reports, and the Controller General brings His Majesty a list of disbursements, which the King authorizes. On Tuesday, the Chancellor hardly stays at the Council of Finances because that day he holds his own Court. M. De Seignelai [Colbert's son and minister of the Navy] alone attends with the King the Council of the Navy after dinner; twice a week in ordinary times, sometimes more often, M. de Louvois is granted private audiences after dinner which he accounts for the army, the forts, and buildings in general. On Monday, after dinner, there is a Council for the Affairs of the Protestants; the King does not attend it, but he is given an account of any important business transacted there."

Two things are obvious from these highly-routine, set-the-clock-by-it meetings and movements: 1) Louis XIV was a man of incredible energy with an eagle eye view of all the minutiae his reign encompassed; and 2) anyone with nefarious intent would know exactly where he was at any given moment of the day. His routine was known to foreign powers and the inmates at Versailles as well. He offered the world, with the arrogance of one who feels he is invincible, a literal blueprint of his daily life. While Louis XIV never came under attack, his successor, Louis XV did feel the sting of an assassin's blade.

We must give the man his due. He never took a day off. He was on constant show from eating his meals, to his amusements, hunting, gambling, dressing, and undressing. It was a staggering 20 years of uninterrupted success. Yet, in 1685, there was a change of heart from this most visible of monarchs. His open-door policy was taking a toll on him. "The King," Dangeau wrote, "who could no longer walk in his gardens without being mobbed by the multitudes which came from everywhere, and especially Paris, ordered the guards to allow only the courtiers and their guests to enter. The populace which had come in before had spoiled many statues and vases."

Louis's sudden need for a retreat would be understood by any privy to his relentless public display, but what did confuse was why not chose one of his already lavish palaces? Why not head to Fontainebleau or Saint-Germain, or Compiegne? No...the Sun King wanted a new sanctuary: one nearby that would allow him a select guest list and a reprieve from the mind-numbing routine and crowds of Versailles. The King turned to a wooded area that had already featured prominently in his grand design for Versailles: Marly.

## Marly

In 1679, the works at Marly, what would later become known as the Marly Machine, was begun. This was three years before the court was moved permanently to Versailles. Providing a sufficient water supply for the copious fountains at Versailles had been a problem from the outset. The construction of the Marly hydraulic machine, actually located in Bougival (where its inventor Rennequin Sualem died in 1708), driven by the current of the Seine moving fourteen vast paddle wheels, was a miracle of modern hydraulic engineering, perhaps the largest integrated machine of the 17th century.

The Marly Machine on the Seine River

The Marly Machine pumped water to a head of 100 meters into reservoirs at Louveciennes (where Madame du Barry, Louis XV's mistress, had her chateau in the 1760s). The water then flowed either to fill the cascade at Marly or drive the fountains at Versailles—the latter after passing through an elaborate underground network of reservoirs and aqueducts. The machine could only deliver sufficient pressure to satisfy either Marly or Versailles, and invariably the King's demands received priority. In the nineteenth century, various other pumps replaced the originals and the last was taken out of service in 1967.

The King was now looking for a retreat on well-wooded royal lands between Versailles and Saint-Germain-en-Laye that were well-watered and provided a grand view. Marly was chosen.

Robert Burger had demonstrated that the design of Marly was a full collaboration between Jules-Hardouin-Mansart and the *premier peintre* Charles Le Brun, who were also working on the Hall of Mirrors at the time at Versailles. Mansart's elevations for the pavilions were to be frescoed to designs adapted from a suite that Le Brun had recently drawn. The frescoed exteriors of the otherwise somewhat severe buildings created a richly Baroque ensemble of feigned sculptures against draperies and hangings with vases on feigned sculptural structures against the piers—all in the somewhat eclectic Olympian symbolism that Le Brun and the king favored everywhere at Versailles.

The décor of the pavillon du Roi featured Apollo, the Sun King's iconographic persona, and Thetis. Other pavilions were dedicated to other Olympians, but also to Hercules, and to Victory, Fame and Abundance. Construction was completed by 1684, two years after the court was moved to Versailles. The Sun King attended the opening of the completed hydraulic works in June 1684, and by 1686, development was sufficiently advanced for the king to stay at the new Marly lodgings for the first time, with a selected entourage. The theme of Marly was that it was a simple hunting lodge, just enough to accommodate the Royal Hunt. In 1688 the *Grand Abreuvoir á chevax* was installed on the terrace, a mere "horse trough."

Marly became more than just a retreat for the king. It was yet another way to keep the nobility jostling for recognition. Only the chosen elite were invited to join Louis at Marly. An announcement would be made to the Court that the King would be going to the new estate and the thundering of noble feet could be heard hurrying to his bedchamber door. Louis XIV would then fling open the door and shout "Marly, Sire, Marly!" The King would then closet himself in his room and make out the much-coveted guest list.

Marly, with the horse trough in the foreground.

Throughout the rest of his life, Louis continued to embellish the wooded park with wide straight rides, in which ladies or the infirm might follow the hunt at some distance, in a carriage, and with more profligate waterworks than waterless Versailles could provide. Saint-Simon wrote in 1715, Marly's heyday was ending, with the death of Louis XIV that year. Louis' heirs found the north-facing slope made Marly damp and dreary, and rarely visited. The last days of Marly have been described earlier in this book in Chapter One.

## Colbert Dies

Jean-Baptiste Colbert served as First Minister of State for Louis XIV from 1661 until his death in 1683. His lasting impact on the organization of the country's politics and markets, known as Colbertism, a doctrine often characterized as a variant of mercantilism, earned him his nickname *le Grand Colbert*—the Great Colbert. His relentless hard work and thrift made him an esteemed minister. He achieved a reputation for his work of improving the state of French manufacturing and bringing the economy back from the brink of bankruptcy. Historians note that, despite Colbert's efforts, France actually became increasingly impoverished because of the king's excessive spending on wars.

Colbert worked incessantly hard until his final hours. Work was his religion; he once pondered whether it was better to rise early and work or to retire very late and work. He concluded rising early and retiring late would be the ideal combination. Towards the end of his life he suffered from stomach aches, which caused him much distress. He was reduced to eating moist bread dipped in chicken broth for his meals.

By 64, he was bedridden and died shortly after his birthday. The surgeons who examined him found he had been suffering from kidney stones. A huge stone was found in his urinary tract, which would explain his pain.

The list of artistic and literary organizations Colbert founded or supported is lengthy. His vast collection of manuscripts was donated by his grandson to the Bibliotheque Royale in 1732. His collection of paintings and sculpture can be seen at the Louvre.

The death of his dear and constant minister must have come as a blow to Louis. They had often butted heads on the expense of Versailles. Colbert would have rather the King remain in Paris at the Tuileries. Louis's letters to his friend show a constant regard even when reminding him of who was in charge. It may have been a great comfort to have Colbert's son, Jean-Baptiste Colbert, Marquis de Seignelay follows in his father's footsteps as Secretary of State of the Navy, while Jacques-Nicolas Colbert was Archbishop of Rouen.

Colbert (left of the King) presenting the Members of the Royal Academy of Sciences to the King in 1667.

# Chapter Twenty-One
## Marriage, Lies & Religion

Mme de Maintenon was slowly but surely making headway at Versailles. The pious widow crept from the shadows daily, mainly by the king's design. On May 29, 1684, the Dauphine's dame d'honneur, the duchesse de Richelieu, died. Louis went to Maintenon without hesitation and offered her the esteemed role. Where was the hierarchy pecking order that the rest of the court was forced to endure in order to secure such a position? Normally, only a grand duchess would be offered a role like the Dauphine's lady in waiting. Yet, the Dauphine was shocked to hear the widow Scarron, recently the marquise de Maintenon, refused the position.

The court scribe Dangeau reported, "Mme la Dauphine went to Mme de Maintenon's room to ask her to accept the office of dame d'honneur but was unable to sway her. Mme de Maintenon received with respect this obliging request but remained unmoved; she had asked the King not to mention the honor he had done her in offering her this office, but His Majesty was unable to refrain from talking about it and the story after his dinner." If the King's offer to Maintenon was not a clear enough indication of his regard for her, his next move was—he offered the position to the duchesse d'Arpajon, whose brother had once been Maintenon's close friend.

That Louis XIV had been regularly visiting the widow's rooms was a poorly kept secret within the gossip-laden walls of Versailles. Maintenon maintained her innocence and declared she acted solely as the king's friend and confidant. Many believed her confessor had encouraged her to engage in intimate acts with the king in an effort to finally drive him from the arms of Montespan and end his double adulterous affair with his mistress of ten years. And so, the clandestine meetings continued until a very monumental event took place—the death of Louis' queen on July 30, 1683. Now, if there were carnal dealings with Maintenon, it would not be considered adultery as they were widow and widower.

With the Queen's death, new doors opened for the king. With his new desire to regain his religious standing in the Church and at Court, Maintenon was the perfect partner. She was everything Montespan was not—pious, mature, and devoted to the king's religious wellbeing. While the bishops, in particular Jacques-Benigne Bossuet, wished the king to remarry, the object of his desire posed a huge problem. Mme de Maintenon was not of royal blood. She had come from obscurity and only Louis' generous title had raised her from the *bourgeoisie*. That his feelings for her went beyond the sensual was new for the king. He adored her mind, her confidence, and her desire to see him become, once again, the "God Given."

There was only one way to bring about Louis' desire to marry this woman—it must be done in private. He would be the laughingstock of Europe if he married a commoner. Yet, he must have her. She would be his wife, but not his queen. Marrying her would mean he would no longer be living in sin, and he would have the strength of this formidable woman at his side.

Their marriage was so secret that the exact date is not known. All that mattered was that it was valid in the eyes of the Church and God. The ceremony took place before Louvois (his Minister of War), his confessor, his valet de chambre (Alexandre Bontemps), and the marquis de Montchevreuil, one of Mme de Maintenon's relatives. The year was no doubt 1684, perhaps just after Maintenon turned down the offer of the Dauphine's lady in waiting.

One of the traits Louis valued was discretion. His new wife had it in spades. She held his secrets close to her heart and even destroyed every note he had ever sent her after his death. In her, he found a confidant without rival. He was so secure in her unfailing devotion to him and his matters of state, that he began holding his meetings with his ministers in her apartments. Typical of Louis, he listened to her advice but seldom took it. It was the same stance he had taken with Colbert and with Philippe, his younger brother. No matter the respect he held for someone, he was the king. It is not clear if his refusal to listen to the advice of others came from a pig-headed ego that would have seen placing another's idea above his own as weakness or a sign of his intellectual lacking, or if he just felt the need to heed his own compass. Perhaps, it was a little of both.

The only ground Maintenon gained was in her whisperings in the king's ear of certain appointments she would like to see given. An example is that of duchesse d'Arpajon being granted the esteemed office of dame d'honneur. Other of her friends prospered. The Dauphine moved into the queen's apartment and took it upon her shoulders to act in the departed woman's stead. She reinforced the Court etiquette and supported him as Monarch.

The Place Vendôme with Louis' towering statue.

Louis XIV, feeling that all had aligned with his wishes, upped his game once more. On December 2, 1684, the King returned from the hunt and changed into a suit with over 12 million livers' worth of diamonds sewn into its cloth. Even for Louis, this was audacious. He followed this by desiring his likeness to be cast in a large statue of bronze in the heart of Paris. In 1685, two new squares in the city were begun. In April, "it became known that the King had bought M. de Vendôme's house in the rue Saint Honoré in Paris, and that it was to be torn down, and replaced by a square something like the Place Royale in the middle of which there will be a statue in bronze;

and that His Majesty would give the plots around the square to build houses of similar design," De Sourches scribed. Today, the Place Vendôme still stands and is considered one of the loveliest in Paris.

The maréchal de La Feuillade, one of Versailles' courtiers, decided to honor the King with a statue as well. He bought a square in Paris of his own and began, but the Square (the Place des Victoires) was not completed. The statue was however, and La Feuillade took pomp and circumstance to the hilt when he circled the statue three times at the head of the Guards regiment, he himself acting colonel. The statue depicted Louis XIV on foot with Fame holding a wreath above his head. It was reminiscent of rituals of old where pagans paid homage to their gods. Louis's Sun was in full zenith.

To underscore the pulling force of his self-ordained planet, the Doge of Genoa came calling in May of 1685. The great man came in response to Louis' demand that he come in person to ask for pardon for the unfriendly way France's expeditionary corps were treated in Italy. Even Genoa's constitution forbidding the Doge to leave its boundaries bent beneath the will of Louis XIV. The constitution was changed, and the Dodge headed for the fabled Palace of Versailles.

The Doge of Genoa paying his respect to Louis XIV.

De Sourches recorded that "The Court was lined up in two rows from the second salon to the end of the Hall of Mirrors where the

King was sitting on a thronelike silver chair, and that was on a platform covered with a Persian carpet. On this platform were Monseigneur (the Dauphin), Monsieur (Philippe), M. le duc de Chartres (Philippe's son), M. le duc de Bourbon, M. le duc Maine, and M. le comte de Toulouse (the illegitimate sons of Mme de Montespan), and behind the King were all the officers of State and his Household who were entitled to be present."

This was the first time the King had presented his illegitimate sons as equals with the royal family. While the Doge paid his respects to the platform of the king, he did not honor Montespan's sons with a visit later.

Dangeau recorded that "At noon, the Doge came in with four senators and many other people who were part of his suite; he was dressed in red velvet with a hat of the same, the senators in black; he kept his hat on while speaking with the King, but often took it off and put it back on; he did not seem embarrassed."

Louis' illegitimate children continued to be included in the dazzling light that surround the greatest monarch in Europe. On July 24, 1685, thirteen-year-old Mlle de Nantes, one of Montespan's illegitimate daughters by the King, was wed to the duc de Bourbon, the grandson of the great Condé, a Prince of Royal Blood. The duc de Bourbon was higher in rank for succession to the throne than the prince de Conti. This marriage secured Nantes place as third lady in France. Only the Dauphine and Madame (Philippe's wife) were higher.

The king's dowry to his daughter was enormous: one million livres, 300,000 livres in jewels, and a yearly pension of 100,000 livres. Her husband also received 100,000 livres in pension, the governorship of Burgundy, and the title of Grand Master in the King's household. A sumptuous wedding banquet followed the ceremony and Louis, with supreme fanfare, made it quite clear that the days of illegitimate children remaining in the shadows was over. They were invited to dine at the king's table. Although they had not been officially legitimized, the duc de Maine and the comte de Toulouse were given the same precedence as the Princes of the Blood.

## Of Lies and Religion

The Protestant question had been a thorn in Louis' side for some time. The Edict of Nantes put forth by Henry IV of France in 1598 granted Calvinist Protestants of France, known as Huguenots, substantial rights in a predominantly Catholic nation. Through the edict, Henry aimed to promote civil unity. The edict treated some, not all, Protestants with tolerance and opened a path for secularism. It offered general freedom of conscience to individuals and many specific concessions to the Protestants, such as amnesty and the reinstatement of their civil rights, including the right to work in any field or for the state, and to bring grievances directly to the king. It marked the end of the religious wars that had afflicted France during the second half of the 16th century.

The edict gained a new significance when Louis XIV broke the post-Nantes tradition of relative religious tolerance in France and, in his efforts to centralize the royal power, began to persecute the Protestants.

Louvois, his Minister of War, had been given the job of Superintendent of the King's Buildings, putting him ever closer to Louis' inner circle. Louvois believed in force, not surprising for a military minister. Louvois, knowing Louis' desire to reduce if not eradicate the Protestant religion from France, padded the numbers of those who were converting to Catholicism. He took upon himself to begin tactics to force the Protestants in France to convert. In France, as in most of Europe, it was acceptable to quarter regiments inside the homes of private citizens. This was a tremendous financial hardship on the host. In 1681, Louis signed an ordinance that excluded recent converts to the Catholic church from having to house these sometimes-tortuous residents. Louvois jumped on this and basically told the Protestant households, you can convert and not endure these dragoons, or refuse and take your chances with these soldiers whose brutality was well know.

When Louis realized what Louvois was doing, he ordered it stopped. Instead, the resisting Protestants were hit with ruinous lawsuits. Next came a declaration stating that seven-year-old children could convert to the Catholic church despite their parent's wishes. What followed was a horrendous battle between child and parent as some were literally ripped from their homes.

These tactics, along with others, saw between 300,000 and 400,000 Huguenots convert, as this entailed financial rewards and exemption from the *dragonnades*. Louis also redacted the promise that Protestants could emigrate if they refused to join the Catholic church. He now insisted that all Protestants must be converted.

It was in 1685 that Louis issued the *Edict of Fontainebleau*, which cited the redundancy of privileges for Protestants given their scarcity after the extensive conversions. *The Edict of Fontainebleau* revoked the *Edict of Nantes* and repealed all the privileges that arose therefrom. By this edict, Louis no longer tolerated Protestant groups, pastors, or churches to exist in France. No further Protestant churches were to be constructed, and those already existing were to be demolished. Pastors could choose either exile or a secular life. Those Protestants who had resisted conversion were to be baptized forcibly into the established church.

The result would become a crushing blow to France and its King. Some rulers, such as Frederick Willhelm, Duke of Prussia and Elector of Brandenburg, encouraged the Protestants to seek refuge in their nations. Historians cite the emigrations of 200,000 Huguenots (roughly one-fourth of the Protestant population), who defied royal decrees. As many of those who fled France were skilled workmen and business owners, France was deprived of many of its citizens who were the backbone of the community. They took their tax paying dollars with them, as well.

Protestants across Europe were horrified at the persecution of their fellow members by the King of France. Louis's public image in most of Europe, especially in Protestant regions, suffered greatly. Most Catholics in France, however, applauded the move. The experiment of religious toleration in Europe was effectively ended for the time being. However, French society would sufficiently change by the time of Louis's descendant Louis XVI to welcome toleration in the form of the 1787 *Edict of Versailles* also known as the *Edict of Tolerance*. This restored to non-Catholics their civil rights and the freedom to worship openly.

## A Visit from Siam

On September 1, 1686, a Siamese embassy arrived at Versailles for the very first time. This was a rare nod to the King's reach from a dignitary who had not acknowledged France before. In Louis fashion, the wine flowed, the tables exploded with fine food, and the court dazzled. The King, dressed in a suit of gold covered with huge diamonds, perched once more on his silver throne atop a tiered dais in the Hal of Mirrors and received the visiting dignitaries. Sources commented that the diamonds were worth more than the entire kingdom of Siam.

Reception of the Siam dignitaries at Versailles.

Louis' wish to dazzle his entourage of nobles continued in 1686. His largesse seemed to know no bonds. Madame de Montespan, still very much on the sidelines was even allowed to attend some of the festivities. On January 4, 1686, "the King and Monseigneur went to Marly for dinner. Mme la princess de Conti (Montespan's daughter), Mme de Montespan, and Mme de Thianges (Montespan's sister) were with them... Monsieur and Madame (Philippe and Charlotte) arrived around five with many ladies and courtiers; the house was brightly lit; and in the salon, there were four shops, one for each season of the year.

"Monseigneur and Mme de Montespan kept that of autumn; M. du Maine and Mme Maintenon that of winter; M. le duc de Bourbon and Mme de Thianges that of summer; Mme la duchesse de Bourbon and Mme de Chevreuse (Colbert's daughter) that of spring. There were splendid fabrics, silver, and what is proper to each season, and the courtiers played cards for them and were given whatever they won. It is thought that there was at least 150,000 livres' worth of clothes; playing went on until supper and after that the king and Monseigneur gave away whatever was left in the shops. Those who won took their winnings; those who lost were forgiven their debt." Thus reported Dangeau of the special evening at Marly.

## Chapter Twenty-Two
## **The Sun Begins to Dim**

The Great Sun King had accomplished everything he set out to do. Only a few regrets or missteps nettled his conscience at night. He was considered Europe's premier monarch. Sitting atop his silver throne he looked down upon the world's reigning royalty and dazzled them with his jewel-encrusted clothing and sumptuous feasts. It was if the fireworks that exploded above the palace were just a climatic exclamation point to the man who had created this oasis of power.

If Louis XIV felt invincible, who could blame him? But Fate had a way of laying low those who thumb their nose at it. "Pride goeth before the fall" should have been lettered on the ceiling vault in the Hall of Mirrors along with the painting title *"The King Governs by Himself."* Common men have felt the sting of a sudden reversal of fortune. For a King, one who claims he is an extension of God's rule on earth, it is a dire tempting of the Universe, to be sure. The sentence would be handed out in a way Louis had not anticipated. It did not come from an enemy camp or a civil uprising. The great Sun King was attacked by his own humanity.

In October of 1685, a sharp pain in his foot suddenly stopped the King's confident gait in its tracks. Louis was now forty-seven; not old by today's reckoning, but in the $17^{th}$ century a male reaching the age of 50 was not the norm. Most lived only to the age of 35-40, although the high mortality rate of children during that era impacted the data. Lower classes were more susceptible to plagues and disease than the nobility. So, when the Sun King was suddenly relegated to the palace and limited activity, it was a rude awakening.

While it may have only been gout, gout is extremely painful.

What followed next was unimaginable. Louis had been dealing with a painful tooth, and the King's First Physician, d'Aquin, declared the only remedy was to remove it. With pliers in hand, the king's head was held secure, and the tooth was wrenched from its socket without anesthesia. Due to the clumsy procedure, and perhaps due to lack of sanitation of the instruments used, an abscess formed, causing Louis even more distress. Aquin, in a startling prognosis, decided the only thing to be done was to remove all of the king's upper teeth! Imagine each tooth pulled without the benefit of numbing the area. It must have been excruciating. To add to the horrific outcome, d'Aquin accidentally removed part of Louis' upper palate. New abscesses coated the roof of his mouth and bleeding sockets. These were cauterized with a red-hot iron.

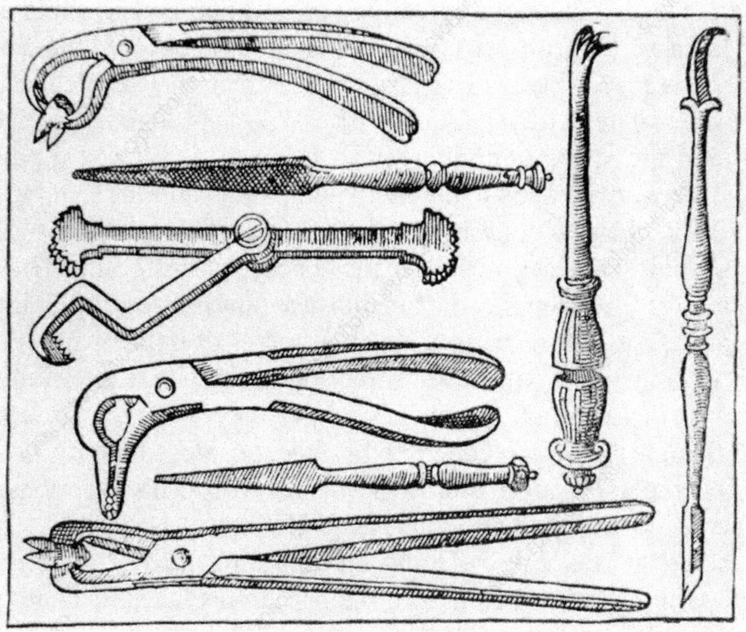

Dental instruments from the 17th Century.

To the court's astonishment, the King kept with his exhausting schedule, never faltering. It wasn't until February of 1686 that he began to worry that his health was in decline. Missing teeth and a throbbing foot were one thing; a tumor was something else.

M. de Sourches wrote "At the beginning of the month the King fell ill with a tumor which came out where the thigh meets the buttock, and since it was so painful as to prevent him from riding, he had it examined by Félix, his First Surgeon, and began to think seriously of having it treated.

"Since he was unaccustomed to pain, he decided against an incision and his physicians and surgeons obeyed him, perhaps too readily. They tried to treat the tumor by inducing sweating, which all those who knew about the disease thought both ridiculous and dangerous.

"…since the King's illness continued, the tumor was cut open to help Nature, which was pushing the infection out…and Félix used a cautery to widen the wound."

By early March, the abscess was still there and routine treatments of cauterizing the open wound took place. Louis spent most of March in his bedchamber as walking caused him considerable pain. On March 13th, the abscess finally burst, and it appeared the wound was beginning to heal. The last of the infection was cleaned out three weeks later.

Within the space of four months, Louis had endured a painful foot, the removal of his upper teeth and palate, and the lancing and burning of a large wound in his buttock area. This trifecta of health issues would have set most humans aback, but not Louis. The fear of someone else stepping in for him was unthinkable. If Philippe, his brother, or Louis, his son, saw a glimmer of hope of improving their situation by taking over some of the king's responsibilities, they were dead wrong. Louis XIV attended every Council meeting, even though they were conducted at his bedside. To him, his son was incompetent, and his brother was a slave to his emotions and temper. Versailles had only one ruler. It would remain so.

Whether it was due to facing his mortality through a series of health issues, or just the onset of old age, Louis became a hardened monarch. His treatment of the Protestants had shown a complete lack of compassion or the ability to look with an open perspective at the suffering of his people. His portraits aged along with him. The nose took on a more aquiline appearance and there is a decided hardness in the angles of his face. Perhaps to prove that the old dog could still hunt, he seems to be putting forth an even more indomitable persona.

Louis XIV in his 40's.

Yet, from 1686 on, the King's health deteriorated. For a man who loved the hunt and had a passion for the dance, his body's betrayal was worse than if he been stabbed in the back by a confidant. Over the years, Louis performed 80 roles in 40 major ballets, often appearing in God-like portrayals. Throughout the 1660s he founded the Academie Royale de Danse and the Academie de Opera, two critical elements in the evolution of French Ballet.

A European military giant could not afford to be seen as infirm. Louis had led an aggressive foreign policy. From 1667 to 1697, his army grew from 30,000 to 400,000 soldiers in just three decades. So it was with some alarm that the King began to show symptoms of illness. He repeatedly broke out in fevers and there was a change in his physical appearance. He lost weight, which also showed in his face. The angles and mouth lines deepened. Sourches wrote in August of 1686, "Although it was never very high [the fever], it still caused the King to become much thinner and changed his face visibly."

It soon became apparent that the fevers were indicative of a much worse condition. Physicians announced that the King was suffering from an anal fistula.

"The King," wrote Sourches, "who was suffering more and more from his fistula, had been resolved, for two months, to undergo the great operation; but he had confided this secret only to Monseigneur,

Mme de Maintenon, M. de' Louvois, his First Physician, Félix, his First Surgeon and the Père de La Chaise, his confessor; and even so Monseigneur did not know the King had decided it would take place on November 19.

Louis XIV before the operation with Mme de Maintenon and his confessor, Père de La Chaise.

"On the seventeenth he strolled in several places in Versailles and finding himself in great pain, although he did not show it, he decided to have the operation the next day…"

Louis developed the tumor in the crotch area. It was described in detail by his personal physician Antoine Daquin (1629 – 1696): "On 15 January, His Majesty complained of a small lump in his crotch, two fingerbreadths in front of the anus, which was not painful to the touch, with no redness or throbbing."

Most likely, the lump was caused by an inflammation of one of the glands in this area. Glandular inflammation was apparently common in the 17th century. The king's physicians started their treatment with various kinds of compresses, including sugar compresses. When a perianal abscess developed, it was punctured to let the pus flow out. In some way, it proved possible to dry out the wound applying compresses soaked in extracts from various leaves as well as from roses cooked in red wine (Burgundy). The doctors also succeeded in filling the cavity that had formed by injecting various substances, a process that caused the king great pain.

His Majesty became increasingly irate over the abscess which continued to leak pus, forcing him to change clothes two or three times every day after dinner. His afflictions continued over many months. The pain was pronounced, but every time he felt better, the doctors continued their treatment sessions consisting of enemas and laxatives, which only served to aggravate the misery. After four months, the formation of a fistula was suspected. Most likely, the constant treatments with a red-hot iron had helped increase the size of the crater.

After having struggled with pain and other discomfort for many months, the king realized that the physicians were powerless. He decided to undergo surgery. In the meanwhile, he isolated himself in his private Versailles' apartments, sullen and cantankerous. Even the court saw very little of him. He had to abandon riding, and every time he was seen out in the gardens, he was sitting in a sedan chair.

No surgeon dared lay hands on the Sun King without prior practice. The great operation was planned in detail and in complete secrecy. The surgeon decided to operate on others suffering from the same affliction first.

The identity of the guinea pigs has remained unclear, but patients from hospitals in the town of Versailles have been mentioned. Historians have unsuccessfully attempted to find out how they fared – or more correctly, how many of them died – but to no avail. It was rumored that the deceased were buried at sunrise and with no tolling of church bells, to prevent anybody from getting wind of what had happened. One patient is thought to have survived.

Charles-François Félix (junior) (1635 – 1703), the king's chief surgeon, had not performed this kind of surgery before, but gained first-class experience over the months he was permitted to experiment. He was especially concerned with finding the correct type of instrument. He gradually developed the instrument that was used on the Sun King, called "le bistouri royal" (the royal probe). This was a long, curved silver probe, now on display in the medical history museum in the rue de l'École de Medécine (Medical School Street) in Paris.

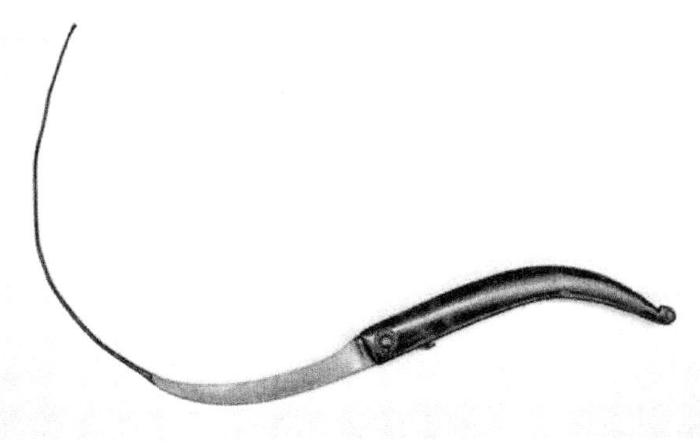

The Royal Probe

On the day before the operation, the king inspected his gardens, monitored the ongoing works, ate his evening meal with his family, and after another round of excruciating painful treatments made the final decision to undergo surgery the next day. On 18 November 1686 at seven a.m., His Majesty was accompanied into "le salon de Bassans" as it was known before the reconstruction in 1701 – today it is equivalent to "le salon de l 'Oeil de Boeuf" (the Bull's Eye salon), the antechamber of the king's bedroom.

The parties involved were already in place. His doctor, chief physician Antoine Daquin and his successor Guy Crescent Fagon (1638 – 1718), chief surgeon Félix as well as four apothecaries had arrived at five in the morning through different doors, so as not to arouse suspicion. The king had been administered a pre-operative enema. He appeared to have his nerves under control and took a great interest in the various instruments that were to be used.

He was then placed on a bed with his face towards the window. A pillow was placed under his stomach while his thighs were spread and held up by two apothecaries. Towards the end of the operation, he asked: "Is it over, gentlemen? Finish. Do not treat me like a king, I want to recover as though I were a peasant."

Although this was to become the most famous surgical operation of the 17th century, it was not granted more than one sentence, admittedly running to half a page, in the king's health records. Daquin, with his condescending attitude to surgeons, would most likely have preferred not to mention this episode at all. He made sure to add that a bloodletting was also performed.

That Félix, the operating surgeon himself, felt the need to write a more detailed description of this spectacular operation is more understandable. On the following day he wrote a full 18 pages. The whereabouts of this document in subsequent years is unknown, but in 2007 the papers resurfaced and were put up for auction with an asking price of EUR 4000. Given the present interest in objects with a connection to royalty, the final price is likely to have been far higher.

The three-hour long operation was performed without any form of antiesthetic. Louvois, the Minister of War, held the patient's hand during the entire procedure, while Mme de Maintenon stood next to the fireplace. The king is said not to have complained of any pain, but on two occasions he is reported to have exclaimed "Mon Dieu.". The pain must have been excruciating, but Louis needed to keep a brave face for the sake of his own and the nation's dignity.

And not only did the king survive – the operation must be called a success, because he was cured. Admittedly, he needed two repeat surgeries, but he was quite naturally very relieved and happy after the first major operation. At ten o'clock the news had spread through the palace and the king himself held council from his bed, "singing all day and in surprisingly good spirits." He was back on his feet no more than two days later.

Louis XIV showed great courage in letting himself undergo surgery. To be sure, he was cornered – he really had no choice, either politically or personally. In 1686 France was in a difficult position, isolated and resented, and facing an alliance of the majority of European countries (the League of Augsburg).

A surgical intervention was the last resort, and the decision was not taken until months of other unsuccessful treatments had been attempted. For Louis, whom we know was anxious of smaller surgical procedures, such as bloodletting, this must have been a difficult decision. He must be deemed to have shown great courage to undergo such an extensive and potentially dangerous operation (risk of bleeding) with no anesthetic.

The fistula operation had a number of consequences. The surgeon's efforts were rewarded with a noble title, a palace, and great wealth. To all those who suffered from a fistula, the operation brought hope of a cure, and like everything else that the Sun King undertook, this also became fashionable in Versailles. The courtiers lined up to have the same procedure done, whether or not they had a fistula. Those with no fistula were turned away by the surgeons.

Like the Sun King, the surgeon also deserves to be termed courageous. The consequences of a failed operation, not to mention the death of the monarch, would certainly have been less pleasant. This joint display of heroism and courage caused French surgical medicine to flourish. Rumors of the successful operation spread throughout Europe, and people flocked to France to be operated on by the skillful French surgeons. From being virtually unnoticed in the shadow of the physicians and dominated and scorned by them, the surgeons stole the limelight in a way never before seen.

On several occasions, not only during the operation of the anal fistula in 1686, but the Sun King's surgeons had also come to his aid. He had to reposition an arm after a riding accident in 1683. Surgical assistance also became necessary later because of an abscess on the back of his neck. It was provided by his deputy chief surgeon Georges Mareschal (1658 – 1736), who took over this position in 1703 and was later appointed chief surgeon to Louis XV. Georges Mareschal was known all over Europe for his skills in operating on bladder stones. (Ellen Jorum, Oslo Medical Hospital)

It wasn't until December of 1687 that Louis finally left his room and walked out among his adoring courtiers. He had defeated the odds and had not died, much to the chagrin of his enemies. Many wondered whether he truly was God-given and impervious to the slings and arrows that would have defeated other men. While he was back among his people, he was not able to sit a horse until March of that year. A celebratory hunt must have ensued. Louis was back—still indefatigable, indomitable, and grandiose in his behavior. It was time for the next move.

# Chapter Twenty-Three
## More Building and War

There comes a time when a creator looks with growing apprehension at the thing he has created. Perhaps the crushing crowd and responsibilities of Versailles became Louis XIV's Frankenstein monster. True, he had demanded the suffocating routine that kept him perpetually in the spotlight, and it was he who so thoroughly tied the noble's hands and purse strings to the point they had become dependent upon him. Now, after a year of pain and limited activity, the king craved freedom and space.

In the summer of 1687, Louis walked the elaborate halls of Marly and was pleased with the results. Yet, it was still the hassle of moving select members of the court and himself to yet another palace with all that that implied. Moving a household of staff each time you felt the wanderlust itch was expensive and laborious. A new thought formed in this restless monarch's head. Why not build something within strolling distance of Versailles, inside the garden confines, which would offer him a sanctuary as well as a retreat where he controlled the number of attendants. Enter the **Grand Trianon**.

During the romantic interlude with Madame de Montespan between 1663 and 1665, Louis commissioned Louis Le Vau to design a porcelain pavilion (*Trianon de porcelain*) to be built in a small hamlet abutting Versailles called Trianon. Louis purchased the town and his plans rolled out in 1670. The façade was made of white and blue Delft-style porcelain (ceramic) tiles from the French manufacturers of Rouen, Lisieux, Nevers, and Saint-Cloud.

Construction began in 1670 and was finished in 1672. Since it was made of porcelain, the building suffered from deterioration. Louis XIV ordered its demolition in 1686 and replaced it with a larger building. Gone were the memories of the king's trysts with Madame de Montespan at the Trianon de porcelain. Now, he would build a residence for his new wife Madame de Maintenon and members of his family and entourage.

Architect Jules Hardouin-Mansart's new structure was twice the size of the porcelain pavilion, and the material used was not ceramic but durable marble from Languedoc. Begun in 1687, the new construction was finished in January 1688. It was inaugurated by Louis XIV, his secret wife Maintenon, and his son The Grand Dauphin during the summer of 1688.

Hardouin-Mansart's early plans for the building were substantially altered during construction, with original intention of keeping the core of the *Trianon de porcelaine* intact vetoed in favor of an open-air peristyle with a screen of red marble columns facing onto the garden. At least three other structures were built at the center of the new building and then torn down before the peristyle was settled on, during the frantic building period of the summer of 1687. The sloping Mansard roof of the original design, meant to harmonize with the roof of the *Trianon de porcelaine*, was vetoed by the king, who felt it looked too "heavy" on the structure. The long interior gallery which forks west from the main wing was built on the spot of a favorite outdoor promenade that Louis enjoyed at the old *Trianon de porcelaine*.

Mansart knew what La Vou knew before him—everything was subject to change. Louis' plans came with a big eraser. Unfortunately, he often changed his mind after the structures were completed. M. de Sourches tells this story relating to the creation of the new Trianon:

"Since the year was well under way when he gave the orders to begin this [the new Trianon], and since he wanted it finished before the winter, he pressed the work and often went to spend the afternoon under a tent, where he worked with M. de Louvois [Minister of War] and looked at the work from time to time as to make it go faster." It was during one of these visits that the king became embroiled in a debate with Louvois concerning a window in one of the newly constructed walls of the Trianon that was not spatially correct. Louvois, who had been overseeing the building work, felt slighted, as if the king was questioning his prowess. He assured Louis that the window was true, but the king demanded proof. Louvois grabbed some measuring tools and to his dismay, it turned out the window was a fraction off from being plumb. Down came the wall and it was redone.

The Trianon with its open peristyle gallery.

The finished Trianon was a confection of pink marble and pale ochre stone. Two wings flanked the main courtyard and led to the open peristyle. Paired pink marble columns ran the length of the open gallery. Tall, arched windows of the wings were topped with carved shells and trophies and separated by pink marble pilasters. Running along the top of the building was a stone balustrade sporting vases, trophies and sculptures of children. The Trianon was a triumph for Mansart who designed the wings, and Robert de Cotte, who was responsible for the peristyle.

The open peristyle at the Trianon.

The interior design theme departed significantly from what Louis XIV and his architects had established at the Palace of Versailles. Louis reputedly ordered the architects to "Paint everything white. No gilt or color for the walls of Trianon." This was a departure from the variegated marbles, rich colors, and gilding which defined the interiors at Versailles. Instead of the heavy ornamentation on display in the palace, the walls of the Trianon were covered in delicately carved wood *boiseries* (ornate and intricately carved wood paneling), with plaster friezes, pilasters, and capitals of noticeably more refined, delicate appearances.

Inside the Trianon with its white walls

The Trianon became home to Louis' extended family housing his son and heir le Grand Dauphin from 1703 to 1711. The domain was a favorite retreat of the Duchess of Burgundy, the wife of Louis' grandson Louise de France, the parents of Louis XV. In the later years of Louis XIV's reign, the Trianon was the residence of the king's sister-in-law Elizabeth Charlotte of the Palantine after the death of the king's brother Philippe, in 1701. Her son, Philippe d'Orleans, future son-in-law of Louis XIV (when he married Françoise Marie, Montespan's daughter by the king) and Regent of France, lived at the Trianon with his mother.

Louis ordered the construction of a larger wing for the Trianon, which was begun in 1708 by Mansart. This wing was called the Trianon-sous-Bois and housed the Orleans family, including Louis legitimized daughter Françoise-Marie de Bourbon who was then married to Philippe d'Orleans, Louis' nephew. The king's youngest grandson, Charles de France, and his wife Marie Louise Elisabeth d'Orleans, also resided there. The Orleans family, who had apartments at Versailles, were later replaced by Françoise-Marie's sister, the Duchess of Bourbon, Madame la Duchesse, who lived at the Trianon and later built the Palais Bourbon in Paris, the design of which copied the Trianon. Many of Europe's greats also copied the lowriding structure, and it became the seat of Napoleon's campaign when he became Emperor. In 1717, Peter the Great of Russia, who was studying the palace and gardens of Versailles, resided at the Trianon; the Peterhof Palace was inspired by Versailles.

The Peterhof Palace in St. Petersburg, Russia

Louis XV, Louis XIV's successor, did not bring any changes to the Grand Trianon (as it was called after the Petit Trianon, built between 1762 and 1768, was created). In 1740 and 1743, his father-in-law, Stanislas Leszczynski, former king of Poland, stayed there during his visits to Versailles. Later, it was during a stay at Trianon that Louis XV fell ill before being transported to the Palace of Versailles where he died on May 10, 1774.

No more than his predecessor had, Louis XVI brought no structural modifications to the Grand Trianon. His wife, Queen Marie Antoinette, who preferred the Petit Trianon, gave a few theatrical representations in the galerie des Cotelle, a gallery at the Grand Trianon with paintings by Jean l'Aine Cotelle highlighting the *bosquets* of Versailles and Trianon.

During the French Revolution of 1789, the Grand Trianon was left to neglect. At the time of the First French Empire, Napoleon made it one of his residences, and he furnished it Empire Style. Napoleon lived at Trianon with his second wife, Marie Louise of Austria.

The next royals to live at the Grand Trianon were the King and Queen of the French—Louis Philippe I and his Italian wife Maria Amalia of the Two Sicily's. He was a descendent of the Regent Philippe d'Orleans, and she was the niece of Marie Antoinette.

In October 1837, Marie d'Orleans (daughter of Louis Philippe) married Alexander of Württemberg at the Grand Trianon. In 1920, the Grand Trianon hosted the negotiations and signing of the Treaty of Trianon, which left Hungary with less than one-third of its pre-World War I land size. To Hungarians, the word "Trianon" remains to this day the symbol of one of their worst national disasters.

In 1963, Charles de Gaulle ordered a renovation of the building. It is today one of the French Republic's presidential residences used to host foreign officials.

In 1685, Louis once again dazzled the court, the newspapers, and Europe at large when he hosted a carousel of magnificent splendor. A carousel was an event of elaborate horsemanship with spectacular costumes. This was not Louis' first "rodeo" hosting such an event. Performances often carried a storyline and functioned as a form of equestrian ballet. This particular event was called the Carrousel of the Civil Wars of Granada, also called the 1685 Carrousel of the Gallant Moors, one of the first major spectacles staged at Versailles by Louis XIV. The theme was derived from a Spanish sixteenth century epic recounting the civil wars in Granada between Abencerages and the Zegris. Jean Berain designed the elaborate and costly costumes for the horses and riders with richly patterned and colorful silks. The Marble Court was chosen for the parade led by trumpets and the display of costumed riders.

The Carrousel of the Civil Wars of Granada painting.

These years had been relatively peaceful for the King of France. The reprieve from fighting wars had allowed him to use his military manpower as tradesmen building extensions of Versailles, Marly, and the Trianon. If they had been at war, the building campaign would have been put on hold. In only ten years, Louis had built Versailles, Marly, and the Trianon. Not too shabby.

## War

1688 marked a turning point on the European landscape. Things were happening outside Louis XIV's control; this in itself was not a welcome course of events to a king with an ego the size of his palace. In 1685, Charles II's death had placed a new king on the throne of England: James II. While James was an honorable and kind man, he lacked the intelligence and fire that a ruler truly needed. France had been on good terms with England and Louis saw no reason why this change of rulers would impede that. Both Louis and James were Catholics, so Louis was content. The English Protestant subjects however were putting their hopes on James II's two Protestant daughters, Mary, Princess of Orange, and Anne, Princess of Denmark to one day take over the throne.

It is here that the proverbial fly enters the ointment. James II's son-in-law, William of Orange (Mary's husband), had long desired a united league of countries to take control of Europe and crush his enemy, Louis XIV. In William's scope of hoped-for allies were the Emperor Leopold, Spain, certain German princes, and England. With a Catholic king on England's throne, there were challenges to his campaign. If, however, Mary, William's wife and the next heir in line to the English throne were to ascend, the league would be a certainty. If James felt the threat of assassination breathing down his neck, who could blame him. But then fate stepped in.

Mary of Modena, James II's wife, had given birth to two daughters but no sons. Several miscarriages during fifteen years of marriage had not produced a male heir. In England, a female could become queen and sit a throne. Suddenly, to the astonishment of all, Mary gave birth to a healthy boy! The large Protestant body of English subjects began to worry. What if this new heir embraced the French king's inclination for an absolute monarchy. Therefore, when William of Orange landed in England, it became apparent that the loyalties of the English people lay with his Protestant son-in-law and James fled. Boarding a ship with his wife and son, he sailed off in a state of rage, confused at the sudden turn of events. Hotly, he tossed the Great Seal of England overboard into the churning sea.

Louis XIV, one moment content with the anointing of a Catholic king in England, now looked with trepidation at the possible rise of Mary II to the throne, especially since she insisted that William of Orange be crowned king alongside her. The custom, as it is with Elizabeth II today in England, is for the queen's husband to take a relatively moot title of Prince or Consort. It gives him some status but no real power. William, his power restricted by an at of Parliament, lost no time in joining the anti-France alliance known as the League of Augsburg. The German princes were in, and when Sweden switched its alliance from France to the new League, Louis was now looking down the barrel of most of Europe.

Louis had warned James about William of Orange and that an uprising could very well overturn his throne. The king had simply told the Sun King to mind his own business. Louis could have turned his back on the exiled king, but he didn't. Perhaps watching a fellow king be thrown out of his own country prickled his conscience or he felt a need to keep the English king close in case of a reconciliation with his country. Louis offered James sanctuary. He, his wife Mary, and their newborn son were offered opulent accommodations at Saint-Germain. "I render you a sad service, Madame," Louis told Mary, "but hope soon to render you greater and happier ones." This comment shows Louis' belief that he would someday be able to offer the newly reinstated James II his military aid and support. Louis had not given up hope that James would one day rule England again and bring the country into the Catholic faith.

Louis closeted himself with his Minister of War, Louvois, and discussed their next move. Oddly, the idea of meeting with William III in some hope of reconciliation was not even put forth. Why not? The French military had beaten him handily at each confrontation. Louvois' suggestion to the king that he believed there might be a civil war uprising in England could have factored into Louis' desire to attack. He was, after all, the ruling monarch in Europe with an army that many feared. This pride and hubris did not take into account the fact that he would be taking on a League of great force. Louvois pushed his advantage and encouraged Louis to pick them off one at a time, beginning with the Emperor, Leopold I. He pointed out that Leopold was currently at war with Turkey, depleting his resources.

Louvois laid out his defense for his plan to attack the emperor. Firstly, Madame (Philippe's wife) was entitled to part of the Palatine as heiress to her late father. This inheritance was negated when Charlotte married Philippe, if her dowry was paid in full by her father, which it had not been. Louis pounced on this and demanded her share of the Electorate without consulting her.

Secondly, Louis was encouraged by Louvois to put pressure on the Bishop of Cologne (Prince Elector of the small state) to appoint his nominee, Cardinal von Fürstenberg, as successor to the bishop. Once that was accomplished, in September of 1688, Louis demanded that the cardinal be elected, and that the emperor approve the election. This would impact the Rhine area greatly. Louis gave the emperor three months to comply to both ultimatums: Madame's claim to her inheritance, and the approval of Cardinal von Fürstenberg.

It was here that Louis XIV made a tragic mistake. Perhaps lulling the emperor into a false sense of security that he had three months to respond to the French king's demands, Louis instead, only one day after dispatching the ultimatum, went on the attack. It was customary to make a declaration of war. Without even a hint of his intentions, Louis XIV plunked his son, Louis, the Grand Dauphine, on a horse and made him the figurehead for an attack on the Rhine. In reality, the hapless heir gave way to the marchal de Duras and Vauban, two great military engineers. Without hesitation they took over the left side of the Rhine and set siege to Philipsburg, which they conquered on October 22, 1685. Louis XIV, who was safe in the palace attending mass, received the news with exultation and announced the triumph to the court.

Next, Mainz and Heidelberg were taken. Mannheim was added to the victories on November 11. Speier, Trier, Worms, and Oppenheim surrendered on the 15th. While Louis celebrated, the rest of Europe looked on with disgust and the court of public opinion toward this mighty French monarch changed. It was basically dirty pool, even if it was served with a lace cuff. These were the fortresses of the Palatinate, a small and unaggressive state. Louvois was calling the shots, while Louis accepted the credit for yet another victory. He had conquered the Rhineland. It was Louvois's idea that they would go in aggressively, showing no mercy, as a warning to the rest of the League. He therefore went for the jugular.

Louis Louvois, Minister of War

The celebration was short-lived. The manner in which the Palatinate was attacked elicited horror and anger throughout Europe. Cities were burned to the ground, farms destroyed, and churches desecrated. Rape and murder occurred as the energy-fueled troops plowed through the small towns. That it was Louvois, that power-hungry Minister of War who gave the orders did little to save Louis' image from this blood bath. The ferocity of which France's enemies came after the monarch had much to do with their anger at this unwarranted attack.

If Louis tried to resurrect his image in the world's opinion, he had a harder time on the home front convincing a tearful sister-in-law that he had not issued the command to destroy her people. Madame heard the news of her homeland's destruction with absolute horror. She had not been asked about Louis' decision to go after her inheritance. It's possible she would have asked him to leave it alone. Now, many of her family and friends were without homes, and some had been violated or killed.

The whole affair backfired. All of Europe was incensed, and Palatine fought back in the spring of 1689. This coincided with the arrival of Emperor Leopold's armies; the Duke of Lorraine commanding their troops. This was the same duke whose state had been appropriated by Louis, and therefore, he was a man on a mission. In June of 1689, Mainz was retaken and Bonn in November. One of Louvois' favorite commanders, the marechal d'Humieres, was defeated by the Prince of Waldeck in June at France's northern border. The Sun King, finally seeing the machinations behind his Minister of War, took back his authority. Remembering how Louvois had made an enemy of his new wife Madame de Maintenon by warning Louis not to marry her, the king saw finally the minister's feet of clay. He therefore replaced d'Humieres with the marechal-duc de Luxembourg, one of Louvois' most hated enemies.

To add further insult to the humiliated Louvois, Louis gave Luxembourg permission to write to him personally, bypassing the Minister of War. Louis placed his military heads in prominent positions across Europe: Catinat was sent to the Italian front; marechal de Lorges headed for Germany; and the duc de Noailles took a small army to invade Catalonia. By the spring of 1689, Louis had 300,000 soldiers and was running out of money to fund the costly war. He therefore ordered the *Garde-meuble* (head of the furnishings at Versailles) to take all the silver—furnishings included—and have them melted down into coin. The once shimmering Hall of Mirrors and the grand State Apartments at the palace were stripped of many of their most-valuable décor. It all added up to about 2.5 million livres. When more was needed, the church furniture went into the melting pot.

All the expense of this wide-ranging war took its toll on Louis' treasury. It was now that the king truly missed Colbert, who had died in 1683. His successor as Controller-General of Finance was Le Pelletier who proved incompetent to run such a vast enterprise. The king replaced Le Pelletier with Louis Phélypeaus, comte de Pontchartrain. After the death of Colbert's son, Seigelay, in 1690, Louis also gave Pontchartrain the Navy. He eventually became Chancellor, remaining in that office until shortly before his death in 1727.

Pontchartrain went after taxes to help with the ruinous cost of war. He made sure everyone paid, even the untapped nobility who were asked to pay 5% of their income. But, as always, it was the poor who suffered the most. When a poor man, ruined by the taxing came to Pontchartrain and begged for relief, the General of Finance merely smiled and said, "Monsieur, you must pay."

In another effort to raise money, Pontchartrain created obsolete offices for purchase by the nobility. Many, such as Wig Carrier to the King, were laughable. He did, in fact, raise money, but it was negated by the fact that those holding these faux offices were now employees who had to be paid. Over time, the burden of these obscure offices added up.

With newly added funds, Louis' fleet returned James II to Ireland where he was greeted by a large Catholic gathering. On July 10, 1690, a French fleet commandeered by Tourville defeated the Anglo-Dutch navies off Beachy Head. Louis' exiled French Protestants raised their heads when they joined with William of Orange the next day at the Battle of Boyne where they demolished James II's army. James grabbed his luggage and fled back to France. Louis' hope of reinstating the deposed King of England had failed.

Things were faring better on the northern front where the French won the Battle of Fleurus; and in August, Catinat defeated the Duke of Savoy near Saluzzo. It was at this time that Louvois objected to further invasions for a time. The fleet was expensive, Ireland had been a failure, and the French armies were victorious. This time Louis listened and ordered the ships back into the harbor. The season of Carnival was approaching. It was time to have fun.

## Chapter Twenty-Four
## **Feuds and Family**

For Louis XIV, there was always room for celebrations and festivities. Despite the ecliptic cost of the war in which he was entangled, he deemed the annual celebration of Carnival would continue. The Paris rag, the *Mercure* reported in January 1690, "The King has, as is his custom, given splendid suppers since the beginning of Carnival and no evening was spent at Versailles without a masquerade or some other amusement. Monseigneur the Dauphin also attended several balls in Paris and having particularly enjoyed the first one Monsieur [Philippe, his uncle] gave him asked His Royal Highness to give him another one." Philippe, with his love of fine clothes and parties, was in his element during Carnival. His wife, Charlotte of Palatine hated them. Perhaps to spite her or to simply enjoy it all over again, Philippe gave a lavish ball.

In February, "Monseigneur the Dauphin came to a ball given by his Royal Highness Monsieur. From the beginning until the end at four in the morning, eight to ten thousand masked dancers were counted. Monseigneur was given yet another ball on the last Sunday of Carnival. On Monday there was a ball at Versailles at M. le duc du Maine's [the eldest son of the king and Montespan] where the entire court was present, and on Tuesday at the King's where Monseigneur the Dauphin appeared in four different costumes. On that same Tuesday, M. le duc de Chartres [Philippe's son] gave a ball for Mademoiselle at the Palais Royal."

How these lavish balls were viewed by a country embroiled in war, who had followed the king's example and donated their own silver to be melted down for the war effort, is not clear. It is amazing how removed from the public's opinion of him and his continuous building and parties Louis really was. He would do as he pleased, despite the suffering of the people he taxed.

Louis XIV continued to advance the needs of his illegitimate children. It was no longer shocking to the court to see them seated at the royal table or strutted about the balls. The king now set his sights on his eldest son by Madame de Montespan, Louis Auguste, the duc du Maine. The boy had grown up with some physical challenges. One hip was a little shorter than the other, resulting in a limp. Hunting and military endeavors were difficult for him, and possibly a royal thorn in Louis' backside. The hunt was everything to him, and a son leading a victorious army would be a credit to him. Louis Auguste lacked friends as he was prone to gossip and was void of a moral backbone. The king, therefore, decided off the army he should go.

"I am sending my son, the duc de Maine, to the army you command," he wrote the maréchal d'Humiéres on May 21, 1689. "You know how fond I am of him and how very much I wish him to be worthy of this position. I have ordered him always to believe what you tell him, as I feel sure you will advise him to do what he must and even a little more. Allow the duc de Maine to see everything but avoid whenever possible his fighting in small engagements where he might be captured." Translation: give him some victories without getting him killed. Humiéres need not have feared for Louis Auguste's safety as he had a hard time getting the reluctant soldier anywhere near the fighting.

## Intrigue and Infidelity

Throughout 1689 and 1690, resentment was building throughout France due to the economic climate. The ongoing war with the rest of Europe had placed a huge burden on the people of France through taxes, sacrificing their silver, and the collateral damage that always came with warfare. Yet, they read of the wanton expense of opulent balls during the first month of 1690 as Louis and his court held not one, but three masquerade balls. As they did in the middle 1860s, pamphlets began appearing ridiculing the king and his constituents.

These amateur pages, consisting largely of cartoon drawings and sarcastic quotes, found their way inside the golden gates of Versailles. Louis' wife, Madame de Maintenon was one of the more prolific roasts. Louis was featured as adding Mary of Modena to his long line of mistresses as his reasoning for supporting her husband, James II. These pamphlets were mild compared to the ones that would circulate during Marie Antoinette's time on the throne.

In this pamphlet, Louis XIV is seen seated in the center of the sun. Each of the 24 rays emanating out from him is said to be a crime he committed. It is written in Dutch and French.

Meanwhile, the intrigue at Versailles continued. The Dauphine, Marie Anne Christine Victoire of Bavaria died. She had never been a favorite at court, least of all with the king with whom she had debated and criticized his policies. The Dauphin, who had been involved in an affair with the maid of honor to his half-sister the princess de Conti, was relieved as the news of the Dauphine's passing was announced. Mlle Choin, whom the Dauphin adored, was a simple-minded woman, well endowed, and compliant. As it was necessary for the twenty-eight-year-old heir to the throne to marry again, he settled on the obtuse Mlle Choin. He secretly married Marie Emilie de Joly de Choin and she became his morganatic spouse.

A morganatic marriage is sometimes called a left-handed marriage. It is a marriage between two people of unequal social rank, which in the context of royalty or other inherited title prevents one spouse's position or privileges being passed on to the other spouse and/or any children born of the marriage. Usually, neither the bride nor any children of the marriage have a claim on the bridegroom's succession rights, titles, precedence, or entailed property. The children are considered legitimate for all other purposes and the prohibition against bigamy applies.

This marital loophole begs the question: would any issue from the Dauphine's marriage to Choin have been eligible for the throne? As Louis XIV himself had entered into such a marriage with Madame de Maintenon, who also was denied the title of Queen as Choin was denied the title of Dauphine, were these wise unions?

The marriage almost didn't occur. What is Versailles without its salacious back story? At the same time Mlle de Choin was horsing around with the Dauphine (before the death of the Dauphine), she was in a relationship with Count François Alphonse de Clermont-Chaste, a member of the entourage of the marechal de Luxembourg. Luxembourg advised Clermont-Chaste to marry Choin in order to acquire power over the Dauphin through her. It was rumored that Marie Emilie and Clermont-Chaste planned to dominate the throne by producing a child, which they would present as the child of Louis, the Dauphin. When these plans were discovered, after the correspondence between Marie Emilie and Clermont was presented to the king (those pesky letter spies), they were both exiled from court, which did not, however, permanently end her relationship with the Dauphin.

Marie Emilie Therese de Joly Mademoiselle de Choin

Marie Emilie married Louis secretly in 1694. No details are known of the ceremony, but on July 19, 1694, the Dauphin referred to her as his legal wife in a letter to his father's morganatic wife, Madame de Maintenon. Nonetheless, the marriage was not officially recognized. Marie Emilie did not acquire the title of Dauphine, continuing to be referred to as Mademoiselle de Choin. She did not participate in court life, which must have been a blow.

The new wife of the Dauphin resided in a palace of Meudon, within which she imitated the role played at court by Madame de Maintenon, with whom she got along well, acting as her husband's hostess, receiving dukes and foreign diplomats. She was allowed to sit in a chair in the presence of members of the royal house and to call them by their names rather than by title. Sitting in a chair with arms was a privilege given only to royalty; all other others sat on a stool, so it was a symbolic nod to her marriage to the Grand Dauphin. Yet, she dressed simply, took no further advantage of the marriage and did not participate in politics.

A Louis XIV armchair & a stool from that era.

Despite the minimal clout given to her as the dauphin's wife, Marie dressed simply, took no further advantage of the marriage and did not participate in politics. Pregnant at the time of her secret marriage, she gave birth to a son who was sent to the countryside and died at age two in 1697 without receiving a legal name. No further children are known to have been born to the marriage.

It is a paradox the Sun King and his only rightful heir had both married women who could not be officially recognized and whose ranking qualified any nobleman of low standing to marry. Versailles, the symbol of wealth, power, and European royalty's role model, closeted the women in secret who were married to the two most powerful men at court. The third most-powerful, Philippe, the king's brother, was still madly in love with the chevalier de Lorraine. He could see nothing but his love for the ambitious young man who had becoming increasingly crueler in flouting his desire for both other men and other women alike. As an angry cast-off female lover would do, Philippe enlisted the company of any young male in the court. The courtiers watched; a parade of lanky, pubescent men ascended the stairs to Monsieur's rooms. It was the delicious fodder of gossip and giggles at the gambling tables of Versailles.

While the antics of the glittering court continued to amuse, including the antics of the king's granddaughter, the duchesse de Bourbon, who resembled Princess Margaret (Queen Elizabeth II's sister) in her wanton desire for entertainment, the war continued.

It is in letters Louis XIV wrote during the war to his wife that we get a glimpse of the depth of his affection for her. "I take advantage of Montchevreuil's departure," Louis wrote in April, 1691, "to assure you of a truth which pleases me so that I can never tire of telling you; it is that I always cherish you and care for you beyond expression; and that, in a word, no matter how much you may love me, I love you still more, my whole heart being yours."

If Madame de Montespan had hung around the court in hopes Louis would return to her, as a mistress if nothing else, this devotion to his wife seems to have sealed her fate. In March 1691, Montespan's apartments were given to her son du Maine by the king. She left the palace that had held so much romance and intrigue and went to her apartment in the Convent of Saint Joseph, occasionally visiting Clagny. It was the end of an era that had identified Louis as a double adulterer and wanton Lothario. He may have breathed a sigh of relief at her departure as it had been a constant reminder of his division from the Church.

## The War Continues

Louis XIV's decision to park his fleet at the end of 1690 enabled William III to land in Ireland with a further 15,000 men. With these reinforcements William III secured a decisive victory at the Battle of the Boyne and once again forced James II to flee back to France. Following the Earl of Marlborough's capture of the southern ports of Cork and Kinsale—thereby confining French and Jacobite troops to the west of the country—William III now felt confident enough to return to the Continent at the beginning of 1691 to command the coalition army in the Low Countries, leaving Baron van Ginkell to lead his troops in Ireland. After Ginkell's victory over the Marquis of Saint-Ruth at the Battle of Aughrim on July 12, 1691, the remaining Jacobite strongholds fell in rapid succession. Without the prospect of further French assistance, the capitulation at Limerick finally sealed victory for William III and his supporters in Ireland, resulting in the signing of the *Treaty of Limerick* on October 3rd. English troops could now return to the Low Countries in strength.

The war continued on throughout 1691 and 1692, with each branch of the Alliance backing their own agenda. Victories teetered back and forth to the point that one wondered if the gaining of one town and the loss of another made the entire thing a moot point. By 1693, the French army had reached an official size of 400,000 men (on paper), but Louis XIV was facing an economic crisis. France and northern Italy witnessed severe harvest failures resulting in widespread famine which, by the end of 1694, had accounted for the deaths of an estimated two million people. It would not be the last time France faced the fallout of a depleted grain supply.

1691 also marked an abrupt change in Louis' government—Louis Louvois, that adversarial Minister of War, died on July 16. Instead of looking outside the Le Tellier family (they had ruled the army for three generations), Louis promptly elected Louvois' ill-tempered son, the marquis de Barbezieux, to replace him as the military head. As it became apparent that Barbezieux lacked his father's thirst for warfare or his brains, Louis began to take over more and more of his government's duties.

Early in June of 1693, Louis dropped the ball as he concentrated on the increasing demands of his role running his government. William III found himself trapped before Louvain by two vastly superior French armies. Louis, instead of capitalizing on his enemy's dilemma, split his forces and sent one army off to Germany under Monseigneur's (the Dauphin) nominal command while he himself returned to Versailles. Sounding as if he needed to validate that decision, Louis wrote to his brother Philippe, "I gave in to the strong remonstrances which were made and to the conclusions of my own reason, and I sacrificed with pleasure my own preference and my satisfaction and what would have been more flattering to me to well-being of my state."

Louis' decision to back off from Louvain when he effectively had William III cornered did not sit well with the Princes of the Blood. To them, it smacked of cowardice. Their murmurings found their way back to the king, and Louis retaliated, as he always did when his authority and pride were attacked. He bypassed them for military advancement. Instead, he chose his illegitimate children by

Montespan. In 1693, he turned his back on his royal bloodline and appointed the duc du Maine (his favorite) to Grand Master of the Artillery and the come de Toulouse Grand Admiral of France. These positions had always been relegated to the royal family. The duc de Chartres' (Philippe II d'Orleans, the King's nephew and son of his brother Philippe and Charlotte) would have been the likely candidate for either post and was imminently qualified, yet he, like his father, was put on the back burner in favor of Louis' own issue…bastards or not.

Saint-Simon, the court scribe, who was clearly antagonistic toward the King, wrote, "The King, preoccupied with the position of his bastards whom he raised higher day by day, had married two of his daughters to two princes of the blood royal. For a long time already, Madame de Maintenon, even more than the King…had wanted to wed Mlle de Blois, the King and Madame de Montespan's second daughter, to M. le duc de Chartres. He was the King's only nephew, and much above the Princes of the Blood, both by his rank as Grandson of France (as Grandson of Louis XIII) and by the splendid Court which surrounded Monsieur (Philippe, the King's brother). The marriage of the two princes had scandalized everyone. The King knew it and realized the effect to be expected from a marriage so much more dazzling."

Louis went first to his brother Philippe to gently broach the subject of marrying off his son to Montespan's daughter. Typical of the king, he backed his efforts with some slick maneuvering. Louis reached out to the one person who had the most influence over Philippe—not his wife, but his longtime lover, the chevalier de Lorraine. The King gave Lorraine the order of the Saint Espirit, and his brother, the comte d'Armagnac, the King's Grand Equerry. Lorraine reasoned with Philippe, who put up little resistance. That left Madame, Charlotte, Princess of the Palatine. As expected, the lady exploded. This was her only son in whom she had high hopes of a royal marriage befitting his rank. Her son was not pleased either and resisted. His tutor, the abbé Dubois, took him aside and pointed out the advantages of the young man giving into the king's wishes. The duc de Chartres began to soften, which only increased his mother's rage.

Philippe II, duc de Chartres

Saint-Simon was swift to report the salacious gossip: "Madame heard about it. She spoke to her son about the indignity of this marriage with all her strength, a quality in which she was not deficient, and made him swear not to give in." The rift this must have caused between herself, and her husband can only be imagined as his lover's advancement to the Saint Espirit hung in the balance."

The scribe continues, "One early afternoon, as I was walking through the Upper Gallery, I saw M. le duc de Chartres coming out of one of his apartment's back doors, looking very sad and embarrassed… I asked him where he was rushing to at this odd hour. He answered, with a hurried and unhappy look, that the King had sent for him… M. de Chartres found the King alone in his cabinet with Monsieur (Philippe), whom he had not expected to see there. The King was friendly to M. de Chartres, told him he wanted to take care of him; that the war which was raging on every side made otherwise suitable princesses unavailable; that he could not better show his affection than by offering him his daughter, whose two sisters had married princes of the blood; that this would make him not just the King's nephew but his son-in-law as well; but that, although he wanted this marriage with a passion, he did not wish to force him, and left him free to decide."

The shy young man played his only card. He said he would abide by his parent's wishes. The King, having already procured his brother's favor of the idea, said, "You are quite right to say so, but if you consent, your father and mother will do the same; and turning to Monsieur: 'Is that not true, brother?' Saint-Simon goes on to note, "Monsieur consented to the marriage… so the King promptly said that the only question now lay with Madame; and he had her sent for… Madam arrived, and immediately the King told her that he expected she would not be opposed to a proposal which Monsieur desired and to which M. de Chartres had agreed: that it was this marriage with Mlle de Blois, that he wanted passionately, and he then added all the same things he had just told M. le duc de Chartres, all in the most imposing way, but looking as if it had not occurred to him that Madame might be anything but delighted, although he knew very well the opposite was true. Madame, who had been counting on the refusal her son had promised he would make, and which, in fact, he had tried to carry out by his embarrassed and conditional answer, found herself trapped and speechless. She looked furiously at Monsieur and M. de Chartres, said that, if they were agreed, she had nothing to say, curtsied and left. Her son followed her, but she carried on with such vehemence that he was not able to tell her what had happened."

As usual, Louis got his way. The betrothal was announced and what followed was, by all accounts, a pitiable sight. Saint-Simon wrote that he saw "Madame, walking in the Hall of Mirrors…her handkerchief in her hand, sobbing openly, speaking quite loudly, gesticulating, the very image of Ceres, after the rape of her daughter, Proserpina, looking for her with fury and asking Jupiter to give her back…Nothing could have been more ashamed than Monsieur's expression…His son looked desolate and even his fiancée seemed extremely embarrassed…

Françoise Marie de Bourbon

"The next day, the whole Court visited Monsieur, Madame, and M. le duc de Chartres, but without saying a word: we merely bowed or curtsied in the deepest silence. After this, we went to the Hall of Mirrors as usual, to await the end of the Council and the King's mass. Madame was there. Her son came to her as he did every day to kiss her hand; at that moment Madame slapped his face with such strength that the noise was heard a little distance away, dreadfully embarrassing the poor prince and causing countless spectators, among whom I was, an indescribable amazement."

Perhaps to appease his family for his selfish insistence on the marriage, the king gave Mlle de Blois the unprecedented dowry of 2 million livres, a pension of 150,000 livres, and jewels worth another 600,000 livres. This was a great deal more than her older sister, Louise received upon marrying the duc of Bourbon, and at a time when the war had emptied the coffers. Louis, probably in gratitude for his complicity in the affair, gave his brother the Palais

Royal, where he had been residing. Philippe's lover Lorraine received 100,000 livres for his role in the duplicity. The young bride was also to receive a household consisting of a dame d'honneur, a dame d'atours, and a chevalier d'honneur, all attendants who were commonly reserved for a king's legitimate daughter.

On 22 November 1681, at the age of four-and-a-half, Françoise Marie was legitimized by Louis XIV and given the courtesy title of *Mademoiselle de Blois*, a style held previously by her older half-sister, Marie Anne de Bourbon, a legitimized daughter of the king by Louise de La Vallière. The name of her mother was not mentioned in the act of legitimization because Madame de Montespan was still married to the Marquis de Montespan, who might have counter-claimed paternity and custody of his wife's children. By the time of her birth, her parents' relationship was coming to an end because of Madame de Montespan's possible involvement in the *Affaire des poisons*.

Her older siblings, Louis Auguste and Louise Françoise, had been legitimized on 19 December 1673 by letters patent registered at the *Parlement de Paris*. Her younger brother, Louis Alexandre, was legitimized at the same time as she and given the title of *comte de Toulouse*. She remained close to him all her life, as well as to their older brother, Louis-Auguste de Bourbon, *duc du Maine*. She was never close to her legitimate half brother, Louis, Dauphin of France. Françoise wielded little political influence considering her near relationships to France's rulers during most of her life. She was involved in the botched Cellamare Conspiracy in 1718 which was supposed to oust her own husband as regent in favor of her full brother Louis-Auguste de Bourbon, Duke of Maine.

She inherited her mother's beauty, Madame de Caylus commented that Françoise was *naturally timid and glorious* and was "a little beauty with a beautiful face and beautiful hands; completely in proportion." She was proud of her royal ancestry and of the royal blood of the House of Bourbon she inherited from her father: Later, it was joked that she would "remember she was a *daughter of France*, even while on her *chaise percé* (toilet). The marquis d'Argenson said she was very like her mother, but had also Louis XIV's orderly mind with his failings of injustice and harshness.

Françoise and Philippe d'Orléans were married on 18 February 1692 in the chapel of the Palace of Versailles. The service was conducted by the Cardinal de Bouillon – a member of the House of La Tour d'Auvergne. In 1685, the Cardinal de Bouillon had refused to take part in the marriage of the Duke of Bourbon and Françoise's sister, *Mademoiselle de Nantes*, and, as a result, had been sent into exile, but he was recalled for the wedding of Françoise and the Duke of Chartres. After the ceremony, a banquet was given in the Hall of Mirrors with all the princes and princesses of the blood in attendance. Other guests included the exiled James II of England and his consort, Mary of Modena. At the newlyweds' bedding ceremony later that evening, Queen Mary handed the new Duchess of Chartres her night shirt. Madame de Montespan had not been invited to the wedding of her daughter.

As her new husband was a legitimate grandson of a king, Françoise assumed the rank of *petite-fille de France* ("Grand-Daughter of France"), and was addressed as *Royal Highness*. Furthermore, the newlyweds traveled and lodged wherever the king did, dined with him, and were entitled to armchairs in his presence. As the new *duchesse de Chartres*, Françoise Marie was next in precedence behind only the Duchess of Burgundy, and her own mother-in-law, the Duchess of Orléans.

Her mother-in-law wrote the following in her memoirs: *"All the ladies in waiting have made her believe that she did my son honour in marrying him; and she is so vain of her own birth and that of her brothers and sisters that she will not hear a word said against them; she will not see any difference between legitimate and illegitimate children."*

Not long after their marriage, Philippe openly ridiculed his wife's bad temper, nicknaming her *Madame Lucifer*. Her mother-in-law said that during the early years of the Chartres' marriage, Françoise was as "drunk as drunk" three to four times a week. That the marriage was a miserable one was well-known. All that mattered was the Sun King got his way. One month after the nuptials, on March 19th, the duc de Maine was married to one of Monsieur le Prince's daughters, Anne Louise, who was a petite spitfire. All of the illegitimate children were now married and moved into the royal family, with the exception of the comte de Toulouse, who was only 14.

## Chapter Twenty-Five
## War and Peace

The sometimes-confusing maneuvers of the Sun King have been put down to ego, self-aggrandizing, an overwhelming need to dominate and conquer at all costs. Yet, if one looks closely, one can see the equivalent of a small child checking the closet for boogeymen. The fear he felt during the upheaval of the Frondes when he was a youth never left him. His relentless drive to bring the nobles to their knees and insulate his palace from the capital city had been his goal from the moment he went over the first blueprint with La Vou. Now, in the 1690's, we see a new strategy: to elevate his illegitimate children to ranks only slightly lower than those of the royal bloodline. True, they were left out of the line of succession, but they were given titles, military posts, and power.

On May 4, 1694, Louis XIV created for them an intermediary rank that basically leveled the playing field for all middle class. Was this an extension of the King's perpetual distrust of the aristocracy? He had surrounded himself with not those of royal lineage in places of power, but those whose talents and loyalties suited him. Colbert, Mazarin, etc. were considered *bourgeoise*. That he kept his own brother beneath his heel was born of fear of a royal coup. Now, the lines between the duc du Maine and comte de Toulouse, and the ducs d'Orleans, de Chartres, de Bourbon, the princes de Condé and de Conti blurred to the point that as the days passed, the court recognized them all as on equal footing.

On a roll, Louis took another slap at those who had represented the inner workings of the Fronde uprising: the Parlement and the nobles. In an unprecedented act in 1694, the King instituted a tax that was revolutionary. The capitation (head tax) was imposed on nobles of the Second Estate and the commoners of the Third Estate alike. It was now that for the first time ever, the nobility, who had always been tax-exempt were told they would heretofore be assessed 5% on their income. Of course, this new tax hit the poor much harder than it did those with jeweled fingers, but it was still enough to send the nobles reeling. Parlement, who was mostly composed of the middle class, must have felt the sting as well, as many of them, were noble by law by carrying a noble estate or from the lineage of an individual parent. Oddly, not one objection was levied at the King from this usual cantankerous body of men. If the cowed silence following what should have been an explosive edict wasn't evidence enough that Louis had succeeded in becoming the government, not just running it, then nothing would.

By the 1690s, Louis XIV had been ruling for over thirty years; the ministers who had been older and wiser when he was younger were gone, replaced largely by their children who were younger than the great Monarch, and who seemed incompetent as the king aged and took on more and more of the responsibilities of his court. He was fulfilling the title of the painting that adorned the ceiling of the Hall of Mirrors…in essence, "he governed by himself."

The late Louvois's son, Louis François Le Tellier of Barbezieux was a case in point as to Louis's loyalty to departed ministers. Barbezieux had succeeded his father as Minister of War, but the twenty-one-year-old man lacked his father's work ethic and dedication to the job. He partied more than parlayed, drank more than directed, and womanized more than putting his energies toward warfare. Finally, Louis reached out to the young man's uncle, the Archbishop of Reims, rather than humiliate him at court. Louis wrote:

"I know what I owe to the memory of M. de Louvois," he wrote in 1693, "but if your nephew does not behave better, I will be forced to make a decision. I will be sorry to do so; but I will have to. He has talents but does not use them well. He asks the princes to supper too often instead of working, he neglects his business for pleasure; he keeps the officers waiting too long in his antechamber; he speaks to them with disdain and sometimes with cruelty."

That the Archbishop must have remanded the young man shows in Barbezieux's improved behavior, which did not last long. On

Friday, October 28, 1695, the king returned from a stay at Fontainebleau, and again put pen to paper and this time handed it to the archbishop in person.

Louis Francois Marie Le Tellier of Barbezieux

"The way your nephew lived in Fontainebleau," Louis wrote, "is not bearable, it has scandalized the public. He spent his days hunting and his nights in debauchery. He does not work, and that has very serious consequences… He is a liar, obsessed with women, always about, hardly ever to be found…If he does not change completely, he cannot remain in office…his work cannot be successful when he neglects it so. I wish him to amend himself without my being involved. It is impossible to make mistakes when the work is so neglected; and they must cost me much."

The cost, in this case, was of utmost importance. Barbezieux was the Minister of War, and France was deeply embroiled in one that lasted nine years. This letter to the archbishop was penned in 1695.

The war would rage on for two more costly years. It is interesting that the great king took a rather passive approach in his hopes of improving his minister's efficiency. It may have been out of respect for a family that had served him for so long that he reached out to the archbishop instead of calling the lazy youth into his chambers. It may have been to send a message to the powerful Tellier family that their days in the sun could be numbered if this member of their branch did not shape up.

Whatever the outcome, the French army marched on and took Gerona in May 1694, when the marechal de Noailles crossed the Pyrenees. Barcelona was next in the marechal's crosshairs, but the city prevailed, and the siege was abandoned. To those looking on, this lengthy and costly war seemed like a Shakespearian quote: "Full of sound and fury, signifying nothing." Victories were chalked up and erased; one side prevailed only to have the other rear up and take their piece of the geographical pie.

## Death of a Queen

Back in England, a large shake-up was happening. In February 1689, while James II was in exile, a special Convention Parliament held that the king had "vacated" the English throne, and installed William III and his wife Mary II as joint monarchs. Mary II had been dealing with smallpox in late 1694. A tall woman for that era, 5'11", she was considered to be fit and would regularly walk between her palaces at Whitehall and Kensington. Many believed she would outlive her husband, William II, and her estranged younger sister, Anne, both of whom suffered from ill-health. When the telltale pustules appeared on her skin, Mary sent away all who had not previously had the disease, to prevent the spread of the infection.

Several days into the course of her illness, the smallpox lesions reportedly disappeared, leaving her skin smooth and unmarked, and Mary said that she felt improved. Her attendants initially hoped she had been ill with measles rather than smallpox, and that she was recovering. But the rash had "turned inward," a sign that Mary was suffering from a usually fatal form of smallpox, and her condition quickly deteriorated. Mary II died at Kensington Palace shortly after midnight on the morning of December 28, 1694, at the young age of 32.

William of Orange, who was away at war and had grown increasingly reliant on his wife, was devastated by her death, and said that "from being the happiest," he was "now going to be the miserablest creature on earth." Mary was widely mourned in Britain. During a cold winter, in which the Thames River froze, her embalmed body lay in state in Banqueting House, Whitehall. On March 5, 1695, she was buried at Westminster Abbey. Her funeral service was the first of any royal attended by all the members of both Houses of Parliament.

William III of Orange and Queen Mary II of the House of Stuart

On January 4, 1695, Louis was dealt a blow with the death of the king's last great generals: maréchal de Luxembourg. He was replaced by the maréchal de Villeroy who was an old friend of the king's. While the tall general towered over the 5'4" monarch, the two shared a love of fashion and a seductive way with women. Louis wasted no time in appointing the duc de Maine, his favorite of his children by Madame de Montespan, as second in command with Villeroy. The Princes of the Blood were once again sidelined by this advancement.

The Sun King's choices to head his military were under scrutiny. Rather than choosing men for these key positions due to skill, merit, and their ability to lead, Louis was favoring handing out these posts to friends, their offspring, and to raise the rank of his own son. Barbezieux's embarrassing conduct and inefficiency did nothing to sway the king from making ill-advised choices when it came to his military posts. Villeroy proved to be incompetent and the duc de Maine was indecisive, cowardly, and frightened of responsibility. These misappropriated appointments may have had something to do with the loss of Namur to William III on September 1695, and subsequently, the Spanish Netherlands. For the first time, Louis found himself on the defense, scrambling to protect his own land, instead of conquering other's. His ego suffered a tremendous blow, one which surfaced in a rare public display of rage.

When the duc de Maine disgraced himself in July, Saint-Simon was there to report on it: "It was for M. du Maine that he [the King] had taken such care. At that moment he saw that it had all availed nothing, and the pain of it was unbearable to him. He felt, for this beloved son, all the weight of the spectacle given the army, and the mockery he read in foreign gazettes, and his disappointment was inconceivable. This King, so even tempered, so much the master of his smallest movements, broke down on this single occasion. Coming out of table at Marly, with all the ladies, and before all the Court, he saw a footman who, as he cleared the table of the dessert, put a biscuit in his pocket. At that moment, forgetting his dignity, holding the cane he had just been given together with his hat, he ran to the footman, who no more expected something of the kind than those he pushed away as he went to him, cursed him, and broke is cane over his shoulders. In truth, it was a reed and did not last long. From there, the broken cane still in hand, with the look of a man beside himself, and still cursing the footman who was long gone, he crossed the small salon and an antechamber and went into Mme de Maintenon's as he often did at Marly after his dinner.

"When he left her to return to his own apartment, he came across the Père de La Chaise [his confessor]. As soon as he saw him standing there among the courtiers, 'Father,' he said in a loud voice, 'I have just given a good beating to a rascal and broken my cane across his back; but I do not think it offended God,' and he went on to talk about the so-called crime. All those who were there were still trembling either from what they had seen themselves or from what they had been told. Their fear redoubled upon this speech: the closest to the King started buzzing about the footman."

The explosion was probably due to more than the king's disappointment in his son. For the first time Louis saw fate treat him as mortal and fallible. In a hasty move to regain some headway, Louis attacked Brussels. It was looked upon as destruction for destruction's sake, and it did little to improve his image on the European front. 1695 had showed the weaker underbelly of the great Sun King. The war had drained the treasury and he was losing ground...and face. He decided to focus on another cog in his royal wheel...the church.

In 1691, Innocent XII Pignatelli was elected Pope and was determined not only to reform the administration of the papal states but also to end the estrangement of France and its clergy. In 1693, he ratified the appointment of the bishops nominated since 1682, provided only that they had not participated in the Assembly of that year. On his side, Louis XIV revoked the obligation for the clergy to subscribe to the Four Articles. Both parties had apparently retaliated; in fact, the Pope lost a good deal more than the King: he accepted the King's view of his regalian rights; and while it was no longer enjoined that the clergy subscribe to the Four Articles, they were not forbidden to do so of their own free choice. Still, for the first time, Louis XIV had publicly acknowledged an error. (*Louis XIV, A Royal Life.* Oliver Bernier)

As the war continued on in 1695 and 1696, Louis began to sense the futility of it all. It had now spread across the ocean to the French colonies in the Caribbean, while in France, Dieppe was largely destroyed by a bombardment from the sea. The king began to have thoughts of a peace treaty, knowing he might not come out on top. Louis chewed on his feathered quill and thought of ways to split up the coalition as one takes apart a whole chicken. He settled on the Duke of Savoy as his best shot at beginning.

Vittorio Amedeo II ruled over Savoy and Piedmont. He was at this time the generalissimo of the Imperial Army. Louis knew the Duke of Savoy could be swayed to switch teams if it suited him, so the king put together a Godfather proposal—one the duke couldn't refuse.

"The comte de Tessé," Voltaire wrote, "a clever and amiable man, with a pleasing sort of genius, which is the most essential talent for a negotiator, first acted secretly in Turin. The maréchal de Catinat, as gifted for making peace as for making war, concluded the negotiation. There was no need for two clever men to join in the convincing the Duke of Savoy to follow a policy advantageous to him. His country [which was occupied by a French army] was returned to him; he was given money; he was offered the marriage of his daughter with the young duc de Bourgogne, son of Monseigneur [the Dauphin] and heir to the French Crown: an agreement was quickly reached... The Duke of Savoy joined the French army with his troops... and... in less than a month had gone from being the emperor's generalissimo to being Louis XIV's generalissimo."

While this new alliance shook Leopold I to his core, it was William III that Louis needed to acquiesce to a peace treaty. This was a tough one. He would need to approach his mortal enemy, a man who spent his entire life trying to defeat him and ask him how he felt about ending it all in the name of peace. To his surprise, William II agreed to meet with him in secret at Ryswick in Holland. The talks drug out. Several times the two adversaries walked away from the table with heated exchanges. William had the Parliament back in England hissing in his ear to end the war, Louis had offered to return all his conquests since the Peace of Nijmegen with the exception of Strasbourg, and the duc de Vendome had just taken Barcelona. William saw the writing on the wall and on September 20, 1697, the terms were at last agreed upon.

Louis had also agreed not to help in the restoration of the Stuarts to the English throne, but he refused to kick James II out of Saint Germain where he would live out the rest of his days. Louis returned his duchy to the Duke of Lorraine and gave him Monsieur's daughter as a wife; he abandoned Catalonia, which he had just conquered, along with the cities in Spanish Netherlands which he had seized since Nijmegen. To the Emperor, he turned over Brisach, Kehl, Freiburg, and Philipsburg. William III recovered his principality of Orange in southern France, and the Rhine forts [a feat of which Louis had been particularly proud] were destroyed.

If the King thought his people would celebrate the new *Peace of Ryswick*, he was mistaken. France, far from being the conquering hero of a war that had lasted nine long years and created taxes and sacrifices in order to finance it, had basically returned every conquest. While the people were eager for peace, this one had come at a dear cost. The treaty brought about a much longed-for stretch of quiet. In its wake were ruined homes and farms, destroyed cities, and treasuries, widowed wives and fatherless children. It had all been for naught.

*Treaty of Ryswick*, by Granger
Fineartamerica.com

## Chapter Twenty-Six
## **Children of the Realm**

While the rest of France was not enchanted with the king's *Peace Treaty of Ryswick*, Louis was feeling the first real freedom he had felt in years. In 1696, the great Sun King was now almost 60 years old. Louis XI was the last king to reach this age and that was in 1483. Louis XIV continued to struggle with bouts of gout, and in the fall of 1696, an abscess formed on his neck resulting in a high fever and immediate surgery. Perhaps the king's feeling of invincibility had been diluted with the sting of ending of a war that had cost him more than he gained, and his continual health issues. Old age was knocking on his palace door and so he did what so many do in this time of life, they drink in the energy of youth.

Marie-Adélaide de Savoy was to be the next pawn in the European game of chess. Keeping his promise to Vittorio Amedeo II of Savoy, as part of his package to win the generalissimo of the Imperial Army during the recent war, Louis welcomed Amedo's daughter to his court. She was only twelve years of age and was now betrothed to the Dauphin's son, the duc de Bourgogne. Expecting another dull, dim-witted, and unambitious princess, the court of Versailles began their gossip mills as news of the engagement was made known.

Court scribe Saint-Simon sharpened his quill and duly noted that "The Court had long been without a queen or a dauphine. All the ladies of a certain position and those in favor bustled and plotted, many of them against one another; anonymous letters, denunciations, and calumnies flew about. All the decisions were taken solely to the King and Mme de Maintenon, who never left his bedside while he was ill [with the abscess on his neck], except when he allowed himself to be seen, and who was often alone with him. She [Maintenon] had decided to be the real governess of the princess, and to create strong enough a tie so that she could use her to amuse the King without fearing that, as she grew up, she might become dangerous. She also wanted to have a hold, through her, on the duc de Bourgogne for the future."

Those who had looked at Mme de Maintenon as a meek, pious, governess had misjudged this woman's scheming mind. Madame de Montespan realized it too late, after the woman she had advanced and thought of as a friend, supplanted her and married the king. Maintenon knew how to remain in the background, away from the finery of the court, and weave her web amid the shadows. With quiet and reason, she entangled Louis and those around him with envious cunning. Now, it was the new Princess of Savoy who became trapped in the sticky threads as Maintenon decided on her ever-important attendants.

"Mme de Maintenon," Simon continued, "therefore sought out, for the princesses' entourage, persons who were either wholly devoted to herself or so stupid that she would have nothing to fear from them."

And so, without hesitation, Maintenon began recruiting the dumb, the malleable, and the close ties, as the new Princess's entourage. The marquis de Dangeau was appointed chevalier d'honneur. He was an old friend of the King's with a reputation at being fiercely adroit at playing cards without cheating. He was outgoing and well-liked. The duchesse du Lude who was appointed dame d'honneur, was rich, pleasant, virtuous, and extremely dim-witted. She was surprised at the post, ignorant of the fact that she had been chosen for her lack of little gray cells than any outstanding attributes. The Comtesse de Mailly, the dame d'Atours, won the appointment due to her close friendship with Maintenon; and the comte de Tessé, was *énegotiations* with duc de Savoy. The ladies-in-waiting were chosen for similar traits, and Louis' wife was now confident that she was fully in charge of this new young pawn.

Louis XIV rode off to Montargis, a little past Fontainebleau, to meet this new lady who would play such an important role at court. With the queen and dauphine deceased, Marie would hold considerable power. She was marrying the heir to the French crown. The king met the young woman on November 4, 1696, and wrote dutifully to Maintenon, who must have been waiting on pins and needles to hear his assessment of her new charge.

"I arrived here before five," the King wrote, "the princess only arrived around six. I went to meet her at her carriage. She let me speak first, but then answered me very properly and with a touch of shyness you would have liked. I took her, across the crowd, to her room, showing her off from time to time by bringing the torches closer to her face. She bore this march and these lights with grace and modesty. We finally reached her room, where the crowd and heat were enough to kill you; I showed her from time to time to those who came close…

Marie Adélaïde of Savoy

"She is very graceful and has the best shape I have ever seen; beautifully dressed and coiffed; her eyes are very beautiful and lively; admirable dark eyelashes; a fine pink and white complexion which is just as one would desire; the finest fair hair and in great abundance. She is as thin as she should be at her age; her mouth is very red, big lips, large white and very jumbled teeth, pretty hands but of the color to be expected at her age. She speaks little, at least in my presence, is not shy about being stared at, and behaves like someone who is accustomed to the great world. Her curtsey is not good, and too Italianate; there is also something Italian about her face, but it is pleasing, I could see that in everyone's eyes. As for me, I am delighted with her… I find her just as she should be and would not want her to be more beautiful."

The King's description of the young princess is akin to a man checking over a thoroughbred horse. One can almost picture him prying open her mouth to check her teeth. It is interesting that the first thing Louis comments upon is her "shape." This scene would play again with another King Louis and another young princess arriving in France to marry nobility. Louis XV met Marie Antoinette at the Handing Over in later years. His first comment was "How are her breasts?" What came next would play out in both young ladies' arrivals. They were stripped of their country's clothing and put immediately into French gowns. The message was that you are France's now and all your allegiance to another country is forsaken. Marie Antoinette's was Austria, and Marie Adélaïde had just arrived from Italy. Louis XIV describes the scene:

"I saw her being undressed; she had a very good body, one might even say a perfect one, and is modest enough to please you…We took supper together; she did not make a single mistake and is always amazingly polite, but especially in regard to me and my son she did not make a single mistake and behaved as well as you would have done."

One must wonder how Madame de Maintenon received these effusive compliments of the young girl. While pleased, no doubt that she would be an asset to the court, to be told that a 12-year-old was as adroit as a middle-aged widow in handling the king and royal dinners may have stung.

The next day Marie attended Mass with the king, and they then traveled on to Fontainebleau. The fourteen-year-old duc de Bourgogne arrived to meet his fiancé at Nemours. At Fontainebleau the future queen was given the departed queen's apartments which must have been opulent. Due to her age, she was allowed only the company of her ladies of her Household and those given strict permission to visit her. Her fiancé could only visit her every other week. Finally, she was taken to Versailles where she received the gift of the late Anne of Austria's apartments. Here, she was introduced to the courtiers that had not been present at Fontainebleau.

The duc de Bourgogne, the Petit Dauphin

"The King and Mme de Maintenon made the princess into their doll," Saint-Simon wrote. "Her insinuating, flattering and attentive spirit pleased them infinitely and, little by little, she took liberties which the king's grandchildren never dared to attempt, and which charmed them. It became clear that M. de Savoy knew our court well… but what was truly astonishing was how thoroughly she used that knowledge, and the grace with which she did everything: there can be nothing like the cajoling with which she bewitched Mme de Maintenon, whom she always called "my aunt," and respected and obeyed more than if she had been her mother and queen; all with a familiarity and apparent freedom which enchanted her and the King both."

It is no wonder that this foreigner came to court and took on the king and his wife with such confidence and security that she would be well-received. Louis' own grandchildren, raised in a palace where their grandfather was remote and stern, always leery of letting his own issue too close for fear of some kind of uprising, had no such relationship with the king. They may have looked on in jealousy and awe at this delightful creature who knew how to use her charm and subservient nature. Perhaps, Maintenon was not the only female at court who instinctively knew how to ensnare.

If Louis' son seemed remote to the king, it can come as no surprise. It was a mixture of his own lack of deference toward the boy and his lack of qualities that would have endeared him to his father. The legitimate heir, Monseigneur, was a dull, slow-moving boy with a lumpy appearance and none of his father's charm and gusto. The king's grandchildren fared no better in his eyes. The duc de Bourgogne, the eldest, was an incongruous blend of violence and piety; a serious boy who lacked in gaiety and the verve the king so admired. Next in line was Philippe, duc d'Anjou, who Louis had deliberately subdued so that he would never be a threat. Due to that retarding of his education and advancement, he was depressed and reclusive. The youngest, Charles, duc de Berry, was only ten, and was a noisy whirlwind of activity. The duc de Maine had proven a disappointment during the war. So, it was with this new Princess of the Court that the King finally found a child to give his heart to.

In 1691, a cousin left the chateau of Choisy to Monseigneur. For the first time, the thirty-four-year-old had his own residence where he could escape the court, his father's watchful eye, and the constant knowledge that he was a disappointment. He went there often with a few chosen friends. Louis was not happy with this arrangement. The rule at Versailles was that everyone was gathered around the king where he could keep an eye on them and dictate their every move.

In a move to bring his son closer to the palace, the king offered Barbezieux Choisy and 900,000 livers in exchange for his chateau at Meudon. An exchange was arranged but not before Louis cleared it with his son. He may not be living beneath his father's roof, but he was much closer. Louis now turned his attention to his illegitimate daughters. They came with their own assortment of disappointments.

The princesse de Conti hated the other two daughters of the king and delighted in the company of low-born officers; the duchesse de Bourbon composed scandalous songs about her other two sisters and loved performing them for the court; and the duchesse de Chartres could be found tipping a glass from morning until bedtime. They were an embarrassment to the king, who would reprimand them when they went too far. For lesser offenses, it was Mme de Maintenon who scolded them. It seemed all around him were apples who had fallen from the royal tree and were rotting in the monied soil of Versailles.

For Mme de Maintenon, the fact that the royal brood were not disciplined, pious children worked in her favor. Louis relied on her to keep them in tow and refine their rough edges. If they had been exemplary role models of the French royal realm, her role in the King's life would have been diminished. With subtle cunning, she spun the web tighter, and looked for opportunities to make herself indispensable to her husband. While Louis often asked her opinion in matters of religion and politics, he seldom heeded it. He deferred to Bossuet and the Pére de La Chaise for religious matters and his ministers for the running of the state. But where the family was concerned, Maintenon found her power.

While her marriage to the king was never recognized, she was treated with all respect and love Louis could give her. She sat in the queen's chair at Mass, and in a chair with arms even though the royal princesses stood. Louis always removed his hat in her presence. Once, when a play mocking Maintenon was playing in Paris, the king had it kicked out in April 1697, despite the play's popularity. It was called *The False Prude* and the wrath of the king was felt throughout the city.

In August of 1698, Louis hosted the war games at Compiegne.

Troops competed for prizes. The colonels and many captains held open tables "that were abundantly served with delicacies," wrote Simon. At the climax of the games, a mock siege of Compiegne was conducted in full regalia. The king and his entourage watched from the top of a rampart which formed a terrace for the chateau.

Saint-Simon wrote of the extraordinary attention Louis paid to Mme de Maintenon in front of all present. "Mme de Maintenon was sitting in her sedan chair in front of the plain and the troops; the glass in her three windows was up and her porters were gone…The King stood next to the right window of the sedan chair, with, behind him a half-circle of the most distinguished men there. The King was always hatless and was constantly bending over to the window to speak to Mme de Maintenon, to explain what she saw and the reason for it all. Each time, she was polite enough to lower the window down by four or five fingers' breadth, never even halfway…almost always it was he who, without waiting for her to speak to him, would bend over to explain something; and sometimes when she did not notice him, he would knock again against the glass." Maintenon was the only person the King spoke to with very few exceptions, including shouting out a few orders. Those around them were shocked at the deference he paid her. Her place in the court was without question.

Shortly before the war games, a monumental feat took place. On Saturday, December 7, 1697, the duc de Bourgogne and Marie Adelaide de Savoy were married. She was thirteen and the groom was fourteen, too young for the marriage to be consummated. Marie Antoinette was only 14 when she married Louis XVI, who was also very young at only 15. Due the young age of Marie Adelaide and the Duke, the bedding ceremony took place, with all the usual onlookers, but they only remained there for 15 minutes. Monseigneur sat next to his son on the bed, after which Bourgogne left his virgin bride.

The next day, the duchesse held court and many marveled at how poised she was, handling all the details with more grace and ease than the late Dauphine. It was now that the court split into two camps. Many left the Monseigneur's side and rallied instead to his newly married son's. This young man was in line for the throne and the king wasn't getting any younger.

Louis XIV was enjoying a rare spate of calm. With the long war over, he continued to govern as he always had—by himself. Colbert's brother, the foreign minister died in 1696 and was succeeded by his son, the marquis de Torcy. In the beginning, he shared the office with Pomponne, whose daughter he married at the king's order, and eventually took over that post.

1698 had been a good year for the Sun King. His Versailles and the Royal Court sparkled. He was still considered the richest and most-powerful ruler in Europe, despite the ending to the war of the League of Augsburg. He could look at the male heirs lined up to further his legacy and feel secure that his throne was safe. *The Treaty of Ryswick* had also left no outstanding contentions as everyone got what they wanted. He had maneuvered weddings to his liking, and he was truly in love with his wife. The plans for Versailles were near completion. The north branch of the Grand Canal ended at the Grand Trianon, allowing happy courtiers to sail along the water, dock, and get out at yet another party. It was akin to a magical theme park, with fountains shooting up into the starlit nights.

A view of the Grand Canal from the Grand Trianon

Yet, somewhere beyond the lush gardens of Versailles, the distant clap of thunder could be heard. A storm was coming, and its origin was Spain. News was out that the childless King Charles II was on his death bed. Negotiations between France, England, and the Empire were under way. A great canvassing was going on to see who would rule the empty throne of Spain. No one wanted another war after what they had just been through. If Louis ignored the rumblings building up around the imminent death of Charles II, it would be at his own peril.

## Chapter Twenty-Seven
## All the King's Children

As 1698 dawned, the now 61-year-old Louis XIV drank in the admiration of his court. The festivities continued, France was still the undisputed military force of Europe, a new Dauphine graced the hallways and salons, and all seemed right with the world. While some grumbled at the repetition of the daily routine, missing the variety Paris offered, they realized that all paths lead to Louis. To be absent from court was unheard of. Indeed, the competition for advancement continued on, sans poisonings.

The Sun King had only one itch left that needed scratching: the question of who would be appointed to the throne of Spain when Charles II died. The fact that Charles had been sickly and expected to die since his birth thirty-seven years prior was a minor steppingstone. Charles II was a product of inbreeding of major proportions. The Habsburgs were notorious for marrying uncles, aunts, cousins, whatever, to keep the power in the family. All of Charles' great-grandparents were descended from the same parents: Philip I and Joanna of Castile. Basically, their children had all married their cousins, who had all married their cousins (or someone of a close relation). By the time Charles came along, he was more inbred than if his parents had been brother and sister. His face had distorted features, many believe because of the inbreeding, and he was cruelly nicknamed "El Hechizado"—the Bewitched.

It was apparent to all; the childless monarch was indeed going downhill and all of Europe wanted in on securing his successor. Louis looked at his best bets for getting his foot in the door. He needed to avoid a war over it and realized it was his arch enemy, King William III, whom he had just spent 9 years battling, that would need to be dealt with. Like it or not, he would have to reach out to England to negotiate on the subject. Surprisingly, that hot head William was open to it. He too was sick of the expense that war brought with it.

In 1698, there were three candidates to fill the vacancy the death of King Charles II would affect. Louis XIV's late queen had been Marie Thérèse of Spain and therefore her offspring could lay claim to the Spanish throne. That meant one of Louis' grandsons was a likely candidate. Next, was one of Emperor Leopold's sons, whose claim came through the bloodline of the grandmother; and thirdly, was one of the Elector of Bavaria's sons, whose mother was also in the Spanish line-up as Marie Thérèse's youngest sister. The cards were now on the table and the game was *Name That Heir*. The problem with appointing one of Louis' offspring, a Bourbon, or one of the Emperor's, a Habsburg, would give them too great a power. These young men were also in line to inherit their respective thrones and to have them in charge of two countries was unthinkable. Therefore, the Bavarian male seemed to be the best choice. He was only three, but he seemed the perfect compromise.

William and Louis agreed that the boy was the only choice, and he would rule Spain and the Indies. Spanish possessions in Italy would be split between France and Austria. Even the Emperor agreed to the choice (everyone was eager to avoid another conflict), and the three leaders breathed a sigh of relief. Charles II's ministers saw the wisdom in the selection and forced their point to the king. He capitulated and in November of 1698, he signed a will leaving his crowns to the young child Joseph-Ferdinand of Bavaria. It had all been so easy. Yet, it's usually when no one expects a storm that one appears on the horizon.

Inconveniently, the little boy died only three months after the will was posted. Now what? Charles was faltering daily, and many feared his death was near. Who would rule Spain and the Indies? Louis paced his antechamber and came up with a new plan. As there was not a new heir to recommend that would suit everyone, why not divvy up the goods? Let France and Austria split the Spanish possessions. Once again, William agreed, and they had only to get Emperor Leopold on board. Unfortunately, he had had time to think, and greed set in. He turned down the proposal.

Time was running out. Charles II's wife, who was of German nationality, pressed her husband to declare the emperor's youngest son, the Archduke Charles, the rightful heir. Charles' ministers advanced their own candidate, Louis XIV's grandson, the duc d'Angou, who was Monseigneur's second son. The problem was, if either of these candidates was chosen, war would break out. Each ruler went to their ministers and haggled over what was to be done, while keeping a finger on the pulse of the king who lay dying in Spain.

King Charles II of Spain

Meanwhile, back at court, Louis was embroiled in yet another challenge. The Abbé de Fénelon, a friend of Mmm de Maintenon's and Louis', was appointed Preceptor to the duc de Bourgogne, the next heir to the throne after his father, Monseigneur, the Dauphin. This was a position of power as it gave Fénelon full control of the future King's education and enabled him to somewhat mold his opinions and perspectives. François de Salignac de la Mothe-Fénelon was tall, charismatic, handsome and popular with the more religious ladies at court. He was an astute teacher and literally turned the young rebellious heir from an aggressive and lazy pupil into one exhibiting self-control, an attentiveness to his studies, and one the king would be proud to call his grandson. The young seven-year-old Duke of Burgundy found in the Abbé a man who offered much of the positive attention he had not found in his father and grandfather. They formed a bond, much to the happiness of the duc de Beauvillier, the grandchildren's governor and friend to Fénelon.

Fénelon with the Duke of Burgundy by Neuville

As tutor, Fénelon was charged with guiding the character formation of a future King of France. He wrote several important works specifically to guide his young charge. These include his *Fables* and his *Dialogues des Morts*.

But by far the most lasting of his works that Fénelon composed for the duke was his *Les Adventures de Télémaque* [The Adventures of Telemachus, Son of Ulysses], written in 1693–94. On its surface, *The Adventures of Telemachus* was a novel about Ulysses' on Telemachus. On another level, it became a biting attack on the divine right of absolute monarchy which was the dominant ideology of Louis XIV's France. In sharp contrast to Bossuet, who, when tutor to the Dauphin, had written *Politique tirée de l'Écriture sainte* which affirmed the divine foundations of absolute monarchy, while also exhorting the future king to use restraint and wisdom in exercising his absolute power, Fénelon went so far as to write "Good kings are rare and the generality of monarchs bad."

French literary historian Jean-Claude Bonnet calls *Télémaque* "the true key to the museum of the eighteenth-century imagination." One of the most popular works of the century, it became an immediate best seller both in France and abroad when it was finally published in 1699, going through many editions and translated into every European language and even Latin verse (first in Berlin in 1743, then in Paris by Étienne Viel [1737-87]). It inspired numerous imitations, such as the Abbé Jean Terrasson's novel *Life of Sethos* (1731), which in turn inspired Mozart's *Magic Flute.* It also more directly supplied the plot for Mozart's opera, *Idomeneo* (1781).

Scenes from *Télémaque* appeared in wallpaper. The American president Andrew Jackson wallpapered the entrance hall to his slave plantation, The Hermitage, in Tennessee, with scenes from Telemachus on the Island of Calypso.

Yet, before the treasonous novel was published, the tutor was highly praised at court. Most believed Fénelon's tutorship resulted in a dramatic improvement in the young duke's behavior. Even the memoirist Louis de Rouvroy, duc de Saint-Simon, who generally disliked Fénelon, admitted that when Fénelon became tutor, the duke was a spoiled and unruly child; when Fénelon left him, the duke had learned the lessons of self-control as well as being thoroughly impressed with a sense of his future duties. *Telemachus* is therefore widely seen as the most thorough exposition of the brand of reformism in the Beauvilliers-Chevreuse circle, which hoped that following Louis XIV's death, his brand of autocracy could be replaced by a monarchy less centralized and less absolute, and with a greater role for aristocrats such as Beauvilliers and Chevreuse.

In 1693, Fénelon was elected to Seat 34 of the Académie française. In 1694, the king named Fénelon Abbot of Saint-Valéry, a lucrative post worth 14,000 livres a year.

The early- to mid-1690s are significant since it was during this period that Mme de Maintenon began to regularly consult Fénelon on matters of conscience. Also, since Fénelon had a reputation as an expert on educating girls, she sought his advice on the house of Saint-Cyr which she was founding for girls.

In February 1696 (three years before the offensive *Telémaque* was published), the king nominated Fénelon to become the Archbishop of Cambrai while at the same time asking him to remain in his position as tutor to the duke of Burgundy. Fénelon accepted, and he was consecrated by his old friend Bossuet in August. The post was an advantageous position. It came with the title of *duc et pair* and an income of some 200,000 livres a year—one of the largest in France. The downside was that the king expected Fénelon to live in Cambrai for 9 months of the year.

Throughout all of this, Madame de Maintenon had plotted to further her cause—chiefly to have the decisive voice concerning the distribution of ecclesiastical patronage. That her husband often asked her advice in matters of religion, only to ignore it and trot over to his confessor, the Père de La Chaise (a man Maintenon hated), and the Archbishop of Paris, Harlay de Champvallon, chaffed. Her hopes lay with Fénelon to join her in her cause. Fénelon, in the 1690s, protected an old religious sect founded by a mystic, Mme Guyon. He was instrumental in advancing her ideas to Mme de Maintenon.

Maintenon had recently founded and run a school for girls from noble families who had fallen on hard times. It gave the former governess a chance to educate and offered her a refuge and reprieve from the Court of Versailles. She had skated perilously close to the edge when, besides her early endorsement of Fénelon, she had hired his friend, the mystic Mme Guyon to teach some rather unorthodox ideas at her school. Guyon taught that messages came from above (thereby sidestepping a divine King) and one could live in "pure love." When the King was shown some of the mystic's writings, Mme de Maintenon, frightened that he could shut down her precious school, removed her support of Fénelon and the mystic. Rather than wait for the King's judgement, Guyon left quietly, and retired to a convent. Two of the carefully woven threads in Maintenon's web had snapped.

Things went from bad to worse. In 1699, Fénelon, the now Archbishop of Cambrai, published his *Telémaque,* which had originally been written only for the eyes of his beloved pupil, the Duke of Burgundy. When it reached Louis XIV, he exploded. He reached out to Pope Innocent XII on March 12, 1699, who published his own pamphlet, the brief *cum alias* denouncing twenty-three principles from Fénelon's *Explication des maxims des saints*. The former tutor reached out to the Holy See, but the damage had been done. He was forbidden to return to court or to communicate with the young heir to the throne.

Maintenon had dodged a bullet, yet there was another in the king's crosshairs. The duc de Beauvillier, Fénelons'friend, and the only great noble to be called to the *conseil d'en haut* by the king, felt his position might be in danger. Saint-Simon wrote that during all the upheaval, the "King, coming back from Mass, found M. de Beauvillier waiting in his cabinet for the forthcoming Council. As soon as he saw him, he went to him and said: 'Well, M. de Beauvillier, what do you say now? M. de Cambrai [as Fénelon was now called] has been well and thoroughly condemned.'

"'Sire,' the duke answered respectfully and yet in a firm voice, 'I have been, and will always remain, M. de Cambrai's close friend; but if he does not submit to the Pope, I will never again communicate with him.' The King remained speechless, and those present much admired so firm a generosity on the one hand, and so clear a declaration on the other."

Only the support of the Archbishop of Paris saved Beauvillier. Mme de Maintenon had managed to discard the poisoned players as one lays down the unwanted cards in a game of poker. Her power remained unchallenged and the young duke, who had loved his tutor and found in him stability and a friend, was once more left to other's devices.

Meanwhile, the Sun King continued to advance his children born on the other side of the royal duvet. The duc du Maine and the comte de Toulouse walked the halls of Versailles with all the apparent privileges of the royal princes. Their sisters were also given more and more perks, such as having their ladies-in-waiting ride in the royal coaches—a privilege reserved for the Daughters of France. The melding of children and titles had all but eradicated the usual definitive lines of hierarchy at the palace. Louis had maneuvered it all in such a seamless manner that it was hard to pinpoint when the actual eraser was used to abolish the royal constructs.

In the north wing of the palace, other news of import was spreading through the twittering court: On October 22, 1699, the duc and duchesse de Bourgogne were finally allowed to sleep together. The duc was seventeen and now allowed to enter into the *conseil des dépêches*. It was not a council of major importance, but it was a beginning and a nod to the young man's station. It did nothing to endure him to his father, Monseigneur, the Grand Dauphin, as he had had to wait much longer for the same honor. The young duchess de Bourgogne still fascinated the King with her verve and happy ways. It was well-known she was his favorite at court. This only further alienated the Dauphin from his son and daughter-in-law.

Sadly, the court at Versailles had splintered and were championing their own hopes for the future. The Dauphin's half-sister, the princesse de Conti, and Mlle Choin (secretly), were now opposing the new married couple. If the duc de Bourgogne did indeed succeed as heir to the throne after his father Louis, the Grand Dauphin, he was in for a bumpy ride.

## 1700 Dawns on Versailles

January of 1700 brought with it the usual excitement of the Carnival season. There was more to celebrate this year as peace was once again in place, thanks to Louis XIV's treaty. The treasury, still shaky from the war effort, was rebounding steadily and the king decided it was time for the festivities to begin. Versailles and Marly glittered with candles and bonfires as one ball followed another. With all the pomp and costume for which the court was renown, they paraded their lavish outfits throughout the salons, along the Hall of Mirrors, and to nearby Marly. Louis opened his purse strings and rewarded them all with an array of masquerades, operas, plays, and endless food and drink. This was the time to be in the king's good graces and to receive the coveted invitations to the more-private enclave of Marly.

The duc de Bourgogne had always been appreciative of the king's largesse. Louis continued to offer him more money, upping the 36,000 livres a year that the duke and duchesse received yearly from the Treasury. The duke would politely decline and say if he needed more, he would certainly let his grandfather know. That the king told him to always come to him directly without need of an intermediary was a rare compliment. Saint-Simon states the king told the duke "to play at cards boldly without fearing any lack of money, for it was of no importance when people like him lost. The King liked people to feel easy with him, but he also liked to be feared, and when shy people who had to speak to him grew embarrassed and had difficulty with their speech, nothing pleased him more." For the eldest of Louis XIV's grandsons, all looked rosy on the inside. But shortly, the second oldest, Philippe d'Anjou, would take center stage.

The Hall of Mirrors filled with dancers.

## Chapter Twenty-Eight
## **A Question of Inheritance**

Many families face difficulties when it comes to the subject of wills. It would be fair to say that the events following the death of little Prince Joseph Ferdinand to smallpox in 1699 set a record for the resulting fallout.

Charles II was the last of the Spanish Habsburgs. Louis XIV's carefully laid out plans, in alliance with William III, had just fallen apart with the death of Prince Joseph. To recap, in an effort to regulate the impending succession, to which there were three principal claimants: England, the Dutch Republic, and France, had in October 1698 signed the *First Treaty of Partition*, agreeing that on the death of Charles II, Prince Joseph Ferdinand, son of the elector of Bavaria, should inherit Spain, the Spanish Netherlands, and the Spanish colonies. Spain's Italian dependencies would be detached and partitioned between Austria (to be awarded the Duchy of Milan) and France (Naples and Sicily).

In February 1699, after the death of young Ferdinand, a second treaty, signed on June 11, 1699, by England and France, and in March 1700 by the Dutch Republic, awarded Spain and the Spanish Netherlands and colonies to Archduke Charles, second son of the Holy Roman Emperor Leopold I, and Naples, Sicily, and other Spanish territories in Italy to France. Leopold, however, refused to sign the treaty, demanding that Charles receive all the Spanish territories intact. The Spanish grandees likewise did not recognize it, being unalterably opposed to partition. Charles II, still breathing, allowed himself to be convinced that only the House of Bourbon had the power to keep the Spanish possessions intact, and in the autumn of 1700, he made a will bequeathing them to Philippe, duc d'Anjou, grandson of Louis XIV of France.

On November 1, 1700, Charles II died. The inevitable had finally happened and the European continent would soon taste the aftermath of his passing. On November 24, only three weeks after the Spanish King's death, Louis XIV proclaimed his grandson King of Spain, as Philip V (the first Bourbon King of Spain), and then invaded the Spanish Netherlands. It was agreed that if Philippe accepted the throne of Spain, he and his male lineage would forever forfeit their right to be heirs to the crown of France.

The Proclamation of Philip V as King of Spain
at Versailles, November 24, 1700.

An anti-French alliance was formed (September 7, 1701) by England, the Dutch Republic, and the emperor Leopold. They were later joined by Prussia, Hanover, other German states, and Portugal. The electors of Bavaria and Cologne and the dukes of Mantua and Savoy switched sides in 1703. Louis had thrown France right back into what felt like a global war. The few years of peace his country had enjoyed were ended.

William III of England, now once again opposed to his former ally, died in 1702, but the government of his successor, Queen Anne, upheld the vigorous conduct of the war. Her champions were John Churchill, duke of Marlborough, and the imperial general Prince Eugene of Savoy. The military acumen of Churchill and Eugene allowed them a series of victories over France from 1704 to 1709. A Franco-Bavarian offensive in Germany was smashed at Blenheim in 1704. The French were driven out of the Low Countries by the battles of Ramillies in 1706 and Oudenaarde in 1708. The French were also expelled from Italy after their attempted siege of Turin was broken (September 7, 1706) by Eugene's brilliant campaign. The only theatre of the land war in which the alliance had no real success was Spain, where Philip V successfully maintained his position.

Louis sought to end the war from 1708 and was willing to give up the Spanish inheritance to the House of Habsburg. The British, however, insisted on the unrealistic demand that Louis use his army to remove his own grandson from Spain. Louis refused, broke off negotiations, and resumed the war. Two developments in 1711 altered the situation in favor of France. On April 17, 1711, Archduke Charles became heir to all the Austrian Habsburg possessions. Britain and the Dutch had no intention of continuing the war in order to give him the Spanish inheritance as well and thereby resurrect the old empire of Charles V.

In Britain, the enemies of Marlborough won influence with the queen and had him removed from command on December 31, 1711. With the collapse of the alliance, peace negotiations began in 1712. Because of conflicts of interest between the former allies, each dealt separately with France. The group of treaties was signed at Utrecht in April 1713. These and the later treaties of Rastatt and Baden ignored the will of Charles II and divided his inheritance among the powers. Louis XIV's grandson remained King of Spain, but the treaties of Utrecht marked the rise of power of Britain and the British Colonial Empire at the expense of both France and Spain.

## Philip V Marries

Before the great war of the Spanish Succession, many pieces of the puzzle were being put into place. In 1700, the Spanish throne sat empty as Charles II was put to rest. It could not remain so for long, and the court readied itself to say goodbye to Philip d'Anjou, the new King of Spain. Philip's (as his French spelling of Philippe had changed) two brothers hugged him tearfully and accompanied him to the border of France and Spain. The three took with them fifteen carriages, fourteen post chaises, and forty-six baggage carts, all pulled by 818 horses. What the young King must be feeling as he envisioned a new life as leader of a country where he could not even speak their language must have been terrifying. His grandfather, Louis XIV had even found it necessary to translate the speech made by the Spanish ambassador who was sent to acknowledge Philip at the scene of his proclamation.

The Duke d'Anjou, Philip V, King of Spain in 1700.

The Sun King, while dreading with his entire soul the promise of another war upon his grandson's acceptance of the crown, could only look at this moment as historic for his reign. As he bid Philip farewell, he reminded him to always remain a friend to France. He gave the young 17-year-old a set of instructions with thirty-three admonitions. They began with "Always do your duty, especially to God," and ended with "Do not allow yourself to be ruled. Be the master; never have either a favorite or a prime minister. Consult your Council, listen to it; but decide yourself. God, who has made you King, will give you all the understanding you need as long as your intentions remain good."

This was the creed by which Louis himself had governed. He was passing along his life lessons from the Fronde and from the days he was governed by ministers such as Richelieu and Mazarin. His fears, his perspectives, and his objectives were now in paper form and crossing the border to become the mantra of another country.

Despite his sudden rise to fame, the new King of Spain was ill-prepared to handle the job. He was the second eldest son of the Grand Dauphin. His older brother was first in line to inherit the throne of France, after, of course their father, the Grand Dauphin (Monseigneur). Just as Louis XIV's brother Philippe had been deliberately held back so as to never offer a threat to the Heir Presumptive, so Philip had been. He was lazy, not the brightest torch at court, indecisive, and suddenly infatuated with sex.

1701 had dawned and it was obvious this new King of Spain required a queen; hopefully one a bit brighter than he was and perhaps able to show him the ropes. So, Louis did a repeat and turned to the Duke of Savoy who had already provided him with a daughter for the duc de Bourgogne. Maria Luisa, the sister of the duchesse de Bourgogne, was decided upon. The Duke of Savoy, however, known for his unscrupulous dealings, began making demands that Louis was not prepared to offer. The Sun King therefore wrote to his grandson on July 29, 1701, saying, "I have thought it best to delay your marriage because I have been advised that the Duke of Savoy was not sincere. You know what he is like. I had written to the marquis de Castel Rodrigo to suspend negotiations but have learned that they are already concluded. Do not be surprised, though if he creates some difficulties…"

Despite the hiccups, the marriage took place by proclamation on September 11, 1701, at Versailles. The other ceremony was held at the city of Turin in the Duchy of Savoy on November 2. The bride was only 13 and the new King of Spain was about to turn 18. Philip fell madly in love with the energetic young woman, and to everyone's delight, Maria was intelligent and showed a bold personality. She would fill the bill nicely for satisfying her young husband in bed, but far too young to take on the role of queen without advisors and people in powerful positions around her to help her rule. It was almost a foregone conclusion that she was the horse to bet on in this royal marriage as there were no high expectations of Philip V.

Marie Luisa's new Camara Mayor, the chief female court official, was a lady with a huge desire to please Louis XIV. She was intelligent and energetic. The fifty-nine-year-old princess des Ursins had been a close friend of Mme Scarron, now the wife of Louis XIV. When Scarron became Maintenon, and hence married the king, she remembered her old friend and recommended her highly to Louis. The Sun King agreed and once again, Maintenon put her people in place. She was not the only one conniving for placement, however. The princess des Ursins was also hoping for a reward if she pleased the King of France with her prowess in helping to govern the new Queen of Spain: her own principality.

Marie Ann de la Trémoille, the princess des Ursins.

Mme de Maintenon's power continued to grow throughout 1700. The king had been holding Council meetings in her apartments for some time now, but it was at a meeting where Charles II's will was read that something significant changed. For the first time, Louis XIV not only asked for her advice, but followed it. This was done in front of an all-male committee. Maintenon was at her zenith. She and Mme des Ursins (the Camera Mayor for the new Queen of Spain) corresponded regularly and it wasn't long until Louis relied upon their news of how things were going in several arenas.

On March 19, 1702, William III died and was succeeded by his sister-in-law, Princess Anne. Now with a female queen on the throne of England, Mme de Ursins basically running the Queen of Spain, and Maintenon pulling the king's strings, the War of the Spanish Succession became decidedly estrogen induced.

In 1701, Barbezieux, Louis' Minister of War, was suddenly taken by apoplex, a gross hemorrhage into a cavity or into the substance of an organ. As Louis was not fond of Barbezieux, he was no doubt somewhat relieved and promptly appointed Michel Chamillart, a French statesman who already held the office of Contrôleur Géneral. Chamillart was a hardworking man, eager and honest to a fault. Louis had admired his skill at billiards, which first drew the king's attention. Michel already had his hands full with balancing the treasury during yet another war, and he told the king in all candor that he felt ill-equipped to handle both posts. It is possible Chamillart also felt himself unequal to the tasks the Minister of War would need to fulfill, especially with a full-scale war raging.

His honesty endeared him to the king even more, and Louis saw in this new recruit someone he could maneuver and outshine. All glory would therefore remain with Louis, not with some minister who happened upon a clever idea.

## The Death of Philippe, duc d'Orleans, the King's Brother

While the War of the Spanish Succession tore apart the European powers, another battle was raging within the sagacious halls of Versailles. Louis XIV, ever obtuse to the feelings of those closest to him, blatantly overlooked his brother's son for advancement once again. As Philippe had been stripped of his chances at military victory by his royal brother, so now, was his son, Philippe II d'Orleans, duc de Chartres. Chartres was Philippe's second oldest son, but after the death of his first son, Alexandre Louis, at the age of four, Chartres remained his only heir by his second wife, Charlotte, Princess of Palatine. Monsieur's only son by his first wife, Henrietta of England, had died in 1666. Philippe II was his last hope of continuing his lineage and his glory, and his own brother was retarding his progress.

Instead, the Sun King continued to advance his children by

Montespan, whom he had legitimized. The duc du Maine and the comte de Toulouse were given commands, even though du Maine had proven a coward in a former battle and disgraced the king. The duc de Toulouse was generally known to be incompetent, yet Louis pointed out his position on the war map and encouraged him to bring home the glory. As for Philippe's son, Chartres was told to remain at Versailles, despite the fact that he had shown real military prowess. He fought with great distinction at the Battle of Steenkerque on 3 August 1692. In the same year Chartres also served at the Siege of Namur. The following year he served at the Battle of Landen; he fought alongside the *prince de Conti*, who was wounded. The royal princes of the blood, de Condé and de Conti, they too were sidelined in preference for Louis' favorites. The ministers may have looked on in horror at these erroneous decisions. France was not in a great position with this war, and Louis was pushing his weakest links to the forefront.

In retaliation, Chartres acted out. He was known for his extra-marital affairs, and one of the ladies had become pregnant. Chartres, who had never loved his wife, and nicknamed her *Madame Lucifer*, flaunted the pregnant Marie-Louise de Sury in front of her. His debauchery fueled rumors throughout Paris, including one that alleged he had an incestuous affair with his daughter, Marie Louise Elizabeth of Berry. The gossip was never proven, but it was rampant enough to inspire several bawdy songs and poems that were trumpeted in the back alleys and taverns of France.

The young Chartres was living at Saint-Cloud with his father and mother. The King's brother loved the chateau with its view of the Seine. He and his lover the chevalier de Lorraine were fond of hosting large parties there, away from the Court of Versailles where his royal brother reigned. Now, upon learning that his son had been held back from the all-important war that had erupted over the Spanish Inheritance, the King's brother headed over to Marly in a white-hot rage. The date was June 8, 1701. Monsieur found the King at lunch. He erupted and the two royal brothers went head-to-head in an argument that had been in the making since their youth. With spit flying, Philippe unleashed the pain he had felt since childbirth as he watched the same ruler measured against his only surviving son.

It only took one remark from the king for the powder keg to

explode. Louis angrily criticized Philippe's son, Chartres, for his wanton infidelity to his wife. Saint-Simon reported that Philippe spat back that fathers who had themselves led loose lives were hardly in a position to blame their children who did the same. Louis volleyed with at least his daughter should be spared the knowledge of her husband's behavior, upon which Monsieur reminded the king that he, himself, had so little spared his wife as to have his mistresses travel in their very carriage! The shouting escalated and was heard by everyone in the next room. Louis played his trump card and stated that as he was cutting back on expenses due to the war, the first pensions he would cut would be those allotted to Monsieur and his family.

Philippe left Marly infused with hate and the all-too-typical feeling that he had been bested and was as ever reliant on his brother's purse strings. Back at Saint-Cloud, still smoldering, he was seated at dinner when he was suddenly hit with a massive stroke. Word was immediately sent to the king, who hastened to his brother's bedside. It was too late to communicate with him, as Philippe had sunk into a coma.

Philippe, duc d'Orleans, Louis XIV's brother

According to Saint-Simon, "Around eight in the morning, since there was no hope, Mme de Maintenon and Mme la duchesse de

Bourgogne urged the King to leave. [It was mandated that a King was never to be in a room with a dying person for fear of catching some disease.] As he was about to leave and was talking in a friendly way to M. de Chartres, both being awash with tears, that young prince made use of the moment. 'Ah, Sire, what will become of me?' he said, holding the King by the legs. [He had fallen to his knees.] 'I am losing Monsieur and I know you do not like me.' The King, who was surprised and touched, embraced him and said many tender things to him…

"The next day M. le duc de Charles came to see the King, who was still in bed and the King spoke to him in a very friendly manner. He told him that he must henceforth consider him as his father, that would look after his greatness and his interests, that he had forgotten all the little reasons he had had to be annoyed with him, that he hoped that, on his side, he would also forget them, and that he trusted that the friendship he was showing him would attach him anew, and cause him to give his heart as he [the King] was giving his…

"After so sad a spectacle, so many tears, so much tenderness, no one doubted that the three days remaining of his stay at Marly would be extremely sad, when, that very day after Monsieur's death, ladies-in-waiting heard Mme la duchesse de Bourgogne [Marie Adelaide of Savoy, the King's favorite] singing opera prologues. A little later, the King, seeing her looking sad, asked Mme de Maintenon with surprise why she was so melancholy…

"After dinner that night, Monseigneur the duc de Bourgogne [Louis' grandson, the Petit Dauphin], asked the duc de Montfort whether he wanted to play cards. 'Cards!' said Monfort in extreme surprise, 'You cannot be serious! Monsieur is still warm.'

"'Forgive me,' the prince answered. 'I am perfectly serious. The King, who does not want people to be bored at Marly, ordered me to have everyone play and, for fear no one would dare to start, to begin it myself.'"

Philippe II d'Orleans, duc de Chartres, was now the new duc d'Orleans. On the death of his father in June 1701, Philippe inherited the dukedoms of Orléans, Anjou, Montpensier, and Nemours, as well as the princedom of Joinville. The King kept his promise and paid Chartres all the pensions that had been allotted to his father. His greatest role was yet to come, as through a chain of unbelievable events, he became regent to Louis XIV's successor—Louis XV.

## Chapter Twenty-Nine
## **Who Is Governing Whom?**

The only time in his life Philippe may have come first as the brother of the King of France was in the juxtaposition of a painting.

Philippe first on the left, and Louis XIV on the right.

It was clear from the king's surprise at seeing people sad or insisting on the continual playing of cards while Philippe's body was "still warm" that the duc d'Orleans' passing was not worth altering life at Versailles where all must be festive, and the courtiers entertained. Yet, with the death of his brother, the Sun King was now facing a very altered reality. All who had grown up with Louis, known him as a youth, and advised him during his early reign, were gone. He looked about him at grandchildren and a court filled with nobles young enough to be his own children. Mme de Maintenon, three years his senior, was ever more important to him as a wise counselor, but even she had been there during the terrible days of the Fronde or shared in his rise to glory.

In essence, Louis XIV had gone beyond even his wildest dreams of conquest. He was King of France, still a powerful military force, envied throughout Europe for his Royal Court and his impact on the fashion scene. Now, through the advancement of his grandson, Philip, to the throne of Spain, he had his hands on Madrid and other Spanish territories.

Louis wrote to the duc d'Harcourt on December 15, 1700, and gave him a gentle warning: "I think it necessary to warn you that the King of Spain's intentions are good. He wants to do well and will if he knows how, but he lacks knowledge in many fields. He has learned little, even less than would be normal at his age. It will be easy to rule him if in the beginning you are careful to prevent any prejudice people may try to give him… He will trust you and follow your advice." Harcourt was the French Ambassador in Madrid and a man Louis had set up to advise his young grandson who was now King of Spain.

Philip had taken on a broken government left behind by the Habsburgs. The Spanish monarchy had been a decadent one and Louis set about tackling it from Versailles. He had Mme des Ursins as his go-between. Her role was to convey orders through messages from Louis XIV to his grandson in Spain. The transfer of letters in those days was a slow and tedious one, and, as we've learned, open to spying. It didn't take long for Ursins to form a bond with Philip and the young Maria Luisa. As time passed, the older woman began encouraging the malleable couple to develop their own policies.

Personal letters from Louis to his grandson were also arriving at the Spanish court on a regular basis. The poor young king was constantly encouraged to rule and behave as a leader, yet he was clearly the puppet of Louis' wishes on one hand, and his wife's (through the admonishments of Mme de Ursins) on the other. The Sun King would repeatedly assure him of his love and desire for his glory, and then lay down a lengthy declaration of etiquette Philip was to employ for the Spanish court. "I love you dearly…now do this," was basically the message instilled by Louis. Meanwhile, Ursins had so ingrained herself in the life of the Spanish Queen, that Maria became the vessel for ruling the king. If Philp waffled over a directive from his young bride, she simply withheld sex for a night and by the next morning, the lustful monarch capitulated.

When Louis began to get wind of the power the young queen was wielding over her husband, he quickly wrote to him on November 13, 1700: "It is essential for your happiness and hers that the Queen be disabused of the notions she may have been given according to which she can govern you. Surely Your Majesty would never allow it.… The Queen is your first subject; as such, and as your wife, she must obey you."

The following year, Maria's mettle would be tested when Philip went off to war. Louis hastened to console Maria in a letter, encouraging her to dry her tears and think of her husband's glory above all else. He went on to flatter her intelligence and spirit. Perhaps, not to anyone's surprise, the young queen took up the challenge and proved she was the stuff of which the Sun King spoke. In many cases, she was more courageous than her husband and was his backbone during difficult times. Her youthful energy made the couple vastly popular. It was she that determined the course of the monarchy. Alone, Philip probably would have floundered. When he did misstep, the letters of admonishment from Versailles were prompt in arriving.

As already reported earlier, the War of the Spanish Succession tore Europe apart and finally ended in 1712 with the signing of the Treaty of Utrecht, followed by the Treaties of Rastatt and Baden on March 7, 1714, and June of 1715, respectively. Article II of the Peace of Utrecht was aimed at the recent event of Louis XIV's grandson succeeding to the throne of Spain:

"Because of the great danger which threatened the liberty and safety of all Europe, from the too-close conjunction of the kingdoms of Spain and France… the same person should never become King of both Kingdoms."

While the War had ended, the premise of the above article was basically a moot point, as the King of Spain was essentially being governed by France, both through Louis XIV, and by Mme de Ursins's influence on the wife of the Spanish ruler.

Throughout the War of the Succession, the indefatigable King of France carried on as usual. The Carnivals, balls, and other festivities were held, and Louis splurged as if the war were not emptying the royal coffers. He and his Court bounced around from Versailles to Marly, to Fontainebleau, and the Trianon with all the heady joviality of a prom party. Not that ill-health didn't continue to knock at the Sun King's door. In 1705, he dealt again with gout and a prolonged period with a bad case of diarrhea that lasted for two months. At one point, he vomited up dead worms, yet he continued on. As did the insidious practice of bleeding and purging him monthly.

It was in 1706 that the Court began to notice a difference in the royal protocol. The gout that had plagued the king for some time now in his foot was growing worse. For the first time, he decided to forego his nightly ceremony of disrobing for bed in front of the entire court. Instead, the *coucher* was held in front of only a small gathering.

The beginning of the next year, 1707, also saw a difference. The continuing war had greatly impacted the treasury and the king, much to his embarrassment, he had to reduce the cost of the New Year's presents he annually gave out to the royal family. 1707 also marked the long-awaited advancement, not of one of Louis' children by Montespan, but of his own nephew, the duc d'Orleans, Philippe's son. The young man was put in charge of the French army in Spain, no small post.

1707 also marked the passing of two important people in Louis XIV's life. His great engineer, Sebastien Le Prestre Vauban died, as did the woman who had been the king's longest reigning mistress and mother to six of his children, Madame de Montespan. There is no mention of Louis' reaction to the death of the woman for whom he had created the Porcelain Trianon and a solid marble octagon bathtub he had transported across France to the first floor of Versailles. With his usual callousness, the King barely marked the day.

Madame de Montespan when she was young and adored by Louis XIV and in later years after the birth of six of his children.

Madame de Montespan with four of the six children born to Louis XIV.

Even the death of the great architect Francois Mansart, who had put his mark on so much of Versailles, including the great Hall of Mirrors, the Royal Chapel, and the Ambassadors Staircase, did nothing to slow the pace of the indomitable King of France.

If these funerals did not showcase Louis' fundamental lack of concern for anything that did not advance the world's view of himself and his empire, or that interrupted his flow of entertainment or plans, the next incident in 1708 would.

Marie Adelaide of Savoy, that dear creature who had won the king's heart and married his grandson, the duc d' Bourgogne, had wonderful news. Saint-Simon stated, "Mme la duchesse de Bourgogne was pregnant. She was feeling very unwell. The King wanted to go to Fontainebleau, against precedent, at the beginning of the good weather [rather than October when he usually went] and had said so. In the meantime, he wanted to make stays at Marly. His granddaughter [Marie] amused him, he could not do without her, but so much movement did not suit her condition. Mme de Maintenon was worried about this, Fagon [the King's First Physician] kept tactfully mentioning her fragility: this bothered the King, who was accustomed to having his own way in everything, and had been spoiled by the fact that his mistresses traveled when pregnant or just after they had given birth, and wore court dress throughout it all. The remonstrances about the trips to Marly annoyed him but he did not cancel them... The Saturday [following one of these trips], the King was taking a walk after Mass... when he saw the duchesse du Lude coming alone, on foot, at a time when there was no other lady with the King... He understood she had something urgent to tell him: he went toward her and when he was close to her, we stopped and left them alone. The conversation was short. She left and the King came back to us... without saying anything. Everybody had guessed what the matter must be, and no one was in a hurry to say anything. In the end, the King... looking at the most important people there but without speaking to anyone in particular, said, looking annoyed: 'The duchesse de Bourgogne has miscarried.'

"Immediately, M. de La Rouchefoucauld began to lament, M. de Bouillon, the duc de Tresmes and the maréchal de Boufflers joined him, then M. de La Rouchefoucauld went on to say, louder still, that it was the greatest misfortune in the world, that having had other miscarriages she might not have any more children.' And even if it were so,' the King, who until now had said nothing, interrupted angrily, 'why should I care? Doesn't she already have a son? [The second duc de Bretagne, born in 1705]. And even if he died, is the duc de Berry not able to marry and have children of his own? And why should I care which of them succeeds me! Are they not all equally my grandsons?' And immediately, he went on impetuously: 'Thank God she has miscarried, since she was going to miscarry, and I will no longer be annoyed about my trips by the representations of the doctors and the reasonings of the women. I will come and go as I please and will no longer be bothered.' A silence such that one could have heard an ant walking followed this outburst."

That Louis was dealing with several defeats in the War of the Succession during this time, a faltering treasury, and a pain in his foot that would not subside, can all be attributed to this brutal and unfeeling outburst. Unfortunately, this was not an isolated occurrence. The king would have what he wanted and all else be damned. In this case, even his favorite at court had diminished his fun and his plans by being inconveniently pregnant and unwell. You can see by his statements that all he cared about was healthy heirs who would succeed him and carry on his glory; nothing for the pain the young duchesses were going through over the loss of a child.

As mentioned earlier, 1708 brought with it a fatal cold spell. By the beginning of 1709, the freeze had devastated much of France's agriculture. On January 19, 1709, Madame [the widow of Philippe, the King's brother] wrote her cousin: "Nobody can remember its being so cold. For the last two weeks there have been reports every morning of people who have died of the cold; partridges are found frozen in the fields. All the theaters have closed, trials are postponed, neither the presidents nor the conseillers can remain in their courts because it is so cold." Madame also wrote to her aunt, the Electress Sophia of Hanover, "The cold is so horrible here that nothing like this, they say, has happened since 1606. In Paris only, 24,000 people have died between January 5 and today [February 2]."

Versailles was freezing. The giant fireplaces did little to mitigate the temperatures pressed against the glass and finding its way into cracks and open doorways. Even the ink froze in Louis' inkwell. The cold attacked the grain, the lifeblood of a country known for its bread, and it was surmised it would impact the following year's growth. The famine swept across the frozen villages and the death toll rose. Madame again wrote to her cousin on June 8th, "The famine is so violent now that children have eaten one another. The King is so thoroughly decided to continue fighting the war that this morning he sent his entire gold service to the Mint, plates, platters, salt cellars, in a word all the gold he had, to be coined into louis."

The devastation the cold spell took on France cannot be understated. Businesses were ruined, goods could not be moved, taxes went unpaid, and the royal treasury sat as empty as a newly dug grave. Madame de Maintenon took the opportunity to point out to the king how right she had been in her frequent admonishments to avoid the war at all costs. Now, with the ruin of France about them, encased in icicles, she lamented even louder that this was God's punishment for the war, and begged Louis to call it off.

Even though 1710 proved disastrous for France, Louis insisted that the festivities at court continue, despite the fact there was no money to do so. There were no New Year's presents this time, and the guests at Marly were asked to provide their own food. On February 15$^{th}$ of that year, the duchesse de Bourgogne gave birth to a healthy son, the duc d'Anjou. He was second to his brother, the five-year-old duc de Bretagne, and for the first time in the history of France, Louis XIV became the only king to have two living great-grandsons in line for the succession. Perhaps now, he could be happy for his hapless favorite.

With the *Treaty of Utrecht* signed in 1712, peace came once again to Versailles. The great King, now seventy-four, limped along on his platform shoes and took stock of what he had just gone through. If he felt pain at the passing of so many of those who had been close to him, it barely appeared on his wrinkled face. The murals adorning the ceiling of the Hall of Mirrors, touting his many glories in battle, were what mattered. More than ever, he was in charge now, and the mantra "The King Governs by Himself," never appeared more prophetic. That he only had three years to live was not a deterrent to a king who believed he was the direct line to God and immortality.

# Chapter Thirty
## The Crumbling of an Empire

The sun rose on the frozen dew of the gardens of Versailles, and it sparkled in the golden rays as if by demand of the royal king who lived within the palace walls. The fountains, still and quiet in their winter habitation, seemed to be waiting for the rebirth of Spring. The large bronze centerpieces looked out with empty eyes upon the manicured walkways and towering edifices of the grandest estate in Europe. How many festivals had these metal giants been privy to? How many secret rendezvous in the shadowed corners of the *basquets* had their sculpted ears eavesdropped upon? From the long-forgotten Thetis Grotto to the famous Menagerie and Labyrinth, these grounds had seen seasons of unequaled splendor, and the funeral marches of the royalty that had called Versailles home.

1711 brought with it a new dawn—one that would set off a chain reaction throughout the French monarchy. *The Treaty of Utrecht* would soon be signed, and Louis XIV breathed a sigh of relief that the war was near its end. The king was now seventy-three, an age well beyond the average lifetime in that era. His son, the Dauphin, was fifty, and while Monseigneur was still without much of a voice in the palace, he was the successor to the throne, and as each year passed, so did the expectation that he would soon be wearing the crown. The king had not slowed in his daily routine and went right on governing with minimal help from the others who often felt their jobs were empty titles.

While the court's eyes were on the king's health and his advancing age, something no one expected happened. On April 9, 1711, Monseigneur fainted during his dressing ritual. By the following day, a high fever saw him confined to bed, and then the dreaded news camc. The heir to the throne was suffering from smallpox. At first, it did not look like the harshest form of the disease, and Madame [Charlotte, Philippe's widowed wife] seemed confident he would recover. On the 12$^{th}$, she commented, "Up to now, the illness is going as it should, the fever is abating, the pustules are beginning to whiten, so we hope all will be well." Monseigneur was at Meudon, and the king went to him, having already had smallpox and thus immune to the disease. It was noted that the Bourgogne's, whom Louis had ordered to remain at Versailles, seemed to be holding court with their supporters surrounding them as if their position of next in line was already decided. As Louis, the duc de Bourgogne was the Dauphin's son, it appeared to be a callous unconcern for his father's well-being. Such was life at Versailles.

Monseigneur seemed to hold his own with the illness, to the point that many anticipated a full recovery. On the 14$^{th}$, Madame went to Monseigneur and reported, "I went to Meudon to congratulate the King on M. le Dauphin's being so much better. I saw the King, who received me very graciously; he told me I should not have complained so much when I had smallpox myself and said that M. le Dauphin felt no discomfort. I answered that was yet to come, that the pustules would swell up and be painful. As I was about to leave, it was announced that M. le Dauphin was worried, that his head was much swollen; everybody thought that meant the pustules were beginning to suppurate and that was a good sign… At nine, [three hours later after Madame had returned to Versailles] news came again that all was well; but at ten there was a message that M. le Dauphin was beginning to be afraid, that his face was so swollen as to be unrecognizable; it was added that the eyes were especially affected. That was still not alarming; I supped at ten as usual;" Madame continued, "at eleven, I undressed and spoke for a moment with maréchale de Clérembault [her chief lady-in-waiting]; I was then going to say my prayers and go to bed but, at midnight, I was very surprised to see the maréchal return in a very upset state; she said that M. le Dauphin was dying… A moment later, they came to me to tell me that it was all over, that M. le Dauphin was no longer alive."

Louis XIV was ushered from Meudon, where he had sat in the room next to his son until the end. As stated, a king cannot remain in the same house with a deceased person and so Louis was escorted to his carriage, where he faltered. Saint-Simon, that ubiquitous scribe, was there and reported, "As he came out to get into his carriage, he found Monseigneur's berlin [carriage] before him; he waved it away because he could not bear to see it. He was not so stricken, however, that he did not call Pontchartrain to tell him to warn his father and the other ministers to come a little later than usual to Marly for the Council…He then had difficulty getting up into the carriage, being supported on both sides; Mme de Maintenon got in immediately after him… A crowd of officeholders from Monseigneur's Household were kneeling all along both sides of the courtyard [at Meudon] as the King went by, begging him with strange shouts to have pity on them who had lost everything and would be starving."

Louis XIV Leaving the Deathbed of Monseigneur

That the Dauphin's Household feared the future now that their source of income was dead, was nothing compared to all those who had backed Monseigneur as the next king and planned their advancement accordingly. The Dauphin's private cabal had made their dislike of the duc de Bourgogne known, and now, he was next in line to the throne. The assignations at court were fast and furious as the Dauphin's protagonists met in secret while looking down the barrel of a bleak future.

While Louis had tried to stoically hide his feelings the day of his son's death, he could no longer contain them later. Madame wrote to her aunt, "He is afflicted by such sorrow that would soften a rock, and yet he does not give in but speaks to everyone with a settled sadness, but then the tears often come to his eyes, and he swallows his sobs. I am terribly worried he may become ill himself because he looks so terrible."

The marquis de Torcy saw the King the next day and reported, "We went to the King's lever at Marly. Once it was over, His Majesty called in M. e Chancelier. He then had the other ministers come in but was hardly able to speak. His sorrow and his tears cut him short every time he tried to explain himself. He even said that, although deeply moved by his loss, he could not understand his condition, that yesterday he had not shed a tear, and that, right then, he could not stop himself from shedding them in abundance."

Typical of the Sun King, he squared his shoulders and moved on with surprising speed. In that same meeting with Torcy, he announced that the title of "Monseigneur" would be retired, and the duc de Bourgogne would henceforth be called M. de Dauphin. Louis' son's wife, Mlle Choin, who was his morganatic wife, just as Maintenon's was the King's, received a 12,000-livre pension, and the late Dauphin's personal belongings were divided up. This was all done within a day of his passing. He, like the ineffectual title of Monseigneur his father had given him, were replaced. Saint-Simon commented, "Never was a man so easily given to shed tears, so inaccessible to real sorrow or so quickly back to his normal condition. He must have been strongly affected by the loss of a son who, although fifty years old, was still six as far as he was concerned… On Thursday already, he was amusing himself with the lists of Marly."

Perhaps it was all an act put forth by a king who could not appear weak or vulnerable. Perhaps his need to distance himself from his late son had to do with a certain degree of regret for the way he treated him. Or it was the face of a man who could internalize his emotions. Was it that inner containment that led to his headaches, and relentless constipation only days after the passing of his heir?

## A Deluge of Death

The dazzling court of Louis XIV found itself in uncertain times. The duc and duchess de Bourgogne, now the Dauphin and Dauphine, were courted shamelessly by those who hoped to endear themselves to the future King and Queen of France. Sycophants could be found in every alcove and banquet. The Dauphine, who had always been the King's greatest amusement at Court (except for her inconvenient miscarriage), had grown along with her new title. She became the hostess her station required, while enchanting all those around her. Madame noted, "People are quite right to praise M. le Dauphin. He deserves it. Mme la Dauphine is endearing herself to all by her politeness. Last Monday, I was invited to have dinner with them; no one could have been more polite than they were: they served me themselves. A whole dozen duchesses were also there; they spoke to everyone."

And so it was, that when the new Dauphine began to suffer a variety of fevers, no one was particularly alarmed; she often had them. The doctors bled and purged her, constant in their barbaric beliefs that often hastened the death of their patients. On February 5, 1712, the Dauphine's fever worsened. She sent her regrets to the king for not attending dinner with him as she usually did. The fever came and went throughout the next day, and everyone assumed it was nothing to worry about. That evening, around six, she was suddenly beset with a violent headache and encouraged the king, who had come to check on her, not to come into her room. Over the next few days, the headache and fever took turns with her body, until on the 10th, telltale spots began appearing, resembling measles. The disease, along with scarlet fever, was plaguing Paris at this time, resulting in many deaths.

The Dauphin kept constant vigil at his wife's side, despite the fact that the illness was contagious. The Dauphine was repeatedly bled and purged, weakening her still. He was still by his wife's bedside on the 11th. Her fever had risen to the point that the doctor's advised the Dauphine should be read the last rites. Louis XIV, who had remained nearby throughout, watched as the Dauphin was suddenly taken ill and put to bed in his own chambers. The following evening, on the 12th, the Dauphine passed away. It is perhaps with her passing that we see Louis' depth of emotion.

The King wrote to his grandson, Philip V, King of Spain, and lamented, "Although you knew how very much I loved her, you still cannot begin to imagine how deeply her loss afflicts me."

Saint-Simon took to his pen and wrote, "With her, vanished joy, pleasure, amusements even, and graces of all sorts. Darkness covered the entire Court. She had animated it all by herself; she was everywhere at once; she fascinated everyone; she understood all its innermost secrets. If the Court survived her, it was only in the most languishing way. Never was a princess so missed, and so deservedly."

Simon's words bring to mind a quote from Charles Dicken's *David Copperfield* when he wrote of the impact the young Dora Spenlow had upon him: "She was more than human to me. She was a Fairy, a Sylph, I don't know what she was—anything that no one ever saw, and everything that everybody ever wanted." It seemed Marie Adelaide, the Dauphine, had that effect on an entire court, and had captured the heart of a king who was as dismissive of his relations and loyalties as he was of a damaged garment.

Louis, accompanied by the ever-faithful Madam de Maintenon, rode off to Marly, as he had done after the death of his son only ten months before, but this time, his demeanor was one of total devastation. On the next day, the 13$^{th}$ of February, the Dauphin came to Marly to see the king. Still dealing with a fever, he had distanced himself from the funeral arrangements at Meudon, as he could not bear to hear of the plans for his wife's final services. The king took one look at him and called for the doctors who immediately sent him to bed at Marly. The fever rose throughout the next two days. The young Dauphin complained that he feared he had been poisoned. On the sixteenth, the small blemishes that had appeared on his wife, now began to dot his skin. The Dauphin had the measles. Only one day later, the weakened heir to the throne died. He was only twenty-nine-years-old.

The King and Queen of France's successors were both dead, within days of each other. The blow for Louis was too much this time. There would be no brave face, no card playing, and no routine. He hid himself away in his private apartments, seeing only Mme de Maintenon and his ministers. His world was crumbling, and the once unfaltering king left the court to its own devices. If Maintenon worried about the impact the dual death of his heir and favorite would have upon him, the next blow was enough to fall a mighty oak.

With black crepe still adorning Versailles and the funeral ceremonies barely concluded for the two coffins, news came that the newly deceased Dauphin and Dauphine's eldest living son, six-year-old duc de Brittany, who was now to be heir to the throne, had also contracted measles. He died on March 8th, 1712, less than a month after his father's passing. The King reeled, as did the court. Was this a punishment from God? The first of the Dauphin's three sons, had died at only one-year-old. Now, the second in line, was gone. That left their last remaining son, Louis, duc d'Anjou, who at the time, was only two years old.

Did the great Sun King think back to his derision at the miscarriage by the duchess de Bourgogne, when he proclaimed that he "cared not if she miscarried…she had born two other sons who were alive and heir to the throne?" Did he now wonder if he would run out of heirs, and wish that miscarriage had never happened, and that fate may have allowed her to produce yet another male?

As for the young Louis, duc d'Anjou, he perhaps owed his life to the woman who rescued him from the hands of the doctors who wanted to bleed and purge him just in case he too had contracted the disease. This protective governess, Mme de Ventadour, hid him away. The little Dauphin, as he was now known, survived, but many wondered for how long. In less than a year, the king who held the record for living during three generations of descendants, had suddenly lost his son, a grandson, and a great-grandson in under a year.

Louis wrote to his grandson in Spain, Philip V, and lamented, "You will understand the excess of my sorrow, when I tell you that the Dauphin [Louis, Duke of Brittany] is dead. In a few days God has demanded of me two terrible proofs of my submission to His commands. I pray that he will keep me Your Majesty and console us of the tragedy I will feel acutely as long it will please Him to keep me alive."

# Chapter Thirty-One
# **Versailles's Shadows**

Somewhere, in the jeweled bowels of Versailles, a two-year-old boy with bouncing golden curls played unaware of the cards Fate had just dealt him. Through an unprecedented series of deaths, the child was now heir to the throne of France. The crown would sit heavy upon his head, and he would inherit along with the royal stables and mirrored halls, a crippling debt and unhappy citizenship left by his great-grandfather, Louis XIV.

For now, in 1712, the Sun King was alive and reeling from the sudden deaths of the Bourgogne's family. At one moment he was celebrating the signing of the *Treaty of Utrecht*, the next, he was attending the funerals not only of his heirs to his throne, but of a family he cherished. It would not take long for the gossip mill at Versailles and throughout Paris to begin churning out rumors of their own concerning the strange line-up of coffins. It was not the first-time poison had been suspected of untimely deaths at Versailles, and now the target of suspicion was planted firmly on the back of one man—Philippe II, the duc d'Chartres, and now the duc d'Orleans, after the passing of his father, the king's brother.

If the young Louis duc d'Anjou were to die also, and most feared the little two-year-old might not make it—due to the mortality rate of children in that era and the recent attack of measles in his family—the next in line would be the duc d'Orleans, as the only remaining living heir. If the little boy's governess, Mme de Ventadour, had not hidden Louis in an effort to save him from the bleeding and purging afflicting his family members, would another child-size casket have been added to the Bourgogne's vault?

Others who fell under the umbrella of suspicion concerning the recent rash of deaths was the brother of Louis, duc de Bourgogne (now deceased), the duc d'Berry, and the son of Madame de Montespan, the duc d'Maine (who was a favorite of Madame de Maintenon). Maine had yet to be legitimized and so the nod would still go to the member of the royal blood line, and that would be the duc d'Orleans. The duc de' Bourgogne's second oldest brother, Philip V, was King of Spain and therefore, under the Treaties signed, could also not sit on the throne of France. Females were out of contention for the throne.

It did not help the duc d'Orleans' cause that it was well-known he loved to experiment with chemistry. It would not be surprising to find Maintenon spinning her web of deceit and fueling the rumors of poison in an effort to see her favorite, the duc d'Maine inherit the throne. If Orleans was found guilty of poisoning the royal family, he would probably be executed or find his new living quarters to be that of the Bastille.

Whether the rumors were true or not, the gossip had its effect. He found himself ostracized from those at the Court of Versailles and in Parisian society. He was met with jeers as his carriage traveled through the streets of Paris and the duke began to fear for his life. Louis XIV listened to his distraught nephew who was fearful the rumors would alter the king's opinion of him. Louis quickly assured him that he gave the gossip no credence but did advise the young man to get rid of Humbert, the chemist whom he had on his Household staff. The duc d'Orleans assured the king that Humbert was just as innocent of the charges against him and begged the Louis to have the chemist questioned at the Bastille.

Madame, the duke's mother and widow of the king's brother, wrote, "My son having sent his Humbert to the Bastille to be examined, the King forbade his being received there; first because his Majesty does not believe what is said about my son, and also because all the doctors who were present at the autopsy of the two bodies say they neither showed any trace of poison, that Mme la Dauphine died of measles, and M. le Dauphin of bad air and sorrow." While Louis was never close to his nephew, remembering his days of debauchery at Fontainebleau and elsewhere, he kept the promise he made on his brother's deathbed: he would care for the duke. While Louis did not believe the rumors of poison, it was an allegation that followed the duc d'Orleans to his grave.

It would be wonderful to be a fly on the wall when Mme de Maintenon and the duc d'Maine found out the plot to take the duc d'Orleans out of the running had failed. We do know the king continued to spend more and more time with Maintenon as he fought to deal with the toll the tragic deaths had taken on him. If he suspected her of dirty dealings in the background, we do not get a sense of it. The great Sun King was now seventy-four and he ran the court more from rote than enthusiasm as he watched the shadows of the past waltz across the parquet floors of Versailles. Gone was the gaiety and energy for which he had been known. The Royal Court, once dazzling and fueled by endless wine and gambling, seemed to incorporate his sadness and lack of verve as if by osmosis. Versailles had changed.

With the lengthy War of the Spanish Succession at an end, there was one more matter of business. It was mandated by the other countries that not only would Philip V renounce his claim as successor to the throne of France, but his brother, the duc de Berry and the king's nephew, the duc d'Orleans, would likewise renounce their right to succeed to the Spanish throne through their Hapsburg lineage. Thus, on March 15, 1713, the two French princes went to Parlement and signed the agreement. Philip V sent his agreement via carrier.

While the war had depleted the Treasury of France, it was generally agreed in 1714 that the king had made the right call to put forth the *Treaty of Utrecht.* Spain had been neutralized and was no longer a threat. Because Emperor Leopold had refused at the last minute to be part of the Treaty, it allowed the offering of Strasbourg to remain in Louis' pocket. While there were those who still grumbled that the war had been a waste of time and money, historians would look more to the ill-advised revocation of the *Edict of Nantes* that incited the vast exodus of the Protestants from France as the Sun King's biggest mistake.

The Salons at Versailles—the King's apartments—were void of the weekly festivities of cards and entertainment. The long-held routine of the *appartements* were no more. Gone were the fireworks and lavish festivals. The groomed groves of the gardens were enjoyed only by those who wandered there. Madame de Maintenon wrote in 1713, "All is dead, here, life is gone."

With the Bourgogne's gone and Phillipe V tied to the throne of Spain, the final son of the Dauphin, Charles, the duc d'Berry and his wife, the duchess d'Berry took over the helm at court. She was notorious for her riotous parties and philandering. She had a faithful following who were delighted to attend her soirees at her own palace, away from the fading light of Versailles. The Condés and the Contis followed suit, inviting their circle of friends to their residences instead of their apartments at the palace. The duc and duchesse du Maine were throwing lavish parties at their castle of Sceaux, and the nobility hastened there. It was as if Versailles, without its pomp and festivities, had been left to a lonely king and his manipulative wife.

In 1713, two marriages of the king's children saw the only spark of the festivities to which the palace had once paid homage. Monsieur le Duc married Mlle de Conti, and the prince de Conti married Mlle de Bourbon. The duchesse de Berry took advantage of the occasion to adorn herself with diamonds, as did the newlyweds. Auxiliary parties were also held elsewhere as everyone celebrated the only happy spot of the year.

Louis spent much of his time in his grand chapel that had been completed during the war, in 1710. Robert de Cotte had completed the work Mansart had begun in 1701, after the head architect died in 1708. Madame de Maintenon, always reminding the king of his inherent glory, no doubt reveled in her husband's revived interest in God and what comes after this life. It was an odd juxtaposition to limp through the glittering jeweled rooms and halls of Versailles to sit in the upper sanctuary of this massive chapel and contemplate his mortality. Perhaps, he could live out the rest of his days in peace and without further heartbreak. It was not to be.

The dark cloud of death was not yet finished with the children of the crown. The duc d'Berry, Louis' grandson, was out riding in the hunt when his horse reared up and the saddle's pommel hit the young man squarely in the stomach. While the impact was fierce,

Berry brushed it off, until the next day, the young 27-year-old prince began vomiting dried blood. On May 4th, he was dead from the hemorrhaging of the internal injuries sustained by the blow. Of the Dauphin's three sons (and Louis XIV's grandsons), the duc de Bourgogne and the duc d'Berry were dead. Only Philippe V remained, and he was irrevocably tied to the throne of Spain.

Charles, Duke of Berry

While the Sun King had never really warmed to the lackluster prince, it was a blow. Madame, Elizabeth Charlotte, the widow of Philippe, Louis' brother, was also the grandmother of Berry's wife, Marie Louise Elisabeth d'Orleans. The marriage resulted in a miscarriage, and the premature birth of a son who lived only a few weeks. She was pregnant at the time of her husband's death but miscarried a daughter one month later. The duchesse was unfaithful to Berry and at one time threatened to run away with her lover, La Haye.

Madame wrote of Berry, referring to him by his nickname she had given him, "Berry Bon Coeur" (Berry Good Heart"). Her thoughts on their marriage were as follows:

"At first, he was passionately fond of his wife; but at the end of three months, he fell in love with a little, ugly, *femme de chambre* (a housemaid or servant). The Duchess, who had sufficient penetration, was not slow in discovering this, and told her husband immediately that, if he continued to live upon good terms with her, as he had done at first, she would say nothing about it, and act as if she was not acquainted with it; but if he behaved ill, she would tell the whole affair to the King, and have the *femme de chambre* sent away, so that he should never hear of her again. By this threat, she held the duke, who was a very simple man, so completely in check, that he lived very well with her up to his death, leaving her to do as she pleased, and dying himself as fond as ever of the *femme de chambre*.

Marie Louise Elizabeth, Duchesse of Berry

"A year before his death [Berry] he had her married [the servant], but on the condition that the husband should not exercise his marital rights. He [Berry] left her pregnant as well as his wife, both of them lay-in after his decease. Madame de Berry, who was not jealous, retained this woman, and took care of her and her child. One month later, the Duchess gave birth prematurely to a girl who died the next day. During the regency of her father, [duc d'Orleans], the young widow became known as Messalina, ill-reputed for the debauched life she led in her Luxembourg Palace. Her health, rapidly undermined by gluttony, alcoholism, and a series of clandestine pregnancies, Madame de Berry died on July 21, 1719. The autopsy revealed that the princess was again with child although she had almost died at the end of March 1719, when giving birth to a still-born child allegedly fathered by her captain of the guards."

And so, it was down to the little boy with the golden curls, the last of Louis XIV's great grandsons.

No one could blame the King of France for looking with fear at the small child with whom everything rested. The little boy, now four, was not of robust health, and the average life span of children in that age was not great. Add to that the machinations of greedy relatives who may have found it all too tempting to help the little fellow out of this world, the king looked about him at the emptying of his blood line and panicked.

It was time, in his eyes, to back his bets. He did have healthy sons born on the wrong side of the blanket; sons he had steadily promoted up the ranks of his family tree. The way things were in 1714, the line of succession was the little Dauphin; his uncle the duc d'Orleans; Orleans's son Monsieur le Duc; his children; the Prince de Conti; his son, etc. If Madame de Maintenon and the duc de Maine held their breath after the sudden death of du Berry, they came close to their ambitions. Louis, who could have given Maine the right to succeed as if he were of proper royal blood, putting him after the little Dauphin but before the duc d'Orleans, stopped just short of Maintenon's hopes. In July 1714, the king issued an edict that the duc du Maine and the comte de Toulouise, along with their male heirs, could succeed to the throne but only after all the princes of royal blood. The edict was filed on August 2nd and the princes were given the same honors and rank as those of royal blood, but with precedence following only after them.

As was typical of the day, this bold move infuriated many who were appalled that the King's new edict aggrandized the bastards from an affair consisting of double adultery and placed them alongside those of royal blood born of sanctified marriages. In grand Louis-style, instead of taking note of the shock his edict has caused his subjects, he upped the ante, and legitimized du Maine and de Toulouse on May 23, 1714. They were now princes of blood in every aspect. Late in July, the king turned to the duc de Maine and told him in front of several attendants: "You wanted this; but you will be nothing once I am gone, it will be up to you then to defend what I have done for you if you can." Saint-Simon's notes ring an ominous bell. It bespoke of a king tired of the fight and of the backlash his unpopular decisions brought. Did it also show a man who was perhaps angry at being manipulated by his wife into doing something he knew would reflect badly on his reign? This edict was flying in the face of God. How far could he take his claim to deity when he was due to meet his maker only one year later?

One has to wonder if Louis would have taken this last daring move if he had not just lost most his royal blood line in such rapid succession. Was it partly to do with the constant hissing of Madame de Maintenon in his ear as she championed her favorite, du Maine? Was it the hubris of a man who saw his sons, *any* sons, as a direct line to himself and therefore as *fils de France* (sons of France)?

## A Regent for the Child King

Little Louis d'Anjou was now four years old. The King recognized that the little heir would need a regent to guide him and rule in his place until he became of age. Whether the king liked it or not, the next in line, should the child die, was his late brother's son, the duc d'Orleans. It's true the duke had improved and was showing Louis that his kindness to the young man had been warranted. In the other wing of the palace, however, a distraught Madame de Maintenon paced and stewed. She finally went to the king with a proposal that she hoped would find its way into his will. Well aware that at the king's passing, the only thing that would bind his wishes were the words he put down in writing, Maintenon pressed her point. Of course, everyone was aware that royal wills could be broken, as was the case with Henri IV and Louis XIII. In both cases, the regency was broken by Parlement, and the power given to the Queen-Mother.

Maintenon persisted, until the poor man capitulated. That it was to favor the duc de Maine surprised no one. Louis was tired, and the one person with the closest access to him hounded him until the ink was dry on the great monarch's will. So, on August 26, 1714, Louis XIV handed his will, sealed with seven seals, to the Premier President of the Parlement, M. de Mesmes.

"Messieurs," Louis said, "this is my will. I alone know its contents. I entrust it to the Parlement, to whom I cannot give a greater proof of my esteem and my confidence… The example of the Kings, my predecessors, and that of the will of my father show me what may become of this [the canceling of Louis XIII's wishes in his will after his death]; but they wanted it; they tormented me; they would leave me no peace, no matter what I said. Well, then! I have bought my rest. Here it is, take it; happen what may, I will have peace and hear no more on the subject."

The following day, Saint-Simon went on to report that Louis turned his wrath on the woman who made his recent days hell: "Madame," he said angrily, "I have bought some peace. I know how useless and powerless it is. We can do anything we want while we live; afterwards, we are more limited than private people; one only has to look at what became of my father's will, immediately after his death, and at those of so many other kings. I know it all; but despite all this they wanted it; I was given neither peace nor rest until it was done. Well, then! it is done, Madame, happen what may, I will no longer be tormented about it."

What's interesting is Louis' repetitive use of the phrase "they wanted it." Was the "they" his way of encapsulating Maintenon and du Maine into one lump, rather than use the more accusatory term "YOU wanted it!" Maintenon was all he had left. Was he couching his words in an effort to keep her close, no matter the stress she had caused him? The will was sealed into one of the walls of the Parlement's tower in Paris until after the King's death.

# Chapter Thirty-Two
# **"Le Roi Est Mort!"**

Louis XIV in his 70's.

On 29 July 1714, upon the insistence of his morganatic wife, the marquise de Maintenon, Louis XIV elevated his legitimized children to the rank of Princes of the Blood, which "entitled them to inherit the crown if the legitimate lines became extinct." Thus, Louis-Auguste de Bourbon, *Duke of Maine* and Louis-Alexandre de Bourbon, *Count of Toulouse* were officially inserted into the line of hereditary succession following all of the legitimate, acknowledged *princes du sang*.

Mme de Maintenon would have preferred Philip V [King of Spain] to be regent and the duc du Maine to be Lieutenant Général and consequently in control. Fearing a revival of the war, Louis named the duc d'Orléans joint President of a Regency Council. He realized this institution would be packed with Orleans' enemies, reaching its decisions by a majority vote that was bound to go against him. The real power would be in the hands of the duc du Maine, who was also appointed guardian of the young sovereign.

Once the will was sealed away, the King began to take stock of his last days. He knew his health was failing. The courtiers and ministers noticed his loss of weight and strength. The pain in his foot had taken on horrendous proportions and he walked with a cane.

In February, the ministers were approached by an ambassador of Persia who wished to pay his respects to the King. The "ambassador" was thought to be a merchant with a ruse to get close to Louis' purse strings. Even though the ministers were on to the possible imposter, they kept quiet, feeling the aging monarch would be pleased to have a Persian dignitary visit him. It was the last ceremony held at Versailles under the reign of Louis XIV.

Bets were placed in London on how much longer the King would live. Louis was at Marly, weakening by the day. The bets were a callous thing to do, and they found their way into the Dutch gazettes. Louis found out about it after he forced Torcy to read it aloud to him one morning after the gentleman stuttered over the captions. The king pretended not to mind, but many noticed at dinner that evening, he couldn't keep his food down.

Louis returned to his precious Versailles on August 10, 1715, and held his councils as always. The next day he visited his Trianon for the last time. He returned to Versailles where he would remain until his death. By now, the pain from his foot had spread to his leg. August 13$^{th}$ marked the last time he would dine in public.

Fagan, the chief physician, had misread the king's symptoms, thinking it was nerve damage due to sciatica. He had put the king on a diet of overripe fruit and all manner of sweets for the prior two years. He missed the fact that pain in the feet or neuropathy are the first sign of diabetes. He was therefore prescribing a diet of even more sugar to a monarch that gorged himself routinely on the rich fare of Versailles. The result soon became obvious—Louis was secretly suffering from gangrene in his leg.

On August 14$^{th}$, Louis could no longer walk. He was carried in a salon chair to Mass and later that evening to a concert in Mme de Maintenon's apartment. He later allowed the court to watch him at his supper in his room, one of the last remaining rituals he could hold onto. He held his Council meetings from his bed for the next eight days, and all in attendance realized that the king's days were numbered.

When on the 22$^{nd}$ he was not able to review the *gendarmerie*, he sent the duc de Maine instead, cementing the young man's authority in the court's eyes. The ever-greedy sycophants now stayed close to Maine's heels, as they did also to the duc d'Orleans, just in case.

August 24$^{th}$, the proud king once again allowed the court to enter his bedchamber to watch him dine, but when he could no longer swallow, he asked them to leave. When he returned to bed, he saw with horror the blackening of his leg. There was no doubt now that Louis was infected with gangrene, and it was eating away at his body. It had, in fact, penetrated to the bone.

On 25 August 1715, a few days before his death, Louis XIV added a codicil to his will:

In the presence of Mme de Maintenon, he sent for his Chancellor and wrote a last codicil to his will. He was yielding, out of sheer fatigue, to his wife and confessor, probably with the reservation that his extraordinary action would be set aside after his death, like the will itself. Otherwise, he would have been deliberately condemning his kingdom to perpetual strife, for the codicil appointed the duc du Maine commander of the civil and military Household, with Villeroy as his second-in-command. By this arrangement they became the sole masters of the person and residence of the king; of Paris ... and all the internal and external guard; of the entire service ... so much so that the regent did not have even the shadow of the slightest authority and found himself at their mercy.

The evening of August25th, Louis XIV had a private audience with the Duke of Orléans, his nephew and son-in-law, re-assuring him:

"You will find nothing in my will that should displease you. I commend the Dauphin to you, serve him as loyally as you have served me. Do your utmost to preserve his realm. If he were to die, you would be the master. [...] I have made what I believed to be the wisest and fairest arrangements for the well-being of the realm, but, since one cannot anticipate everything, if there is something to change or to reform, you will do whatever you see fit..."

Louis ordered his musicians to play…there would still be music at Versailles. It must have been a very somber moment for all involved. The King took communion and received the last rites. He then called in each family member alone. Madame de Maintenon remained at his bedside and was privy to each conversation as he received the duc d'Orleans, the duc du Maine, the comte de Toulouse, the king's daughters, and the Princes of the Blood.

August 26th saw the courtiers of the great palace shown into the king's bedchamber for his public farewell. Dangeau recorded that "At noon, His Majesty had the little Dauphin brought into his room and, after having kissed him, he said, 'Sweet child, you are about to be a great King, but your whole happiness will depend on your submission to God, and on the care you take to relieve the people of their burden. In order to do this, you must, whenever you can, avoid making war: it is the ruin of the people. Do not follow the bad example I have given you on this point. Often, I have started wars without sufficient cause and continued them to satisfy my pride. Do not imitate me, be a peaceful ruler, and let your main object be to look after your subjects. Take advantage of the education Mme la duchesse de Ventadour [the Dauphin's governess] is giving you, obey her and follow the advice of Father le Tellier when it comes to serving God. I give him to you as your confessor.

"'As for you, Madame [speaking to Mme de Ventadour], I owe you much gratitude for the care with which you are bringing up this child and for the tenderness you show him. I ask that you continue in the same fashion, and I urge him to give you every possible proof of his gratitude.' After this, he kissed the Dauphin twice and gave him his blessing."

Philippe's widow, Madame, wrote that "he called for us, the duchesse de Berry, myself, all his daughters and grandchildren. He bade me farewell with words so loving that I still cannot understand why I did not faint dead away. He assured me that he had always loved me, and more than I had thought, that he was sorry he had sometimes caused me sorrow."

The brave princess who had come from a different country to marry the brother of the King of France, only to find her new husband preferred the company of men; who had looked with disdain upon the frivolousness of an overly-dressed and bejeweled court, and worn what she wanted; who threw etiquette to the wind and out-rode and out-hunted many of the men at court; was still there to bid the King farewell. Did it cross her mind at this moment that her own departed husband could have been the next to sit the throne and she might have become Queen of France? Many, many thoughts were no doubt going throughout the mind of each person paying their last respects to a monarch that had defied the odds and lived into his seventies.

Louis called in the duc d'Orleans and gave him his first order as the boy's regent. He was to take the little Dauphin away from Versailles to the palace of Vincennes and keep him there until after his death, at which point, he was to have the entire palace of Versailles thoroughly cleaned out, and then return the new monarch to his place of reign…Versailles.

The king continued his messages to his devout courtiers. He gathered them around him and said, "Messieurs, I am pleased with your services; you have served me faithfully and with the desire to please. I am sorry I could not reward you better; these last few years have not allowed me to do so. Serve the Dauphin with the same affection you have shown me; he is only a five-year-old child who may have many setbacks, for I remember having had many myself when I was young. I am going, but the State will remain. Be faithful to it and let your examples inspire all my other subjects. Always remain united in accord—that is the strength of a state—and always obey the orders my nephew [the duc d'Orleans] will give you; he will govern the kingdom. I hope that you will do your duty and also that you will remember me sometimes."

Dangeau reported that "we all burst into tears, and nothing could begin to describe the sorrow and despair of all those present."

On August 27th, only Louis' Confessor and his wife, Maintenon were allowed into his room. On the 28th, he told her that he hoped to see her again soon, given her advanced years, which may or may not have been a compliment the lady wanted to hear. Three times, Louis bade farewell to Mme de Maintenon and twice to the court. In the afternoon of the 27th, a man came to the Palace claiming he had a cure for gangrene. He was allowed to give it to the king, who admitted to feeling a bit better the next day, but it was too late. The black disease was in his bones and nothing short of amputation would have cured it. Given the king's age and his other health issues, it was perhaps never suggested that the remedy be advanced. The pain increased and it was only a matter of hours, or so thought all those present.

Madame de Maintenon, perhaps wishing to save herself from the last tearful vestiges of her husband's life, left the palace and headed for her private school, Saint Cyr, where she kept an apartment. The king that evening fainted, and upon coming to was asked by Fagan, his physician, if he was in great pain. Louis answered, "No, and that annoys me. I would like to suffer more for the expiation of my sins."

The Sun King, Louis "the God Given," was now more than ever conscious of his impending reunion with God, and desired to be punished with excruciating pain. Better to pay retribution here than throughout the eternities. That he was suffering was clear. The gangrene had now traveled up to his thigh and he fainted several times. In a panic, he called for his wife, but was told she had gone to Saint Cyr, which was close by. He ordered her return. Maintenon returned; we are not told if this was with reluctance. All through the 30th, Louis was in and out of consciousness, and remained half-coherent. Maintenon left again for her school.

Throughout August 31st, his physician kept vigilance, expecting at any moment to announce the king had breathed his last. Early that evening, rallying once more after the prayers for the dying, he cried out, "O God, come to my help, please relieve me soon." God obliged him, and the great King of France sank into a coma and died at eight-fifteen the following morning.

## The Sun Sets at Versailles

Louis XIV died at Versailles on 1 September 1715 and was succeeded by his five-year-old great-grandson, Louis XV. His council room door overlooking the Marble Court was thrown open and the announcement was given to those waiting below, "Le Roi Est Mort!"—the King is dead!

Without wasting any time, the King's desires were put to naught, just as he predicted they would.be. On September 2nd (only one day after the King's death), the Philippe, the Duke of Orléans went to meet the *parlementaires* in the *Grand-Chambre du Parlement* in Paris in order to have Louis XIV's will annulled and his previous right to the regency restored. After a break that followed a much-heated session, the *Parlement* abrogated the recent codicil to Louis XIV's will and confirmed the Duke of Orléans as Regent of France.

Also ignoring the late King's command that the Dauphin (now the new King) be returned to Versailles after it had been cleaned, the regent decided to bring the young Louis XV from the château de Vincennes to the Tuileries Palace in Paris instead, in December of that year, 1715. The small king lived at the Tuileries until his return to Versailles in June 1722 at the age of 12. The regent governed from his Parisian residence, the *Palais-Royal,* just around the corner from the Tuileries.

Orleans disapproved of the hypocrisy of Louis XIV's reign and opposed censorship, ordering the reprinting of books banned during the reign of his uncle. Reversing his uncle's policies again, Philippe formed an alliance with Great Britain, Austria, and the Netherlands, and fought a successful war against Spain that established the conditions of a European peace. During this time, he opened up diplomatic channels with Russia which resulted in a state visit by the Tsar Peter the Great, who reportedly picked up the young king and kissed him on the cheek, ignoring all royal protocol.

The new regent acted in plays of Molière and Racine, composed an opera, and was a gifted painter and engraver. Philippe favored Jansenism which, despite papal condemnation, was accepted by the French bishops, and he revoked Louis XIV's compliance with the bull *Unigenitus*. *Unigenitus* was an apostolic constitution in the form of a papal bull promulgated by Pope

Clement XI in 1713, opening the final phase of the Jansenist controversy in France.

At first, Orleans decreased taxation and dismissed 25,000 soldiers. But the inquisitorial measures which he had begun against the financiers led to disturbances, notably in the province of Brittany where a rebellion known as the Pontcallec Conspiracy unfolded. He countenanced the risky operations of the banker John Law, whose bankruptcy led to the Mississippi Bubble, a disastrous crisis for the public and private affairs of France. It was an early example of the bursting of an economic bubble.

On 6 June 1717, under the influence of Law and the duc de Saint-Simon, the regent persuaded the Regency Council to purchase from Thomas Pitt for £135,000 the world's largest known diamond, a 141 carat (28.2 g) cushion brilliant, for the crown jewels of France. The diamond was known from then on as *Le Régent*. This rare diamond found its way into the coronation crowns of Louis XV and Louis XVI, and then into Marie Antoinette's hands where she wore it until it was stolen during the French Revolution. It was later found in the attic of an abandoned house in Paris where it was acquired by Napoleon Bonaparte, who set it into the hilt of his sword.

The Regent Diamond in Napoleon's sword hilt.

After Napoleon's death, Archduchess Marie Louis of Austria, brought the stone back to Austria, but it was later returned to the French Crown jewels where it was then mounted in the crowns of Louis XVIII, Charles X, and Napoleon III. Many rumors circulated that the diamond was cursed.

For a king who had reigned for 72 years and had only missed his 77th birthday by four days, his funeral was, at first, supposed to be a simple affair. The Master of Ceremonies oversaw a tribute that was prolonged and imposing.

For the first twenty-four hours the King's body was exposed on his deathbed. The tradition at the time was that if poison had been used to cause death, it would leave telltale black marks on the victim's face. Throughout the day, courtiers, members of the Household, and the public filed past the corpse, reposing in the opulent King's bedroom, situated in the very heart of his palace. Nun's chanting were the only sounds heard other than soft sobs.

The following day, Louis XIV's body was taken to the room next door called the Bull's Eye Room and placed upon an operating table for the customary opening of the body. This was done with due ceremony in front of a Lorraine prince—the duc d'Elboeuf—a senior military figure—the maréchal de Montesquiou—and various members of the Household. There were precise religious ceremonies associated with the autopsy of a royal corpse: the heart and intestines were removed, embalmed, and sent in a royal procession to Paris. The intestines were taken to Notre Dame by the archbishop of Paris. Enclosed in a golden urn, the heart sat on the lap of a French cardinal in a coach escorted by thirty bodyguards to another Parisian church, Saint-Antoine.

For eight days, the body of the Sun King lay in state on the official bed behind the balustrade in the Salon of Mercury. The Mercury Room was originally the royal bedchamber in the King's State Apartment. The bed was removed in winter to make room for the game's tables. The alcove was separated from the rest of the room by a balustrade made from silver. The Duke of Anjou, Louis XIV's grandson, slept there for three weeks before traveling to his new country as King of Spain.

And so, this room who had once vibrated with the sound of laughter and bets called out during card games, was cloaked in somber overtones. Four altars stood within the window embrasures.

From here, the clerics addressed their non-stop daily masses for the royal soul to the king's empty armchair and praying stool. The abbé Besongne, who was there, described it "as if the king full of life was still there." On the ninth day, the coffin was hoisted onto the shoulder of twelve bodyguards who carried it down the Ambassador's Staircase where once the Sun King had dazzled all the visiting dignitaries of Europe and beyond. The coffin was loaded onto a royal coach and the cortége went directly from Versailles to the Abbe of Saint-Denis in Paris, where royal burials took place.

It was evening, and the trip took 12 hours due to the enormous train of coaches and to allow the arrival to coincide with the abbey's prayers who were to begin as soon as the coffin arrived. The path bypassed the capital of Paris, denying the Parisians the traditional royal procession which included the king's death mask, borne aloft as it traveled through the streets. Louis XIII's funeral in 1642 had followed this tradition and it is unclear why it was not recognized for Louis XIV. Was the royal family concerned about Louis' faltering popularity in later years?

It is true his subjects saw him as the king who had bankrupted France and lived large while they starved. He had committed adultery over and over again, while deeming himself an extension of deity. To top it all off, he had elevated his illegitimate children to ranks of glory, while installing a protocol at the palace that turned away those not worthy to enter.

Versailles sat empty for seven years as the seasons turned the flower parterres into an array of colors. The nobility returned to their homes, feeling as if they had awakened from an odd dream where they were held captive in a golden palace. The sound of a housemaid's mop echoed in the empty salons where once raucous card games filled the night with laughter and jeering. The sight of elegant ballgowns and glittering jewels were no longer reflected in the glass of the Hall of Mirrors; only the sunlight from the exterior gardens found its way in. The Governor of Versailles, Blouin, continued to maintain the palace and run the jets of water through the myriad garden fountains once every fortnight.

Gone were the sound of pounding horse hooves through the forests of Versailles. Gone was the hunt. Gone were the Carousels where nobility and royalty alike paraded about upon costumed horses. The marble tub that had enchanted Madame de Montespan sat empty and void of the Sun King's orange blossom-scented water. It was a memory now. Yet, it would forever be known as the most-influential reign in French history.

The Last Journey of Louis XIV. His funeral procession.
His coffin is the square box at the left.

# Chapter Thirty-Three
# The Reign of Louis XV Begins

Louis XV as a child, circa 1720, about 10 years old.
Studio of Pierre Gobert.

Philippe de Courcillon, marquis de Dangeau was a French officer and author most remembered for keeping a diary from 1684 until his death in 1720, much of which dealt with the events surrounding Louis XIV and Louis XV. It is to him we owe the first historic moment when a small boy with dark eyes and hair, dressed in black velvet learned that his life would never be the same. From within his sumptuous room in the south wing of the palace of Versailles, he heard a loud commotion outside his door. Suddenly, the doors burst open and there, bowing to him, was his great-uncle, the duc d'Orleans, along with the Princes of the Blood and a herd of curious court members. "As soon as the child heard himself called 'Sire' and 'Your Majesty,' he burst into tears and sobs even though no one had told him that Louis XIV was dead," Dangeau wrote.

It was not that the little dauphin had been close to his great-grandfather. The Sun King, in his typical fashion, had been a remote father and grandfather, seeing his offspring and their offspring mainly on court occasions. He had given the young boy his blessing and admonitions for running his country only days before. It may have been a rare moment when the King kissed the future monarch of France. For Louis XV, as the boy would know be known, death had become all too familiar for one so young. Only three years prior, he had lost his mother, father, and brother in a matter of weeks to measles. The only person he was close to, was his governess, Duchess de Ventadour. She had shown him love and devotion that the boy had been missing.

What must it have been like to look out at the sea of faces who were eagerly vying to catch the new king's eye? The avarice of the Court would become his daily challenge, yet for now, it was merely a blur of powdered wigs, glittering jewels, and forced smiles. The duc d'Orleans was a man he barely knew, yet he was now to rule France for him until the child came of age in eight years' time, when he turned 13. This cavernous palace with its soaring ceilings and crammed hallways was his inherited domain. For a child who recognized his surroundings from the eye level of knees and waists, it had to be a daunting place to take on. And it had been thrust upon him within a blink of an imperial eye.

Louis XV was a sole survivor of a once numerous family of royals. No one foresaw the surreal deaths of so many of his family in such a short period of time. The child himself was considered sickly and rumors swirled that he would not last long. If he were to die, two men had claim to the throne: Philip V, King of Spain and the Indies, who was the second of Louis XIV's grandsons, or Philippe, duc d'Orleans, the son of the king's late brother and hence, Louis XIV's nephew. These two candidates clearly showed the delineation of the royal blood line. Philip V represented the eldest branch of the Bourbon family, and the duc d'Orleans that of the king's brother, the younger branch. Philip V was out, as the *Treaty of Utrecht* had required his resignation as a successor to the crown of France. That left Philippe, the duc d'Orleans, a man who had never been close to Louis XIV, and one basically hated by most at court. It was his lack of popularity that caused many to wonder if he might try to harm the young boy and take the crown for himself.

The five-year-old king inherited much more than a title and a crown. His great-grandfather had left behind a mountain of debt from the wars, and a court that revolved around strict etiquette never before seen in Europe. Here, rich nobles fought over who would hold the king's candle as his night shirt was handed to him. His every movement had been done in public, with great ceremony and ritual. The courtiers even bowed as the royal food made its way to the royal table. There were *levers* and *couchers* to be performed, council meetings that never ended, and fashion statements to be upheld. To say all the eyes of the world were on this little boy would not be an exaggeration. Louis XIV was a tough act to follow.

Would Louis XV follow his great-grandfather's example and "Rule Alone" without a prime minister, or would he have his Mazarin or Richelieu? Whom would he marry? Would there be the usual line of mistresses? And the question on everyone's lips, would this king rule from Paris or remain at the sanctuary the Sun King had created in Versailles?

Louis XV had just been thrust into an unenviable situation. Already, intrigues were swirling around him. Thanks to the late king's will, and his ruling that his illegitimate sons were now elevated to true heirs to the crown after the royal bloodline, there were new players in the ranks. The duc du Maine, the son of Madame de Montespan, had been given authority in the will to command the Household troops and was appointed Superintendent of the future king's education. By controlling both the troops and Louis XV's personnel surrounding the little boy, he was in a powerful position. The duc d'Orleans may have been named the new king's regent until he came of age, but Maine had the power to have the regent arrested if he suspected him of endangering the boy's life. It was a deadly game, played out by the two factions of the royal family, and in the center stood a frail youth whose only occupation should have been to play with wooden horses and choose a dessert of his liking.

Louis XIV was dead. Paris waited with bated breath to see if the Parlement would annul his will as it had the wills of Henri IV and Louis XIII. The duc d'Orleans obviously wanted to be affirmed as the little king's regent until the little boy's thirteenth birthday. The Parlement, however, wanted to regain its rights to remonstrate on any edict given by the king and to delay its registration on the record. In the beginning, these remonstrances were of a technical nature. The Parlement would diplomatically ask the king to reconsider what they thought was a faulty decision or one concerning a burdensome tax. The king was free to reject their remonstrances, and if he did so, the Parlement was forced to register the new edict. If there was further dispute, the king would appear before the body of conseillers during what was called the *lit de justice*, the "bed of justice," so named because the King sat on a mound of cushions beneath a canopy. He would then demand that the edict be published, and as ruler and absolute monarch, his orders were carried out.

The fear now was the Parlement would take advantage of a minor and try to regain its power. It was therefore not surprising to find the regent, the duc d'Orleans, holding a private conference with the Premier President of the Parlement. The announcement was made that the king's will would be taken from its hiding place the next morning and read before the Parlement and Peers. The duc du Maine seemed confident that Orleans would be overturned as regent. The duke had appointed the Premier President in the past and he was a big supporter of the greedy legalized son of Louis XIV.

By seven the next morning, the great hall of the Parlement was abuzz with excited voices. The légitimés (Louis XIV's legitimized children) entered, followed by the duc de Bourbon and the regent. Louis Henri, the duc de Bourbon, was a member of the reigning House of Bourbon and a Prince of the Blood. He was head of the Bourbon-Condé cadet branch and ended up serving as Louis XV's prime minister. The Peers sat up on their high benches, the conseillers and presidents sat below, dressed in scarlet robes. With the accustomed ceremony, the King's will was taken from its hiding place and read by the Premier Président before the people gathered there. After the reading, the Président turned to the regent, Louis XIV's grandson, bowed and offered him the floor. It became clear within minutes what his course of action would be.

Referring to the late king's codicil where he set up a Council to oversee decisions concerning the new king, Orleans decided to use the Louis XIV's own words uttered to him on his deathbed. He pointed out the impracticality of the government set up in the will and related the words the late King had said to him. Orleans explained the Sun King had said, "Nephew, I have preserved for you the rights your birth gives you. I think I have arranged everything for the best, but since one cannot foresee everything, you will make whatever alterations or additions you think fit. I ask that you relieve the State." The regent added, going for an emotional approach to underscore his closeness to the late king, that "he also said several things so flattering to myself that I cannot repeat them." He then proposed the annulling of the will as not the practical thing to do, but in keeping in accord with the king's dying wishes. It was not lost to many of those present that Madame de Maintenon and the duc du Maine had harassed and pressured Louis to amend his will to their demands.

This same duc du Maine now rose heatedly and tried to interrupt. The regent, using a tone one would to an inferior member of his family, told him to wait his turn. With that, Orleans turned back to the packed hall and demanded that a full, unrestricted Regency with the right to govern as he saw fit, to make appointments and order punishments, and the disposition of Household troops [the authority that had been given du Maine] and finished with, "I want to be free to do good, and consent to be so tied that I cannot treat anyone badly."

It this last part of his speech was to give all present the peace of mind that he had no intention of harming the young king, as the vicious rumors had stated, it seemed to hit home. The next to speak was one of the Royal Princes, the duc de Bourbon. If ever the du duc Maine's rank in the Bourbon family was made apparent, it was by this order of who was authorized to speak first. Without hesitation, Bourbon supported the regent, and the power shift was palpable. The duc du Maine raised his voice in support of keeping the will intact, but the hostile whispers from those around him drowned him out. He went pale and collapsed into his seat. The final coup de grâce was the Premier Président, along with the Parlement, awarding Orleans the title and investitures of regent. The defeated duc de Maine announced hotly that if that were the case, he could no longer guaranty the new king's safety, as he had just been released as commander of the Household troops. With perhaps a smirk of victory, the regent bowed and said he was happy to accept the role and the responsibility for Louis XV's safety.

The duc d'Orleans had just been given the full powers of the monarch. But to the surprise of many, he did nothing to punish those who had worked so hard to defeat him. The duc du Maine remained Superintendent of the King's education and a Prince of the Blood as Louis XIV had wanted. He showed compassion to Madame de Maintenon and honored her pension left by the late king. He took her first pension installment in person to the widow at her apartment at Saint Cyr and gave her his assurance she would be taken care of. To all who were beginning to understand the new regent's reign, it was clear that his ways of dealing with people were different from that of Louis XIV. The Sun King had led with manipulation, the offering of titles and comfort based on strict obedience, and a system of advancement that was not only demeaning, but at times, cruel. Orleans' was giving a snapshot of a new reign, one governed with kindness. It would remain to be seen if the young Louis XV followed suit.

## Louis XV Begins His Reign

On September 12, 1715, young Louis XV performed his first royal duty as King of France. The Parlement and Peers once again met in the great hall and this time the small monarch would preside. As the regent remained in close proximity, "The King went up the great staircase on foot; M. le duc de La Trémoille, First Gentleman of the Bedchamber, carried the train of his cloak…Once everyone was in place, the King said very graciously: 'Gentlemen, I have come here to assure you of my affection for you. My Chancellor will tell you what I have decided'… During this sitting, which lasted for a full hour, the young King did not look embarrassed; he was quiet and firm in his place, only he was terribly hot and wiped his face now and again with a handkerchief Mme de Vetadour [his governess] gave him and which he returned to her while apparently paying attention to what was being said and done." This was dutifully recorded by Dangeau.

And so, this small young monarch was already imitating a scene cut from his great-father's diary: he was seated upon a pile of satin pillows beneath a royal canopy, presiding over the powerful Parlement while a regent retained temporary control. For Louis XIV that regent has been his mother; for Louis XV, it was his great-uncle, Philippe, duc d'Orleans.

As for the regent, he gave the Parlement what they had been hungry to receive. During this session, he announced his first edict to be registered: that the Parlement would once again, retain the right to present remonstrances to the king. It looked like the beginning of a new reign, and throughout France, there was a feeling of hope.

Louis XV was from that day forward thrust into the royal limelight. People sought out any chance to get a look at him. He was a very handsome child, with dark wavy hair, dark eyes and delicate features. His portraits show a confident face looking back at the painter—almost whimsical. While he was still somewhat fragile, plans were in the making to strengthen his constitution. In the forefront of that campaign was his beloved governess, the duchesse de Ventadour for whom the child was excessively fond. He had begun calling her "Maman," and it was clear she offered him the rare nurturing and consistent care he craved. Only a year earlier, she had hidden him away in some obscure room deep in the bowels of Versailles to save him from the bleeding and purging that weakened and finally killed the boy's father, mother, and older brother. The little King was saved as he watched his family perish from measles and the hapless doctors' ineffectual remedies for the disease.

Now, this surrogate mother took over the boy's health. She made sure he ate the right food, wore the correct clothing as per the climate, got his daily exercise and rested. And to the surprise and happiness to all those close to the new king, his regent became an indispensable source of comfort and encouragement. The duc d' Orleans came daily to see Louis, and they began to form a bond. Here was the boy's last living biological relative and the regent was devoted to him. Philippe duc d'Orleans was forty-one in 1715 as he stepped into the royal shoes of Regent of the King of France. Saint-Simon took to his quill to describe the man who was temporarily ruling France:

Philippe 11, the duc d'Orleans, Regent of France

"M. le duc d'Orleans," Simon wrote, "was of only ordinary tallness at most, quite fleshy without being fat; he had an easy expression and way of carrying himself; his face was wide, pleasant, quite ruddy, his hair black as was his wig... His face, his gestures, all his manners were imbued with the most perfect graciousness, and it came to him so naturally that it adorned even the least and most common of his actions. With great ease of manner, when not feeling constrained, he was kind, open, welcoming, easily accessible and charming, with a pleasant tone of voice and a gift for words which was particular to him…

"The great figures of history and their lives were familiar to him, and so were the intrigues of earlier courts and of the one he lived in. To listen to him one would have thought he was very well read, but nothing could be further from the truth. He skimmed rapidly but his memory was extraordinary, so that he forgot neither the incidents nor the name nor the dates… He was extremely witty, and in several ways…No one had a more respectful look or air when he was with the Royal Family or the king, and yet this was blended with great dignity. He was naturally kind, humane and accessible to pity…"

High praise for the man Louis XIV had dressed down for his immoral and embarrassing conduct at the festivities of Fontainebleau and other places. And while the accolades given by Saint-Simon seemed well-founded, the duke had not entirely changed his spots. It was well-known he conducted orgies at his Palais-Royale nightly; inviting in all the lovely young ladies and handsome gentlemen he could line up. His mistresses were legion, and his reputation for drunken sexual parties well-known. Yet, he was known to be a good and loving father who single-handedly saved his daughter Elisabeth when she caught smallpox and was given up by the doctors.

This man of many faces was now the regent and Louis XV's role model. The debauchery may have been kept from the small king. We do know Orleans stepped in to save him from the corrupt influences of a new man about to enter the young boy's life.

## Chapter Thirty-Four
## **The Making of a King**

Louis XV was living in a world of contradictions. He was a king, but he was a child not yet of age to be one. He was powerful in title only while his uncle wielded the power the king rightfully owned. He was five years old, yet he could not relate to others his own age (nor them to him), in fact his days were encapsulated with adults giving him no end of direction. It was a lonely existence; a golden island of rich draperies and jeweled clothing, bereft of family, leaving only an uncle who had, until very recently, been a remote figure in the little boy's life. It was to his governess, MMe la duchesse de Ventadour, that he clung as the only lifeboat anchored to that island of plenty.

The regent began his duties by honoring Louis XIV's wish that the new king be taken to Vincennes where the air was healthier than that of Versailles. The swamps the Sun King had tamed into submission were not altogether gone, and the diseases carried by mosquitoes were still a real threat. There was also the fear of any vestiges of the disease that had caused the great King's gangrene. Versailles was to be thoroughly cleaned, and then the boy returned there. And so, on September 5, 1715, only four days after Louis' death, Orleans called a meeting of the court doctors to consult with them on the merit of removing the child to Vincennes, and they agreed, the palace would be a better option.

The Château de Vincennes was in fact, a grim fortress. Severe in its façade, it had its origins as a hunting lodge constructed for Louis VII in 1150 in the forest of Vincennes, to the east of Paris. In the 13th century, Philip Augustus and Louis IX erected a more substantial manor. In the 14th century, the castle was greatly enlarged replacing the earlier site. A *donjon* (tower), 52 meters high, the tallest medieval fortified structure in Europe, was added by Philip VI of France around 1337. The tower served as a residence for the royal family, which included a library that had belonged to Charles V. In the 17th century, Louis Le Vau built for Louis XIV a pair of isolated ranges mirroring one another across a parterre to one side of the keep, suited for the Queen-Mother and Cardinal Mazarin, but once Versailles took over the king's attention, nothing more was done to enhance the bleak chateau.

Château de Vincennes

On September 9th, the little King was loaded into a coach and left Versailles, the only home he had known. He was cutting the strings to the place he associated with his father and mother, and an older brother who had played with him within the rooms of the palace. It must have felt like losing the last thing familiar to him or that was tied to his memory of life to this point. Dressed in purple velvet, he "left Versailles at two in the afternoon and arrived at Vincennes in excellent health," Dangeau noted. "With him in his carriage were M. le duc d'Orleans and Mme la duchesse de Ventadour sitting with him in the backseat, M. le duc de Maine and M. le maréchal de Villeroy [the King's Governor] in the front seat, with M. le maréchal de Toulouse at the door… All along the road and especially near the walls [of Paris], there was an infinity of carriages and people. One could hear people shouting, 'Long live the King!' even in the streets on the other side of the walls."

Louis XV entered into a new home, one less opulent, to be sure, and without the myriad windows overlooking elaborate gardens and fountains. Dangeau noted on October 1, "The King is getting stronger and enjoys the best of health, but since the bad weather will soon be here, it is thought that he will be more comfortable in the Tuileries for the winter." The fortress must have been a cold, sad place to be in the winter months. The regent asked the doctors for their advice. Moving the boy to Paris would be a great deal easier for him, as the ride from his Palais Royal to Vincennes was a daily ninety-nine-minute ride. The doctors discussed the move and opined it would be better to wait until after the first freeze to move the little king to the capital city.

On January 1, 1716, four months after Louis XIV's death, the late king's wishes were ignored. Rather than return the boy to Versailles, as per the Sun King's desire, Louis XV was taken to the Tuileries in Paris—that great palace connecting to the Louvre, enhanced by Catherine de' Medici after the accidental death of Henry II of France. The difference between Vincennes and the Tuileries could not have been more dramatic. Here, famous gardens stretched as far as the eye could see. The Seine was viewable from balconies on the one side, and the city of Paris on the other. The energy of the city was palpable. Dangeau note, "The King is in the best of health and shows much pleasure at being in Paris."

The regent had gotten his wish. His Palais-Royal was just around the corner. He could have his orgies throughout the night and be at the little king's side the following morning. There was also a very important statement this move made to the people of Paris: by installing the king here, it sent a message that he might govern from the capital, rather than remove himself from his subjects as his great-grandfather had done when he secluded himself and the court at

Versailles. This was a new reign, and it brought much hope to a citizenship who had seen wars, crippling taxes, and starvation. It would remain to be seen if this young boy would endure the debacles that sent his great-grandfather, Louis XIV and his mother fleeing when the late king was only ten. The first Fronde had frightened the Sun King so badly, that it was his major impetus for creating Versailles, and he built the walls and gates around himself as protection from ever being within striking distance of a civil uprising again. For now, his successor was happy with his new home and the people seemed happy to have him there.

The Parlement, that body who had been so engrained in the Frondes of the mid-1600s, also seemed content with the olive branch the regent had extended to them under his new role. They were now authorized to offer remonstrances once more, and they were allowed to do so before the edict was registered, giving them a temporary veto. The regent did instill a time limit however for this privilege: the remonstrances had to be made "within a week at most for the courts which are located in the place of our residence." Unless forced to call a *lit de justice*—a last ditch measure—it seemed the monarchy and the government were going to play nice.

Another new change to this burgeoning realm was the abolishment of the ministries Louis XIV had always relied upon, replaced by a series of councils, each staffed with an inferior group of men than the late king had encircled himself with. Gone were the likes of the great Colbert and Louvois. In place were a group of aristocrats who knew as much about the machinations of government as they did about handling household chores themselves. They focused on the running of their own estates rather than the State. In defense of Orleans, it was the late father of the little king who had proposed the idea of a Council, and it was out of respect for the late duc de Bourgogne, that the regent put into place this new body of advisors.

The Council of Regency, as the new platform was called, was comprised of councils for the War, Navy, Finances, Interior and Church Affairs. Mainly, the men holding the titles to these factions spent their time at Council arguing with one another. It was soon apparent the structure was not working. Each council was presided over by a Prince of the Blood or a duke whose lack of competency was only nullified by their rank and title. It was a fiasco that lasted an amazing four years. In secret, the regent, who had abandoned confidence in it, was dealing directly with the professional civil servants.

The fact that the Council of Regency showed a fairer approach in the governing of the people may have been somewhat responsible for its popularity and longevity. Here, rather than a despotic structure where a monarch governed alone, the people saw a body of men who represented both the Parlement (a body made up of the nobility, the clergy, and the common folk) and the royal family. It was as close to a democracy as they had come.

Perhaps the biggest display of change under the new rule, was the emptiness of Versailles; that once-great hive of people and pomp. With the ruling king now back in Paris, the Hall of Mirrors emptied as the nobles went back to their estates. Louis XV retained a small Household, as he must, and the duc d'Orleans was happy to dispense with the etiquette he had seen as ridiculous. The nobles, freed from their constant requirement to be within the king's eyeline at all times, now piled into the streets of Paris to resume their fun. Gone were the restraints of etiquette, both in fashion and Louis XIV's demands for strict regulation of their personal habits and obedience to his routine.

Suddenly, the dress code came tumbling down. Light silks, pastel colors, and voluminous skirts replaced the stiff brocades and straight lines of Louis XIV's court. The poufs of towering hair built upon wire infrastructures was replaced by short curly hair, covered in white powder. Theaters filled, dances and balls appeared nightly, and Paris saw a surge in new décor. Just as modern-day eras had signaled a new wave of freedom and free thinking, so did the post-Louis XIV timeline. Talent was worshiped while strict censorship was tossed out with the ruined vegetables.

From his balcony overlooking the parterres of symmetric gardens, a young boy watched from afar as Paris filled with revelers and sounds of music. For him, he was encased in a glass bubble that everyone feared would break should he become ill or assassinated. All around him treated him with solemn diffidence—bowing, respecting, keeping their distance—while children his age were sliding along iced over sidewalks with squeals of laughter, and darting into candy stores with chubby hands clutching a few coins bearing the image of the late King.

The hopes and fears of an entire population, indeed of Europe itself, were all drawn up in one small frame who was trying to understand his role in it all. The mindset of the people was perhaps best summed up in a somewhat callous remark by the regent's mother, who said "The King might well die, but it would be a terrible misfortune, even for us [her son the regent would take over the throne], for I think there would be a terrible war." This dehumanizing assessment of this young boy's station and purpose in life was not that uncommon. Rulers came and rulers went. One day's glory was the next day's disaster. It was all fleeting and fearful, jubilant and wonderful, but transitory. This was the world Louis XV had inherited.

## Tutors and Treachery

"Our young King is at the Tuileries and, thank God, in good health; he hasn't been sick for a moment," the regent's mother declared. "He is allowed to do anything he wants lest a refusal make him ill. I am sure that if he were punished, he would be less passionate… but everyone wants to remain in the King's good graces, no matter how young he may be." And therein lies the rub. This was a child. A child with the title of King of France. He is surrounded by elders, many, no doubt, finding cause to discipline him as one would any child acting out. But with this child, a wrong move now could be your undoing later. No one wanted to the one to be remembered for causing the young boy angst, let alone punishing him. It was another example of the parallel worlds in which Louis XV found himself.

Part of Louis' education was of necessity, not that of an ordinary child. At six he was taught how to be on display, exhibiting majestic politeness and adroit conversation for which his great-grandfather, Louis XIV had been renowned. Say what you will about the Sun King, he had Kingly protocol down to a science. Never rude or dismissive, his worst slight was to give a cool "We shall see," if he was not of a mind to grant a favor at the moment. One never felt snubbed in the king's presence. He doffed his hat for all females, not just the nobility, and handled awkward moments with deft wit. Little Louis must learn this rare art of dealing with people. He must remember myriad names and keep his personal feelings to himself; something he would learn in spades.

The pressure was immense for a six-year-old. At one point he fainted beneath the pressure of being in the spotlight of a large group of people. His loving governess took care of his well-being, to be sure, but she also remembered the late king's admonitions to her, and she repeated them often to Louis XV: to always serve God; to always remember who he was and behave; accordingly, and he must learn discretion—to keep a secret and never let others know his true feelings. The words of his late great-grandfather burned into his malleable brain, and by the time he was seven, it was inviolable.

By the time Louis was seven, he had been inundated with the mantra to "trust no one." It was not his governess, Ventadour, alone who drummed this into his nubile mind. His great-uncle, the duc d'Orleans, the regent, had grown up around the nefarious court of Versailles, with its pernicious and greedy social climbers. He was the epitome of a man who trusted absolutely no person. While this barrier could serve its purpose for a king who would be daily commissioned for favor by sycophants with an agenda, it also caused a jaded outlook on the world. It was a harsh thing to continually show a child the face of a crooked realm and teach him that most were not interested in him, but only what he could give them.

The lesson was so profound that even when an occasional child was brought to play with the young king (after being indoctrinated with how to treat his Royal Majesty), Louis had no idea what was expected of him. Rather than play with the boy one-on-one, he gave the young man a watch. After being told repeatedly that people would only seek him out for favors and gifts, he dutifully fulfilled that image and replaced common interaction with presents. If he took a misstep, he was reminded immediately of who he was. Expected to act as an adult without the benefit of an adult's maturity or ability to control emotion, he was in constant fear of "messing up."

As if this were not enough of a hardship, a new change came into his life when he turned seven. According to tradition, when a young prince turned seven years of age, he was taken away from his governess and put in the charge of a Governor—in this case, a man chosen by the late king, the maréchal de Villeroy. Villeroy was in his seventies and the opposite of Ventadour's mindset or warmth. In February of 1717, Louis XV was stripped naked before a group of courtiers with the regent presiding. The doctors prescribed him as healthy and ceremoniously handed him over to old Villeroy. For the little boy, it was too much. Mme de Ventadour had basically replaced his parents in terms of warmth, love, and constant care. She had saved him. His life was nothing but a continual upheaval and loved ones lost. Louis cried throughout the day, refused to eat, and called out for the governess repeatedly. Instead of having her returned to him, he was given a casket of jewels which included a necklace of pearls and a diamond cross to hand to the governess as her reward. It was another lesson in exchanging goods for affection. As Louis presented her with the gift, he told Mme de Ventadour the present paled in comparison to the gratitude he owed her.

Enter François de Neufville, duc de Villeroy, perhaps the worst man the late king could have nominated to be in charge of the royal ward. He immediately began to undo all the regent and Ventadour had told the boy in respect to his calling. Where Ventadour had impressed upon him that he was to serve God, Villeroy repeatedly placed the boy where he could see his subjects and reminded him, he was ruler of all he could see. He flattered Louis (never forgetting the powerful position this close proximity to the king gave him) and missed no occasion to parade him about while the public gawked. The governor utterly neglected the boy's education and focused more on building him up and reminding him of his power. He was also angling to set himself up to replace Orleans as regent.

Saint-Simon described Villeroy as "tall and well built, with a very pleasant face. He was strong, robustly healthy, and could do anything he wanted to his body without fear. He had no difficulty in spending fifteen or sixteen hours on horseback and stayed up all night. All his life he lived and prospered in the highest society. The son of [Louis XIV's] Governor, he was brought up with the King and was his familiar friend from his earliest youth. A lady's man by profession, he knew all about all the love affairs of both court and town, with which he used to entertain the King, whom he knew thoroughly and whose foibles he was able to exploit… He lived in great style and had very noble manners… was never gratuitously nasty… excessively proud by nature, but also humble to excess whenever it could do him any good…

"He had the kind of wit one learns at court and in society and spoke the fashionable jargon… He was a man born to preside over a ball…

He understood neither people nor events… was incapable of giving good advice… incapable also of attending to business of any kind, or even of understanding anything in depth, stopping always at the surface… He was the least-liked of anyone at Court because people found in him only a mass of fatuousness, of self-interest and smugness, of boasting about the King's favor and about his great successes… He had read nothing, knew nothing, was completely ignorant in every field, given to shallow jokes, much wind and all completely empty."

François de Neufville, duc de Villeroy

Not the best description of a man who was now in charge of the young King's indoctrination into the world. To Louis XV's credit, he saw through the flattery and had a keen insight into people, even at the age of seven. Unfortunately, Villeroy's constant parading of the boy before immense crowds of people caused Louis to develop a debilitating shyness that stayed with him the rest of his life. The ceremonies of the *lever* and *coucher,* instigated during the reign of Louis XIV, were also performed daily in front of large crowds. The boy was dressed and undressed as strangers ogled him in his bedchamber. All the while, Villeory looked for more ceremonial occasions to display his new toy. In November of 1717, the mother of Orleans wrote, "The young King is good-looking and very intelligent, but he is not a nice child. He loves no one but his former governess; he takes a dislike to people for no reason and is already fond of making sharp criticisms… He would really be nice if only he spoke a little oftener, but one really has trouble getting him to say a few words."

The regent continued to visit the young King daily, but due to the myriad responsibilities of running France, his visits were short, lasting under 45 minutes. He had no authority over how Louis XV was brought up as that fell to his governor; a matter Villeroy was prompt to point out. As for the governor, he was often absent when there was no occasion to flaunt his young charge. This was all for the good, as a new man had now entered the young king's life—one he would spend considerable time with—the M. de Fréjus.

## Chapter Thirty-Five
## **A Wealth of Advice**

When one is born a king, yet too young to rule, his days are filled with an overwhelming avalanche of advice. Every dichotomy of conduct was thrown at him: "be available to the people but remain remote;" "listen to those you have appointed as counselors but make the decision alone;" "show compassion but restraint;" "serve God first but you are all magnificent." For a child not yet ten to cut his way out of the thorny maze of contradictions was not only unfair but put an agonizing amount of weight on his young shoulders. The governess he trusted had been removed and he had been saddled with an egocentric man who only wanted the glow from the boy's crown to shed light and infamy onto himself. The regent was attentive and respectful when he was around, but rumors of his great-uncle's nocturnal antics abounded. It was a lonely and confusing time for the boy king.

A last-minute addition to the codicil Louis XIV made to his will would bring some semblance of order into Louis XV's life. André-Hercule de Fleury, Bishop of Fréjus, was appointed tutor to Louis. Here was a man who was chaste, sober, modest, and liked children. He took over the young boy's education in February 1717 and was the exact opposite of Villeroy's method of molding a king. Louis XV warmed to Fleury almost immediately as the bishop went about gaining the little boy's trust. Here was the warmth the child had been missing since his governess had been removed. Fleury turned his back on his other duties and devoted every moment to the King. He then presented the child's lessons in an entertaining way to keep the bright little boy's attention. He saw quickly that Louis lost interest when he was merely required to memorize dull lessons and recite mindless quotes.

Fleury, Bishop of Fréjus

Fleury's insistence on daily exercise not only resulted in a healthier and more robust young man, it incited Louis XVs life-long love affair with the hunt. He took to riding a horse like a bird to flight. It was often hard to get him out of the saddle as he outrode and outlasted others who accompanied him. But it was Louis' excellence in his academics that gave his tutor immense pride. He was taught grammar and spelling, and it shows in the few errors found in his writings. Geography, mathematics, history, Latin, and the foundation of politics were all on the daily menu. One might wonder at the differences between Fleury and Villeroy as the little boy studied a map of Europe for his lessons. You can almost hear

Villeroy saying, "And you own that piece, and that country, and that inlet, and that castle…" Whereas Fleury often recited things to the boy such as "No one is greater than a kind and hardworking king; no one, on the other hand, is more despicable than a lazy and cowardly king."

Fleury pounded into the little boy's brain the concept that serving God was everything. Little by little, he overrode the wiring Villeroy had installed in Louis' psyche and replaced it with sound wisdom while warning him repeatedly of the dangers of submitting to flattery. By the time he was ten, in 1720, he was studying with specialized teachers in the fields of astronomy, drawing, mathematics, the natural sciences, geography, more Latin, the art of war, and dance steps for the popular dances at court. Unlike his great-grandfather who adored the dance, often performing lead roles and composing several himself, Louis XV found no joy in it. His predecessor had also created a culture unlike any other. Etiquette was everything; perhaps more than any other government seat in Europe, thanks to Louis XIV.

The boy was never given a day off from his organized routine. He had a quick intelligence and was soon drawing maps, running a little printing press, and engraving stones. His lifelong love of botany and astronomy no doubt stemmed from these early lessons.

The fact that Fleury was in his mid-sixties when he took over the king's tutorship may have presented the young boy with a father figure he desperately needed. While du Maine, d'Orleans, and Villeroy were preoccupied with women and pleasures, Fleury had no ambition other than to serve the new king, and he did this without agenda, a rare thing in the Court of a French King. It soon became apparent to many that the little monarch loved this Bishop, but some were too busy positioning themselves for favor to notice. He was still a little boy—a puppet King. He was not a threat, other than what he might exact once he came to power. It was much like a dutiful pat on the head, and "now go play" type of association.

Here we see the daily contradiction little Louis lived with. When the Tsar Peter the Great visited in 1717, he totally broke with the protocol demanded for meeting the king of the most powerful county in Europe, yet, because Louis XV was a child, the rules seemed malleable. To pick up a small king and kiss him repeatedly was a rare sight to see. No wonder Louis XV grew up with a need for privacy and a sense of mistrust. Rules, at least at this age, seemed flexible to all but himself. He had watched his great-uncle, the regent, negate the duc d'Maine's power, and yet the cousin was allowed to remain Superintendent of the King's Education. It was an empty title really. Villeroy paraded the boy and Fleury taught him, but du Maine appeared each morning at the *lever* and told the little king funny stories. This is the kind of thing a little boy likes, especially as it broke the monotony of endless studies and court etiquette. Maine was known for his charm, even more so for his ambition.

The Tsar Peter the Great lifting Louis XV up to kiss him.

Ambition wasn't lacking in the king's entourage. When it became known to the regent that the duc du Maine had been plotting against him from his castle at Sceaux (just outside Paris), and had recruited several men who opposed Orleans, the regent called a *lit de justice*. The result was that du Maine lost his capacity to succeed to the throne. He was no longer a Prince of the Blood, merely a duke again, and he lost his post as Superintendent of the King's Education. Waiting in the wings, drool dripping from his lips, was the greedy Louis Henri, duc de Bourbon. He was the eldest son of Louis XIII, Prince of Condé, and Louise Françoise de Bourbon, the eldest legitimized daughter of Louis XIV and his mistress, Madame de Montespan. He was born at Versailles and saw it as his rightful heritage. He was third in line for the throne, behind the regent of little Louis XV. This made him a dangerous piece in this royal game of chess.

Once again, the players in the young King's life changed. He was perhaps becoming accustomed to the perpetual flux of intimates. Saint-Simon noted that upon hearing of du Maine's release, "He only mentioned the duc de Maine's name once, after his dinner that same day, and then he asked where he was going in the most indifferent way." We see here a boy who was already beginning to insulate himself from the constant giving and taking of the people who played a huge part in his life. Like a vest of armor, Louis may have felt the need to protect his feelings at all costs. Like many who suffer unrelenting loss, we see a withdrawal from portraying his emotions or easily giving of his trust.

Louis Henri, the duc d'Bourbon (M. le Duc)

The duc d'Bourbon, or M. le Duc, was the head of the Condé branch of the Bourbons and the First Prince of the Royal Blood. He was an enemy to the Orleans' branch, and thus promised to bring conflict in his wake. He was known to be greedy, dishonest, and unpleasant. He was extremely wealthy and desired to surpass the regent and even the king himself on the way to the throne. For a man who was only in his mid-twenties, he was possessed of an air of entitlement and terrorized everyone around with him with his vile temper and mood swings. He owned several estates and had several massive pensions totaling 1,800,000 livres. Yet, it was never enough.

M. le Duc was described as tall and lanky, smug-faced, and grandiose. He wore a patch over one eye due to a hunting accident. What the young king must have thought of him, after the departure of the amusing du Maine, remained to be seen. With the young monarch, M. le Duc reined in his tendency to be quick-tempered. He was affable and amiable, but absent much of the time. This only increased the influence and closeness Fleury had with the boy. In this pool of young, spoiled royals, the elderly Bishop was a breath of fresh air.

It was perhaps his unsullied closeness with the king that caused some to worry about his influence. Thus, in 1721 the bishop was suddenly offered the Archbishopric-Duke of Reims. This title went to the man who would actually crown the king upon coronation day. Fleury's first assumption was that the offer had come from the regent, in hopes of getting him out of the way. He was wrong. The instigator had been the regent's past tutor, the ambitious abbé Dubois. He recognized the closeness forming between Fleury and the king and wanted a powerful role for himself. Dubois gained the favor of Louis XIV by bringing about the marriage of his pupil with Françoise-Marie de Bourbon, Mlle de Blois, a natural but legitimized daughter of the king and Mme de Montespan; and for this service he was rewarded with the gift of the abbey of St. Just in Picardy.

"The abbé Dubois was a little man, sharp, hypocritical, with a blond wig, the face of a weasel and a look of wit," wrote Saint-Simon. "All the vices fought within him. Avarice, debauchery, ambition, these were his gods… He excelled at low intrigues… but always had a goal to which all his stratagems were directed, and this with a patience whose only bound was success." This was the newest member to be introduced into the young King's realm. Dobois had encouraged d'Orleans' intellect when he was his tutor, but he tempered it by introducing him to the brothels of Paris and to orgies.

It soon became apparent what role Dubois wanted to play in the new reign…Prime Minister to the King of France. He knew the regent wouldn't be an obstacle to his goal, but he feared Fleury might. Fleury understood what lay behind the sudden offer of power made when the title of Archbishopric-Duke of Reims was dangled before him. He would be sent away to Reims, his influence over the king with him. Dubois was running out of time. The boy would ascend to the crown once he turned thirteen. He feared Fleury must have the same aspirations of becoming prime minister, and as of now, Louis XV was closer to the bishop than anyone. Greedy people always assume others are cut from the same cloth. He could not have been more wrong when it came to the mild Bishop.

Guillaume Dubois, the abbé Dubois

Fleury turned down the offer of Archbishop, much to the surprise of the regent. Knowing the little king would have been devastated by losing yet another close advisor, the bishop opted to stay by his side, for which Louis was immensely grateful. He became even closer to the older man. Fleury was now sixty-seven and seemed less of a threat as far as the regent was concerned. How much longer could he live?

The regent continued to show his affection to the king. He treated him with respect and fondness. In August 1719, the duc d'Orleans offered the young Louis his very own hunting lodge in La Muette, just outside Paris. Saint-Simon noted, "The King was delighted. He thought something at last belonged to him personally, took great pleasure in going there, obtained bread, milk, fruit and vegetables from his garden and indulged in all the games which amuse one at that age."

La Muette during the reign of Louis XV.

Dubois had the opposite effect on the king. Louis did not like him—a feeling Villeroy, and Fleury encouraged. Dubois spoke to the king without the diffidence and respect the regent and Fleury used. He was condescending and treated the king with a familiarity that annoyed the young boy. Louis XV had had etiquette drummed into him from his birth. To have an elder treat him without the respect his title afforded him showed a lack of respect he could not tolerate. If Dubois thought a young child of ten would not notice this flippant air of easy familiarity, he was wrong. Louis wasn't in a position yet to use his power, but it was coming soon.

The duc d'Orleans, whether in public or private, showed the young king all the respect he deserved. He never took liberties, talked down to him, or pressed his opinion. He always behaved as if he was the king's minister and there to advise, but also to obey. If an office or gift was to be given, he might propose a worthy candidate, but then immediately informed Louis the ultimate decision was his and his will would be carried out. The regent encouraged Louis to make his own decisions, and the young king appreciated it. He began to feel like a king as Orleans continued to teach the monarch about the government.

Meanwhile, all throughout 1720 and 1721, Fleury continued to teach Louis and ready him for taking over his role as King of France. His lcssons on serving God continued, as well as warning the king repeatedly to beware of flattery. "He who knows himself well sees with his own eyes and has not taste for the praise of other men," was one such quote.

Villeroy continued to display the ten-year-old King as his prize pet. In 1721, he decided Louis should dance a ballet, something that would have been torturous for one so shy. It only made him more self-conscious, and he shunned such entertainments for some time. Saint-Simon stated, "The King did not dance with any vivacity, he looked serious."

On January 10, 1721, Marais, a court reporter, relayed an interesting story concerning the young King's early display of authority:

"The King attended the play *Dom Japhet* by Scarron, which is very amusing and made him laugh. There has been a quarrel about it which the King resolved like a second Solomon. The dud d'Aumont, First Gentleman of the Bedchamber, whose year is ending and who had ordered the Cardenios's new ballet to be performed, claimed that if it was still being danced, he must oversee the performance even though his year was over. The duc de Mortemart, whose period of office began with the year 1721, said on the contrary that it was his duty to oversee them, and that no one would usurp any part of his year. The regent told them to settle the dispute themselves, and that he had more important business to attend than their ballet. They went to see the King, who told them that in order to solve their problem, he no longer wanted to see the ballet, which had bored him, and that he wanted performances of *Dom Japhet*, which had made him laugh. And so, this frivolous dispute has been solved by a child."

The old duchesse d'Orleans gave an appraisal of the young king as he turned eleven: He is "the handsomest child anyone has ever seen," she wrote. He was tall for his age, with a generous mouth, and clear complexion, a trait appreciated during an age when smallpox scars marked many a cheek. Something unexpected happened during his 11th year, the King entered puberty. At first, the young man thought he was ill, as a nocturnal occurrence frightened him to death. The doctors had to reassure him that what was happening to him was normal, albeit a tad early. Marais noted that the people began to laughingly refer to it as the "King's disease."

On July 31, 1721, Louis XV was taken ill. "He was seized by a fever as he attended the Mass and was forced to leave it," a diarist named Barbier noted. "He has been bled from the arm. On August 1st, "his fever doubled and even made him delirious, so the doctors have had great disagreements about bleeding him from the foot… The King almost fainted at the end of the bleeding. All the Court was in great fright, but he soon regained consciousness, and then he slept for eight hours." Next, the doctors purged their patient and gave him two grains of emetic which brought about, one observer noted, "a charming evacuation." The fever soon broke and the king slept. The next morning, he was up on his feet and all of Paris erupted in celebration. Everyone had been watching with fear, thoughts of the deaths of Louis XV's father, mother, and brother in their mind. Their young King had been delivered back to them and the streets filled with gaiety, bonfires, fireworks, dances, and song. The fishwives took an eight-foot sturgeon to the Louvre (next to the Tuileries), the butchers brought an ox and a sheep, and everywhere were shouts of "Long live the King!" One observer noted that the "nobility has spent a prodigious amount on fireworks." This was evidence tattooed across the sky in exploding rockets of the love and hope the people of France had for this young King—Louis XV.

## Chapter Thirty-Six
## **A King Comes of Age**

On August 12, 1721, Louis XV made a rare public appearance in order to attend a thanksgiving service at Notre Dame. He was still recovering from his recent bout of sickness, and it was noted that "he looked very pale in his carriage," according to Marais. "The people, showing its joy anew, shouted more than ever. It is impossible to describe the full extent of their celebration." Barbier, known for his drole interpretation of things, may have come close to a very real reality: "One can tell how much we need him to live, and how deeply the regent is hated, by the way everyone worries about his health, for, as to himself, we have yet no reason to love or hate him."

Summed up in one succinct sentence was a prophecy for any king, especially one so young who had yet to please or displease his subjects. It was a precarious position. This "let's wait and see if we like him or not" attitude would leave one fearing a misstep or a reign that proved unpopular. While this would not affect Louis XV to any great degree, it cost his successor and the queen their lives.

Louis XV had reached puberty earlier than most youths and therefore it was advised to get him "breeding" as soon as possible. The royal blood line had been seriously depleted with so many sudden deaths. Those who feared the regent, the duc d'Orleans, taking the throne should something happen to the new king, wanted him to sire a son as soon as he had reached the age to claim his crown.

Due to a ping-pong style short-lived war with Spain, where Philip V was trying to indulge his second wife's greed for more property, France prevailed and alliances were made, linking France, Spain, and Great Britain. One of the results of this alliance was, as usual, political marriages. One of the regent's daughters was betrothed to the Prince of Asturias, the Spanish Heir Apparent, while the Spanish infanta was sent to France as a wife for Louis XV. They met in March of 1722. There was one hitch: Mariana Victoria of Spain, the infanta, was only five years old.

While this hiccup was being discussed, another drama was playing out. Villeroy was doing everything in his power as governor to keep the regent from having any private audience with the king at all. Repeatedly, Orleans had tried to wrangle time alone with Louis, but was thwarted at each turn by Villeroy's insistence in being in attendance. Many who hated Orleans, and who were still positing the claim that the regent would one day poison the youth to claim the throne, gathered around Villeroy with their support. It came to such a head, that in a surprise move, the regent decided it was time to take Louis XV to the home from which he would rule for the rest of his life: Versailles. This would remove Villeroy from his Parisian nest of supporters. All the regent would give as his explanation for the move was that it would afford the king the pleasures of the hunt, fresher air than the polluted fumes of Paris, and better security than a court in the midst of the capital could afford.

And so, on June 15, 1722, at the age of twelve, Louis XV was led to his new quarters at the massive chateau of his great-grandfather. The very next day, his happiness at being there was making the scribes quills quiver: "The King is very fond of Versailles, so fond, in fact, that it has been decided to leave him there all winter," Marais wrote. Three weeks later: "The King is in splendid health; he goes up [probably referring to the massive staircases], he comes down, he runs, he walks and is becoming healthier-looking and stronger." The old duchess d'Orleans commented a week later, "Our King is a very handsome and very pleasant young man, but he is too silent. When he doesn't know people intimately, one can get nothing out of him."

Louis was growing into a tall and robust young man, with a built-in distrust for flattery and the forced attentions of the court, who had followed him to Versailles. Where Louis XIV had craved the attention of the nobles and their subservience, his great-grandson wished only to be left alone.

The Palace of Versailles had always been home to intrigues. Within weeks of moving into his new home, the king was privy to his first taste of the debaucheries of the court. At the end of July 1722, with Louis' succession to the crown only six months away, a scandal erupted at the Court of Versailles that would have long-reaching implications. Villeroy's granddaughter was the source of the more scandalous affront. Marias was on hand to give out the details concerning the new Court of Louis XV: "They live in the most open debauchery at Versailles," Marias reported. "The Princes have declared mistresses, politeness, manners and good order are a thing of the past… The maréchal de Villeroy has been pained to learn that the duchesse de Retz, his granddaughter, has had lovers of every social condition since she's been at Versailles... She tried to seduce the King himself… and attempted to handle him in a very hidden place. Upon which the maréchal exploded with anger against the duchesse and sent her away from Court on the spot… There are also orgies of young gentlemen together which they don't bother to conceal."

To make matters worse, one of Villeroy's grandsons was accused of trying to rape a young man in the seclusion of a nearby wood. Louis XV, who had reached puberty, was now within the proximity of all this wanton sex. The regent feared what might happen if the young man were to be brought into homosexual encounters, or other affairs that could affect his marriage and the siring of heirs. The fact that two of Villeroy's grandchildren had been involved in such inappropriate behavior was all the fodder Orleans needed to rid himself of his enemy.

The regent had the governor arrested on August 10, 1722. The two grandchildren who had been accused of their individual acts of debauchery were exiled from court, along with two other young nobles who had taken part in the rape of the young duke. When Louis XV asked why all these young noblemen had been exiled, he was told they had been caught tearing down railings in the park. When the king heard Villeroy had been arrested, he was deeply affected. The governor had become a large part of his life, and as he matured, he had learned to like the man. The greatest hit came next. Bishop Fréjus, who had pronounced that should Villeroy ever be asked to leave, he would have to leave as well, was now forced to honor that pledge and Fleury disappeared.

Marais penned Louis XV's reaction to both of the sudden voids in his life: "As soon as he heard, the King blushed; his eyes grew moist; he hid his face against the back of an armchair, without saying a word, and would neither go out nor play. He barely ate a few mouthfuls at supper, cried and stayed awake all night. The next morning and dinnertime that day were hardly marked by any improvements…The King's tears had been much increased by the absence of M. de Fréjus, who had disappeared."

Villeroy was replaced by a weak, yet honest man—the duc de Charost. Louis ordered the return of Fleury, who was all too happy to comply. The regent and the bishop were the only two anchors to which the young man could cling. As if there had not been enough change, the hated abbé Dubois was made cardinal, and then achieved the post he had so coveted: he became the prime minister.

Fleury continued to teach his young pupil, reinforcing good morals, tempered behavior and suspicion of anyone seeking favor from the king through flattery and manipulation. Cardinal Dubois now began his part in readying the young man to become king. The duc d Villars noted, "Cardinal Dubois had become accustomed to coming in with the regent at the end of the King's morning study period, and, in the presence of M. le Duc [Bourbon], de Charost and the Bishop of Fréjus, he would bring in a memorandum which it would only take him a little over fifteen minutes to read. The memoranda contained brief instructions to start informing the king of several details regarding the Army, the finances, and the current negotiations. From the beginning of the year, the regent, after the evening study period, would come in alone. Everyone withdrew and gave the King information without any witnesses."

### "Long Live the King!"

On October 25, 1722, Louis XV was crowned King of France in the Gothic cathedral of Reims. Fleury, who stood in for the Bishop of Noyon, carried the monarch's sword belt. There had not been a coronation for three quarters of a century, thanks to the long reign of Louis XIV. The ceremony was a bit unorganized, yet grand. The shy young King was anointed with the holy chrism that noted his divine representation of heaven, and then he was crowned. He was now the chosen of God and King of France at the age of thirteen.

On February 16, 1723, before the assembled Parlement, a *lit de justice* was called to declare the King of age. The Regency was now at an end. The statement "on the advice of our uncle the Regent" was dropped from future official acts. The Council of the Regency now became the King's Council, which was headed by the duc d'Orleans (the former regent) while Dubois remained prime minister. The rest of the Council included the duc de Chartres [Orleans' son], the duc de Bourbon as First Prince of the Blood, and in an unprecedented move, Fleury was added to the board. No tutor had ever been included in the body of government before.

The Coronation of Louis XV

On August 10, 1723, the Cardinal Dubois suddenly died of a syphilitic infection. Perhaps a life of orgies had exacted their toll on the cardinal. Before his body was cold, Orleans hurried to the king and asked to take over Dubois' vacated post as prime minister. Without hesitation, Louis granted him the prestigious title. His haste in nabbing the office for himself was perhaps from fear that M. le Duc would beat him to it.

As it turned out, all the maneuvering and stratagems came to naught. On December 1, 1723, the duc d'Orleans was sitting by the fireplace of his drawing room at Versailles. He seemed to be in a depressed mood and asked the duchesse de Falaris to amuse him with some titillating piece of court gossip. She had only begun when the duke suddenly fell forward. She fled from the room in a panic, screaming for someone to help her. The doctors arrived within minutes, but it was too late. The forty-nine-year-old uncle of the king was dying. They stretched him out on the floor before the fireplace. He died soon after.

Louis mourned with a sadness few around him shared. Philippe, the duc d'Orleans had been more than a regent to the young King; he was the son of Louis XIV's only brother, and therefore, his uncle. When all he saw was the death of family members, Orleans had been a true relation and one who had shown him great love and respect. It came as no surprise that the great Hall of Versailles resounded with the sound of platform shoes hurrying toward the private apartment of the king. It was M. le Duc, panting and perspiring who burst in upon Louis and asked for the appointment of prime minister.

If the thirteen-year-old king was repulsed by the obvious greed of this twenty-one-year-old First Prince of the Blood (just after the duc de Chartres), we don't know. Upon the death of Orleans, the duc de Chartres became the new duc d'Orleans. Louis tried to keep up with the changing faces about him. As for the late uncle, "The King, who felt deeply his unchanging respect, his attempt to please him, his manner of speaking to him and working with him, mourned him and was truly moved by his loss, so much that he has only spoken of him since then… with esteem, affection and regret." As for the new duc d'Orleans, he may not have been a likely contender for his father's office. He was overweight and slow-witted, and incapable of running a government. He bragged of his cousinship to the king but lacked ambition of any kind.

And so, M. le Duc became the new prime minister, and Fleury remained close by. M. le Duc awarded Fleury the authority to dispense all French ecclesiastic preferments, which meant, no archbishop, bishopric, or abbey could be given without the consent of Fleury. It may have seemed to some a generous gift from a duke who had once tried to move Fleury to Reims. With this new gift of power, the Bishop of Fréjus was now the second most-powerful man in France after Louis XV and the prime minister. The Church played a major role in the life of the French people. The king used its benefices to reward not only clerics but also members of the Royal Family. Fleury's luck continued as he was admitted to a Secret Council composed of the king, the duc de Bourbon, and the old maréchal de Villars. All the years of steadfast loyalty to the king had paid off for Fleury. He had always been there, and he had the king's trust and affection—two things no other could claim. And though the apartments of Versailles were redistributed, and M. le Duc took over the regent's rooms just below the king's apartments, this young monarch was not naïve to the machinations going on around him. To underestimate Louis XV, at any age, was a foolish risk.

M. le Duc, acting as Prime Minister, was the opposite of his predecessor. Where Orleans had been kind, M. le Duc (Chartres) used force. Ever since the War of Succession had ended, Paris had been deluged with beggars. It was a scourge to those trying to navigate the streets of Paris without being accosted by someone begging for food and money. Chartres' answer to this was to have them all arrested and put into workhouses where there was no food, heat, or bedding. The result was that they died. He inflicted the death penalty on anyone caught stealing, no matter the amount. In this same edict of March 4, 1724, he went after the Protestants, and instated sever penalties on anyone not conforming to the Catholic Church precepts. The prime minister rewarded his supporters with offices at court that carried with them pensions, which raised the public expenditure and the taxes.

To be fair, M. le Duc did reform the prison system, increasing the care of the prisoners. A stock market was founded in Paris and a new canal was begun to link the Somme and Oise Rivers. To cut salaries, he abolished the office of Governor, with the exemption of a dozen major cities, along with a large number of municipality offices and around 100 secretaries to the king. Most cities were given back the right to elect their own mayors and municipal councils. It was a start, but for the unpopular M. le Duc, it was still not enough. He remained all-powerful as prime minister, but the king could dismiss him at will. There had to be a way to get closer to the king, without Fleury sidelining him. He went for the obvious.

Louis XV's love of the hunt was well known throughout France. It was a passion that the young king indulged at every given chance. Even in the winter when the ground was hard, he rode indoors. M. le Duc saw a way to get close to the king through his love of riding, and presumably, through the common love of women all men at Versailles encompassed. He offered the setting of his Chantilly estate and invited a bevy of willing young women to attend. He and his mistress, Mme de Prie (whom the king loathed), put the fete together. Presenting the king with a possible mistress offered the prime minister one more avenue to Louis, and he hoped the romp at Chantilly would do just that. With Chantilly's excellent hunting, the king agreed to go there for a month, and of course, the court went with him.

To say the "Court" went with the King was no mere entourage. It was reported that in 1722, Narbonne, the police commissioner at Versailles, counted 8,254 heads, including 4,000 said to be living inside the palace proper! As there were only 364 lodgings offered at that time at the palace, we can see a lot of families crowding in together! How many of that Court went with Louis to Chantilly, we don't know, but we can assume the cost of the month-long party was astronomical!

Chateau de Chantilly, the Conde's grand estate

Mme de Prie was suspicious of Louis' acquiescence when the invitation was extended. He already had the reputation of being highly secretive. The hunting trip was just a guise for the real purpose of the party—to hook up the young king with a mistress that could be manipulated by M. le Duc and possibly report back with State secrets divulged during pillow talk. If Mme de Prie thought she was being crafty, it seemed Paris was way ahead of her. A ribald song of which the *bourgeoise* were so fond, made its way around the city: "Margot the seamstress said to her lover, 'What's the use of strumpets they take to Chantilly?' 'What, for one virgin must they send a whole troupe of seventeen whores?'"

The "whores" were actually nobles in their fanciest dress, all hoping to seduce the king. Louis was now fourteen-and-a-half, and with his height and well-formed body, looked older. It was to the dismay of M. le Duc and Mme de Pried, and to the delight of Fleury, that the well-hatched plan fell through. Paris was already abuzz with the gossip. Barbier noted, "The main purpose of the trip to Chantilly has apparently failed. The King does nothing but hunt and does not want to try [intimacy]…" Louis's abstinence could be the result of his shyness, or his anger at the obvious plot, or the knowledge that any of his sexual exploits would soon be all over France. Whether one or all of these reasons, he cut the visit short. The death of the duc de Chatillon by an enraged stag had put a damper on all the festivities. No number of fireworks, hunts, banquets or entertainment would prompt the king to stay.

In a last-ditch effort to woo the king, Prie convinced her lover, the prime minister, to move the court to Fontainebleau in October and November for the good hunting. Learning her lesson, she planned not a single ball, only hunting, music, and gambling. Louis attended and it seemed to work. He became cordial to the couple, and they relaxed. But they were not finished with their scheming. If the young king could not be tempted with a mistress, well then, a queen must be provided, and they set off to find one.

## Chapter Thirty-Seven
## **Marriage, Ministers, and Mistrust**

The summer of 1724 saw an unusual revolution of young females coming and going beneath Louis XV's radar. There were behind-the-scenes manipulations, as well as those right before his eyes. It was time to find the king a wife, young though he might be. Producing an heir was critical. No one was more cognizant of the ramifications of securing the right bride than M. le Duc. He and his mistress, Mme de Prie had already hatched a plan. Why not offer up one of the duke's own daughters? There were three to choose from.

One small problem—Louis was formally engaged to the now seven-year-old infanta of Spain, who had been waiting in the wings for two years. The King of Spain, Philip V, was pressuring M. le Duc to have the marriage formally declared. M. le Duc looked at the cards laid out on the table and pondered the choices.

If he broke the engagement with the young infanta, it would provoke a major meltdown with Spain. The little girl was far too young to marry, let alone bear children, and if the King were to die before an heir was born, the crown would go to the duc d'Orleans; a thought that made many shudder. Due to the animosity between the Orleans' clan and the Bourbons, M. le Duc could count on a life in exile.

The campaign to find a replacement for the little infanta began and she was sent back to Madrid. If she was to be sent back to Spain, it needed to be because an older candidate was found that was of childbearing age. Surely, the King of Spain would understand that. Names were put into the hat: Mlle de Vermandois, one of M. le Duc's sisters (currently living a pious life in a convent), and his other two sisters, who were not so pure of heart and body, were proposed.

Before these three ladies could be considered, Fleury interfered and stated under no uncertain terms would Louis marry into the Bourbon-Condé branch of the Royal Family. Louis still trusted the bishop, even though he was no longer his tutor, and the prime minister backed off. Next, Mme de Prie proposed the Grand Duchess Elizabeth of Russia, but her rank was not sufficient for the role of Queen of France. Her father was Peter the Great, but her mother had begun life as a prostitute.

As the net for a queen for Louis was cast far and wide, the king suddenly came down with another of his severe bouts with indigestion. While he recovered quickly, it only escalated the duke's fear of something happening to Louis before an heir was in place. The search for the right lady continued in earnest. New princesses were put under the glass, including George I's daughter, but she was Protestant; a princess of Savoy, who was Louis V's first cousin, but she too proved unsuitable due to her father's alliance with the Habsburgs; the Princess of Hess-Rheinfels was a "No," and so the search continued.

Marie Leszcznska, the daughter of Stanislas, the dethroned King of Poland, was eagerly proposed by Mme de Prie. She was twenty-one, six years older than Louis who had turned fifteen in 1725. The lady was pious, kind, and had high morals. The downside was that she was rather dowdy, plain, and not the brightest candle in the candelabra. Her father, the past king, came from one of the best families in Poland and was related to the Sobieskis, who often held positions on the throne. Now, as a dethroned king, Stanislas and his family were living in poor economic conditions and a marriage between their daughter and the King of France would be a Godsend. Obviously, Mme de Prie could see her future in glowing tones if Marie were accepted, as the young princess would be forever grateful to her for championing her for the French throne. Being buddies with the queen came with many perks.

It was decided, Marie Leszczynska was it! A messenger was dispatched to Wissembourg with the good news. On May 27, 1725, the declaration of a wedding was made public. By June, the ladies of the Queen's Household were named. To no one's surprise, M. le Duc got one of his sisters in the door after all. Mlle de Clermont was made *surintendante*; the duchesse de Boufflers was made *dame d'honneur*, despite her reputation for a plethora of lovers and being affiliated with the Bourbon branch. Mme de Prie wormed her way in as one of the ladies-in-waiting, along with her close friends, the duchesse de Villars, the marquises de Nesle, de Ruppelmonde, de Matignon, and the Comtesse d'Egmont. Joseph Pâris-Duverney was elected as the new queen's private secretary.

The court and general public were not generous in their response to the selection of Marie Leszczynska. Not only was her appearance nothing to brag about, but she was a penniless Polish princess without a throne. Nevertheless, the wedding was set to take place on September 5$^{th}$. Back in Wissembourg, the ex-King of Poland fell to his knees and praised God when he heard his daughter was to be the next Queen of France. After thanking the deity repeatedly, he then proceeded to gush over the lady who had made it all possible—Mme de Prie.

In only a matter of days, the Leszczyńska's were taken to Strasbourg. The young princess, who had known the struggles of poverty only days before, was now inundated with boxes of fancy brocade dresses, the finest lace and silk, furs, and jewels. It was a fairytale. A marriage by procuration would occur, as was usual with royal marriages where someone was chosen to stand in for the king before the official ceremony would be performed at Fontainebleau. As if to rub salt into the wound, the duc d'Orleans was chosen to fulfill the role of proxy. Off the disgruntled Orleans went, leading a dozen golden carriages and surrounded by a military escort. And where was Mme de Prie? Way ahead of them.

The wily de Prie was already ensconced with the queen-to-be and had been there since May. She had personally carried the king's gifts to Marie herself at Wissembourg. She remained, supervising the trousseau, instructing the new queen on how the etiquette at Versailles' Court worked, basically taking over the naïve and slow-witted princess's life. And for this, Marie was effusive in her gratitude. Her father had reminded her often that she owed this miraculous marriage to the efforts of de Prie.

When the duc d'Orleans finally arrived, pudgy and pouting, all Marie saw was an entourage of glittering coaches, jewels, and dignitaries. Men in regal regalia doffed their plumed hats and bowed to her. It must have been a surreal moment. It continued as the marriage by procuration was celebrated in an elaborately decorated cathedral, followed by the parade of the golden carriages heading to

Fontainebleau for the official wedding. They stopped at every town where they were wined and dined, speeches made, and fireworks launched. It was merely the prologue of what was to come as the prancing horses entered the courtyard at Fontainebleau. A bevy of jeweled beauties and handsome nobles greeted her, jostling for position to get a look at the lady chosen to be their Queen. There were the usual catty remarks made by the powdered and rouged lovelies who let their eyes travel over every inch of the Polish Princess. It is rumored that one remarked it was obvious "the only cosmetic the pale woman had ever known was snow." Welcome to the Court of Louis XV!

The Wedding of Louis XV and Marie Leszczyzńka

Louis XV greeted his new bride. He was tall, handsome, and composed. There is no mention as to what he thought of her initially.

The ceremony took place without delay. According to Chevalier Daudet, Marie wore "a royal cape of purple velvet, held by gold fleur-de-lys, bordered and lined with ermine; her skirt was of the same material, with the bodice and the front of the skirt covered with precious stones and clasps made of the rarest diamonds... On her head she carried a diamond crown... The King was in gold brocade enriched with diamonds and precious stones, a cloak covered with gold embroidery, a white plume and a huge diamond in his hat."

Marie Leszczyzńska, the Queen of France

After the wedding, the newlyweds were honored at a huge banquet followed by a grand display of fireworks. The festivities lasted into the night, but it was finally time for the bedding ceremony. As the doors to the royal couple's bedchamber finally closed, it must have been an awkward moment for a virgin king and queen; both professed to shyness and neither knowing what to expect. The courtiers may very well have been listening outside the door. The

French Court was never shy about sex, and the king's sex life was often the topic of conversation. The following morning, it was announced that, not only had the evening been a success, but that Louis had "honored his wife seven times!" Whether or not that is to be believed, we do know that Louis found something he enjoyed as much, if not more so, as hunting! He slept with his new queen every night, eager to give siring an heir "another go."

M. le Duc, Mme de Prie, and indeed the rest of France waited with bated breath for news of a pregnancy. It was still early days, and while Louis seemed happy with the intimate part of his marriage, he soon realized that his wife had no interest in…anything. She was extremely pious, shunned frivolity, liked neither the hunt nor the theater, and looked with horror at the thought of hosting some gala or loud supper party. Her only interests seemed to be in trying to master a variety of musical instruments, resulting in sounds coming from her apartments resembling the torture of small animals. Chatting with her ladies-in-waiting or playing a tame game of cards were her daily routines. It was clear this lady would never be any kind of political threat to the throne—she lacked the brains and ambition to stage any coup against the king. For that, Fleury was grateful.

Fleury remained close to Louis. He had agreed to the marriage, and as his reward, M. le Duc offered him a prestigious court appointment, that of Almoner to the Queen. The bishop was no longer the king's tutor, and this post helped to fill that void. Smelling a rat, Fleury turned it down. M. le Duc kept after him to accept, and finally, he gave in, on the understanding that he was opposed to pretty much every other appointment to Marie's Household. He came down especially hard on le Duc's mistress, Mme de Prie, telling the prime minister he did not feel she was fit to attend Her Majesty. M. le Duc ignored him. Fleury decided to bide his time, stick close to the king, and live for the day the prime minister would be gone from court.

In June 1725, Louis held a *lit de justice* to impose the registration of a 2 percent tax on most incomes. The Clergy were not included in that edict, and as that body was comprised of three quarters of the nobility, the peasants once again felt the sting of it. When in July, a pitiful crop production hit the lower class, widespread riots ensued. The outcry and starvation were so vast, that an Assembly of the

Clergy appealed to the king to withdraw the new tax. M. le Duc stepped in and rather than help the stricken population, he abolished the Assembly instead. Louis, who had not yet found his voice, let it go.

Fleury continued to press for the release of Mme de Prie and added the queen's private secretary, Joseph Pâris-Duverney to the list. Mme de Prie was detested throughout France, and true to form, the downtrodden people took to verse to show their displeasure. Fishwives and merchants could be heard bellowing: "De Prie is clever, the Queen docile, the King too easygoing, Le Duc an imbecile!" M. le Duc, seeing now that Fleury had to go, closeted himself with Mme de Prie to come up with a plan. This one was to involve the new queen.

Only twelve days after the royal marriage, M. le Duc and Mme de Prie called in their bargaining chip. The prime minister could never get the king alone without the Bishop Fleury being there, so they went to Marie and asked her for a favor. The English Ambassador takes up the tale: "On Monday, in the evening," he reported, "as soon as Her Majesty had notice of the King's return from hunting, she quitted her cards and desired to speak to him in the closet [her private study]...The Queen took that opportunity, in the presence of M. le Duc, to press him most earnestly, and in the most insinuating and flattering ways possible to do business with M. le Duc alone, that night; which he would by no means consent to, notwithstanding her repeated instances for above an hour, when His Majesty said he must got to the Bishop."

The scheme had backfired dismally. Here it was! All that Fleury had warned his young pupil about. Flattery for the purpose of advancing one's own goals. And it had come at the hands of his new wife and his prime minister. Louis was furious. He went straight to Fleury and told him of the clandestine trap. Fleury, never one to be incited to rash decisions, took it all in. It was obvious the prime minister was angling to get the king alone in an effort to rid himself of the bishop who held so much power over the teenaged monarch. He could have taken the moment to press for the removal of his enemy, but he wasn't ready to assume the role of prime minister for himself, nor take on the backlash from the duke's powerful family should he be suddenly exiled. Instead, he calmly advised the king to return to his queen (after Louis threatened to never see her again), and to retain the prime minister.

In a clever move no one saw coming, the following morning while the King was out hunting, Fleury played his trump card. He wrote a letter to Louis stating he had decided to retire from court in order to avoid further conflict and stress for the king. He left for his country house in Issy (just outside Paris). While M. le Duc celebrated the sudden absence of his advisory, Fleury sat before crackling fire of his cozy home as a storm rattled the windows. He smiled. Without a doubt, he knew this move would force the king to realize just how important he was to him, making Louis all the more cognizant that M. le Duc was nothing but divisive in his court.

When Louis returned from hunting, he was handed the letter from Fleury. Only one floor up from M. le Duc's apartments, the King went to his bedroom, and then to where his *chaise percée* was kept (the only place where he could find privacy), where he remained for over an hour. As the court began to worry about the King's absence, the duc de Mortemart, the First Gentleman of the Bedchamber opened the door to the toilet and told the King he felt he should order M. le Duc to recall Fleury to court. That the valet took it upon himself to burst in upon the king while he sat upon his toilet shows not only the precedence this post took over other members of the King's Household, but that he understood the situation was grave. Louis, looking grateful, asked the duke if he would go to the prime minister and give him that message, which Mortemart did.

The *chaise percée* of Louis XV

Realizing he had underestimated Fleury and was in danger of being kicked out, M. le Duc drafted a letter to Fleury which was sent by messenger to Issy: "Your letter, Monsieur, has surprised me to a degree I can hardly express. The King desires your return and orders me to tell you that he wants you back. Having no time to say anymore, I will wait until the first time we meet again and limit myself to carrying out His Majesty's orders." The sound ringing in M. le Duc's ears was that of the gauntlet Fleury had thrown down. He was now more irreplaceable than ever, and the prime minister knew it.

As for the queen, she was caught in the middle between her loyalty to the king, and her appreciation to M. le Duc and Mme de Prie for getting her the crown. A more astute woman would have realized the choice was not a hard one, but she anguished on. Louis was now angry at her for trying to manipulate him and more infuriated at M. le Duc for using his wife to advance his cause. Perhaps it reminded Louis of his younger days when the duke treated him with casual disregard, like a child to be indulged. He had not forgotten the lack of respect le Duc showed to him when his uncle was still regent. Now, to bring in a woman to manipulate him into doing something he did not want to do, was the last straw.

As for Mme de Prie, the king snubbed her entirely. In a court where His Majesty's every nod, smile, and indifference is noted as favor or disfavor, it was an embarrassing position in which to be. The gossip flew. The court waited, believing the dismissal of the prime minister and his mistress was only days away. Meanwhile, the in fatigable court went on gambling, partying, and feasting. The card playing and betting took on new proportions. It was reported the king and queen lost 200,000 livres ($900,000) in two months' time. Marie Leszczynska was put on the sidelines by her husband. He still slept with her at night, anxious to father an heir, but otherwise, he distanced himself from her. He found her boring and plain, and her partnering with the prime minister behind his back was still uppermost in his mind. He would go off to La Muette and hunt, taking along a small group of people. M. le Duc continued to govern France but within the range of Fleury's influence.

M. le Duc, feeling the king's hostility toward him daily, finally gave in and asked to be released from his post as prime minister. Louis, taking a sudden unexpected turn, denied the request and actually began to treat the duke with warmth and friendship. The king even invited the prime minister to join him at Rambouillet, the residence of the comtesse de Toulouse, where he had been invited to hunt and dine that evening. Looking surprised and relieved, M. le Duc thanked him and said he would be along shortly, that he had some work to finish. As Louis stepped into his coach, he said affably, "Hurry up and finish your business, then, and come early to Rambouillet, as I intend to have supper at eighty-thirty…Don't keep me waiting at supper."

At eight o'clock that evening, the prime minister walked to his coach to follow the king, as invited. Suddenly, the duc de Charost, the Captain of the Guard, asked M. le Duc to follow him. He then whispered something into the prime minister's ear and handed him a letter. After reading it, the arrogant Duke seemed deflated and simply said, "Accustomed as I am to command everyone's obedience to the King, I will now offer up myself as an example of this same obedience." He asked to be allowed to burn some papers and was shortly put into a carriage under guard. The letter handed to him had been from the king. It read: "Mon cousin, as I desire to govern by myself in the future, I am abolishing the post of prime minister; I thank you for the care you have taken of my affairs and order you, on pains of disobedience, to go to Chantilly and stay there until I command you otherwise. I forbid you to see the Queen."

Conflicted as to her loyalties, Marie called in Mme de Prie to break the bad news that M. le Duc had been banished to his chateau at Chantilly. It was perhaps a bit naïve of the queen to think the duke's mistress didn't already know. Louis had Fleury deliver a letter to the queen during her supper that evening, instructing her to obey Fleury's orders that she was not to communicate with the ex-prime minister from that day forward. The letter had gone on to say that Mme de Prie was to be removed from Versailles and that she could not keep the duke company at Chantilly. The duke's mistress was instead sent off to her castle Courbépine in Normandy. The queen cried for three days over the exile of the duke and de Prie. Louis continued to distance himself from her.

If the scene played out by the sixteen-year-old king when he blindsided the prime minister sounds familiar, it is eerily reminiscent of the subterfuge Louis XIV used when he caught Fouquet unaware and had him arrested after playing up to the money-embezzling Superintendent. While M. le Duc was not stealing money from the Royal Treasury, he had been plotting against Fleury. Both Kings chose to pretend friendship just before the axe fell. Cowardly, manipulative, vengeful, or shrewd? The bottom line was that the trap was sprung both times when the arrogant ministers of the King's Court thought they were untouchable.

On June 13, Louis XV wrote to his cousin the Elector of Bavaria. "Having decided to take the government of my realm in hand, I have abolished the post of prime minister, while at the same time admitting to the knowledge of the most particular business and to my most intimate confidence the former Bishop of Fréjus [Fleury], who, ever since my earliest youth, has given me proof of his zeal and attachment to my person… This new disposition will entail no change in the general conduct of business…I want to follow the example of the late King, my great-grandfather, in every way." The new Council now consisted of d'Aguesseau as Chancellor; Le Péletier des Forts as Controller General of Finances; Le Blanc—War; Saint Florentine as head of the Navy and Royal Household; Maurepas as head of Church Affairs and Fluery was Minister of State.

The changing of the guard reached the ears of Paris. Unlike their usual inclination to complain or compose some ribald ditty in protest, the general population seemed pleased. M. le Duc had been universally loathed, as had his mistress, de Prie. They were beginning to see signs of a strong king—a teenager though he may still be. The subjects in Paris lit bonfires in the street to celebrate; something that probably did not go without notice at the nearby chateau of Chantilly.

Barbier was quick to print the king's response to the new structure: "The King, like the man he is, has made a speech at the first council held since the exile M. le Duc. He declared that what he had done in no way lessened the friendship he felt for his cousin, but that he was pleased to put things back in the same condition as during the reign of Louis XIV… that people should now speak to him directly about any favor and that his ministers would work with him accordingly to a regular schedule, in the presence of the former Bishop of Fréjus, who will be there for everything."

Fleury had acquired, in essence the role of prime minister without the title. He was also given the postal service. Just as in Louis XIV's day, there was a *cabinet noir*, or secret police who opened and copied any letters of interest. This gave him a special keyhole through which to view any potential plots or intrigues at court. When he was ordained a cardinal on September 11, his power was complete. From then on, he had a public *coucher* just like the king where his evening undressing was open to special entrees.

Fleury was tutoring the young king as surely as if he was still his pupil. Louis learned a lot about government. Fleury also taught him that no war was worth the cost. The new cardinal set about to balance the budget. The 2 percent tax was abolished, and the currency was refined: a standard gold coin, the *louis*, was now worth twenty-four *livres*; the silver *écu* was the equivalent of three *livres*. With the stabilization of currency, trade began to flourish. The cardinal set an example for bringing down costs by living modestly himself. Unlike Richelieu and Mazarin, he lived off the income he received from two abbeys. While still offering the ceremonies for which Versailles was famous, he cut back on the things that he did not feel were necessary, such as the cascade at Marly due to the cost to run it.

Fleury continued to improve the conditions of Louis XV's realm. The roads had become a sorry state and he set about having them fixed and new ones built, thus improving the speed and safety of trade routes to the palace. He reduced the Navy yet increased the merchant marine from 300 to 1,800 ships for commercial trade. Goods were taxed, hence, the improvement of the roads and increase in shipping added to France's coffers. As France was not at war, and due to its alliance with England, it didn't appear to be a candidate for one in the foreseeable future, the Army's soldiers were reduced from 150,000 to 100,000 men—again cutting immense cost. Thanks to the *Treaty of Utrecht* by the great Sun King, peace had been enjoyed for a relatively long stretch of time. There were other factors to thank for the lack of warfare: Spain was dependent on France, thanks to a recent war; Leopold I of Habsburg was drowning in debt; Sweden had lost its war with Russia and wanted peaceful times; Italy had been divided up to the extent that it was not much of a military threat; and Prussia was allied to France and Great Britain, which kept Germany stable by providing a threat to Austria's flank.

At Versailles, peace also reigned, as much as it was possible in a

Court built upon rivalry and scandal. The divisive tactics of M. le Duc were gone. Louis began to enjoy himself. He attended dinner parties at the Comtesse de Toulouse at Rambouillet, hosted his own at La Muett and Choisy, hunted, and began to feel like a king. At this time, a great shift had also occurred in the culture of Europe. There was an awakening of creativity and self-expression, which Louis whole-heartedly supported. Louis XIV had set the stage during his reign with new advances in architecture, décor, and art. The Gobelin Factory rivaled the once-unchallenged genius of Italian craftsmen. His Petit Gallery housed such works as the Mona Lisa and works by Bernini, Titian, and Veronese. His gardens with their symmetry and fountains, were being copied all over Europe. Now, Louis XV jumped into the cultural scene with both feet, patronizing such artists as Antoine Gaudreaux, who created a remarkable medal chest for the King in 1728 that can still be seen at Versailles. It was for Louis' study and was a marvel of inlaid woods, and sculpted gilt bronzes, all in the rococo style.

Medal Chest created for Louis XV by Antoine Gaudreaux.

Like his great-grandfather, he surrounded himself with the great painters of the era. Where Le Brun had been the Sun King's go-to, Louis XV was fond of John Baptiste Oudry, who was a master of depicting animals and the hunt. Other artists such as Nicholas Lancret and John Baptiste Joseph Pater also found favor. To be endorsed by the king was to have arrived. There was no end of craftsmen offering their talents to the king. Only a few were chosen.

The young king flourished, with no small thanks to the efforts of his capable sidekick, Fleury. Daily, it was noticed that his confidence grew. While he would remain secretive and introverted throughout his reign, he was coming into his own. He was emulating the great Louis XIV's pattern of running the State, which no doubt gave him the confidence that he was on the right track. But he was also falling into the pitfalls his great-grandfather had found out too late—Versailles was insulated, and its false façade of gilt and pomp were not the realities that faced the everyday citizen of Paris. He was removed from his subjects' travails, other than what was reported to him second-hand. The consequences had not yet reared their ugly head, but it was coming.

Meanwhile, as 1727 loomed on the horizon, Louis had much to be proud of. His newly felt confidence could be seen in his tall, florid handwriting. In an era, rife with misspelled words, the King excelled in his grammar, a lesson well-learned at the knees of his governors.

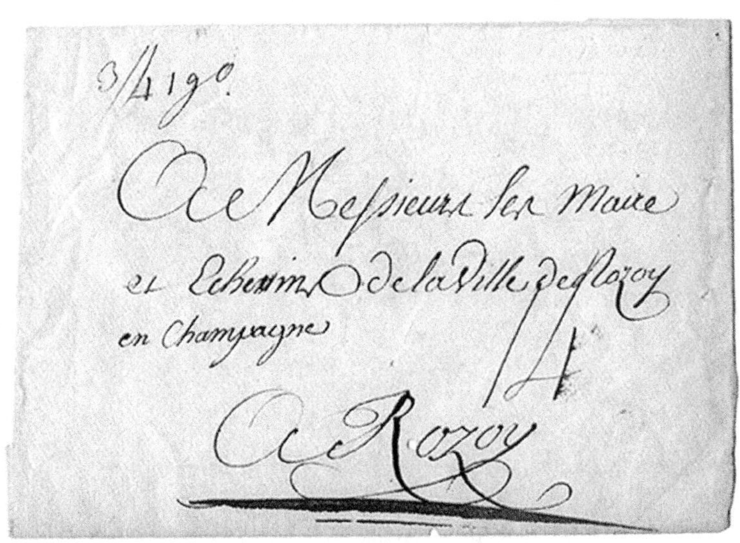
A Messieurs les Maire
et Echevins de la Ville de Rozoy
en Champagne
14
A Rozoy

Handwriting sample of Louis XV

The beginning of 1727 brought the news the entire country had been waiting for. Fleury had convinced the King to forgive his wife for her interference in the contrivances of M. le Duc and Louis had favored her bedchamber once more. The marriage was still a dull and uninspired one, but Marie accomplished the part for which she was brought to the court to fulfill—she was pregnant.

# Chapter Thirty-Eight
# Versailles—Meet Louis XV!

Louis XV began 1727 as a seventeen-year-old absolute monarch who had banished his foes from court, created (via Fleury) a new system of economics, and had now fathered a child. For a youth living beneath the formidable shadow of Louis XIV, it was not a bad start. The shadow of the former king was forever looming over him. Symbols of the Sun King were everywhere: adorning the gates, Salons, and the Hall of Mirrors. The God Apollo, with whom Louis XIV aligned himself, roared up from the great fountain at the end of the *tapis verte*. It may have been a wish to emulate the conqueror of Europe by copying his policies and etiquette. One area in which this Louis would upstage his predecessor was in fathering children.

Marie Leszczyńska had done her duty. She had delivered not just one child, but two twin girls. While it was not an heir to the throne, Louis was thrilled to be a father. This orphan was anxious to have a family of his own. This one act changed his feelings toward her. She had earned his lasting affection and he shunned all beds but hers; something unheard of for a French monarch. He was entertained by his female cousins, Mlle de Clermont and the Comtesse de Toulouse at their estates, and he found great pleasure in their witty company. He felt relaxed in their homes, away from the temptations and machinations of the unsavory goings-on at court, and he remained true to his Queen.

This is one case where Marie may have wished for his absence from her bedchamber. The sexually enthusiastic king kept her pregnant for a decade. In ten years' time, the queen gave birth to ten children: 8 girls and 2 boys. She was literally delivering a baby each year. She was exhausted. Rather than risk another pregnancy, she hit upon a plan to delay the king's visits. According to Lisa Hilton, a biographer in the documentary *The Rise and Fall of Versailles*, she the queen, being very pious, began telling Louis that he could not come into her bedchamber on certain Saint's Days. "The Saint's Days became more frequent," according to Hilton, "and the Saints became increasingly obscure." It was this refusal of sex that turned the once virtuous king onto a course of endless affairs.

Before the mistresses began lining up, Louis worked hard. He met daily with his minister and made sure to oversee the actual running of his government. A torrent of documents found their way across his desk daily, and he read them all, initialing where it was required. These forms ran the gambit from complicated foreign affairs to the maintaining of structures. It was his handwritten letter with his signature that went out to foreign leaders. Lastly, he kept a close eye on the treasury. From the larger payouts to the money spent on the court's daily expenses, nothing was paid out without Louis' autograph *bon* ("good") in the margin.

The king kept a keen eye on the debt owed. Perhaps not wanting to go the way of his great-grandfather, who had left France 2 billion *livers* in debt at the time of his death, Louis tried to keep up with what was an avalanche of expenditures at the palace and for the State. Most years, the treasury was at least six months—and often a year or two—behind in meeting unpaid bills. In February 1733, when the budget was almost balanced, the treasury still owed 54,434 *livers* for the Queen's Household in the July quarter. Despite this, Louis retained the expectations of the court by hosting occasional celebrations, such as Carnival on each January 1st, the king's birthday, and ceremonial occasions. On the 14th of August when the queen gave birth to twin daughters—Mesdames Elisabeth and Henriette—there was a celebration at court, albeit not as grand as the festivities heralding the birth of a dauphin on September 4, 1729.

Between August 14, 1727, and July 15, 1737, Marie gave birth to ten children: Elisabeth, Duchess of Parma; Princess Henriette; Prince Marie Louise; Louis, Dauphin of France; Philippe, Duke of Anjou; Adelaide, Duchess of Louvois; Princess Victoire; Sophie, Duchess of Louvois; Princess Therese; and Louise, Prioress of Saint Denis. It was the birth of the Dauphin that cemented Louis XV's reign. Upon the baby's arrival, the room filled with the Princes of the Blood, Fleury, and assorted dignitaries who kissed the queen on the forehead and thanked her. After that, the Cardinal de Rohan, Grand Almoner of France, put a drop of Holy Water on the Dauphin's forehead and presented him with the blue sash of Saint Esprit. As was usual, the governess would arrive to take over. In this case, it was the beloved Governess who had saved the king's life and been so indispensable to him, the duchess de Ventadour. A wet nurse was usually provided as well. The queen's never breast fed their babies.

Fireworks and bonfires erupted throughout Paris where the party went on for three days. The rooftops of Versailles sparkled in the bursting light of a thousand rockets, their bright colors reflecting in the glass surface of the Grand Canal. The celebration was repeated on August 30th, 1730, when the queen gave birth to a second son, Philippe, the duc d'Anjou. The King's crown was secure. He now had an heir and a spare.

## Versailles Changes Costume

A lot had happened on the social scene as Versailles sat empty for seven years following Louis XIV's death in 1715. When the nobles were released from their Versailles "captivity," they went through a period of self-realization and pushing the envelope as far as social limits allowed. The result was an awakening akin to an Enlightenment Era where the arts flourished, and fashion took a hard look at the late Sun King's dictates. When Louis XV took over, the face of fashion at Versailles and Paris changed a great deal.

By 1730, although etiquette at Versailles was still mandated as per Louis XIV's code of manners, the old ways of the court had evolved in very overt areas. Known for its fashion, and copied all over Europe, Versailles and Paris ruled during this era for its sheer beauty and use of fabric and lace.

Under Louis XV, the dresses began to follow straight lines. In 1716, the panier appeared—a hoop worn under the dress to broaden the skirt. Obviously, as Louis was still a child in 1716, this new fashion statement can hardly have been said to bear his influence, but it was credited to the era of his reign. The problem with the panier was that it expanded skirts mostly in a sideways direction, unlike the round bell hoops called crinolines found under the skirts of southern belles and women of the 1800s. As the skirts grew wider, they were often split in the front center, showcasing a contrasting or matching underskirt, usually adorned with lace, ribbons, and even artificial flowers. These paniers would increase the width of the dress sometimes as much as six feet!

Panier gown showing slit in the middle.

Going to extremes.

Paniers during Louis XV, circa 1715-1774

As women hurried to emulate the current fashion trend, the clergy were not impressed. They attacked the new fashion violently. An Orator named Duguet published "*Traité des l'Indécense de Paniers,*" reflecting the clergy's distaste for the "baskets," stating it was a fashion born of the devil. The plunging necklines also drew fire. While the ladies ignored these dispersions on their attire, they did heed the recent admonishment against wearing diamonds and jewels during the madness over Law and the Mississippi Bank debacle that had embroiled Fleury in 1716. The fear was the jewels could be exchanged for shares or notes of the Mississippi Bank. Therefore, in place of the eye-popping diamond necklaces worn during the Sun King's reign, ribbons began to appear adorning swan-like throats.

The fashion was attacked from many sectors, none so much as the clergy, as they continued to rail against the fashion for many years. In 1735, a pamphlet was published in Paris assailing the panier, saying it "takes the room of at least six persons." It went on to say, "Is it not the said panier that makes your carriages groan, and that bulges through them like the sails of a ship, while you are holding your noble wooden hoop in both hands, and displaying it beneath a costume that is a scandal to the Church, and a laughing-stock to the whole world, and that insults the magnificence of our altars by its audacious splendor?"

An interesting point is that the French did not invent the panier. The fashion infrastructure began in Italy and Spain under the name of a *vertugadin*. The French renamed it a *panier*. It did not take long for the exaggerated width of the skirt to begin causing problems at the Court of Versailles. Cardinal Fleury was not a fan. According to the lawyer Barbier, "It is hard to believe, but true, that the cardinal has been embarrassed by the paniers women wear under their skirts to make them wider," he stated in 1728. "They are so ample that when women sit down the stays are pushed out and take an amazing amount of space, so that now they have to make special armchairs. Only three women can fit in the boxes at the theatres… This fashion has become so exaggerated… that the princesses who sit next to the Queen were covering her skirt with their own. This seemed impertinent, but it was difficult to find a remedy, so the cardinal, after much pondering, decided there would always be an empty chair on either side of the Queen to prevent her from being bothered; and the pretext is that the two chairs are being kept for Mesdames de France, her daughters."

The seated dilemma.

As always, nothing was ever simple at Versailles. Fleury's attempt to remedy the situation backfired. According to Barbier: "The story about the paniers has some consequences," he reported a month later. "Since there is now a space between the Queen and the Princesses of the Blood Royal, these last have demanded that the same sort of distance be established between them and the duchesses and, in fact, their request has been granted… That has greatly annoyed the ducs. A manuscript is circulating throughout the court. It attacks the Princes of the Blood Royal and is both clever and strongly worded, so that it has been burned by the executioner."

The pecking order at Versailles had been installed as a means to subjugate the nobles and keep them under Louis XIV's thumb. This new upheaval over something as ridiculous as a skirt was nothing new to the inbred need at the court to claim their rank. The upside to this strange fashion accessory was a sudden boom in the whaling industry, thanks to the whalebone used to build these voluminous hoops. The trade with Holland was materially augmented. In June 1722, the States-General of the Netherlands authorized a loan of 600,000 *florins* in support of "a company established in East Friesland for the whale fishery, the trade in which increased daily by reason of the demand for whalebone used in the construction of hoops for women."

While the hoops went wider, the hair became shorter and closer to the head than the days of the Sun King. Louis XIV's massive leonine wig was replaced by a new look where men wore their hair flat on the top with short curls next to the ears and the rest pulled back in a ponytail, tied with a ribbon. White or grey powder blown onto the hair was now the rage. While some sported wigs, many powdered their natural hair. Women were sporting shorter hairstyles with flattering curls. This style was called the *Téte de Mouton* or "sheep's head." Women didn't begin wearing wigs until 1770.

The men didn't cause the stir the women did with new fashion trends, although they did begin sporting a new look. Their coats were shorter and fuller, and lace flowed profusely from cravats and cuffs. Stockings, once of various colors, were now predominantly white. The waistcoats often rivaled the gay colors of women's fabric, as floral patterns ran riot. The buckled platform shoes were still in vogue, while the three-sided hat—the tricorne—usually trimmed with lace and often sporting a plume, was seen everywhere.

Typical men's fashion under Louis XV (1740)

Powdering the hair.

The *Téte de Mouton* (sheep's head) hairstyle

Louis XV wearing the fashionable shorter hairstyle wig.

Another change at the Court under Louis XV was the desire for more intimate gatherings rather than the use of the large, usually cold common areas of the palace. Women were now receiving guests in their private apartments, and it was fully acceptable for them to entertain while reclining on their made beds. The large skirts may have made it necessary. In 1730, private parties were held in the boudoir, a small, sometimes oval room, and the larger Salons were reserved for more formal and grand occasions. A special room was incorporated for the most-anticipated part of the day: the supper. Dinner was usually at 4:00 o'clock, while supper began around 9 pm and involved a smaller circle of intimate guests. Here, wit and elegant attire were the rule of the day. Laughter, amidst sumptuous food and drink, was the prevalent atmosphere. Gossip from politics to new scandals at court dripped from tipsy tongues.

Within the palace, Louis XV's preference for lighter colors, soft curves, and Rococo styling, was beginning to appear. The overly gilded walls and loud brocades seemed to thunder down on his head as he strolled through the ornate Salons and Hall of Mirrors. While he left most of his great-grandfather's brainchild untouched, he put his stamp on other parts of the palace that were his private domain, with one gigantic exception—the Ambassador's Staircase.

# Chapter Thirty-Nine
## Versailles Evolves

Louis XV continued to try and emulate his predecessor, the great Sun King. Yet, he loathed the court life Louis XIV had created. Still agonizingly shy, he endured the ceremonies over which he was forced to officiate; received the courtiers who were mostly strangers to him and pressed their advantage simply because their birth had landed them in noble families. The *lever* and *coucher* were things he dreaded and eating in public while everyone else stood and watched him caused him no-end of anxiety. No wonder he lost himself in the hunt or the company of a select few.

It wasn't long before the king set about doing a little remodeling at the cavernous palace. While leaving the ceremonial great rooms alone, he turned his attention to the king's private quarters. He had long disliked the massive bedroom his great-grandfather had used that sat in the heart of Versailles. It was accessed from the anterooms that opened off the Hall of Mirrors and was a thoroughfare of people. It was drafty, too ornate, and freezing in the winters. Louis XV decided to move into a smaller bedroom connected to a series of cabinet rooms.

The large bedroom of Louis XIV was still used for the morning *lever*, but Louis XV did not sleep there. He had usually been up for hours when he returned to his great-grandfather's bedroom and lay down upon the bed for the hated morning ritual. Each evening he told the Premier Valet du Chambre the hour the *lever* would commence on the following morning. As the mantle clock struck the hour, the bed curtains were pulled back, exposing the king who had only just climbed into the bed. Then, the entrées were allowed in from where they had been waiting in the antechamber. They entered in order of precedence; a valued order as it gave you a couple of spare moments to address the king, usually for a favor.

The duc de Luynes, a very important noble at court, and also the husband of the queen's dame d'honneur, wrote about the importance of the order of the entrées in his diary:

"The entrées in the King's bedroom," Luynes wrote in 1737, "are the familieres [family], the grandes entrees, the Premieres entrees, and the entrees of the chamber. The entrees familieres come in the moment the King is awake and while he is still in bed. All the Princes of the Blood, except M. le prince de Conti, and also M. le de Cardinal [Fleury], M. le duc de Charost [former King's governor], Madame de Ventadour [his former governess], and the wet nurse are the only ones who have them. The grandes entrees, when the First Gentleman of the Bedchamber come in, are when the King has just risen from his bed. The Premieres entrees are when he is up and wearing his robe. The entrees of the chamber are when he is in his armchair in front of his toilette; and after that, all the courtiers come in.

"All these entrees, in the evening, are exactly the same for the King's *coucher*, which is to say that the familieres, the grandes and the first entrees stay for what is called the *petit coucher*, that is, until the King is actually in bed. The others leave when the King's armchair is brought near the toilette [a table where he attends to his person, the way a woman attends to her makeup and hair]. When the crowd has left, the Premier Valet de Chambre, on the King's order, gives the candlestick to whichever one of the courtiers is allowed to stay. One keeps the candlestick until the King rises from his armchair to get into bed. Then one gives it back, but one stays on after having given it back until everyone is out… In the evenings, the King comes out of his study, goes over to his prayer stool within the balustrade near the bed, and then he takes off his blue ribbon [of the order of Saint Esprit] and his coat. That is the moment when the First Valet de Chambre holds out the candlestick and the King says the name of the person to whom it shall be given. The King takes his chemise from the hands of a Prince of the Blood, the Grand Chamberlain, the First Gentleman of the Bedchamber, or the Grand Master, or Master of the Wardrobe. Then he takes his robe; he sits down, and his shoes are taken off; the pages of the chamber give him his slippers; then the armchair is brought near the toilette and the Valet says: 'Proceed Gentlemen' and all leave the room." While the duc repeats himself, it is clear to see that the hierarchy involved in the *lever* and *coucher* was of huge significance; not just in proving you were above the next guy in rank and important, but in the chance it gave you to be in close proximity to the king and have an opportunity to speak to him. The opportunity given to the noble chosen to hold the candlestick was immensely important—he remained after others were excused.

It is easy to see how bickering and outright brawls broke out due to wanting access to the first entrees or to be included at all. Some nobles, after having been invited once, argued vehemently when turned away on a subsequent occasion that they had been allowed in before. When you have thousands of courtiers crammed into a palace, obviously you have to pick and choose who is granted entry into the private domain of the King.

Once the *coucher* ended and the bed curtains were closed, Louis hurried back to his private sanctuary only a few rooms away from the giant King's bedchamber of Louis XIV.

The King's bedchamber of Louis XIV

Louis had varied interests, thanks chiefly to the studies of botany and science he had been introduced to in his childhood. He took the king's private apartments of Louis XIV and arranged them to suit his needs.

The King's Cabinets under Louis XIV

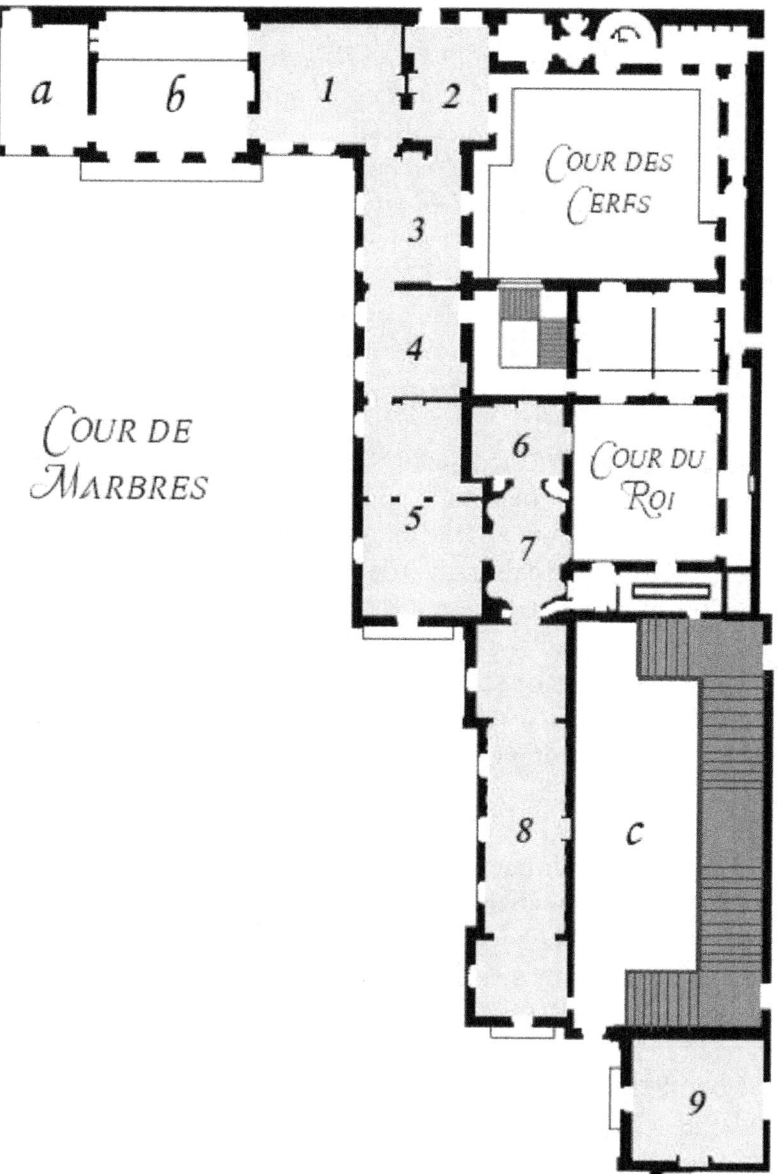


Courtesy of www.thisisversaillesmadame.blogpost.com.

**Key to Louis XIV's floorplan:**
1) The King's Cabinet/*Cabinet du Roi*
2) Cabinet of the Wigs/*Cabinet des Perruques*
3) Billiard/*Cabinet de Billiard*
4) Salon of the Small Staircase/*Salon de Petit Escalier*
5) Cabinet of Paintings/*Cabinet de Tableaux*
6) The Cabinet of Shells/*Cabinet de Coquilles*
7) The Oval Cabinet/*Cabinet Ovale*
8) The Small Gallery/*Petit Galerie*
9) Cabinet of Curiosities/*Cabinet des Curiosities,* and *Cabinet des Médailles*

a) Antechamber of the Bull's Eye
b) The King's Bedchamber of Louis XIV
c) The Ambassador's Staircase

At the top of the Ambassador's Staircase was the entrance to the long line of Salons, or King's apartments. This grouping is a suite of rooms used by Louis XIV, Louis XV, and Louis XVI. Located on the first floor of the palace the rooms are found in the oldest part of the palace dating from the reign of Louis XIII. Under Louis XIV, these rooms housed the king's collection of artworks and books, forming a museum of sorts. Under Louis XV and Louis XVI, the rooms were modified to accommodate private living quarters. At this time, the rooms were transformed, and their decoration represents some of the finest extant examples of the style Louis XV and style Louis XVI at Versailles.

Louis XIV was immensely fond of billiards. To be invited to play with the king was a great honor. He also kept several of his hunting dogs here, giving the room a second name—*cabinet des chiens*. The Cabinet of Paintings showcased from the Italian schools of Correggio, Raphael, Giorgione, and Titian. There were also cabinets arranged to hold his collection of carved rock crystals. The Cabinet of Coquilles and the Salon Oval along with the Cabinet des Medailles, formed the main rooms of the King's Cabinets de Curiosities. The Salon Oval housed in four niches four bronze sculptural groups: Jupiter and Juno, the Abduction of Orethyia and the Abduction of Persephone. The Cabinet of Shells housed his rare gem collection, it was later converted to a library of rare books.

Number 8, the Petit Gallery, was a long hallway where his great works of art were on display for the chosen few, he allowed to accompany him there. Here were the creations by the greats of the world. It was famous for housing the Mona Lisa by Leonardo Da Vinci. This long grouping of several rooms was formed from rooms once given to the marquise de Montespan before she was moved to the apartment of the baths on the ground floor after losing favor with the King.

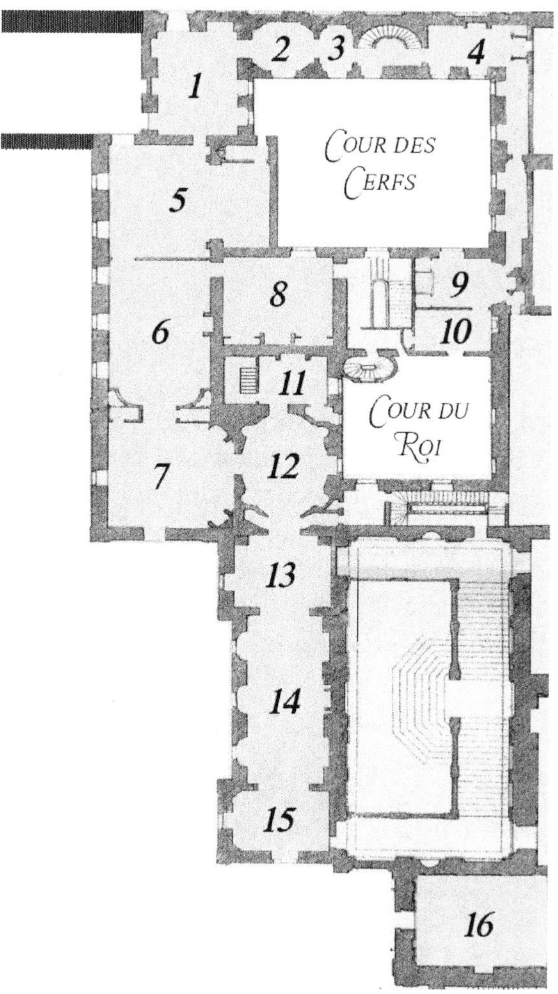


Louis XV's first modification in 1740.
Courtesy of www.thisisversaillesmadame.blogpost.com

**Key to Louis XV's floor plan of the King's cabinets (1740):**

1) Cabinet of the Wigs/*Cabinet des Perruques*
2) Cabinet/*Antechambre des Chiens* (dogs)
3) Toilet/*Chaise Percée*
4) Golden Cabinet
5) Louis XV's Bedchamber/*Chambre de Coucher*
6) The Clock Chamber/*Salon des Pendules*
7) Dining Salon/*Salle de Manger/Cabinet intérieur*
8) Antechamber
9) Bath Chamber/*Chambre du Bains*
10) Bath/*Bains*
11) Cabinet
12) Oval Cabinet
13) Petite Gallery/*Petit Galerie*
14) Small Gallery/*Petit Galerie*
15) Salon
16) Cabinet of Medallions/*Cabinet des Medailles*

Louis XV ordered a new bedroom in 1740, constructed on the site of Louis XIV's billiard room, which was enlarged to the north into the *cour du roi* to accommodate an alcove for the bed. In the same year the *degré du roi* (private staircase) was demolished and a new staircase was built to the north of the old location. A new room was constructed on the site formerly occupied by the *degré du roi* of Louis XIV, the ***antechamber des chiens***. As with Louis XIV, Louis XV kept some of his hunting dogs in this room.

Degré du roi (King's private staircase)

Further modifications of the *petit appartement du roi* ("roi" means King) at this time included the creation of the *salon des pendules* and the *cabinet intérieur*. These rooms were created when the *salon du degree du roi* and the *cabinet au tableaux* of Louis XIV were destroyed.

The ***salon des pendules*** (also called the *salon ovale* due to its elliptical shape) was given this name due to the dials arranged in the apsidal recess of the eastern wall that showed the times of the rising and setting of the sun and the moon.

The ***cabinet intérieur*** served a number of purposes: it housed part of Louis XV's numismatic (coins and other currency) collection and collection of miniature paintings; it served as a dining room; and it served as a workroom. Of all the rooms of the *petit appartement du roi* during the reign of Louis XV, this was perhaps one of the most richly decorated and opulently appointed.

The ***cabinet des livres***, ***salon ovale*** of Louis XIV, the ***petit galerie*** with its two salons, and the ***cabinet des médailles*** were retained.

By 1740, the *petit appartement du roi* had expanded to such an extent into the *cour du roi* (courtyard) that the eastern part became a separate courtyard. This new courtyard was called the *cour intérieur du roi* and the *cour du roi* was renamed the ***cour des cerfs***, due to the two dozen sculpted deer heads that Louis XV ordered placed on the walls of the courtyard.

The Cour Des Cerfs Courtyard

Louis XV extended these first-floor rooms to the upper floors where he created new rooms, libraries, scientific galleries, and laboratories, along with work cabinets and a dining room. We see here a king wishing to disappear into a warren of small rooms where he could indulge his love of the sciences and art. Where Louis XIV had lived his life entirely in the spotlight, Louis XIV valued privacy and a place to entertain a small group of intimate friends. His shyness and a lack of trust were paramount in his need to create a sanctuary away from the fickle and demanding court.

In 1730, when Louis XV was twenty, he approved the completion of the work on a large salon that was to be a ballroom. It was scrapped in 1669, but now Louis completed the grand Salon of Hercules. It was now the first salon one entered from the Chapel and in keeping with the other salons in the king's apartments, the ceiling was painted by François Le Moyne with the classical myth that gave the room its name.

The Salon of Hercules

While the King paid homage to his great-grandfather in his desire to keep Versailles the showcase it had always been, he often spent time at Fontainebleau, Marly, and Compiegne, as well as other palaces that gave him some distance from the madness of the court. These palaces were Choisy, La Muette (the treasured gift from the late regent), Saint-Hubert and Bellevue.

In the gardens of Versailles, which remained largely unchanged from the time of the Sun King, the *Basin de Neptune* was created between 1738 and 1741 and was the most important legacy Louis XV made to the gardens. The **Neptune basin** is an artificial basin located in the park of the Palace of Versailles and named after Neptune.

It is located in the alignment of the Allée d'Eau_and the Dragon Basin, at the northern end of a south-north axis encompassing the Swiss lake, the Orangerie and the Parterres d'eau.

The Neptune Basin

It was built between 1679 and 1681 under the direction of Le Nôtre at the lake under the Dragon. Under the reign of Louis XV, the basin was modified. In 1736, Ange-Jacques Gabriel changed the route a little and in 1740, three groups of lead sculptures were installed: Neptune and Amphitrite (his divine wife) by Lambert Sigisbert Adam, Le Dieu Océan by Jean-Baptiste Lemoyne, and Protée by Edmé Bouchardon. The new basin then offered large and varied water games arousing the admiration of the court.

With his love of botany, Louis XV encouraged scientific expeditions to bring back plant specimens from distant places with climates differing from France. In the gardens of the Trianon, he created a Botanical Garden where he used a system of plant classification developed by the Swedish botanist Linné. This incredible garden of exotic plants, covering acres of ground, was replaced with rambling vistas, winding paths, and wildflowers when Marie Antoinette took over the Petit Trianon and wanted to emulate the then popular untamed English gardens. She was met with initial resistance at the undoing of all Louis XV's hard work and the scientific significance of the catalog of botanical species.

Louis XV's love of science took him into the newly emerging field of electricity. In 1746, Abbé Nollet performed a Leyden Jar experiment at Versailles before the King, resulting in an electric charge.

The Leyden Jar Experiment

Louis XV also collected clocks and precision instruments. His geographers worked with astronomers to map the country. He had a telescope and often walked along the rooftops of Versailles studying the stars and contemplating the mysteries of life.

As for the royal children, of the ten born to the king and queen between 1727 and 1737, six daughters and one son survived to adulthood. They lived in the Princes' Wing, now known as the South Wing, as children. At the age of six, the Dauphin, the only surviving son, was moved to the main wing of the palace where a suite of rooms were created on the ground floor. Recent excavation at the palace has shown some interesting earthworks below the Dauphin's room that intimate an interior passageway for coaches may have one time run through there.

# Chapter Forty
## All's Fair in Love and War

While the king's remodeling of the old Sun King's cabinets stretched on until roughly 1740 (for the first phase), other events had been going on at Versailles. There was the usual political intrigue, usually involving Cardinal Fleury and the Parlement. It was becoming clear that the once-powerful Parlement had lost its popularity. In the same vein, Fleury, who had been possibly the most popular minister to head a French King's Court, was falling in the ratings. It was largely due to his age and his apparent hold on the king.

In 1732, Louis was twenty-two-years-old, and Fleury was pushing eighty. Many had supposed the cardinal would be long gone by now. There were those anxious to take his place, such as the ambitious d'Argenson. With its usual zeal for dissing the latest topic, the *bourgeoise* of Paris sang: "O King born to hunt deer, will you always be the slave of an octogenarian prelate?" No matter: Louis XV continued to look to Fleury for guidance and was devoted to him. The prime minster/cardinal had been paramount in the years of peace France had been enjoying.

Sadly, that era was coming to an end. A war was on the horizon, and it involved Louis' wife, Queen Marie Leszczynska. King Augustus II of Saxony was on his death bed. When he died, there would be a new election in which France would be naturally involved. France and Poland had been allies against the Habsburgs before Augustus II came onto the scene. It would be to France's benefit to place their own king upon the throne of Poland, and Louis did not have far to look. His wife's father, the deposed Stanislas Leszczynska would be a perfect choice to be reelected as King of Poland.

There were a lot of people hoping to thwart his attempt to gain the crown, however. The dying Augustus II wanted his son; the Emperor Charles VI wished nothing more than to keep the French out of Poland, while the nobility in Poland had been bribed to vote against Stanislas. Once again, the outcome would probably erupt in war with Austria and the other powers. France's alliance with Britain had been strained in recent years, partly because of commercial rivalries and partly due to England's evolving need to balance the power between the Continental states. If France pushed the envelope by backing Stanislas, it could, with all probability, force a British-Austrian alliance.

Louis and Fleury chewed on the new dilemma. War was expensive, always resulting in increased taxes, something sure to cause a revolt among the citizens of France. This would mean reinstating the 5% income tax that had caused so much upheaval before. Add to that, 139 counselors of the Parlement were scattered throughout the Providences due to the last conflict between the cardinal and the government body where a Declaration of Discipline had been instated, and you had a sticky conflict to overcome. Fleury had no choice. On November 11, 1732, he began recalling the conseillers back to Paris.

The Declaration of Discipline had been imposed by the king on August 18th of the same year. It proclaimed that all edicts registered in the course of a *lit de justice* would become executory at once; remonstrances could only be made once; they could not thereafter be renewed without the king's express permission; and the Parlement was forbidden to ever again go on strike. This caused an immediate backlash from the conseillers who refused to register the king's edict. Louis returned on September 3rd and held *another lit de justice* to enforce his ruling. The next day the younger members constituting a part of the Parlement called the Enquêtes et Requêtes went back on strike. Louis and Fleury struck back, exiling 139 conseillers.

Now, the king and cardinal needed them back. Popular opinion was turning against the Parlement, who many thought held too much power and disrupted the running of the State. As a resolution to the issue with Parlement, and reinstating the 139 exiles, the King came up with a compromise, no doubt scripted by Fleury. On December 4$^{th}$, the chancelier announced that the Declaration of Discipline would be temporarily suspended. This allowed the king to save face by not repealing it entirely, and the Parlement read it to mean the suspension would probably be permanent. Peace resumed just in time. Less than two months after the reconciliation, Augustus II, King of Poland and elector of Saxony, died on February 1, 1733.

Louis quickly backed his father-in-law, Stanislas Leszczynska and made the announcement. There was one hiccup. How to get the unpopular former King of Poland to Poland. He had enemies everywhere along the route in Russia, Prussia, and Austria. It was soon announced that Stanislas would travel by boat instead of land, and by late Spring, he was seen to board the ship amongst a trumpet and gun salute. It was a hoax. An imposter had boarded the ship disguised to look like Stanislas while the real King-apparent was actually traveling through Germany disguised as a vagabond merchant. On September 11, 1733, he reached Poland and was elected King.

No sooner was the election announced but Russian and Austrian troops invaded Poland where a new Diet, accompanied by six thousand nobles, attacked and gave the crown to the Elector of Saxony, who, upon placing the stolen crown upon his head, became Augustus III. Stanislas, who had not had time to organize an army, or man one to the extent his assailants had, disappeared. He donned yet another disguise and made his way to Danzig where he found refuge temporarily. News of his whereabouts had leaked out and Danzig was under siege. Danzig put up a valiant effort to resist the onslaught, but it was clear Stanislas would have to surrender. He finally made his way back to Paris and embroiled Louis XV in a minor war.

France became involved in the War of the Polish Succession where it tried to restore the queen's father to the Polish throne. The attempt failed, but France gained the Duchy of Lorraine. The war took place in Poland, Rhineland, and Italy. It resulted in the *Treaty of Vienna*. Augustus III gained the throne, and France and the Habsburgs gained territory. The result was that Austria lost the crowns of Naples and Sicily to Charles of Parma yet was awarded the Duchy of Parma; Poland lost direct control over the Duchy of

Courland and Semigallia; and the Duchy of Lorraine went to the hapless Stanislas Leszczynska, who left it in his will to his daughter, Louis' wife, the Queen of France. In one war, Louis XV and Fleury had added as much in land conquests as Louis XIV had during his long years of battle.

As for the immortal Cardinal Fleury, in 1738, he went right on, defying the odds of remaining upright at the age of eighty-five. He had been ruling alongside the king for twelve years. While Louis' fondness for him was unabated, he was finding himself more and more situated to be his own man and began making decisions without running them by the elderly prime minister. In April 1738, Barbier noted: "The King now works every day with each of his ministers in private, and he asks about details. He also works almost every day at the Cardinals." Fleury now asked the king for his consent for major appointments where he had heretofore advised Louis on who was the best candidate. He may have been surprised to have the king actually negate his suggestions and put forward his own.

Many were beginning to notice the change in the king. Although still secretive and preferring time in his inner sanctum of cabinet rooms to the hustle of court life, he was taking on more responsibility. He still listened to his minister's advice and valued it—he was after all only twenty-eight, but the court saw a difference. In March of 1739, the ambitious d'Argenson (who waited hopefully for Fleury to breath his last), wrote: "The King writes a lot in his own hand, whether it be letters or memoranda, and makes many a summary of what he has read… It is quite possible that Louis XV will surprise the world by showing himself a very great King."

It was becoming clear that Louis had found his stride. He immersed himself in the economics of his State, asked penetrating questions rather than having the situation skimmed over, and treated the people around him with respect. One did not see a dictator whose first impulse was to go for the jugular. He had become a loved ruler, and he was not yet 30. So far, Louis XV had found a rhythm to his life. It was balanced between running his country, hunting, family time with his children, visiting the queen, and a newfound pastime—extra-marital affairs.

## Mistresses

No one could fault the queen for needing a respite from back-to-back pregnancies. Whether she was using Saint's Day or poor health, she had forced the king from her bed. Perhaps due to a rather slow-witted mentality or the complacency that a faithful husband brings, she underestimated the needs of such a virile King. The lawyer d'Argenson, whose younger brother was the Minister of War for the king, noted: "A lady-in-waiting has told me that it was all the Queen's fault if the King had taken a mistress… She [the Queen] said: 'What, always in bed, always pregnant, always giving birth!' As a consequence, she forced the King to abstain for long periods of time, giving her poor health as a pretext, and disdained what today she bitterly regrets. One must also know that the Queen is afraid of ghosts; even when the King is lying at her side, she had to have a maid who held her hand all through the night and told her stories to make her go to sleep; and when the King wanted to used his conjugal rights, that maid barely went away. Besides, the Queen hardly sleeps at all; she gets up a hundred times a night, sometimes to piss, sometimes to look for her dog; besides, she practically puts mattresses over her because she is so afraid of being cold, so that the King died of the heat and left in a sweat without having done anything. He would withdraw to his own bedroom… so as to get a good night's sleep and find a solitary relief for his sensual ardors, and this finally induced him to take a mistress."

If one wonders how the lady-in-waiting would have known what the king did in his bedroom, such as finding "a solitary relief," it was the custom to exam the royal bedsheets each morning. His secret was then part of the data regularly recorded. Ladies missing their periods were also noted and pregnancies suspected in advance. There were no secrets at Versailles.

The queen amused herself throughout the day with a routine that would have bored the king. She was either reading, embroidering, practicing the guitar, violin, or harpsicord, or engaging lady friends in conversation, dining, or playing cavagnole. Cavagnole, also called Biribi, was a board game along the lines of roulette where pieces were placed on numbered sections from 1 to 70. It was a low stakes game, which was prohibited by law in 1837.

Cavagnole board game from the late 18th Century.

The queen enjoyed her own company and read the Bible and other moral literature daily. Dull, though she appeared, she was always pleasant, refrained from gossip, was not interested in the intrigues of the court, and detested talk of politics. At first, the relief of not being taken to bed with the subsequent repercussions may have felt like freedom. It would soon become apparent she had taken a once-faithful husband and pushed him to find sexual fulfillment elsewhere.

The first mistress appeared on Louis' radar in 1732. It was while he was dining with a small circle of friends at his great-aunt's chateau at Rambouillet, that he first noticed a rather unremarkable lady seated at the other end of the table. The hostess, the Comtesse du Toulouse, had invited the duc de Penthievre (her son); the duc de Gesvres, First Gentleman of the Bedchamber; the duc d'Epernon, the marquis de Meuse; and a few young virtuous women, with the exception of M. le Duc's sister, Mlle de Charolois, whose affairs were legendary, and who had set her cap for the King.

Louis was too shrewd to fall for the overt temptation put before him in the guise of this Princess of the Blood, and so, he found himself watching the young woman who was no real beauty, rich, or of any acclaim. She and Louis were close to the same age (he was 22 in 1732). Her family, the Mailly-Nesles, had roots that went back to the eleventh century, but they were poor. The thorn in the situation was that the young woman was married to the comte de Mailly, a lieutenant in the Scottish Guards belonging to the King's Household *and* she was a lady-in-waiting to the queen.

At first, the affair was as secret as the young king. The queen was among the first to find out and she wrote her father, Stanislas, about it. The king, feeling great guilt over the affair, went to great lengths to hide it and tried to call it off three times. Louise Julie de Mailly saw no advancement at court, as those honored by Louis XIV's attention had always done. There were no jewels or apartments or fine clothes. The king's need to call off the affair regularly, happened to coincide with Easter so that he could take communion in public. Once the religious rites were over, he was back with his mistress. He was, at that time, still sleeping with the queen, who bore him three daughters between 1734 and 1737. By the last birth, which resulted in a miscarriage, the secret was out and the King's desire to bed his queen over. That year, the King did not attend the Easter communion.

Barbier was quick to note Mlle de Mailly's appearance. He stated she had "a long face, a long nose, a large and high forehead with slightly flat cheeks, a large mouth, a white complexion, rather beautiful large eyes with a lively expression, a very rough voice, ugly breasts and arms, but fine legs. She was tall, without grace or presence, but very elegant; amusing, cheerful, good-tempered, a good friend, generous and kind." For the shy king, perhaps a plain woman was less intimidating. He would progress to court beauties later in his philandering years. Plus, de Mailly was lively, witty, and entertaining—the traits lacking in the forgotten queen.

The "secret" was of course, no real secret at court. In September 1736, d'Argenson noted: "The King…took as his mistress some six months ago, Mme de Mailly, daughter of M. de Nesle. Thus, M. le Cardinal has consented to the arrangement, seeing that the King needed a mistress. He had 20,000 livres [$90,000 dollars] given to her…" In July 1737, he added: "When they came to tell the King about the birth of another daughter, they asked him whether she should be called Madame Septiéme [Madame the Seventh], and he answered Madame Derniére [Madame the last] from which people have concluded that the Queen will be neglected indeed."

Louise Julie de Mailly

While de Mailly was now recognized at Louis' mistress, many were surprised that other than the small pension Fleury had given her, she was never given a higher position or dripping in jewels. While the queen was no doubt suffering from the humiliation and pain of seeing her own lady-in-waiting paraded around as her husband's new love interest, the rest of France saw the affair as a good thing. In 18th-century France, kings were expected to take mistresses. It was a sign of masculinity and virility. Indeed, Louis XVI, Louis XV's successor was ridiculed for remaining faithful to Marie Antoinette throughout their marriage. Mistresses had also been known to add polish to man's sensibilities and social etiquette. It was noticed that Louis appeared more at each in public and was coming out of his shell.

The affair was still going strong in 1739, when Barbier commented: "Mme la comtese de Mailly is still thought to be the King's favorite. There are now many suppers, either at La Muette or at …Madrid; the King is beginning to have a taste for ordinary pleasures. There is nothing wrong with his being a little less passionate about hunting... which might have made him too somber and wild. The frequencies of women and the experience of pleasure will take him less time and improve his mind and feelings."

The King proved to be restless in his choice of residences as he sought out places where he could enjoy "ordinary" pleasures. It was noted by Narbonne, the Versailles Chief of Police in 1730, that Louis spent 86 nights at Marly, 50 at Fontainebleau, 46 at Comiègne, 52 at La Muette, and 33 at Rambouillet, leaving only 98 nights for Versailles. While Louis XIV had enjoyed his Marly, Fontainebleau, and Saint-Cloud, he was predominantly at his Palace of Versailles. For the more reserved Louis XV, taking small groups of people to the less crowded and theatrical chateaus was more to his liking. It is why, in 1739 and 1740, he remodeled the king's cabinets and moved his bedroom to that labyrinth of rooms away from the traffic flow of the courtiers.

Louis XV had remained faithful to his wife for a decade—a record for a French monarch. Louis XIV had taken a mistress only two months after marriage. Louis XV, King of France and Navarre remained a kind friend to his wife and demanded her respect at court. He was a devoted father, visiting the South Wing regularly to see his brood of children, again, not the usual. The Sun King had been a remote figure in his children's lives until they were needed later for reasons of politics or heritage. And breaking with tradition, was the closeness between the king and his son, the dauphin. Louis spent copious amounts of time with the boy in his private apartments on the ground floor of the main wing. He gave him presents, oversaw his education, gave him mementos of personal value, kept a close eye on his health, and praised him for his achievements.

When the dauphin was nine, the young boy suffered from an abscess at the juncture of the cheek and the jaw which would have to be incised. Without the benefit of anesthesia, the operation was extremely painful, and Louis insisted on staying by his son's side throughout. The king was so affected by his son's cries of pain, that he grew quite pale and began shaking to the point many feared he would faint. When, for reasons of economy, Fleury suggested five of his seven daughters should be sent off to a convent for a few years, the two eldest were allowed to stay in hopes that marriage was on the horizon. The sisters, Elisabeth and Henriette (the twins) were eleven. Madame Adelaide, six at the time, burst into tears and flung herself into her father's arms and begged him to let her stay. The king relented and allowed her to stay, despite the cost of maintaining separate households for each of the girls. In May 1738, Mesdames Victoire, Sophie, Félicité, and Louise went off to the convent of Fontevrault.

Devoted to his children, he was. But he reserved time to enjoy life as the thirties were drawing to a close. He loved champagne and owned ten underground ice houses which in total contained some four hundred cubic feet of ice. He still indulged his love of hunting, and his various passions such as science, botany, and the arts. He collected his clocks and tinkered with experiments coming of age in the Enlightenment Era of France. He was enjoying Mlle de Mailly greatly, but even so, as with all kings, he was not wanting of a wandering eye. That his fancy should hit so close to home for de Mailly was a surprise.

In 1738, de Mailly had finally been given a suite of rooms: one a bedroom, the other a study in which the king would bring his work and spend time with her. Suppers took place in the king's cabinets in which a small select group of people gathered between seven and eight at least once a week. His spirits seemed high, indeed he seemed like a new king with a sense of humor and ease that had not been seen before. The duc de Luynes noted in 1737 that "For some time now he has been going up after supper onto the roofs of the castle, takes walks with those who have the honor of being invited to sup with him, sometimes all the way to the end of the new wing, and from there to the wing of the Princes [south wing]. Several times, he went into Mme de Chalais's apartment for a chat, entering through her window which looks out onto the roof, and to Mme de Tallard's, down the chimney. There was even a rather pleasant conversation at Mme de Tallard's...The King spoke quite naturally about his tastes and his character as they relate to life in society."

Louis' friends began to talk about this new pattern of his to drop in on them without notice. Luynes noted with pleasure that "The King...after supper came for a walk in the gallery and the corridor which run around my apartment; he had someone scratch at one of the back doors and had me called. Mme de Luynes came to the door; the King came in and played cavagnole until almost three in the morning."

While the positive effects of Louis's affair with Mme de Mailly were apparent to all, she had not been given the official title of maîtresse déclarée, although she appeared to be taking on airs as such. She was still miserably poor, despite the station of her famous lover. Her gowns were worn, and she was unable to honor her gambling debts to friends. It was during this time that she noticed the king's affections were waning. In fact, Louis was paying attention to another lady at court, and it was none other than Louise Julie de Mailly's sister, Pauline-Félicité de Nesle, marquise de Vintimille.

Pauline was the second oldest of the five de Nesle sisters. Louise was the oldest, and then Pauline, next was Diane Adelaide, and then Hortense Felicitie, and finally Marie Ann. Louis had affairs with all of them in their turn, with the exception of Hortense. It was even rumored that Pauline shared his bed with her sister Louise after gaining Louis' favor in 1740. One would think this audacious behavior would shock the Court, but we are talking about Versailles.

Pauline-Félicité de Nesle

Diane Adelaide de Nesle

Hortense Félicité de Nesle

Marie Ann de Nesle

Louis continued to frequent his friends' suppers, and as some fell away, new faces emerged, including the prince de Conti whose popularity fluctuated at court. He was a distant cousin of Louis with high ambitions. Some thought he had re-emerged to be near the king in case Fleury died and he would be in a prime spot to submit his name for the role of prime minister. He was now showing up at the small dinner parties Louis attended. On the king's arm was the new mistress, Pauline-Félicité de Nesle, Mme de Vintimille. She was described as taller than her sister Louise, just as plain, very witty, and able to converse on a plethora of subjects. She was fun, animated, elegant, and a joy to be around. With her, the king could recede into the background of conversations, as he was wont to do when his shyness overcame him. He was content to let her shine.

At the January 1st Carnival of 1740, Mme de Vintimille was the only person outside the king's immediate family to receive a present. The new mistress was presented a gold box set with diamonds. There was no hiding it—the king had a new mistress. Despite the gift of the gold box, nothing had changed in Louis' proclivity to keep a tight rein on the finances. Pauline was no more lavished with gifts and jewels than her older sister had been. The king, on the other hand, made sure his royal presence was appropriately lavish. At a ball in 1739, he was dressed in a blue velvet frock coat lined with white satin. The coat and waistcoat sported diamonds, as did his hat and shoes. He positively sparkled.

The duc de Luynes reported that the king's new bedroom was a thing of beauty. There were hangings [tapestries and bedcurtains] of "a gold and crimson fabric on which they had been working in Lyon for five or six years. The taste, the design and the texture of this fabric are admirable. The furniture is covered with crimson velvet enriched by a very wide, very thick gold embroidery in superb pattern of flowers and green-gold ornaments."

Another splurge of the money-minded king was the purchase of a little chateau in Choisy in November 1739, just outside Paris. He spent 300,000 livres on it [$1,350,000]. "The King is very pleased with his new acquisition. The furniture is handsome, the dining room very pretty and the view admirable." Choisy soon became one of his favorites places to go.

The Chateau of Choisy

In August of 1739, Louis had the opportunity to celebrate the engagement of his first daughter, Elizabeth. It was again, a political marriage between the King of France's daughter and the son of Philip V of Spain. The palace was ablaze with balls and banquets, and the ubiquitous fireworks over the opulent gardens of Versailles. In Paris, a special island was built in the middle of the Seine, filled with symbolic fictional figures denoting love and the joining of two powerful families. Elizabeth would become known as Madame Infante. She wore a gown of sliver cloth covered in diamonds. The Court of Versailles unpacked their best gowns and jewels from their trunks in their palace apartments or rode over from their nearby estates. It was a fine moment for the King and Queen of France.

As 1740 rode up the *Avenue de Paris* to the Palace of Versailles, past the manicured grounds and glistening buildings, it looked as if Louis XV had achieved everything a king could wish for. But it is in complacency we are typically thrown into chaos. The world was about to change. Many were agog that Fleury was still around to see it. For Louis, it proved his mettle and tested the love of his people.

# Chapter Forty-One
# **The World is Watching**

1740 would prove a turning point in the reign of Louis XV. His trusted advisor and prime minister were still at his side, but it was noted that between 1737 and 1738 the cardinal was constantly suffering from digestive issues. While Louis continued to enjoy the company the Nesle sisters, war was brewing that would engulf France and end the peaceful lull it had been enjoying.

Maria Theresa Walburg Amalia Christina was the only female ruler of the Habsburg dominions, ruling from 1740 until her death in 1780. Due to the result of a war which began in 1740, she became the sovereign of Austria, Hungary, Croatia, Bohemia, Transylvania, Mantua, Milan, Lodomeria, Galicia, the Austrian Netherlands, and Parma. By marriage, she was Duchess of Lorraine, Grand Duchess of Tuscany, and the Holy Roman Empress.

Maria Theresa, circa 1759

Maria's father, Emperor Charles VI died in October 1740. He paved the way for his daughter's succession with the Pragmatic Sanction of 1713 and spent his entire reign securing it. He ignored the advice of Prince Eugene of Savoy, who believed that a strong military and a rich treasury were more important than mere signatures. Eventually, Charles VI left behind a weakened and impoverished state, partially due to the *War of the Polish Succession* and the Russo-Turkish War (1735-1739). It was upon his death that France entered the picture in hopes of securing the empty throne.

Louis XV was not the only one to jump into the fray. Saxony, Prussia, and Bavaria all repudiated the sanction they had recognized during Charles VI's lifetime. Fredrick II of Prussia (who would remain Maria's rival throughout most of her reign) promptly invaded and took the affluent Habsburg province of Silesia in the seven-year conflict known as the *War of the Austrian Succession.* During the course of the war, Maria Theresa successfully defended her rule over most of the Habsburg Monarchy, apart from the loss of Silesia and a few minor territories in Italy.

While the pretext was Maria Theresa's right to inherit from her father, Emperor Charles VI, in reality, France, Prussia and Bavaria saw an opportunity to challenge Habsburg power. Maria was backed by Britain, the Dutch Republic, and Hanover, collectively known as the Pragmatic Allies. As the conflict widened, it drew in other participants, among them Spain, Sardinia, Saxony, Sweden, and Russia. These principal players took turns trying to ally with France. Louis XV took to his pen rather than his sword in the beginning, hammering out details and compromises, but in the end, it was looking as if France itself would be attacked.

Louis XV, at the age of 33 in 1743, decided to lead his troops into battle, much to the applause of the Parisians who saw this as a king taking literally the reins of his country and riding off under the mantle of acquiring territory and protecting their borders. It was what kings did. It was his foray into war. His decision to take along his mistresses was less popular. He was also dealing with the death of his longtime counselor, Cardinal Fleury, who finally passed away on January 29$^{th}$, 1743. Louis, rather than giving the post of prime minister to someone else, declared he would be his own prime minister, thereby adding to the burden he was now facing.

There were four primary theaters of the war: Central Europe, the

Austrian Netherlands, Italy, and on the seas. Prussia occupied Silesia in 1740, then repulsed Austrian efforts to regain it, while between 1745 and 1748, France conquered most of the Austrian Netherlands. Elsewhere, Austria and Sardinia defeated Spanish attempts to regain territories in Northern Italy, while in 1747, the British naval blockade was crippling French trade.

Under the 1743 *Treaty of Fontainebleau*, Louis XV and his uncle, Philip V of Spain, agreed on a joint action against Britain. This included a proposed invasion of Britain, aimed at restoring the exiled Stuarts, and over the winter 12,000 French troops and transports were assembled at Dunkirk.

In February 1744 the *Battle of Toulon*, a combined Franco-Spanish fleet fought an indecisive action with a British naval force commanded by Admiral Mathews. Although Mathews prevented them from exiting the Mediterranean and supporting the invasion attempt, he was forced to retreat, which led to his dismissal. Success allowed Spain to land troops in Northern Italy, and in April, they captured the important port of Villefranche-sur-Mer, then part of Savoy.

However, storms sank or severely damaged many French ships, while most of Louis' ministers opposed what they considered an expensive and futile diversion of resources. The invasion was cancelled on March 11$^{th}$, and Louis formally declared war on Britain. In May, a French army invaded the Austrian Netherlands. The Dutch were reluctant to fight and unsuccessfully tried to persuade Louis to withdraw.

The French made rapid progress, quickly capturing most of the Dutch-held Barrier fortresses along the border, including Menen and Ypres. Paris cheered its conquering hero. When an Austrian army under Prince Charles of Lorraine invaded Alsace in June, Louis went on the defensive in the Southern Netherlands, and traveled to Metz to meet this threat. While there, in early August, he fell dangerously ill with what some assumed was smallpox—a disease often fatal at the time. The doctors bled him, and it was feared he might die. Louis had taken on another of the Nesle sisters as his current favorite and it was Marie Ann, Mme de Châteauroux, who was with him in Metz. She had become such a necessary companion, confidant, and advisor to the king, that he had ordered a special wooden gallery built over the street that separated the two houses they were occupying in Metz during the war campaign. She could now go back and forth to be with her lover without the prying eyes of all around them. Many were appalled that the king was not putting all his attention toward the battles being played out. The fact that this was now the third sister of the Nesle family he was bedding was also causing the gossip mills to grind.

As Louis fever rose on August 8th, he was given repeated enemas, thinking it was perhaps another of his indigestion issues. His fever and headaches worsened and Mme de Châteauroux nursed him. The fever continued and a series of remedies were instigated: emetic to make him vomit, enemas, and more and more bleeding. In the meantime, word had reached Paris that the king was in serious peril. The people panicked and prayers were said. While in the king's bedroom at Metz, a dilemma of another kind was playing out. Not just the king's life was at stake, but his very soul.

Louis was told if it looked as those he might die, he would need to have the last rites administered and repent in order for his soul to be accepted by God in heaven. This was a big deal to a king who was the acclaimed extension of God while on the throne. In order to repent, he must send away his mistress and forsake all such adulterous and lewd behavior. On the 12th, the Bishop of Soissons, the First Almoner told the king under no uncertain terms he would need to repent and send his concubine away. Louis fudged, thinking he might survive his maladies, and told the bishop a full confession was too taxing right now with such a fever and headache. The bishop volleyed back and told him he could start the confession now and finish tomorrow. Louis, after much waffling, called Marie Ann to him and kissed her hand, telling her they must separate. When she tried to kiss him, he pushed her away.

Marie Ann finally left in a borrowed carriage and under disguise, but it was found that she was still hanging around in the town of Metz. Bishop Soissons told the king this would not do, and he could not administer the final rites until she departed the city. Louis ordered her to leave. He was in such a weakened condition by this time, that he was in no condition to argue. Taking advantage of the fact, the bishop went a step further and told the king he needed to apologize to his subjects for living in sin and ask their forgiveness, which the king did. This was overstepping his authority, and the bishop knew it.

Louis's condition worsened, and he was repeatedly bled. It was not until August 26th that any improvement was seen. The military had been advancing during his two-week ordeal and had beaten the Austrian army before it could cross the French border. In Paris, the people continued to hold their breath for the king's recovery. There were tears and lamentations the likes of which had never been seen.

It was finally announced the king was out of danger. An explosion of joy was heard throughout France. Bonfires blazed, fireworks lit up the skies, and everyone illuminated their windows to show their happiness. It was now that Louis XV received the moniker for which he would forever be known: "Louis the Beloved."

The war blazed on with the usual collateral damage. During 1746, the French continued their advance into the Austrian Netherlands, taking Antwerp and then clearing Dutch and Austrian forces from the area between Brussels and the Meuse. After defeating the Jacobite Rebellion at Culloden in April, the British launched a diversionary raid on Lorient in an unsuccessful attempt to divert French forces, while the new Austrian commander, Princes Charles of Lorraine, was defeated by Saxe at the Battle of Rocoux in October.

The Dutch Republic itself was now in danger and in April 1747, the French began reducing their Barrier Fortresses along the border with the Austrian Netherlands. At Lauffeld on July 2, 1747, Saxe won another victory over a British and Dutch army under the Prince of Orange and Cumberland; the French then besieged Maastricht and Bergen op Zoom, which fell in September.

These events lent greater urgency to ongoing peace talks at the Congress of Breda, which took place to the sound of French artillery firing on Maastricht. Following their 1746 alliance with Austria, an army of 30,000 Russians marched from Livonia to the Rhine but arrived too late to be of use. Maastricht surrendered on May 7 and on October 18, 1748, the war ended with the signing of the *Peace of Aix-la-Chapelle*.

The *Treaty of Aix-la-Chapelle* (1748) reflected a stalemate; the commercial issues that led to the war were left largely unresolved and many of the signatories were unhappy with the terms. Despite nearly bankrupting the state, Louis XV withdrew from the Low Countries for minimal benefit, to the dismay of the French nobility and populace. The Spanish considered their gains in Italy inadequate (they had failed to recover Menorca or Gibraltar) and viewed the reassertion of British commercial rights in the Americas an insult.

Despite their victories in Flanders, French Finance Minister Machault repeatedly warned of the impending destruction of their financial system. The British naval blockade led to the collapse of French customs receipts and caused severe food shortages, especially among the poor; after Cape Finisterre in October, the French navy could no longer protect their colonies or trade routes. Due to this and ongoing threats, Louis agreed to return the Austrian Netherlands, whose acquisition had cost so much. He could not afford to engage in more conflicts. France, who had been so joyful at his recovery from a life-threatening illness, not erupted in protest. How could he give back what they had all paid so dearly to win? Combined with the lack of tangible benefits for helping Prussia, a new phrase of displeasure rolled throughout Paris: "as stupid as the Peace."

Louis' popularity at home plummeted. The tally of losses associated to the *War of Austrian Succession* did not help things:

France sustained 158,400 casualties, lost 20 ships of the line, 16 frigates, 20 minor ships, 2,185 merchant ships and 1,738 naval guns. The Habsburg Monarchy came in second with 148,000 casualties. Compared to the numbers of casualties suffered by the other military forces, it was a dismal tally. Prussia suffered 23,100 casualties, Spain 3,000, Great Britain 26,400, the Dutch Republic 14,630 and Savoy-Sardinia 7,840. It had cost France dearly, and Louis had given back the victories that had sunk the country into debt and cost so much in human life and military acquisitions.

Although Maria Theresa was acknowledged as her father's heir, she did not consider this a concession and deeply resented Britain's role in forcing her to cede Silesia to Prussia. Her determination to recover Silesia led to the Seven Years War, where France, would once again, take up arms in 1756.

Even as the war continued in 1744, Louis went back to Versailles to regain his strength after his near-fatal illness. The king was greeted with fanfare all along the route home with voices calling, "Long live the King!" This was before the final outcome of the *War of the Austrian Succession,* when the fickle crowds of Paris turned against him. For now, he was hailed as the "Beloved" of the people.

Once Louis was home for a few days, reality sunk in as to the events at Metz. He began chaffing at the humiliation of the public apology he was forced to offer via the Bishop of Soissons in Metz. To compound the embarrassment, the king was unaware that his son, the Dauphin had been there to witness it. The Dauphin's Governor, the duc de Châtillon, had ignored Louis's orders not to bring his son to Metz. The family had panicked over his illness and wanted to rally around him. In his feverish condition, the king was not even aware the Dauphin was in the same house. Not only was there the fear the next in line to the throne could contract the disease afflicting the king, but Louis had not wanted his family there, especially with his mistress holding court in the midst of a war.

Early in November of 1744, the duc de Châtillon found himself exiled from court. There were also rumors that letters had begun again between the king and his favorite mistress, Marie Ann, Mme de Châteauroux, who was at her house in Paris. In all fairness, the king, still contrite about his sinning, and having the public made fully aware of his contrition, tried to approach the queen. On November 15, he went to her door. "Last night," the ubiquitous Lynes writes, "someone came three times to scratch at the door between the Queen's apartment and the King's. The Queen's ladies warned her about this, but she answered that they were mistaken, and that the noise they heard was due to the wind. That noise having occurred a third time, the Queen, after waiting awhile, ordered the door opened, but no one was there." The king, feeling rebuffed had given up and gone away. [Scratching at a door with one's little finger instead of knocking was considered a more refined way to alert someone you were at their door.]

By the 28th of November, the word was out. Things were being put in place to have Mme de Châteauroux return to Versailles. Her office as Superintendent of the Dauphine's Household, which had been revoked at Metz, was given back to her. Louis then singled out his Minister of the Navy, Maurepas, to be the personal messenger to go to Marie Ann and tell her that her rooms were once more available to her at court. Maurepas, a man known to have despised the mistress and her divisive whisperings to the king, was not thrilled to be the messenger boy for this particular errand. But he went.

He needn't have feared the return of the Nesle sister to Versailles. She had been feeling unwell shortly after her return from Metz.

During the next three days her fever rose, and her head pounded—the same symptoms Louis had displayed in Metz five months prior. On December 1st, it was worse, and on the 3rd the king was too worried to go hunting or hold court. He locked himself away in his labyrinth of cabinet rooms and waited for reports brought to him. By December 6th, he was told there was no hope. Wracked with stomach pains, a burning thirst, and convulsions, Marie died on December 10. If this had been the Court of Louis XIV, poison would have been expected. Oddly, there was no rumor of it associated with Marie Ann's death.

The king fell into a deep depression and left for La Muette where he could weep in private. He hardly ate. One cannot put the duties of the king on hold for long, so, on December 18th, he returned to Versailles, but holed up in the Trianon, where he stayed until the 22nd.

Only two things seem to draw him out as 1744 came to a close: his son, and a new woman who had slipped in under the radar.

## Chapter Forty-Two
## **Marriage, Mistresses and Politics**

In 1744, Louis XV negotiated a marriage between his fifteen-year-old son and the nineteen-year-old Infanta Maria Teresa Rafaela of Spain, daughter of King Philip V and his Italian wife, Elisabeth Farnese, and first cousin of Louis XV. The marriage contract was signed December 13, 1744. The marriage was celebrated by proxy at Madrid December 18, 1744, and in person at Versailles on February 23, 1745.

On December 28, 1744, the king celebrated his son's marriage with the usual full-blown festivities, but he also gave him something on a more meaningful level. Louis XV presented the young Dauphin with a diamond plaque of the Saint Espirit. The Dauphin was touched, and while Louis had always been an affectionate father, the young man blushed at the gift. Louis told him he must learn to relax in his father's company. Something not easy to do when Dad is the King of France and surrounded by sycophants begging to be near him.

Louis, Dauphin of France

Marie Teresa, Dauphine

The *War of the Austrian Succession* was still going on at this time, but it didn't keep Louis XV from celebrating the marriage of this only surviving son. The other son had died as a toddler, leaving the King with a plethora of daughters and one Dauphin. Therefore, no expense was spared for the festivities celebrating not only the union of the two young people, but a strategic alliance with the Spanish Crown. Despite the fact that Philip V of Spain was a blood relative of Louis', history had proven that when it came to crowns and politics, family ties went by the wayside.

The three days of parties planned were not the only sign of expense for the wedding celebrations. The courtiers and royals were determined to show up in dazzling splendor. Barbier reported, "Some men's suits cost up to 15,000 livres [$67,000]; they will need three, one for each day. M. de Mirepoix… has rented three suits that he will only wear one day each and then return to the tailor for 6,000 livres [$27,000]. M. le marquis de Stainville has a suit of cloth of silver embroidered in gold and lined with marten. The lining alone is said to cost 25,000 livres [$112,000]."

As for the Infanta, the Dauphin fell in love with her instantly. Due to the looks that passed between them during the dinners, the feelings were mutual. The wedding night seemed to only heighten their affection for each other. The following evening there was a *bal pare,* the grandest balls put on at Versailles. This was hosted in the sparkling Hall of Mirrors, where reflections of jewels and gold silk vied with each other for attention. The next evening, a masked ball was held where the queen appeared as a shepherdess, but far from representing a simple peasant, she was covered in diamonds. The king had other plans for disguising for his identity.

Midway through the masquerade ball, the mirrored doors of the king's antechamber burst open, and eight yew trees danced onto the Hall of the Mirrors parquet floor. To the amusement of all, the costumed dancers mingled with the others, one in particular made a beeline for a very pretty young woman dressed as Diana the Huntress. To the astonishment of all, the yew tree removed his mask of leaves to reveal Louis XV, King of France. And the woman to whom he was paying homage was a middle-class beauty by the name of Jeanne Antoinette Poisson, Mme d'Etioles.

## Madame de Pompadour Enters the Scene

The Masquerade Ball in the Hall of Mirrors (note the eight yew trees).

If the court was surprised at the king's choice of dance partner, it might be even more intrigued to find this was not his first encounter with Mme d'Etioles. Due to the lady's involvement in Paris salons, as well as her grace and beauty, Louis XV had heard the name of Jeanne Antoinette mentioned at court as early as 1742. The ambitious Mme d'Etioles had already set her cap for the king, although she was married and from the *bourgeoise* side of the tracks. One person who did take note of her was the late Mlle de Châteaurox, the King's previous love who had recently died. Before her death, Marie Ann had warned Jeanne Antoinette to leave the king alone. Jeanne's response was to go for it!

The king was riding in a hunt in the forest of Sénart in 1744. Because Jeanne occupied an estate close to where the king was hunting, she was allowed to follow the royal party at a distance. However, wanting to attract the king's notice Jeanne Antoinette drove directly in front of Louis XV's path; once in a pink carriage called a phaeton, wearing a blue dress, and once in a blue phaeton wearing a pink dress. The King sent a gift of venison to her. On February 24, 1745, Jeanne received a formal invitation to attend the masked ball to be held on February 25$^{th}$ at the Palace of Versailles. This was no ordinary woman. She quickly seized on the perfect attire—Diana the Huntress, to remind him of their encounter in the forest of Sénart. It was probably an inference of her intentions to hunt the prey of choice, the King of France.

Madame de Pompadour as Diana the Huntress

The court was suddenly rife with gossip. True, the lady was beautiful and witty, but she was of low rank. Luynes noted that people "have been speaking of the King's new love affair, and mostly about a Mme d'Etioles, who is young and pretty. Her mother was called Mme Poisson. They say that she has lately been much time in *ce pays-ci* [at Court] and that she is the King's new choice; if that is true, she will probably be just a passing fancy and not a proper mistress." The rest of the court seemed to agree with Luynes. How could this lady of inferior rank fit in with the rigid etiquette of court, or hold her own in the often witty and knowledgeable conversations of the Salons? Would she know how to glide (one did not walk at court, one glided!), or bow properly? Surely, this was a casual fling to help heal the king's heart from the loss of Mme de Châteauroux. After all, the Nesle's sisters had been presented at court and therefore worthy of the king's attentions. This woman, who had not been officially presented, could not hope to measure up.

In 1745, Louis was thirty-five-years-old, still considered the most-handsome monarch in Europe, athletic and strong. Jeanne Antoinette quickly realized he was also extremely kind, intelligent, and open-minded. Louis, for the first time, was taking on a real beauty. His confidence had come a long way from selecting plain women who posed no threat to his insecurities. He also found in Jeanne a lady who was amusing, amiable, intelligent, and loved art and the theater. In a nutshell, she loved life, and she was kind—one thing Mme de Châteauroux had not been. The more time Louis spent with her, the more alive he became. For a king, who had been known to go through bouts of melancholy and depression, she was the perfect remedy to pull him out of his shell.

When February of 1745 melted into March, the court began to worry that this was no passing fancy. This woman had no title! How could she compare, let alone rule over the courtiers at Versailles who held the required 400 years of nobility? Yet, in April, they wondered no more. Word was out the Mme de Mailly's apartment above the king's was being redecorated.

It was true. As early as March, she was the king's mistress, installed at Versailles in the apartment directly above Louis'. On May 7, the official separation from her husband was announced. But the affair was put on hold when the king rode off to join his army on May 6. The Dauphin, the ducs d'Ayen, de Richelieu and the marquis de Meuse rode with him. Mme d'Etioles went back to her estate while her husband was sent away on business. She called in her close friend to keep her company—the emerging poet, Francois-Marie Arouet, known for his nom de plume as Voltaire. Jeanne had already introduced him to the king and Louis was quick to award the writer a pension of two thousand livers a year, the office of Royal Historiographer, and the title of Gentleman of the Bedchamber in Ordinary, which afforded the holder a cherished patent of nobility.

Voltaire was not the only one invited to stay with Etioles while Louis was away. She took the time to learn the ways of court by inviting two courtiers, the marquis de Gontaut and the abbé de Bernis to teach her all about Versailles etiquette and how to behave. Louis wrote long love letters to her from the battlefield, all addressed to Mme d'Etioles. On one occasion, as Jeanne was about to slip a polished nail beneath the seal of the king's latest letter, she noticed her name was different. On the envelope, in Louis' tall, elegant hand was the name "Madame la marquise de Pompadour.

Enclosed in the letter was a patent for the new title. Jeanne Antoinette Poisson was now part of the ranks of titled nobility.

She had done it. Those who had laughed at her behind her back, making fun of the fact that her last name Poisson meant "fish" in French, were now put in a position to kowtow to the king's favorite, or be kicked out of court. Whether or not Pompadour, as she was now called, could hold her own at court, bow correctly, glide and follow the rigors of court, was soon put on display for all to see.

Jeanne Antoinette Poisson, Madame de Pompadour

On September 7, 1745, Louis came home from the *War of the Austrian Succession*. "He drove in his carriage to the Tuileries, where he met the Queen, the Dauphine [no doubt happy to have her husband back as well], and Mesdames [Louis' daughters]. The Royal Family having thus gathered, they all attended a *Te Deum* at Notre Dame. That night, there were illuminations all over, and especially at the Tuileries; the King, the Queen and the Royal Family went to the Hotel de Ville, watched handsome fireworks display and had supper with forty ladies. On the ninth, there was a royal banquet at the Tuileries and on the tenth Their Majesties arrived back at Versailles," the duc de Cröy wrote in the *Nouvelle Revue*.

Four days after returning to Versailles, the court was gathered and the marquise de Pompadour was officially presented to the king, queen, and mesdames by the king's cousin, the Princess of Conti. Pompadour looked regal and beautiful. The envious ladies of court angled for a better position in hopes of seeing her make a guffaw or botch the royal bow. They were to be disappointed. Madame de Pompadour glided up to the dais, curtseyed with the deep bow taught to all nobles, and backed elegantly away, kicking her train gracefully as she went. She was the epitome of elegance, presenting as a woman to the Palace born.

If the faces of the ladies at court had taken on a sickly pallor of green, they became positively ashen as the new marquise continued to dazzle. Barbier noted as early as October that "The Court at Fontainebleau is brilliant; Madame la marquise de Pompadour holds her rank well to the great regret of the ladies of the Court; they say that she behaves beautifully to the Queen."

Indeed, Madame de Pompadour became a champion of the queen from the moment Marie Leszczynska addressed her. In French protocol, one must be addressed first by anyone ranking above them. To be the first to begin a conversation if you were of an inferior rank was to be branded a social pariah. Even more so with the Royal Family. Therefore, it was with pure delight that Pompadour received the queen's initiation at conversation when Marie enquired after a mutual acquaintance, Madame de Saissac. That the queen recognized her was momentous occasion—to Jeanne and to the others watching. This was not to be a rivalry between queen and mistress. Pompadour was so moved, that she pledged her loyalty to the queen.

Marie, the neglected queen, was suddenly surrounded with attention she had never before been afforded. Pompadour gently told the king that he needed to treat his wife better. An odd thing for a mistress to do, but there it is. Jeanne was probably also aware that being friends with the queen was a good thing, but it does seem that she took on the queen's happiness out of kindness. Marie suddenly found herself being invited to Louis' precious Choisy, a chateau she had never set foot in. Debts she had run up by donating to charities, and which had weighed heavily on her mind, were suddenly paid off by the king. Her apartments at Versailles were redecorated with new tapestries, bedcurtains, furnishings, and objects d'art. And, for the first time, she was sent flowers. A queen residing over the most-splendid gardens in Europe, now received flowers, and it was all thanks to Madame de Pompadour.

It was Louis in whom the courtiers saw the most dramatic change. He seemed to come to life. Mme de Pompadour put on plays for him, taught him about gardening (not the structured gardens of Versailles, but the simple joys of gardening), and introduced him to areas of decorating and the arts he had missed. Her suppers for him always involved the intelligent and witty nobility. Gone was the mindless gossip that pervaded the usual court gatherings. Here, people discussed the sciences and current events of the world.

This was all noticed, not just by those at Versailles, but by visitors. The duc de Cröy from Belgian, who regularly attended court noted, "The King was now ordinarily freer and more talkative since the campaign and seemed to be much in love... with Mme de Pompadour... She gathered the whole Court into her apartments and almost presided over it... the King usually hunted three or four days a week, took supper, on those days, upstairs in her rooms and spent most of his time there... He worked much and assiduously with his council and each one of his ministers, most especially M. d'Argenson...who took precedence over all the others because of the war... I found out that the marquise de Pompadour was very powerful and that everyone paid court to her, so I arranged to be presented to her...I found her charming, both in looks and character...and full of amusing talents so that the King seemed to love her more than he had the others... She always played cards at the Queen's games, behaving with grace and dignity, and I noticed that when the time came [to join the King] in his private apartments, she asked the Queen for permission to leave the game, and the Queen would say, in a kind manner: 'Go'... the King seemed to me infinitely improved in his manner, in the best of health, looking cheerful and decisive, having fun, which he hadn't much seemed to do until then, speaking much and in a very obliging manner."

The Dauphin also had reason to appreciate her involvement at Versailles. All through 1746, she grew in popularity and position. Noticing that the Dauphin seemed to be intimidated by the king, she set about arraigning occasions for them to be together. The duc de

Cröy noticed that on November 23, 1746, "the King left for Choisy…riding in a *vis-á-vis* [a couch where only two people can ride facing each other—in this situation it was the Dauphin and the King], which … was the work of the clever mistress who was traveling with the Queen's ladies."

Mme de Pompadour next tackled politics in December. Once again Cröy reported, "She managed affairs with gaiety and endless grace. I saw her receiving many petitions. She lived in the upstairs apartment… which was much adorned…As the marquise had much influence, the ministers feared and respected her."

The king's favorite wielded a lot of power. She was closest to the King and those hoping to advance their position, or a cause would often seek out the mistress in order to get close to the monarch. For this reason, Mme de Pompadour was soon being asked to speak to the king about political affairs, many of which were over her head. The ministers began resenting her as they saw her as competing with their offices and the advice they were there to proffer. A cabal against Pompadour began forming at court, primarily lead by Jean Frederick Maurepas. For now, they remained in the background, but it was safe to say, all eyes were on the king's *maîtresse-en-titre*.

## Chapter Forty-Three
## **Peace and Pompadour**

While the *War of the Austrian Succession* continued to leave scarred countryside across Europe, death hit much closer to home at Versailles. In July of 1746, after only a little over a year of marriage, Marie Therese Raphaelle, Infanta of Spain, the Dauphine, died. To add to the Dauphin's sorrow, his wife had just given birth to a baby girl only three days before her death. The child was baptized Marie Therese and was styled as Madame Royale. The Dauphin's despair was intense. He had deeply loved his wife and he went into mourning.

Louis XV, deeply ensconced in war and needing to find a new bride for his son as soon as possible, turned to d'Argenson who suggested Marie-Josèpha of Saxony. By offering to put a Saxon princess on the throne of France, they would gain an alliance with Saxony, which until then had been tied to Austria. They would kill two birds with one wedding: a new wife to give birth (hopefully) to an heir, and a strategic alliance that just might alter the outcome of the war.

In December of 1746, Louis made the announcement that his son was to marry the Princess of Saxony. Six months later, the wedding took place. It was said the Dauphin was still mourning his wife and that the king had to practically drag him down the aisle. His grief was very public, but Maria Josepha was praised greatly for her conquering the heart of the Dauphin "bit by bit". When the

Dauphin's daughter by his late wife died in April of 1748, at the age of five, his grief worsened. Maria Josepha later commissioned a painting of her stepdaughter to be left over her cradle.

Maria Josepha of Saxony

As it turns out, Madame de Pompadour had also been influential in the selection of the Saxon princess for the Dauphin, and the young 15-year-old was grateful. Like the Dauphin, the new Dauphine was very devout. The couple were not fond of the various entertainments held at Versailles every week, preferring to stay in their apartments which can still be seen on the ground floor of Versailles overlooking the Orangery.

The couple's first child was a girl, born in 1750 and named Marie Zephyrine. The birth was greeted with much joy by her parents, but the king was disappointed the child was not male. She died in 1755. Their second child, Louis Joseph, Duke of Burgundy, was born on September 15, 1751, and the court erupted with celebration. The little boy died on March 22, 1761, after falling from a toy horse. After the accident, he started limping as a tumor began to grow on his hip. He was operated on, but he never recovered. The couple's second son, Xavier, was born in 1753, and died a year later. The king, along with his son and daughter-in-law, felt as if a curse lay upon the offspring of the royal couple. Finally, a third son, Louis

Auguste was born on August 23, 1754, and became second in line to the French throne, after his father, the Dauphin.

To everyone's delight, the child grew, and the future looked promising. Maria also gave birth to Louis (Louis XVIII), Charles X, Marie Clotilde (Queen of Sardinia), and Elisabeth of France. There were sadly many children who died:

The children were as follows:

Stillborn son (January 30, 1748)
Stillborn son (May 10, 1749)
Marie Zephyrine of France (Aug. 1750-Sept. 1, 1755) died at 5
Louis Joseph of France, Duke of Burgundy (Sept. 13, 1751-March 1761) died at the age of 9.
Stillborn daughter (March 9, 1752)
Xavier of France Duke of Aquitaine (Sept. 8, 1753-Feb. 22, 1761), died at 7.
Louis XVI of France (Aug. 23, 1754-January 21, 1793) married Marie Antoinette of Austria)
Louis XVIII of France (Nov. 17, 1755-Sept. 16, 1824), married Princess Marie Josephine of Saxony.
Stillborn son (1756)
Charles X of France (October 9, 1757- Nov. 6, 1836), married Princess Maria Theresa of Savoy
Marie Clotilde de France (Sept. 23, 1759-Nov. 6, 1836), married Charles Emmanuel IV of Sardinia
Stillborn son (1762)
Elisabeth of France (May 3, 1764-May 10, 1794, died unmarried.

The Dauphin's second wife was pregnant fourteen times during their marriage. The Louis XV's Queen, who knew all too well what it was like to have multiple back-to-back pregnancies was, no doubt, a great consolation to the young woman. Five stillborn children would be incredibly hard, let alone to lose others in their infancy as you watched them grow with hopes for their future. Marie Josepha did become close to the queen, who also detested the court activities and preferred her private apartments and chosen gatherings of friends. The Dauphin also learned to love her, and it was a happy union.

On October 18, 1748, the long *War of the Austrian Succession* ended with the signing of the *Treaty of Aix-la-Chapelle*. As reported earlier, the result of the war resulted in an uproar from France who felt the king had needlessly given back Netherlands and undone all the French had fought so hard to win. Louis had looked down the road and realized the cost of an ongoing war and did what he thought was best for his country. Prolonging the fight would see the increase of taxes and endless wars of revenge and loss of life. When advised to give the people an explanation for the Treaty and his decisions, Louis scoffed and said the king did not need to offer explanations for his actions. He was not a "merchant" and therefore chose "not to bargain," was his retort as he walked away to the seclusion of his cabinets.

Peace at last reigned, and Louis settled into a delightful routine of suppers with close friends and the company of his ever-present mistress, Madame de Pompadour. In December of 1748, his eldest daughter Elizabeth, Madame Infante, came to Versailles and stayed for a year. Seeing Madame de Pompadour as the gateway to her father's continued good graces, she treated the mistress with courtesy. It seemed Pompadour had found herself accepted at Court with surprising amiability from the women in Louis' life who should have resented her most. The queen still welcomed her to her suppers, appreciative of all the interloper had done to elevate her treatment at court. Only the Dauphin kept his distance, due to religious reasons. He was civil and kept his feelings hidden.

The marquise continued to expand her influence over the King. She introduced him to more of the arts and encouraged him to patronize architects, painters, and sculptors. She entertained him with her wit and charm, challenged him mentally, and surrounded him with great minds and easy conversation. If the ladies at Court had thought this beauty was but a royal roll in the hay when she first set foot upon the parquet floors of Versailles, they had long resolved themselves that they had been outmaneuvered by a superior mind.

Despite an unpopular peace treaty, Louis XV was still considered the most powerful monarch in Europe in many respects. The military genius Frederick II ruled over a tiny county of six million or so. Maria Theresa of Austria was still a force to be reckoned with, but she was still chaffing over losing Silesia to Prussia. England had lost much in the recent war, and Spain had continued to struggle and was in a decline. Italy had been so chopped up that it proved to be no threat. Russia was too distant and primitive. France still sparkled in every arena, and while it too was licking its wounds from the long and costly *War of the Austrian Succession* (it had been hit hard in its Navy), it still had a lot to crow about. In 1748, Louis XV was thirty-eight years old and still considered the most-handsome ruler in Europe. Young, strong and virile, he emulated royal branding. No other palace or court rivaled his, indeed, his Chateaus and gardens were copied all over Europe. To add to it, he had a mistress who had made a name for herself, not in the bawdy sense, but as a lady with a mind and a heart who had become the closest the king had to a true friend and someone Louis could trust.

Louis XV circa 1749

With the end of the war, Louis decided to take the opportunity to reduce the debt and modernize the system of taxation of the Kingdom of France. The package of reforms was put together by his finance minister D'Arnouville and was approved by the king and presented in two decrees issued in May 1749. The first measure was an issue of bonds, paying five percent interest, to pay off the 36 million livres of debt caused by the cost of war. This new measure was an immediate success. The second measure was the abolition of the *dixième*, a tax of ten percent on revenue, which had been created to finance the war, and its replacement by the *vingtième*, a tax of five percent on net revenue, which, unlike the *dixième*, taxed the income of all French citizens, including for the first time the income from the clergy and the nobility.

While the tax was supported by many, including Voltaire, it met immediate and fierce resistance from the both the nobility and the church. When on May 5, 1749, it was presented for formal registration to the Parlement of Paris—the assembly composed of high nobles and wealthy Parisians who had purchased seats—it was rejected by a vote of one hundred and six to forty-nine; the majority asked for more time to consider the project. The king responded by demanding immediate registration, which was done on May 19th.

Resistance to the new measures grew with the church and in the provinces, which had their own parlements. While the Parlements of Burgundy, Provence, and Artois bowed to the King's demands, Brittany and Languedoc refused. The royal government closed down the Parlement of Brittany, ordered the members of the Parlement of Languedoc to return to their estates and parishes, and took direct control of Provence.

Within Paris, the battle between the King and Parlement was fought over the status of the *Hôpital Gènèral*, a semi-religious organization which operated six different hospitals and shelters in Paris, with a staff of some five thousand persons. Many of the hospital staff and officials were Jansenists, while the board of directors of the hospital included many prominent members of the Parlement of Paris. In 1749, the king decided to purge the hospital of Jansenists and corruptions, appointed a new "Superieure" against the will of administrators, who resigned, then appointed four temporary administrators, and asked the First President of the Parlement of Paris, Rene Nicolas Charles Augustin de Maupeou, to implement his decree for the reorganization of the hospital. De Maupeou refused to carry out the decree without the authorization of the Parlement, and the Parlement, without taking any action, went on vacation. On November 20, when the Parlement returned, the king again summoned Maupeou for an audience and again demanded action without delay. This time the Parlement members met but refused to discuss the *Hôpital*.

On January 28, 1752, the king instructed the Grand Council to change the administration of the *Hôpital* without the approval of the Parlement. Voltaire, describing the affair, wrote, "Never before has such a small affair caused such a great emotion of the spirit." Small or not, it was the first overt disobedience of the legislature against the king, and one of the first signs that the Parlement believed they, not the king, was the legitimate source of laws in the nation.

The king's original plans to tax the church also ran into difficulty. A royal decree ordered all the clergy to submit a declaration of their revenue by February 17, 1751, but that day passed without any declarations given. Instead, it became known that the king had quietly issued a new decree in December of 1750, canceling the tax and relying again, entirely, on the "don gratuity," the voluntary donation by the church of 1,500,000 livres. Under the new decree, instead of a tax, the church would each year collect a comparable sum and donate it freely to the government. His support of the church came both from the teachings of Cardinal Fleury, and his gratitude to Archbishop de Beaumont, who defended him against the attacks of Jansenists and the criticisms of the Parlement, and the for the archbishop's tolerance of the king's own personal life and mistresses.

Back at home, Madame de Pompadour continued to advise Louis XV, helping him choose or demote ministers. Her opinions led to the downfall of some very competent ministers including Machault d'Aurnouville, and the Marquis d'Argenson, and to the promotion of a number of incompetent military commanders. Her most successful choice was the promotion of the Duc de Choiseul, who became one of the king's most effective ministers. Being the catalyst for the dismissal of ministers does not win one popularity contests. The comte de Maurepas, who had served continuously since becoming Minister of the Navy, at the age of 14, back in 1715, was suddenly dismissed. With his family ties to prominent Parlement members and his lengthy amount of time as minister in Louis' government, many who were on the outside were shocked at his firing. On the inside, it was all too clear who was behind it. Maurepas headed the anti-mistress campaign and went as far as to write derogatory pamphlets about Mme de Pompadour. It was after a particularly denigrating poem written by Maurepas that he was ousted. It read, "Once it was from Versailles, that good taste came to us. But today the riff raff preens and rules over us. If the Court is vulgar, why should that surprise us? Isn't it from the market that fish comes to us?" The correlation between Pompadour's last name of Poisson (French for "fish'), and the fact that the fish wives were coarse and vulgar in the marketplace, left no doubt that the prose were meant to offend. Oddly enough, the bawdy pamphlets and songs did not come from the lower or middle classes. They came from the heart of the palace—the nobility, who had recently been harnessed with an income tax that was hitting close to home.

As Parisians read the pamphlets and heard of the king's anger and sudden state censorship on such pamphlets, there began a stirring. A shift of opinion had begun against Louis. Still stinging from the *Treaty of Aix-la-Chapelle*, more taxes, rumors of a mistress who danced the King of France at the end of her strings, dismissals of loyal ministers, and now a censorship that curtailed their freedom of speech...Parisians were beginning to rethink the name: "Louis the Beloved."

## The Children Come Home

Louis XV's children were grown. On January 20, 1751, his daughter Elizabeth, Duchess of Parma, gave birth to an heir, Don Ferdinand. On December 9, Maria Luisa was born. In the summer of 1748, Madame Victoire returned from Fontevrault, where she and two of her sisters had been sent upon the suggestion of the late Cardinal Fleury. Following her home was Mesdames Sophie and Louise in 1750. Madame Henriette, Elizabeth's twin was there, but tragedy struck in 1752. The King had asked his daughter Henriette to accompany him on a snow sledge for some winter fun. It was February and bitterly cold. Henriette had not been feeling well, but flattered at her father's offer, went along. It was soon ascertained that the 24-year-old had smallpox. She died three days after the outing with the king. Louis went into deep despair. He ordered the finest funeral and had the body sent to the Tuileries for her wake memorial to honor her. It was said she was made up to look alive and dressed in the finest silk. To the king's dismay, rather than a solemn occasion marked by saddened crowds, the Parisians laughed, drank, and partied. It was a clear indication that Louis had lost favor in their eyes, and they saw the death of his daughter as punishment from God for his transgressions with a mistress they loathed. Another daughter, Madame Sixième had died in 1744 of smallpox at the Convent of Fontevrault. She was only eight and had not seen her parents since she was sent there at the age of two. Princess Sophie and Princess Victoire were the other daughters that went to the convent with her.

The people of Paris were not the only ones who detested Madame de Pompadour. Although she tried to win the approval of the returning daughters to court, the only one who warmed to her eventually was Elizabeth, and that was to further her political ambitions. Like their brother, the Dauphin, they loathed the favorite. The daughters were jealous of her. None of them had her beauty, wit, or knack for entertaining. They had been away from court since they were young, living at a convent. They were described as "dull, mean-spirited, jealous, and lazy." They and the Dauphin didn't like the time Pompadour took away from his mother. In no time, they had come up with a nickname for the *maitrese en titre*: "Maman Poutain" (Mother Whore).

The Dauphin was vastly aware he was not the man his father was. The duc de Cröy noted, "He waddled when he walked and was careless about time, so that he was twice as difficult to serve as the King and one never quite knew how to treat him. He was often closeted with Madame la Dauphine, the rest of the time with his gentlemen who had taken him over; beside that, he was neither easy nor pleasant of access." The poor Dauphine was described as overweight, plain, clumsy, and lacking in charm or the ease of conversation that draws people in. The Dauphin's wife was extremely jealous of him. There were occasions when he had mustered up the courage to flirt, but he was caught by the dauphine, and it ended there. She rarely let him out of her sight.

With the return of three of his daughters to court, Louis began looking about for a place to put them. Not just any hole in the wall would do. He wanted to please them. He looked at the outdated Ambassadors Staircase that had been one of the highlights in Versailles during Louis XIV's reign, and saw wasted space, a deteriorating skylight, and royal pomp for which he had no use. He ordered it destroyed to make way for royal apartments, a long suite of rooms on the ground floor of the Palace, decorated in the latest fashion. Madame Victoire's and Madame Adelaide's suites of rooms can be toured today.

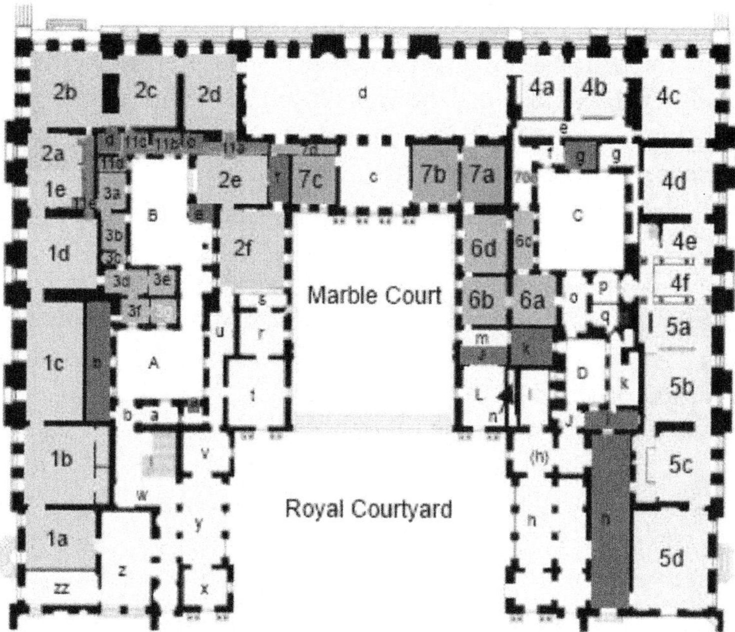


**Ground floor of Versailles during Louis XV**

4a-4f are Madame Victoire's apartments; 5a-5d are Madame Adelaide's suite of rooms. 1a-1e are the Dauphin's rooms, and 2a-2f are the Dauphine's apartments. (Courtesy of www.thisisversaillesmadame.blogspot.com.)

Louis continued to juggle the changing dynamics at home and with the Parlement, who went on strike more than once. The tension between the king and his people was building, as was the friction between the rulers of Europe.

# Chapter Forty-Four
## When is Enough, Enough?

Madame de Pompadour continued on with her dizzying daily schedule. One would think she was Queen of France as she juggled relationships, politics, and keeping Louis amused and happy. In September of 1751, she wrote Mme de Lutzelbourg: "On Monday I go to Crécy for five days… I am having a wedding for the girls of the villages and will show it all to the King. They are coming tomorrow to eat and dance in the courtyard of the chateau." Crécy was one of the castles Pompadour owned. Offering the lower-class girls of the village a place to celebrate their weddings was a kind gesture, and one that Louis approved.

Yet, as the year wore on, Pompadour noticed her health was failing. In one letter she stated, "We are so often on the road that I have given up hunting…I need some time to think," she wrote in December of 1751. In October of the following year, she wrote, "I have had a fever for ten days…bled and have had a terrible headache…I am overcome with visits, with letters and still have at least sixty more letters to write." "The life I lead is terrible," she complained. "I scarcely have a minute of my own; rehearsals and performances, and twice a week a trip…Indispensable and considerable duties: The Queen, the Dauphin, the Dauphine, who, luckily, is consigned to her chaise lounge, three daughters [Mesdames], two Infantas, see whether I can find time to breathe."

It was at this time, 1750-1751, that Mme de Pompadour and the king's relationship changed. Louis's sexual appetite had long been a concern of Mme de Pompadour's. She admitted to "the misfortune to be of a rather cold temperament" when it came to lovemaking. To please Louis, she tried a number of aphrodisiacs to increase her libido, including a diet of truffles, celery, and vanilla. During the early fifties, she was also suffering the aftereffects of whooping cough, recurring colds, and bronchitis, spitting blood, headaches, three miscarriages to the king, as well as an unconfirmed case of leucorrhoea (a white, yellow or greenish vaginal discharge, often attributed to an estrogen imbalance. It can have an unpleasant odor.)

With all these things taken into account, Madame de Pompadour encouraged the king to indulge his sexual desires elsewhere, and even offered a name or two of plain, dull ladies of the court that she knew would be of no threat to her. Pompadour took on more and more of a role as friend and confidante; someone the king could trust. She was already indispensable to him. She felt safe in the knowledge he could not do without her. She came close to losing him when a conspiracy of Pompadour's enemies at court put the tempting 18-year-old Mme de Choiseul in Louis' path. The young beauty began a campaign of seduction, and the king finally caved. Once Choiseul figured she had Louis in the palm of her hand, she began the sabotage of Pompadour. She told the king she would leave her husband for him, but only if Pompadour left. Louis, his sexual desire blazing for this new lovely, finally said, "Non." Pompadour and her friendship were too important to him.

The marquise and the king had come close to losing each other. Many at court were holding their breath that the favorite would be exiled, but she stayed. This was a lesson to both. Pompadour realized that if she were to forego Louis' lovemaking, she would need to oversee his conquests so that the likes of Mme de Choiseul did not happen again. For Louis, it underscored his need for the marquise. There were beautiful women everywhere throwing themselves at him, but none had created a home for him. It was her advice he sought in everything, for he trusted her honesty and lack of an agenda toward her own ambition. Louis would need her now more than ever as the peace throughout Europe was beginning to erode, the Parlement was rebelling again, and his belief in his ministers was luke-warm.

Due to his respect for the woman who remained by his side, in 1752, The king declared Mme de Pompadour—the former Mlle Poisson—a royal duchess. This was a monumental title and one that came with envied perks. The "honors of the *tabouret*" meant she was now entitled to a stool in front of the Majesties, rather than stand.

She would now proceed all ladies without title while entering a room or walking down a hallway; she would wear a ducal coronet and mantle on her coat of arms at a time when the latter were everywhere, from one's carriages to one's bed linens, as well as on private salon chairs that carried the privileged about Versailles. Pleased as she was to be recognized, Mme de Pompadour kept her name of marquise, rather than use the title of duchess. It was a statement, perhaps toward the snobby ladies at court, that titles were not what mattered to her—it was the king's happiness.

On February 8, 1756, Louis announced a new title for Pompadour. The marquise-duchesse de Pompadour was appointed a supernumerary dame du palais de la Reine (lady-in-waiting to the Queen). If some thought making his *maîtresse déclarée* a lady-in-waiting to his wife callous and unfeeling, they were late on getting the news. In October of 1755, Mme de Pompadour had officially ceased being the king's mistress.

Besides abstaining from sex with the king, Pompadour stopped eating meat on Fridays and Saturdays due to her recently found connection to the church after the loss of her daughter Alexandrine. Now that she was no threat to the royal family as the king's mistress, the need to plot against her and have her removed from court eased. As the king's close friend, she was afforded constant contact with him. She relaxed knowing she would no longer have to suffer through sexual encounters for which she found no pleasure, and that her frequent illnesses would not cause her the guilt they had before when Louis was kept from her bed.

Pompadour may have found relief in the new twist on she and the king's relationship, but his needs had not changed. The queen had aged, and not in an appealing way. She was as dowdy and dull as ever, so that avenue was closed to him as well. And so, Louis seized upon a plan. Not wanting to go through the whole mistress scenario again, he opted for casual sex under the cloak of secrecy. He chose a small house with five or six rooms just outside the park of Versailles at a location called the Parc aux Cerfs. He purchased the house, put in a few select and discreet servants, and began having a succession of very young, lower-middle class girls brought in from Paris. These girls were in their mid- to late-teens, sexually inexperienced, and were told they were visiting a foreign dignitary. Contrary to popular belief, this was not a harem of girls entertaining the king all at once. One girl occupied the house at a time, usually for a month, and then was replaced.

Mademoiselle O'Murphy, by Francois Boucher (1751)

One such lovely was an Irish girl by the name of O'Murphy. Her portrait was painted by Francois Boucher. The Deer Park, as it became known, was a secret for some time and the girls were brought in under the cloak of darkness. Madame de Pompadour has been accused of procuring the girls for the king, but there is no solid evidence to support that assumption. She was probably relieved that these nymphettes could not possibly pose a threat to her station or winning the king's heart. She stated, "It is his heart I want! All these little girls with no education will not take him from me. I would not be so calm if I saw some pretty woman of the court or the capital trying to conquer it."

By 1755, Europe was crackling with tension. The peace had broken down and France was now standing alone without an ally it could depend on. Waiting in the wings was the Parlement, hoping for a chance to undermine the king. Raising taxes for another war would do the trick. The ministers bickered. Its chief member, d'Argenson, was a known enemy of Madame de Pompadour. Louis was now 46. He was known to be kind, still favored secrecy, and held only a few people close to him; Pompadour led those in favor.

## The Seven Years War

1756 found France participating in the *Seven Years War* which lasted until 1763. France entered the war with the hope of achieving a lasting victory against Prussia, Britain, and their German allies and with the hope of expanding its colonial possessions. While the first few years of war proved successful for the French, in 1759 the situation reversed, and they suffered defeats on several continents. In an effort to reverse their losses, France finished an alliance with their neighbor Spain, in 1761. In spite of this, the French continued to suffer defeats throughout 1762, eventually forcing them to sue for peace. The 1763 *Treaty of Paris* confirmed the loss of French possessions in North America and Asia to the British. France also finished the war with very heavy debts, which they struggled to repay for the remainder of the 18th century.

The *War of the Austrian Succession* had ended leaving many of the parties dissatisfied with the outcome. Many believe the *Seven Years War* was just a continuation of the former war after a short half-time. France and Britain were engaged in an intensifying global rivalry after they superseded Spain as the leading colonial power. Hoping to establish supremacy, both countries engaged in several minor wars in North America. French colonies in Louisiana, Illinois, and Canada had largely surrounded British colonies strung out in a narrow strip along the coast. All the French needed to totally envelope the British was control of the Ohio Country. Attempting to gain control of this territory, France built a complex system of alliances with the area's Native American tribes and brought them into conflict with Britain.

Throughout the war, Madame de Pompadour was asked by the king to meet with certain key players as she could do so in secrecy while he was always surrounded by people. The power went to her head, and she begin to see herself as a huge political mediator, when in fact, she was out of her depth. Criticism was hurled at the king and Pompadour as missteps were made. Louis's other advisors rose and fell with rapid succession, continuing the lack of stability which had plagued the monarchy in the early 18th century.

While the *Seven Years War* began in North America, in 1755 France became drawn into a major war in Europe. Recently allied to Austria, Sweden, and Russia, the French tried to defeat the Prussians who had only the British as major allies. Despite repeated attempts between 1757 and 1762, the French and their allies failed to win the conclusive victory against Prussia despite a constant war of attrition. They were partly frustrated by an army led by the Duke of Brunswick made up of British forces and troops from the smaller German states which operated in West Germany.

France had opened the war against Britain in Europe by capturing Menorca and until 1759 they believed they held the upper hand. The British navy, however, had initiated a tight blockade of the French coast which prevented supplies and troops moving freely, and sapped morale. Realizing that Prussia was unlikely to be defeated until its ally Britain was, the French foreign minister, Choiseul developed a plan to invade Britain in three separate places at Portsmouth, Essex, and Scotland. He oversaw the construction of a massive fleet of transports to convey the troops during 1759. Defeats of the French navy at Lagos and Quiberon Bay put an end to these plans and he was forced to call off the invasion in late autumn.

The Battle of Quiberon Bay in Nov. 1758

A diversionary force under François Thurot had managed to land in Northern Ireland before he was hunted down and killed by the British navy. In the wake of the disaster at Quiberon, Thurot was lionized as a hero in France.

François Thurot

By this time, France's finances were in poor condition, despite the efforts of Silhouette to keep down expenditure, and France was only kept afloat by a major loan from neutral Spain. Despite the Spanish government's official policy of neutrality, they were slowly shifting towards supporting an outright pro-French position, encouraged by Choiseul. In December of 1761, war finally broke out between Britain and Spain—but the Spanish involvement did not provide the relief to the French that had been hoped for. Instead, French troops were needed to bolster Spanish efforts to invade Portugal and became bogged down there. Spain also suffered defeats in Cuba and the Philippines in 1762, and by the end of the year, both Spain and France were urgently seeking peace.

The War continued in North America, Asia and in Africa. In April 1758, a British expedition conceived by the merchant Thomas Cumming captured the French settlement of Saint-Louis in Senegal. The scheme had been so successful and profitable that two further expeditions were dispatched the same year which captured the Island of Gorée and the French trading station on the Gambia. The loss of these valuable colonies further weakened France's finances. In 1762, a force was prepared to retake the Senegal territories, but had to be abandoned.

The French began negotiations in Paris in late 1762. Because of a change in the British government, they were offered more lenient terms than might otherwise have been expected. While they lost Canada to the British, Martinique and Guadeloupe were returned to them in exchange for Menorca. The French defeat had a devastating impact on French political life, and a number of senior figures, were forced out of public office. Realizing the deficiency in the French navy, Louis XV began a massive rebuilding program to match British naval strength. Choiseul drew up a long-term plan to gain victory over the British which was partially put into action during the *American War of Independence* after France joined the conflict in 1778 (under the reign of Louis XVI), as did its ally Spain.

Back at Versailles, Louis's popularity was waning along with the daily reports of losses on the front lines. Pamphlets against himself and Pompadour continued, and notes found their way into the palace and garden grounds; many with threats. The King, with his usual disdain for such things, merely crumpled them and tossed them aside. A horrific wake-up call came when on January 5, 1757, an assassination attempt was made on the King.

"This day," Barbier exclaimed in his diary, "has witnessed the most dreadful of events. The King has been assassinated, knifed…by a scoundrel. On Thursday morning, consternation was widespread in Paris, everyone was crying in the churches; but by the evening we had the happiness of learning with certainty that the blow was neither deadly nor even dangerous."

The duc de Cröy, who was in Louis XV's suite, saw what happened: "Around six in the evening, the sky being rather light but cloudy, there being a full moon and torches which dazzled the eyes, the King decided to return to Trianon, wherc everybody had remained. As he came down the last step of the small guardroom to step into his carriage, leaning on his Grand and First Equerries, the duc d'Ayen and M. le Duc following him, the Captain of the Swiss Guard walking before him, a sufficient number of troops being lined up, a man sprang forth between two guards, whom he pushed, one to the right, the other to the left; he struck an officer with such strength that he made him fall, and came up, partly from behind, and struck the King on the right side with a knife that had a folding blade, using such force that the knife pushed the King forward, prompting him to say, 'Duc d'Aynes, someone has just punched me.'

Staircase to the King's Private Apartments

Louis felt the place where he thought he had been punched and saw his hand covered with blood. "I am wounded. Arrest him but do not kill him," he said to the guards. They seized the man and the king turned back. His attendants wanted to carry him, but he said, "No I am still strong enough to go up myself," and he walked back up the staircase near the Marble Court. When he finally got to see the wound back in his room, and saw the blood pouring out, he said, "Oh! I have been struck. I will not recover!" He began asking for a priest and a surgeon. Unfortunately, his entire household was at Trianon awaiting his return. There were no sheets on his bed or a fresh shirt. A robe was finally procured for him. The king, weakened by loss of blood and fear, thought he was dying. He asked urgently that a priest be brought to him to hear his last confession.

The almoner on duty came in and the king hurriedly confessed, saying he would do more if he was still alive later. A surgeon came in and washed the wound. The First Surgeon La Martinere came over from Trianon and probed the wound. He pronounced that while the wound seemed superficial, he was worried that the tip of the blade may have been poisoned, as it was a major concern in those days. The mesdames [Louis' daughters] rushed in upon hearing the news and fainted at the sight of their father covered in blood. The queen also came in, and likewise fainted at the sight of the blood.

The knife that had inflicted the wound had a three-and-a-half-inch long blade and was very sharp. It was long enough that it could have hit a major organ. What had saved the king was the many layers of clothing and the thick coat he was wearing in the January cold. After a few days of fever and feeling weak, the King was told he would fully recover. The household returned from Trianon, and news that the knife was not poisoned seemed to put an end to it. This was far from the truth. When an attendant said to the king that the wound was not very deep, Louis replied, "It is deeper than you think, for it reaches the heart." Knowing his people hated him enough to try and kill him, he sunk into a deep depression. He felt he was no longer "Louis the Beloved", but "Louis the Hated."

## Chapter Forty-Five
## The View from the Window

Louis XV had been attacked. The wound had impacted his psyche far more than it had his body. The would-be assassin turned out to be a man who was mentally unbalanced. Robert-François Damiens had been a footman for the counseiller Béze de Lys, an official of the Parlement. Often hearing the denigration of the king from de Lys (of the taxes and other "wrongs" the Parlement were levying at the Crown), this slow-witted man took upon himself to teach the king a lesson so that he would listen to that inciteful body of the government. He went to threaten Louis but not to kill him. One Mme de Lutzelbourg summed it up: "The monster is a dog who will have heard a few dogs of the *Enquetes* barking and will have caught rabies from them."

The often-fickle Parisians were once again on the king's side; horrified at the attack. If Louis felt they no longer loved him, he had only to hear the song being sung in the capital city: "In vain an execrable monster, spewed up by a raging hell, Strike the most lovable of kings…From high above, God who protects the King, beloved of his subjects, holds back the sacrilegious arm. Tender subjects, dry your tears, Louis will not forsake the light. God only permitted your alarms to increase your love."

What followed would lead to the king's undoing where it should have signaled the fall of the Parlement. Damiens confessed to his reasons for attacking the king: that he had heard all the accusations from his superiors and acted upon them, hoping to frighten the king into listening to the Parlement (who were, at this time, still on strike). As the assault had taken place at the Royal Palace, it was now in the jurisdiction of the *prévot de l'hôtel*, a special official who had no reason to suppress Damiens' damning confession and hence allow the Parlement to save face. Though still on strike, they reached out to the king and begged him to let them put the attacker on trial. Louis XV could have broken them by refusing and allowing the world to know who had incited the attack. But he had just been given the last rites when he thought the wound would be fatal, and part of those rites was to forgive your enemies, which he declared. The popularity of the Parlement was already at an all-time low; the news of Damien's impetus would have killed it in the court of public opinion.

The king granted them permission to conduct the trial themselves. In spite of being relieved at the king's acquiesce, they announced they would only break their strike long enough to hold the trial, but then would resume their protest until the king withdrew his Declaration of December 13 where more restrictions had been levied against the members of Parlement. Louis maintained his stance on the Declaration and the Parlement went on with its trial of Damiens. It was to their benefit to do so and squelch his reports as much as possible.

What the king did not know was the methods this corrupt body would go to in order to alter the reality of the events leading up to the attack on the monarch. Louis XV had specifically told his guards to "arrest the man, but do not hurt him."

The Parlement's method of justice began with questioning the prisoner, torturing him when his answers were detrimental to them, questioning him again, and torturing him again. It began with the man being strapped to a board and hot irons applied to the bottoms of his bare feet. He had already told them the truth, and his impaired mind didn't know what else to do. On March 28, he was taken to the Place de Grève, in front of the Hôtel de Ville, there to have his right hand cut off, boiling lead poured over his body and his tongue cut out. All of this was being done in a public square where a mixed crowd watched: some in horror, some with base excitement. Finally, the poor man, still alive, was laid on the ground between four horses. His wrists and ankles were tied to long ropes, each rope tied to a horse. It was the archaic practice called "drawn and quartered." The horses were incited to run in four different directions, the purpose to tear the limbs from the body. But Damien had a strong body, and through his wails of pain, his limbs held. The executioner finally took up an axe and chopped at the joints of his shoulders and thighs until the limbs flew off. Even then, he lingered on before finally dying.

This gruesome torture would come back to haunt Louis, when the tide of popular opinion turned against him once more. It was assumed by the general citizenship of Paris that the king had ordered the heinous execution in retribution for his attack. Nothing was further from the truth. When the King was read the report from the local gazette, he froze in horror. The Parlement had betrayed him and in their need to save face, had mercilessly tortured a man beyond reason.

The King's family remained by his side as he recovered from his wound. Because of the last rites administered to him while he lay wounded, Madame de Pompadour was kept away. Alone, she wondered at her future. Would this be a repeat of Metz where Louis' mistress was ordered exiled? Her only trump card was that it had been openly declared before the incident that she was no longer the king's mistress, but only his friend. Would that save her from being dismissed from Court? The fickle courtiers, assuming she would be sent packing, kept their distance, and she waited in agonizing solitude.

Louis leaned on his family throughout his depression and physical pain. It wasn't until January 16, 1758, eleven days after the attack, that he borrowed a cape from the duchesse de Brancas, who had been visiting him with the Dauphine, and, still in a nightcap and robe, he ascended the stairs to his private apartments, leaning upon a cane. He had gone to visit Madame de Pompadour.

With repulsive speed, the courtiers beat a path to Pompadour's door once the word was out that she was staying and still acting as the king's friend and advisor. While she treated them with courtesy, her mind was determined to rid herself of her enemies at court. It was therefore not surprising that within twenty-four hours of the king's visit to her door, a letter was given to Monsieur d'Argenson, signed by the king, asking him to resign his office as Secretary of War, and his other offices, and "withdraw to your estate of Les Ormes." Marchault followed next, and while the two exiles were met with favorable applause, the ministers replacing them were not exactly top shelf. Peyrenc de Moras, lacking in enthusiasm for the post and having no idea how the deficit should be handled, replaced d'Argenson.

## Death Comes to Versailles

In 1764, dissention had broken out between the Pope and Jesuits of France. Louis XV became embroiled in the dispute, when he was asked to defend the Jesuits' right to worship and teach in their churches and houses. In March of that year, they were banished from the Kingdom of France, infuriating the king who posted an edict dated November 1764, allowing individual Jesuits to live in France as a private person. Choiseul actually joined with the Parlement in its war against the Jesuits. The dauphin, mesdames, the queen, and the anti-Pompadour faction were incensed at Choiseul's support of a cause that they saw as sacrilege. Widely thought to be Pompadour's man, the Court of Versailles was split over the matter.

Louis XV, despite the continual upheaval around him, tried to maintain some semblance of order at court by maintaining the usual routine. He dined in public and had the strange reputation of being able to crack off the top of his soft-boiled egg with unrivaled elegance. Many came to Versailles just to watch this royal achievement. The *lever* and the *coucher* continued, he hunted and gave ample attention to new buildings going up. Madame Infante, Louis' favorite daughter was back again at court for an extended stay, looking as always for a way to add to her holdings by exchanging Parma for a bigger state. Louis would often be found in her apartments discussing business. The *Seven Years War* brought her no nearer to her pursuits, but to Louis' delight, she stayed on at Versailles.

Suddenly, in November of 1759, Elizabeth caught smallpox. It was an aggressive case, and it was soon told to the king that there was no hope. His eldest daughter, and twin of the late Henriette, died on December 5$^{th}$. Louis went into mourning and was seen to grieve for months. Finally, he rallied and transferred his affection to her son and his grandson, Don Ferdinand, who was in Parma. The boy was only eleven years old when Louis wrote to him in September of 1762, assuring him of his love for him and his pride in how well people spoke of the boy. When in July 1765, Don's father, Don Philip, died, leaving the boy an orphan, the letters from his grandfather Louis XV, sealed in red wax and dried with gold sand, became more frequent. Don Ferdinand was now 14 and Louis pledged to help him. In a letter, the king wrote to him, "You are now in a great position, though at thc hcad of a very small state; always ask your Sovereign Judge for his help in governing it wisely. I wrote to Spain as soon as I heard about your father's death and how that the King, your uncle, will not forget in his nephew the love he had for his brother. I kiss you most tenderly, my very dear grandson." Louis was no doubt remembering the feelings he had when he was orphaned so suddenly at a tender age.

The double deaths of his daughter and son-in-law were not the only shadows hanging over the Court of Versailles. Madame de Pompadour, only 42 years of age, had not been well for some time. By the winter of 1763, it had become obvious. She was constantly out of breath, had swollen legs, had visibly aged and was in a weakened state. Her portraits had also changed. In twenty years, she had gone from the slender beauty at court to a more matronly version of herself.

Madame de Pompadour in her early years at Court, and in 1764

Madame de Pompadour continued to maintain her hectic schedule, stubbornly refusing to show any signs of frailty. Her only concession was a sort of elevator—called a flying armchair—to transport her up the stairs. It relied on a pulley system and servants to man it. She was tired and had relied on Choiseul to handle the political side of things to which she had once involved herself. Finally, in early 1764, she became seriously ill.

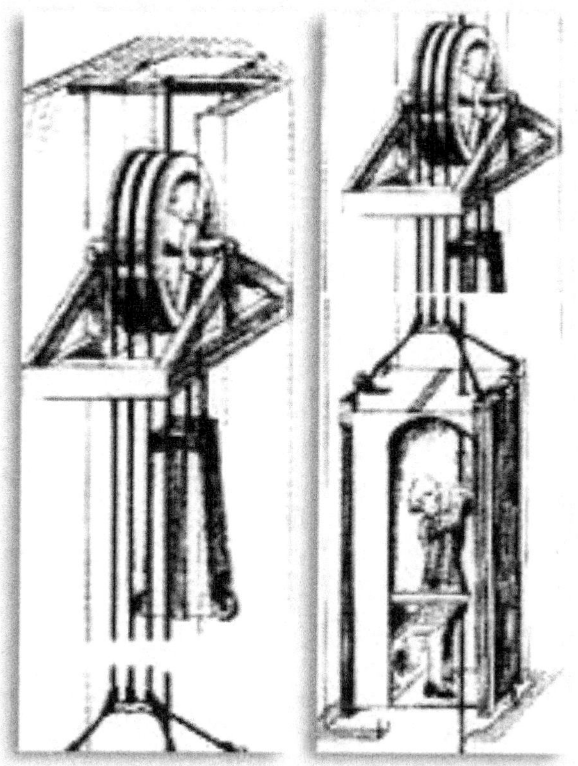

The Flying Armchair built for Pompadour.

The duc de Cröy penned, "At Court, Mme de Pompadour's illness stopped everything. It had begun, on February 29, by a bad cold on the chest. The seventh day of the illness, she was thought to be safe when she developed a strong miliarial fever, and on the eleventh a strong putrid fever was noticed. She was very ill, the worry grew, the King was almost always with her. On March 10, she was near death; they say that on the ninth day of her illness she confessed to the priest from the Madeleine… Everybody agreed that she was kind and seemed to take an interest in them…

"On April 13, her situation looked absolutely desperate…During the night of the fourteenth to the fifteenth she was given the last rites even though she was at Versailles…. She showed much courage and ready acceptance of death.

"His Majesty had seen her the day before, but he no longer saw her after she had received the last rites. For a long time, she had been merely his friend, and he was the one who told her she needed the last rites. She could no longer remain in bed because her chest illness choked her: she always sat in an armchair unable to breathe.

"A little before her death, the marquise said good-bye and sent away MM. de Soubise, de Gontaut, and de Choiseul, saying: 'It is coming close; leave me with my confessor and my maids.' She called back M. de Soubise and gave him her keys. She arranged everything, called back her business manager and told her to call her carriage so that she could be taken to her Versailles house.

"She died on April 15…at seven at night…She was widely regretted, for she was kind and had helped those who had come to her."

Louis XV was not allowed to be with her in the end, and the moment she died, etiquette demanded that she be removed from the palace. It had been an unprecedented move to allow her to die there in the first place. That right was reserved for the royal family. It is a testament to the love Louis bore her.

Dufort described what happened next: "The duchesse de Praslin told me, "I saw two men pass by carrying a stretcher. When they came closer (they passed right under my window) I saw that it was the body of a woman covered only with so a thin a sheet that the shapes of the head, the breasts, the belly and the legs were clearly visible. I sent to ask: it was the body of that poor woman who, according to the strict rule that no dead person can remain in the Palace, was being carried to her house."

Dufort continued to report on the King's whereabouts as the body was leaving the Palace: "It was six o'clock at night, in winter, and a dreadful storm was raging. The King took Champlost by the arm; when he arrived at the mirrored door of the *cabinet intime* which gives out onto the balcony facing the avenue, he told him to close the entrance door and went with him out onto the balcony. He kept absolutely silent, saw the carriage drive into the avenue and, in spite of all the bad weather and the rain, which he appeared not to feel, he kept looking at it until it went out of sight. He then came back into the room. Two large tears were still running down his cheeks, and he said to Champlost only three words, 'These are the only respect I can pay her.'"

The queen wrote to a friend on April 20 of the following year, "There is no more talk of her who is gone, than as if she had never existed." A cruel summary, but accurate. Madame de Pompadour's body had barely left Versailles before ambitious females began jockeying to replace her as the king's mistress, including Choiseul's sister, the duchesse de Gramount, who failed. Madame de Pompadour's possessions were sold at auction, including the gold-and-lacquer desk Maria Theresa sent her. Her chateau at Bellevue was returned to the Crown.

One of Madame de Pompadour's apartments above the King's at Versailles.
(Photo courtesy of www.thisisVersaillesmadame.blogspot.com.)

Jeanne-Antoinette was gone. Her patronage of the arts was also gone. She was a noted art collector with a particular love of porcelain and owned hundreds of objects of all shapes and sizes; she supported the development of the porcelain foundation at Sèvres. She had a wide range of interests and helped the king with his many architectural pursuits, including the laying out of the Place Louis XV, now the Place de la Concorde, in Paris. She also encouraged the Encyclopédie project of Diderot and d'Alembert and helped with the editing of the book. Louis had been opposed to the new Encyclopedia project until one day at a supper party someone asked how gun powder was made. Madame de Pompadour exclaimed that if they could look it up in the Enclopédie, they could find out. The king became fascinated with the wealth of information he saw there and changed his mind about the book. She was said to be fond of truffle soup, chocolate, and champagne.

On Madame de Pompadour's suggestion, her brother was appointed director of the king's buildings and made the marquis de Marigny. Together they built the Ècole Militaire, most of the palace of Compiegne, the Petit Trianon, a new wing at Fontainebleau, and the exquisite Chateau de Bellevue for Pompadour, which sat on a hill above where the Eiffel Tower is today. The Petit Trianon was in the process of being built when Pompadour died. It was to be her special retreat. It was later given to Louis's next mistress, Madame du Barry, and finally to Marie Antoinette under Louis XVI's reign. Pompadour, Marigny, and Louis XV also built many pavilions and summer houses.

Madame de Pompadour's apartments were said to be decorated with exquisite taste. It was built in the attic above the Mars, Mercury, and Apollo rooms of the king's apartment. A private staircase led from the king's rooms up to Pompadours' apartments. Her rooms had a wonderful view from their windows of the North Parterre and the forest of Marly. Around 1750, when the king's relationship with Pompadour became platonic, she moved from the attic and into a large apartment on the ground floor of the palace, where she died in 1764. This apartment was later given to Louis' new mistress, Madame du Barry.

This later apartment opened onto both the Marble and Stag Courtyards and can be reached by the King's Staircase. There is a sequence of rooms, including a dining room, an antechamber, and a bedchamber, which was connected to the King's Private Apartments by a hidden staircase. A bathroom, library, and some service rooms are over the Stag Court.

Louis XV grieved in private. As the carriage wheels bearing his friend of twenty years crunched through the gravel of the avenue leading away from the palace, did he walk back through the mirrored door out into the Hall of Mirrors and remember removing his yew tree headdress before a stunning beauty dressed as Diana the Huntress? Surely, everywhere he looked about his massive palace were memories of trysts, laughter, comradery, and love. He felt utterly alone.

The Chateau de Bellevue of Madame de Pompadour

## Chapter Forty-Six
## **Where To Now?**

Madame de Pompadour had done much more to influence the king other than encouraging him in his patronage of the arts and architecture. She had given him the confidence he had lacked his entire life. Always shy in speaking with others, he had turned Jeanne into a kind of private secretary, and asked her to engage with dignitaries and officers, the unfortunate result leading to bad political endeavors. As the days passed after Pompadour's death, the court watched and waited. Many supposed he would spend more time with his daughters and the dauphin, or with the queen. But Louis had been introduced to a society of wit, charm, and stimulating conversation, thanks to Madame de Pompadour. While remaining a dutiful father and husband, he found their company lacking. In short, he was bored.

His daughters tried to provide him with some distractions, but to no avail. Madame Louise was forever engulfed in religious exercises; Mesdames Victoire and Sophie were dull, slow-witted, and spent their days indulging themselves with the rich fare of Versailles. That left only Madam Adelaide. This daughter was the only of the girls who was a reactionary. She loved to stir the pot, was forever spouting ultra-Catholic viewpoints, and had hated Pompadour (it was she who gave the mistress the nickname "Mother Whore"). Perhaps the brightest of the bunch, she was also foul-tempered and lacked persistence. She would begin a new campaign, only to abandon it.

Louis maintained his routine of work, hunting, and writing letters. He wrote copious correspondence, all in a tall, elegant hand. Many went to his orphaned grandson, Don Ferdinand, Duke of Parma. He continued to assure the boy of his affection. On August 25, 1765, his letter to the duke was merely to tell him how hot the weather had been. To all around the king, it looked as though he had rallied from the loss of Pompadour. He still held suppers with friends such as Ayen, Richelieu, Meuse, and Soubise. He played with clocks and studied the stars and botany. He oversaw his building campaigns at Versailles, including the ongoing work on the Petit Trianon which sat outside his botanical gardens behind the Trianon.

It was therefore a cruel twist of Fate when in October of that year the Dauphin became gravely ill. He had once caused Louis great alarm when he had earlier contracted smallpox. This, however, was something more serious. The heir to the throne was suffering from consumption, a deadly disease that was usually the death knell for those afflicted with it. Throughout October and into November, he became increasingly worse. Louis, distraught and rudderless without Pompadour's shoulder to lean on, took to his pen. He wrote to Don Ferdinand on November 17, and said, "I am your grandfather by a daughter whom I loved dearly and lost. I am about to lose my son as well: last Wednesday he received the last rites; imagine how I must feel."

On December 20, 1765, Louis Ferdinand, the Dauphin of France, died of what is today known as tuberculosis. It was surmised it was that same disease that took Madame de Pompadour. The dauphin died at Fontainebleau at the age of 36. At his passing, his eldest surviving son, Louis-Auguste, duc de Berry, became the new dauphin, and would later become Louis XVI. The dauphin was buried in the Cathedral of Saint-Ètienne in Sens. His heart was buried at Saint Denis Basilica.

The death of his son and heir pushed the often-melancholy king into depression. His letters to Don Ferdinand showed a man reeling and unable to face the court festivities: "...his loss has been a dreadful blow to me and the whole Kingdom," Louis wrote in late December. "I am going to Choisy to avoid the [New Year's] compliments which this year, I could hardly bear." In another letter he wrote on January 6, 1766, "...we are deep in winter, and without an end in sight..." Two weeks later, he writes, "I try distracting myself as best I can since here there is no remedy, but I cannot get used to not having a son, and when they bring my grandson, what a difference for me… Our winter is terrible and refuses to end."

The grandson was Louis-Auguste, the new dauphin and twelve-years-old. Louis XV was now fifty-six. It was a terrible thing to outlive a child, let alone one who was destined for the throne. While France was finally at peace, the work continued to pile up on the king's desk. Parlement was still a thorn in his side. It did not help that Choiseul was a liberal freethinker and was on friendly terms with the Parlement, not the least reason being that his wife was related to a number of the great Parlement families. It too served his purpose to keep the religious upheaval over the Jesuits simmering. It meant he would be needed by the king to try and resolve the issue. One was always in fear of being replaced, and his biggest supporter, Madame de Pompadour was gone.

Louis-Auguste, the new Dauphin of France

As the controversy with two Parlements raised their ugly heads

(Paris and Rennes), Louis' late son, the dauphin, spoke from the grave. Louis reread a letter his son had written to him years earlier: The Parlements, the Dauphin had written, were trying to "convince the kingdom that, oblivious to the people's misery, you waste their blood and their treasure; that, considering only you own pleasure, you are establishing a crushing despotism; that without [the parlements] all the laws would be annulled and the State in an uproar…An unbreakable firmness is the only way to preserve…your authority; it is sad to have to make others fear you, but sadder still to be in fear yourself."

The letter must have had tremendous impact on the king. It had the importance of being timed with his grief for his son, adding immediacy to the words. On February 28, March 1 and March 2, 1766, Louis could finally face the course he must take by addressing three successive councils. The *lit de justice* that followed on March 3rd left no one in doubt as to the king's resolve. Although written by the king's Attorney General Joly de Fleury, Louis had modified it and now read it out to the waiting Parlement. It was to be his last attempt to settle the long, disruptive assaults on his government.

Louis XV spoke at length in a clear, firm tone, with the authority France had been waiting to see from their reclusive king. He said in part, "I will not suffer anyone to introduce into the monarchy an imaginary body [the illegal alliance of the Parlements of Paris and Rennes] which could only disrupt the harmony. The magistrates do not constitute a body or order separate from the three orders of the realm [the Estates General consisting of the clergy, the nobility, and the common citizens]. The Magistrates are my officers…

"It is in my person only that the sovereign power resides; its particular characteristic is the spirit of wisdom, justice and reason; it is from myself alone that my courts hold their existence and their authority; the plentitude of this authority, which they exercise in my name, remains always within me; it is through my authority alone that the officers of my courts proceed, not to make but to register and publish my laws, and that they may remonstrate whatever is part of the duty of good and faithful advisers; the public order in its entirety emanates from me; I am its supreme guardian; my people are one with me only; and the rights and interests of the nation, which some have dared represent as a body separate from the monarch, are necessarily with mine and rest in my hands alone."

The Hall of the Parlement was hushed as the king drove home his final point in response to that body's continuous refusal to register his edicts, go on strike, and other disruptive measures to undermine his authority. Voice thundering, the king wrapped it up:

"If, after I have scrutinized your remonstrances, and in full knowledge of the question, have persisted in my intentions, my courts should persevere in their refusal to obey instead of registering by the King's express command, the formula used to express duty and obedience; if they try to annihilate by their own efforts laws which have been solemnly registered; if finally, when my authority has been forced to show itself to its fullest extent, they still dare to fight on by using defensive decisions, suspensive oppositions or through the irregular method of cessation of service or resignations, then confusion and anarchy will replace the legitimate order and the scandalous spectacle of a contrary rival to my own power will reduce me to the sad necessity of using all the power I have received from God to preserve my people from the fearful consequences of such attempts.

"Let the officers of my courts, therefore, weigh attentively what I am still good enough to tell them."

The people's reaction in the streets was immediate. Tired of the Parlement and its shallowness, joy erupted, and approval of the speech was widespread. The king's speech to the Parlement was dubbed *le discours de la flagellation* ("the flagellation speech") as it was akin to the whipping of a small irretractable child. All at once, the people saw a king who was united with them. They had seen the wealth heaped upon the nobles who constituted the majority of the seats in Parlement; they were rich, feudal and powerful. Louis XV had put them on notice, and the everyday merchants, artisans and middle class approved.

In the background, as ever, rumblings of discontent sounded from the different European alliances. By 1766, it was becoming obvious that Catherine II and Frederick II were eyeing each other as allies, which would likely result in serious territorial losses for Poland. In February 1767, a number of Polish nobles rose up against the Russians. Austria stayed out of it and Prussia watched from the sidelines. The Poles and the Turks were crushed by the Russian army, and a fissure began forming between Austria and France, due to Choiseul's interference.

While France had dodged becoming involved in another war, deaths at Versailles piled up, hitting close to the heart of the king. In March of 1768, only a year-and-a-half after the death of her husband, the Dauphine died of consumption, leaving her five children in the king's care. Three of her sons became Kings of France: Louis XVI, Louis XVIII, and Charles X.

Only three months later, the Queen, Marie Leszczyńksa, died on June 24; she was sixty-five. She was buried at the Saint Denis Basilica, and her heart was entombed at the Church of Notre-Dame-de-Bonsecours in Nancy (Lorraine).

The king had been extremely fond of his daughter-in-law, the Dauphine, the Duchess Maria Josepha of Saxony. He was known to have remained affectionate with his wife, although it was the affection one would offer an older aunt, as the queen was ten years his senior. Thanks to the efforts of Madame de Pompadour, Marie had found a new station at court and her circumstances bettered. Her passing represented the last vestiges of the Regency created in Louis' earlier years. So many had died who had been there with him. The loss of so many family members, advisors and dear friends left him feeling untethered and vulnerable.

## Madame du Barry

Madame du Barry, circa 1770

Jeanne Bécu, Comtesse du Barry was the last *maitresse-en-titre* of Louis XV. She was born on August 19, 1743, at Vaucouleurs, France, as the illegitimate daughter of Anne Bécu, a seamstress. Jeanne's father was possibly Jean Jacques Gomard, a friar known as *frère Ange.* During her childhood, one of her mother's acquaintances, Monsieur Billiard-Dumonceaux, took both Anne and three-year-old Jeanne into his care when they traveled from Vaucouleurs to Paris and installed Anne as a cook in his Italian mistress's household. Dumonceaux funded Jeanne's education at the Couvent (convent) de Saint-Aure.

At the age of fifteen, Jeanne left the convent, for she had come of age. She had nowhere to go after her mother was thrown out of Dumonceaux's house, and she wandered the dingy streets of Paris carrying a box full of trinkets for sale. Over time, she worked at different occupations; she was first offered a post as assistant to a young hairdresser named Lametz. Jeanne had a brief relationship with him that may have produced a daughter, though it is thought improbable. She was next employed as a companion to an elderly woman, Madame de la Garde. Later, she worked as a milliner's assistant in a haberdashery shop.

Jeanne was a remarkably attractive blonde woman with thick golden ringlets and almond-shaped blue eyes. Her beauty came to the attention of Jean-Baptiste du Barry; a high-class pimp/procurer nicknamed *le roué*. Du Barry owned a casino, and Jeanne came to his attention in 1763 when she was entertaining in Madame Quisnoy's brothel-casino. She introduced herself as Jeanne Vaubernier. Du Barry installed her in his household and made her his mistress. Giving her the appellation of Mademoiselle Lange, Du Barry helped establish Jeanne's career as a courtesan in the highest circles of Parisian society; this enabled her to take several aristocratic men, even courtiers, as brief lovers or clients.

As Mademoiselle Lange, Jeanne immediately became a sensation in Paris, building up a large aristocratic clientele She had many lovers from the king's minsters to his courtiers. Even the old Maréchal de Richelieu, Louis' friend, became one of her recurring lovers. Because of this, Jean due Barry saw her as a means of influencing the king, who became aware of her in 1768 while she was on an errand at Versailles. The errand involved the duc de Choiseul, Minister of Foreign Affairs (and currently skating on thin ice with the King), who found her rather ordinary, in contrast to what most other men thought of her. The king took a great interest in her and obtained her identity with the help of his personal valet and procurer of ladies, Dominique Guillaume Lebel.

Jeanne was escorted to the royal boudoir frequently, and it was soon becoming a worrying issue to Lebel when this liaison was seemingly becoming more than just a passing fling. In any case, Jeanne could not qualify as a *maitresse-en-titre* unless she had a title (as was the case with Madame de Pompadour); however, after divulging to the king that Jeanne was nothing but a harlot, the king ordered Jeanne to wed a man of high lineage so she may be brought to court as per protocol. This was solved by her marriage on September 1, 1768, to du Barry's brother, Comte Guillaume du Barry. The marriage ceremony included a false birth certificate created by Jean du Barry himself, making Jeanne younger by three years and of fictitious noble descent.

Jeanne was now installed about the king's quarters in Lebel's former rooms. She lived a lonely life, unable to be seen with the king since no formal presentations had taken place as yet. Very few, if any, of the nobility at court deigned to become acquainted with her, for none could accept the fact that a woman of the street had the audacity to mingle with those above her station and thrive in trying to become like them. Comte du Barry constantly pestered Jeanne and urged her to speak of presentation with the king. Louis XV, in turn, asked her to find a proper sponsor to be able to be presented at court. Richelieu offered to pay ladies of the nobility to perform the task. They all asked for too much money. Finally, Madame de Béarn took the role as Jeanne's sponsor after her huge gambling debts were paid off.

On the first occasion when the presentation was to take place, de Bèarn was panicked by fear and feigned a sprained ankle. On a second occasion, the king was badly hurt when he fell off his horse during a hunt and broke his arm. Finally, Jeanne was presented to the court at Versailles on April 22, 1769; an occasion which was long-awaited by the gathering crowds outside the palace gates, and by the gossiping courtiers within the Hall of Mirrors. Not all the noble ladies attended. They heard the description of the gown and jewels she wore, however: Jeanne wore a gown of silvery white with gold brocade, bedecked in jewels sent by the king the night before.

The dress, ordered by Richelieu especially for the occasion, had huge panniers at the sides.

The fact that Madame du Barry was beautiful was never disputed. She was fond of wearing her lustrous blond hair unpowered and showing off her ample bosom in plunging necklines. Jealous tongues described her as "pretty as a flower and dumb as a basket." It was true, Jeanne had no ambitions for the political arena, and talk of business bored her. She was the exact opposite of Madame de Pompadour. The king seemed fine with the arrangement. What du Barry offered him, at thc autumn of his life, was youthful lustiness, bawdy jokes, and a return to the days when he was a virile monarch adored by every woman at court.

Madame du Barry

Choiseul took an instant dislike to the new mistress on several grounds: one, was that his own sister had gone after the king as Madame de Pompadour's body was being wheeled away from the palace and had failed to attract his interest. Secondly, mistresses were known to execute influence over the king, and this was the last thing he needed; and thirdly, Richelieu was a supporter of du Barry, and he had been anti-Pompadour, Choiseul's backer. He made his dislike known the day after du Barry's presentation at court by hosting a large reception filled with the ladies of the Court—du Barry was not invited.

Jeanne quickly accustomed herself to living in luxury. Louis had given her a young Bengali slave, Zamor, whom she dressed in elegant clothing to show him off. She rose at nine and Zamor brought her a cup of chocolate. Her hairdresser Nokelle dressed her hair for special occasions, or Berline took up the comb and powder for everyday outings. She would receive friends (the anti-Choiseul set began to gather around her), invite in the Paris merchants who would display their latest stock and jewelry in hopes of her buying them. She quickly gained a reputation for her excessive spending, but she also showed a good heart when she intervened twice for people headed for the gallows for what she felt were unfair reasons.

While Louis was surprised at her appealing to him so soon for favors, he said, "Madame, I am delighted that the first favor you should ask of me should be an act of mercy!" The parties in question were pardoned. Still, she continued to spend. The gowns became more opulent and the Treasury more depleted. Louis had now officially declared her the *maîtresse déclarée* and she proved worthy of the name as she appeared dripping in diamonds from her neck and earlobes. She made enemies at court, not the least was the lady Louis had spurned, Choiseul's sister, the Duchesse de Gramont. She and her brother had plotted from the beginning to have du Barry removed from court, going as far as composing slanderous lies on Paris' famous gutter pamphlets.

Jeanne was finally introduced to the Duc d'Aiguillon, the nephew of Richelieu, who sided with her against the opposing Duc de Choiseul. As Jeanne's power at court grew, Choiseul could feel his waning. His final misstep was to disobey Louis' orders. He decided France was capable of war again and sided with the Spanish against the British for possession of the Falkland Islands. After the horrible *Seven Years' War* incident, Louis had had enough. When the plot came to light to the du Barry clan, the mistress exposed all to the king and, on Christmas Eve of 1771, Choiseul was dismissed from his ministerial role and from court; ordered by His Majesty to exile to his Chanteloup property along with his nefarious sister and wife.

Louis XV, dressed in armor and holding the baton in later life.

The pamphlets that had circulated under Choiseul's malevolent hand had done much harm to the king's reputation. He was seen as a lecherous, old, impotent debauchee. Memories of the Deer Park reignited and vile songs of his relationship with du Barry were sung with gusto in the Paris pubs: "You will see the dean of Kings, at the knees of the countess, who once would have become your mistress for a small coin, making a hundred efforts, on the road of sex, to move the springs of his ancient machine, but in vain, he has recourse to the grand priestess, right in the midst of his discourse, he lapses back feebly." It was tawdry and worthy of the back street Parisians who found glee in the scandals at court.

It wasn't just the lower class of Paris who were teasing the king about his taste in mistresses. At Versailles, Louis said to the duc de Noailles that with Madam du Barry he had discovered new pleasures; "Sire"—answered the duke— "that's because your Majesty has never been in a brothel."

While Jeanne was known for her good nature, she was constantly in debt, despite the generous monthly income from the king of up to three hundred thousand *livres*. Her spending added to the reversal of the king's popularity with his people and to her own. To add to Madame du Barry's problems, a new lady was coming to court.

# Chapter Forty-Seven
# The Wedding of the Future King of France

Before Choiseul was banished from court, he managed to pull off a major coup. Following the *Seven Years War* and the *Diplomatic Revolution* of 1756, Empress Maria-Theresa decided to end hostilities with her longtime enemy, King Louis XV of France. Their common desire to destroy the ambitions of Prussia and Great Britain, and to secure a definitive piece between their respective countries, led them to seal their alliances with a marriage. None other than Choiseul orchestrated the Franco-Austrian alliance. The dauphin was to marry the Austrian Archduchess Marie Antoinette.

Her mother, Maria-Theresa of Austria, was fully aware that her daughter was virtually illiterate, and asked Choiseul (who was still at court and hanging on by a thread) to recommend a tutor who would improve Marie's French and instruct her in the ways of Versailles' formidable court. Choiseul recommended the abbé Vermond. Vermond arrived in Vienna and was told to devote one hour of the day to teaching the future dauphine 'religion, the history of France, a knowledge of the great families and especially those who occupy positions at court…and the French language and spelling.' After a year of tutelage, she still wrote 'inexpressibly slowly' and when signing her marriage contract, she made two spelling errors in writing her own Christian names. Her writing was the despair of Vermond.

While Choiseul's involvement in the royal marriage may have earned him some points, it was not enough to erase the damage he continued to create. Madame du Barry was one such error in judgement. Dufort wrote, “As for the duc de Choiseul, [Mme du Barry] showed regret that she couldn’t have been his friend and told us about all the efforts she had made to win him over; she told us that without his sister, the duchesse de Gramont, she would have managed it. She complained about no one and never said anything nasty… ‘I only wanted to oblige everyone,’ she said.

The marriage contract: You can see Louis XIV’s signature at the top, followed by Louis Auguste and Marie Antoinette.

Marie Antoinette's signature. She pressed too hard on the pen from nerves causing an ink blob, and misspelled Johanna. She wrote Janne.

It was Choiseul who did his best to make sure no one at court would sponsor du Barry at her presentation to the king and queen. Vile pamphlets and songs were instigated by the minister and his sister. Even after the king reprimanded him, Choiseul continued on with his anti-du Barry campaign. He was also encouraging the Parlement with its antagonism toward the king, all the time his foreign policy was meeting with disaster. Feeling that his help with the future dauphine's education in preparation for her attendance at Versailles made him indispensable, he went recklessly on with his egotistical actions. As we have seen, it backfired.

Back in Vienna, the Austrian Ambassador to France, Mercy-Argenteau, was appointed Marie Antoinette's unofficial guardian. Vermond told Mercy that Marie's handwriting was the field in which he had been most tormented. (Twenty years later she would be writing copious coded letters using invisible ink.) Vermond added that 'a little laziness and much flightiness have made it more difficult to teach her… I can't get her to go deeply into a subject though I suspect she can.'

Marie was not the only one in the upcoming marriage to be disparaged. Vermond gave Mercy a pen-portrait of the dauphin: thin, pale, slightly bow-legged, blond hair, high forehead, large but not disproportionate nose. The dauphin's eyes in the portrait were commented upon, noting that while they were a lovely deep blue, but they lacked fire. Vermond offered that the smile suggested kindness rather than gaiety, and that this, coupled with the lack of animation in the eyes and a certain nonchalance, gave an appearance of stupidity. According to Vermond, the dauphin 'had not liking for the arts and a special loathing of music.' He was known to be clumsy and people who witnessed him in action called him 'a dancing bear.'

'The Navy,' Vermond continued, 'is his favorite study and on this subject, he possesses as much knowledge as can be acquired without having gone to sea.' He had no 'love of luxury even that associated with his station in life.' The final assessment was that Louis Auguste possessed 'firmness or, if you prefer, stubbornness.'

The Dauphin, Louis Auguste (16) & Marie Antoinette (14)

As the wedding festivities plans went forward, Choiseul (not yet exiled) oversaw the details and spent lavishly. Louis XV had decided earlier to finish work on the Opéra Royal which Louis XIV had begun and abandoned during the *War of the Spanish Succession*. The work had begun in 1765 and was completed in 1770 in time for the wedding of Louis Auguste and Marie Antoinette. It was designed by Ange-Jacques Gabriel. It was also known as the Theatre Gabriel. The interior decoration by Augustin Pajou is constructed almost entirely of wood, painted to resemble marble in a technique known as *faux marble*. The excellent acoustics of the Opera Royal are at least partly due to its wooden interior.

The Opera Royal is located at the northern extremity of the north wing of the Palace. Lully's Persée, which was written in 1682 to commemorate Louis XIV moving the court to Versailles, was the play that inaugurated the Opera on May 16, 1770, in celebration of the marriage of the dauphin—the future Louis XVI—to Marie Antoinette.

The mechanical wonders of the Opera Royal are that it can serve as a theater setting, accommodating an audience of 712, or as a ballroom when the floor of the orchestra level of the auditorium is raised to the level of the stage. On these occasions, the house can accommodate 1,200 people! It was a technical marvel, yet expensive to use. The theatre burned ten thousand candles in one night. At the time, it was the largest theatre in Europe.

The Opéra Royal at Versailles.

The wedding wasn't until May, but signs of the royal union were being seen about Versailles. According to Louis Petit de Bachaumont, "There are two berlines [coaches]...One is covered with a flat velvet, crimson on the outside, on which the four seasons are embroidered in gold. There are no paintings at all, but the work is of a fineness, a subtlety which makes it practically a fine art. The roofs are very rich; one of the two even seems too heavy. The imperial is topped by bouquets of flowers in gold of every shade; they are worked with just as much care. The carriages are so well suspended that they sway with every move... M. le duc de Choiseul, as Foreign Minister, has ordered these magnificent coaches."

The coaches appeared in January of 1770 and were about to head to Vienna to be used by the Archduchess Marie Antoinette for her trip to France. Before she would make her debut at Versailles, there would be the marriage by proxy, which took place at the Habsburg Court Church of St. Augustin, on April 19, 1770, at six o'clock in the evening. It was a proxy wedding as her bridegroom, the dauphin, was awaiting her in France. He was represented by Maria Antonia's (Marie Antoinette would become her French name) brother, the Archduke Ferdinand, at the altar. The royal couple would not meet until Marie Antoinette arrived at Compiegne, where the marriage, already celebrated by proxy in Vienna, would enable the two to finally meet for the first time.

Marie's departure from her home was an emotional one. She was going to a foreign country to marry a man she had never met, and she was only 14 years old. The imperial procession departed from Vienna at nine o'clock on April 21, 1770, and the famous long neck of Marie Antoinette was reported by the son of her wet-nurse, Joseph Weber, as "craning" out of the window again and again to take a last look at the sight of her summer palace of Schönbrunn. The Marquis de Durfort had brought with him the two carriages which would transport Marie Antoinette personally to France—one decorated in crimson, the other in blue. Maria-Theresa finally broke down, and clasping her daughter to her, she cried, "Farewell, my dearest child, a great distance will separate us. Do so much good to the French people that they can say that I have sent them an angel."

The wedding procession was composed of much more than the two coaches provided by Louis XV. 21 state coaches, followed by 36 fine carriages, 450 horses (2000 counting the replacement horses that were stationed along the route of the two-and-a-half-week journey), and 250 people which included hairdressers and seamstresses, cooks and servants. The dauphine would literally travel across the whole of Central Europe. The ride was laborious, some days they traveled for over nine hours. From time-to-time, she would open the small portrait given to her of her future husband and study his face.

There were many stops along the route as the wedding was celebrated in town after town. Her reception was always enthusiastic but repetitious. They finally reached Munich on April 26 where she was given a day of rest at the Nymphenburg Palace, home of the Elector of Bavaria, Maximillian Joseph, a cousin on her mother's side. The next stop was Augsburg, where she was made honorary member of the Academy of Sciences and Fine Arts. Next came Günzburg and another two-day stopover with her father's sister, Princess Charlotte of Lorraine. Her reception was extravagant and filled with celebration—after all, Marie was 'de Lorraine' as well as d'Autriche.'

After that, it was on to Ulm and then Freiberg. It was May 6 when, having passed through the Black Forest, the dauphine reached the abbey at Schüttern where she was to spend her last night on German soil before the handover. This was also the night Marie Antoinette would meet the first of the French court officials who were intended to guide her inexperienced footsteps at Versailles. The first to bow to the new dauphine was the Ambassador Extraordinary of Louis XV, Comte de Noailles. The next day, she met his wife, the formidable Comtesse de Noailles. She would act as Mistress of Marie's Household and take charge of her at Versailles. The Noailles were rigid and proud, in their fifties and were the epitome of etiquette and fidelity. If Marie had dreamed of being met with warmth and hugs, she was rudely awakened. She made the faux pas of throwing herself into the arms of the horrified Comtesse de Noailles, who immediately backed away and reminded her of court etiquette.

The "handover" (the official ceremony denoting Marie leaving behind her Austrian roots and becoming the property of France) took place on an island in the middle of the Rhine near Kehl. Marie was told to turn and say farewell to her Austrian attendants, none of whom, except for the Prince Starhemberg, were to travel on to Versailles. Amid tears and hugs, she begged the departing friends to send her love to her family. When her favorite little pug was taken from her, she was desolate. Why couldn't she keep Mops? She was told she would be given a French dog, if she liked. Count Mercy, her Austrian ambassador did manage to get Mops back after the de-Austrification was over.

Here, within a tent made of tapestries and a dais, Marie was stripped of her Austrian clothing, down to her stockings and underwear, and a French gown was dropped over her shoulders. It was her first glimpse of the nonchalant view the French took when it came to nudity. Versailles would be an even greater shock.

Marie's French attendants were then presented to her on the French side of the "handover" location. Her ladies had originally attended the late Queen, Maria Lesczcyńska, who had died two years earlier. They were the Duchesse de Villars, the Marquise de Duras, the Duchess de Picquigny and the Comtesse de Mailly. The fact that the Duchesse de Picquigny had been appointed had raised some eyebrows—she was known to have a disreputable private life. Other various Ladies of the Bedchamber and lesser waiting-women were chosen for her.

Marie spent the night in the episcopal palace of the Cardinal Louis Constantin de Rohan. The next morning, she continued on her way across north-eastern France. There was still 250 miles to go before reaching Versailles. Finally, on the afternoon of May 14, in the forest near the King's chateau of Compiegne, the fabled meeting of the future king and queen took place. In the forest outside the chateau, Louis XV arrived in a carriage that contained his grandson, the dauphin, and three of the King's four surviving daughters. Looking forward to finally seeing the new dauphine, Louis XV had already asked his ambassador to Austria about her bosom. The ambassador blushed and said he had not looked at the archduchess's bosom. "Oh, didn't you? That's the first thing I look at," the king replied jovially.

As the dauphine stepped out of her carriage onto the ceremonial carpet that had been unrolled for just this purpose, the Duc de Choiseul stepped up and greeted her. It had been his instigation that brought her here, and she was quick to tell him, "I shall never forget that you are responsible for my happiness," she told him. He replied, "And that of France."

When the duc de Cröy presented Marie to the king, she flung herself to her knees in front of him, calling him *'cher granpére'*, "dear grandfather." She would later call him "Papa" or "Papa-Roi." She saw before her a tall man with "large, full, prominent black piercing eyes and a Roman nose', a king that was still handsome and imposing in his sixties. Next to him stood a mirror opposite: the dauphin was already portly at fifteen years of age, with heavy-lidded eyes, thick eyebrows and a sulky expression. He appeared awkward and unsure of what to do. The miniature portrait Marie had admired during the long carriage ride through Europe had been given a royal polish of sorts, not unlike today's Photoshop.

The two finally embraced in a short, nervous gesture beneath the approving gaze of the king, and the jealous glare of the three "Aunts": Madame Adelaide, Madame Victoire, and Madame Sophie. Their nicknames were 'Rag', 'Sow', and 'Grub' respectively. Horace Walpole had described the king's daughters as 'clumsy, plump old wenches.' Unbeknownst to the new dauphine, they were intent on using her in a campaign to get rid of their father's hated mistress, Madame du Barry. If they could get Marie Antoinette on their side, they might find a way to end the affair they found so disgusting. They were not excited to find an Austrian dauphine in their midst, but they did see her as a possible ally for their purposes.

Marie was described by those who first saw her as lovely, undeveloped (compared to the bosomy ladies at court), possessing a lovely complexion of white with natural color on her cheeks, rather than the rouged faces at Versailles. The king, disappointed with her flat chest, reminded himself of her age, and decided she would 'fill out' later.

After celebrations and introductions at Compiegne (where Marie fist laid eyes on Madame du Barry and thought her eyes very pretty) and a banquet at La Muette, amid a lightning storm, it was finally time to go to Versailles for the royal wedding ceremony. It was hard to deduce the dauphin's impression of his new bride. His entry in his hunting journal was brief; it said merely, 'Meeting with Madame de Dauphine.'

Marie was presented with the magnificent jewels, diamonds and pearls that were her due as dauphine. They had belonged to the late Maria Josepha; the value of the gems listed at nearly 2 million livres. Marie Antoinette also received a collar of pearls, the smallest 'as large as a filbert nut.' More gifts poured in provided by King Louis XV, including a diamond-encrusted fan, and bracelets with her cipher MA on the blue enamel clasps. Presents for her attendants were also included in in the six-foot-long coffer in crimson velvet.

It was time. At 1 pm, she entered the King's Cabinet. The dauphin was there, dressed in the gold and diamond-covered habit of the

Order of the Holy Spirit. He took her hand, and they crossed the crowded State Apartments, thronged with excited courtiers. The king and the Prince of Blood followed behind as they made their way to the Royal Chapel. The pomp and glory of Versailles was released on this one long-awaited occasion. All eyes were on this tiny woman who, in the words of one observer, was so small and slender in her white brocade dress inflated with its vast hoops on either side that she looked 'not above twelve.' Her bearing was also commented on, and it was the general consensus that she was every bit the archduchess who had been trained with rigorous grooming since her childhood. The dauphin, unfortunately, was reported to look aloof, cold, sulky or listless throughout the long Mass. They knelt before the altar from where the Archbishop of Reims took over the ceremony. The dauphin trembled as he placed the ring on her finger.

The Wedding of Marie Antoinette and Louis Auguste

Versailles was ablaze with feasting, dancing and music. It was said to be the finest wedding anyone had ever seen. Despite the continuing rain, lanterns hung from illuminated boats along the Canal. The massive fireworks were canceled due to the deluge, but inside, there was nothing but celebration and high hopes for the new royal couple of France. Marie Antoinette and Louis Auguste attended the ambassador's reception before going to the Hall of Mirrors which was lit up for the occasion. The day ended with a sumptuous feast in the newly completed Opera Royal where the stage had been elevated to provide a large flat area for the banquet tables and chairs. 3,000 candle flames reflected off the dazzling jewels, silver, and gold accoutrements that filled the hall.

The celebrations continued throughout Paris and Versailles until May 30, when fireworks on the Place de Concorde killed 130 people. For some reason, workmen had dug three deep and wide trenches, blocking the exits. As the fireworks procession moved from place to place within the Place de Concorde, the massive crowds moved with it. Men, women, children and coaches fell into the deep trenches. The corpses were so high that many could not get out of their carriages. Was the thunderstorm the day of the wedding and the death of the Parisians during the celebratory fireworks display an omen of what was to come for this hopeful couple?

As the night waned, it was time for the final (and to the dynasty) most-important moment of the wedding—the bedding ceremony. The usual rituals were maintained: the Archbishop of Reims blessed the nuptial bed. Louis XV handed his grandson his nightgown, the young Duchesse d'Chartres gave the dauphine hers. The king then took his grandson's hand and handed him formally into bed. Chartres did the same for Marie. The large gathering of onlookers, all there based on birth and their position at court, smiled at the couple, bowed and left the room. It is reported that before drawing the bedcurtains closed, the king whispered a few pieces of advice to his grandson.

The room finally hushed, only echoes of laughter and celebrating coming from outside. The timid couple lay there, both virgins and neither knowing what to do next. This was all too clear when the next morning it was found out that nothing had taken place. It was the beginning of a long seven-year ordeal that would see Marie Antoinette lambasted by her mother back in Austria, and the king's growing concern and impatience. Unfortunately, he would not live long enough to see the birth of his future heir.

## Chapter Forty-Eight
## 'LE ROI IS MORT! Vive le roi!'

The dauphin and dauphine were not compatible in many ways. He had inherited his grandfather's shyness and secrecy while she was outgoing, loved society, balls, the opera, and the theater. He detested all such outings. Louis Auguste kept a hunting journal for which he was famous for his daily succinct comments. They might pertain to the weather, the hunt, a new mechanical wonder he had discovered, or a significant event at court. He was an avid reader, while Marie Antoinette rarely cracked a book, and her handwriting was still littered with strikeouts and ink blobs. The children of the court loved her for her childlike enthusiasm, and she was constantly playing with her dogs.

On June 15, 1770, the Austrian Ambassador Mercy-Argenteau, who was in essence Marie's overseer at court, wrote home to her mother, Maria Theresa: "The King finds her [Marie] sprightly and a little immature, but that is right for her age." The letters from Mercy to Marie's mother would be frequent. The young dauphine felt spied upon, and for a long time could not figure out how her mother always knew what was going on with her activities at Versailles. It took 8-10 days one way to get a letter from Vienna to Versailles. Marie Antoinette was ordered to write her mother once a month. The response from the Austrian Queen was usually a mixed bag of complementing her daughter, followed by recrimination and admonishments concerning her behavior and what became known as the "Great Work."

Royal marriages had two purposes: political affiliations and to produce an heir to the throne. A marriage could be annulled if the wife failed to fulfill her obligation of delivering a prince. This particular issue would be the bane of Marie's existence at Versailles. Mercy reminded her repeatedly of the dangers of her barren state, while her mother back in Austria asked for monthly accounts of Marie's bedsheets—to see if a period had been missed. The court was flummoxed as to why the youthful couple didn't seem to be engaging in sex. Marie was admonished by her mother in letters to handle the dauphin with "caresses and redoubled caresses!" In another letter Maria Theresa writes "Everything depends on the wife, if she is willing, sweet and *amusante* [amusing]."

The problem didn't seem to lie with the young dauphine. For whatever reason, be it shyness, a lack of knowing what to do, a medical condition, or something else, Louis Auguste didn't seem interested in sex. It didn't help that the path to his wife's bed had to be traversed beneath the watchful eyes of the courtiers, or to their sniggers as he passed them on the way back to his own bedchamber. This became such an ordeal, that Louis regularly stopped visiting his wife's bedchamber.

Marie had been staying in temporary quarters until her proper apartments could be completed. The architect Gabriel, Louis XV's favorite, had been pushing for the usual overkill of gold gilt and ornate opulence. Marie Antoinette wanted something simpler. Finally, a compromise was reached and roses and fleur-de-lys alternated, together with sphinxes holding the arms of France. The great double-headed eagle of Austria loomed above the bed. Louis Auguste left the fine touches to his wife's bedchamber to her. He had his own private suite of rooms, much to the anger of Maria Theresa who thought the couple should share a double bed to inflame the passions.

The years passed and in 1773 the King ordered a doctor to "check out" the Dauphin for any medical issues that might be preventing him from instigating intercourse. This came on the heels of a nasty outburst from Marie's mother who snapped, "The Dauphin is not a man like others!" The doctor found nothing wrong with him, although phimosis had been suspected by some—a tightness of the foreskin that would make intercourse painful. It was the doctor's diagnosis, after the examination and discussing sex with the dauphin, that the marriage had not been consummated due to the young man's shyness and clumsiness in bed.

For Marie Antoinette, who constantly had to watch the antics of

Madame du Barry as she stroked the king in public and made known how frequent their sexual liaisons were, it was torture. She was also reminded by her mother how horrible it would be if the dauphin's brother, the duc de Provence and his wife became pregnant before her. The pressure was all around her. If she made a misstep at court, Mercy was there to reprimand her, and within two weeks a corresponding letter arrived from Vienna, filled with criticism. Once, Marie had joined the hunting party's luncheon. She was trying to support her husband's love of the hunt and mingle with his friends as they spread out a blanket beneath a large tree. The servants brought the plate of meats, fruits, breads, and other eats. Marie handed around the plate of meats to the party. Mercy was at once at her upon her return to court, telling her it was not her place to hand meat to a member of the court—that was a servant's job.

As for the hunt, Marie Antoinette was told not to participate as riding a horse could induce a miscarriage. She found that laughable as her husband had yet to perform the act. Still, her mother admonished on about the dangers of riding. The irony was, that Maria Theresa's favorite portrait of her daughter painted while she was at Versailles, shows Marie in a riding habit. The Empress praised the portrait by Joseph Krantzinger in 1771, saying it is "very like" her. Maria Theresa kept it in her study hanging on a wall, 'Thus, I have you always with me, under my eyes." That Marie Antoinette was "always under her eyes" was never in question!

Maria Theresa's favorite portrait of Marie Antoinette.

As Marie Antoinette navigated the tricky etiquette of Versailles, it was becoming more and more obvious that Madame du Barry would have to be dealt with. "The Aunts" as they became known at court, were obsessed with getting their father's "harlot" tossed from court. They used the excuse that his continuing affair with her would cause him eternal damnation in the afterlife and the refusal of the last rites upon his deathbed. He had already gone down that road in Metz with the Mailly sisters. There was also some truth in the fact that the daughters of Louis XV were spinsters, unattractive, mean-spirited and bored. Stirring up trouble through gossip and encouraging the "new lady" to snub the king's favorite became their fulltime activity. Madame Adelaide was the main instigator of the malicious assault on du Barry. For some reason, she even encouraged Marie to dislike Louis' other daughter, her sister, Madame Victoire, out of boredom perhaps. Mercy was appalled and increasingly concerned, as Marie continued to ignore du Barry and even turn her back to her in pubic. To show indifference to Louis XV's chosen *maitresse en titre* was to cast dispersion on the king.

Mercy and Maria Theresa implored Marie to acknowledge du Barry, no matter how small, as the mistress, due to protocol, could not talk to her first. Mercy advised Marie to distance herself from the aunts for a time, but the dauphine was lonely and homesick, and the aunts offered her comradery and her first inclusion at court. Despite the warnings, she spent a good deal of time with the nefarious spinsters, going to their private apartments as much as four times a day. While the aunts certainly encouraged Marie's dislike for du Barry, the dauphine made it clear in a letter to her mother dated July 9$^{th}$: "The King is infinitely kind to me and I love him tenderly, but what a pity that he should have such a weakness for Mme du Barry, who is the most stupid and impertinent creature imaginable." What the naïve dauphin did not realize, was that the aunts were making fun of her as well behind her back, usually despairing remarks about her Austrian heritage, including her German pouting lower lip.

It was in 1770, that Marie lost her first ties to Versailles. Choiseul was finally exiled from Court. It was he who brought about 'her happiness…and that of France.' Du Barry's hatred for the man had played a part in his removal from Versailles, but as stated earlier, he had himself to blame for misguided moves during the *Seven Years*

*War*, and in his secretive support of the Parlement.

### The New Parlement

The Parlement had continued to cause trouble for Louis XV. They once again went on strike with 132 judges out of the 170 refusing to obey the king's orders to state without delay whether they would be returning to work. More than half the magistrates ignored the order or answered in the negative. They were all exiled to tiny villages whose inns lacked the luxuries to which they had become accustomed. Louis XV set up a new court called the Council of State. Through his chancellor René Nicolas Charles Augustin de Maupeou, Louis attempted to centralize political control by abolishing the parlements (1771) and substituting law courts that had no influence over policy. The new judicial system eliminated the sale of magistracies with judges becoming appointive salaried officials.

On January 29, 1771, the king addressed this new Council: "Messieurs, I need you so that the course of justice in my Parlement be interrupted no longer. I know your zeal and your attachment to my person and count on them. You may count on my protection as you carry out your new functions, and on the marks of my affections." Most assumed the old Parlement would return, but the new Council of State faced a hostile opposition through the Princes of the Blood: the duc d'Orleans, the prince de Conti, the comte de Clermont, and the comte d'Eu announced publicly they refused to be judged by the new Council. They had always counted on the old Parlement to defend their privileges. They went so far as to send the king their remonstrances, but he refused to read them. Everyone knew the parlements favored their relatives and friends.

On February 25, Maupeou spoke to the Council of State and made it clear the old Parlement would not be returning. The new Parlement would still register the king's edicts and keep the right to present remonstrances, but it lost the right to defer registration after the king had either accepted or refused the remonstrances. New geographical locations for a compartmentalized Parlement were also implemented to speed up communications. A Parlement would still sit in Paris, but it would be augmented by five councils located in Blois, Chalons, Clermont-Ferrand, Lyon and Poiters. Two other parlements of Rouen and Douai were abolished and replaced by councils. A number of other outdated institutions were dissolved.

To Louis' credit, the new Parlement proved superior in a short amount of time. It was smaller, with only 75 judges, yet they accomplished more than the previous 170. If the former Parlement saw their exile as just another threat by the king, they were rudely awakened when the new Council was met with relief from the people, or a shrug. There was no hoped-for revolt or uprising to come to the banished Parlement's defense. A new ministry was instated. Maupeou remained chancellor; the abbé Terray kept his post as controleur general. Bertin stayed on as the Minister of Agriculture, Mining and the Merchant Marine, and Saint-Florentin (now the duc de La Vrilliere) stayed as Minister of the King's Household. The duc d'Aiguillon became Foreign Minister. This may not have surprised anyone as d'Aiguillon was a close friend of Mme du Barry. As Minister of War, Louis chose the marquis de Monteynard, taking over for the exiled Choiseul, and the Navy went to Bourgeois de Boynes.

The Council of State first tackled the always violent question of taxation. Terray was already trying to balance the budget early in 1771. For many years, the Treasury had suffered from the fact that the poor paid taxes and the rich did not. Therefore, in 1771, Torray reinstated the vingtiémes on a new basis. This 5% income tax was to become permanent. A second veintieme was to last only ten years and it meant everyone in France would pay a 10% income tax, but it would go back down to 5% in 1781. As expected, the rich nobility, who were used to being exempt from taxes, let out a great howl. To show he meant business, Torray ordered that all France be surveyed, while checking income tax returns and prosecuting fraud. Within months, the Treasury began to see its coffers fill.

Lastly, Torray eliminated hundreds of unnecessary offices whose only purpose had been to sell them to nobles wanting rank and pensions and to put money in the Treasury though the sales. Once again, the gilded hallways of Versailles echoed with angry shouting as many saw their pensions and official titles stripped away. By 1774, the debt was shrinking, and the balance was largely in balance. Louis XV had, in his august years, finally learned to trust his own instincts. He had not merely tamed the Parlement but ended it; his government was on a course of progress and new ideas, and Torray had restored the State's finances. The dauphin was married and hopes of a royal pregnancy still prevailed. Mme du Barry made him feel like a young man, and he ruled without the unapproving glance of a queen. The king saw only a bright future.

## The End of a Reign

As always, the eyes of Europe were upon Versailles. In the early 1770s, the glamour continued. Not only did Louis XV show no signs of slowing down, but he went into overdrive in indulging Madame du Barry. She was the opposite of Madame de Pompadour. She loved money, jewels, sex, opulent apartments and furnishings, and was hoping for the adoration of the court—in particular, the acceptance of Marie Antoinette, who was still snubbing her at every opportunity.

Word got out about the king's expenditure on behalf of his mistress. It was staggering sums! Her annual pension was 1,200,000 *livres* ($5,625,000), plus an annual income of another 150,000 *livres* ($675,000). She was allowed to draw from the Treasury for her household expenses, such as expensive clothing for her slave Zamor, and other servants. She ordered fine carriages and the most-expensive service ware from Sèrves.

Madame du Barry's Sèrves service with her initials

Her absorptive spending continued on gowns (170,000 *livres*/$765,000), and jewels. One diamond-encrusted bodice of flowers, bows and ribbons cost over 2 million in American dollars. The necklace made to go with it became part of the undoing of Marie Antoinette in a nefarious subterfuge called The Diamond Necklace Affair, which will be covered later.

Madame du Barry's diamond necklace, which later figured in a scandal under the reign of Marie Antoinette (left).

Of course, the gossip vines of Versailles made their tangled way to the Parisian salons, and all were buzzing about the extravagance while many were starving in the capital city and in the beleaguered farmlands. The king's popularity had still not rebounded from the unfortunate outcome of the *Seven Years War,* and the *War of the Austrian Succession*. France thought the king had betrayed them and their pocketbooks by handing back all they fought so hard to win. An alliance with Austria was untenable and now, there was an Austrian Archduchess about to become Queen of France! Continued news of the old king cavorting with a harlot and spending enough on her jewels, pensions, and gowns to feed the poor of Paris had taken its toll. And now, new taxes, which had the nobility in an uproar. These platforms would become the springboard for the French Revolution inherited by the king's grandson, the future Louis

XVI.

Marie Antoinette was still dealing with the pressure of her lack of marital intimacy, and the demands that she begins treating the king's mistress with some symbol of civility. The king did not wish to admonish her directly (du Barry was whining in his ear that she was being snubbed by the new dauphine), so he appealed to Mercy. When Mercy gently addressed the dauphine again on the matter, stressing that her marriage was by no means on solid ground as she had not become pregnant, Marie erupted and reminded him of to whom he was speaking. Mercy bowed himself out of the room, and turned it over to Maria Theresa, who was swift in dashing off a letter that brooked no more refusal on the matter:

"The Ambassador," the Empress wrote, "has confirmed that you are entirely led by your aunts [Adelaide and Victoire] … I respect them, I like them, but they have never known how to earn the respect or affection of their family or the public and you want to go the same way… You must know and see the Barry only as a lady received at Court and in the King's circle. You are his first subject; you owe him obedience and submission. You must show the Court and courtiers that your master's will is done… Let us see now for whom you have done this; it is through a shameful compliance to people who have subjugated you, treating you as a child… these are the great causes which make you prefer them [the Mesdames] to your master and which, in the long run, will make you ridiculous, so that you will be neither liked nor respected…Your only goal must be to please and obey the King."

Basically, this was a "Don't make me come over there!" remonstrance, and Marie chewed on it. She feared her mother. Madame Adelaide, fearing she was losing her best mouthpiece, redoubled her efforts to keep Marie in the anti-Barry camp by telling Marie that the King really didn't care if people liked du Barry or not…he wasn't paying attention to the court and gossip, which was a total lie. The king had gone to Mercy on the matter. Marie, still naïve as to the viciousness of the king's daughters, bought it and wrote her mother, saying, "I have good reason to believe the King does not want me to speak to the Barry; besides, he never talked to me about it… I do not say that I will never speak to her but cannot agree to speak on a precise day at a precise time because she would mention it in advance and look triumphant."

The two stubborn Austrians, mother and daughter, locked horns, but the king became increasingly annoyed. It was clear Marie didn't want to announce when she might speak to du Barry for fear the lady would make sure all were gathered around to witness her triumph. Finally, without warning, on January 1, 1772, at the Carnival Ball, Mme du Barry, like the rest of the court, filed past the receiving line which included the dauphine. An awkward pause followed, with a good many people watching, no doubt the aunts among them. With obvious vexation, Marie Antoinette looked at the hated woman and managed the least comment she could think of: "There are many people at Versailles today, Madame." The Comtesse du Barry, known for her kindness, if not for her greed for money, seemed pleased, but did not gloat. The king beamed.

The court rambled on for another two years. There was a youthful feeling to the fêtes and festivities now as a new generation was holding court. Not only the youthful appearances of the dauphin and dauphine, but the two brothers of Louis August: d'Provence and d'Artrois, gave a feeling of a new hope for the future. Artrois took a bride in 1772 and Versailles was ablaze with celebrations. Louis XV was 62 and still a very handsome man. By 1774, his new Parlement was running smoothly, the debt was shrinking, but it was still a formidable amount. Europe was at peace with no crisis looming on the horizon. Louis XV maintained his vigorous hunting schedule, traveled from chateau to chateau and presided over his private suppers with friends. He was now spending more and more time at the Petit Trianon, his gift to Madame du Barry.

The Petit Trianon had been built for Madame de Pompadour by Louis XV, but she died before it was completed. The king gave this garden jewel, just behind the Trianon (now the Grand Trianon) to du Barry. Here, with a handful of servants and invited friends, they could carry out their trysts without the prying eyes of the massive Versailles Court.

The king was at the Petit Trianon on April 26, 1774, with du Barry and several nobles from his entourage, when he suddenly felt ill. He went ahead and participated in the hunt the next day but rode in a carriage rather than on horseback. That evening, he was still feeling ill, and sent for the court physician, Le Mariniers. At the surgeon's insistence, the king was brought back to Versailles for treatment, uttering the ominous words, "Versailles is where you must be ill."

At the end of the day, the king was put into a carriage at the Petit Trianon, wearing his robe with a coat over it. The duc d'Cröy recorded that, "As he entered the carriage, the King said, 'At the gallop' and in fact, he went from the courtyard of the Petit Trianon to that of Versailles in just three minutes…All night his fever was high and accompanied by a severe headache… to ease the pain, he was given opium.

"The King was in a small camp bed in the middle of the room… The Royal Family came in and out often during the day…"

Finally, the tell-tale pustules appeared on the king's face. He had smallpox. The physicians attending the king now had decisions to make. He had now been sick for three or four days and there was a good chance that he would recover if he did not have the more virulent form of the disease. Yet, if he worsened, there was the problem of du Barry, who would have to be removed from court in order for the king to renounce her and receive the final rites. No one wanted to be the one to tell the favorite to leave, and then have the king recover and face his wrath. The court divided into the camps for and against du Barry, and all waited.

To the court's surprise, the Mesdames, who had never had smallpox, moved into their father's room and kept him company. To their chagrin, du Barry also remained near his side, risking her renowned beauty and her life should she contract the disease. Oddly, the physicians kept reassuring the king that he was probably suffering from a military fever, and all would be well. When Louis showed them the pustules forming on his hands or what he saw in his reflection in "the glass," they lied to him and tried to show him the confidence they were not feeling. As no one had mentioned last rites to him, the king remained assured he would be alright.

Louis XV was also deceived by his condition. He repeatedly said, "If I hadn't had smallpox when I was eighteen, I would think I had it now." Finally, even his bravado couldn't mistake the appearance of the disease. On May 3, he looked at the pustules on his hands and studied them. He finally said, "It is smallpox."

Once the King confirmed the disease, he turned to du Barry and said, "Now that I know what my condition is, I will not repeat the scandal of Metz. Had I known what I know now, you would not have come in. I owe myself to God and my people. You had, therefore, better leave tomorrow." She fainted. When she finally left his room, she hurriedly packed her trunks and went to her carriage, rather than wait for the following day.

That night, the king wanted to see her. "Towards midnight [the King] said, 'Go and get Mme du Barry.' Laborde told him, 'She has left.' 'Where has she gone?' he asked. 'To Rueil, sire.' 'Ah, already,' the king replied, and two large tears ran down his cheeks.

The duc d'Cröy reported the sad events, and continued, "That night, he asked to get up, but the pain from the pustules on the soles of his feet made him faint…

"On Friday, May 6, during the night there was some agitation, with moments of delirium… At nine in the evening, the face seemed darker, which might have been due to the scabs on the pustules…"

On Saturday, the King confessed, received absolution and was given the last rites. The Cardinal de la Roche-Aymon went into the king's bedroom's antechamber, the Oeil-de-Boeuf, where the court was assembled, many holding handkerchiefs to their noses as the smell from the king's illness was beginning to permeate the rooms. The cardinal, in a clear voice, said, "Gentlemen, the King has asked me to tell you that he begs God's forgiveness for having offended Him, and for the scandal he caused his people [du Barry]; if God gives him health, he will look to penitence, to sustaining our religions and to relieving his people." Louis, who had heard the words spoken, merely said in a hoarse voice, "I wish I had had the strength to say it myself." He later told his daughter, Madame Adelaide: "I have never felt better, or more at peace."

Later that day, he worsened. The fever rose and his face changed. On the 9th, "he got much worse," d'Cröy wrote, "the scabs and dried pustules became black… and it was noticed that an inflammation of the throat prevented him from swallowing." Scabs began forming on his eyelids and he could no longer open them. "His face, swollen by the scabs, was the color of bronze… His chest was immobile, his mouth open, but his face was not misshapen and showed no agitation; in short, he looked like a Moor's, dark and swollen." The windows were opened, and the smell from the room wafted out to the Marble Court.

"On May 10… he remained conscious until noon and showed, as before, the greatest patience, firmness, quiet and acceptance. At three-fifteen, he expired." Immediately the courtiers ran out of bedroom where the body had already begun to decompose.

Across the courtyard, alone in the dauphin's room, Louis Auguste and Marie Antoinette watched the candle flame in the window of the king's bedchamber. The flame suddenly went out, as the announcement was made: "Le Roi is mort! Vive le roi!" (The King is dead! Long live the King!" It was a symbolic transition from one king to another in the short time it took a heart to stop beating.

Suddenly, a noise like thunder filled the Hall of Mirrors as thousands of courtiers ran toward the dauphin's room, each wanting to be the first to show their face to the new king. As the doors to his room were flung open, the crowd hushed as they saw the dauphin and dauphine kneeling upon the floor, tears streaming down their cheeks. The dauphin cried, "Protect us, O God, we are too young to reign." In actuality, Louis Auguste was older than his predecessors when they inherited the throne: Louis XIII had been 10, Louis XIV and Louis XV were five. Louis Auguste, at age 19, had a distinct advantage on them.

Louis Auguste and his brothers had been kept from the king's room during the ordeal, for fear they might contract the disease. The closest the dauphin was allowed to his grandfather's room was to stand at the bottom of the King's staircase. The three grandsons were the future of France. There were no last words of wisdom from grandfather to grandson, no warnings or guidelines on how to rule. Suddenly, the nineteen-year-old king was untethered from the one man who could help steer him through what was to come.

Louis XV's body was hastily prepared. "The usual autopsy was omitted for fear of contagion. The King's body was hurriedly encased inside a lead coffin into which was poured a mixture of lime, vinegar, and camphor. No one at court would shroud the gangrenous body and solder it into its lead casing. Laborers were paid extra to do the job, and one was said to have died from retching. The coffin was then placed in a hermetically sealed oak casket filled to the brim with earth. It spent the night in the Feuillants monastery near the Tuileries… Next day, the cortege set off for the basilica of Saint-Denis… The cortege consisted of only three carriages: the first two contained officiating priests and household officers on duty that day—there were no volunteers, no mourners—the last carried the coffin, draped in a blue velvet mantle strewn with the lilies of France and topped with the crown….There was a fine drizzle, and the light was fading as they arrived at the basilica. The service was perfunctory, and, as an extra precaution, Louis XV was bricked up in his mausoleum. It was a solitary end to what had always been a solitary life." (Excerpt in italics courtesy of *The Life of Louis XVI*, by John Hardman.)

Louis the Beloved had died detested by people across the wide range of nobility and peasant. Madame du Barry, the Deer Park, the taxation and earlier imprisonment of people at will, copious amounts of money spent on splendor and mistresses…it had all culminated in a king who was anything but loved. To many, the legacy he left behind was one that his successor could not overcome.

As for the young man who would now have that mantle of the late king placed firmly upon his shoulders, his diary entry noting the passing of his grandfather was succinct and without emotion:

"May 10: Death of the king at two in the afternoon and departure for Choisy."

Louis XV, a year before his death

That was it. The king was a footnote in his own death. Within thirty minutes of Louis XV's passing, a messenger pressed his way through the courtiers crowded into the dauphin's apartment. He bore a note from the Minister of the Interior, the duc de la Vrilliere. As the duke had been at the king's bedside during his illness, he, and the other ministers were in quarantine, forcing him to communicate by messenger. Louis Auguste answered the questions Vrilliere put to him in the letter as follows: He would be known as Louis XVI, not Louis Auguste; he would retain his grandfather's ministers and keep in touch with them via letter until their 10-day quarantine was over and "if anything crops up, the matter should be sent to me." This statement was in reply to the question of whether or not the ministers should form committees to deal with foreign and home affairs during the 10-day lapse.

## Chapter Forty-Nine
## **Youth and Indecision**

The new king and queen left for Choisy that very afternoon. The rest of the court crammed themselves into carriages to follow them away from the contaminated halls of Versailles. The palace would have to be thoroughly cleaned. By the time Louis XVI returned to the Versailles three months later, Louis XV would be merely someone who had once tried to live up to the Sun King and failed.

Louis XVI traveled in the same coach as his two brothers, Provence and Artois, and their wives (the daughters of the King of Sardinia and the duke of Savoy). Louis Auguste was now king, and he struggled with the new protocol where his brothers should now address him in more "regal" terms. After Marie Antoinette pointed out this protocol to him, Louis complained to his foreign secretary, "I am not happy with the way in which… [the duke of Parma, cousin to Louis XV] has been writing to me since I became King. He has not asked my permission to write informally."

As for Madame du Barry, out of respect for the late king, Louis granted her a pension, but she had to spend it in a convent. Louis XVI, feeling woefully inadequate for his new role, had advice handed to him from many arenas. The voice whispering the loudest was that of his Aunt Adelaide; his grandfather's daughter had been pulling Marie Antoinette's strings since the Austrian lady arrived at court. Adelaide now put forth her candidate for an advisor to the new king, as Louis XVI was determined to rule without a prime minister. For now, he would keep the *parlement* and the ministers, but he wanted a wiser head to advise him.

Here we have the first subterfuge of Louis XVI's reign. The new King had wanted Machault, the finance minister who had introduced the *vingtieme* tax under his grandfather Louis XV. The late king had said, 'the parlements have forced me to dismiss Machault, the man after my own heart. I will never get over it.' Louis XVI wrote to Machault at Thoiry, Machault's estate, only one day after his grandfather's death:

'Monsieur, overwhelmed as I am by the proper grief which I share with the kingdom I nevertheless have duties to perform. I am king. The word implies a multitude of obligations, but I am only twenty. I do not think I have acquired all the necessary knowledge. Moreover, I cannot see any of the ministers, since they were all interned with the king in his illness. I have always heard you well-spoken of for your probity; and your reputation for a deep understanding of affairs of state is well deserved. This is why I am asking you to be so good as to come to assist me with your advice and understanding. I would be obliged, Monsieur, if you come to Choisy as quickly as possible where I will be delighted to see you.'

This letter was signed Louis Auguste. The intrigue begins with the ambiguous use of the term 'Monsieur.' As soon as Aunt Adelaide heard that Louis had mailed off the letter, she was furious. She hated Machault for trying to tax the clergy and was happy when he was exiled. She went to Louis to persuade him to ask for Maurepas instead. The problem was, the letter was on its way via carrier to Toiry. The courier had been delayed with a broken spur, and Louis instructed La Vrilliere to intercept the letter to Machault, replace the envelope and address it to Maurepas' estate in Pontchartrain. The wording of the letter and the address of 'Monsieur' could apply to both men. It would be left for history to decide if this broken spur played a part in the Revolution that was to follow.

Maurepas had been in exile for twenty-five years and was now instructed to return to court. He was seventy-four and one would need to look at his hatred for Louis XV for exiling him during his most-productive years as a minister. Louis XVI's letter, meant for Machault, may have rankled Maurepas even further: "well spoken of" and "reputation for deep understanding of affairs of state are well deserved" would be hard to swallow under the conditions the former minister had found himself. Was the new king naïve enough to think that the passing of Louis XV was mourned by all?

Still, Maurepas ordered his carriage and set off for Choisy early in the morning of May 13$^{th}$, 1744. As he approached the chateau, he had to wrangle his way past the coaches of courtiers still arriving from Versailles. Where would they possibly put them all? The elderly former minister bowed to his new king and jumped right in:

'I will be nothing in the eyes of the public. I will be for you alone: your ministers will work with you; I will never speak to them in your name, and I will never undertake to speak to you on their behalf. Just defer decisions that are not of a routine nature. We will have a chat once or twice a week and if you have gone too quickly, I will tell you.' He then pointed out how the reign of Louis XV had been happiest when Cardinal Fleury had been the prime minister (1726-43), and that he felt it was essential for a 'centre,' a prime minister to be in place. It was obvious he was the best choice for the post. 'If you will not or cannot be such a man, you must necessarily choose one.'

Maurepas had overshot the mark. Louis had not called him there to offer him the post of prime minister, indeed, he did not want one. He was perhaps just looking for someone in the wings who might share his advice on how the late king would have handled it until the young king found confidence in his own wings. Maurepas had spoken as a man with an agenda, and even had the audacity at this first meeting to hint that he would reign the king in if he had "gone too quickly." His speech was met with what would become Louis XVI's signature reaction: total silence. Unlike Louis XIV, who would diplomatically respond to a delicate situation with "We shall see," this shy and indecisive new ruler dealt with situations he was not prepared to handle with silence.

Louis XVI called his first council, the *Conseil des Dépêches* to discuss home affairs on May 19. The quarantine had ended for the ministers, but a new one had begun. The aunts, who had stubbornly stayed by the late king's bedside, had contracted smallpox, so Louis had to leave Choisy for La Muette to conduct the *Conseil*. Rather than move the entire court again, Adelaide and Victoire were quarantined in another building on the grounds of Choisy.

The ministers waited for the uncomfortable new king to gather his thoughts. He was nothing like his late grandfather in looks or composure. To be fair, the ministers were older men, and not much to look at either. They were greedy for power and took this opportunity to size up the tall king before them. Louis XVI grew to be 6'4" tall—the tallest of the French monarchs. He may have felt uncomfortable with this in an era where the average height of a man was 5' 7". It may be why he slumped, giving him the bear-like appearance, along with his lumbering gait. For a shy man, standing out in the crowd was probably not a welcome trait.

Maupeou was present at the *Conseil*, acting as chancellor. He took precedence after the king and acted as proxy in his absence. Louis XV had been fond of him and called him his 'little Seville orange' due to his complexion and his short stature. Also present was the duc d'Aiguillon as Minister of War and Foreign Affairs. The abbé Joseph-Marie Terray was seated and acted as the Controller-General of Finance. He was a brilliant if ruthless finance minister who enjoyed the income from the abbeys of Saint-Martin de Troarn and Notre-Dame des Molesmes. Finally, there was La Vrillere and Bourgeois de Boynes, the Minister of Marine, who had run down the navy during Louis XV's reign to the point where there was now only one ship-of-the-line in service.

This was the motely crew Louis XVI sat before in that first council meeting. Men all older than himself, greedier and desiring the power and riches that came with their titles. For Maurepas, who had come away from his lofty speech to the king with no particular role other than advisor, he now sat across the table from men who had maintained their power while he cooled his heels for almost thirty years at a chateau in Toiry. He was related to La Vrilliere and d'Aiguillon but had not been in their confidence for some time. His first address to the king in regard to them was: "Concerning your present ministers, I shall say nothing: some are close relatives, the others are known only to me by public repute."

In truth, Maurepas knew his voice at these council meetings would amount to nothing. He would be outvoted by Louis XV's old ministers every time. If he wanted any chance at advancement, he would need to somehow "winkle the existing ministers out." He wasted no time. At first, he kept silent as to his disagreements with their policies, but as the summer continued, Louis XVI realized his special advisor was advocating to dismiss the existing ministers and recall the old parlement that Louis XV had worked so hard to end.

The King and his Aunt Adelaide were shocked at Maurepas's advice; the latter regretting she had recommended him to the King. Louis XV would have turned over in his bricked-up coffin. News got out to the sitting ministers that mischief was afoot, and that the king's advisor was against them. On June 2nd, the duc d'Aiguillon resigned, fearing his dismissal was eminent. This left two offices open—foreign affairs and war. It was hinted that Marie Antoinette's dislike of d'Aiguillon for his links with Madame du Barry may have played a part in the duke's retreat. The duke had often referred to the new queen as a 'coquette.'

The duc d'Aiguillon was replaced by the comte de Vergennes, who would prove a poor alternative where Marie Antoinette was concerned. He was to prove to be an insurmountable obstacle to her brother Joseph's territorial designs and she was often embroiled in hot debates with the new minister. The other appointment for minister of war was the comte du Muy. All the counsel members were elderly in terms of the era. They had figured into past king's and dauphin's lives in one way or another. They were familiar, if not remarkable.

Louis Auguste would not officially be crowned King of France for another year. As summer had donned at Versailles, and the court had been reinstated, it was time to move again. Versailles was not the best place to be in the sweltering French summers. Its rudimentary sanitation was a constant complaint at the palace. In the eighteenth century there were public latrines placed along hallways and stairwells of the palace, the Grand Commons, and other annexes. These latrines consisted of a room with a wooden seat, or *lunette*, closed by a cover in a vain attempt to shut in the odors, and connected by a waste pipe to a cesspit. Some were kept locked, and the keys given to only the nearby lodgers at the palace.

The complaints of the smell from these *lunettes* were legion. In 1785, under Louis XVI, seven lodgers in the attics of the Grand Commons, among them the king's dressers and one of the queen's chaplains, petitioned for the closing down of a fourth-floor privy because 'the smell penetrates the lodgings…and infects furnishings, clothes and linen," as well as "serving certain riff-raff who use it as a meeting place."

The nobility didn't fair much better, other than their 'closestools' usually had padded seats. In 1766, under Louis XV, the king's daughter Madame Adelaide, demanded new rooms for a lady-in-waiting lodged above the queen's apartment with the complaint it was "far too near a privy." Two years earlier the Comtesse du Chatelet, who lived in the attics of the south wing, complained of the smell from the nearby privy and also—a glimpse of the "cheek-by-jowl" living at Versailles—of the fact that she could be seen in her cabinet from its window. Adding to the smell were the leaks of latrines through the floor to lodgings beneath them. Iron or lead pipes were prone to blockage and corrosion, one leaking into Marie Antoinette's kitchen, poisoning everything.

If a latrine was not handy, the courtiers and staff would simply find a place in the public corridors. In 1762, the comte de Compans complained about the passerby and kitchen boys who "attended to their needs" in an inner courtyard. Chamber pots were common, and it was an ongoing patrol to keep servants from dumping their contents out windows into the courtyards below. Marie Antoinette, before she became queen, was once hit as she crossed the king's inner courtyards beneath the numerous windows of Madame du Barry. Marie never believed du Barry's assault with a dumped chamber pot to be an accident.

To add to the discomfort of Versailles, the unfinished Gabriel Wing under Louis XVI was an ongoing building site, whose exterior wouldn't be completed until 1780. The noise and the sanitation issues prompted moving from chateau to chateau based on the season, the hunting, and the gardens. It was customary for the kings to spend a month or two in the smaller royal chateaus, such as Compiegne or Marly; and in the autumn they went to Fontainebleau. It was recorded that Louis XVI spent fifty-seven nights away from Versailles in 1775; one year after the late king's death. When the news came that the court could return to Versailles after the quarantine, and Versailles had been deemed ready to reinhabit, Louis did not immediately return. He visited his other chateaus: Choisy, La Muette, Marly, and Compiegne. He finally returned to Versailles on September 1$^{st}$. By October 5$^{th}$, he's traveling again to Fontainebleau for the hunting; and to La Muette in November.

For each of these trips, the King's linens, plate, bed, household, etc. had to be moved along with him. The packing and unpacking of trunks were a tedious affair for the servants. The copious amount of time spent at the smaller chateaus did work out well for Maurepas, as he was able to closet himself more with the king. Away from Versailles, ministers had to ask permission to visit the king. With the advantage of having the king's ear, Maurepas put forth his idea that the decision-making power of the *Conseil d'Ètat* be given instead to ad hoc committees, from which ministers who were against Maurepas's policy could be excluded when it was a matter of general policy.

Maurepas pointed out that this had been used under Louis XV (always a good ploy) when committees had prepared work for the council, but the decisions had not been taken in the council. Adding honey to the deal, the advisor tried to hit the king at his most vulnerable point—his lack of experience. He pointed out that smaller informal committees would make it easier for the new king to learn his craft. It wasn't a hard sell, as Louis XVI hated the large council meetings. On one occasion, the tension of arguing and butting heads got to him and he stormed out without saying a word. Maurepas had to bring him back so that another meeting might be scheduled.

While Louis chewed on Maurepas's plans, he took an important step based on the late king's demise: On June 18th, at Marly, he had himself vaccinated against smallpox. While vaccinations were still risky, Louis wanted to set the example for his subjects. Following the vaccination, many panicked when the smallpox pustules erupted on the king's nose, fingers, and stomach, but by June 30h, he was clear, and the vaccination considered a success. Following suit, Louis' brothers, Provence and Artois also received vaccinations, much to the duc de Cröy's chagrin who felt it insanity to risk wiping out the entire Bourbon dynasty with one giant procedure and leaving the door open to the Orleans branch who had been wrangling for the crown ever since the sickly Louis XV was up for the throne.

If the woes of the ministers were not enough for the new king, his cousins joined the fray by presenting Louis with a petition to reinstate the old parlement. The current duc d'Orleans and his son, duc de Chartres, were circulating the petition and Louis acted without hesitation. He exiled them to their estate at Villers-Cotterêts. Meanwhile, Maurepas' plan for the system of smaller committees was taking place by the start of August. On July 20, Turgot replaced Bourgeois de Boynes as the Minister of the Navy. Due to Boynes mishandling of the Navy (a passion of Louis XVI's), it was an easy choice to dismiss him. It didn't take long for Maurepas to begin his next sabotage with his criticism of Terray, and he threw Maupeou into the mix. To keep Terray, the finance minister, restrained in his official capacity, Maurepas resurrected the *Conseil royal des finances*, which met for the first time on July 19th.

An anonymous letter to the king in July came as a boon to Maurepas' cause. The letter accused the king of personally benefiting from Terray's grain monopoly, the *régie des grains*. On July 30th, Louis wrote to Maurepas: "Whilst you are in Paris, try to get to the bottom of the so-called grain treaty—and find me a *contrôleur-général*. Adieu and good night till we meet at Compiêgne.' The grain issue would continue to hang like the Ides of March throughout the reign of Louis XVI, eventually leading to the French Revolution and the death of the new royal couple.

# Chapter Fifty
# **Troubles At Home**

To look at Louis XVI under a microscope in his first years after the death of Louis XV is to see a frightened young man who is convinced, he is too young to rule. He waffles on decisions, remains silent when faced with confrontation or a topic he feels inadequate to address. His gangling lope when he walked, stooped-shouldered, with the look of a man who wished he could disappear into the woodwork did little to inspire. He was happiest closeted away in his private rooms where he tinkered with locks, clockworks, and read copious books on the sciences, botany, and the Navy. Hunting was a passion. There, on horseback, surrounded by wilderness, he was free. Not necessarily free from courtiers and family who followed along in carriages or rode next to him, but free from the crushing hallways at Versailles.

Louis XVI

Louis was intelligent, but his sense of inferiority for the job caused him to defer to advisors, clergy and his own wife. Marie Antoinette played a precarious role in his life, however. He had been raised to hate Austria and mistrust the Habsburg dynasty. He would therefore often keep his wife at arm's length when it came to matters of State. Whether he worried she would relate private French affairs to her mother or ambassador is not known. It is known many Parisians worried that the new queen could be a spy.

Never is Louis XVI's frame of mind in 1774 more apparent than the meeting he had with his advisor Maurepas on August 23$^{rd}$. Maurepas was agitated that Louis had yet to get rid of the chancellor Maupeou. Louis had waffled and said he needed to keep him on for a bit as it was customary for the chancellor to preside over the privy council to review judicial decisions which had been taken by the parlement over the past year. Maurepas, his patience at an end, went for his *travail royal* [one-on-one] meeting with the king that morning:

'You don't have your portfolio,' said the king, 'do I conclude there is not much business?' 'I beg your pardon, Sire, but the matter about which I must talk to you has no need of papers. It is a question of your honour…if you do not want to keep your ministers, say so…and appoint their successors.' 'Yes, I have decided to change them, said the king, 'it will be on Saturday, after the *Counseil des Depéchés*.' 'No, Sire,' the minister replied with some petulance, 'that is not how to govern a state! I repeat: time is not a commodity with which you can dispose at pleasure. You have already lost too much for the good of affairs and I am not leaving until you have decided…' 'But what do you expect me to do,' replied the king; 'I am overwhelmed by business, and I am only twenty. It's all getting me down." 'You have always said you want an honourable ministry. Is yours so? If not change it. That's what you are there for. These last days the abbé Terray has given an opportunity by asking you after his travail whether you were satisfied with his administration.' 'You are right,' said the king, 'but I was scared. It's only four months since I've been accustomed to being frightened when I spoke to a minister.'

This conversation is shocking and revealing. Would Louis XIV have ever allowed a minister, or anyone, to speak to him that way? As Louis XV began to feel his oats in later life, he too would not have tolerated such disrespect. Maurepas is literally demanding that the king make a decision. "This is not how you govern a state!" has the sound of an adult chastising a child. And to Maurepas, in his seventies, the young king of twenty probably did look like a child, with his chubby cheeks, cherubic mouth and hooded eyes. That Louis not only took the remonstrances but agreed with him— "You are right"—shows a vacillating, ineffectual king who fears confrontation or the responsibility his decisions might bring. And, above all, he wanted to be loved.

With a heavy heart, Louis finally bent to Maurepas' will and dismissed Maupeou and Terray. The time he took to decide, however, turned the public opinion against him. They wanted a king who would take an active role in deciding the question of parlement. As Louis came back from Saint-Denis on July 25 for the memorial service for Louis XV, he was met with a glacial silence. His opponents gleefully pointed out in essence that "what goes around comes around," meaning he was known for handling things with silence, and now the people were using his own weapon against him.

His decision to reinstate the parlement, undoing what Louis XV had fought to put in place, was the sticking point. When the perils of reversing the former king's accomplishments were pointed out to him, Louis XVI said, "That may be true. It may be considered politically unwise, but it seems to me to be the general wish and I want to be loved."

Maupeou's carriage was stoned as he left Compiegne where the council had been held. His effigy was burned on the Place Dauphine. He never relinquished his title as chancellor, even when offered a dukedom. A trial would have to ensue to strip him of his title and Louis was not willing to go that far. Therefore, Maupeou was the last chancellor of France. He died in 1792, shortly after the Revolution broke out in 1789. His anger concerning the verdict was shown in his final declaration: "I have won the king a lawsuit which has been dragging on for three hundred years. If he wants to throw it all away that's his look-out; he is f----d'.

Terray was dismissed on the same day. Maurepas wasted no time in replacing the two empty seats. As Maupeou retained the title of chancellor, Maurepas chose the title Keeper of the Seals and appointed Armand-Thomas Hue de Miromesnil, who was accused of being a 'cunning Norman.' Louis XV had been displeased with de Miromesnil during his reign. Miromesnil had taken it upon himself as premier president of the parlement to be mediator between the parlement and the king, and the king and the parliament, thereby speaking in the king's name. Louis XV had dressed him down, saying, 'M. le premier president I am very displeased with you—personally displeased; you have not carried out my orders; do not let this happen again.' Miromesnil was a 'lifelong friend' of Maurepas', which gives us a glimpse behind the curtain. Louis XVI would come to believe that Miromesnil betrayed him in his hour of need.

While Miromesnil was informing Maurepas of his plan to reinstate the old parlement Louis XV had abolished, he added his caveat: they would impose conditions on it that would not cause any trouble. Meanwhile, the other appointment was announced: Anne-Robert-Jacques Turgot was to move from the marine to the finance minister. Turgot swallowed his doubts about restoring the parlement out of gratitude to Maurepas for giving him the appointment.

Louis XVI wanted desperately to be a good king, a beloved king. He looked always to the public as a barometer of how he was doing. He said that he "must always consult public opinion; it is never wrong." It was, unfortunately, those a little closer to home who were working with agendas of their own. The disenchanted princes of the blood, most of the dukes and most of the philosophers (excluding Voltaire) were opposed to Louis XV's old policies. This group, along with the exiled *parlementaires* and others, began calling themselves the "patriot party." They would be instrumental in opposing the king during the pre-Revolution crisis.

Within the king's inner circle was more dissatisfaction. Aunt Adelaide regarded Maurepas as a traitor, brought back from the exile her father had imposed upon him. Two princes of the blood, along with the king's brother, Provence, who was now called 'Monsieur' as brother to the king, were also not keen on recalling the old parlement. Provence was next in line to the throne if Louis XVI and Marie Antoinette did not produce an heir.

During a full council, Vergennes took it upon himself to address the elephant in the room. He asked the king and those in attendance: 'Did the former parlement deserve the late king's punishment? Was it permissible for the king to suppress the parlements by virtue of his authority? In both cases, would it not be more dangerous to recall the exiled parlement than to let the new one remain, even with the faults it contains?'

One can picture the culmination of swiveled heads as all looked to Louis XVI for his reply. One of those present, Soulavie, reported on the buffeted king's response:

'He was 'a silent spectator during the debates which tore to pieces the royal authority and analyzed it before the eyes of the people. In the progress of this transaction, the king was not destitute either of information or advice; he classed them in his cabinet with particular attention, and he wrote on the covers of the memoirs of the two parties the words: 'opinions favourable to the return of the old parlements'; 'opinions favourable to the existing parlements'; and he embraced that which was to him the most fatal.'

It is apparent that Vergennes questions were put in rhetorical form, as one positing an opinion to be chewed upon. Louis, with his usual need to procrastinate and remain silent, merely filed them under 'pros and cons', and waited. A select cabinet of four members—Maurepas, Miromesnil, Turgot and Sartine (who had just taken over as naval minster to free up Turgot as finance minister)—met in complete secrecy to discuss the question of parlement. It was decided to put forth 'all that has been said, written, thought and circulated, for and against, on this subject. The ministers wanted to know his opinion on everything and establish the most detailed discussion with him...This method has had the desired effect which was to make him regard the plan which has been determined as his own—and able to circulate his opinion among the public.'

It was a form of brainwashing, or coercion, handled with kid gloves. Louis needed to feel the ideas were his own 'in order that he may bring to bear the degree of warmth and involvement necessary in all large-scale operations of this kind.... As this decision is different from the ideas he had before ascending to the throne, he has himself confessed his astonishment: 'Who would have said, a few years back when I went to the *lit de justice* with my grandfather that I would be holding the one I am about to hold?'

The ploy had worked. Veri's account of 're-education' of the king as to all things parlement led to the *lit de justice* on November 12, on the very day Louis stopped his non-stop chateau trips and returned to Versailles.

The gentle massaging of the ministers seems to have found their way into the parlement now present. The parlement would be divided into several chambers: The *Grand' Chambre* and several *chambres des enquètes* (investigation) and *requètes* (pleas), which did the preliminary work. The *Grand' Chambre* was staffed by more senior, established members, the *enquétes* with younger blood, hot to make a name for themselves. A key element of this 1774 settlement was to increase the powers of the *Grand' Chambre*, whose key features could be bought with royal patronage, at the expense of those of the *enquétes.* The parlement could be forfeited if it broke certain conditions, recalled by the princes and dignitaries of state. If that happened, it would automatically be replaced by a Grand Conseil. Once an edict was registered, only one further remonstrance would be heard.

Louis XVI rose to read off the new rules of the old parlement, and the reaction was one of shock: "We were astonished," wrote Veri in his journal, "at the tone of firmness and personal volition which the king brought to his speech. The ministers of the committee did not expect it…he learned his speech by heart." As Louis walked from the Palais de Justice after the *lit*, he was greeted with thunderous applause. At the base of the statue of Henry IV, the first and most popular king in the Bourbon dynasty, someone had written 'Resurrexit'— 'he is reborn.' For a young king, so unsure of himself, this was a tribute that hit home. 'What a splendid conceit,' he said humbly, no doubt bursting with pride, 'if it's true," he added modestly. 'Even Tacitus could not have written anything so laconic or so fine.'

The fact that Louis had hidden the plans for the *lit* from the proponents of the new parlement Louis XV had put in place was a bit surprising. Hearing rumors that he might be making an announcement at the *lit* in favor of reinstating the old parlement, they had written to him at Fountainebleau where he was staying before returning to Versailles on November 12. They were reassured that he was keeping his grandfather's parlement. Louis' passive aggressive answer to them was 'that he was surprised that…[it] make any remonstrances to him upon mere public reports.' The king's duplicity in not acknowledging that he had indeed made up his mind to recall the old institution is a further sign of his reluctance to take a stance and risk disapproval or confrontation. It smacked of both of his successors who had used subterfuge rather than confronting opponents face-to-face on egregious matters.

It was Louis' brother, Monsieur, comte de Provence, in a memorandum presented to his brother, who summed up the disloyalty many were feeling in the king's kicking to the curb of the parlement his grandfather had put in place:

'Will the king confiscate the places of an obedient parlement, which had re-established the crown on the king's head, only to give them to a parlement which had attempted to dethrone him? Will he abandon the members of a faithful parlement to public scorn, to the outrages of a parlement vindictive and flushed with victory on its return?'

Julian Swann wrote of the psychological damage done by recalling the old parlements and the late king's 'good servants' who filled the seats: 'Whilst undoubtedly a minority…[they] were still sufficiently numerous to provide a functioning judicial system between 1771 and 1774. Had Louis XVI given them the opportunity they would have continued to do so.' Along with the members of the rejected parlement were also ministers, military commanders, and intendants who had helped the late king recover his authority. Louis XVI had cut the cords. Would he regret it when he would need the support of true and loyal men when the mobs were at his door?

## Louis XVI's Private Domain

Louis XVI was now back at Versailles and for the first time saw it as *his* palace. While murals of the Sun King's glory glowered at him from every formal ceiling and in works of art, vestiges of Louis XV were not as ubiquitous. The Royal Opera bore his stamp, as did the ongoing building of the Gabriel Wing. There was "the Beloved's" botanical garden behind the Trianon, and his recreated private apartments, but it was Louis XIV's presence that still pervaded the interior and exterior of Versailles.

The private apartments (*interior du roi*) were really a misnomer during the Sun King's time as they were open to the roving crowds. Louis XV chose to have private suppers for a select group of friends. He had passed his love of secrecy and mistrust of others down to his grandson. And so it was, that Louis XVI peered into the late king's private enclaves and went about making them his own. The king's royal business: his *lever* and *coucher*; meetings with the ministers and affairs of state, were held in the three rooms flanking the Hall of Mirrors. These rooms overlook the Court de Marbre (Marble Court) and have balconies leading from their tall windows. It was here that Marie Antoinette bowed before the thundering crowd on the eve of the Revolution.

Besides the king's royal bedchamber (where the *levers* and *couchers* were held), there was a giant antechamber, the Oeil-de-Boeuf (the Bull's Eye) because the window was shaped like the eye of an ox. It was here the courtiers gathered, handkerchiefs pressed to their noses, awaiting news of Louis XV's state of health. On the other side of the King's bedchamber was the cabinet du conseil. Here, Louis XVI made his first remodeling attempt: he installed a bathroom with two baths next to the council chamber.

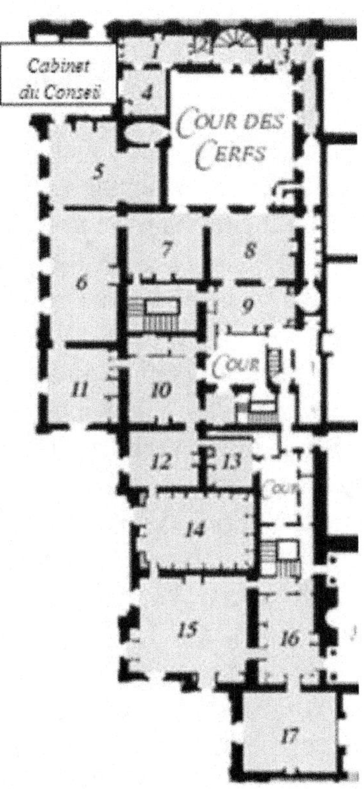


Louis XVI's private apartments floor plan.
(Map courtesy of www.thisisversaillesmadame.blogspot.com)

Key to map: Louis XVI Private Apartments.

1) Bath

2) Toilet

3) Golden Cabinet

4) Wardrobe

5) Louis XV's Bedchamber

6) The Clock Chamber

7) Antechamber

8) Salon of the Hunt

9) The Buffet Salon

10) Cabinet of Dispatches_

11) Interior Cabinet

12) Pièce de la Vaiselle d'Or

13) Cabinet de la Cassette

14) Library

15) The Porcelain Salon

16) Billiard

17) The Gaming Salon

Louis XVI did little to alter the rooms of Louis XV. He mainly changed their purpose.

Several rooms along, in what had been Adelaide's gilded study, Louis had his working library with his travel and science books and periodicals including the English Review, the Annual Register, and French-language journals produced in the Low Countries and half-heartedly banned by his own censors and foreign secretary, Vergennes. These included the *Gazette de Leyde*. "There was also the official *Gazette de France*, which served as a court circular, whose entries Louis monitored and sometimes wrote. Louis did most of his work here, seated at a small bureau made of acajou, a tropical wood favored by the court *ébénistes* such as Riesner, who made this desk in the classical Louis Seize style." (Courtesy of John Hardman, *The Life of Louis XVI*)

Louis XVI's library at Versailles.

Above the *interieur du roi* were several floors dedicated to Louis XVI's truly private rooms. The new king left Louis XV's rococo furnishings and décor. The king did add his own touch to the stairway leading to the private enclave by hanging hunting trophies from his days as dauphin. The first floor of the king's private rooms housed his drawing room where engravings of the French canals hung. Above this room was the geography room, filled with maps, navigational instruments and globes. The third floor showcased Louis XV's collection of wood-working tools made of rosewood and silver mounts. To this collection Louis XVI added his extensive array of barometers, chronometers, telescopes, scientific instruments and other new age wonders. The room also housed a rose lathe used to create amazing snuff boxes in gold that Fabergé tried to emulate later. Louis XVI did repurpose Louis XV's game room on the fourth floor, turning it into his main library. It was a beautiful room filled with everything published in France during his reign. It also showcased some 586 English books in his collection.

According to John Hardman's wonderful book, *The Life of Louis XVI*, 'On the fifth floor was a smithy where Louis indulged his passion for locksmithing. An interest in the mechanical arts was quite usual for the period and was made fashionable by Rousseau's educational treatise, *Émile*, in accordance with which, for example, Louis's young cousin, Louis-Phillipe of Orléans, had dutifully learned how to use a plane. Nevertheless, Louis was made to feel ashamed of his 'mechanical pursuits', as Marie Antoinette described them, and either practiced them in secret or abandoned them for months on end. His valet-de-chambre credited himself with a *bon mot* which is too neat and too insulting for him ever to have uttered to a king: 'Sire, when a king does the work of the people, the people will seize the functions of the king.'

'Right at the top of his wing of the palace was a small turret, or belvedere, just large enough to contain an armchair and a telescope, through which Louis liked to watch arrivals and departures at Versailles. Sometimes the king clambered over the roofs and chimneys of the chateau to watch the tilers and chimney sweeps at work. Then at night he would chase away stray cats. On one occasion, though, he shot the pet Angora belonging to Madame de Maurepas, herself a somewhat feline, manipulative individual, who used the wiles of the species to get her way with her husband. Fortunately, Louis was able to source an identical replacement for the animal.'

The image of a lumbering 6'4"-tall man scampering over the rooftops of Versailles like the Hunchback of Notre Dame is one that is rarely associated with the French monarchy. And then, to picture his horror at finding he has hastened Madame de Maurepas' prized pet to the afterworld, and his endeavors to find an exact replacement, borders on a hilarious satire. This was a ruler unlike those who had gone before him. We see a young man fascinated by the simple workings of the tilers, finding respite among his gadgets and books, that one can only refer to as the "reluctant king." Sex with his wife had yet to find its way into the inner sanctum of his preferred pastimes. Despite the gossip and twittering at court, Louis XVI seemed devoid of the lustful appetite attributed to his predecessors.

## Chapter Fifty-One
## **A Diminished Versailles**

Louis XVI acceded to the throne in 1774 at the young age of nineteen. The government was deeply in debt and resentment of a despotic monarchy was on the rise. He felt woefully inadequate to resolve the situation. As a result of this, he spent much of his time in his private apartments. In his hunting diary, which carried a daily entry, he would simply write *rien*, meaning he had spent the day hidden away in his enclave of private rooms.

The new king's distaste for public appearances was obvious. While audiences with his ministers were a necessity, displays of pomp or festivities were regulated to only the most important of occasions, and he dreaded those. He stated that the nobility could go elsewhere if they desired, the exact opposite of Louis XIV's commandment that all were to be in attendance under his watchful gaze. Louis XVI stipulated that court services were to be 'reduced to what is absolutely necessary.'

John Hardman writes in *The Life of Louis XVI*, 'The ceremonies of the *lever* and the *coucher* remained the focal points of the court's day, but there was no life to them. The *lever* was at eleven o'clock, but the king had already risen at seven, been shaved, put on a simple grey coat, possibly slipped into the queen's apartments, and had also done three hours' work. Then he took off his coat, put on his night shirt and was formally handed his day shirt, in the presence of the select few who had the *grandes entrées,* and then, before a larger gathering, his brown coat and silver-hilted sword. (On ceremonial occasions he would wear blue velvet and crown jewels, such as the large diamond known as the regent, in his hat and another attaching *cordon bleu* of the Saint-Espirit, the highest order of the chivalry.)

Then the king passed into a small room to have his natural ash-blond hair powdered (he wore no wig). At the *coucher* at night the ceremony was performed in reverse order, ending with the night shirt.'

King Louis XVI of France wearing the Order of the Golden Fleece, the Order of Saint Esprit and the Order of Saint Louis, with an embroidered drape over his right shoulder.

The king held sumptuous private suppers in his apartments to select honored guests. The public dinners found him picking at his food as the court watched. He would then retire privately to the billiard room where a plank was placed across the game table and he would be served cutlets, pâté, and water, which he guzzled down. The reviews are mixed as to whether Louis was fond of alcohol. One camp is of the opinion he abstained, while rumors swirled that he could be found in "his cups." Véri recounted a hunting incident in

1775 when 'he [the king] was surprised by drink...[and] the officer in attendance had the quick wits to bundle him into his carriage without anyone noticing or at least daring to speak of it.' Louis may have enjoyed the occasional glass of wine, and that may be why the word "surprised" was used when one too many affected him.

Versailles had changed. The glamor, balls, fireworks, sumptuous feasts during *the apartment's* festivities three times per week, were for the most part, gone. The nobility, so used to scheduling their days around the movements of the king, looked around and could not find him. If he wasn't closeted in a private room tinkering with locks, then he was out riding, reading in his library, or taking off for another chateau. As a result, the numbers at court began to dwindle. Even when the king did make an appearance, his shyness and silence did little to enliven the room or cause a courtier to seek him out.

For a man so shy, it is interesting that he loved to play practical jokes. Unsuspecting pages and courtiers could bear the brunt of some antic he thought particularly funny. It showed a childlike quality about him that was frowned upon by the likes of the duc de Cröy, the marshal of France, who 'would have desired a better tone from him.' The king sought out peasants and the hunt servitors rather than the nobles to get a sense of their daily lives. He may have felt the weight of propriety lifted when he spoke to the lower classes. As mentioned earlier, he would watch the tilers and workmen around the chateaus. It was here he felt the weight of the crown lift, and he could be himself.

In the wings was Maurepas, Louis' advisor, still advocating that the king calls a prime minister. It may have been one of the failures that haunted Louis' reign that he did not choose to. The ministers he had called were forever at each other's throats, turning *counseil* meetings into verbal brawls. They spent money with abandon, despite what funds were available, and tried to sabotage each other's policies. For Louis, it was agony to sit at the head of the table and try to bring some order to a room of bellowing ministers while he was stilled cowed by them.

## Marie Antoinette and Challenges at Court

As Louis struggled to find his way, his wife Marie Antoinette faced her own albatrosses. As she aged, she became even prettier, her once adolescent form filling out, including the bosom Louis XV had hoped to find. She had lovely eyes, blue grey in color and spaced widely-apart. Marie was short-sighted and it often gave her a remote appearance. Her hair had darkened from blond to brown and was abundant. One drawback physically was an aquiline nose (eagle-like) that became more prominent with age. But it was the Habsburg lower lip that diminished her beauty. It sunk under while the chin jutted forward, giving her a pouting or disapproving attitude. Portrait artists usually played it down by concentrating on her upper lip. It is the marble bust of Marie that shows this facial 'defect' more than her portraits.

Bust of Marie Antoinette by Louis-Simon Boizot

In Antonia Fraser's wonderful book *Marie Antoinette: The Journey*, she writes, 'The radiance of the Queen's smile was celebrated; it contained 'an enchantment,' which the future Madam

Tussand, an observer at Versailles, would say was enough to win over 'the most brutal of her enemies.' But the Comte de Tilly, who first saw Marie Antoinette in 1775 when he was fourteen, and judged her with the critical eye of youth, thought it ridiculous to pretend that the heavy 'and at times drooping underlip' lent nobility and distinction to the Queen's appearance. Whatever the sweetness of her smile, it was a mouth that only came into its own when the Queen was angry.'"

It was perhaps that very Austrian facial trait that reminded the court daily that a hated Habsburg was sitting the throne. It was never far from their minds, even as they fawned over her and complimented her gown. Marie was noted for her fine white complexion, causing the famous artist Madame Vigée Le Brun (who painted some of the most famous portraits of the queen) to say Marie's skin was 'so transparent that it allowed no shadow'. The artist thought the queen prettier before the French nightly ritual of rouge marred her perfect complexion.

Marie Antoinette by Vigée Le Brun.

Baron de Besenval described Marie's bearing as perhaps her best asset: 'Something delightful about the carriage of her head, a wonderful elegance in everything, made her able to dispute the disadvantage with others better endowed by nature and even beat them.' Besenval's wording gives us a glimpse of the general consensus: while considered very pretty, she was obviously not portrayed as a stand-alone beauty. Her own mother wrote to her, 'It's not your beauty, which frankly is not very great,' Maria Teresa wrote. 'Nor your talents nor your brilliance (you know perfectly well that you have neither).' It was Marie's great desire to please and her winning smile and bearing that saved her in the eyes of the court and her mother. She was famous for her 'glide,' a way of walking where one never saw the movements of her gait, only a gliding motion that made one wonder if her feet touched the ground.

But from the beginning of Marie's marriage to Louis XVI, while they were still dauphine and dauphin, the letters from home haranguing her about her lack of pregnancies flooded in. Her mother, Maria Teresa, kept the mail couriers between Austria and Versailles at a constant gallop. After admonishing her daughter to 'encourage his affections' by caresses' and being pleasing, Teresa, out of frustration over the continuing sexual debacle, turned her tirade on Louis. 'He is not a man like others!' she complained in a letter to her daughter. Mercy, the Austrian ambassador sent to give Marie Antoinette advice (and report all to her anxious mother) tried to soothe the Austrian Empress's fear. 'There can be no doubt that with a little caution, she will be able to dominate him completely.'

Yet, as the years went by, and the queen's situation did not improve, the pressure on Marie Antoinette was heightened. It was feared that Louis XVI's brother, Provence, and his new bride may become pregnant first, not only providing an extra heir to the throne should something happen to Louis but underscoring the fact that the Queen of France remained barren. In an effort to facilitate more private and frequent visits to the queen's apartments, Mercy arranged construction of a secret passage connecting the queen's and king's apartments in 1775. This secret passage, hidden by a panel next to the queen's bed, would later save her life.

Empress Maria Teresa's fears that Marie could be sent packing if she did not provide children, was not her only concern where her willful daughter was concerned. In 1775, at the time of the king's coronation in Rheims, Marie was still campaigning to keep Choiseul, as it had been he who orchestrated her marriage to the dauphin. Marie decided to give Choiseul a long audience, knowing Louis' dislike for him. It was her way of establishing her own 'character.' She thought to trick Louis and boasted to a childhood friend: "You will never guess the artifice I employed in seeming to ask for the [king's] permission. I told...[him] that I wanted to see M. de Choiseul and that the only problem was finding the right day. I succeeded so well that despite the poor man [king], he himself arranged the time which suited me best to see him. I think that I have made a suitable use of a woman's prerogative on this occasion—I bet old Maurepas can't sleep in his bed tonight."

'Pride goeth before the fall' was an appropriate saying as Marie's blustering led to disaster. Her friend showed the letter to the Empress Maria Teresa who erupted. She wrote a blistering letter to her daughter accusing her of acting like a Pompadour or du Barry rather than a Habsburg. She accused her of wanton frivolity, saying 'you dare to busy yourself with matters of state, with the choice of ministers.' As for Choiseul, Louis snubbed him. After the coronation, when it became Choiseul's turn to kiss the king's hand, Louis withdrew it and looked away, a 'terrible grimace' creasing his face. Choiseul recognized the death knell when he heard it. He turned his involuntary exile into a permanent one. He died in 1785, embittered and bankrupt.

Over the years, Maurepas and Marie butted heads. He constantly worried that she was seeking his dismissal. He told Véri, 'The capital point is not to allow the queen to choose ministers or direct major affairs.' Marie's mother had to take her daughter in tow when Marie had refused to acknowledge du Barry, the king's favorite. The young dauphine had finally bowed beneath the barrage of letters from her mother, reminding her that with her barren condition she could not afford to insult Louis XV. Now, the new queen was playing Russian roulette with her husband's closest advisor; a man with a connecting staircase to the king's apartments and in constant consultation with him. The pressure on Marie Antoinette was crippling.

If the queen felt the weight of all the demands placed upon her, it paled to the situation facing her husband. This time it was not the nobility nor warring ministers that were circling the wagons—it was the humble farmer.

## The Flour War

The Flour War refers to a wave of riots from April to May 1775, in the northern, eastern, and western parts of the Kingdom of France. It followed an increase in grain prices, and subsequently bread prices; bread was an important source of food among the populace. Contributing factors to the riots include poor weather and harvests, and the withholding by police of public grain supplies from the royal stores in 1773-1774. This large-scale revolt subsided following wheat price controls imposed by Louis XVI's Controller-General of Finances, Turgot.

The Flour War was part of a broader social and political crisis during the Ancien Régime. Recent analyses treat this event not only as a revolt caused by hunger, but also as a prelude to the French Revolution. The grain market was subject to harsh rules to ensure the quality of the bread and its availability at all times. The king was required to ensure the food supply of his subjects, nicknamed *le premier boulanger du royame* ("prime baker of the kingdom"). Police held responsibility over the food supply, under the king's orders. In order to maintain social order, the grain market was subject to harsh rules to ensure the quality of the bread and its availability at all times and for the entire population.

Grain merchants were viewed with suspicion; they were called "the cruelest enemies of the people" as they were suspected of mixing flour with other products (such as chalk or crushed bones) or of hoarding grain to artificially raise the price of this vital commodity. The king favored a "moral economy" where cupidity was moderated by strict regulations. The police controlled the purity of the flour and made sure that no one would hide grain to drive up prices. To alleviate hoarding, the grain police would forbid exports from regions enjoying overproduction. It could also force a merchant to drop the price of his flour (he was later compensated for his loss in times of abundance).

Louis' Finance minister, Torgot had other thoughts. He was of the mindset that if you leave it alone, it will pass. Despite the riots beginning as shortages and raised prices swept across France, he abolished police regulations and established free trade in grain on September 13, 1774. It could not have come at a worse time.

During the period before the spring harvest of 1775, the cereal reserves were exhausted while new crops had not yet arrived. In spring, 1775, famine arose: before Turgot's edict, every region faced its own shortages, so that some would have suffered a genuine famine while others would have been totally spared and supplied through state-ensured stable prices. A royal intervention would have been requested, and without a doubt obtained, to assure the supply of the regions most affected, thus mitigating the most severe effects of the famine. However, with liberalization, owners of grain started to speculate by storing grain and acting with astute business acumen in efforts to corner the market. They also tended to buy *en masse* in areas of good harvests to sell in areas of bad harvests where profits could be greater, causing significant price increases and shortages countrywide (less grain in good-harvest regions led to higher prices there as well) as opposed to being confined to local food disruptions.

Consequently, the food shortages of early 1775 affected more people more quickly, and the king was faced with a national crisis as opposed to several small local disturbances. This conflict was known as the "Flour War of 1775". Reports from those that controlled the flow of grain stated there were problems with the grain harvest, causing shortages and less grain availability. News of a grain shortage was met with skepticism and frustration rose from higher prices, which many were unable to afford. Those in opposition of the reform rioted, and seized grain that came in shipments. They offered what they felt was the "just price" for it. This demonstrated a way in which the people took some power back into their own hands. This practice was known as "taxation populaire", or popular taxation.

While there were documented efforts to deal with the grain shortage problems, such as increasing shipments from foreign countries, beliefs that the famine was intentionally orchestrated by Louis XVI, through the "*Pacte de Famine*" emerged. Turgot repressed the riots and restored control over the grain market. The idea of free trade of grain was discredited and the economic experiment distanced the masses from the government in Versailles. The Flour War can be seen as the prelude to the French Revolution.

The rioters reached Versailles on the morning of May 2, 1775. Most of the ministers were in Paris, where they had their main offices while maintaining smaller headquarters at Versailles. The situation is eerily familiar to the circumstances that led up to the storming of the Bastille on July 14, 1789. Here, we see a difference in how Paris fit into the uprising. When Turgot liberated the grain trade in 1774, he made an exception of Paris which was heavily policed. Therefore, the Parisians in the 1775 riots hid in their homes and watched as rioters from the surrounding countryside pillaged the markets and bakeries. 'They barred their doors but leaned out of their windows to watch the riot going by as if had been a procession'. In 1789, the Parisians were out in full force when they stormed the Bastille for ammunition during another famine and civil unrest.

The Flour War as rioters attack the Bakeries

Louis XVI seems to have handled the attack on Versailles with calm, despite the fact that Maurepas and Turgot were absent from the palace that day. The king gave detailed orders to the troops and wrote to Turgot on May 2nd at 11:00:

'I have received your letter... Versailles is under attack, and it is the same men from Saint-Germain; I am going to liaise with... [the war minister and the colonel of the Swiss Guard] to see what is to be done. You may count on my firmness. I have just sent troops to guard the market. I am pleased with the precautions you have taken for Paris…I have just given orders here concerning the markets and mills in the surrounding areas.'

25,000 soldiers were sent out, resulting in 162 arrests, and the hanging of two rioters (a 28-year-old wigmaker and his 16-year-old companion) for 'having spoken of a pretended plot to assassinate the king.' They were executed as examples in the Place de Greve. A return to order was helped along with the assistance to the population by the organization of food supplies to provinces in need as well as obligations placed on supply owners to sell their product at a fixed price. The king sent an increased number of messages to the peasant masses, in particular through the preaching of the clergy.

Louis XVI had had his first taste of a king's precarious standing when the masses are frightened or angry. France had a long history of grain shortages, and this was not the last, or the most volatile of uprisings the young king would face on this matter. As it was his first, and perhaps due to his very young age, he shows more confidence in bringing the unrest to a conclusion than he would when faced with the events on the eve of the French Revolution, when he had been disgraced and undergone a long period of depression. Here, in May of 1775, he writes to Turgot: 'Sometimes good can come out of evil and people will have seen from all this that I am not as feeble as they supposed and that I will know how to carry through what I have resolved to do. This knowledge will make it easier for you to do what has to be done. The truth is that I am more embarrassed dealing with one man that fifty."

This is a rare look at Louis' need to show himself as effectual and worthy of his crown. It almost reads like a student writing home to his parents from college assuring him of how well he is doing on his own and perhaps hoping for a pat on the back and a "well done!" What he doesn't see, as well as his predecessors, was the danger ruling from Versailles had always brought. Where the Sun King created this golden fortress in response to the Fronde Wars and childhood trauma, it had always been a slap in the face to Paris and distanced the monarch from his people. Louis XIV, XV, and now the XVI were not in the capital to see events firsthand nor to associate with their people. The nobility that filled the chambers of

Versailles were not a true barometer of the masses, and it was that very 12-mile distance from Paris that led to many of the uprisings. Gossip was the main grapevine connecting Versailles to the populace of the capital, and the people tended to believe the more salacious and negative reports.

Five months were needed to put a definitive end to the trouble, but most of the problems were over by May 11, 1775. But there was an underlying danger connected with the Flour War that would raise its head in insidious and fatal results in 1789 when the monarchy fell. 25,000 troops had been deployed to quell the riots of the Flour War. Louis wrote to Turgot in response to rumors that the king had been 'too heavy handed' in sending out so many soldiers to quell a bread riot. 'It is certainly true that at present we have too many troops in the environs of Paris but at first we couldn't know how things were going to turn out,' Turgot replied in defense of the troops.

The seeds had been sown for a future event the king could never have predicted. The guards, now housed in Paris to keep up a street patrol, began to fraternize with the Parisians. If the king had been in residence in Paris instead of 12-long miles away in Versailles, would the troops have felt free to 'hang out' with the denizens of Paris? It reached a head in 1789 when the Parisians attacked the Bastille as the troops looked the other way. The ultimate result was the execution of Louis XVI and Marie Antoinette.

## Chapter Fifty-Two
# Exit Turgot—Enter America

Anne Robert Jacques Turgot owed his appointment as Minister of the Navy in July 1774 to Maurepas, the "Mentor" of Louis XVI, to whom he was warmly recommended by the abbé Very, a mutual friend. A month later in August, he was appointed Controller-General of Finances. His motto was: "No bankruptcy, no increase of taxation, no borrowing." In the face of the desperate financial situation in which France found itself, he wanted to enforce the most rigid economy in all departments. The king assured him repeatedly he had his back, even over some controversial policies. This was not new for Louis—he usually bowed to those he felt superior to him in matters of state.

Anne Robert Jacques Turgot

One of the new reforms was directed at the king. Turgot appealed personally to Louis against the lavish giving of places and pensions. Turgot put forth his 'six edicts' to the *conseil du roi* in January 1776 and before the parlement in February. This was to be Turgot's swansong. Of the edicts, the most important was the suppression of the *corvée* (established in 1730) and turning it into a money tax. The *corvée* required non-noble country dwellers to provide their 'arms or horses' for several days a year to make the network of roads France still enjoys. Nobles, clerics, and town dwellers were exempt. They would not have been exempt from the new tax that would replace the *corvée.*

The second edict to meet with hostility was his recommendation to suppress the jurandes and maîtrises, by which the craft guilds maintained their privileges. The abolition of the guilds struck at the heart of the corporate organization of the ancient régime, a system in which the government has dealings not with individuals but with 'corps' such as a guild, a municipality, a village or a province.

But the loudest bellowing came from the nobility in response to Turgot's suppression of the *corvées.* Turgot boldly announced as his object the abolition of privilege, and the subjection of all three Estates of the realm to taxation. The nobles erupted. They were already subject to the *vingtième*, but that had from its inception been a universal tax: the labor on the roads had only ever been performed by those subject to the taille (the poll tax paid by the peasantry, the staple tax of the monarchy since the Middle Ages). This was a slap in the face to the nobility as they were now, in effect, no better than the peasantry and taxed equally. The clergy, who had been exempt from paying the *vingtième*, were also now to pay the new tax.

Louis listened to the uproar and took to his private apartments to think it over. On the one hand Louis's father, the dauphin, had believed that the nobility should be preserved in the property and status; on the other he believed that fiscal privilege 'makes the whole burden fall on the poor people.' He told the parlement, 'I have no intention of blurring the distinctions between the Estates or of depriving the nobility of my kingdom of the distinctions it has acquired by its services…which I shall always maintain. It is not a question here of a humiliating tax but of a simple contribution which everyone should take pride in sharing, since I am myself setting the example by contributing in virtue all of my domains.'

Louis decided the clergy were to remain exempt from the taxation, but the rest of the edicts were registered by the *lit de justice* on March 12, 1776. The other four edicts related to the grain trades were not met with the same opposition. By now, almost everyone was against Turgot. His attack on privilege had won him the hatred of the nobles and parlements; his attempted reforms of the royal household and that of the court; his free trade legislation; his views on tolerance for the Protestants; and his edicts on the *jurandes*, that of the rich *bourgeoisie* of Paris and others, such as the prince de Conti, who interests were involved. Marie Antoinette disliked him for opposing the grant of favors to her proteges, and he had offended her dear friend Mme. de Polignac in a similar manner. The queen played a key role in his dismissal.

It is perhaps here that we hear Louis' refrain, "I just want to be loved." He looked around at the outrage of the nobles and waffled. After all, these were the people who inhabited his cloistered world at Versailles. Many were his friends, and all family members were used to the privileges that set them apart from the common man. He knew nothing of the people of France who worked their farms, sold their goods, or swept his streets. Louis could not fail but see that Turgot had not the support of the other ministers, and he had incurred the hatred of the nobles at court. The queen was railing against him behind closed doors. Even the king's friend, Malesherbes thought Turbot was too rash, and was, moreover, himself wishing to resign. The alienation of Maurepas was also increasing.

Whether it was through jealousy of the ascendancy which Turgot had acquired over the king, Maurepas took sides against him. A pamphlet appeared around this time entitled *Le Songe de M. Maurepas*, generally ascribed to the comte de Provence (Louis XVIII), containing a bitter caricature of Turgot. It was also Turgot's unpopular remonstrances against France becoming involved with the American Revolution that found many wishing for his removal. As Minister of the Navy from 1774-1776, he opposed financial support for the Revolution between the new American colonies and England. He believed in the virtue and inevitable success of the revolution but warned that France could neither financially nor socially afford to overtly aid it. French intellectuals saw America as the hope of mankind and magnified American virtues to demonstrate the validity of their ideals along with seeing a chance to avenge their defeat in the *Seven Years' War*.

The immediate cause of Turgot's fall was a multi-faceted one. Some speak of a plot, of forged letters containing attacks on the queen shown to the king as Turgot's; or of a series of notes on Turgot's budget prepared, it is said by Necker, and shown to the king to prove his incapacity. Others attribute it to the queen, and there is no doubt that she hated Turgot for supporting Vergennes in demanding the recall of the comte de Guînes, the ambassador in London, whose cause she had ardently espoused at the prompting of the Choiseul clique. Others attribute it an intrigue of Maurepas.

On the resignation of Guillaume-Chretien de Lamoignon de Malesherbes, minister of the *maison du roi*, in April of 1776, whom Turgot wished to replace by the abbé Very, Maurepas proposed to the king as his successor a nonentity named Jean Antoine Amelot de Chaillou. Turgot, on hearing this, wrote an indignant letter to the king, in which he reproached him for refusing to see him, pointed out in strong terms the dangers of a weak ministry and a weak king, and complained bitterly of Maurepas's irresolution and subjection to court intrigues. He asked the king to keep the letter confidential, but Louis showed it to Maurepas, whose dislike for Turgot was further embittered. With all these enemies, Turgot's fall was certain, but he wished to stay in office long enough to finish his project for the reform of the royal household before resigning.

To Turgot's dismay and surprise, he was not allowed to do that. On May 12, 1776, he was ordered to send in his resignation. He at once retired to La Roche-Guyon, the chateau of the duchesse d'Enville, returning shortly to Paris, where he spent the rest of his life in scientific and literary studies, being made vice-president of the Académie des Inscriptions et Belles-Lettres, in 1777. Turgot died in 1781, before the French Revolution and the conclusion of the *American War of Independence*. He never doubted the Revolutionary victory. Within a few weeks of his dismissal, his legislation was very largely revoked. The nobility had won.

## Louis Enters the American War of Independence

France bitterly resented its loss in the *Seven Years' War* and sought revenge. It also wanted to strategically weaken Britain. Following the Declaration of Independence, the American Revolution was well received by both the general population and the aristocracy of France. The Revolution was perceived as the incarnation of the Enlightenment Spirit against "English tyranny."

At first, Louis XVI struggled with joining in the war between the American colonies and England. How does a monarch support the insurrection of a people who are forcefully taking control from another monarch and governing themselves? What message would that be sending? Louis' foreign secretary, Charles Cravier, chevalier, comte de Vergennes, pressed the king to become involved in the Americans' cause. Other ministers were also in favor of joining the fray. Still Louis resisted.

In the last quarter of the eighteenth century, two events, more than any other, shaped the modern world: American independence, achieved with the aid of France, followed by the French Revolution six years later. Louis XVI, when able to take stock and look back at the two events, believed they had a causative link.

Boston Tea Party

The restraints on the new American colonists from England were harsh. They were only allowed to trade with the motherland, buying her goods and quid pro quo supplying her with their raw materials. The eastern coast of North American, where the colonies were spread, was filled with rich timberland, animals and hence, fur. But

England's regulations were one-sided. They held all the cards, which meant fluctuations in taxation and other restraints. The colonists revolted. One December 16, 1773, fifty Bostonians dressed as Mohawks attacked three East India Company ships in the harbor and dumped 342 cases of English tea into the sea. Other attacks on British ships had already occurred, including one that was smuggling from the French sugar islands—they set it on fire. King George III was swift to react closing the Boston port and putting the town under military rule.

In 1775, when Louis was dealing with the Flour War, the war between England and America was underway in Lexington, twenty miles from Boston. While only a skirmish, it was regarded as the start of the *War of Independence*. Four weeks later the Continental Congress asked George Washington to form an army. On July 4$^{th}$, 1776, Congress declared American independence. King George III promptly declared the colonists rebels to his crown. As things heated up "across the pond," Louis XVI's ministers looked heavily at the situation. In March 1776 Vergennes, Louis' foreign secretary, put forth his document known as the *Considérations* to his fellow ministers at court. He advocated in this proposal that France should supply clandestine aid to the Americans and should rearm her navy and put her own colonies in a state of defense against an English attack.

On top of his ministers favorably supporting the secret aid to the colonies, France's Bourbon ally, Spain, threw its hat into the ring. Spain was involved in a dispute with Portugal over the border between Brazil and Spanish America along the River Plate. Spain falsely believed that England was secretly egging on her oldest ally, Portugal, to resist Spanish claims. They advocated a Franco-Spanish invasion of England. Louis chewed on this, his instincts telling him that it was a bad idea. Wars were expensive, and France was not in a great financial situation. He was still dealing with the repercussions from the grain shortage and the civil unrest of his people.

Louis did what he always did: he waited to see what the general consensus would be from his ministers. On May 2, 1776, Vergennes 'had the honor of placing at the feet of Your Majesty the paper authorizing me to furnish a million *livres* for the service of the English colonists, providing Your Majesty deigns to affix his *approuvé.'* Marie Antoinette spent that much for her balls the previous year, so it was not the amount that continued to give the king pause. He would also be responsible for the 'laundering' of a further million from Spain and allow the Americans to trade in French ports and purchase arms and munitions. Vergennes had his fifteen-year-old son, Constantin, write up the order, bypassing his own secretaries in an effort to keep the entire enterprise secret.

Secrecy was Louis's strong suit. He had created a life around it. His grandfather, Louis XV had a *secret du roi*, and he would follow suit during the Revolution. Vergennes stressed that 'It was essential that his operation cannot leak out or at least not be imputed to the government.' Papers relating to the House of Austria's family archive were found in 1792 under the king's anvil in his 'mechanical arts' room, because he knew it was the one place Marie Antoinette would never look. She despised his preoccupation with all the tinkering of locks and gizmos. Yes, he knew how to do 'secret.'

Pierre-Augustin Caron de Beaumarchais, the author of the *Barber of Seville* was chosen as the perfect mole to navigate between France and America. More than a playwright, he was also a forger, financier, and polemicist. In April of 1776, Vergennes wrote to Beaumarchais:

'It is necessary that in the eyes of the English government and of the Americans the operation should have essentially the aspect of an individual speculation to which we [France] are strangers…We will secretly give you one million…We will try to obtain a similar sum from Spain…with these two million you will establish a big commercial house, and at your risk and your peril will supply the Americans with arms, munitions, equipment and all other things that they will need to maintain the war. Our arsenal will deliver to you arms and munitions, but you will either replace them or pay for them. You will not demand money from the Americans, since they do not have any, but you will ask in return the produce of their soil which we will help you sell in this country…'

Benjamin Franklin traveled to France in December 1776, in order to rally the nation's support, and he was welcomed with great enthusiasm. He had been named an agent of a diplomatic commission by the Continental Congress. He set sail from Philadelphia for France, hoping to secure a formal alliance and treaty. Known for his accomplishments in scientific and literary circles, he was touted throughout Paris and quickly became a fixture in high society. His goal of securing a treaty, however, was slower in coming. Although France had been secretly aiding the patriot cause since the outbreak of the American Revolution, France felt it could not openly declare a formal allegiance with the Americans until they were assured of a victory over the British. It was not until the American victory over the British at the Battle of Saratoga in October 1777 that France felt an American victory was possible.

A few short months after the Battle of Saratoga, representatives of the new United States and France, including Benjamin Franklin, officially declared an alliance by signing the *Treaty of Amity and Commerce* and the *Treaty of Alliance* on February 6, 1778. The French aid that these agreements guaranteed was crucial to the eventual American victory over the British in the *War of Independence.*

The shipments of military aid to the patriots were primarily gunpowder and it was done through a company called *Rodrigue Hortalez et Compagnie* beginning in the spring of 1776. Estimates place the percentage of French supplied arms to the Americas in the Saratoga campaign at up to 90%. By 1777, over five million *livres* of aid had been sent to the American rebels.

If enough stress were not already resting on the shoulders of a man who had only been king for a few short years, his wife's relatives came calling for his support. When the international climate at the end of 1777 became more tense, Habsburg Austria (Marie Antoinette's mother and brother) requested the support of France in the *War of the Bavarian Succession* after the death of the Bavarian ruler. It was the battle of the Spanish Succession all over again. This new war was against Prussia in line with the Franco-Austrian alliance. France refused, causing the relationship with Austria to sour. Marie Antoinette was caught in the crosshairs as she was pressured to bring Louis around. Louis longed for his private enclave of rooms where could play with such things as a wooden Egyptian lock and forget it all.

Wooden Egyptian lock

Jacques Necker was a Genevan banker who served as Finance Minister to Louis XVI after the dismissal of Turgot. He warned the king that if they were to get into a full-fledged war with England, instead of only surreptitiously suppling the United States with ammunition, it would be very expensive for France's wobbly system of taxation and fiancé. The king had ordered that the French Navy be rapidly rebuilt after its diminished line of ships resulting from the *Seven Years' War*. He was hoping it would be ready if needed, but there were doubts if it could stand up to a serious conflict. England was heralded for its navy, considered the finest in Europe.

Meanwhile, behind the scenes at Versailles, Marie and Louis continued to struggle with their intimacy issues. Letters from Austria continued to bombard the hapless Queen of France; first concerns about her barren womb, and secondly reminding her of her loyalty to Austria amid the Bavarian crisis. It was a miserable time and one about to hit a new challenge. Maria Therese, desperate to see her daughter pregnant, sent Marie's brother, Joseph to Versailles to have a little man-to-man chat with Louis to see if he could ferret out the problem in the marital bedroom. Louis despised his brother-in-law, and with the king's recent decline to get involved in the Bavarian debacle, the feelings of Joseph toward him were mutual.

Joseph arrived at Versailles in 1777 and quickly ascertained that the problem concerning the sexual problem between king and queen was nothing medical—astonishingly the direct descendant of the two most lustful kings in France was ignorant of how to 'do it.' By nature, shy and secretive, he had never admitted that intercourse was a mystery to him. He had married a young virgin, who had anticipated her husband would take charge, and so, for seven long years, nothing had happened. Joseph II reported the situation in graphic terms to his brother (and Marie's) Archduke Leopold: 'Imagine, in his marriage bed—this is the secret—he has strong, perfectly satisfactory erections; he introduces the member, stays there without moving for about two minutes, withdraws without ejaculating but still erect, and bids goodnight. It's incredible because he sometimes has night-time emissions; it is only when he is actually inside and going at it, that it never happens. Nevertheless, the King is satisfied with what he does.' Louis merely marked his conversation with Joseph in his diary of May24th, as 'Walked alone on foot with Emperor.'

It appears Joseph gave Louis the" Birds and the Bees" talk, afterward disparaging him as 'sluggish in body and mind' and said that if Louis had been a donkey his problems could be solved by smacking him on the backside. Joseph in his visit to France noted with envy how homogenous and compact Louis' dominions were. That was why he wanted Bavaria, which would round off his territories. Louis did not want Austria to be once more the dominant force in Germany. He had been a guarantor of the *Peace of Westphalia* and he wanted a balance of which he could be the arbiter.

If it seemed that all the world was at his door with its hand out, and his subjects had turned against him, there was finally some good news at court, and it came in the form of a baby.

# Chapter Fifty-Three
# **Marie Antoinette**

Portrait of Marie Antoinette, by Jean-Baptiste Gautier-Dagoty, 1775, Palace of Versailles, France.

For months Marie Antoinette had struggled with the realization that the wife of Louis' brother, the Comtesse d'Artrois was with child. What she had feared had come to pass. Letters from home intensified as rumors swirled about the apparent coolness of the royal marriage. She responded to them with increasing spirit, no longer the cowed little girl. She wrote to Count Rosenberg (an Austrian correspondent who reported back to the Empress) in April 1775, 'You know Paris,' she wrote, 'and Versailles, you have been here, you can judge.' She went on the defensive when once again remonstrated for her marriage's lack of love. She said in her defense, 'For example, my tastes are not the same as the king's who is only interested in hunting and metalworking. You will agree that I would cut an odd figure at a forge; I am not one to play Vulcan [the god of Fire] there and if I played the role of Venus that would displease him a great deal more than my actual tastes of which he does not disapprove.'

These "tastes" were turning more and more to gambling and spending on lavish wardrobes, jewels, and gifts for her friends. It was her way of dealing with her emptiness and the stress always upon her. Her husband had distanced himself, preferring the hunt or his private apartments. They had so little in common. Many who visited Versailles committed on Marie's moodiness and disinterest in conversations of current events, science, or other topics that were of vast interest to her husband. This was the Age of Enlightenment and conversations swirled around daily discoveries and experiments. She would yawn behind her fan and look for ways to escape the gathering. She came alive around her close friends, or in the company of her many pet dogs, or with small children whom she always stopped to enjoy.

A short glimpse of joy was had on the New Year of 1776 when the palace had been hit with six weeks of snow. The king ordered that the ancient sledges, last used by Louis' father in his youth, be brought out from their cobwebs. For Marie, it also brought back memories of her childhood and she felt her heart leap. The sound of sleigh bells filled the air and the horses pranced with gold-decked harnesses and white plumes. Masked ladies from the court rode all the way to the Champs-Elysées. But Marie's joy was cut short as reports got back to her that the sleigh rides were too 'Viennese.' Shortly after, she abandoned riding them. Her Austrian roots were constantly thrown at her, no matter what she did to support France and her husband, the king.

Marie's desire for a child overshadowed everything. One incident brought it home with astounding clarity. She had been riding in a coach near Louveciennes when a little village boy ran out and fell beneath her horses' hoofs. He was of about four or five with big blue eyes and fair hair. Although he was unhurt, Marie cradled him, beside herself. The little boy's grandmother came out from a cottage to find the Queen of France clutching the boy to her bosom. 'I must take him. He is mine,' Marie exclaimed. While shocked, the old woman, who was already taking care of five other orphans, put up no argument. The little boy's mother had died and left the poor woman shackled with six mouths to feed. Marie promised to financially take care of the entire family and bundled the confused little boy into her carriage. She took him to the palace and had him scrubbed and put into fine lace. The boy, Jacques, howled his displeasure. He wanted to go home. Undaunted, Marie shared her food with him and supervised his education. She kept her promise to Jacques' grandmother.

Such an impulsive move shocked the court. The more scurrilous remarks came from the aunts, especially Adelaide who secretly detested the little Austrian, while smiling to her face. The remark that Marie had stolen someone else's child because she could not have one of her own, made the gossip mills. The queen's unhappiness was apparent to all, and it worsened with every new marriage in the royal family, both in France and Austria. Maria Therese never faltered to alert Marie as to how well her brothers and sisters were doing and who was pregnant "again."

And so, the dreaded day arrived on August 6, 1775, when the Comtesse d'Artois gave birth, not just to a child, but a boy! Louis XVI immediately gave him the royal title of the Duc d'Angouléme. This little baby was the first Bourbon prince born to the new generation, a blow to the Orleans family, as he now took precedence to the succession to the throne. As the bells rang, excited courtiers hurried to the bedchamber door. Those with Rights of Entry, including Marie Antoinette, were present at the birth. As the pitiful queen looked on, she witnessed the birth of a son, an heir to the throne as Louis' nephew. To add to her misery and humiliation, she witnessed the uncontrolled joy when the Cometesse, seeing it was a boy, cried out to her husband, 'My God, how happy I am!'

Marie kept her poker face, and hugged her sister-in-law, congratulating them all. She then exited the room, and still with her head held high made her way hurriedly to the safety of her apartments. Sadly, this meant walking past the market women who were allowed to hang about the palace. Cat calls of 'When will you give us an heir to the throne?' followed her. Finally, the queen reached her rooms, walked calmly inside and collapsed in tears. Her First Lady of the Bedchamber, Madam Campan, wrote: 'She was extremely affecting when in misfortune.' The tears flowed unabated. Letters from her mother would certainly be written with all the vitriol to which she had become accustomed.

There now appeared in the queen a certain kind of desperation. Her gambling increased, as did her pursuit of pleasures. On her 21$^{st}$ birthday, the gambling lasted for two days, from October 30$^{th}$ into October 31$^{st}$. When it flowed into All Saint's Day until 3 a.m., Louis brought it up to her. Marie replied coquettishly, 'You said we could play, but never specified for how long.' The king laughed and said cheerfully, 'You're all worthless, the lot of you.'

At the same time Marie's brother, Joseph II was instructing Louis about sex, he was also lecturing his sister about her mad passion for gambling, her unsuitable friends, and her neglect of the king. He adored Marie, and they were very close. Yet, he took it upon himself to tell her of his distaste for the French love of rouge, which was not a mainstay in Austria. Sarcastically he cried, 'A little more! Go on, put it under the eyes and the nose, you can look like one of the Furies if your try!' He also made fun of her towering hairstyles and headdresses. To the Emperor Joseph, who had no children, his sister, fifteen years his junior, was very dear. He called her 'my dear and charming Queen and my little sister.'

It was this brother's visit that brought about the miracle all had been praying for. Maire increased her warmth toward her husband, and Louis, now knowing what he was doing wrong, did at last stop being 'two thirds of a husband.' After seven years and three months, the 'Great Work' was accomplished. On August 10, 1777, an ebullient Marie Antoinette wrote to her mother that she was experiencing, 'the most essential happiness of my entire life—beginning eight days ago!' Obviously, Louis got the hang of it for Marie wrote the 'proof' of Louis' love had now been repeated and 'even more completely than the first time.'

While the queen was not yet pregnant, she was hopeful. Having an irregular period did little to alleviate the anticipation her mother was now feeling, as she prayed for a pregnancy. Marie's bedlinens were checked each morning, and each time the telltale red stain appeared, Marie's and her mother's moods dampened. The good news was that Louis and Marie had grown closer due to their newfound intimacy. Even when it was announced that a second son had been born to the Comtesse d'Artrois on January 24, 1778, it didn't carry the pain the first announcement had brought the queen. She was hopeful she would soon be with child.

Benjamin Franklin returned to France in 1778, and a lavish party was thrown for him at Versailles. In support of the war against England, the courtiers all wore the map of England pinned to their backsides. The great man was surrounded by adoring Parisians who treated him like an 18$^{th}$ century Rockstar. For Louis, who loved all things mechanical and scientific, it was a wonderful opportunity to discuss some of his favorite topics. As for Marie, she invited Franklin to stand behind her chair as her supporter during her game of cards.

Benjamin Franklin Returns to Versailles in 1778

This visit may have been the time that the royal couple came together and finally conceived. On May 16, 1778, Dr. Lassonne made an examination of the anxious queen and pronounced himself satisfied that she was with child. To celebrate and alert the public to her good news, Marie asked Louis for 12,000 francs to send to the relief of those who were being held in debtors' prison in Paris. Her chosen recipients were aligned with children: those who were in jail for failing to pay for their children's wet-nurses, as well as the poor of Versailles. 'Thus, I gave to the charity and at the same time notified the people of my condition,' wrote Marie Antoinette.

With the cruelty known to be a trademark of the Parisian pamphleteers, they ignored the queen's happy news and philanthropy and attacked her pregnancy. Losing the fodder that had provided them with jokes about the king's impotency, the illustrated pamphlets turned their attention to the upcoming baby and suggested names for who the father might be. It was a seditious and disgusting thing to do, yet nothing compared to some of the illustrations that would follow. A few of the names put forth were the duc de Coigny and most repugnantly, the king's brother, the duc d'Artois, with whom she was close, sharing more common interests than she did with the king. An affair had been hinted at before.

Marie, who had been faithful to Louis, ignored the spurious pamphlets and focused on her immense joy at the impending birth. Marie began preparations with enthusiasm. She chose the Abbé de Vermond to be her *accoucheur* (a male midwife), passing up the one who attended the Comtesse d'Artois, Sieur Levret. She then selected a wet nurse, an apartment for the baby on the ground floor of Versailles where she felt the air was better, swaddling clothes and other essentials. She was heard to say there were 'moments when I think it all a dream…[I've] lived for so long without hoping to be so happy as to bear a child…the dream continues.'

Marie continued to revel in her happiness. She announced by the end of May that she was getting fat, putting on four inches, mainly in her hips. At five months, she was declared rather large for her stage in mid-August. Along with her burgeoning belly came a new wardrobe. Her favorite seamstress and designer, Rose Bertin, created flowing silk garments in Marie's favorite colors of pale blue, turquoise and soft yellow. These flowing garments were known as *Lévites*, and in the summer heat were a wonderful replacement for the tight gowns, hoops, other restrictive clothing and accoutrements.

She continued her walks in the cool of the evening, finding Versailles' gardens and their lush foliage a welcome respite. The spray from the fountains and the stars overhead all found symbolic meaning to the new mother.

Marie's hairdresser Léonard had to deal with the challenge of the queen's changing hair. During 1776 when she was depressed over her current state of affairs in her marriage, the stress had caused her usually luxurious head of hair to thin dramatically. The daily ritual of teasing the hair to new heights, powdering and applying pomade, did little to help the situation. Now, changing hormones due to pregnancy added to the problem. Luckily, wigs were all the rage, and the queen's health was otherwise good. She was given iron and bled once or twice.

The baby's name was chosen well in advance as baptisms were usually immediate and a lavish celebration would be warranted. Marie's mother Maria Theresa had been named godmother while Charles III of Spain was the godfather. Maria Theresa was given the right to name the child. If it was a boy (crossing fingers) he would obviously have some variation of the name Louis. If the child was a girl, she would be christened with the French version of Maria Theresa's name, as the Empress of Austria required all first-born daughters to be named after her.

The *American War of Independence* was still raging across the sea, but at the court of Versailles, other events eclipsed the news of victories and defeats. A musical prodigy appeared at court, none other than Wolfgang Amadeus Mozart. Marie had first met him as a child in Vienna, and Mozart had been smitten with her. Now, at twenty-two, he arrived in Paris in late March 1778, along with his mother who was hoping for 'a letter of introduction from someone in Vienna to the Queen.' She was hoping that her standing as a Habsburg might wrangle such a letter. Alas, due to the queen's pregnancy, he was not given an audience, or the patronage he was hoping to secure. He was offered the post as organist for Versailles, but he refused it as unworthy of his talent. Leopold Mozart advised him to take it saying an appointment of that kind would be the best way to win 'the protection of the Queen.'

The great composer left France in late September without gaining an audience with the queen. Other of his rival composers, such as Gluck and Piccinni met with similar rejection, leading Gluck to announce five years earlier that where music was concerned, the French 'are and always will be asses, and as they can do nothing for themselves, they are obliged to have recourse to foreigners.'

On August 23rd, as Marie struggled to maintain her famous glide beneath the weight of her prodigious belly, she sat before a crowd of people being presented to her. There, she saw a familiar face. The handsome man who caught her eye was Count Axel Von Fersen whom she had last seen four and a half years ago at the end of the reign of Louis XV. He had recently returned to France from Sweden after failing to convince an English heiress to marry him. Her money had been his object and so there was no love lost on his behalf. He had decided to pursue a military career and told his father, 'I am young and have a great deal to learn.' He wrote home that upon being presented to the queen, she had exclaimed, 'Ah, it's an old acquaintance!" He seemed thrilled that she had been happy to see him, but then added that 'the rest of the royal family did not speak to me.' Marie Antoinette had an adoring circle of handsome young men whom she considered friends. At this time, she may have eyed Fersen as just another addition to that group. He, however, was smitten.

Axel Von Fersen

It was during this time that another familiar face made its appearance. The return of Philippe d'Orleans, Duc de Chartres, returned from a self-proclaimed naval victory against the English off the coast of France. The Battle of Ouessant was celebrated as a French victory, with the duke taking the bows for its success. He arrived at Versailles at 2 in the morning and had to wait for Louis' *lever* that morning to make his announcement. While Louis was probably thrilled by the victory, the duc d'Orleans had lost none of his pompous air and was not a favorite of the king's. The duke headed over to the Palais-Royal, the royal Parisian residence, where he was met with celebration. That night at the opera, he was given all of the accolades of a returning hero.

As it was found out later, it was a lie. Rumors of cowardice and incompetence began to flood in. The fact that he had left the battle in order to return to Paris and garner all the fanfare for himself was soon put to verse, in the ubiquitous Parisian fashion:

'What! You have seen smoke!
What a prodigious achievement…
It is absolutely right
That you should be an august sight
At the opera.'

At a ball a few months later, he pushed his luck. Known for his unfiltered and rude manner, he made the mistake of denigrating a noble lady's looks as 'faded.' The lady whirled about to face him, and retorted, 'Like your reputation, Monseigneur.' The Duc d'Orleans enmeshed himself in some squalid affair that had to do with ministers and corruption, and Louis had enough. Despite the pleadings from the duke's father, Louis exiled him from court for a month. While Marie had always found the dashing, rebellious cousin a fun companion, her husband had other views.

None of this mattered as December rolled around and the birth of the king and queen's child was imminent. Finally, on December 19, 1778, Marie Antoinette's long hoped for baby was born. She had gone to bed at eleven o'clock without any signs of labor starting. Just after midnight, the unmistakable tightening of the stomach and resulting pain ensued. She rang her bell at 1:30 a.m. Princess Lamballe, Superintendent of the Household, held the right to be told first, as did others who were privy to the 'honours.' At three a.m., the Prince de Chimay went to alert the king.

The pecking order of who was given notice of the impending birth went into action. Princess de Lamballe personally gave the news to members of the royal family that the queen was in labor. These included the Princesses and Princes of the Royal Blood who were mainly housed in the South Wing. Pages were then sent to Saint-Cloud to inform the duc d'Orleans, the Duchesse de Bourbon and Princess de Conti. The disgraced duc de Chartres, the duc de Bourbon and the Prince de Conti were in Paris when they got the news.

While order had been maintained at this point, it fell by the wayside as the cry went out throughout the gilded hallways of Versailles that 'The Queen is in labor!" There was a mad dash of hurriedly dressed bodies toward the queen's apartment. While only those with Entrée privileges would be allowed in during the birth, it did not stop most of the palace from crowding into anterooms and some, including a couple of Savoynards, gaining access to the birthing room and garnering a perch for the best view.

Marie walked about the room until around 8 in the morning, until the pains became too much. She finally laid down upon the small white delivery bed in her room. Around her was the anxious king, the Prince and Princesses of the Blood, and Yolande de Polignac, who had the right to be there. Louis, while exhibiting all the traits of a nervous husband awaiting the birth of his child, had the clarity of mind to insist that ropes be attached to the tapestry screens surrounding the birthing bed for fear the crush of people might send them toppling over onto the queen.

As other members of the household crammed into the Grand Cabinet, a cheer came from the delivery room. At 11:30 a.m. on December 19, 1778, Marie Antoinette gave birth to a healthy Bourbon baby.

# Chapter Fifty-Four
# **The Petit Trianon & Scandal**

Marie Thérèse Charlotte entered the world without the exaltation a male heir would have been provided. The little girl was healthy and flawless, and quickly became the apple of her mother's eye. Her father, the King of France, while thrilled to have a princess, was vastly aware that his brother, Provence, was still in line for the crown, with Artois and his two sons breathing down his neck. Without a male heir, Louis XVI would have his crown handed over to a brother or to a brother's offspring.

The little girl was christened Madame Fille du Roi (daughter of France). That name was eventually shortened to Madame Royale. The moniker 'Madame' was retained by Provence's wife, further establishing his status in the realm. It was interesting that the scientific mind of Louis XVI would have a superstitious side, but it is said he warned Marie Antoinette during her pregnancy to prepare for a girl, 'because two Kings would not have two sons in the same month.' He was referring to the birth of the King of Sweden who was born just before Marie went into labor.

The little princess was handed to the Princesse de Guéméné, who was the Governess to the Children of France. It was at that moment that Marie Antoinette went into distress and began to convulse. The room was stifling hot with the throng of people pressed into every available square inch. It had been a twelve-hour-long labor and the queen had hemorrhaged, causing her to faint. At first, no one noticed. The scene was so loud and chaotic that Madam Campan noted, 'anyone might have fancied himself in a place of public entertainment.'

It is here the recounting of what happened next changes depending upon the narrator. Several accounts have the king dramatically pushing his way through the throng of people to open the window and allow air into the room to revive the queen. One statement even said he 'smashed the window glass with his fist' to get air into the room. Another account says several strong men at the scene ripped off the boarded-up shutters to allow in the cold December air. It was customary to shut up a room during a delivery to alleviate the threat of bacteria entering in. Whomever was responsible for opening the window, it seemed to help.

Marie was not told the sex of the child for about an hour. When she heard it was a little girl, she wept. It was not put down as her response to the child not being a boy, but rather to exhaustion and the news that the child was healthy. When she did finally address her precious little bundle, she tenderly said: 'Poor little girl, you are not what was desired, but you are no less dear to me on that account. A son would have been the property of the state. You shall be mine; you shall have my undivided care; you will share all my happiness's and you will alleviate my sufferings…'

In France, where a female could not sit the throne, the Parisians were quick to remind the queen of that with their usual propensity to put it to verse:

A Dauphin we asked of our Queen,
A Princess announces him near.
Since one of the Graces is seen
Young Cupid will quickly appear.

In other words, 'Good job, you finally had a baby by the Grace of God. Now get back in there and give us an heir!' But it was Comte de Provence who took the low road during the baby's baptism, at which, gratefully, Marie was not present as she was confined to bed for eighteen days. Provence approached the archbishop at the baptism and under the mask of concern for propriety, protested that 'the name and quality' of the parents had not been formally declared, as was customary in these procedures. It was a not-so-subtle allusion to the gossip that the baby may have been sired by someone other than the king. His meaning was not lost on the courtiers in attendance.

The king's cousin, the Duc de Chartres, who had been banned

from court, retaliated by decorating the family residence of the Palais-Royal with minimal illuminations. The king, no doubt, was hurt by the actions of his family, but the queen was spared as she was not in attendance. It was not the joyful celebration given to the birth of children to former Kings of France. For a man who already suffered from an inferiority complex, it made its mark. If Louis was not aware yet, his dismissal of the duc de Chartres had split the royal family down the middle, furthering the divide between the Orleans side and that of the Bourbons. While many would put the French Revolution down to the fish wives and peasantry, it was the nobility that brought Versailles to its knees.

Marie decided to breastfeed her daughter in accordance with theories of natural healthy motherhood. If the child had been a boy, he would have been handed to a wet nurse. In this concession, Marie's promise to the little girl that 'you are mine' was fulfilled. Unfortunately, the never-content Maria Theresa soon sent off letters of disapproval, saying breastfeeding was a natural contraceptive. The Empress appealed to the king and Marie's doctors, but in this case, Marie won out. A wet nurse was also employed, but the queen continued to breastfeed her daughter for a time.

## The Petit Trianon

Shortly after Louis XVI was crowned king in 1774, he gave his nineteen-year-old bride a wonderful gift. Built on the site of part of the botanical gardens of Louis XV, it was a chateau in Neoclassical lines, designed by Ange-Jacques Gabriel. As it fell within the grounds of the Grand Trianon, it was called the Petit Trianon. It had originally been created for Louis XV's long-term mistress Madame de Pompadour, but she died four years before its completion. It was subsequently occupied by her successor, Madame du Barry. Louis XVI's gift of this chateau and the surrounding park to Marie Antoinette was a gesture of love, yet it would lead to rumors of debauchery and excessive spending.

Marie Antoinette would come to the Petit Trianon to escape the formality of court life and those of royal responsibility. It was her haven that she could decorate as she pleased. It was an "invitation only" arrangement and many nobles who were excluded from that list complained. Even Louis XVI was to drop by only if invited, fueling rumors of clandestine affairs behind the columned facades. It was Marie's inner circle of friends who were constantly in attendance there: the princesse de Lamballe and Yolande Martine Gabrielle de Polastron, duchese de Polignac. Polignac had been presented to the queen in 1775, the year after Marie became Queen of France. She was considered one of the great beauties of society, but her extravagance and love of gossip and intrigue gained her an unfavorable reputation. She was Marie Antoinette's favorite and was quickly installed in the palace. The queen paid off her family's debts and appointed Polignac's husband a post. Others in the Polignac family prospered to the point that Mercy wrote home to Marie's mother, 'It is almost unexampled that in so short a time, the royal favor should have brought such overwhelming advantages to a family.' The princess de Lamballe was just the opposite of the flamboyant Yolande. She was shy, retiring and pious. She and Polignac had a calming influence on the queen and Louis XVI welcomed their company.

It was Marie Antoinette's favoritism to Polignac that fueled the queen's unpopularity at court and with the Parisians. When Yolande's husband was given the title duc de Polignac in 1780, it further alienated the courtiers. This close friendship would lead to some of the most lewd and pornographic pamphlets in the late 1780s, shortly before the eve of the French Revolution.

The Petit Trianon was to be a house of intimacy and pleasure. Marie's need for privacy was so great (after being on constant display at Versailles and subject to gossip and sniggering) that she devised ways to have as little contact with the servants there as possible. To that end, the table in the *salle â manger* was designed to be mobile, mechanically lowered and raised through the floorboards so that the servants below could set places unseen. The tables were never built, but the delineation for the mechanical apparatus can still be seen from the foundation.

Within the queen's apartment, her boudoir features a device that fueled the gossip of wanton sexuality, orgies, and affairs going on withing the little chateau. Unique to the age were mechanical mirrored panels that could be raised from the floor to cover the windows. By turning a crank, the panels rose, and no one could see into her private rooms. It was a contrivance necessitated by a need for privacy, but it led to some of the more salacious twittering. The mirrors reflected the candlelight within the room, giving it a dazzling appearance and increasing the illumination. Her bedroom was simple but elegant, with furnishings from Georges Jacob and Jean-Henri Riesener. The wallpaper was painted by Jean-Baptiste Pillement.

The interesting architectural aspect of the Petit Trianon is that it has four distinctive facades, each thoughtfully designed according to the part of the estate it would face. The Corinthian order predominates, with two freestanding and two engaged columns on the side of the Formal French Garden, and pilasters facing both the courtyard and the area once occupied by Louis XV's greenhouses. Overlooking the former botanical garden of the king, the remaining façade was left bare. The subtle use of steps compensates for the difference in level of the chateau's inclined location.

It was the west elevation that most guests approached the chateau, and it was here, in 1901, that Versailles' most famous ghost story played out.

West Façade of the Petit Trianon

North Façade of the Petit Trianon

East Façade of the Petit Trianon

South Façade of the Petit Trianon

The *salle â manger* (dining room)

The Salon

Mechanical mirror panels rising to cover the windows in Marie Antoinette's bedroom.

After the French Revolution, when many entered the Petit Trianon, they were surprised to see how simple it was in its elegance. It was just another misconception about this French Queen with an Austrian heritage. She was hated and much of the information enflaming that hatred was false. It was at the time of the Flour War that Marie Antoinette was accused of saying, 'Let them eat cake' (*Qu'ils mangent de la brioche*). This is something Marie would never have said. She had a huge heart, as demonstrated when she rescued the small boy who had fallen beneath her horse, her love of animals and children, and her kindness to others. She wrote to her mother during the grain shortage and said, 'It is quite certain that in seeing the people who treat us so well despite their own misfortune, we are more obliged than ever to work hard for their happiness. The king seems to understand this truth; as for myself, I know that in my whole life (even if I live for a hundred years) I shall never forget the day of the coronation.' This was the woman who refused to ride over the peasant's cornfields because she was aware of the minutiae of the lives of the poor.

In April of 1779, while the Empress of Austria was regaling her daughter with letters entreating her to try again for a male heir, Marie Antoinette came down with an 'exceptionally severe' case of measles. As Louis had never had measles, the queen opted to spend her three-week quarantine at the Petit Trianon. As the chateau was so small, Marie's household stayed in the nearby Grand Trianon. She was obviously not in pain as she spent her days boating on the Grand Canal, drinking asses' milk and chatting to a few aristocratic ladies from Paris who dropped by to keep her company. It isn't noted whether they had already had the illness.

But it was the company of four young men that gave Marie's Austrian ambassador, Mercy, heart palpitations. The duc de Coigny, the duc de Guines, Count Esterhazy and the Baron de Besenval, had come to amuse the queen. She lounged upon cushions as they regaled her with amusing stories and played musical instruments to her delight. The Princess Lamballe and the Comtese de Provence also arrived, until what was an innocent party became the gossip of Paris. Can you imagine the king having four pretty young things attending him if he were to be sick? It was the same scurrilous reports that followed the queen everywhere.

If Mercy did report the entourage at the Petit Trianon to the Empress, it does not seem to have stirred the pot. She was happy to hear that Marie and Louis' relationship had become deeper since the arrival of their child. This was evidenced by the king going to the little chateau while his wife was ill and waiting for a quarter of an hour in a private courtyard while Marie leant out a window to speak with him. He missed her and their tender words to each other were enough to allay Maria Theresa's fear on that count. It did not, however, stop the letters from flying concerning the need for another pregnancy, ASAP.

For the Queen of France, the Petit Trianon offered a sanctuary like no other. It wasn't long before Marie began to take over the park upon which her little chateau resided. She began with the **Temple of Love.**

Set on an island in the river only steps from the Petit Trianon stands a circular platform with seven steps. Atop this dais are twelve columns supporting a domed cupola. The floor is in veined white, Languedoc red and Flanders marble while the ceiling is covered in carved rosettes and caissons arranged around a centerpiece sporting a quiver, arrows and flames, all a tribute to cupid and burning love. In the center of the temple is a sculpture copied from Boucharadon's *Cupid fashioning his bow from Hercule's club.* (1750) Sculptor Louis-Phillippe Mouchy produced the replica of the statue that was originally to appear in the Hercules Salon at Versailles. After the Revolution, it was returned to Saint-Cloud, where it had been since 1752 before Marie had it transferred to the Louvre for the reproduction process.

The Temple of Love at the Petit Trianon

The Temple itself was designed by Richard Mique in 1777. Marie approved the design immediately, contrary to her usual back-and-forth on designs. On May 5, 1777, he showed the queen a model created to the exact specifications of the sculptor Joseph Deschamps. The construction was completed in July 1778. With the arrival of a long-awaited baby in December of that year, the Temple probably symbolized love for the queen in more than just romantic affiliations.

**The Belvedere** is also found on the Petit Trianon grounds and was completed in 1781, only eight years before the fall of the monarchy. Its lovely setting atop a hill overlooks the lake. The octagonal design is topped again with a cupola, restrained by a balustrade that encircles it. Relief sculptures of the four seasons top the four windows, one on each side. The folly was designed by Richard Mique, the same artist as the Temple of Love. Patio doors on each side of the building open to an interior decorated in intricately detailed murals by Sebastien-Francois Le Riche. Lagrenee painted the ceiling where cherubs frolic in a blue summer sky. The floor is of marble mosaic. Marie Antoinette loved the Belvedere in the summer where she could open the windows and doors and lounge beneath the natural light, sounds from the lake, and fluttering shadows from the surrounding woods.

The Belvedere next to the Grotto

**The Grotto** is a magical rock formation seemingly formed by fairies sits next to the Belvedere at the Petit Trianon. This enchanted enclave of lumpy rock is found at the end of a path that leads down into a small valley where a stream flows. A tiny doorway leads into a grotto, big enough to house only three people standing. Secluded and shadowed, the only light entering the enclave comes from openings in the rock. A rough-hewn stone bench sits within, once covered with a green blanket to resemble moss. In a corner, the whimsical notes of a waterfall can be heard as it tumbles along the crags. At the other end of the grotto is a staircase that leads up to a hidden entrance at the peak of this artificial tumble of stones. It was this entrance and exit from a secluded 'cave' that sparked rumors of intimate dalliances between Marie Antoinette and lovers--in particular, Axel de Fersen. The Grotto was completed in 1782, one year after the finished work on the Belvedere.

Marie Antoinette's Secret Grotto

After the Revolution, when the commoners were released to look about Marie's haven at the Petit Trianon, the Grotto was one place they were eager to see. The fact that these artificial stone outcroppings appeared in many gardens did little to slate their thirst for salacious gossip. They may have been disappointed to see how ordinary and sparse it really was.

Marie Antoinette was a great enthusiast for the theatre and opera. She was often found in Paris attending a new play or operetta. She was known to clap at the end of a performance, something not typically done in that era. While a grand Opera Royale was housed within the palace of Versailles, Marie deigned that one on a much smaller scale should be built within her Petit Trianon sanctuary. Monsieur Campan had been giving her the basics in acting for her more amateurish productions within her apartments. Now, she was hungry for something with a stage, seating, backdrops, and the accoutrements of a small theater.

Entrance to Marie Antoinette's theater at the Petit Trianon

Interior of the Theater

Richard Mique was once again chosen to design the new

addition to the Petit Trianon grounds. On June 1, 1780, the new theater was inaugurated. Its décor reflected the queen's favorite colors of blue and gold, with blue velvet and blue moiré, along with paper-mâchéto simulate marble. Backdrops of woodlands, the interior of a simple maiden's hut, and other whimsical facades were painted on large canvases. This large scenery was raised and lowered by a series of mechanical pulleys hidden in the rafters.

**The theater** could accommodate only 100 guests, and invitations to her performances were considered an honor. Louis XVI is reported to have loved watching his wife perform, and she improved through the hiring of professional acting coaches.

The wooden mechanical machinery for stage backdrops

While Marie kept the cost down for her theatre by using wood and paper mâché to simulate marble, it seemed an unnecessary expense at a time when the lower classes were still struggling, and a finance-draining war was going on. The queen was a controversial figure, not only in Paris but at court, where her Austrian heritage had always made her a suspicious character. While many aristocrats had small theaters on their country estates to pass the time performing plays and operas, Marie was maligned for spending money on what many considered frivolous and self-aggrandizing. She further alienated many nobles at court who were not proffered a private invitation to her plays. In 1780, she and her friends performed Pierre-Alexandre Monsigny's *Le Roi et le fermier* (The King and the Farmer) in the new theater. Marie was in a simple shepherdess costume and sang.

As if the war, famine, ongoing struggles to raise money to support the French involvement in the *American War of Independence* was not enough, Marie had suffered a miscarriage the year before in the summer of 1779. The dreaded letter to her mother met with less anxiety than it would have if she had not already given birth to a healthy baby. The Empress still implored her daughter to put forth all her efforts to produce an heir to the throne. These were to be the last communiques from Maria Theresa to her beleaguered daughter. Her last letter was dated November 3, 1780, the day after Marie Antoinette's twenty-fifth birthday. She had not seen Marie for over ten years and the note showed her thoughts and feelings: 'Yesterday I was all day more in France than in Austria.'

Although only sixty-three, she had been suffering from dropsy which affected her legs. Shortly afterward, her lungs began to harden, and she complained of a burning sensation inside, repeatedly ordering that the windows be opened. She sent away the daughters who had been in attendance with her as she worsened. The Archduchesses Marie Christine, Marianne, and Elizabeth were asked to leave her room as she did not want them to see her die. They were also forbidden to attend her funeral. The Empress, fearful, for perhaps the first time in her willful life, refused to go to sleep, saying, 'At any moment I may be called before my Judge. I don't want to be surprised. I want to see death come.' And it did, on the morning of November 29, 1780.

1780 marked the beginning of a decade where insidious minds were at work to overthrow the monarchy. As the tension mounted, and Louis XVI found himself more and more in the crosshairs of those whom he relied upon for support, it all came crashing down. The French Revolution would end the Sun King's dreams of a lasting legacy at his beloved Versailles. In nine years, rebels would crash through the golden gates, tear down his velvet curtains, destroy valuable furnishings, murder guards and seek out Marie Antoinette's head. They would pillage the kitchens, and steal whatever they could get their hands on. Nine short years. As the new decade began, unaware of what Fate was aligning for them, Marie Antoinette was planning more building at the Petit Trianon, ministers were hounding the king about a peace treaty with England, and news of Maria Theresa's death was heading to Versailles.

## Chapter Fifty-Five
## Ministers, Marie and Mistresses

It took a week for the news of Maria Theresa's death to reach Versailles. Marie Antoinette was devastated. She wrote to her brother, Joseph II, on December 10, 1780, expressing the depth of her despair: 'Devastated by this most frightful misfortune, I cannot stop crying as I start to write to you. Oh, my brother, oh my friend! You alone are left to me in a country [Austria] which is, and always will be, so dear to me…Remember, we are your friends, your allies. I embrace you.'

Louis XVI declared a grand mourning for his mother-in-law and fellow sovereign. The king asked Vermond, the queen's personal advisor, to tell her of the plans. Louis even thanked him for doing him this service, something the reclusive king was not apt to do. Marie saw it as a great act of tenderness on her husband's part. The couple had grown much closer since their conjugal visits continued on a regular basis, and a child had graced their alliance.

The death of the Empress had brought about a change in another respect. There would be no one for Mercy to report to concerning Marie Antoinette's behavior. It would take a while for the queen to realize her mother's passing brought a sort of freedom. Her brother Joseph became even more of a close confidant, but it was now her choice to alert him of news. There was no secret pipeline via carrier to spread gossip or mishaps to Austria.

It may have been Marie's closeness to her brother that made him take a closer look at the political intrigue playing out between England and the United States. Joseph II had toyed with joining up with England, but a letter to Louis XVI, his brother-in-law, gave a more welcome assurance. Joseph wrote at the beginning of 1781, 'Our links with France are natural, advantageous and infinitely preferable to those with England.'

As 1781 began with new hope for peace and comradery between her homeland and that of France, Marie Antoinette had another reason to feel joyful. As of February, she was beginning to suspect she might be *enceinte*, pregnant. On March 17th, when she reached the two-month mark, she began to let the news leak out to a chosen few. She told the Princess Louise of Hesse who prophesied it was a boy. On May 7, she reported that health was perfect and that she was 'putting on a lot of weight.' It was now and in the coming months that perhaps she missed the letters she would have written to her mother, keeping her apprised of her progress.

As Marie's mid-section grew, she would have been grateful for the new style of dress she adopted a few years later. Along with her gardens and privacy at the Petit Trianon, the queen had desired clothing to complement her simpler way of life. Tired of the rigid court dress with its restrictive panniers and other instruments of torture, she had designed a dress of plain material, often white, that was put on over the head and tied with a drawstring at the neck. It was complimented with sashes and ribbons, sometimes flowers. It was a nod to a peasant's life, without the poverty and toil. A straw sunhat completed the ensemble. It was called the *robe en chamise*, for indeed, the dress looked like a chamise worn beneath a gown.

It was this style of dress that was seen in the painting of 1783 by Madame Vigée Le Brun. Marie, finding the portrait lovely and a tribute to her new lifestyle, was surprised to find that the general public hated it. It was not 'the look of a queen,' they shouted. 'She looks as if she is wearing undergarments!' It was vulgar and not befitting the Queen of France. Not only were the Parisians unimpressed, but the silk manufacturers were livid. They depended on the wealth of silk dresses ordered by the queen, the nobility and all that copied her style of dress, which were legion. In one fast stitch of muslin, they saw their output and revenue shredded. As always, Marie could make no decision without it being an unpopular one.

The portrait, which was hanging in Le Brun's first Salon, was so scorned that the artist was told to remove it from the exhibition. Le Brun painted a new portrait of Marie Antoinette, once again in the fashionable silk gown of a queen, with the jewels and finery expected of her.

The hated chamise portrait by Le Brun

The approved portrait by Le Brun

For all the controversy leveled at the queen's choice of dress, the loose design of the chemise dress was to become the popular thing to wear by the end of the 18th century.

## Necker and Financial Scandal

While Marie Antoinette reveled in her pregnancy, France was still entangled with the *American War of Independence*. It was now in its fourth year as wars erupted along the eastern coastline of the United States. Necker, Louis XVI's banker friend, and in whom he had placed all his hopes for financial relief through the influential banker's loans, was putting forth ideas that were meeting with resistance. Taxing the nobles would never be a popular move, as Turgot and the king had already found out. The mere mention of possibly imposing a tax on the nobility had made many enemies for Necker.

Wars could not be financed by increased taxation alone. It represented a dilemma not easy to reconcile. Either raise the taxes by 50 per cent (ruining the peasantry) or forcing 500,000 members of the privileged classes (i.e., the nobility and clergy) to bear the entire burden. The mere thought of how the nobility would revolt under that edict was enough to make Louis hide amongst the rooftop chimneys. So, how does one acquire a balance between the loans Necker had garnered from constituents, and taxation? With the king and Necker delaying taxation over and over again, creditors began to worry that they would not get their money back and began to demand a higher rate of return.

Where once Necker had been the white knight riding in to solve the king's needs for financing to back the French involvement in the war between England and the United States, it was now looking as if the knight might sink the kingdom. Necker, during his time in office, borrowed a total of 530 million *livres* at a 6 percent interest rate. England, on the other hand, was operating at a 3.5 percent interest rate for the money it borrowed backed by its parliament. Now, in 1781, Necker was looking down the barrel of a 10 per cent rate.

The pamphleteers in Paris were alive and well as they spread their smear campaigns against Necker in a "Taxes vs Loans" theme.

Maurepas, stinging from Necker's ministerial changes, did nothing to discourage the mudslinging.

It is here, in February of 1781, that Necker made his fatal mistake. In an effort to put himself in a good light and regain the people's confidence in his endeavors, he published his infamous *Compte rendu au Roi,* which was an overview of the royal revenue and expenditure. This was never done. The royal finances were not made public, but it was about to get worse. Necker tried to validify his decision for making the reports public knowledge by pointing out that England had been able to borrow more cheaply by publishing its accounts. The problem here was that Necker's reports were a lie.

Necker, in a nutshell, claimed that despite four years of a costly war, and *without* taxation, the royal treasury was actually showing 10.2 million *livres* in surplus! It was a total lie. In reality, there was an annual deficit of around 70 million. When the true numbers were reported in 1787 and 1788, it would be a huge component in the revolution that exploded the following year. But this deception, in 1781, worked. 20,000 copies of the *Compte* were made available, and a false sense of 'All is Well' swept through the country. The loans Necker needed for the king were soon fully subscribed. After all, 10 per cent tax-free returns from a government showing themselves to be in the black, even in wartime, was a bargain!

Necker went on to downplay the expense of the war from the French side. Not only downplay it but ignore it. He put expenditures at around 254 million *livres*, when in fact, in 1780, the total debt was 677 million; 146 million of that went to the navy alone. Necker had introduced 'charlatanism into the administration.' Louis XVI had always trusted that his ministers, and in this case, his financier, knew more than he did. Almost without fail, he bowed to their "expertise." If he felt that by doing so, he could point the finger at someone else if it all went south would have been naiveite in the extreme. When you're a monarch, "the buck stops here."

Due to several reasons, not the least of which was his reputation for dishonesty and his ongoing acrimonious relationship to Maurepas, Necker resigned his post. Louis was furious. His ministers did not just resign, especially the man who was supposed to finance the war. If Necker had hung in there, he would have been in a position of extreme power, as Maurepas' health was failing, and the war effort needed him. If Maurepas died, Necker would have been impregnable.

Both Turgot and Necker had advocated the taxation of the people who could afford it—the nobles and the clergy. Both men had been symbolically stoned for suggesting such a thing, and in both cases the king had refused to act upon their suggestion out of fear of the repercussions of his friends and family. Necker was succeeded by the *conseiller d'état* Joly de Fleury. He was a dour man and in precarious health. For Maurepas, he was a welcome sight as the minister watched with glee as Necker departed the premises for good. Marie Antoinette, biding her time in hopes that the birth of a dauphin would strengthen her role in the political arena at court, watched from the sidelines and waited for Maurepas' imminent death.

## A Dauphin is Born!

On the morning of October 22, 1781, the queen went into labor. She still took her morning bath and walked about a little. Louis canceled his shoot to be held at Saclé. The labor pains increased in the next half hour and the invited party of those closest to the queen assembled in her room. These included the Princesse de Lamballe, the Comte d'Artois (who had become a close friend of the queen's and acted with her in plays), Mesdames Tantes, the Princess de Chimay, and the Comtesse de Tavannes. The Princess de Guéméné was also there and would be in charge of the newborn as the Royal Governess. She was currently caring for little Marie Therese who was almost three years of age. This time, Louis made sure the windows were open to allow air into the room.

It was time. The queen was escorted to the small delivery bed where she laid back. The king uncharacteristically wrote in his journal: 'At exactly a quarter past one by my watch she was successfully delivered of boy.' In the antechambers, all waited in suspense. Fifteen minutes went by. Finally, one of Marie's women ran out into the crowd and exclaimed, 'A Dauphin! But you must not mention it yet!' (This is Versailles! Are you serious?) There was still silence in the room, and the queen feared it meant the child was another girl. The king approached her and tearfully said, 'Madame, you have fulfilled our wishes and those of France, you are the mother of a Dauphin.'

Marie, anxious to see the child, said to Louis, 'You can see I'm behaving very well. I'm not asking you anything.' Louis, holding the baby, tearfully said, 'Monsieur le Dauphin asks to come in.' After eleven-and-a-half years, she had accomplished what she was supposed to do. Her mother's wishes were fulfilled, and those of France and Austria. This little baby boy was of the Habsburg and Bourbon blood.

The good intentions for secrecy that the woman had desired when she announced to those waiting not to 'mention it yet,' were for naught. The palace went crazy with the news. The Royal Governess was carried in a chair to her own apartments with the new Dauphin in her arms. The people pressed in on her, eager to just touch her chair or the child. Clapping and shouts of joy were everywhere. 'We adored him,' wrote Count Curt Stedingk, a great favorite of the queen's. 'We followed him in a great crowd.'

According to Antonia Fraser in her wonderful book, *Marie Antoinette: The Journey*: 'Marie Antoinette described the birth of her son in a letter to her friend, Princess Charlotte of Hesse-Darmstadt. Such a jubilant reaction was not confined to the baby's mother. The baptism, according to custom, was performed in the afternoon following the birth. The child was named Louis Joseph (for his Bourbon forefathers and his Habsburg godfather (and uncle) with the additional names of Xavier and François. The king wept throughout the ceremony. Soon, as Madame Campan noted, he was framing his conversation so that the words 'my son the Dauphin' could be introduced as frequently as possible.

'Oh Papa!' exclaimed the little Duc d'Angoulême when shown the Dauphin. 'How tiny my cousin is!'

'The day will come,' replied Artois with meaning, 'when you will find him great enough.'

The birth of the dauphin had removed Artois's sons from the next in line to the throne, but more importantly, Louis' other brother, Provence had just moved down the ranks, behind three young male heirs. It was noticed that he remained quiet at this baby's baptism, omitting the snarky comment he had made at the previous royal ceremony, when he hinted at the child's paternal origin. You don't slander a long-awaited dauphin.

Marie Antoinette, despite wishing with all her heart that her mother was here to celebrate the birth of a future king, was perhaps the happiest she had ever been. The ever-fickle Parisians celebrated with grand operas and fireworks. She was hailed everywhere as wonderful, beautiful, and admired. Where were the scandalous pamphlets? Where were the ribald songs strung with salacious gossip? For now, the queen rode high. It was if France needed desperately to return to the old days of celebrating their king and his heir. The war, the famine, the threats of more taxes…it all taken a toll. Here was something with which to feel happy! Back in Vienna, the celebrations went on as well. This little boy would be the salvation of France and a cornerstone of a strong Franco-Austrian alliance.

The King and Queen with the baby Dauphin and little Marie Therese

As if to give a nod of approval to the controversial queen, now that she was mother of the future king, many courtiers and 'town people' began to emulate her new hairstyle. Leonard had cut Marie's hair to a shorter length to offset her thinning locks. It was of a slightly more frizzy, curled look and the ladies reached for their scissors, called their hairdressers, or ordered wigs in the new 'fashionable' style named *coiffure á l'enfant*. Gradually, her chamise dress would catch on as women were tired of wearing all the gadgetry that pushed their skirts to ridiculous widths. The queen was advocating simplicity and in the Age of Enlightenment, it was right on track. That is not to say that the queen's every move was not still dissected and commented upon. Gossip was the order of the day, and the ones with targets on their backs were usually the ones running the government—not much different than today.

Marie Antoinette's shorter hair style

Yet, there was one thing the wagging tongues were bereft of—any form of disparaging rumor of the king taking a mistress. Louis, disgusted by what he saw with Louis XV, refused to even entertain the notion. Sadly, many nobles had tried to tempt him by putting young lovelies in his path in the hopes he would take a mistress. The reason was quite simple: a mistress could become an ally; a mistress could be bought; a mistress could bestow favors and gain the king's ear in your favor. But Louis refused, sometimes with an angry retort. He, like Charles III, remained loyal to his wife.

To underscore his resolve to rule without a mistress, Louis XVI had an iron gate installed at the bottom of the staircase that was Louis XV's causeway for his chosen favorites. It shocked France. This was unheard of. While some saw it as admirable, many lusty Parisians deemed it a sign of weakness. Kings were supposed to be virile and surrounded by adoring women. It was just the expected thing to do.

The Mistress Gate, blocking the stairway used by Louis XV

Louis XVI was a happy man. His confidence grew and the usually glum expression for which he was known was replaced with a smile. If it were not for the ongoing war and inner strife of his ministers, he might have been able to enjoy this wonderful little miracle. As it was, the *American War of Independence* and its crippling cost took center court.

# Chapter Fifty-Six
## **The Underpinnings of Disaster**

The *American War of Independence* was like a vortex pulling the French under. French participation in the conflict transformed what might otherwise have been a lopsided colonial rebellion into a significant war, with potential to become another global conflict. The British had little appetite for this—especially when other European powers such as Spain and the Dutch Republic proved willing to support the colonists.

Meanwhile, Benjamin Franklin had garnered clandestine support from Louis as France picked up the tab for military engineers, along with clothing, arms, and ammunition for 25,000 soldiers. Ultimately, France provided about 1.3 billion *livres* of desperately needed money and goods to support the rebels. The October 1777 victory at Saratoga, a turning point in the war, saw 90 percent of all American troops carrying French arms, and they were completely dependent on French gunpowder, housed mainly in the Bastille.

The triumph at Saratoga was encouraging and Louis borrowed more money to help the American colonists. Once the French and the American alliance was formalized in twin agreements early in 1778 (the *Treaty of Alliance* and the *Treaty of Amity and Commerce*), the flow of supplies soared, along with the number of soldiers and sailors crossing the Atlantic to fight the American cause. Roughly 12,000 French soldiers served the rebellion, along with 22,000 naval personnel, aboard 63 warships. Lafayette was one of the earliest and the most prominent French officers to join. The comte de Rochambeau, commander in chief of all French forces, played a crucial role in containing the English fleet and in the final campaigns. The comte de Grasse reinforced revolutionary forces in Virginia with French troops from Saint-Domingue (now Haiti) in the Caribbean, then dealt the British navy a decisive defeat at the 1781 Battle of Chesapeake. It would be a battle led by Washington, Lafayette, and Rochambeau together that struck the final blow at Yorktown.

Without France's aid, American revolutionaries might have been seen by other major powers merely as treasonous subjects rebelling against their rulers. Indeed, it was something Louis XVI struggled with in the early stages. Would this 'idea' that citizens could decide to rebel and separate themselves from their monarch hit home? While his ministers pointed out that America was a long way away, Louis retorted those ideas can travel swiftly.

French willingness to negotiate with Silas Deane, Benjamin Franklin. and their successors conferred legitimacy on American leaders. If France had not sided with the colonists, the history books would have shown a different ending. The *Treaty of Amity and Commerce* of 1778 formally acknowledged the United States as an independent nation and opened the way for Americans to continue trading internationally. Over time, France also enlisted the aid of other major European powers (Spain allied itself with the United States in 1779) while sidelining Austria, which never joined the war but made clear it would back France in any wider conflict.

Baron George Brydges Rodney's victory at the Battle of Saintes changed the overall enthusiasm of France. The news of the French defeat arrived nearly six weeks later in Paris and was met with dismay. The defeat was costly, both militarily and financially. The Royal Navy now had the strategic initiative, and as a result, British demands at the peace talks were greatly strengthened in 1783. France was approaching its limits of its ability to borrow money and now sought a quick end to the war. The defeat also signaled the end of the Franco-American alliance—as a result, Benjamin Franklin never informed France of the secret negotiations that took place between Britain and the United States.

Following the Yorktown surrender, France's diplomatic support (and yet another loan) proved critical in reaching a formal end to the conflict, with the 1783 *Treaty of Paris*. Both the French and the Americans refused British offers of separate peace agreements, and French foreign minister Vergennes took a key role in brokering the treaty. Ultimately, it wasn't until Britain and France settled their differences that the Americans finally signed the *Treaty of Paris*. They had also signed a preliminary peace treaty with Great Britain. Britain acknowledged that the United States owned all the land south of the Great Lakes and east of the Mississippi River, except for Florida (which went to Spain). The French accepted the preliminary with protests but no action. Since France was not included in the American-British peace discussions, the influence of France and Spain in future negotiations was limited.

The 1.3 billion *livres* France spent to support America almost bankrupted the French treasury. It raised France's debt to 3.315 billion *livres*. France's status as a great modern power was reaffirmed by the war, but it was detrimental to the country's finances. Even though France's European territories were not affected, victory in a war against Great Britain with battles like the decisive siege of Yorktown in 1781, had a large financial cost which severely degraded fragile finances and increased the nation's debt. France gained little except that it weakened its main strategic enemy [England] and gained a new, fast-growing ally [America] that could become a welcome trading partner.

However, the trade never materialized. In what was perhaps the biggest betrayal from the young rebels to the nation that financed their victory for independence, the United States proclaimed its neutrality between Great Britain and the French Republic. To top it off, they began trading with England again, leaving France out in the cold. By the time the French Revolution occurred, in just six short years, England's trade with her former colonies had reached 90 per cent of their pre-war level and soon surpassed it. To add salt to France's wound, America, now free and on its own, developed much faster and created a bigger market just as the Industrial Revolution was gaining momentum in England, providing the goods America needed. It was a blow. Benjamin Franklin, the man for whom Versailles had rolled out the red carpet, was instrumental in putting together the peace talks with England. Louis looked around at a devastated treasury and a mound of loans that had to be repaid.

In the end, George III and Louis XVI remained on friendly terms. They both shared similar values. George praised Louis for a 'sense of justice, candour and rectitude' and the 'simplicity and purity of his morals and private life.' Louis wished George *'jusq'au bout'* (success).

The war's tragic ending for France in terms of financial loss and the trade they were counting on from America, weakened Louis XVI's reputation. It had never been great to start with, as he came across as shy, reclusive, indecisive and clumsy. With his dismissal of Turgot, Marie Antoinette had informed him that she had overheard gossip while at a Parisian gambling salon that the 'town people' wanted an explanation for why the finance minister was dismissed. Louis' cold response mirrored Louis XV's: he was the king; he did not need to explain himself or his actions to anyone. This mind-set had always come at a cost. With the king so far removed from the heart of Paris, his silence only served to distance his subjects from him and form their own opinions, which they did, and served them up in scandalous pamphlets. Looking back, it seems amazing that these monarchs misunderstood the role Versailles played in their loss of support and popularity.

While France began to recover in trade efforts elsewhere, it was going to take a while to recoup the money and pay off the loans. Necker was kicked to the curb, Joly de Fleury took his place and Charles-Alexandre de Calonne became the new Controller-General of Finances, in 1783. He owed the position to the Comte de Vergennes, who for over three years continued to support him. According to the Habsburg ambassador, Calonne's reputation was very poor, and he was noted as using unscrupulous means to get results. He approached the king with a radical proposition to inspire the nation's confidence and fill the treasury. The king should spend more, not less! Louis was dumbfounded. Calonne reassured him that by a series of building projects and spending, it would show that France was in good shape, which was chiefly designed to maintain the crown's capacity to borrow funds.

He presented the king with his plan on August 20, 1786. At its heart was a new land value tax that would replace the old *vingtième* taxes and finally sweep away the fiscal exemptions of the privileged orders. The new tax would be administered by a system of provincial assemblies elected by the local property owners at parish, district and provincial levels. This central proposal was accompanied by other reforms meant to further rationalize the French economy, a package that included free trade in grain and abolition of France's myriad internal customs barriers. It was, in effect, one of the most, if not *the* most, comprehensive attempt at enlightened reform during the reign of Louis XVI.

## The Hamlet of Marie Antoinette

It is doubtful that Calonne's new building program involved the queen's sudden need to add an ambitious array of small cottages to her Petit Trianon enclave. That she chose to begin the construction in 1783, just as the war was ending, is also interesting. Was she counting on an influx of cash from the promised American trading, or a new confidence in the treasury's health now that the tug on its purse strings from the *War of Independence* was over? It may have been the same question the lower classes were asking, and France in general, who had to bear a good deal of the financial loss. Nonetheless, from 1783 to 1786, Marie worked with designers, architects, and landscapers to create her dream: her *Hameau de la Reine* (the Queen's Hamlet).

The Hamlet served as a meeting place for the queen and her closest friends. Here, they would dress in simple chamises with straw hats and be at their leisure. A rumor that they were insensitively mocking the peasantry was ill-founded. It was designed by Marie's favorite architect, Richard Mique with the help of painter Hurbert Robert. It contained a meadowland with a lake and various buildings in a rustic or vernacular style, inspired by Normand or Flemish design, situated around an irregular pond fed by a stream that turned a small mill wheel.

The building scheme included a farmhouse, (the farm was to produce milk and eggs for the queen), a dairy, a dovecote, a boudoir, a barn that burned down during the French Revolution, a mill and a tower in the form of a lighthouse. Each building is decorated with a vegetable garden, an orchard, or a flower garden. The largest and most famous of these houses is the "Queen's House," connected at the center of the village to the Billiard house by a wooden gallery. A working farm was close to the idyllic, fantasy-like setting of the Queen's Hamlet.

Other nobilities were building small hamlets on their estates. The English Garden style was now in vogue, instead of the formal parterres for which Versailles is known. The Prince of Condé had his *Hameau de Chantilly* (1774-1775) built which was the inspiration for Marie's version. They were fashionable with aristocrats at the time, but for a queen slandered for her spending, it was perhaps not a prudent move on the heels of a ruinous war.

In spite of its idyllic appearance, the hamlet was a real farm, fully managed by a farmer appointed by the queen, who oversaw its vineyards, fields, orchards, and vegetable gardens that produced fruit and vegetables consumed at the royal table. Animals from Switzerland, according to instructions of the queen, were raised on the farm. For this reason, the place was often called "the Swiss Hamlet".

Marie and her young friends would walk lazily through the tall grass and wildflowers, dressed in flowing gowns of soft muslin, sometimes adorned by a *fichu*. Marie would often wear a Polonaise gown; the term Polonaise referring to the dress of Polish shepherdesses who would hoist and drape their overskirts in two or three loops in order to keep their dress clean while farming. In this sense, Marie was copying the peasantry.

The Hamlet was completely enclosed by fences and walls, and only intimates of the queen were allowed to access it. While it had been created as a harmless agglomeration of playhouses in which to act out a Boucher pastorale and escape the rigors and lavish dress of Versailles, in the eyes of the French people, the queen seemed to be spending copiously and wantonly merely to amuse herself.

The Queen's Hamlet. The Marlborough Tower & Working Dairy

The Mill and Water Wheel

One of the Flower Gardens of the Hamlet

The Queen's House & the Stove Room

Dovecote and Guard House

The Queen's Boudoir

Aerial view of Marie Antoinette's Hamlet

Interior of the Hamlet cottages was not as rustic as the outside.
Photo courtesy of dailymail.co.uk

Marie Antoinette took her children to the Hamlet to educate them about nature. Here, they learned to milk a cow, gather eggs, pick strawberries and discover a wide variety of flowers. It was also here that the queen was enjoying an autumn day on October 5, 1789, when a page ran to her admonishing her to return to the palace as an angry mob of people were on their way, seeking her head.

## Chapter Fifty-Seven
## **Diamonds and the Queen's Fall**

The Queen of France was losing in the popularity poles. Her exclusive clique of friends had alienated many nobles at court and rumors of affairs and even orgies circulated around her secret grotto and mirrored panels at the Petit Trianon. Her interference in the government's politics had garnered her powerful enemies and the people of France saw her as extravagant, arrogant, and a wanton queen who was an Austrian outsider. Nearly every move she made was misconstrued and characterized in pamphlets for the amusement of the masses.

In the midst of her waning popularity, the queen gave birth to her third child, a healthy baby boy. There was now an "heir and a spare" and the king was overjoyed. Marie had been so large with this pregnancy that many suspected twins. But it was Louis Charles, the duc de Normandie, who screamed into the world on Easter Sunday, March 27, 1785. By this time, the queen's favorite friend, the Duchesse de Polignac, had been awarded the position of Royal Governess, and she dutifully took responsibility for the child.

The usual rumors circulated as to whether or not the king was the father. Oddly, Count Fersen (who was enamored with Marie) was not among the accused. As it was, this very count arrived at Versailles only two months after the birth of Louis Charles, in May of 1785, and remained until June before joining his regiment in Flanders. He noted the cool reception of the queen when she visited Paris; 'not a single acclamation' broke 'the perfect silence'. Yet, Fersen claims she was applauded for a quarter of an hour—in tribute to the birth of another son. It may be that the 'silence' in town came from the lower class who had begun to hate the queen, while those in attendance at the opera were the nobility. The fickleness of the French people toward her had always been confusing and hurtful.

She had become the scapegoat for all that was wrong with the current financial crisis. It was easy to point to her love of chocolate (an extravagance at the time), dresses, jewels, and her spending for her Petit Trianon fantasyland. She was now the symbol of the growing hostility toward the government. What happened next would be the final undoing of the Queen.

### *Affaire du colier de la reine*

The Affair of the Diamond Necklace, or Affair of the Queen's Necklace (*Affaire du colier de la reine*) was an insidious plot carried out between 1784 and 1785 at Versailles, involving Marie Antoinette. Her reputation, already tarnished by gossip, was ruined by the false implication that she had participated in a crime to defraud the crown's jewelers in acquiring a very expensive diamond necklace she then refused to pay for. She had in fact, rejected the necklace when it was shown to her by the creators: Parisian jewelers Charles Auguste Boehmer and Paul Bassange.

The necklace had originally been commissioned by Louis XV to grace the neckline of his favorite, Madam du Barry, in 1772. The cost was 2,000,000 *livres* (approximately $15 million in US dollars in 2021). To create the massive piece, it would take the jewelers several years and a great deal of their money to amass an appropriate set of diamonds. In the meantime, Louis XV died of smallpox and his grandson banished Madame du Barry from the court. The necklace was described as 'a row of seventeen glorious diamonds, as large almost as filberts… a three-wreathed festoon, and pendants enough (simple pear shaped, multiple star-shaped, or clustering amorphous) encircle it… around a very Queen of diamonds.'

The Diamond Necklace

The jewelers, after losing Louis XV's commission, hoped that Marie Antoinette would buy it. It was shown to the queen who refused it on two counts: 1) it had been originally commissioned for the late king's mistress, not a queen; and 2) with the recent war financial fiasco, Marie stated, "We have more need of Seventy-Fours [ships] than of necklaces." There was also the rumor that it had been shown to Louis XVI and he had considered it, but eventually thought better of it with the current financial climate. At any rate, the jewelers were sent away without a buyer—a huge problem, as who else could afford to pay for it and they were out the money for its creation.

Boehmer and Bassange tried in vain to find a buyer outside France and failed. Upon the birth of Louis Joseph, Dauphin of France, they again approached the Queen and she again refused.

The diamond necklace scandal all began with one woman: Jeanne de Saint-Remy de Valois (Jeanne d la Motte). Valois was a descendent of an out-of-wedlock son of Henry II of France. She had married an officer of the gendarmes, Nicholas de la Motte, the self-proclaimed "comte de la Motte." She was living on a small pension granted to her by her by the king. She hatched a plan to use the necklace to gain wealth and possibly power and royal patronage.

In March 1785, Jeanne became the mistress of the Cardinal de Rohan, a former French ambassador to the court of Vienna, and hence to Marie Antoinette's mother. He was known for making many conquests among the sweet young things at court. Marie Antoinette had never liked him, as he had spread gossip about her behavior to the Holy Roman Empress, her mother, Maria Theresa. Marie had also learned of a letter in which the cardinal spoke of the Empress in a manner that Marie found offensive.

Cardinal de Rohan

At this time, the cardinal was trying to regain the queen's favor in hopes of becoming one of the king's ministers, and hopefully, his Prime Minister. Jeanne de la Motte (Valois) had entered the court by means of her lover named Rétax de Villette. She persuaded Rohan that she had been received by the queen and enjoyed her favor. It is doubtful Marie Antoinette even knew who she was. On hearing that, Rohan resolved to use Jeanne to regain the queen's goodwill. Jeanne assured the cardinal that she was making efforts on his behalf.

Thus began an alleged correspondence between Rohan and the queen. In truth, Jeanne de la Motte was writing the letters on forged stationary showing the queen's letterhead. Rohan would hand her his response to give to the "Queen" and la Motte would answer them, the tone becoming more and more friendly and warm. The cardinal became convinced the queen was in love with him, and he, in turn, became enamored with her. Marie Antoinette was totally in the dark as to all that was going on behind her back.

The cardinal begged Jeanne to arrange a secret night-time meeting with the queen, face-to-face. The meeting was set for August 1784, in the shadowed gardens of Versailles. At the appointed time, a nervous cardinal stood in the shadows and awaited the arrival of his former enemy. Shortly, a woman stepped from a pathway shrouded in towering hedges and walked slowly toward him. Heavy with anticipation, Rohan stepped toward the veiled woman, believing it was the queen. In fact, the woman was a prostitute, Nicole Le Guay d'Oliva, whom Jeanne had hired because of her resemblance to the Queen. She had often parodied Marie Antoinette in the back streets of Paris, to the delight of the rabble. Rohan offered the "Queen" a rose. She, in return, offered in a soft voice to forget their past disagreements.

The happy cardinal was most grateful to Jeanne for the reconciliation between himself and the Queen. He allowed la Motte to borrow large sums of money from him, stating that it was for the queen's charity work. Rohan began to see the medal of the prime minister placed about his neck in the very near future. Jeanne used the money to buy fancy dresses and weave her way into respectable society. She openly boasted about her closeness to the queen, and many nobles believed her, inviting her into their company.

It is here where the diamond necklace enters the picture. The two jewelers, Boehmer and Bassenge, heard of Jeanne's closeness to the queen and approached her about once again putting the necklace before Marie Antoinette. They offered Jeanne a large commission for her help if the queen were to buy the necklace. At first, Jeanne demurred at accepting the money, feigning her respectability, but then agreed to take it. According to Madam Campan, Jeanne, pretending to be the queen, sent several letters to Cardinal Rohan asking him to buy the necklace. The pretense was that the Queen desired the expensive necklace, but due to the financial crisis and her shaky popularity, it would come back at her if she were to spend such a sum on a necklace. If he would consent to be the buyer, she would repay him "under the table."

The letters to Rohan were always signed 'Marie Antoinette de France.' If Rohan had been on his toes, he would have realized that royals sign only with their given name. Tricked into believing the content of the letters, Rohan negotiated the purchase of the necklace for 2,000,000 *livres*, to be paid in installments. He told the jewelers he had the queen's authorization for the purchase and showed the jewelers the conditions of the bargain in the "Queen's" handwriting. Rohan took the necklace from the ebullient jewelers and went at once to Jeanne de la Motte's house. There, a man Jeanne declared as a valet to the queen, took the heavy box containing the most-handsome necklace in France. Rohan departed and Jeanne la Motte went to work.

The diamond necklace "was promptly picked apart, and the gems sold on the black markets of Paris and London" by Madame de la Motte. In the meantime, the promised installment payment for the necklace came due. Rohan, who not heard from Jeanne in a while, reached out to her to ask what the plans were for the queen to pay the installment. When the silence continued, Rohan became nervous, and the jewelers began to panic, until Boehmer complained to the queen. Marie Antoinette erupted, feeling as if the desperate jewelers were trying to corral her, but when she heard the story of Rohan's involvement, she was convinced it was he who was trying to ruin her with the scandal. If the public believed she had dropped 2 million *livres* for baubles to hang about her neck, she would be maligned to such a degree she would never recover.

Retribution came swiftly. The cardinal was arrested in the Hall of Mirrors at Versailles. On August 15, 1785, the *Feast of the Assumption of Mary*, Rohan was taken before the king, queen, the Minister of the Court Louis Auguste Le Tonnelier de Breteunil and the Keeper of the Seals Armand Thomas Hue de Miromesnil to explain himself. Rohan produced a letter signed "Marie Antoinette de France". Rohan did not realize that royalty signed with only their baptismal name (in Marie's case, her birth name was Maria Antonia. It was changed to Marie Antoinette when she became French.). This prejudiced Louis against the cardinal who he 'could not understand how a courtier, and above all a Rohan, a member of a family so keen on the details of status, could make such a mistake.'

Rohan was arrested and taken to the Bastille. On the way, he sent home an order to destroy all his correspondence. Jeanne was not arrested until three days later, giving her a chance to destroy her papers. The police arrested the prostitute Nicole Le Guay, as well as Jeanne's lover, de Villette, who confessed he had helped to write the letters and forge the queen's signature. To add spice to the uproar, an occultist, Alessandro Cagliostro, was also arrested for what was believed to be a small part he played in the deception.

The trial was conducted before the Parlement de Paris who would act as judges. The outcome was that the cardinal was acquitted (infuriating the queen). Lequay and Cagliostro were also acquitted on May 31, 1786.

Jeanne de la Motte was found guilty and condemned to whipping. She was branded with a hot iron in the shape of the letter 'V' (for voleuse, 'thief') on each shoulder, and sent to life imprisonment in the prostitute's prison at the Salpêtrière. In June of the following year, she escaped prison by disguising herself as a boy. Meanwhile, her husband (who had fled when things went south) was tried *in absentia* and condemned to be a galley slave. Jeanne's lover, Villette, was banished from France. All the news was publicly posted, exciting the denizens of Paris.

Despite the queen's innocence in the matter, the public turned on her. They believed Marie Antoinette used la Motte as an instrument to satisfy her hatred for Rohan. The queen's disappointment in his acquittal and his quick exile by the king to the Abbey of la Chaise-Dieu confirmed their belief. Besides, hadn't the Parlement pardoned the cardinal by acquitting him. That caused tongues to wag that it was he who was innocent in all this and not the queen. The masses also believed Marie had wanted the expensive necklace and went about getting it with the demise of her enemy. All those factors led to a huge decline in the queen's popularity. She was labeled a manipulative spendthrift, more interested in vanity than the welfare of her people.

After her escape, Jeanne de la Motte took refuge in London, and in 1789, published her *Mémoires Justificatifs* in which she once more libeled the Queen Marie Antoinette.

*The Diamond Necklace Affair* was important in discrediting the Bourbon monarchy in the eyes of the French people four years before the French Revolution. Marie Antoinette's "unpopularity was so great after the *Diamond Necklace Affair* that it could no longer be ignored by either the Queen or the government. Her appearances in public all but ceased." Her reputation was irrevocably destroyed. It never recovered. Her early history of excessive spending caused her public image to be already blemished, but the *Diamond Necklace Affair* catapulted public opinion of her into near hatred since she appeared to have plotted to misuse more of the kingdom's depleting money for personal trinkets.

Paris Pamphlet Entitled "One Beast, Two Heads."

This public relations nightmare led to an increase in salacious and degrading pamphlets, which would serve as kindling for the upcoming French Revolution. It could be said that "she symbolized, among other things, the lavishness and corruption of a dying regime" and served as "the perfect scapegoat of the morality play that the revolution in part became," making her a target for the hatred of the French Republic and groups like the Jacobins and the *sans-culottes*. The only up-side was that the whole affair caused Louis to become closer to her and more protective.

Over the years, the caricatures of the queen's opulent dress and hairstyles had been the original means of disparaging Marie. Perhaps the most famous pouf was one her hairdresser Leonard created to celebrate the victory of the French frigate *La Belle Poule* in a naval battle against the English frigate HMS *Arethusa* on June 17, 1778, at the beginning of the *American War of Independence.* The queen's expenditure on expensive hairdos and gowns began the gossip that led to her demise.

The Frigate Hairdo

As a final note to the events surrounding the *Diamond Necklace Affair,* it was ironic that at the time Cardinal Rohan heard he was to be arrested, Marie Antoinette was on stage at her beloved Theatre at the Petit Trianon. The Queen played the girl Rosina in Beaumarchais' *Le Barbier de Sèville.* The young Duc de Guiche portrayed the guardian Doctor Bartolo, Vaudreuil was Figaro, and her brother-in-law Artrois was the amorous Count Almaviva. It would be Marie Antoinette's last performance at the stage there.

## Chapter Fifty-Eight
## **All the King's Horses & All the King's Men**

Marie Antoinette struggled with her unpopularity and another concern closer to home. On November 2, 1785, the queen turned 30. She suddenly felt old and fat. Her frame was considered more 'stout' than it had been, but she now had three children: Madame Royal, age seven-and-a-half; the Dauphin who was approaching three, and the Duc de Normandie, only fifteen months old. She was therefore surprised, and a bit trepidatious to suspect she was once again pregnant. It was later confirmed. The queen from the outset felt unwell with this pregnancy and worried that all the strain from the trial of *The Diamond Necklace Affair* and France's daily struggle with finances and bickering between countries would make this pregnancy a difficult one.

Louis XVI had departed to Cherbourg and other seaports on an eight-day visit. As he had rarely left the confines of Versailles, he was surprised to be met with cheers and hats waving as his coach passed. Pleased, he began to wonder if all the rumors of his and the queen's unpopularity were true. When it was time to return to Versailles, Louis made the dour comment as the coach moved along: "I can tell we are getting closer to Versailles as the cheering is getting less and less.'

When Louis arrived at the Marble Court of Versailles, Marie greeted him from the balcony of the palace with their three children. The King was touched by the cries of 'Papa! Papa!' A new, more confident Louis emerged from the carriage to embrace his family. The welcome he had received from places such as Harcourt (where they kissed the sheets he had slept upon), along with his naval acumen he had demonstrated during his talks there, gave him a boost with which he was unfamiliar. He resumed his love of the hunt, something he had not done for a while.

Ten days after his return, the queen reported feeling unwell. She attended Mass, and three hours later, at seven-thirty in the evening, a baby girl was born. She was christened Sophie, in honor of the king's late aunt, who had died of dropsy four years earlier. Emperor Joseph (Marie's brother), with his usual lack of tact, was reported to have said it was a pity the child was not another boy. It was not the child's gender that concerned the mother and those around her. The baby was early, not expected until the end of July, which accounted for Marie believing she was simply unwell instead of believing she was in labor. Also, Louis would not have left on his eight-day tour if he thought the birth was imminent.

The baby was not strong and the mood at court shifted. The young dauphin was once again plagued with his frequent fevers, and Marie was in a constant rage over the contuining slander against her in Paris. Why had no one apologized for wrongfully accusing her of The Diamond Necklace Affair? Why the scurrilous innuendo about the paternity of each baby she bore?

## The Assembly of Notables

Louis XVI was in a pickle. Calonne's advice to 'spend more and buy our way out of debt' had failed. France's finances were in a desperate state. The singular cry from the finance ministers Louis had appointed (Turgot, Necker, Calonne) had been the same: tax reform was necessary, and that meant taxing the nobles, which Louis dreaded. To implement tax reform, it first had to be registered with the French parlements. Repeated attempts had failed due to the lack of parlement support, as parlement judges felt that any increase in tax would have a direct negative effect on their own income. As one Versailles documentarian so wittily put it, 'It was like asking turkeys to vote early for Christmas.'

Knowing the climate at a parlement meeting would be tempestuous, Louis' finance minister, Calonne, suggested that the king call an Assembly of Notables. While the Assembly of Notables had no legislative power in its own right, Calonne hoped that it if the Assembly of Notables could be made to support the proposed reforms, then this would apply pressure on parlement to register them.

Calonne proposed four major reforms:

1. a single land-value tax
2. the conversion of the *corvée* into a money tax
3. the abolition of internal tariffs
4. the creation of elected provincial assemblies

The traditional telling of the outcome of this Assembly was to say the plan failed because the 144 assemblymen, who included princes of the blood, archbishops, noblemen and other people from the traditional elite, did not wish to bear the burden of increased taxation. Others, like Simon Schama tells a different story. He wrote:

'Yet what was truly astonishing about the debates of the Assembly is that they were marked by a conspicuous acceptance of principles like fiscal equality that even a few years before would have been unthinkable…Where disagreement occurred, it was not because Calonne had shocked the Notables with his announcement of a new fiscal and political world; it was either because he had not gone far enough or because they disliked the operational methods built into the program.'

The floor of the meetinghouse was a hotbed of debate. Voices were raised and Louis felt thwarted once again. After reports were given of the true state of the debt (which Necker had lied about), the assemblymen exploded and rejected the plan. Finally, the Assembly insisted that the proposed reforms should actually be presented to a representative body such as the Estates-General, which would include the lower classes (third estate).

Calonne was disgraced and Louis had lost all confidence in him. Bowing to the outcry of the nobles filling his halls, he dismissed the finance minister on Easter Sunday, April 8. In his place, Étienne-Charles de Loménie was chosen as the new Controller-General des Finances. As France watched another finance minister leave Versailles in disgrace, the government appeared like a revolving door of fiscal 'experts' coming and going. Once again, the king did not deem it worthy of his station to offer his subjects an explanation. It was left for them to deduce the government of France was like a rudderless ship and it was headed for the rocks.

Vergennes, who had been with Louis XVI since his accession thirteen years earlier, died on February 13, 1787, just as the king's world was unraveling. Marie Antoinette was not among the mourners, as she and the foreign affairs minister had often locked horns. Count Mercy, her Austrian counselor, immediately badgered Marie to influence the choice of a new Foreign Minister. He reminded her that she must perform 'a service to the two courts' of Austria and France. Mercy advocated Comte de Saint-Priest who had been an enemy of Vergennes and was also a close friend of Marie's love interest, Count Fersen. When Louis preferred the Comte de Montmorin, a childhood friend, the queen went along with it without much dispute. Mercy put this down to her 'lack of interest in serious things.' She shot back that it was not right 'that the Count of Vienna should nominate the ministers of the Court of France.' Finally, after years of her mother, Mercy, and her brothers telling her what to do in the interest of Austria, Marie Antoinette was pushing back as the Queen of France. It was sadly, coming at a late stage in the game.

Louis XVI, never seen as an exemplary king, especially in comparison with his predecessors, continued to plummet in the polls. His apathy, indecision, the reports of his falling asleep—and even snoring—during Council meetings, only grew worse. A man who was a foot taller than the Sun King could not "fill his shoes." His despair grew as everything he tried to bring an end to the abysmal financial chaos, failed. By May 1787, he crashed. He began coming daily to the queen's room and crying openly. By August, he was in a full-blown depression and shut down completely. Count Mercy noted that the king's physical appearance was also suffering. Mercy said, he [the king] hunted 'to excess' as an escape measure. His appetite diminished. Mercy also stated that worst of all 'there were occasional lapses of reason and a kind of brusque thoughtlessness which is very painful to those who have to endure it.' Rumors swirled that Louis had also turned to alcohol to numb his mental anguish.

It was now Marie Antoinette who stepped up in an effort to keep the government from crumbling. While not astute enough to carry out political matters, she showed real courage in trying to put a brave face on the situation and bolster her husband as he floundered. At the same time, the queen was losing what had been her closest friend besides Madam Lamballe—Yolande de Polignac. Things had changed at court. With the departure of Colonne, so too went much of the patronage the Polignac set had counted on. The queen no longer entered into Yolande's carefree lifestyle. Marie was now a mother of four and becoming more matronly by the day. Many commented on her weight gain, emerging gray hairs and full chin. King Gustav of Sweden had cruelly said in public that the Queen of France had grown too fat to be any longer counted as a beauty. Marie's own brother, the blunt Joseph II, commented to their sister Marie Christine that Marie had 'the fine face of a good fat German.' Gone were the days of partying with Yolande and the frivolous spending on ball gowns and jewels.

Polignac in return gathered more glittering friends around her at her salon—a salon Marie paid for. The queen sent a page to see who was at these parties. When she made a critical comment to Yolande about the company she was keeping, Polignac retorted, in effect, that she didn't comment on the company the queen kept and Marie should not comment upon hers. It became clear that when the wine was flowing and the balls were plentiful, the Polignac's were there in full force. If the baubles and offices were no longer in the deal, nor was their allegiance.

The decisions made by the royal couple during times of financial duress never ceased to amaze those on the outside. While the dismissal of The Assembly of Notables on May 25, 1787, resulted in the elimination of 173 posts in the queen's household to begin reducing expenditure, other purchases racked up. The king, who was trying to regain his composure, sulked at the reduction in the numbers of his hunting horses. He promptly went out and bought the chateau of Rambouillet for its hunting prospects, and spent to redecorate it, along with his chateau at Fontainebleau. Yet, it was not he but Marie Antoinette who was derisively named 'Madame Deficit' in the summer of 1787. By 1788, court expenditure accounted for between 6 and 7 per cent of the total national outlay, while 41 per cent was put toward servicing the national debt.

Marie Antoinette, in an all-out effort to rebrand herself, began attending committees of the king and his counselors. She also put forth a new campaign to be seen as a wife and mother of the Children of France by hiring her favorite painter Madame Vigée Le Brun to paint her portrait not as the shepherdess of the Petit Trianon in a flowing white chemise, but as the Queen of France. Rose Bertin dressed Marie in red velvet edged in black fur, with white plumes in the matching red pouf. These were reminiscent of the red, black, and white colors of the French royal ancestry. Her children were also painted. It was the epitome of home, wife, Queen and mother.

Portrait of the Queen and her children. Baby Sophie here is the result of Photoshop by some creative artist. The original is missing.
Le Brun

The portrait depicted the baby Sophie in the cradle. Sadly, the baby's image would later be painted over. Noticeably absent was a necklace around the Queen's neck. The painting hung in Versailles until tragedy struck on June 19, 1787, when Sophie died just a few weeks before her first birthday. Her tiny figure was pained out. Now, the dauphin's finger pointing at an empty crib was the young baby's memorial. The autopsy showed that Sophie had never really fully developed. Three small teeth about to cut through the gums sent the small infant into convulsions, ending her life. As the Queen looked down upon her deceased daughter at the viewing at the Grand Trianon, her foster-brother Joseph Weber made the unfortunate remark that as the child had not even been weaned yet, surely the loss could not be felt as much as one who had lived longer. Marie tearfully exclaimed, 'Don't forget that she would have been my friend!' The daughters whom she referred to as "mine," were still strong in her heart. The sons would belong to France.

The revised painting after the death of Sophie. Le Brun.

The new painting was to be hung at Salon of the Royal Academy at the end of August. It was advised that it should not be displayed, due to the hatred the people now felt toward the queen. The curators feared a riot or an unpleasant reaction to the portrait. It was removed, leaving an empty frame in its place. Someone pinned a not to the frame that simply read: "Behold the Deficit!"

Marie Antoinette's happiness would never fully return. Things went from bad to worse. Madame le Motte's escape from prison and subsequent publishing of libelous reports concerning the queen only added fuel to the hatred the French people felt for their sovereign. Le Motte's steamy accounts of lesbian affairs between herself and the queen, aligned perfectly with prior insinuations that the Marie Antoinette had had affairs with Lamballe and Polignac. She had also been accused of intimate relations with the king's own brother, Artois. None of it was true, but it didn't matter. She was called 'the monster that escaped Germany,' and compared to the likes of evil women such as Cleopatra and Catherine de' Medici. She never outran the false publicity aimed at her. Pornographic pamphlets of her cavorting with women, soldiers, and even a dog, littered the streets and signposts of France.

During all of this, Louis' depression continued, and she had to rally to take his place in minor decisions at court. She struggled to support Brienne, agreed to reinstate Jacques Necker in 1788 to help with the financial crisis, while yet another heartrending event was happening. The dauphin was sick.

Louis XVI rallied enough to try desperate means to save his realm. Along with his new *Controller-General des finances*, de Brienne and Necker, he tried to simply force the *Parlement de Paris* to register the new laws and fiscal reforms. Upon the refusal of the members of the Parlement, Louis tried to use his absolute power to subjugate them by every means: enforcing on many occasions the registration of his reforms (August 6, 1787; November 19, 1787; and May 8, 1788), exiling all Parlement magistrates to Troyes as a punishment. On August 15, 1787, the king prohibited six members from attending parliamentary sessions on November 19, arresting two very important members of the Parlement who refused his reforms on May 6, 1788, and finally in a bold move that would sign his death warrant, dissolved Parlement, depriving them of all their power. Louis replaced them with a plenary court on May 8, 1788.

The failure of these measures and displays of royal power is attributable to three decisive factors: First, the majority of the population stood in favor of parlement against the kings, and thus continuously rebelled against him. Second, the royal treasury was financially destitute to a crippling degree, leaving it incapable of sustaining its own imposed reforms. Third, although the king enjoyed as much absolute power as his predecessors, he lacked their image and personal authority crucial for an absolute monarch. In short, he was perceived as weak, vacillating and a despot. Now unpopular to both the commoners and the aristocracy, Louis XVI was therefore only very briefly able to impose his decisions and reforms, for periods ranging from 2 to 4 months, before having to revoke them.

The King of France had only one card left to play: he would have to call an Estates-General, which had not met since 1614 under the rule of Louis XIII. Louis XVI convoked the Estates-General on August 8, 1788, setting the date of their opening for May 1, 1789. How could he know that only five months after the opening session, he, his wife and children would be captured by an angry mob, the queen's guards beheaded, and the family taken away from the Sun King's glittering Versailles forever.

## Chapter Fifty-Nine
## **Countdown to the Revolution**

Among the major events of Louis XVI's reign was his signing of the *Edict of Versailles*, also known as the *Edict of Tolerance*, on November 7, 1787, which was registered in the Parlement on January 29, 1788. Granting non-Roman Catholics—Huguenots and Lutherans, as well as Jews—civil and legal status in France and the legal right to practice their faiths, this edict effectively nullified the *Edict of Fontainebleau* that had been the law for 102 years. The *Edict of Versailles* did not legally proclaim freedom of religion in France—this took two more years, with the *Declaration of the Rights of Man and Citizen* of 1789--however, it was an important step in eliminating religious tensions and it officially ended religious persecution within its realm.

It's evident, in the latter-part of 1787, that Louis XVI was still very much vested in the happiness of his subjects. Perhaps he was still hoping to be "loved." The meeting of the Estates-General would end all hopes of that.

May 1, 1789, dawned with an air of trepidation. Once again Louis placed his image and reputation into the hands of those who were perhaps not as sensitive to the desires of the French population as he was. Because it had been so long since the Estates-General had been convened, there was some debate as to which procedures should be followed. Ultimately, the Parlement de Paris agreed that "all traditional observances should be carefully maintained to avoid the impression that the Estates-General could make things up as it went along".

Things were already off to a bad start when, before the Estates opened, the deputies for the three orders were presented to the king. While he was familiar with the nobility and the clergy, he did not know any of the representatives for the Third Estate and was at a loss as to how to proceed. Rumor spread that he didn't want to receive the "commoner's representatives" at all. When the nobility and clergy members were ushered into the King's Cabinet to be presented, both doors of the room were open. When it came time for the Third Estate's representatives to enter, only one door was open the other firmly locked. It was perceived as a slight…one that would not be forgotten,

At Mass, the day before the opening, it was evident that Marie Antoinette was stressed. Her 'brow was troubled, her lips tight-set, and she made vain attempts to hide her agitation.' Bombelles noted that there were no cries of 'Vive la Reine.' He went on to note: 'Never has a queen of France been less popular; and yet no act of wickedness can be laid at her door. We are decidedly unjust to her and far too severe in punishing her for, at most, a few examples of flightiness'.

At the Estates-General opening, the king agreed to retain many of the traditions, which had been the norm in 1614 and prior convocations of the Estates-General, but which were intolerable to a Third Estate [the common people] buoyed by recent proclamations of equality. For example, the First and Second Estates [the clergy and the nobles] proceeded into the Assembly wearing their finest garments, while the Third Estate was required to wear plain, oppressively somber black clothing, an act of alienation that Louis XVI would likely have not condoned. He seemed to regard the deputies of the Estates-General with respect: in a wave of self-important patriotism, members of the Estates refused to remove their hats in the king's presence, so Louis removed his to them. He feigned removing it to wipe his brow, and then left it off. It is an image no one could picture the Sun King doing.

At this time, the First Estate comprised 100,000 Catholic clergy and owned 5-10% of the lands of France—the highest per capita of any estate. All property of the First Estate was tax exempt.

The Second Estate comprised the nobility, which consisted of 400,000 people, including women and children. Since the death of Louis XIV in 1715, the nobles had enjoyed a resurgence in power. By the time of the Revolution, they had almost a monopoly over distinguished government service, higher offices in the church, army, and parlements, and most other public and semi-public honors. Under the principle of feudal precedent, they were not taxed.

The Third Estate comprised about 25 million people: the *bourgeoisie*, the peasants, and everyone else in France. Unlike the First and Second Estates, the Third Estate were compelled to pay taxes. The *bourgeoisie* found ways to evade them and become exempt. The major burden of the French government fell upon the poorest in French society: the farmers, peasantry, and working poor. The Third Estate had considerable resentment toward the upper classes.

The Estates-General 1789. The Third Estate, all in black, are in the foreground.

The Estates-General would consist of equal numbers of representatives of each Estate. The Third Estate had demanded, and ultimately received, double representation due to its large population of 25 million people. This had been granted to them in provincial assemblies. When the Estates-General convened in Versailles on May 5, 1789, however, it became clear that the double representation was something of a sham: voting was to occur "by orders," which meant that the collective vote of 578 representatives of the Third Estate would be weighed the same as that of each of the other, less numerous Estates.

It was just the beginning of a blocked attempt to rally the nation. Royal efforts to focus solely on taxes failed totally. The Estates-

General reached an ultimate impasse, debating (with each of the Three Estates meeting separately) its own structure rather than the nation's finances. It was the open door the Third Estate needed.

On May 28, 1789, Abbé Sieyès moved that the Third Estate, now meeting as the Communes (English: Commons), proceed with verification of its own powers and invite the other two Estates to take part, but not to wait for them. Here was the opportunity so many had hoped for: the fall of the monarchy. No more absolute ruler. No unfair tilting of the scales in favor of a government that made all the rules and surrounded itself with wealth and tax-free opulence. They proceeded with their plan, completing the process on June 17. They voted a measure far more radical, declaring themselves the National Assembly, an assembly not of the Estates but of "the people." They invited the other orders to join them but emphasized that they intended to conduct the nation's affairs with or without them.

The Tennis Court Oath

Louis XVI was incensed. He had not foreseen such a radical move. Fearing he had lost total control, he responded with force. He shut down the Salle des États where the Assembly met. The Assembly moved its deliberations to a nearby tennis court. They swore the *Tennis Court Oath* on June 20, 1789, under which they agreed not to separate until they had given France a constitution. A majority of the representatives of the clergy soon joined them, as did forty-seven members of the nobility. By June 27, the royal party had overtly given in. Military forces began to arrive in large numbers around Paris and Versailles. Messages of support for the Assembly poured in from Paris and other French cities. On July 9, the Assembly reconstituted itself as the National Constituent Assembly.

That the clergy and nobles joined may not be all that surprising. Louis and his ministers had been trying (in vain) to impose taxes across the board, a highly unpopular move for the rich and entitled. It didn't look like the king would abandon this campaign with the sad affair the treasury was in. The fact that the king's own brothers had often campaigned against him, as had other princes of the blood, contributed to a king without a foundation from any fraction of his kingdom.

Only 5 days after the formation of the National Constituent Assembly, on July 9$^{th}$, the Bastille was breached. It was the beginning of the French Revolution.

The political black clouds gathering over the Versailles' rooftops paled in comparison with the crippling blow that hit the king and queen on June 4, 1789, during the Estates-General meetings. At one in the morning, the frail young Dauphin of France died at the age of seven. His fevers, which had occurred throughout his life from the age of three were finally put down to tuberculosis of the spine. The constant fevers and weakness by the angular curvature of the spine, produced by the gradual crumbling of the vertebrae, caused his deformity to worsen and pressure on his spinal column increased.

He had been kept in a beautifully decorated room at the Chateau de Meudon where doctors tried to keep his fevers down. His wet nurse, Genevieve Poitrine, was accused of transmitting tuberculosis to the young dauphin.

When word came to Louis, who was in the middle of all the chaos emanating from the Estates-General debacle, he was devastated. His love for his oldest son, and his hopes for his future as king, overwhelmed him. The king heard Mass in private on the day of Louis Joseph's death, and again on the 5$^{th}$ and 6$^{th}$. Marie Antoinette was inconsolable and so Louis made all the funeral arrangements. The dauphin's heart was buried at Val-de-Grace, his body at Saint-Denis. The Court went into two months of mourning, except Louis, who was obliged by protocol to dress normally. Villedeuil, as House Minister, informed the little duc de Normandie that he was now the dauphin. The little boy was given the cross of the order of Saint-

Louis. His sister, now eleven, was crying, and so he cried also.

Louis Joseph Xavier Francois, the late Dauphin

The Third Estate, who at this time in June, were forcefully trying to gain entrance to see the king, were turned away as Louis XVI was closeted away in his grief. One deputy cruelly remarked, 'For Heaven's sake, his son is not as sick as the state!' On June 6$^{th}$, several deputies managed to see the king, their lack of sensitivity causing him to remark: 'There are no fathers then among the Third Estate.' It became more difficult to gain an audience with Louis XVI, who finally retreated to the chateau of Marly from June 14-June 21. Even there, manipulations were in play to bring down the crown.

The mood at the palace was bleak. Louis was not happy about Necker's return, declaring he had been forced to take him back. 'They'll soon regret it,' he said. Yet, Necker's reappointment was met with cheers from the populace and a surge in the Stock Exchange. As for Marie Antoinette, after the *Diamond Necklace Affair*, she remained in a melancholy frame of mind. Her hairdresser Leonard, who attended her daily, noted her pitiful state. He stated she would often start a sentence with 'If I began my life again…,' then break off and ask him to amuse her with onc of his stories.

This was all before the devastating outcome of the Estates-General. When Necker was once more let go, it fueled the attack on the Bastille.

The crippling winter at the start of the year that heralded the French Revolution did nothing to help matters. The winter of 1789 was the most severe in recent memory. New Year's Eve was blanketed in a snowstorm, followed by two months of freezing temperatures. The temperatures were so low that couriers between Paris and Versailles froze to death. Thomas Jefferson, in Paris at the time, reported that he felt he was freezing to death, as if in Siberia. As always, it was the poor who suffered most. Bread prices rose and as usual, tongues wagged that it was a plot of the royals, such as Artois and the queen, to produce a shortage in flour and profit by it. The fact the rich were skating and sledging without care did nothing to alleviate the misery of the lower-class subjects of France. Taking advantage of the situation, the manipulative duc d'Orleans donated to the poor's plight, ingratiating himself as the protector of the downtrodden.

## The Storming of the Bastille

There is little doubt that Jacque Necker's dismissal on July 11, 1789, was a turning point for the Revolution. The finance minister had been sympathetic to the Third Estate. When news of his being "sacked" reached Paris on Sunday, July 2nd, the Parisians naturally believed that the dismissal marked the start of a coup by conservative elements. Liberal Parisians were further enraged by the fear that a concentration of Royal troops—brought in from the frontier garrisons to Versailles, Sèvres, the Champ de Mars, and Saint-Denis—would attempt to shut down the National Constituent Assembly, which was meeting in Versailles.

Crowds gathered throughout Paris, including more than ten thousand at the Palais-Royal. Camille Desmoulins successfully rallied the crowd by "mounting a table, pistol in hand, exclaiming: 'Citizens, there is no time to lose; the dismissal of Necker is the knell of a Saint Bartholomew for patriots! This very night all the Swiss and German battalions will leave the Champ de Mars to massacre us all; one resource is left; to take arms!'"

The Swiss and German regiments referred to were among the

foreign mercenary troops who made up a significant portion of the pre-revolutionary Royal Army and were seen as being less likely to be sympathetic to the popular cause than ordinary French soldiers. By early July, approximately half of the 25,000 regular troops in Paris and Versailles were drawn from these foreign regiments. The French regiments included in the concentration appear to have been selected either because of the proximity of their garrisons to Paris or because their colonels were supporters of the reactionary "court party" opposed to reform.

During the public demonstrations that started on July 12$^{th}$, the multitude displayed busts of Necker and of Louis Philippe II, Duke of Orleans, then marched from the Palais Royal through the theater district before continuing westward along the boulevards. The Royal commander, Baron de Besenval, fearing the results of a blood bath amongst the poorly armed crowds or defections among his own men, then withdrew the calvary towards Sèvres. The crowd, desperate for weaponry, even crashed into the Opera House to steal weapons from the plays. They were dismayed to find the swords and guns were props, made of cardboard.

The unrest continued throughout the night as the growing mob attacked any place, they thought might harbor arms or supplies. A rumor ran around that supplies were being hoarded at Saint-Lazare, a huge property of the clergy, which functioned as a convent, hospital, school, and even as a jail. An angry mob broke in and plundered the property, seizing 52 wagons of wheat, which were taken to the public market. That same day multitudes of people plundered many other places including weapon arsenals. The Royal Troops did nothing to stop the spreading chaos in Paris during those days. As mentioned earlier, many of these troops had been confined to their barracks during the initial stages of the mid-July disturbances and, along with the Gardes Françaises, had formed many local ties in Paris for some time, mingling with the everyday people and watching their unrest. Many were sympathetic to their cause. If the royal couple had done the same, by living at the Tuileries instead of Versailles, would the story be different?

The Royal Commander Besenval's withdrawal led to a virtual abdication of royal authority in central Paris. On the morning of July 13, the electors of Paris met and agreed to the recruitment of a "bourgeois militia" of 48,000 men from the sixty voting districts of

Paris, to restore order. Their identifying cockades were of blue and red, the colors of Paris. Lafayette was elected commander of this group on July 14 and subsequently changed its name to the National Guard. He added the color white, the color of the king, to the cockade on July 27, to make the famous French tricolor.

On the morning of July 14, 1789, the city of Paris was in a state of alarm. The partisans of the Third Estate in France, now under the control of the Bourgeois Militia of Paris, had earlier stormed the Hôtel des Invalides without opposition. There, they made off with 29,000 to 32,000 muskets, but no shot. The commandment at the Invalides had in the previous few days taken 250 barrels of gunpowder to the Bastilles as a precaution.

At this time, the Bastille was nearly empty, housing only seven prisoners: four forgers; James F. X. Whyte, a "lunatic" imprisoned at the request of his family; Auguste-Claude Tavernier, who had tried to assassinate Louis XV thirty years before; and one "deviant" aristocrat, the Comte de Solages, imprisoned by his father using a *lettre de cachet*. The famous Marquis de Sade had been transferred out of the Bastille ten days earlier.

The Bastille stood as a symbol of royal tyranny. The regular garrison consisted of 82 *invlaides* (veteran soldiers no longer suitable for service in the field). On July 7$^{th}$, however, it had been reinforced with 32 grenaliers of the Swiss Salis-Samade Regiment from the regular troops on the Champ de Mars. The walls mounted 18 eight-pound guns and 12 smaller pieces. The governor was Bernard-René de Launay, son of the previous governor and actually born within the Bastille.

The crowd gathered outside the fortress around mid-morning, calling for the pulling back of the seemingly threatening cannon from the embrasures of the towers and walls, and the release of the arms and gunpowder stored inside. There were 954 names on the list of those who attacked, and more waiting in the crowd. The majority of attackers were local artisans, some regular army deserters, and even 21 wine merchants. Two representatives from the Hotel de Ville (municipal authorities from the Town Hall) were invited inside to talk over a possible negotiation. As the negotiations drug on past noon, the crowd became restless. Around 1:30, the protestors stormed the unprotected park surrounding the Bastille.

A small party climbed onto the roof of a building next to the gate to the inner courtyard and broke the chains holding the drawbridge to the Bastille, which fell, killing one of their own as it did. Soldiers demanded the crowd disperse, but gunfire rang out and the crowd became an angry, uncontrolled mob by 5:30, as they swept into the Bastille to take it over. The soldiers, realizing they did not have enough water or food to stage a stand-off inside, and fearing carnage if the fight continued, opened the gate. Nighty-eight attackers and only one defender died in the actual fighting, due mainly to the protection of the fortress walls. Governor Launay was dragged to the Hotel de Ville, where he was beaten and finally stabbed to death after he kicked a baker in the groin.

As per the popular tradition of the time, his head, along with that of Monsieur Flesselles, Prévôt des Marchands, were placed on pikes and carried through the cheering crowd. The three officers of the permanent Bastille garrison were also killed by the crowd. Two of the *invalid*es of the garrison were lynched. The blame for the fall of the Bastille would rather appear to lie with the inertia of the commanders of the 5,000 Royal Army troops encamped on the Champ de Mars, who did not act when either the nearby Hôtel des Invalides or the Bastille were attacked.

Storming the Bastille on July 14, 1789

The king learned of the storming the next morning through the Duke of La Rochefoucauld. “Is it a revolt?” asked Louis XVI. “No sire, it’s not a revolt; it’s a revolution.”

## The Fall of the Bourbon Dynasty

Paris was a hotbed of contention following the fall of the Bastille. La Fayette was in charge of a militia for the city while further militia were created all over France. The day after the storming, Louis XVI bravely visited the National Assembly in its salon at Versailles. Mirabeau, upon hearing the king was greeted with applause from some members of the Assembly stopped them, saying, "The people's silence is a lesson for kings." The next day, July 16, he conceded to the Assembly's demands to abandon his new ministers such as Breteuil who had only been in office an abysmal 'Hundred Hours,' and to recall Necker simply because 'the people' wanted him back.

It was then decided in private, that due to the volatility directed at the queen and hence her circle of friends, that many should leave the court. Firstly, was the Polignac family. Yolande, Marie's closest friend, despite their on-again, off-again relationship, was in tears as she and her family packed to leave for thc Swiss border. Members of the royal family were also told to leave, as no one was sure what would happen next. The king's brother, Comte d'Artois and his wife, the Princes of the Blood, Condé and Conti, and the Abbé de Vermond—Marie's confidential advisor for twenty years—packed their trunks.

The tearful scene as Yolande Polignac stopped to embrace Marie before departing across the Marble Court was heartbreaking. At first, Polignac refused to desert the queen, and then begged her to flee as well. Marie, fearful that one more minute could not be lost, said to her dear friend, 'I am terrified of everything; in the name of our friendship go, now is the time for you to escape from the fury of my enemies. Don't be the victim of your attachment to me, and my friendship for you.' Louis XVI appeared, and Marie begged him to help her persuade the Polignac's to leave. The king agreed they should go and added that he had just commanded the Comte d'Artois to depart as well. 'Don't lose a single minute,' he implored them. The king and queen were in tears as they watched those closest to them scurry across the courtyard to the waiting coaches—trunks hastily tied and loaded into others—followed by the sound of horse hooves as they departed Versailles for the last time.

Yolande Polignac traveled disguised as a maid, as Marie's terrified letters followed her. The family arrived safely in Switzerland where Polignac changed her name to Madame Erlanger. Many have wondered why Marie Antoinette, the most hated of the party, did not flee. Her sense of duty as the wife of the king (who refused to leave) and the mother of the dauphin compelled her stay. For all the rumors of her frivolous nature and naiveite, the queen was made of sturdier stuff, as she proved when she stepped up during Louis' depression. La Fayette, who saw the queen as an obvious obstacle to the king maintaining some kind of royal authority, would have wished her departure, if only temporarily as he struggled to cool the fires of Parisian tempers. She refused to leave Louis' side, believing her place was there and that he needed her support.

Breteuil and Artois encouraged Louis to leave with Marie and the children. They recommended they could hurry to Metz, one of the strongest fortresses in Europe and not far from the borders of Germany and the Netherlands. It was the king's other brother, the nefarious Provence (who had remained at Versailles) that told the king he should stay put. The old Marshal de Broglie backed up Provence's advice and encouraged the royal family to remain at Versailles.

It is one of Louis XVI's saddest and most profound statements that he made to Count Fersen when all was lost: 'I should have gone then and I wanted to, but what could I do when Monsieur [Provence] himself begged me not to go, and the Marshal de Broglie, as commander, replied: 'Yes, we can go to Metz, but what shall we do when we get there?' I missed my opportunity, and it never came again,' the King said sadly. Marie had been in favor of the move to

Metz and had even ordered the packing, but Louis called it off.

With the 20-20 of hindsight, can we play armchair quarterback and wonder if Provence encouraged the royal family to stay in hopes of their fall? Not that he wished them dead, but even if they had been deposed or imprisoned, he was next in line to the throne after the 4-year-old Louis Charles. If the entire family were gone, he would be king. At the very least, if Louis XVI were removed, Provence would be regent over the little boy. We do know the king's brother had been stirring the pot of contention for a long time; hinting that the royal children were fathered elsewhere, plotting uprisings in Paris, and undermining the monarchy. He had a great following.

As the pot boiled in Paris, the loneliness and tension that flowed through the hallways of Versailles, where once jeweled gowns and masquerade balls thrived, Marie felt the absence of her circle of friends greatly. There was an air of uncertainty about what would happen next. Had the King's concessions to the Assembly's demands been enough to restore peace? It was a long and sad summer. Alas, it did not have the effect they hoped for. It was too little, too late.

Peasant revolts continued in different regions as what was called the 'Great Fear' permeated France. Stones were thrown through the windows of the Archbishop of Paris on the evening of August 3rd, two weeks after the outbreak concerning the Bastille. Males were recruited everywhere into the National Guard, including valets and musicians from the Royal Chapel at Versailles. At the end of August, La Fayette proclaimed the abolition of all feudal privileges in his *La Déclaration des Droits de l'Homme.*

Marie Antoinette kept as low a profile as possible, turning her attention to her children. Louis hunted three or four times a week, heavily guarded. While the members of the royal family had for the most part all departed, there were still courtiers at Versailles, though in vastly reduced numbers. In one of many ironic scenes, the king still received the market-women, perhaps hoping to reconcile himself with his subjects in France and to assure them that their king was still in residence and vested in his country's happiness. It was a given right that these women could come inside the gilded doors of Versailles and pay their respects. Sadly, it also reinforced that the journey from Paris to the Sun King's palace was only 12 miles.

In the background, the food crisis in France continued. Even in

Versailles, the riots concerning the bread shortages hit home. A baker was almost hanged on September 13$^{th}$, accused of saving his better-quality bread for his more affluent customers. As mentioned before, it had become a prevalent trend for the bakers to add other ingredients to their flour during the grain shortage, including crushed bones, chalk and other fillers. Mothers and wives in Paris were facing their starving families and feeling more and more anxious and angry. These women formed strong bonds and aggressively shouted down the Mayor at Paris, yelling 'Men understand nothing!'

It was in this atmosphere that a new urgency appeared for the king to return to Paris. No one had seen him there since July 17th and it was now mid-September. At Versailles, Louis and Marie were still trying to maintain some sense of normalcy. To replace Polignac as the children's governess, Marie hired the very pious and very stern Marquise de Tourzel, a forty-year-old widow with five children. Her nickname (behind her back) quickly became 'Madame Severe' by the little dauphin, but Louis Charles was actually very fond of her. She absolutely believed in the monarchy. Her motto was 'Faithful to God and the King.' Her eighteen-year-old daughter, Pauline, was of the same mindset and the two of them dedicated their time to the royal children, albeit now, only two remained.

Marie Therese and Louis Charles

The two royal children were treated with love, but Marie had asked the new Governess to make sure she gave equal time to the ten-year-old Marie Therese as there was a tendency to put the next heir to the throne in the preferred position. Marie herself made sure to lavish time on Maire, remembering her own unhappy childhood. Louis Charles was beginning to exhibit some unwelcome tendencies, even though he was not yet five. He repeated everything he overhead, usually embellishing it with relish. He was not beneath telling a lie if it benefited him, causing his mother angst. The dauphin also hated loud noises, particularly that of the many dogs at Versailles.

Louis Charles had his good qualities: he loved his sister and made sure if he received a gift, that she did as well. He was proud, which might serve him well when he became king, as long as it was reined in to show confidence and not arrogance. His biggest pet peeve was to apologize for anything. He would go to the mat rather than say the word 'Sorry'.

It was as October 1789 began, that the world of the royal family would change forever. Fueled by one harmless, yet distorted event, the fuse to the Revolution powder keg was lit.

## The Attack on Versailles

On October 1, 1789, The Royal Flanders Regiment was brought to Versailles from Douai and a banquet was given for them in the theater at the palace. Here, they were seated alternately with the king's bodyguards. Louis and Marie had not planned to attend, keeping a low profile. As the wine poured and the patriotic emotions rose, they called for the king and queen to join them. The royal couple were finally compelled to make an appearance. Marie was in a simple dress of white and blue, with matching feathers in her hair, and a turquoise necklace. She carried Louis Charles in her arms and had Marie Therese by the hand. They were met with drunken adoration as the cheers of loyalty filled the large hall. It was probably an overwhelming thrill to the hearts of the royal couple who had known only hatred of late.

The next day, the Parisian press put out an entirely different account of the banquet. It read: 'In the course of an orgy,' the *L'Ami du Peuple* stated, the tricolour cockade had been trampled underfoot. Madame Campan, who had witnessed the evening, admitted that a few soldiers had turned their coats inside out to show only the white lining in tribute to the royal family, but the other accusations were hotly denied by those who were there. Even the songs played that evening were misconstrued as incitements to counter-revolution. It was the final straw for a populace looking for a reason to attack Versailles, and especially, the queen.

On Monday, October 5th, Marie Antoinette was at her beloved Petit Trianon with her children and a small group. It is possible Count Fersen may have been there at some point as he had returned to Versailles a week earlier at a house he had rented in town for the winter. Louis XVI was hunting in the forests of Meudon. He was having a good day, having bagged eighty-one head of deer when he was sent an urgent message from his Minister of the Household, Saint-Priest. An angry mob of market-women were marching toward Versailles from Paris. They had begun the 12-mile journey at 10:00 that morning. Their purpose was to demand grain or flour from the king and to force him to accede to some constitutional changes he had yet to grant. Louis heeled his horse and made for Versailles.

Louis XVI arrived at the palace at 3:00 in the afternoon. A messenger had been sent to the queen at the Petit Trianon and she too hastened back with the children. The royal couple anxiously deliberated on what to do when the mob arrived. It was pouring rain and fog engulfed the floor of the grounds in an eerie and ominous atmosphere. It was proposed that perhaps the royal family could hurriedly leave for the security of Rambouillet as it was twice the distance from Paris as Versailles and did not have the abundance of doors that were perpetually open. At least send the queen and children there. Marie again refused to leave her husband, and Louis vacillated, not wanting to become a 'fugitive King'.

They took too long to decide. The first group of angry market-women reached Versailles at 4 o'clock, with the larger group arriving between five and six. La Fayette sent a message to the king that he was on his way with the National Guard, and he too arrived at six. For some reason, the doors were left open as always, and a representative group of market-women climbed the stairs to the Hall of Mirrors and entered the King's Cabinet—the Oeil-de-Boeuf (Bull's Eye Room)—where Louis was meeting with his ministers. The king agreed to meet with one of the women, and he chose one whose clothes indicated neither 'misery nor an abject condition.'

The young Marie Theresa remembered the women as barely dressed and had never seen such poverty. The woman, poor or not, let the king know her mind in no uncertain terms. They were there to demand bread or grain—the people of Paris were starving! Louis listened and offered to tell the directors of two granaries to release all possible stores of grain to the people. The woman went away but returned saying they needed what he had just said in writing, no doubt to solidify his promise and to have something to show the granaries as proof of the king's words.

It was a welcome concession, yet the mob lingered, their all-day march still pulsing in their veins. Things were going their way. They decided as long as they were there, with their pitchforks and pikes, they would push the envelope. They wanted the king back in Paris. It was rumored that not all the market-women brandishing weapons were female. Some men had disguised themselves as women and were carrying firearms. The royal family once again discussed if it was too late to make a run for Rambouillet. That question was answered when it was announced the traces (straps that attach the horses to the carriages) had been cut.

Contemporaries of the Duc d'Provence hinted that it was he that had encouraged the march of the market-women to confront the king. The royal bodyguards were becoming increasingly alarmed as they overhead threats from the teaming crowd that they wanted Marie Antoinette's head. Some market-women were said to have bragged about wearing their work aprons in order to disembowel her and use her entrails to create cockades.

At midnight, an eerie calm settled across the palace and La Fayette departed. Marie, fearful of the hatred toward her, refused to share her husband's apartments, despite the fact she would have been safer there.  At 2 a.m., she lay across her bed but could not sleep. The sister of Madame Campan, Madame Augié, and Madame Thibault were in attendance to the queen in her room. The Marquise de Tourzel, shared the dauphin's bed, as was her custom. The queen told her to take the dauphin to the king's room immediately if a crisis should occur. And it did, at dawn, 4 a.m. the following morning.

Madame Auguié heard the shouting as dawn broke across the mansard roofs and glittering gates of Versailles. Madame Royal, the young Marie Theresa later wrote in her memoirs that 'the principal project [of the attack] was to assassinate my mother, on whom the Duc d'Orleans wished to avenge himself because of offences he believed he had received from her.' This rumor was also believed by a good many people, stating they thought Provence had not only encouraged the attack that occurred in the early morning hours of October 6$^{th}$, but that he may even have shouted the words, 'Kill the Queen!'

Madame Auguié ran to the door of the queen's antechamber leading to the guardroom and was shocked to see a blood-splattered guard who cried out to her: 'Save the Queen, Madame, they are coming to assassinate her!' Marie's attendants quickly dressed the queen in haste, missing one ribbon of her petticoat. The women fled to the hidden panel beside the queen's bed that led to a secret staircase connecting to the King's apartments. This was the same staircase and passage that was installed to help the shy king in the early years of his marriage go to the queen's room for conjugal visits without having to make the embarrassing journey past a wall of onlookers. Now, this very passageway would save Marie Antoinette's life.

No sooner had the women entered the passage and closed the hidden door, than the screaming mob attacked and beheaded two of Marie's guards in her antechamber and broke into her bedroom. They stabbed at the queen's bed with pikes upon not finding her there. The royal family gathered in the King's apartments, and they tried to show an outward calm for the children and those assembled. Marie said to the Governess's daughter, 'Don't be frightened, Pauline.' Outside, the noise grew as did the crowd assembled in the Marble Courtyard beneath the balcony of the king's rooms. They shouted out, demanding he make an appearance. Louis XVI stepped out onto the balcony, as did Marie Antoinette and the children. The crowd screamed, 'No children! No children!' The petrified dauphin and his sister were taken back inside but an ashen queen and her frightened husband remained.

Here, history departs on what happened next. Many say the queen, knowing it was she herself they had come to kill, bowed her head upon the railing and spread out her arms in subjection to the crowd. Silence fell over the assassins, and some yelled 'Long live the Queen,' before crying out once more in hatred. Another report has La Fayette bowing before her and kissing her hand on the balcony.

Whichever (or none) is true, the shouts of 'To Paris! To Paris!' filled the air, which at that petrifying moment must have sounded better than gunfire. Louis XVI felt he had no choice. His family's lives were in danger. At 12:30 in the afternoon, with La Fayette and his guards holding the mob at bay, the royal family made their way to the waiting coaches. Walking through the crowd, who were simmering with hatred and bearing pikes, pitchforks and guns, must have been one of the more terrifying moments throughout their ordeal.

Proposed scenario of what may have happened on the balcony

The procession of coaches, followed by thousands of screaming people, set out for Paris. The journey took seven hours to reach the capital due to the people thronging the roadway, as they sang out the popular song 'the Baker, the Baker's wife, and the Baker's boy' and that they were taking them to Paris, meaning bread would be back on the tables now. The procession was led by the decapitated heads of Marie's bodyguards placed upon pikes. It was a hideous site for the queen as these had been her protectors and family companions.

The carriage's occupants of the royal family rode on in horror, listening to the angry epithets hurled at their windows and the repetition of the 'Baker's Song.' Louis noticed his sister, Elizabeth looking out her window as they passed her beloved Montreuil. 'Are you admiring our lime avenue?' he asked her kindly. 'No, I am saying goodbye to Montreuil,' she replied.

At Versailles, the mob sacked much of the building, tearing down tapestries and taking mementoes. They even offered some bloody relic as a souvenir to some members of the diplomatic court who arrived at Versailles for a Tuesday reception. They were horrified at what they saw. The queen's hairdresser Leonard reported that when he later looked into Marie's bedroom, he saw her slippers and stockings in their usual place, waiting for her to being her *lever*. The room however was trashed, and a cold wind blew in through the splintered door to her room.

It was the last royal family to live in the Sun King's magnificent palace. Mistresses of former kings had come and gone, visiting dignitaries, gambling in the Salons, lavish banquets, and parties that lit the night sky with bursting rockets were no more. The Grand Canal reflected only a lonely moon as the Hall of Mirrors echoed with ghosts from the past. Even Napoleon chose to stay at the Grand Trianon during his time as Emperor of France, foregoing the large and ostentatious hallways of Versailles.

## Chapter Sixty-One
## **Escape to Varennes**

Louis XVI noted succinctly in his journal: 'Departure for Paris 12:30, visit to the Hôtel de Ville, dine and sleep at the Tuileries.' These brief words hardly represented the hours of horror accompanying the capture of the royal family. Once the entourage reached Paris, they were taken to the Hôtel de Ville which had been the seat of the Paris City Council since 1357. While Mayor Bailley greeted the king with a reference to Henri IV conquering the city and now the city had conquered Louis XVI, things were more affable when the exhausted king stood before the council and said: 'It is always with pleasure and confidence that I find myself amid the worthy inhabitants of my good city of Paris.'

Affirming the king and queen were to now reside at the Tuileries, Louis XVI, Marie Antoinette, their children, the Royal Governess, and the king's sister, Madam Elizabeth were hastened into the royal palace once owned by Catherine de Medici. The royal bodyguards had been replaced by La Fayette's National Guard as a protection to the sovereigns. As the family entered, they were surprised to see how dilapidated the giant palace had become. Four hundred rooms large, it felt unwelcoming and cold. The long gallery built by Henri IV was still there, linking the Tuileries to the Louvre. The rooms were dark and depressing, faded tapestries and paintings spoke of a happier and opulent past. Workmen's ladders littered the area. The once-beautiful gardens were filled with weeds, the ponds fetid, and prostitutes plied their trade in the foliage at night.

About 120 servants, along with their families, were living there now along with other homeless Parisians who nestled in places where they hoped to escape detection. All were now evicted from the palace.

The first night at the Tuileries was a sleepless one. The Governess Marquise de Touzel perched on the dauphin's ramshackle bed all night, watching the door to his room like a hawk. The threat to the future king of France was a real one. The fact that the door would not latch added to her anxiety and she barricaded it with furniture. The following morning, the little four-year-old said to his mother, 'Everything is very ugly here, Maman.' Marie Antoinette replied, 'My son, Louis XV lodged here comfortably enough; we must not be more particular than him.' Louis Charles then asked, 'Is today going to be like yesterday?'

It was perhaps the most-relevant question ventured by the royal family. What would happen next? Was this a stopping point to somewhere worse? Were the abysmal conditions of their new home meant to be a message of what they deserved after their opulent life at the greatest palace in Europe. No one knew. Nerves were on edge and the parents did what they could to present a calm façade for their children and others held captive there with them.

The following days were spent trying to turn their new arrangements into a home. The Comtesse La Marck, a seventeen-year-old member of the wealthy Noailles family, had recently decorated the ground-floor apartments of the south wing for her own use. The Queen took these over after insisting Louis pay the young lady 117,000 *livers* for the furnishings and mirrors. The children slept above the queen on the first floor and the king set up three rooms on the ground floor, and his bedchamber and cabinet on the first floor. Marie insisted their areas be separated as she still felt the hatred of the people was toward her.

When the always-vigilant market-women came round to jeer and press their faces to the windows, the king's sister, Elizabeth asked to be moved to the Pavillon de Flore. Mesdames Tantes were housed in the Pavillon de Marsan, affectionately named for Louis XVI's Governess. As for Louis' brother, the insidious Provence (who had accompanied them to the Tuileries), he and his wife headed off to their comfortable palace at Luxembourg. Gone were the familiar faces of the Polignac family and Marie's inner circle of friends and supporters. Only one greeted her that day at the Tuileries, and he refused to leave her side.

Count Fersen had never really left the queen and actually rode in one of the king's carriages as they ran the gambit of hateful protestors on the way to Paris. He wrote to his father, 'I was a witness to everything.' Now, Fersen made sure the family was alright at their new 'home' before making arrangements of his own. He sold his house and horses that he had purchased in Versailles and found a place to live in Paris where he could visit Marie, and also keep his father Gustav, the King of Sweden apprised of what was going on. The rest of Europe watched the unprecedented events in France with trepidation as it affected them all.

Another welcome face came to see the Queen and they fell into each other arms. Madam Lamballe, one of Marie's dearest friends and her attendant, had been away due to ill health. Madame Campan also came and was distressed to find the queen shaken, but still treating all around her with kindness. Marie greeted her dear lady's maid with an ominous statement whispered into her ear: 'Kings who become prisoners are not far from death.' She then turned her thoughts to how to make the best of their current situation, stating that 'patience, time, and inspiring [in the French] a great confidence' might make them forget their 'horrible mistrust.' To this cause, she decided to maintain a low profile, fearful of testing their limits by venturing outside with the mobs still simmering like a pot ready to boil over at any provocation.

After they had been there awhile, and nothing else had happened, the inhabitants of the Tuileries began to establish a somewhat "normal" existence. Furniture arrived from Versailles, underscoring they would not be going back. Riesener made furniture for the dauphin's room to help enliven it, and there was even a billiard table in the Gallerie de Diane. Leonard, that fashionista of the hair, came regularly and Marie confided more and more in him. Mademoiselle Rose Bertin still came to attend to the queen's wardrobe although she was doing more mending and alterations of current dresses than creating new gowns. Princess de Lamballe, as Superintendent of the Household, even held a few gatherings in her apartments.

It was then, in this half-world, that the royal family and their attendants found themselves. The oddity of royal hairdressers and seamstresses coming and going as if they were still at Versailles, was a surreal reality. Was it over? Were they out of harm's way? Surely, the hostile Parisians wouldn't condone the queen maintaining her *toilet* with wigs and dresses if they were to be slaughtered?

If the revolutionaries were quiet for now, it was because they were deliberating what to do now that they had their prey in a cage. For as Louis XVI wrote, 'We are in prison.' The Revolution's principles of popular sovereignty, though central to democratic principles of later eras, marked a decisive break from the centuries-old principle of divine right that was at the heart of the French monarchy. As a result, the Revolution was opposed by many of the rural people of France and by all the governments of France's neighbors. Still, within the city of Paris and amongst the philosophers of the time, many of which were members of the National Assembly, the monarchy had no support. As the Revolution became more radical and the masses more uncontrollable, several of the Revolution's leading figures began to doubt its benefits. Some, like Honoré Mirabeau, secretly plotted with the crown to restore its power in a new constitutional form.

Beginning in 1791, as the royal family tried to carve some semblance of a normal routine at the Tuileries, Montmorin, Minister of Foreign Affairs, started to organize covert resistance to the revolutionary forces. Thus, the funds of the *Liste Civile*, voted annually by the National Assembly, were partially assigned to secret expenses in order to preserve the monarchy. Arnault Laporte, who was in charge of the Civil list, collaborated with both Montmorin and Mirabeau. After the sudden death of Mirabeau, Maximillen Radix de Sainte-Foix, a noted financier, took his place. In effect, he headed a secret council of advisors to Louis XVI, which tried to preserve the monarchy; these schemes proved unsuccessful and were exposed later when the *armoire de fer* was discovered.

Regarding the financial difficulties facing France, the Assembly created the Comité des Finances, and while Louis XVI attempted to declare his concern and interest in remedying the economic situations, inclusively offering to melt the crown silver as a dramatic measure, it appeared to the public that the king did not understand that such statements no longer held the same meaning as they did before and that doing such a thing could not restore the economy of a country. At this point, any measures the king made would appear hollow, manipulative and 'too little, too late.'

Mirabeau's death on April 7$^{th}$, and Louis XVI's indecision, fatally weakened negotiations between the crown and moderate politicians.

The Third Estate leaders also had no desire in turning back or remaining moderate after their hard efforts to change the politics of the time, and so the plans for a constitutional monarchy did not last long. On one hand, Louis was nowhere near as reactionary as his brothers, the comte de Provence and the comte d'Artois, and he repeatedly sent them messages to halt their attempts to launch countercoups. This was often done through his secretly nominated agent, the Cardinal Loménie de Brienne. On the other hand, Louis was alienated from the new democratic government both by its negative reaction to the traditional role of the monarch and in its treatment of him and his family. He was particularly irked by being kept essentially a prisoner in the Tuileries, and by the refusal of the new regime to allow him to have confessors and priests of his choice rather than 'constitutional priests' pledged to the state and not the Roman Catholic Church.

As for the children, they began to acclimate to the Tuileries. Louis Charles especially loved to play in the gardens and was known to hand flowers to women passing by. He seemed to thrive in the outdoors and when asked which he preferred, Versailles or Paris, he exclaimed, 'Paris! Because I see more of Papa and Maman!' Marie spent every day with her beloved children, and in this respect, their new home seemed to bring the family together. Madam Royale's First Communion on April 8th was not the usual celebration where the daughter of France was usually given a handsome set of diamonds. In lieu of what was going on, it was deemed an unwise gift. The King told her that there were people who were going without bread, so the small sacrifice of diamonds seemed irrelevant.

It was in February of 1790 that Marie Antoinette was informed her dear brother, Joseph, the Emperor of Austria and the one who had come out to Versailles to give Louis XVI a "sex talk", had died of tuberculosis. He was succeeded by their brother Leopold, with whom Marie had never really gotten along. She, however, assured the new Emperor of her husband's support and her loyalty. Privately, she grieved the loss of her ally and friend, and closest brother. Her confidante and advisor, Count Mercy, was also recalled to Austria by the new Emperor Leopold, leaving the queen without a rudder in a continuing turbulent sea of unrest.

April of 1791 brought fresh problems to the hapless couple. The scandalous pamphlets against the queen had surfaced again, more pornographic and insulting than ever. Princess de Lamballe, residing at the Tuileries as Superintendent of the Household, was once again libeled as the queen's lesbian lover. La Fayette was now added as one of Marie's lovers, and worst of all, she was accused of sexual contact with three quarters of the Gardes Françaises. The pamphlets were hugely popular, and the presses ran day and night printing them.

The king had his own concerns on a religious scale. April 22, 1791 was Easter Sunday and he wished to take Communion. But how was he to take the sacrament from the hands of a juror priest? This was the ultimate betrayal of all he believed in. The King of France, ordained by God, refused to be allowed to partake of the sacrament of the Holy Roman Catholic Church. It was shortly after this that he took to his bed with depression, high fevers and coughing up blood.

As Marie struggled to hold it all together, the Mesdames Tantres—the royal Aunts Adelaide and Victoire—took their leave of the Tuileries for Rome in February of that year. Like rats deserting the sinking ship, the royal couple's circle of supporters either died or moved away. Louis rallied after a week of purges and emetics, but his mental state was a different matter. He wrote to the Duchesse de Polignac a few weeks later: 'How can I have these enemies when I have only ever desired the good of all?' Marie wrote her brother Leopold in October 1790, 'Oh my God! If we have committed faults, we have certainly expiated them.' She called the French 'a cruel and childish people.'

Within the restraints they found themselves, the king and queen were beginning to listen more and more to the pleadings of those in their confidence to escape. Paris was a bubbling cauldron of civil unrest, with the witches encircling it were still cackling for the queen's head. Finally, after much waffling from Louis XVI, who had made indecision an art, they decided they had to leave; for the sake of themselves and their children, and any hope of restoring their throne.

## Escape to Varennes

On June 21, 1791, Louis XVI attempted to flee secretly with his family from Paris to the royalist fortress town of Montmédy on the northeastern border of France, where he would join the émigrés and be protected by Austria. The escape was planned by the Swedish nobleman, and often assumed secret lover of Marie's, Axel Von Fersen.

While the National Assembly worked painstakingly towards a constitution, Louis and Marie were involved in plans of their own. Louis had appointed Breteuil to act as plenipotentiary, dealing with other foreign heads of state in an attempt to bring about a counter-revolution. Louis himself held reservations against depending on foreign assistance. Like his mother and father, he thought that Austrians were treacherous, and the Prussians were overly ambitious.

As tensions in Paris rose and he was pressured to accept measures from the Assembly against his will, Louis and the Marie agreed to escape from France. Beyond escape, they hoped to raise an "armed congress" with the help of the émigrés, as well as assistance from other nations with which they could return and, in essence, recapture France. This degree of planning reveals Louis' political determination, but it was for this determined plot that he was eventually convicted of high treason.

Louis XVI left behind on his bed a 16-page written manifesto, *Déclaration du roi, addressée a tous les François, á sa sortie de Paris*, traditionally known as the Testament politique de Louis XVI ("Political Testament of Louis XVI"). The document explained the king's rejection of the constitutional system as illegitimate. It was printed in the Paris newsletters. Believing he would be far away when the papers were found, he mistakenly played his card prematurely.

Unfortunately, the hasty departure of the king's aunts had caused a stir in Paris. Was the entire family getting ready to flee? Demonstrations once again broke out at the Tuileries. Plans for the escape escalated. It was finally decided they would escape to Montmédy, after other possibilities were discussed. The route was not an easy one: it was 180 plus miles through areas where the loyalty of the people was uncertain. The clear way was to go via Meaux and Rheims which was a straightforward route advocated by Fersen and Bouillé. Louis, fearing he would be recognized in Rheims, due to his coronation ceremony there sixteen years prior, changed the route to the south: Châlons-sur-Maine, then Sainte-Ménehould, then turning north, through a small town called

Verennes on the river Aire, then on to Dun, crossing the Meuse, to Stenay, and then to Montmédy.

While Bouillé was in favor of loyal troops positioned at certain strategic points, Fersen advocated for a clandestine trip without tell-tale sign of troops. The dates for the escape were changed a few times before it was settled. Marie wrote to Mercy, 'All is decided. We go Monday at midnight, and nothing can alter the plan.' It was carried out, with the royal party sneaked through the darkness to the waiting berlins. Marie was in a simple servant's dress, and the others likewise attired in clothing that would not give them away. Food was loaded for the long trip. One of the cases packed into the queen's carriage was a traveling picnic basket of sorts with plates, cutlery, etc. It also doubled as a dressing cabinet with a mirror, pots of makeup and tools. It was called a *néssaire.*

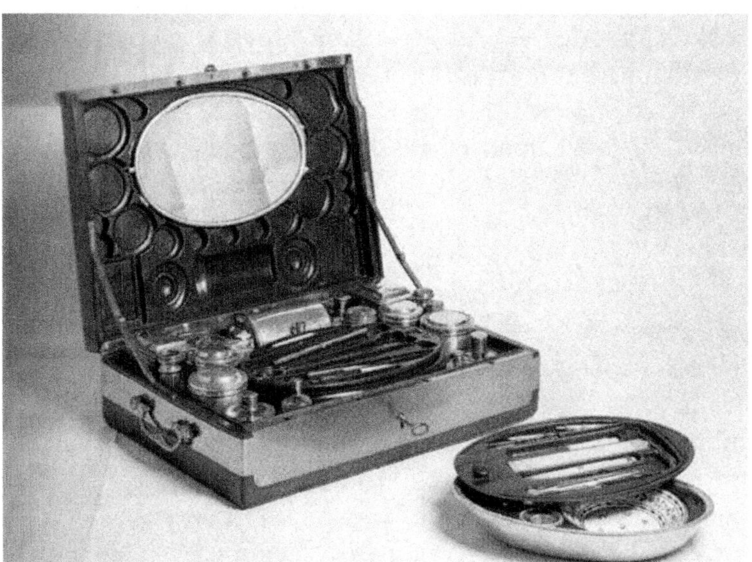

Marie Antoinette's *néssaire* that went with her to Verennes.

The following morning at 7 o'clock, Tuesday, June 21, when the King's valets entered his room as usual and drew back his bed curtains, they were surprised to see the king's bed empty. They went quickly to the dauphin's room and found it empty as well. The quandary came when the valets wanted to send word to alert the queen that the king and dauphin were missing. But the Queen's dressing hour was not until 8 o'clock and no one dared enter her room early. They were told that Madame Royal (Marie Theresa) had also asked for an additional half an hour to sleep in that morning. When the Queen's bedcurtains were finally pulled back, the cry went out, 'They've gone! They've gone!' It was all over Paris in a short order and the Tuileries was attacked and the king's portrait shredded.

It was after one-thirty in the morning when Fersen, who had driven the queen's berlin, reached the berlin waiting outside the city barrier at Porte Saint-Martin. Rather than taking the more public route, he had looped around out of caution, but that action caused an even further delay. When the party reached the first *poste* at Bondy, Fersen left the refugees, as had been agreed in advance. Marie may have felt his departure keenly as he had become her protector throughout these frightening days.

It was around two o'clock when the royal party expected to hook up with the Duc de Choiseul and forty officers at an out-of-the-way *poste* at Pont de Somme-Vesle, fourteen miles past Châlons. They had not arrived, and it had become two-thirty and then four-thirty. The party realized their original schedule may have been a bit optimistic. Still, they felt they were alright, as no one seemed to be following them. But when they didn't arrive, due to several horses stumbling and falling along the rugged route, finally breaking a harness that needed to be repaired, Choiseul, still at the *poste* waiting for them, lost his nerve. He assumed the mission had gone wrong or been aborted.

Choiseul, without waiting for the courier Valory, who was to ride ahead and report progress, took his dragoons and headed back in the direction of Montmédy. Goguelat helped to warn those down the line that something had gone wrong. When the royal family finally arrived at the *poste* at Somme-Vesle at six o'clock, they were shocked to find no Choiseul and no dragoons to provide the promised military escort. They had no choice but to continue. At eight o'clock, they had been traveling for eighteen hours. At Sainte-Ménehould, the king was recognized when he learned from the coach window.

The man claiming to recognize the King was one Drouet, and he said he recognized Louis XVI from his distinctive appearance as it appeared on the *assignat*, a paper bill of French currency. While the berlins were allowed to travel on, an hour-and-a-half later, Drouet, his suspicions aroused, along with another man, Guillaume, set off to follow the party. By now, Louis' entourage had reached Clermont. The Comte de Damas, Colonel of the Dragoons, was to await their arrival here with 140 men. But word had reached him that the mission had been aborted, and so he ordered the horses unsaddled and that the men could go to sleep around 9 o'clock. Drouet and Guillaume arrived soon after the party had decided to move on, afraid of delaying any longer. The king and his entourage finally arrived at Varennes-en-Argonne at about eleven o'clock where they looked in vain for the fresh horses that were to await them there.

Louis XVI's face on the assignat.

Meantime, Drouet had arrived and alerted a few people that the king was there and attempting to escape. The king's party, unaware, were knocking on doors. The bodyguards kept looking for horses. Procurator Sauce was put into a delicate position. His was a little town, and how was he to arrest the King of France in the middle of the night? He, therefore, under pretense that there was an irregularity in their passports, persuaded the exhausted party to accept the hospitality of his home. He told them he was sure it could all be cleared up in the morning and they could go on their way.

By morning, crowds were gathering outside the house where the king had slept in an armchair. Damas had arrived with a small army of loyal troops, but the King told him to stand down. There would be no bloodshed. The King exited the house and stood before the crowd, assuring them he was not going to leave France and he would return to Varennes after he was established at Montmédy. The people were not fooled. Montmédy was too close to the border. One person sarcastically called out, 'And what if your foot slipped [over the border]?'

Arrest in the Sauce house in Varennes

The emissaries from the National Assembly arrived at six in the morning, bringing orders for the return of the king and his party to Paris. It was over. There was to be no escape…no new life. What awaited them in Paris would be the utmost cruelty they had yet suffered, and in the end, it would cost them their lives.

## Chapter Sixty-Two
## **"Goodbye, Papa!"**

The events going on in France were not contained in that beleaguered country. The other monarchies of Europe looked with concern upon the developments in France and considered whether they should intervene, either in support of Louis XVI or to take advantage of the chaos there. The key figure was Marie Antoinette's brother, the Holy Roman Emperor Leopold II. He was hoping to avoid war, but he was becoming more and more concerned.

On August 27, 1791, Leopold and Frederick William II of Prussia, in consultation with the émigré's French nobles, issued the *Declaration of Pillnitz*, which declared the interest of the monarchs of Europe in the well-being of Louis and his family, and threatened vague but severe consequences if anything should befall them. Although Leopold saw the *Pillnitz Declaration* as an easy way to appear concerned about the developments in France without committing any soldiers or finances to change them, the revolutionary leaders in Paris viewed it fearfully as a dangerous foreign attempt to undermine France's sovereignty.

In addition to the ideological differences between France and the monarchical powers of Europe, there were continuing disputes over the status of Austrian estates in Alsace, and the concern of members of the National Constituent Assembly about the agitation of émigrés nobles abroad, especially in the Austrian Netherlands and the minor states of Germany.

In the end, the Legislative Assembly, supported by Louis XVI, declared war on Austria first, voting for war on April 20, 1792. The war began with France providing disorganized troops, thanks to the

Revolutionary uprising. The Duke of Brunswick issued a proclamation on July 25$^{th}$, called the *Brunswick Manifesto*, written by Louis's cousin, Prince de Condé, declaring the intent of the Austrians and Prussians to restore the king to his full powers and to treat any person or town who opposed them as rebels to be condemned to death by marital law.

As with everything else going on in Louis' life, it backfired. Instead of strengthening the king's position against the revolutionaries, the *Brunswick Manifesto* had the opposite effect of greatly undermining his already tenuous position. It was taken by many to be the final proof of collusion between the king and foreign powers in a conspiracy against his own country. Combined with the documents he left behind during the royal party's failed escape, it was his death knell.

The anger of the populace boiled over on August 10, 1792, when an armed mob—with the backing of the new municipal government of Paris (the Insurrectional Paris Commune)—marched upon and invaded the Tuileries Palace where the royal family was once more residing after their capture in Varennes. The Swiss Guard was positioned to protect the king and his family as thousands descended on the palace. It was agreed to take refuge at the National Assembly close-by and the small procession of the royal family now filed its way through the western garden door, across a courtyard, to the site of the Assembly. Six ministers accompanied them as well as Swiss Guards and grenadiers from the National Guard.

Deputies from the Assembly met them and formally offered the King asylum. The group, consisting of all the royal family with their attendants were crammed into the reporters' box behind the chair of the President Vergniaud. Throughout that hot day, stuffed into a ten-foot square space with a grating exposed to the sun, they waited. A sparse meal was rounded up and brought to them at 2 in the afternoon.

Things were much worse at the Tuileries. An hour-and-a-half after the family fled to the protection of the National Assembly, the crowd attacked the palace and gunfire rang out. A massacre resulted, many historians laying the blame at Louis XVI's feet for forgetting to give a cease-fire order to the Swiss Guard before he fled. Instead, the bullets flew, and gunfire was returned by the mob. The Tuileries was, in the end, a scene of carnage such as had not been witnessed here before. Bloodied corpses were everywhere, severed limbs littered staircases and courtyards. Some people were thrown from windows, found hiding in the stables, cellar and even the chapel, and were killed. Furnishings were smashed and the invaders wiped their blood-stained hands on the king's royal garments.

Marie Grosholz, who would later be known to the world as the wax sculptor Madame Tussaud, remembered years later the blood and body parts strewn about the palace. Elsewhere in Paris, fleeing parties, whether the Swiss Guards or others, were killed, and gutters filled with thc bodies of the Guards, stripped naked and mutilated. Many innocent people were beaten to death.

The only concession to human decency that day came when a group of *sans-culottes* (a group of the lower-class people) burst into the dauphin's apartments and found the cowering waiting-women of the queen's that had remained behind. The men saw them and yelled, 'We don't kill women! Get up, you trollop, the nation pardons you!' And thus, Pauline de Tourzel, the daughter of the Royal Governess, and others were spared. What they saw as the sun rose over the carnage the next morning must have been horrific.

The Attack of the Tuileries, Swiss Guard Staircase

That evening, the royal family was moved to the Convent of the Feuillants. They were told the Tuileries was unhabitable, which was an understatement. The Queen’s wardrobe and furnishings were also in a shambles and blood and bodies were everywhere. The Convent was small and spartan. The royal group’s first concern was for fresh clothes as they had sweltered in the heat of the cramped space at the Assembly until their clothes were soaked through. Princesse de Lamballe sent a note to the Princesse de Tarante asking for a chemise since she had not changed clothes for two days. The Duchesse de Gramont provided some. Clothes were also found for little Louis Charles. The little boy had been crying, worried what had become of Pauline, the Governess’ daughter who had remained behind. Eventually, Pauline and others escaped the Tuileries with only the clothes on their backs and made it to the Convent where they were joyfully welcomed by the royal family.

Elsewhere, behind closed doors, it was decided that a National Convention would determine the king’s fate. He was to be provisionally suspended from his powers for a start. They now discussed where to house the royal family until a trial could be planned for the king. The Luxembourg Palace was suggested, the former residence of the Comte de Provence. The Hôtel de Noailles was proffered by the National Assembly, but it too was negated on the grounds that it was not safe enough. Finally, the newly formed revolutionary Paris Commune settled on the Temple: an ancient fortress in Paris used as a prison, in the Marais district.

The place settled; it was now time to discuss how many attendants would be allowed to join them at the prison. In the end, the party consisted of the five royals, the Princesse de Lamballe, the Tourzels (Governess and her daughter), Mesdames Thibault, Saint Brice and Navarre, the valets Chamilly and Hué. They departed for the Temple on the evening of Monday August 13, 1792. The journey took two-and-a-half hours due to the heavy-laden carriages and having only two horses each. Along the route, they passed the statue of Louis XIV, seated upon his stallion. It had been pulled to the ground and smashed. How symbolic for the king who had created Versailles, and which was itself, in shambles.

A satisfied crowd of angry Parisians watched the royal party head for the prison. A member of the mob created a sign and placed it upon the broken Tuileries door: ‘House to Let.’

**The Trial of Louis XVI**

Things escalated quickly once the royal family was imprisoned in the Temple. On September 21, the National Assembly declared France to be a republic, and abolished the monarchy. Louis was stripped of all his titles and honors, and from this date was known as *Citoyen Louis Capet*, declaring him a citizen and not a sovereign. Capet was the surname of the French royal dynasty.

The Girondins were partial to keeping the deposed king under arrest, both as a hostage and a guarantee for the future. Members of the Paris Commune and the most radical deputies, who would soon form the group known as the Mountain, argued for Louis's immediate execution. The legal background of many of the deputies made it difficult for a great number of them to accept an execution without the due process of law, and it was voted that the deposed monarch be tried before the National Convention; the organ that housed the representatives of the sovereign people. In many ways, the former king's trial represented the trial of the monarchy by the revolution. It was seen as if with the death of one came the life of another.

Portrait of Louis XVI at the Tower

At the Temple, the family had been greeted with chants of ‘Long live the nation!’ Even more coldly came the sing-song words of the guards: ‘Madame goes up into her Tower, When will she come down again?’ The word “Tower” referred to one of the many sections of the Temple. It was sixty-feet-high, a foreboding mediaeval edifice that once belonged to the old monastery of the Templar Order. It was divided into a Great Tower and a Small Tower. Not far from the Bastille, it resided in an ancient district unfamiliar to many Parisians. The family was put into the Small Tower as the Great Tower was ‘spruced up’ a little and made secure. Madame Elizabeth (the King’s sister), Pauline de Tourzel, and the waiting-woman Madame Navarre slept in the kitchen.

Security was beefed up with twenty guards stationed at the gate and four commissioners always keeping an eye on the new prisoners. Marie Therese was dismayed at the way her father was treated. Gone were his titles and respect. All who spoke to him called him ‘Monsieur’, or even, “Louis.” Simple deliveries such as books, linens and clothes were searched. The Small Tower was set up to give Louis a bedroom on the third floor and a little study in the turret. Marie and the others slept on the second floor below him. The first floor housed a dining area, an antechamber, and surprisingly, a book-lined turret. The deposed king took to reading a book a day, while Marie, having been allowed the use of her needles and yarn from the Tuileries, took up her tapestry work. Their little dog Mignon was even brought over and allowed to use the gardens.

Clothing received an allotment of 25,000 *livres*, which also went toward sheets, stockings, laundry and hats. Sailor suits were ordered for little Louis Charles and Louis XVI was allowed to have his cobbler, Giot, create a limited supply of shoes. Food was plentiful, as was drink, and Louis took to it, although only having a small aperitif in the evening. A surreal routine settled in with the former king giving Louis Charles his lessons, Marie embroidering tapestries, and spending time with Marie Therese. The small family took comfort in each other’s company and with their small entourage.

That was soon to change. News came from the Paris Commune that they were removing the Princesse Lamballe, the Marquise de Tourzel with Pauline, Chamilly, Hué (the King’s attendants) and the waiting-women, for interrogation. The Commune had set up a special tribunal to try royalists for crimes allegedly committed during the overthrow of the monarchy. Marie begged to have Lamballe stay with them, saying she was part of the family. But they took her away.

The group was greatly diminished. Without the Governess, Louis Charles was moved into his mother's room. Hanet Cléry, who had attended the king at the Tuileries and escaped death by jumping from a window, was now allowed into the prison to act as barber to the king and hairdresser to the ladies. As he cut and trussed hair, he whispered important information from the outside. One such report was that La Fayette had fled France. They also learned that Durosoy, the publisher of the royalist paper, the *Gazette de Paris*, had been executed by a new machine created to replace the executioner's sword: the guillotine.

It was on September 2nd, that the monotonous routine of the royal family was interrupted by the sound of a loud boom of a cannon. Immediately thinking it signaled the end of the king, Marie cried out, 'Save my husband!' while Madame Elizabeth sobbed, 'Have pity on my brother!' It was not for the family in the Small Tower however that the cannon was fired. An assault upon the inhabitants of the La Force prison, where the Marquise de Tourzel and her daughter were being kept, along with the Princesse Lamballe (who had always been touted as Marie Antoinette's lesbian lover) were drug out from the safety of the stone walls. Similar assaults were happening at other Paris prisons and at Versailles and Rheims. The body count was never tallied as the inmates were massacred. It was rumored the death count was around 1,300. Children as young as eight died, along with beggars and prostitutes.

The gory assaults went on throughout the night, while inconceivably, many Parisians went about their lives with indifference, attending the theater and dining at restaurants. At 10 o'clock that night, Commissioner Manuel reassured the queen that the Princesse de Lamballe had survived. Sadly, he was wrong. It was the Governess Marquise de Tourzel who was acquitted before the tribunal and Pauline was spirited away by a mysterious Englishman.

Lamballe's fate was not the same. Before the tribunal she refused to denounce the king and queen, saying: 'I have nothing to reply, dying a little earlier or a little later is a matter of indifference to me.

I am prepared to make the sacrifice of my life.' She was told to 'exit for the Abbaye prison' which was a code for execution. Once she was outside and in the courtyard of La Force, it was reported 'several blows of a hammer on the head laid her low and then they fell on her.' According to the reports, the Princesse was violated, her breasts and private parts cut off, her heart was removed and placed upon a pike. Her head was then cut off and placed on a pike, where it was carried throughout Paris, until the cry came to take it to the Temple Tower and make the queen lean from her prison window to bestow a kiss on her dead lover's lips.

Death of the Princesse de Lamballe

The king and queen were upstairs, playing backgammon, when the head appeared before the dining room window on the first floor. Cléry and Madame Tison saw it, she giving out a loud cry. Upstairs, the municipal officers looked from the window to see what all the laughter was outside and saw the head. Mercifully, they closed the shutters to the room. When Louis asked what was going on, he was told, 'If you must know, Monsieur, they are trying to show you the head of Madame de Lamballe.' Marie fainted. Undaunted, the murderers began to scale rubble in order to set the pike with the head up higher for the queen to see it and kiss it.

The Commissioner Daujon stopped the crowd from entering the Temple, where they wanted to show the royal family not only Lamballe's head, but her heart and bloodied chamise carried on other pikes. He turned them away but allowed them to march around the Tower all day. That night, Marie Therese went to sleep to the sound of her mother weeping.

As the tumultuous and bloody days continued, two events led up to the trial of Louis XVI. First, as the war with Austria and Prussia continued, after the Battle of Valmy on September 22, 1792, General Dumouriez negotiated with the Prussians who evacuated France. Louis could no longer be considered hostage or as leverage in negotiations with the invading forces. He had been stripped of his title, and therefore, his worth. Second, in November 1792, the *armoire de fer* (iron chest) incident took place at the Tuileries Palace, when the existence of the hidden safe in the king's bedroom containing compromising documents and correspondence, was revealed by François Gamain, the Versailles locksmith who had installed it.

Gaiman went to Paris on November 20 and told Jean-Marie Roland, Girondinist Minister of the Interior, who ordered it opened. The resulting scandal served to discredit the king. Following those two events, the Girondins could no longer keep the king from trial.

On December 11th, the Louis XVI was taken from the Temple to a place where he would stand before the convention and hear his indictment: an accusation of high treason and crimes against the State. On December 26th, Louis' counsel, Raymond Desèze, delivered the deposed king's response to the charges, with the assistance of François Tronchet and Malesherbes. Louis had already told his lawyers he knew he would be found guilty and be killed, but to prepare an act as though they could win.

The convention would be voting on three questions: first, is Louis guilty; second, whatever the decision, should there be an appeal to the people; and third, if found guilty, what punishment should Louis suffer? On January 15, 1793, the convention, composed of 721 deputies, voted on the verdict. 693 voted guilty, none for acquittal, with 23 abstaining. The next day, a rollcall was carried out to decide his fate. 288 of the deputies voted against death, advocating exile or life in prison. 72 voted for the death penalty but allowing for several delaying conditions and reservations. 361 voted for the former king's immediate execution. Louis was condemned to death by one vote.

Malesherbes wanted to break the news to Louis and bitterly lamented the verdict, but Louis told him he would see him again in a happier life and he would regret leaving a friend like Malesherbes had been. The last thing the king said to him was that he needed to control his tears because all eyes would be on him.

The night of January 20$^{th}$, after the death penalty had been passed and the king was told he would be put to death the following morning by guillotine, Marie Antoinette learned of his fate. It was the criers beneath her window who told her of the trial's outcome. Louis had asked for three days in which to prepare himself spiritually, but he was denied. At first, Louis was denied seeing his family, but the Convention finally relented and let them downstairs to see him at the Tower. The royal family had been moved up to the Great Tower earlier when its preparations had been completed.

Louis XVI's last evening with his family

They had not seen Louis for six weeks as he went about the trial and imprisonment. Marie Therese said she found her father 'much changed.' The king wept, not for himself, but the thought of being parted from his family. He urged Louis Charles to forgive the people who were about to bring about his death, and then he gave his weeping children his final blessing. Marie begged him to spend his final night with them, but Louis refused, saying he had much to do to prepare for death and he needed peace. It was more likely he wanted to spare them the long hours of pain at seeing him devastated and weeping.

Marie pressed herself against him as he held Louis Charles. The little boy clutched both their hands, kissing them and crying. Louis' sister, Elizabeth clung to him and cried while Marie Therese wailed in agony. Louis finally rose and promised his family he would see them again in the morning, hoping it would give them a final night's rest. He said, 'I am not saying goodbye. Be sure that I shall see you again at eight o'clock tomorrow morning.'

'Why not seven o'clock?' asked Marie.

'Seven o'clock then…'

'Do you promise?' cried the Queen.

'I promise.' He tore himself away from his bereft family and went into his bedroom. He could hear his family wailing through the walls.

The next morning at six o'clock, the queen's door opened, but it was not her husband who stood there. It was a man needing to fetch a prayer book. The gates to the Temple were locked, and the world outside seemed oddly hushed. Just before 10:30 in the morning, the sound of drumming wafted over on a breeze, followed by loud 'shouts of joy' from the howling spectators. It was this herald that informed Louis XVI's family that he was dead. Louis had not been able to keep his promise to his wife and family to see them one last time. He preferred to spare them that last dagger to their hearts.

Marie was speechless as the cheering continued. It was Elizabeth who screamed out: 'The monsters! They are satisfied now!'

On Monday, January 21, 1793, Louis XVI, at age 38, was beheaded by guillotine on the *Place de la Révolution*. As he mounted the scaffold, he appeared dignified and reserved. He delivered a short speech in which he pardoned "…those who are the cause of my death…" He then declared himself innocent of the crimes of which he was accused, praying that his blood would not fall back on France. As the king proceeded to say more, he was cut off by a drum roll ordered by Antoine-Joseph Santerre, a general in the National Guard. Louis was then placed on the guillotine platform, his hands tied behind his back, rolled to the front of the device where a harness was lowered to hold his head still, and the blade dropped. The executioner testified that the former king had bravely met his fate, despite reports that the blade had not cleanly cut through his neck the first time. Many in the crowd rushed forward to dip their handkerchiefs in his blood. Louis' body was taken by cart to the nearby Madeleine cemetery where he was buried in a mass grave. Afterwards, his body, with his head placed between his feet, was buried in an unmarked grave, with quicklime spread over it.

Louis XVI's Execution at the Place de la Revolution

Versailles' last King to sit upon the throne was dead. Dust would gather on his precious locks in his metal craft room where a forge stood silent. If the sound of billiard balls echoed within the Billiard Room, it was a ghostly hand holding the stick. Could the phantom echo of horse hooves sound in the eerie quiet of Louis' favorite hunting grounds? Or…on a moonlit night, when the gold gilding of the palace gates sparkled, could one look up and see the portly king scampering over the rooftops of Versailles? It would not be the first, or the last ghost story told here.

## Chapter Sixty-Three
## **A Sad Ending**

'Unfortunate Princess! My marriage promised her a throne; now, what prospect does it offer her?' These words were written by Louis XVI on the eve of his execution. It is perhaps fortunate he did not live to see what was to befall his "Princess" and his children.

At the moment of the King's death, Marie Antoinette was renamed the 'The Widow Capet.' She asked to see Louis' barber and confidant in hopes the king had left some message for her to assuage her immense grief. Cléry was denied seeing the queen. In due time, after he had left the Tower, the items left by the king were given to the family by a kind heart named Adrian Toulan. He arrived with more than messages from the late king; he came bearing Louis's gold wedding band, engraved *M.A.A.A. 19 April 1770* (the initials were for Marie Antoinette Archduchess of Austria), and the date marked the proxy wedding in Vienna. Toulon relayed the message that Louis said he had only parted with it with his life. A small parcel containing locks of the family's hair, 'so precious to him' was handed to the grieving widow.

Marie asked for mourning clothes in which to show respect to her late husband. Mademoiselle Pion was allowed to come to the prison to begin fitting for a black taffeta cloak, fichu, skirt and gloves, all to be made up in the 'simplest possible way.' Black mourning dresses were also created for the other ladies while a municipal officer watched at all times. Goret, one of the municipal officers was saddened by the queen's state. She was pale and barely ate. Marie refused to go outside to take the air as it would lead her past the king's door. The guard finally arranged a place in the circular gallery of the Tower for her to sit before a window and get some sunshine and fresh air.

Marie Therese said of her mother: 'She no longer had any hope left in her heart or distinguished between life and death; sometimes she looked at us with a kind of compassion which was quite frightening.' The young girl cut her foot on January 25$^{th}$, 1793, and said she was glad of it because it caused her mother to care for her.

As for Louis Charles, he was only celebrated as Louis XVII, 'the little King' abroad in royal circles. To announce his new title in France would have been extremely dangerous. Yet, heir to the throne he remained, and was duly recognized as the new King of France throughout Europe. The Comte de Provence, the late king's brother, was not as shy about announcing his new title. It was one he had been thirsty for since his 7-year-old nephew was born. He proclaimed himself as regent by 'right of birth.' It was not a popular move, especially with the Austrians, who believed it was Louis Charles's mother, Marie Antoinette, who had superiority, despite her imprisonment.

As the days passed since Louis XVI's execution, things began to calm down. The blood thirst of the mobs had been slated. The guards at the Temple did not supervise the Princesses every conversation as before, and the prisoners were treated with more gentility. The municipal officers believed the royal party would probably be traded to Austria in exchange for prominent French captives.

Little Louis Charles sang a song one evening as his sister accompanied him on the harpsicord. It brought tears to the guards' eyes.

> "Everything is fled from me on earth
> But I am still at my mother's side."

Back in Austria, Count Mercy played with asking the French for the return of the queen and her family which bore a precedence that a foreign princess could be reclaimed by her country. In the end, he waffled, stating that 'we should remain passive in this horrible crisis,' for fear of making things worse.

Things did worsen as the war raged on and France found itself on the losing end. Austria was once again the enemy. And the 'Queen in the Tower' represented that hated country. As for the grieving widow of Louis XVI, her health continued to decline. She had always had trouble with her menstrual cycles, which had caused so much concern when she was trying to conceive oh so long ago. It was feared she might have tuberculosis as she repeatedly coughed and ran intermittent fevers. A doctor was called to look at Marie Therese who had begun her cycle at the age of fifteen, and he too voiced concern over the queen's haggardness and ill health.

Axel Von Fersen continued to try for her freedom as he reached out to her powerful relatives in Austria. Sadly, even her brother Leopold II seemed apathetic about her plight. It was Fersen who felt near panic that she would be executed as tensions over the war rose. Rumors of a trial for the queen circulated, to prove her involvement in the "treason" for which her husband had been accused. Exiling Marie and her family had also been discussed—a surely welcome resolve.

A new Revolutionary Tribunal had been set up on March 10 which would oversee the queen's trial. On April 6, a new Committee of Public Safety was formed. The following day, Philippe Égalité (a cousin of Louis XVI's who had advocated for the Revolution and the king's death), and his third son were arrested. Other French aristocrats, the Prince de Conti, Philippe's sister, and Orleans's second son, Montpensier, were arrested and sent to prison in Marseilles. Hatred for all things Bourbon or Orleans was at a fever pitch.

Efforts to exchange Marie Antoinette for French prisoners fell through. Security at the prison was heightened. Bars were placed on the windows and those were often shuttered. Fear was palpable among the small group of inmates. In June, the Pope announced the late King of France a martyr who had been executed solely for his religion: 'O triumphal day for Louis!...We are sure he has exchanged the fragile royal crown and the ephemeral lilies for an eternal crown decorated with the immoral lilies of the angels.'

## The Final Dagger

On the evening of July 3rd, without warning, officers arrived at the Tower to remove Marie Antoinette's son. They stated there had been rumors of abducting the new little king. He was to be taken to 'the most-secure apartment of the Tower.' Louis Charles threw himself into his mother's arms, wailing. The weakened queen aroused herself from her apathy and refused to let him go, even when the guards threatened to kill her. It was only when they announced they would kill her daughter, that the weeping mother released him.

The little boy had spent nearly half his life in prison. He was only eight-and-a-half years old. Marie and the others could hear him sobbing for weeks from his room elsewhere in the Tower. It was the worst pain a mother could endure. Knowing the guards let the child out into the garden for daily exercise, Marie found a window where, if she craned her neck, she could get a glimpse of him. She would often stay there all day in hopes of seeing him.

Louis Charles was put into the care to a cobbler named Simon who guarded him at the Temple and was told to toughen the little boy up. The new "Little King" was beaten when he cried, given wine to make him tipsy, and was taught the obscene language of the guards. After a time, he adopted their ways and their language, to please them. They were all he had now. It was their wish to make him forget who he was and dilute any ties he had to his royal family.

That tie with his mother would become even more fragile when Marie Antoinette was removed from the Temple and taken to a prison known at the Conciergerie. The Austrians and their allies were winning the war and getting closer to the capital city. Whether from fear that they would rescue the queen, or from a distorted view that they appeared weak for having not dealt with her yet, the French decided to up their game where she was concerned.

Her cell was the stuff nightmares are made of. It was damp and dark with a brick floor, a table and prison chairs. A cot with two mattresses were brought in, along with a bucket. Marie was given some semblance of respect by the jailer's wife, Madame Richard, and her maid Rosalie Lamorlié. Where others at the prison had refused to show the queen recognition—she was merely Prisoner 280—these two ladies were cognizant of who she was and her plight. The two women provided Marie with a stool so that she could hang the watch given her from Marie Therese on a nail.

Early in the morning, while still dark, the queen began to undress. Her small bundle contained clothes and essentials, including smelling salts. She declined Rosalie's offer to help her undress, stating she must take care of herself now.

Dressing and undressing would become a humiliating part of the queen's day. The gendarmes had put up a curtain only four feet high for Marie's privacy. They were stationed on the other side of it and frequently peered over at the hapless lady as she tried to use the bucket and dress in privacy. It was a humiliating experience. She grew accustomed to sitting in a chair with her back to them, facing a wall.

Marie Antoinette's cell as replicated at the Conciergerie today.

A certain Mademoiselle Fouché smuggled in a non-juror priest named Abbé Magnin, who had friends among the grenadiers. He would give the queen solace and listen to her confessions. There may have been another reason for Magnin to be there as plots to rescue the queen continued. The so-called *Carnation Plot* of late August and early September was one such attempt.

The plot took its name from a carnation that a certain Alexandre Rougeville dropped at the queen's feet while in her cell. He was there to spirit Marie away in a coach to the chateau of Madame de Jarjayes and then to Germany. Marie recognized him as a Knight of the Order of Saint Louis and became afraid of his intent there. She could not risk any appearance of an escape plan. The queen picked up the flower and found a small note hidden inside its petals. It was reported by Hué, the late king's valet that she pricked out the word, 'No' into the petals with one of her embroidery needles. Gilbert, one of the gendarmes who watched the queen regularly, gave the game away. It was the worst thing that could have happened to her.

The sad irony of this plot, and others like it, by the ordinary citizens within the queen's realm, was that it was the 'little people' who tried to save Marie's life, while the rulers of her home country and others, with their money and powerful armies, sat by and did nothing. Count Fersen, who would never give up trying to negotiate Marie's release, and the Comte de La Marck were driven to a frenzy over the queen's relatives' lack of action on her behalf.

To pour money into the severely depleted revolutionary government, contents of Versailles and the Petit Trianon were auctioned off. Everything from Louis XVI's desks and personal items to the furnishings of the "Widow Capet's" Petit Trianon went on the auction block, bringing in far less than the original price tag. The emptying of the great Palace of Versailles and the queen's beloved Petit Trianon left the royal residences feeling lost in time, the past glory only a memory. As Marie Antoinette's clocks left her Trianon, it was a symbolic ending.

Marie Antoinette was tried by the Revolutionary Tribunal on October 14, 1793. Some historians believe the outcome of the trial had been decided in advance by the Committee of Public Safety around the time of the discovery of the *Carnation Plot*. She and her lawyers were given less than one day to prepare her defense. Among the accusations, many previously published in *libelles*, were: orchestrating orgies at Versailles, sending millions of *livres* of treasury money to Austria, planning the massacre of the *gardes francaises* (National Guards) in 1792, and declaring her son to be the new king of France.

The accusation that all but sent the Queen's to her knees was that her son, little Louis Charles, had made allegations that she had committed incest with him. It was a surety that the radical Jacques Hebert, who was now in control of the boy, had pressured him into doing it. Louis Charles, eager to please his 'new family' went along, perhaps not even understanding what incest was or how damning it would be to his mother. The boy, bolstered by the praise from his guards, also included his sister Marie Therese as one who had 'touched him' during their play. She was incensed and both she and

Madame Elisabeth begged him to retract his statements, but he refused. The breach between himself and his sister and aunt were never healed.

Marie Antoinette reacted as the accusation was made with shock and immediately appealed to the mothers in the room at the trial. The women's sympathetic response would be the only kindness shown her during the allegations against her.

Early on October 16, 1793, Marie Antoinette was declared guilty of the three main charges against her: depletion of the national treasury; conspiracy against the internal and external security of the State; and high treason, because of her intelligence activities in the interest of the enemy; the later charge alone was enough to condemn her to death. At worst, she and her lawyers had expected life imprisonment.

In the queen's final hours, she composed a letter to her sister-in-law, the late king's sister, Elisabeth, affirming her clear conscience, her Catholic faith, and her love and concern for her children. The letter did not reach Elisabeth. Her will was part of the collection of papers Robespierre found under his bed and were published by Edme-Bonaventure Courtois. Marie Antoinette's final words to her daughter were to respect her Aunt Elisabeth and treat her as her second mother.

Preparing for her execution, Marie had to change clothes in front of the guards. This middle-aged, haggard woman was not spared this final indecency. She put on a plain white dress, white being the color worn by widowed queens of France. Her hair was shorn, her hands bound painfully behind her back, and she was put on a rope leash like a common animal. Unlike her husband, who had been taken to his execution in a carriage, she had to sit in the back of an open cart, on full display, during the hour ride to the same guillotine that had beheaded her husband at the *Place de la Revolution*. She maintained her composure, despite the jeers of the crowd that lined the cart's transport via the rue Saint-Honoré. A constitutional priest, not one of the Catholic cloth, sat beside her along the way to hear her confession. She ignored him.

The Queen of France, who had once gambled and partied into the wee hours at the Salons of Paris, and attended its Opera Houses and Theaters, was guillotined at 12:15 p.m. on October 16, 1793. Her last words were to apologize to the executioner for stepping on his toe. Her head was held up to the ecstatic crowd who ran forward to dip their handkerchiefs into her blood. Marie Tussaud, who would become famous for her Wax Museums, was employed to make a death mask of Marie's head. Her body was then thrown into an unmarked grave in the Madeleine cemetery located close by the rue d'Anjou. Because the cemetery had reached capacity, it was closed the following year, on March 25, 1794.

Marie Antoinette riding to her execution.

Both Marie Antoinette's and Louis XVI's bodies were exhumed on January 18, 1815, during the Bourbon Restoration, when the

Comte de Provence ascended the newly reestablished throne as Louis XVIII, King of France and Navarre. Christian burial of the royal remains took place three days later January 21 in the necropolis of French kings at the Basilica of St. Denis.

## The Remains of the Day

The royal children left behind by Marie Antoinette did not fare well. Louis Charles was said to have been kept in a dark room for the rest of his young life. The small area was barricaded, and food was passed to him through bars. He was forced to live among his own filth. According to reports, no one entered the 'Little King's' room for six months. It was only after a new attendant came, Jean Jacques Christophe Laurent, along with a man named Gomin, that Louis was taken out for fresh air and walks on the roof of the Tower. On March 31, 1795, Etienne Lasne replaced Laurent and declared the boy to be seriously ill.

Louis Charles, the boy who would never sit on the throne of France, died on June 8, 1795. His death was put down to tuberculosis (scrofulous). During the autopsy, the physician Dr. Pelletan was shocked to see the countless scars which covered the boy's body, evidently the result of physical mistreatment which the child had suffered while imprisoned in the Temple. He was buried on June 10 in the Sainte Marguerite cemetery without a stone to mark the spot.

On May 11, 1795, Robespierre visited Marie Therese where she remained in the Tower. She was never told what happened to her family. She knew only that her father was dead. The following words were scratched on the wall of her room at the Tower:

"Marie-Therese Charlotte is the most unhappy person in the world. She can obtain no word of her mother; not to be reunited to her, though she has asked it a thousand times! Live my good mother! whom I love well, but of whom I hear no tidings. O my father! watch over me from Heaven above. O my God! forgive those who have made my parents suffer."

Madam Royale finally was told of the deaths of her mother and brother in late August 1795. Reeling with grief and filling the cell of her Tower apartment with great sobs, she could not have seen that the future would be outside these cold walls. She was released on December 18, 1795 and was allowed to leave France. She was 17 years old. She was exchanged for prominent French prisoners and taken to Vienna, the capital of her cousin, the Holy Roman Emperor Francis II, and her mother's birthplace. She later left Vienna and moved to Mitau, Courland (now Latvia) where her father's eldest surviving brother, the comte de Provence, lived as a guest of Tsar Paul I of Russia. Provence had proclaimed himself King of France and Navarre after the passing of the 'Little King' Louis Charles.

Provence had not children of his own and he wished his niece to marry her cousin, Louis-Antoine, duc d'Angouleme, son of his brother, the come d'Artois. Marie Therese agreed. The wedding took place on June 10, 1799. They later moved to Great Britain where the newlyweds settled at Hartwell House, Buckinghamshire. Marie Therese's long years of exile from France ended with the abdication of Napoleon I in 1814. He used the Grand Trianon as his headquarters during his reign, foregoing the vast empty hallways of Versailles. The first Bourbon Restoration followed at that time and Louis XVIII stepped upon the throne of France, twenty-one years after the death of his brother Louis XVI.

Marie Therese returned to France but found it emotionally draining. She visited where her brother had died and wept at the graves of her parents. While in France, Napoleon tried to regain his rule during a period called the Hundred Days. Provence fled France. Marie stayed on with her husband. After Napoleon was defeated at Waterloo on June 18, 1815, the House of Bourbon was restored for a second time, and Louis XVIII (Provence) returned to France. He died however on September 16, 1824, and was succeeded by his younger brother Artois, who became known as Charles X.

Marie Therese's husband was now heir to the throne, and she was addressed as Madame la Dauphine. Through a series of abdications due to a new Revolution of 1830, the French crown finally landed on the head Louis-Philipe, duc d'Orleans. On August 4$^{th}$ of that year, Marie left for a new exile with her uncle, her husband, her young nephew, his mother, and his sister Louise Marie Therese d'Artois. They sailed for Britain on August 16$^{th}$.

Marie Therese's husband died in 1844 and was buried next to his father. She passed away on October 19, 1851, three days after the fifty-eighth anniversary of the execution of her mother. She died from pneumonia and was buried next to her uncle/father-in-law, Charles X, and her husband Louis XIX, in the crypt of the Franciscan monastery church of Castagnavizza in Görz, then in Austria, now in the city of Nova Gorica. She had remained a devout Roman Catholic. Marie's tombstone is marked "Queen Dowager of France" due to her husband's twenty-minute rule as King Louis XIX of France.

## The End of Versailles as a Royal Residence

Under Napoleon's leadership, Versailles, which had survived the Revolution's onslaught, he began to return the gardens and fountains to their past beauty. He had hopes of one day living in the grand palace, surrounded by his new court. He, and his wife Josephine, turned the Grand Trianon into a residence worthy of an Emperor. Napoleon's first wife, Josephine, was unable to produce a child and her marriage to Napoleon I was dissolved. She died on May 29, 1814. The emperor's second wife, Marie Louise married the new ruler of France on March 11, 1810. Marie produced a son, much to the emperor's delight, and outlived both her husband and her son. She died on December 17, 1847, at the age of 56. Napoleon I died May 5, 1821.

Napoleon I and Josephine

Shortly after becoming King in 1830, Louis Philippe I decided to transform the Palace of Versailles into a museum devoted to "All the Glories of France," with paintings and sculptures depicting famous French victories and heroes. Most of the apartments of the palace were demolished in the main building, leaving only the king and queen's apartments intact. Galleries were installed to commemorate Napoleon, battles, and Louis Philippe's own coming to power in the French Revolution of 1830. The overthrow of Louis Phillippe in 1848 put an end to the rest of his grand plans, but the Gallery of the Battles is still as it was.

The Gallery of Battles in the South Wing at Versailles

Louis XVI was the last King of France to sit on the throne and welcome guests and dignitaries to the grand Palace of Versailles. He and his Queen Marie Antoinette were the last monarchs to sleep in the royal bedchambers. The final baby born within the Sun King's walls was the baby Sophie who died in infancy, leaving Marie Antoinette and Louis XVI, heartbroken as her little casket was carried away across the Marble Court. So many intrigues, births, deaths, and scandals had been played out inside the walls of this Pleasure Palace. And many say, the ghosts of the past walk there still.

# Epilogue

The saga of the Sun King's palace will never completely play out on the pages of historical offerings, nor splashed across the screens of today's many media outlets. We are truly indebted to those scribes of Versailles who were eyewitnesses to all the drama and glory. Their quills raced across paper or parchment at maddening speeds to capture dialogues and intrigues, death, births, marriages, and murders. Architectural historians are unveiling Versailles' hidden secrets even today. For the voyeur who wants only to get a first-hand look at the opulent hallways and salons, it awaits with its gilded gates open. It is truly a treasure and a gift to walk there.

And what of one of the many secrets that still tantalizes today? Did Marie Antoinette and the Swedish Count, Axel von Fersen have a romantic affair? Many believe so. Historians believe that Fersen and Marie consummated their long friendship on one fateful evening in February of 1792 when the Count spend a solitary night at the Tuileries. He reportedly had a bedroom above hers. Their letters to each other over the course of many years are legion. They gave pet names to each other to disguise their writings should they be discovered in that ever-present secret service of Versailles' underbelly.

Marie Antoinette wrote several letters to Fersen using invisible (white) ink. Starting in July of 1791, the two began to employ an elaborate, encrypted code. They used a polyalphabetic system that, at times, proved taxing for Marie. In a letter to Fersen dated November 2, 1791 (her birthday), she writes, "Farewell, I am getting tired of ciphering; this is not my usual occupation, and I am always afraid of making mistakes."

In an encrypted letter to Fersen while Marie Antoinette was imprisoned on June 28, 1791, we see a woman who still holds out hope and concern for her dear friend, Fersen. This is the translation of the secret letter:

"I am alive here my beloved, for the reason to adore you. Oh, how anxious I have been for you, and how sorry I am about all you must have suffered in having no news from us. May heaven grant that this letter reaches you. Do not write to me, this would compromise all of us and above all do not return under any circumstances. It is known that it was you who helped us to get away from here [escape to Varennes] and all would be lost if you should show yourself. We are guarded day and night. I do not care. You are not here. Do not be troubled on my account, nothing will happen to me. The National Assembly will show leniency. Farewell the most loved of men. Be quiet if you can. Take care of yourself for myself. I cannot write any more but nothing in the world could stop me from adoring you until death."

From a documented report of a haunting within the Petit Trianon grounds in 1901, it appears that Marie Antoinette's adoration lives beyond the grave. In this eerie excursion that many believe to be an authentic time warp or some paranormal intrusion on a memory Marie Antoinette sent forth from another time and space, we see her love for her precious Petit Trianon—a romantic hideaway she often shared with Axel von Fersen and her circle of friends.

The ghosts of Versailles still wander through the lush gardens and sumptuous rooms of an era never to be duplicated. Come along and see for yourself.

# The Haunting

## The Strange "Adventure" of Charlotte Moberly and Eleanor Jourdain: Ghosts of the Petit Trianon

Charlotte Moberly & Frances Lamont

On August 10, 1901, two mature women from the world of academia were visiting Versailles as tourists from England. These were well-educated, no-nonsense scholars taking in the sights of Paris on a short vacation. Charlotte Moberly was the principal of an Oxford Women's College residence hall in the UK. Eleanor Jourdain was to become her vice-principal. Moberly's father was also of the academic field, acting as headmaster at the Winchester School. He later became the Bishop of Salisbury; something of which Ms. Moberly was immensely proud. Jourdain's father was a vicar of the Church of England. These were two women who had no interest in the realm of ghosts and who had to come to grips gradually with what happened to them on that hot, sultry August day at Versailles.

Let's look at the preface to the book *An Adventure* which was published by the two women under the pseudonyms Elizabeth Morrison (Moberly) and Frances Lamont (Jourdain), in 1910:

'It is a great venture to speak openly of a personal experience, and we only do so for the following reasons. First, we prefer that our story, which is known in part to some, should be wholly known as told by ourselves. Secondly, we have collected so much evidence on the subject, that it is possible now to consider it as a whole. Thirdly, conditions are changing at Versailles, and in a short time facts which were unknown, and circumstances which were unusual, may soon become commonplace, and will lose their force as evidence that some curious psychological conditions much have been present, either in ourselves, or in the place.

'It is not our business to explain or to understand—nor do we pretend to understand—what happened to put us into communication with so many true facts, which, nine years ago, no one could have told us of in their entirety. But, in order that others may be able to judge fairly of all the circumstances, we have tried to record exactly what happened as simply and fully as possible.'

Elizabeth Morrison
Frances Lamont

The strange occurrences began with Ms. Moberly's visit to Ms. Jourdain's flat in Paris where Jourdain was working as a tutor. The visit was for the two women to become better acquainted before the school term began. It was decided a little sightseeing was in order as Paris was awaiting them just outside the window shutters. They made their way to Versailles and toured the main palace. The day was hot, and their thick Victorian dresses felt like weights. As they descended the 100 steps, they investigated the welcoming green foliage of the Trianon area and struck out in that direction.

'Looking at Baedeker's map," Ms. Morrison [Moberly] wrote in their publication entitled *An Adventure,* "we saw the sort of direction and that there were two Trianons and set off. By not asking the way, we went an unnecessarily long way round,--by the great flight of steps from the fountains and down the central avenue as far as the head of the long pond. The weather had been very hot all the week, but on this day the sky was a little overcast and the sun shaded. There was a lively wind blowing, the woods were looking their best, and we both felt particularly vigorous. It was a most enjoyable walk.

'After reaching the beginning of the long water [Grand Canal?] we struck away to the right down a woodland glade until we came obliquely to the other water close to the building, which we rightly concluded to be the Grand Trianon. We passed it on our left hand and came up a broad green drive perfectly deserted. If we had followed it, we should have come immediately to the Petit Trianon, but not knowing its position, we crossed the drive and went up a lane in front of us. I was surprised that Miss Lamont did not ask the way from a woman who was shaking a white cloth out of the window of the building at the corner of the lane, but followed, supposing that she knew where she was going to **[Cottage, Woman and Girl].**

'Talking about England and mutual acquaintances there, we went up the lane, and then made a sharp turn to the right past some buildings. We looked in at an open doorway and saw the end of a carved staircase, but as no one was about we did not like to go in. There were three paths in front of us, and as we saw two men a little ahead on the center one, we followed it, and asked them the way. Afterwards, we spoke of them as gardeners, because we remembered a wheelbarrow of some kind close by and the look of a pointed spade, but they were very dignified officials, dressed in long greyish-green coats with small three-cornered hats. They directed us straight on **[Two Laborers with a Cart].**

We walked briskly forward, talking as before, but from the moment we left the lane an extraordinary depression had come over me, despite every effort to shake it off, it steadily deepened. There seemed to be absolutely no reason for it; I was not at all tired and was becoming more interested in my surroundings. I was anxious that my companion should not discover the sudden gloom upon my spirits, which became quite overpowering on reaching the point where the path ended, being crossed by another, right and left.

'In front of us was a wood, within which, and overshadowed by trees, was a light garden kiosk, circular, and like a small bandstand, by which a man was sitting. There was no green sward, but the ground was covered with rough grass and dead leaves as in a wood. The place was so shut in that we could not see beyond it. Everything suddenly looked unnatural, therefore unpleasant; even the trees behind the building seemed to have become flat and lifeless, like a wood worked in tapestry. There were no effects of light and shade, and no wind stirred the trees. It was all intensely still.

'The man sitting next to the kiosk (who had on a cloak and a large shady hat) turned to look at us **[Man and Kiosk].** That was the culmination of my peculiar sensations, and I felt a moment of genuine alarm. The man's face was most repulsive—its expression odious. His complexion was very dark and rough. I said to Miss Lamont, "Which is our way?" but thought "nothing will induce me to go to the left."

'It was a great relief at that moment to hear someone running up to us in breathless haste. Connecting the sound with the gardeners, I turned and ascertained that there was no one on the paths, either to the side or behind; but at almost the same moment I suddenly perceived another man quite close to us, behind and rather to the left hand, who had, apparently, just come either over or through the rock (or whatever it was) that shut out our view at the junction of the paths **[Rock and Running Man].**

'The second man was distinctly a gentleman; he was tall, with large dark eyes, and had crisp, curling black hair under the same large sombrero hat. He was handsome, and the effect of the hair was to make him look like an old picture. His face was glowing red as through great exertion—as though he had come a long way. At first, I thought he was sunburnt, but a second look satisfied me that the color was from heat, not sunburning. He had on a dark cloak wrapped across him like a scarf, one end flying out in his prodigious hurry. He looked greatly excited as he called out to us, "Mesdames, Mesdames! Il ne faut pas passer par la." He then waved his arm, and said with great animation, "par ici…cherchez la maison." ("Ladies, you must not go that way…this way…look for the house.")

'I was so surprised at his eagerness that I looked up at him again, and to this he responded with a little backward movement and most peculiar smile. Though I could not follow all he said, it was clear that he was determined that we should go to the right and not to the left. As this fell in with my own wish, I went instantly towards a little bridge on the right and turning my head to join Miss Lamont in thanking him, found, to my surprise, that he was not there, but the running began again and from the sound, it was close beside us.

'Silently we passed over the small rustic bridge which crossed a tiny ravine. So close to us when on the bridge that we could have touched it with our right hands, a thread-like cascade fell from a height down a green pretty bank, where the ferns grew between stones. Where the little trickle of water went to, I did not see, but it gave me the impression that we were near other water, though I saw none **[Bridge and Water].**

'Beyond the little bridge, our pathway led under trees; it skirted a narrow meadow of long grass, bounded on the further side by trees, and very much overshadowed by trees growing in it. This gave the whole place a somber look suggestive of dampness and shut out the view of the house [Petit Trianon] until we were close to it. The house was a square, solidly built small country house, and on the rough grass which grew quite up to the terrace and with her back to it, a lady was sitting, holding out a paper as though to look at it at arm's length **[The Lady—Marie Antoinette?].**

'I supposed her to be sketching, and to have brought her own campstool. It appears she must be making a study of trees, for they grew close in front of her, and there seemed to be nothing else to sketch. She saw us, and when we passed close by her left hand, she turned and looked full at us. It was not a young face, and (though rather pretty) it did not attract me. She had on a shady white hat perched on a good deal of fair hair that fluffed round her forehead. Her light summer dress was arranged on her shoulders in handkerchief fashion, and there was a little line of either green or gold near the edge of the handkerchief, which showed me that it was over, not tucked into, her bodice, which was cut low. Her dress was long-waisted, with a good deal of fullness in the skirt, which seemed to be short. I thought she was a tourist, but that her dress was old-fashioned and rather unusual (though people were wearing fichu bodices that summer). I looked straight at her; but some indescribable feeling made me turn away—annoyed at her being there.

'We went up the steps to the terrace, my impression being that they led up directly from the English garden; but I was beginning to feel as if I was walking in a dream—the stillness and oppressiveness were so unnatural. Again, I saw the lady, this time from behind, and noticed that her fichu was pale green. It was rather a relief to me that Miss Lamont did not propose to ask her whether we could enter the house from that side **[Petit Trianon].**

'We crossed the terrace to the south-west corner and looked over into the cour d'honneur; and then turned back and seeing that one of the long windows overlooking the French garden was un-shuttered, we were going towards it when we were interrupted. The terrace was prolonged at right angles in front of what seemed to be a second house. The door of it suddenly opened, and a young man stepped out on to the terrace, banging the door behind him. He had the jaunty manner of a footman, but no livery, and called to us, saying that the way into the house was by the cour d'honneur, and offered to show us the way round. He looked inquisitively amused as he walked by us down the French garden till we came to an entrance into the front drive. We came out sufficiently near the first lane we had been in to make me wonder why the gardener officials had not directed us back instead of telling us to go forward.

'When we in the front entrance hall we were kept waiting for the arrival of a merry French wedding party. They walked arm and arm in a long procession round the rooms, and we were at the back—too far off from the guide to hear much of his story. We were very much interested and felt quite lively again. Coming out of the cour' d'honneur, we took a little carriage which was standing there, and drove back to the Hôtel des Réservoirs in Versailles, where we had tea…

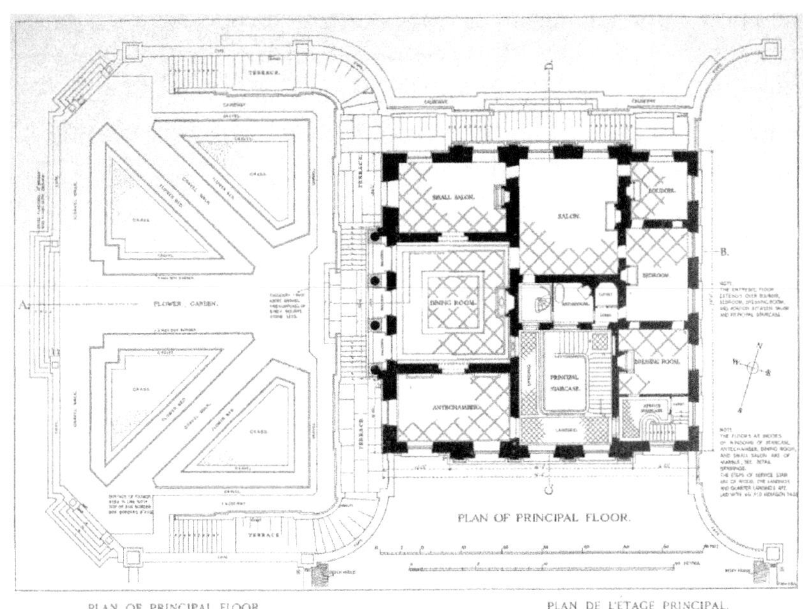


Map of the Petit Trianon, courtesy of ARCHI/MAPS.

'…For a whole week we never alluded to that afternoon, nor did I think about it until I began writing a descriptive letter of our expeditions of the week before. As the scenes came back one by one, the same sensation of dreamy unnatural oppression came over me so strongly that I stopped writing, and said to Miss Lamont, "Do you think that the Petit Trianon is haunted?"

'Her answer was prompt, "Yes, I do." I asked here where she felt it, and she said, "In the garden where we met the two men, but not only there." She then described the feeling of depression and anxiety which began at the same point as it did with me, and how she tried not to let me know it. Talking it over, we fully realized, for the first time, the theatrical appearance of the man who spoke to us, the inappropriateness of the wrapped cloak on a warm summer afternoon, the unaccountableness of his coming and going, the excited running which seemed to begin and end close to us, and yet always out of sight, and the extreme earnestness with which he desired us to go one way and not another. I said that the thought had crossed my mind that the two men were going to fight a duel, and that they were waiting until we were gone. Miss Lamont owned to having disliked the thought of passing the man of the kiosk.

'...Three months later, Miss Lamont came to stay with me, and on Sunday, November 10$^{th}$, 1901, we returned to the subject, and I said, "If we had known that a lady was sitting so near to us sketching, it would have made all the difference, for we should have asked the way." She replied that she had seen no lady. I reminded her of the person sitting under the terrace, but Miss Lamont declared that there was no one there. I exclaimed that it was impossible that she should not have seen the individual, for we were walking side by side and went straight up to her, passed her, and looked down upon her from the terrace. It was inconceivable to us both that she should not have seen the lady, but the fact was clear that Miss Lamont had not done so, though we had both been rather on the lookout for someone who would reassure us as to whether we were trespassing or not.

'Finding that we had a new element of mystery and doubting how far we had seen any of the same things, we resolved to write down independent accounts of our expedition to Trianon, read up its history, and make every enquiry about the place. Miss Lamont returned to her school the same evening, and two days later, I received from her a very interesting letter, giving the result of her first enquiries.

E.M.

Miss Lamont's (Jourdain's) account of their visit to the grounds of the Petit Trianon on August 10, 1901, is almost identical to that of Miss Morrison's (Moberly's) with a few significant differences: Lamont notes that once they reached the Grand Trianon and looked over at the pathways leading to the Petit Trianon, she stated, "Shall we try this path? It must lead to the house," and we followed it. To our right we saw some farm-buildings looking empty and deserted; implements (among others a plough) were lying about; we looked in but saw no one. (This is where Morrison saw a woman beating a rug from the window, but Lamont did not. Morrison did not see a plough, but Lamont did.)

"The impression was saddening, but it was not until we reached the crest of the rising ground where there was a garden that I began to feel as if we had lost our way, and as if something was wrong. There were two men there in official dress (greenish in color), with something in their hands; it might have been a staff. A wheelbarrow and some other gardening tools were near them. They told us, in answer to my enquiry, to go straight on. I remember repeating my question, because they answered in a seemingly casual and mechanical way, but only got the same answer in the same manner.

Versailles Guards circa 1789 holding a "staff" (l)

"As we were standing there, I saw to the right of us a detached solidly-built cottage, with stone steps at the door. A woman and a girl were standing at the door-way, and I particularly noticed their unusual dress; both wore white kerchiefs tucked into the bodice, and the girl's dress, though she looked 13 or 14 only, was down to her ankles. The woman was passing a jug to the girl, who wore a close white cap. (Moberly did not see this woman or girl.)

The Cottage Girl's style of dress, here seen in a painting depicting Marie Antoinette at her Hamlet at the Petit Trianon. Courtesy of CR Fashion Book.

Miss Lamont's account of seeing the dark-complexioned man with a face scarred by smallpox, sitting on the steps of a kiosk, jives exactly with Miss Morrison's. They both felt dread upon seeing him there and hastened away, going to the right. She next recounts hearing the Running Man, and his sudden appearance seemingly from nowhere. She gives the exact report of what he said to them and noted the odd pronunciation of the word *faut*—he pronounced it *fout*. Both women noticed this. They both noted that he wore buckled shoes.

She goes on to state that they crossed a small bridge where a small cascade of water trickled down from a shelf of rocks on their right. They followed a narrow path until they reached the English Garden front of the Petit Trianon (North side). As they approached the terrace on the North side of the building, Lamont writes that she had a feeling as "though someone were near me and I had to make room," and she instinctively pulled her skirts away. This was the place Miss Morrison saw whom she believed to be Marie Antoinette sketching. Miss Lamont did not see the lady sketching.

"While we were on the terrace, a boy came out of the door of a second building which opened on it, and I still have the sound in my ears of his slamming it behind him. He directed us to go round to the other entrance, and seeing us hesitate, with the peculiar smile of suppressed mockery, offered to show us the way. Both women agree on this. They also agree on witnessing the French wedding party and finally taking a carriage ride back to the Hôtel.

"It was not until three months later, when I was staying with her, that Miss Morrison casually mentioned the lady, and almost refused to believe that I had not seen her. How that happened was quite inexplicable to me, for I believed myself to be looking about on all sides, and it was not so much that I did not remember her as that I could have said no one was there. But, as she said it, I remembered my impression at the moment of there being more people than I could see, though I did not tell her this.

"The same evening, November 10, 1901, I returned to my school near London. Curiously enough, the next morning I had to give one of a set of lessons on the French Revolution for the Higher Certificate, and it struck me for the first time with great interest that the 10th of August had a special significance in French history, and that we had been at the Trianon on the anniversary of that day.

"That evening, when I was preparing to write down my experiences, a French friend whose home was in Paris, came into my room, and I asked her, just on the chance, if she knew any story about the haunting of the Petit Trianon. (I had not mentioned our story to her before, nor indeed to anyone.) She said directly that she remembered hearing from friends at Versailles that on a certain day in August, Marie Antoinette is regularly seen sitting outside the garden front at the Petit Trianon, with a light flapping hat and a pink dress. More than this that the place especially the farm, the garden, and the path by the water, are peopled with those who used to be with her there; in fact, that all the occupations and amusements reproduce themselves there for a day and a night. I then told her our story, and when I quoted the words the man spoke to us, and imitated as well as I could his accent, she immediately said that it was the Austrian pronunciation of French. I had privately thought that he spoke old French. Immediately afterwards, I wrote and told this to Miss Morrison.

✦

August 1901

"On receiving Miss Lamont's letter, I turned to my diary to see on what Saturday in August it was that we had visited Versailles and looked up the history to find out to what event she alluded. On August 10, 1792, the Tuileries was sacked. The royal family escaped in the early morning to the Hall of Assembly, where they were penned up for many hours, hearing themselves practically dethroned, and within sound of the massacre of their servants and of the Swiss guards at the Tuileries. From the Hall, the King and Queen were taken to the Temple.

"We wondered whether we had inadvertently entered within an act of the Queen's memory when alive (this is Jourdain's key theory—not that they traveled into the past, but that they somehow walked into Marie Antoinette's memories), and whether this explained our curious sensation of being completely shut in and oppressed. What more likely, we thought, than that during those hours in the Hall of the Assembly, or in the Conciergerie, she had gone back in such vivid memory to other Augusts spent at the Trianon that some impress of it was imparted to the place?

"As Miss Lamont was going to Paris for the Christmas holidays, I wrote and asked her to take an opportunity she might have to see the place again, and to make a plan of the paths and buildings; for the guide books spoke of the Temple de l'Amour and the Belevedere, and I thought one of them might prove to be our kiosk.

E.M.

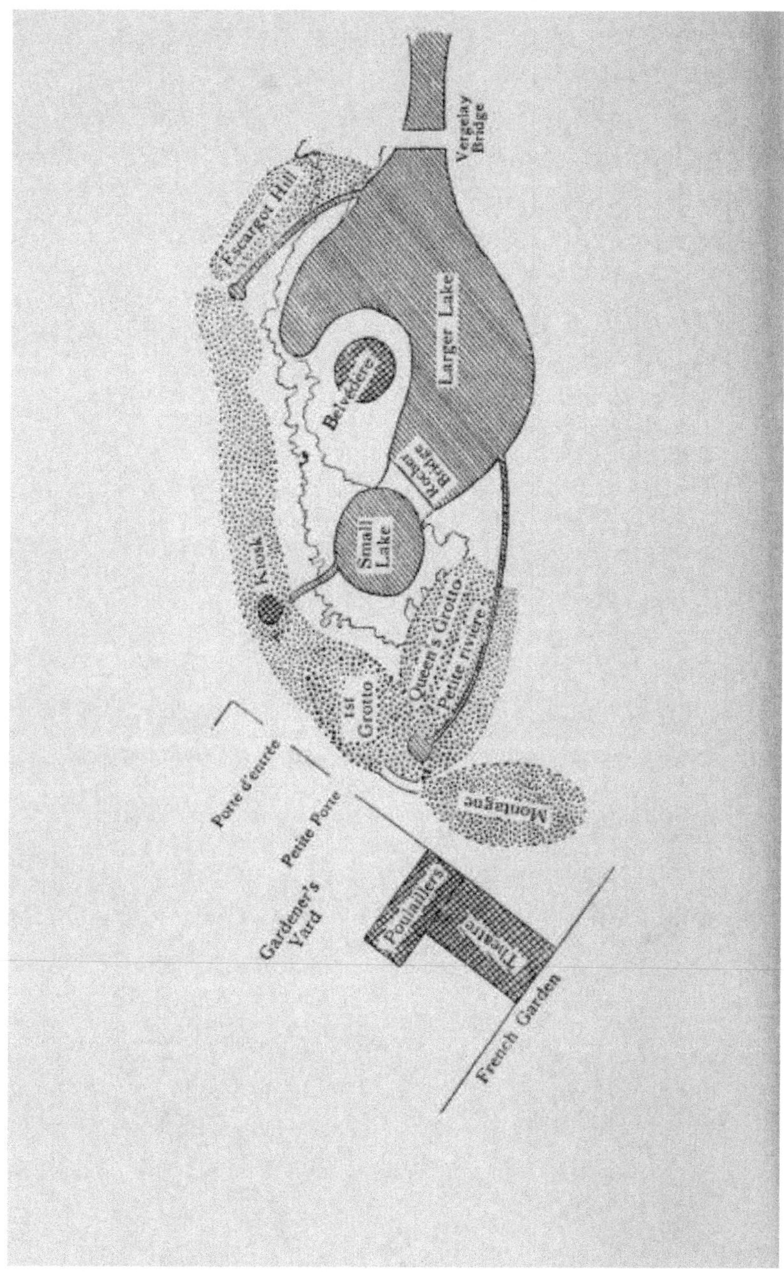


Map drawing from the book *An Adventure*, published in 1910.
This map and those following are from the Internet Archive.

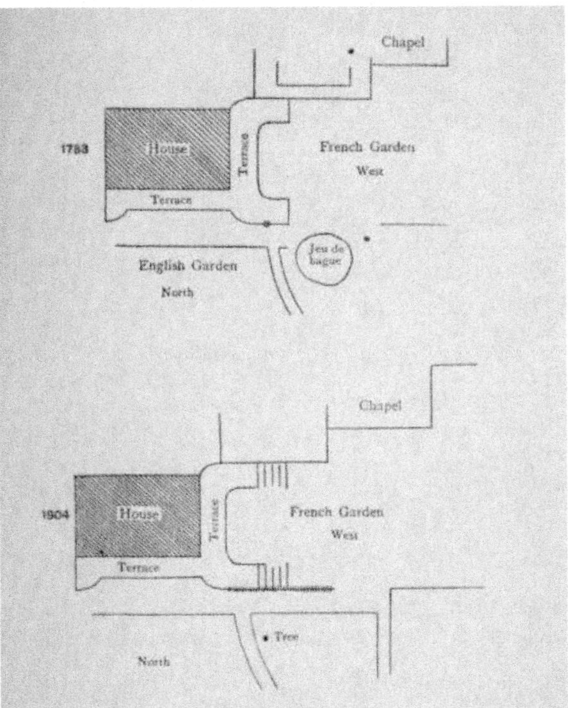


Map drawings from 1783 & 1904 visit. Note the changes.

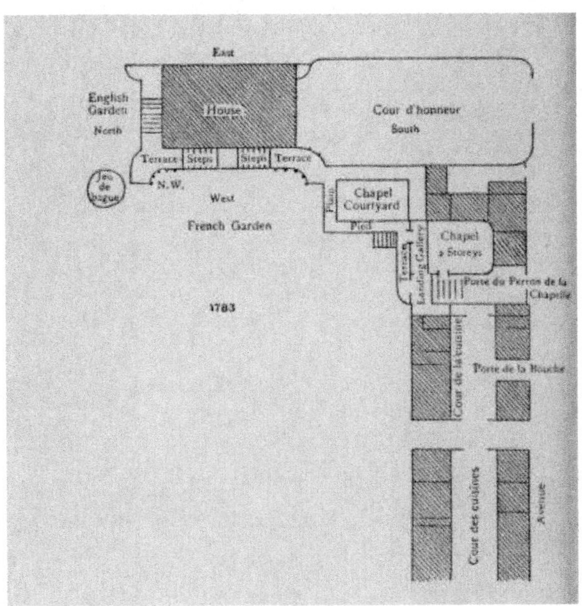


1783 Petit Trianon w/Chapel buildings

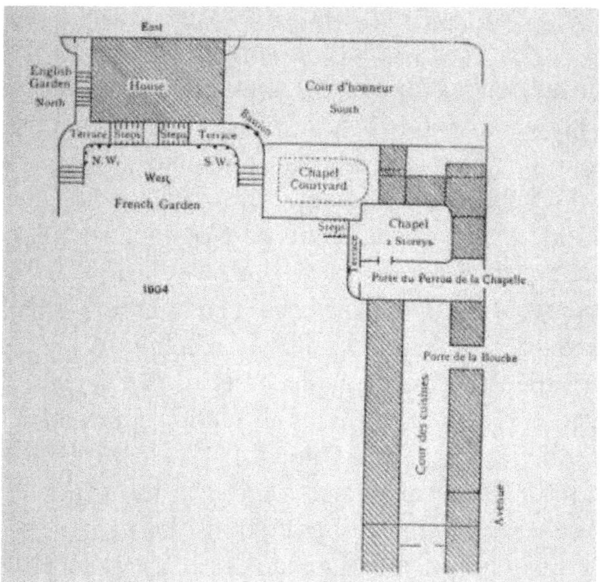


1904 Petit Trianon w/Chapel buildings

## Miss Lamont's Second Visit to the Petit Trianon, 1902

"On January 2nd, 1902, I went for the second time to Versailles…This time I drove straight to the Petit Trianon, passing the Grand Trianon. Here I could see the path up which we had walked in August. I went, however, to the regular entrance, thinking I would go at once to the Temple de l'Amour, even if I had to go no further. To the right of the cour d'honneur was a door in the wall; it led to the Hameau de la Reine. [This is also called the Hamlet. It was Marie Antoinette's private clustering of rustic cottages emulating a small farm.] I took this path and came to the Temple de l'Amour [Temple of Love], which was not the building we had passed that summer. [The kiosk with the man.]

"There was, so far, none of the eerie feeling we had experienced in August. But, on crossing a bridge to go to the Hameau, the old feeling returned in full force; it was if I had crossed a line and was suddenly in a circle of influence. To the left I saw a tract of park-like ground, the trees bare and very scanty. I noticed a cart being filled with sticks by two laborers and thought I could go to them for directions if I lost my way. The men wore tunics and capes with pointed hoods of bright colors, a sort of terra-cotta red and deep blue. I turned aside for an instant—not more—to look at the Hameau, and when I looked back, men and cart were completely out of sight, and this surprised me, as I could see a long way in every direction. And though I had seen the men loading the cart with sticks, I could not see any trace of them on the ground, either at the time or afterwards. I did not, however, dwell upon any part of the incident, but went on to the Hameau. The houses were all built near a sheet of water, and the old oppressive feeling of the last year was noticeable, especially under the balcony of the Maison de la Reine **[The Queen's House]**, and near a window in what I afterwards found to be the Laiterie **[The Diary]**.

"I really felt a great reluctance to go near the window or look in, and when I did so, I found it shuttered inside.

"Coming away from the Hameau, I at last reached a building, which I knew from my plan to be the smaller Orangerie; then, meaning go to the Belvedere, I turned back by mistake into the park and found myself in a wood, so thick that though I had turned towards the Hameau, I could not see it. [**The Wood**] Before I entered, I looked across an open space towards a belt of trees to the left of the Hameau some way off, and noticed a man, cloaked like those we had seen before, slip swiftly through the line of trees. The smoothness of his movement attracted my attention.

"I was puzzling my way among the maze of paths in the wood when I heard a rustling behind me which made me wonder why people in silk dresses came out on such a wet day; and I said to myself, "just like French people." I turned sharply round to see who they were, but saw no one, and then, all in a moment, I had the same feeling as by the terrace in the summer, only in a much greater degree; it was a though I were closed in by a group of people who already filled the path, coming from behind and passing me **[The Crowd]**. At one moment there seemed really no room for me. I heard some women's voices talking French and caught the words "Monsieur et Madame" said close to my ear.

"The crowd got scarce and drifted away, and then faint music as of a band, not far off, was audible. It was playing very light music with a good deal of repetition in it **[The Music].** Both voices and music were diminished in tone, as in a phonograph, unnaturally. The pitch of the band was lower than usual. The sounds were intermittent, and once more I felt the swish of a dress close by me.

"I looked at the map which I had with me, but whenever I settled which path to take, I felt impelled to go by another. After turning backwards and forwards many times, I at last found myself back at the Orangerie, and was overtaken by a gardener **[The Tall Gardener]** and asked him where I should find the Queen's grotto, that had been mentioned in De Nolhac's book which I had procured while in Paris. He told me to follow the path I was on, and, in answer to a question, said that I must pass the Belevedere, adding that it was quite impossible to find one's way about the park unless one had been brought up in the place, and so used to it that "personne ne pourrait vous tromper" [*"no one can mislead you"*]. The expression specially impressed me because of the experience I had just had in the wood. He pointed out the way and left me. The path led past the Belevedere, which I took for granted was the building we had seen in August, for coming upon it from behind, all the water was hidden from me. I made my way from there to the French garden without noticing the paths I took.

"On my return to Versailles I made careful enquiries as to whether the band had been playing there that day but was told that though it was the usual day of the week, it had not played because it had played the day before, being New Year's Day.

"I told my French friends of my walk, and they said there was a tradition of Marie Antoinette having been seen making butter within the Laiterie, and for that reason it was shuttered **[Ghost Story]**. A second tradition they mentioned interested me very much. It was that on October 5$^{th}$, 1789—which was the last day on which Marie Antoinette went to Trianon—she was sitting there in her grotto, and saw a page running towards her, bringing the letter from the minister at the palace to say that the mob from Paris would be at the gates in an hour's time. The story went on that she impulsively proposed walking straight back to the palace by the short cut through the trees. He would not allow it: but begged her to go to the "maison" [Petit Trianon] to wait whilst he fetched the carriage by which she was generally conveyed back through the park, and that he ran off to order it."

F. L.

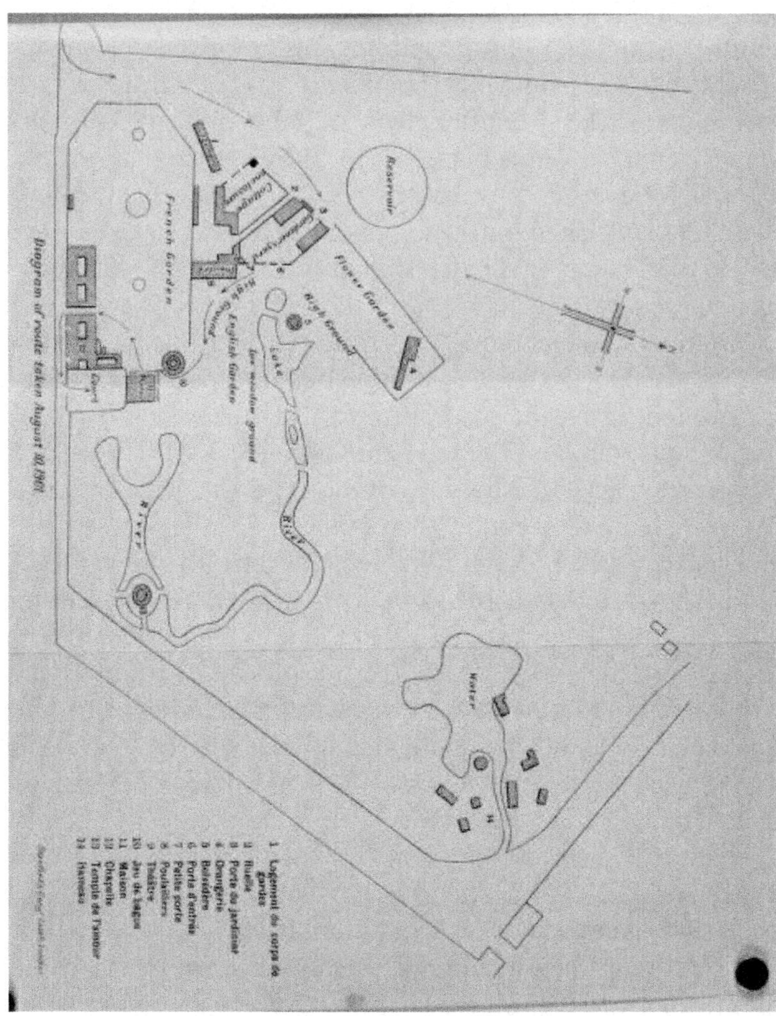


The Path Moberly and Jourdain took & important locations.
Map courtesy of the Internet Archive.

## Their Research and Conclusions

Many have wondered if Moberly and Jourdain had some form of sensitive psyche that enabled them to pick up on paranormal occurrences that happened to them on not one, but two or more visits to the Petit Trianon grounds and house. When Miss Lamont returns on January 2, 1902, it is not the August 10$^{th}$ anniversary of Marie Antoinette's harrowing experience at the Hall of Assembly in 1789.

It's a completely different date, and yet she encounters new 'specters' including two men loading sticks into a cart and a tall gardener who speaks to her. She hears a band playing, voices conversing near her ear, and the feeling and sound of dresses moving past her on the path.

For the next two years, the two women went over their notes and tried to find meaning in the things they saw and heard. "Photographs of the Belevedere made it clear that it was not identical to the kiosk," wrote Miss Morrison. "On the many occasions on which Miss Lamont went to the Trianon she could never again find the places—not even the wood in which she had been. She assured me the place was entirely different; the distances were much less than we had imagined; and the ground was so bare that the house and the Hameau were in full view of one another; and that there was nothing unnatural about the trees.

"Miss Lamont brought back from Paris *La Reine Marie Antoinette*, by M. de Nolhac, and *Le Petit Trianon*, by Desjardins. We noted that M. de Nolhac related the traditional story of the Queen's visit, and that the Comte de Vaudreuil, who betrayed the Queen by inciting her to the fatal acting of the Barbier de Séville in her own theater at Trianon, was a Creole and marked by smallpox.

Compte de Vaudreuil

Turning over the pages of Desjardins I found Wertmüller's portrait of the Queen and exclaimed that it was the first of all the pictures I had seen which at all brought back the face of the lady **[Queen's portrait]**. Some weeks later I found this passage: 'This tableau of the Queen was poorly received by contemporary critics, who found it cold, without majesty, without grace. For posterity, on the contrary, it has very great merit—that of looking like her. Madame Campan said that no good portrait of the Queen existed except that by Wertmüller and that by Madame Lebrun, painted in 1787.'

Detail of Wertmüller's portrait of Marie Antoinette showing her aquiline nose, small mouth, and protruding chin.

"In January, 1904, Miss Lamont went to the Comédie Française to see the Barbier de Séville, and noticed the Alguazils standing round were dressed exactly like our garden officials, but had red stockings added…Also, she reported, that Almaiva was dressed in a dark cloak and a large Spanish hat, which was said to be the outdoor dress of French gentlemen of the period.

E.M.

## Return Trips and Findings

July 4th, 1904, both women return to the Petit Trianon grounds, this being Miss Morrison's second visit. These are the bullet points of their findings:

1. The lane was there, and they turned right at the *lodgement des corps de gardes* which was the same as they saw it before. From there, everything was different from their visit on August 10, 1901.
2. The old wall facing them had gates, but they were closed...and seemed to have been for a very long time.
3. The cottage where Miss Lamont said she had seen a woman and a girl [gardener's house] was quite different.
4. Where they had met the garden officials had also changed; it was "now a parterre with flower beds and a smooth lawn of many years' careful tendance. It did not seem to be the place where we had met the garden officials."
5. They could not find the old paths they had traveled that day and "the distances were contracted, and all was on a smaller scale than I remembered," wrote Miss Morrison.
6. "The kiosk was gone; so was the ravine and the little cascade which had fallen from a height above our heads, and the little bridge over the ravine was, of course, gone too."
7. "The large bridge with the *rocher* [rocks] over it, crossing one side of the lake at the foot of the Belvedere, had no resemblance to it. The trees were quite natural and seemed to have been a good deal cleared out, making that part of the garden much less wooded and picturesque."
8. The English Garden in front of the Petit Trianon now contained less trees and a clear view of the Hameau could be seen. The rough meadow leading to the terrace of the house was now a graveled sweep and the trees on the lawn are gone.
9. Where Miss Morrison had seen the lady sitting and sketching by the terrace now held a large spreading bush "of many years' growth."
10. The staircase to the house at the north-west terrace had changed; an extension of wall had been added which one had now to go to reach the staircase. [Map on pg. 753]
11. They tried to retrace Miss Lamont's steps from her visit on

January 2, 1902 but found no thick wood: all the paths were visible from one another.
12. Returning to Versailles, the women went into a bookseller's shop and asked for a map of the Petit Trianon as it had been in the old days. He showed them one that he refused to part with. On the map was a picture of the *Jeu de Bague* [an old jousting ring, pictured in map on pg. 753 in the 1783 drawing but gone in 1904.]
13. The bookseller said the green uniforms the women described seeing the two garden officials wearing "was one of the colors of the royal liveries" and said it was "impossible" that the women had seen men wearing that livery only three years before during their visit.

**Summary of the Results of Their Research**

1. **The Plough**: In 1905, Miss Lamont was told by a gardener that no plough was kept at Trianon; there was no need of one, as the government only required the lawns, walks, water, trees, and flowers to be kept up. In 1908, another gardener told them that ploughs had entirely altered in appearance since the Revolution, and it was not likely that the old type would be seen anywhere in France now. A list of tools bought for the gardeners showed no mention of a plough from 1780-1789 (the Eve of the Revolution). "We learned," wrote Miss Morrison, "that throughout the reign of Louis XVI, an old plough used in his predecessor's reign had been preserved at the Petit Trianon and sold with the King's other properties during the Revolution.
2. **The Guards**: In 1904, the women were told by well-informed persons at Versailles that it was "impossible" that they saw guards wearing the green liveries that were worn by the Guards of the Sleeve in the reign of Louis XVI. They carried halberds, what Miss Lamont had called staffs or staves. The livery of the Comte d'Artois (Louis XVI's brother), who was colonel-general of the gardes Suisses (Swiss Guards) was green. In 1908, we learned that the *porte du jardinier* at the Petit Trianon was always guarded "dans le temps," (when the Queen was there) and that on October 5$^{th}$, 1789, the guards were two of the three Bersy brothers who, with Bréval, were generally on duty whenever the Queen was in residence at Trianon. "In 1910, we found that they had the title of *garçons jardiniers de la Chambre,* (gardener lads of the Chamber) and they

are said to have been stationed in '*la pepinière proche la maison*' (the nursery near the house). The most ancient *pepinière* (nursery) was close to the gardener's house."

3. **The Cottage, Woman & the Girl**: "In 1908, we discovered from the map of 1783 that there was a building, not now in existence, placed against the wall (outside) of the gardener's yard between the *ruelle* (alley) and the *porte du jardineir*; if our original route lay through this yard to the English Garden, this building would be exactly in the right place for Miss Lamont's cottage" where she saw "a woman in old-fashioned dress handing something to a girl of about 13 or 14, who wore a white cap and skirts nearly reaching to her ankles."

4. **The Kiosk:** In September 1908, "Miss Lamont found in the archives a paper (without signature or date) giving the estimate for a "ruine" having seven Ionic columns, walls, and a dome roof. [A ruin meant a copy of an older building.] If the walls of this building were low, it would correspond in appearance with our recollections of the kiosk. This "ruine" is said to have formed a *"naissance de la rivière,"* (source of the river) suggesting its position above the small lake which fed the principal river. A piece of old water pipe is still to be seen on the northwestern side of the small lake.

I. In 1788, it is stated that rocks were placed at intervals on a path leading from "la ruine" to the 2nd source du ravin" (second spring of the ravine) beyond the wooden bridge. Desjardins considers one of the "sources" to have been close to the theater which was at our right hand; this might have been the second spring.

II. Mique (Marie's architect & map maker) states that in 1780 he placed a small architectural "ruine" above the grotto. A note in the archives, dated 1777, speaks of a *"porte d'entrée au bout du grotte"* (entryway at the end of the cave). If, as we believe, we had just passed out of the gardener's yard by this *"porte d'entrée"* we should have been close to the earliest placed grotto. [It is interesting that the reference to the "ruine" or kiosk, should also contain details of the ravine and small wooden bridge that the two women also saw that day, and were not there on return visits. Author's note]

5. **The Man by the Kiosk:** "Most of the intimate accounts of the period say that the Compte de Vaudreuil was a Creole and marked by smallpox. He was at one time one of the Queen's innermost circle of friends but acted an enemy's part in persuading her to gain the

King's permission for the acting of the politically dangerous play of *Le Mariage de Figaro*. The King had long refused to allow it, saying it would cause the Bastille to be taken. The earlier version of the same play, *Le Barbier de Sèville*, was last acted at Trianon (August 19th, 1785), just at the beginning of the *Diamond Necklace Affair*, when Vaudreuil took the part of Almaviva and was dressed for it in a large dark cloak and Spanish hat. Vaudreuil left the court of France amongst the first party of emigrés after the taking of the Bastille, July 1789.

6. **The Running Man:** The following year of the two women's visit to the Petit Trianon, on October 5th, 1902, they learned there was a tradition that on October 5th, 1789, a messenger was sent to the Trianon to warn the Queen of the approach of the mob from Paris: that she wished to walk back to the Palace by the most direct route, but the messenger begged her to wait at the house whilst he fetched the carriage, as it was safer to drive back as usual by the broad roads of the park. The Queen is reported to have addressed the messenger as "Breton." This was not an uncommon name about the court and old Versailles. The court almanac for 1783 shows that then the Queen had a Page de l'Écurie," called "de Bretagne." Madame Éloffe (the Queen's modiste) mentions a Mademoiselle Breton amongst the Queen's women.

"If "De Bretagne" was 16 years old in 1783, he would have been 22 in 1789—just in the fresh young vigor suitable to our running man." Buckled shoes, such as the ones the two women reported seeing the Running Man wearing, "are expressly mentioned as being very fashionable in 1789, and there was, at that time, a rage for steel ornaments."

7. **Bridge Over Little Cascade:** Neither the bridge, nor cascade, nor ravine that the two women crossed could be found on their return visits. "In 1907 we bought *Souvenirs d'un Page* by the Comte D'Hezecques. He says: "In front of the lawn, which ends at the rock shadowed by pines, by cedars, by larches, and surmounted by a rustic bridge as one might see in the mountains of Switzerland and the precipices of Valais. This rural and wild view is made sweet by the third façade of the castle.' He also speaks of water passing through the moss-lined grotto, which, according to our idea, must have been below us, but close by on our right hand. Madame Lavergne writes of the "petite cascade" (little waterfall) and of the

sound of the grotto.

"In April 1908, extracts from Mique's accounts and plans for the Trianon grounds were procured from the archives, giving the history of the grottos. "June 4, 1780, a clay model was made of the ravine with the little bridges. 1788, a piece at the top of the Rock of the Ravine—the passing of carriages on the wooden bridge. A piece opposite the Rock of the Ravine long the path to the ruine on the wooden way to the second spring of the ravine.' The first source was probably close to the "Ruine" (our kiosk?). The second "source" might coincide with Desjardins' source," which he places a few steps from the *poulaillers* (henhouse) and was probably meant to feed the *"petite riviere,"* which passed through the Queen's grotto, carrying off the water from the stagnant pool between the grottos to the larger lake. That would exactly agree with the position of our little cascade, small bridge, and glimmering pool."

8. **Isolated Rock: "**In 1908 we found a mass of rocks standing in the dry bed of the small lake. On one rock covered with ivy were two full-grown pine trees. It seems unlikely that the trees should have originally been in the small circular basin of water. D'Hezecques says the pine trees were planted high up over the grotto to give the appearance of a Swiss mountain. The grotto was destroyed about 1792, and it is possible that some of the rocks covering it were displaced and allowed to slip into the lake below, and that the present pine trees may have been seedlings at the time, for we were told that the life of a pine tree is from 100 to 200 years old.

"In January 1791, trees were torn up from the *montagnes* [mountains]. In February, March, April 1792, every few days occurs the entry: "A day spent tearing up the cedars on the mountain…" There is now no isolated rock standing up as we saw it behind the Running Man—only mounds covered with shrubs and trees. But in the archives, there is a note saying that in 1788 rocks were placed in various parts, and one especially is mentioned, "a piece overlooking the side of the lake on the old side of the rocks…towards the track towards the Ruine by the wooden way to second spring of the ravine." This would have been the path we were on in 1901."

9. **Pelouse [Lawn]:** "It is easy to suppose that between the years of 1901-1904 trees were cleared away from the rough ground on the north side of the house, which in 1901 had given it the look of an

orchard. So much was this the case that the lady sitting under the north terrace was thought to be making a study of the tree stems; for she was looking into trees, and she held a large paper in her hand, and, as we passed, held it out at arm's length.

"At present, there are trees on each side of the *pelouse* [lawn], and one growing near the site of the old *Jeu de Bague*, but none growing in front of the house, (map pg. 753) and it all looks drier, brighter, and less confined than in 1901. Before the new theater was built in 1779, the old *comédie* was moved; it gave place to a *"pelouse parsemée d'arbres"* (lawn dotted with trees).

10. **The Lady:** "Nothing unusual marked the lady sitting on a low seat on the grass immediately under the north terrace. I remember recognizing that her light-colored skirt, white fichu, and straw hat were in the present fashion, but they struck me as rather dowdy in general effect. She was so near us that I looked full at her, and she bent slightly forward to do the same... The lady was visible some way off; we walked side by side straight up to her, leaving her slightly on the left hand as we passed up the steps to the terrace, from whence I saw her again from behind, and noticed that her fichu had become a pale green.

"In the summer of 1908 we read the Journal of Madame Éloffe (the Queen's modiste). She says that during the year 1789 the Queen was extremely economical and had very few dresses made. Madame Éloffe repaired several light dresses, washing short skirts, and made, in July and September, two green silk bodices, besides many large white fichus. This agrees exactly with the dress seen in 1901. The skirt was not a fresh white but was light colored—slightly yellowish. The white fichu in front seemed to have an edge of green or gold, just as it would have appeared if the white muslin, or gauze was over green. The color would have shown more clearly at the back, but in front, where the white folds accumulated, the green would have been less prominent. The straight edge in front and the frill behind had often puzzled me, but in Madame Éloffe's illustrations of the fashions at that time there are instances of the same thing. There is in the book, a colored picture of the green silk bodice, with all the measurements to enable her to fit the Queen perfectly."

One comment Miss Morrison made in her reports stands out: she saw the lady sitting before the Petit Trianon terrace on the English Garden side of the house, not the side with the French Garden sporting parterres. The English side was more free form with a random appearance of trees and wildflowers. It is this side of the house that others have seen the Queen sitting on a low bench in the garden before the terrace.

11. **Jeu de Bague:** The *Jeu de Bague* was a precursor to today's children's carousel. It was a ring where knights would ride around a circular enclosure and try to spear things as they did in Louis XIV's Carousels. These could be haystacks with fake heads attached, wooden rings, etc. The wooden ring was later replaced by a brass ring on modern carousels that the rider tried to snatch as they rode around.

"As we approached the terrace at the northwest corner of the house, we had some barrier on our right hand entirely blocking the view, so that we could see nothing but the meadow on our left hand, and the house with its terrace in front.

"At present, the pathway which curves towards the house, and is very likely the old one, has a large bare space on the right hand with one beautiful old tree growing on the edge of it; and from some way off one can easily see across it to the chapel beyond the French garden. A long piece of wall extends westward from the terrace, round which one must go into the French Garden in order to find the staircase; whilst the whole length of wall, including part of the north terrace, is hidden by a large old spreading bush, completely covering the place where the lady sat. Originally, we could not see any steps whilst on the path, but after we had passed the barrier on our right hand, we found them at once without going round any wall.

"The map of 1783 shows us that *Jeu de Bague* [erected in 1776] once stood on what is now bare space. It was a circular building surrounded by a wooden gallery, masked by trees. This would have completely shut out the view, and the path was probably curved on its account.

"In 1907, we learned that the Queen had a passage made under the terrace from the to the *Jeu de Bague*; and in 1908 we discovered the old walled-up doorway leading into the English Garden behind the bush…In 1910 we also learned that the bush had been planted when Duchesse d'Orleans occupied the house." (See map on pg. 753. Note the *Jeu de Bague* drawn in 1783 but gone in 1904.)

12. **The Chapel Man**: "Whilst we were standing on the southwest end of the terrace above the French Garden, the door of a building

at right angles to the house suddenly opened, and a young man came out and slammed the door behind him." Miss Morrison goes on to state how he told them "jauntily" that they could not enter the house from that point and had to go around to the cour d'honneur to enter. He then led them around the buildings.

"...in 1906, Miss Lamont had leave to go into the chapel...The terrace door [from which the young man exited to call to the women] of the gallery is bolted, barred, and cobwebbed over from age and disuse. The guide said that the door had not been opened in the memory of any man there: not since it was used by the court of Louis XVI." (See map on pg. 753-54.)

"...In September, 1910...it was explained that above the kitchen passage [at the Petit Trianon] there had been a covered way, by which the Queen could enter the chapel from the house in wet weather. The top of this covered way had been *"de plain pied,"* [the same level] joining the bit of terrace outside the chapel door to the terrace by the house. This would have been the level way along which our man came to us.

13. **Two Laborers with A Cart:** "On her second visit, January 2nd, 1902, Miss Lamont saw in the field near the Hameau, two laborers, in brown tunics and bright-colored short capes, loading a cart with sticks. The capes hardly came below their shoulders and had hoods: one was bright blue and the other red.

"In May 1904, a search was made in the archives with the result that it was clear that carts and horses for the purpose of tidying the grounds were hired by the day in old times and not kept in the farm for constant use. In January 1789, two men, instead of the usual one were hired to collect the caterpillar nests and burn them." Miss Lamont was there in January.

"The entry in the wages book showed that up to 1783, from time to time, a wagon with a horse and a driver were hired for picking up branches and sticks in the parks: but on October 4th, 1789, a cart with two horses was hired for three days for the purpose." [Two horses would require two men, according to Miss Morrison.]

14. **The Wood:** During Miss Lamont's visit in January of 1902, she found herself in a "wood of very tall trees, with such high, thick undergrowth that she could not see through it. [This was winter when the trees should have been mostly without leaves.] Well-kept paths opened at intervals right and left at different angles, and they

gave the impression of being so arranged as to lead round and round. She had the feeling of being in a midst of crowds passing and repassing her, and heard voices and sounds of dresses...After vainly pursuing the confusing paths for some time, she found herself close to the hill leading to the Orangerie...In 1904 and in 1908 we tried to find this wood, without results...In the gardener's wages book, the gathering up and occasional burning of undergrowths in a wood are alluded to.

"In Mique's map (1783) the wood with its diverging paths can be plainly seen. It is approached by two bridges over the river and stretches towards the hill on which the Orangerie stands."

Mique's map from 1783 Miss Morrison refers to. The circular wood can be seen near the large lake in the middle of the map. There is even a spiral depicted. This is by the Orangerie (box shapes at top).

15. **The Music:** "Whilst in the wood, Miss Lamont heard sounds of a band of violins drifting past her from the direction of the house...She could afterwards write down from memory about twelve bars, but without all the inner harmonies. She ascertained immediately afterwards that no band had been playing out of doors

that afternoon at Versailles. It was a cold, wet winter's afternoon.

"In March 1907, the twelve bars were shown to a musical expert, who said (without having heard the story) that the bars could hardly belong to one another, but the idiom dated from about 1780...He said that the bands in the eighteenth century were lower in pitch than they are now. He suggested the name of Sacchini.

They found through further research a melody written by Monsigny created for a performance of *"Le Roi et le Fermier"* opening at the new theater at the Petit Trianon, August 1, 1780, had the first of the twelve bars found in the music Miss Lamont heard. Marie Antoinette acted in that play.

16. **The Gardener:** "Miss Lamont then went along the upper path [on her January 2, 1902, visit], and when between the Escargot hill and the Belvedere, she met a very tall gardener of apparently great strength, with long muscular arms. She thought that with his long hair and grizzled, untidy beard and general appearance, he had the look of an Englishman rather than a Frenchman. He was dressed in a rough knitted jersey, and a small dark blue round cap was set back of his head. She enquired where she could find the Queen's grotto, and he walked a little way beside her to show her the way.

"Miss Lamont expected to turn back to the present grotto, and when she remarked that they were going past the Belvedere, he replied firmly that they must go past the Belvedere and said that it was necessary to have been born and bred in the place to know the way so that "nobody could fool you."

"In August 1908, we were told by a former gardener that their dress now is the same as the traditional dress of the *ancien régime*, viz., a rough knitted jersey with a small casquette on the head. In the old weekly wages book there appears, for several years, the name "l'Anglais" [the English]—probably a nickname.

"We owe our research as to the position of the Queen's grotto almost entirely to the tall gardener's decided directions and guidance to the part of the English Garden between the Belvedere and the *montagnes* [mountains]close to the theater.

E.M. F.L
September 1910

## The Aftermath

The account of Charlotte Anne Moberly (1846-1937) and Eleanor Jourdain (1863-1924) as to their extraordinary experience on the grounds of the Petit Trianon in 1901 and 1902 has been a topic of fascination for many scholars over the years. Was it a shared hallucination between two women caught up in the heat of an oppressive August day? Was it a time warp that they somehow walked through—a parallel dimension into the past? Had they invented it, embellishing their story over the years to fit their "facts?" Here is Charlotte Moberly's (Miss Morrison's) own account of what she believed happened:

"We do not believe in anniversaries in the usual sense. We have tested both our days (August 10$^{th}$ and January 2$^{nd}$), going, as far as possible, under the same circumstances, without any result at the Petit Trianon. Yet, it is possible that if we entered into an act of memory, it may well have been first made on that terrible 10$^{th}$ of August 1792, though the memory itself was occupied (in the central place) with the events of October 5$^{th}$, 1789. The dress of the messenger was more suitable for October than August. At the same time Vaudreuil left France the previous summer and cannot have sat in the Trianon woods after the taking of the Bastille, July 14$^{th}$, 1789.

"There is an incoherence about both the large and small incidents which seems to require combination within a single mind, and the only mind to which they could all have been present would have been that of the Queen. Our theory of 1901, that we had entered within the working of the Queen's memory when she was still alive, is now enlarged. We think that the two first visits to Trianon (August 10$^{th}$, 1901, and January 2$^{nd}$, 1902) were part of one and the same experience; that quite mechanically we must have seen it as it appeared to her more than a hundred years ago, and have heard sounds familiar, and even something of words spoken, to her then."

Convinced that the grounds were haunted, they decided to publish their story in a book *An Adventure* (1911) under the pseudonyms of Elizabeth Morrison and Frances Lamont. The book, containing the claim that Marie Antoinette had been encountered in 1901, caused a sensation. However, many critics did not take it seriously on the grounds of the implausibility's and inconsistencies that it contained.

A review of the book by Eleanor Mildred Sidgwick in the Proceedings of the Society for Psychical Research suggested that the women had misinterpreted normal events they had experienced. In 1903, and old map of the Trianon gardens was found and showed a bridge that the two women had claimed to have crossed that had not been on any other map. The identity of the authors was made public in 1931.

Both women claimed many paranormal experiences before and after their adventure. In one of them, Moberly claimed to have seen in the Louvre in 1914 an apparition of the Roman emperor Constantine, a man of unusual height wearing a gold crown and a toga; he was not observed by anyone else. During the First World War, Jourdain, the dominant personality of the pair, who had succeeded as Principal of St. Hugh's, became convinced that a German spy was hiding in the college. After developing increasingly autocratic behavior, she died suddenly in 1924 in the middle of an academic scandal over her leadership of the college; her conduct having provoked mass resignations of academic staff. Moberly died in 1937.

A friend of this author's, Sandy Lakdar, who lives in Paris and has researched Versailles' history thoroughly, imparted the following information to me regarding Moberly and Jourdain's reviews after the book was published:

"In 1952 a French archivist/archeologist named Leon Rey decided to search out the authenticity of the women's testimony. He found out there was not a Chinese house [kiosk] nor a gardener looking like they described at the Marie Antoinette time period. So, he reported that everything the English ladies said was fake.

"In 1959 Guy Lambert, an historian, is also having a look at the ladies' book and discovers some lost archives from Versailles City. He found that at Louis XV's time period, gardeners were actually looking like the ladies said. He even found two men's names—a father and a son named Claude and Antoine Richard—who were the Gardener of the King Louis XV. Plus, Guy Lambert found a map of the Versailles Garden from 1774 and there is actually a Chinese house on it.

"The ladies wrote in their book in 1910 details that even French historians did not know before 1959. If they were tracking back in the time period of 1774 [like the map shows], not 1789, they didn't see Marie Antoinette, but instead saw Madame du Barry [for whom Louis XV built the Petit Trianon]. Either way, they were historically right and accurate in their descriptions.

"Another story I heard that actually aired on French national TV was a report on all the "little hands" that work at Versailles—all the people who work all year, but you never see as visitors," Sandy told this author. "It's absolutely NOT a TV report about paranormal but really something about the people who work behind the curtains. The report begins with a night watchman with the journalist following him in his night work: "How does it feel to work at night in a place like Versailles?"

"The guard replies, "This is such an honor and I feel so privileged to have access here by myself, but also, it can be very disturbing and scary when we arrive at the Sun King's bedroom." The journalist on the program looks surprised and asks "Why?" The guard looks embarrassed and says, "Well, sometimes we hear a baby crying from the bedrooms but when we arrive, there is nothing. All my co-workers have witnessed it. Only my boss hasn't, and she does not believe us. When the journalist interviewed "the boss" as to the watchman's story, she just laughed and said, "Well, it's funny how the baby cries only when I'm not around. If this story is true, I would hear it also."

"We receive a lot of emails from people who either work there, or used to work there, saying that we should investigate as they often feel uncomfortable or not alone in there."

This author would like to thank Sandy Lakdar for sharing this information with me. She regularly investigates the paranormal and reports on it.

## More Accounts of Paranormal Activity at Versailles Come Forward

The Belgian website for the *Centre of the Study and Research into Unexplained Phenomena* has a listing of other testimonies from visitors to the Petit Trianon area, written by Sylviane Putinier:

"John and Kate Cooke with their son Stephen, were Americans

living near Versailles between 1907 and 1909. On two occasions in July 1908, they say they saw a sitting woman, busy sketching near the Grand Trianon. She had a cream dress, a white fichu, and a broad brimmed hat. John heard old-fashioned music and saw a man with a tricorn hat. The couple saw a woman with old-fashioned clothes collecting wood in the gardens. They waited until 1914 before reporting their visions—of course *An Adventure* had been published by then. The Cooke's also mention an electrical hissing sound.

"In October 1932, Claire Burrow and her pupil Anne Lambert visited Versailles. They hadn't heard of Moberly or Jourdain. They also describe the feeling of depression. They saw a woman and an old man in 18th century dress with a knee-length cloak and a tricorn hat. They spoke to him but couldn't understand his French. They said they'd never heard of *An Adventure*.

"In 1935, Robert Philippe and his parents visited the Trianon. He stayed back a few minutes to light a cigarette. He felt a presence beside him and as he turned, he saw a young woman. They exchanged a few words. The unknown woman spoke with strange, accented French and said she lived at the Trianon—which Robert knew was not inhabited. He turned his head for a few seconds to strike another match and the woman had gone. His parents heard him talking to someone but didn't see the young woman.

"A London solicitor and his wife visited Versailles on 21 May 1955. The weather was close and very heavy—as if a thunderstorm was coming. They saw a woman between two men. She was wearing a very bright yellow dress. They couldn't recall the shape of the men's coats. They came closer, then vanished. The ghosts seemed to be walking in the direction of an avenue in the woods called Onze Arpents [which was mentioned in *An Adventure* by Moberly], but this avenue disappeared in 1786.

"In 1949, Jack Wilkinson, a poultry farmer from Levens in Westmorland, England, saw a woman, but not ghostlike. His wife also saw it.

"In 1938, Elizabeth Hatton saw something. Later, people researching found an experience predating the visit of Moberly and Jourdain from 1870—it was another English person.

"An Alsatian painter called René Kuder also had an experience at Versailles. No date is given, but Kuder died in 1962, so it was obviously before then. He was sketching inside the Petit Trianon about 10 in the morning as a preliminary to illustrating a book about Versailles. Suddenly, he screamed and banged against the door. The guard ran in and found him unconscious on the floor. When he came to, he said he had seen Marie Antoinette coming down the stairs—without her head. He said he even heard the clip-clop of her heels. He made an official report on the event."

While researching and writing this book, many have reached out to this author with their own stories of haunted happenings at Versailles. I'd like to relate a few of them here:

Mary Fashings, USA: "My husband and I were doing the Garden Tour at Versailles in June of 2017. We had seen the palace before and just wanted to take a more leisurely look at the vast gardens. To my disappointment, several of the fountains were not turned on. I was standing, studying the Latona Fountain, which is nearest the palace, counting the number of frogs surrounding it. The water was very still, and I wished I could see it with its jets on. Just then, I heard a great gush of water and jumped back in surprise. I could hear the individual streams of water coming from the frog's mouths, but there was no water flowing in front of me. I looked around for a different source of the noise, but there was nothing near to me to explain it. The pond around the fountain is large, and I could clearly see the calm water in the basin. Yet, in front of me was the loud sound of gushing fountains, some rising up above my head. My heart was pounding. My husband came strolling over and I grabbed his arm. "Do you hear that water?" I asked him, looking somewhat hysterical. He looked at me with raised eyebrows and said, "What water?" "You don't hear that gushing sound of fountains?" He stood and listened, looked around to see if I meant one of the other fountains at a distance, then shook his head. "Do you still hear it?" he asked, puzzled. "YES!" I screamed. "How can you not hear *that*?" He put it down to the heat and my wanting to see the fountains working. I know what I heard."

James Hardy, England: "I got the rare chance to be by the Apollo Fountain without a crunch of people around and was enjoying standing there and taking it all in. Something smashed me in the back. I turned around and there was nothing there. I could still feel the stinging on my back. As I stood there worrying it out in my head, I hear voices going past me talking French. It was like a party of people, went by, their voices faded, and then a new group came by. One batch of people were clearly all female voices, giggling and speaking very quickly and excited like in French. I couldn't see anyone! There was nobody there! Just then, a youngish couple looking at a map walked over, and it was like it broke some kind of spell. I didn't hear anything else. They just stood there looking at the map and talking about the fountain. They were Americans, I think. That's the only haunted thing ever happened to me."

Nixie Blake Adams, England: "A group of us were touring Versailles. It was so --- crowded that I was sorry we came. I was sick of people bumping into me. We were standing in the Hall of Mirrors, and I hear a group of men quarreling behind me. I was pretty much up against the mirrored wall and couldn't figure out who was behind me. I turned and saw just my reflection. They kept yelling in what sounded like French. No one else seemed to notice it. Just then, one of my friends, who was going over some printed guidebook thing, says that I'm standing in front of the mirror door that leads to the Council Room called the Bull's Eye where the Kings held their meetings. Just as she pointed it out, the yelling stopped. It was really creepy."

Michelin Monté, Belgium: "My wife and I have visited Versailles many times. I am reaching out to you because I have purchased many of your books and I saw you were writing a book about Versailles. Make no mistake…it is haunted! Only one time visiting did I not experience something ghostly. May I share two with you?

"It was in April (April in Paris, right?) and I took my bride to see Versailles. We were waiting in a long line in the courtyard, and I was looking up at the busts that sit up by the balconies. Something caught my eye and I looked up to see a woman standing on the balcony in the middle staring down at the people. She was in a long gown, some kind of necklace around her throat that seemed to twinkle in the light, big hair, and a feather sticking out of it that was as least as tall as an ostrich feather. I was about to point her out to my wife when she disappeared! I don't mean she went in the door. She vanished right in front of me. I looked about to see if others had their heads tilted up that way, but no one seemed to have noticed it.

"That same day, we were coming out across the Marble Court and discussing what to do next when the sound of galloping horses and buggy wheels came screeching by me so close that I jumped back, jerking my wife's arm with me. My heart was pounding. Several people jumped and looked at me with surprised expressions. My wife yelled, "What?" She didn't hear it or experience it. Some people had stopped and were waiting to hear what I said. I couldn't say anything. My heart was still beating so fast, but what was I going to say. There was nothing there. Many of my friends who have visited have told stories of hearing laughter inside empty rooms, music, fighting, and one hear glasses breaking when there was no one nearby. I hope they do haunted tours someday. It's an amazing place."

There are many stories of seeing some of the acclaimed visitors to Versailles over the centuries. The ghost of Benjamin Franklin has been spotted on more than one occasion, wearing his ubiquitous spectacles and breeches. His visit to the palace during the *American War of Independence* under Louis XVI's reign certainly impacted the Court. Many people have reported hearing music and the sound of revelry, shouts as though someone has won at a hand of cards, strange bird calls within the palace, shimmering reflections of color in the mirrors when nothing is there to explain it. There are reports of hearing glasses knocking against each other as if a servant is ferrying them on a tray down the hallway. Sounds of laughter, babies crying, horse and carriage noises, and the angry shouting of mobs have all made their way into blog posts and footnotes.

Based on the triumphant and tragic saga of the Palace of Versailles, could anyone expect the hallways, gardens, and private rooms to remain quiet. Thankfully, they aren't.

# Appendix I:

## The Family Tree of Bourbon

## Appendix II:

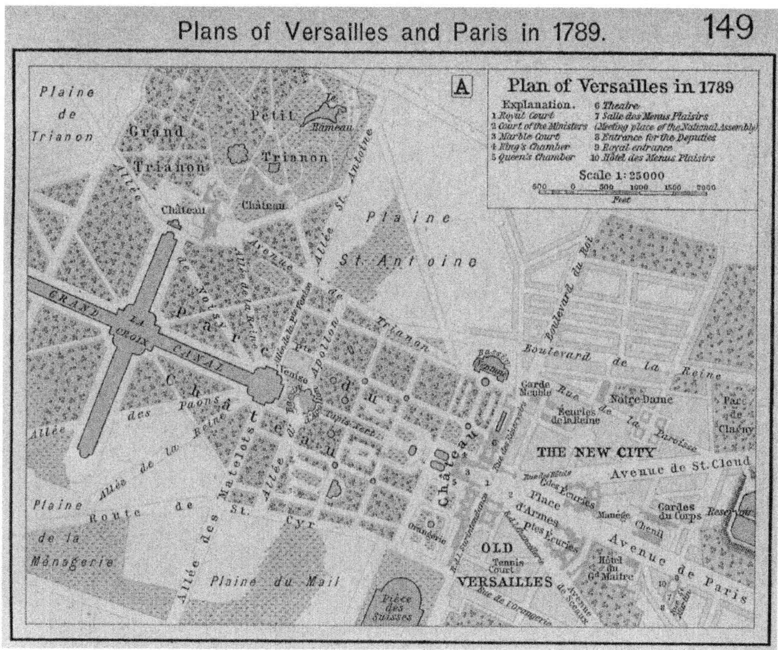


Plans of Versailles & Paris, 1789.

**Bibliography & Recommended Reading:**

1. *Louis XIV: A Royal Life* by Olivier Bernier
2. *Louis the Beloved: The Life of Louis XV* by Oliver Bernier
3. *Versailles: A Biography of a Palace* by Tony Spawforth
4. *Secrets of Marie Antoinette* by Olivier Bernier
5. *The Life of Louis XVI* by John Hardman
6. *Versailles: Tour of the Chateau* by Daniel Meyer
7. *Marie Antoinette: The Journey* by Antonia Fraser
8. *Versailles and the Trianons* (Anonymous)
9. *Marie Antoinette and the Petit Trianon* at Versailles by Martin Chapman
10. *An Adventure* by Eleanor Jourdain
11. *An Adventure* by C.A.E. Moberly and E.F. Jourdain
12. *Madame de Montespan* by Henri Carré
13. *Louis XIV* by Philippe Erlanger
14. *Mémoires* by marquis de la Fare
15. *Mémoires* by Mme de Motteville
16. *Mémoires* by Saint-Simon
17. *Lettres* by marquise de Sévigné
18. *Le Siècle de Louis XIV* by Arouet de Voltaire
19. *Mémoires sur la vie de Marie-Antoinette par Mme Campan* (Paris 1849) by J.L.H. Campan
20. *Louis XVI King of the French* by P.R. Campbell
21. *Mémoires* by P.V. Malouet
22. *Correspondance secrète avec l'Empereur Joseph II et le prince de Kaunitz* by Mercy-Argenteau
23. *Les Devoirs du prince* by J.N. Moreau
24. *De la Révolution française* by J. Necker
25. *Correspondance secrète inédite* by Louis XV
26. *The French Revolution Sourcebook* by J. Hardman
27. *Despatches from Paris* by O. Browning
28. *Mémoires sur la Cour de France* by Baron de Besenval
29. *The Private Realm of Marie Antoinette* by Marie-France Boyer
30. *Le Mariage de Marie-Antoinette* by Maurice Boutry
31. *Les Femmes Bibiliophiles* by Quentin Bauchart
32. *Views and plans of the Petit Trianon at Versailles* by Pierre Clémentel-Arizzoli
33. *The French Revolution as Seen by Madame Tussaud Witness*

*Extraordinary* by Pauline Chapman
34. *Mémoires* by Duc de Choiseul
35. *Relation du départ de Louis XVI* by Duc de Choiseul
36. *Journal inédit 1718-1784* by Duc de Cröy
37. *Maria Theresa* by Edward Crankshaw
38. *Origins of the French Revolution* by William Doyle
40. *Marie-Antoinette: A Portrait* by Ian Dunlop
41. *Royal Palaces of France* by Ian Dunlop
42. *The French Revolution* by Alan Forrest
43. *Journal* by Lady Elizabeth Foster
44. *Rose Bertin: Minister of Fashion* by Madge Garland
45. *The Bourbon Tragedy* by Rupert Furneaux
46. *The Compromising of Louis XVI: the armoire de fer and the French Revolution* by Andrew Freeman
47. *L'Éducation d'un roi: Louis XVI* by Pierette Girault de Coursac
48. *Marie Antoinette* by Joan Haslip
49. *The King's Trial: The French Revolution vs Louis XVI* by David P. Jordan
50. *Souvenirs* by Madame Vigée Le Brun

Other sources too many to list were also consulted for the writing of this book, including digital archives, library websites, internet blogposts, and personal websites. Where possible, they were given accreditation at their source within the book.

**Other books by Rebecca F. Pittman:**

**The History and Haunting Series:**

The History and Haunting of the Stanley Hotel
The History and Haunting of the Myrtles Plantation
The History and Haunting of Lemp Mansion
The History and Haunting of Lizzie Borden
The History and Haunting of Salem: The Witch Trials and Beyond

**Books on Creating Businesses in the Creative Arts:**

How To Start a Faux Painting or Mural Business, Simon and Schuster
Scrapbooking for Profit, Simon and Shuster

**Television Show:** *Troubleshooting Men: What in the WORLD do they want?* based on the book by the same title.

**Juvenile Fiction:**
T.J. Finnel and the Well of Ghosts (Book 1 in a 5-book series)

**Upcoming books:**

**Non-fiction:**
Sarah Winchester and "The House That Spirits Built"
The History and Haunting of Henry XVIII's Hampton Court
New Countdown to Murder Series

**Fiction:**
Don't Look Now!
The Diamond Peacock Club

About the Author:

Rebecca F. Pittman is the author of 16 titles. Her bestselling series, *The History and Haunting Of*, has been featured on TV, radio, and podcasts worldwide. Working closely with the owners of the most-haunted venues in the world, she spends years researching and writing about some of the most-famous people and places that continually capture our imagination.

Continuing the *History and Haunting Of* branding, Miss Pittman created the *Lizzie Borden Paranormal Card Game* as a complement to her book *The History and Haunting of Lizzie Borden*. It contains actual crime scene photos, new evidence, suspects, and alibis, with a supernatural twist. Other games are in the works, along with maps and related merchandise, sold on her website and select retailers.

A new series of non-fiction books in the True Crime genre begins with *Countdown to Murder: Pam Hupp*, released December 2021. *Countdown to Murder: Harold Henthorn* will be released Fall 2022.

On the drawing board are murder mysteries with a supernatural bent, as well as a continuation of more *History and Haunting Of*, and *Countdown to Murder* releases.

Rebecca makes her home in the foothills of the Rocky Mountains in Colorado where she pursues her love of golf, boating, travel, and spending time with her growing family. You can see her website at www.rebeccafpittmanbooks.com where you can sign up for her free newsletter *Ghost Writings*. Each of her books has a corresponding Facebook page with updated information pertaining to each venue, event, or person, based on the books' titles.